"Aimed at educated, experienced travellers, the [Berlitz Travellers] Guides capture the flavor of foreign lands."
—*Entrepreneur*

"Filling a needed niche in guidebooks . . . designed to eliminate the cumbersome lists of virtually every hotel and restaurant . . . . Special out-of-the-way places are detailed. . . . The books capture the personality and excitement of each destination."
—*Los Angeles Times*

"There's a different tone to these books, and certainly a different approach . . . information is aimed at independent and clearly sophisticated travellers. . . . Strong opinions give these books a different personality from most guides, and make them fun to read."
—*Travel & Leisure*

"Aimed at experienced, independent travellers who want information beyond the nuts-and-bolts material available in many familiar sources. Although each volume gives necessary basics, the series sends travellers not just to 'sights,' but to places and events that convey the personality of each locale."
—*The Denver Post*

"Just the right amount of information about where to stay and play."
—*Detroit Free Press*

"The strength of the [Berlitz Travellers Guides] lies in remarks and recommendations by writers with a depth of knowledge about their subject."
—*Washington Times*

"The most readable of the current paperback lot."
—*New York Post*

"Highly recommended."
—*Library Journal*

"Very strong on atmosphere and insights into local culture for curious travellers."
—*Boston Herald*

"The [Berlitz Travellers Guides] eliminate cumbersome lists and provide reliable information about what is truly exciting and significant about a destination. . . . [They] also emphasize the spirit and underlying 'vibrations' of a region—historical, cultural, and social—that enhance a trip."
—*Retirement Life*

"Information without boredom. . . . Good clear maps and index."
—*The Sunday Sun* (Toronto)

CONTRIBUTORS

STEPHEN BREWER is a freelance writer and editor who works on many national magazines and book projects. A long-time New Yorker, he is the editorial consultant for this guidebook.

ELEANOR BERMAN is a widely published travel writer. Her guide *Away for the Weekend: New York* has been a regional best-seller since 1982. She has contributed to major metropolitan daily newspapers throughout the United States as well as to such national magazines as *House Beautiful, Modern Bride,* and *Caribbean Travel and Life.*

DAVID BERREBY is a member of the Outer Critics Circle and the American Theater Critics Association. He reviews theater for the *New York Law Journal,* and his work has appeared in the *Village Voice, The New York Times, Ms., Diversion, New York Newsday,* and other publications.

ANDY BIRSH is a contributing editor at *Gourmet,* for which he writes a monthly column on New York dining. For a decade he edited and published *The Restaurant Reporter.*

STEVE ETTLINGER is an independent book producer with several award-winning books to his credit. He is also a freelance picture editor and was formerly associate picture editor at *GEO* magazine. His most recent photo-book project is *Vietnam: The Land We Never Knew,* by Geoffrey Clifford.

DAVID FRANKEL, formerly an editor of *New York* magazine, has written on music for *New York* and *Rolling Stone.* He is an editor of *Artforum* magazine.

DWIGHT V. GAST has written for numerous publications.

MATTHEW GUREWITSCH has written about music, dance, theater, and film for *The New York Times,* the *Atlantic, Mirabella,* and other publications around the world.

ELEANOR HEARTNEY is a writer and critic specializing in contemporary art. She is a regular contributor to *ArtNews, Art in America,* and the *New Art Examiner.*

EDWARD HERNSTADT, a former contributor to *The Berlitz Travellers Guide to France,* lives in downtown Manhattan.

AMY K. HUGHES, a New York freelance editor and writer specializing in art, nature, and travel, has edited several guides in the Berlitz Travellers series.

BARRY LEWIS, an architectural historian, has created tour programs and produced lecture series for New York's 92nd Street Y. He has also written articles on the city's architectural history for various publications and was a contributor to the Municipal Art Society's *Juror's Guide to Lower Manhattan.*

PATRICIA LYNDEN writes for a wide variety of publications. She is a senior editor of *Longevity* magazine.

LENORE MALEN, a New York artist and long-time resident of SoHo, is the executive editor of the *Art Journal.*

BONNIE ROTHMAN MORRIS is a television producer and writer who has contributed to *7 Days, Food and Wine, Cosmopolitan,* and *Allure.*

MITCHELL NAUFFTS is a freelance writer based in Manhattan.

INGRID NELSON is a freelance writer living on Manhattan's Upper West Side.

JOANNA NEY is a freelance writer specializing in dance. She was formerly dance critic for *East Side Express* and *Other Stages* and has contributed to *The New York Times, Cosmopolitan, Cue,* and *V.* Currently she reviews dance for WBAI radio.

HELEN O'CONNOR was a freelance writer from Ireland who was a frequent contributor to the *Daily News, New York* magazine, and other publications.

RANDALL SHORT is a columnist for the *New York Observer*. He reports regularly on literature and the arts for *The New York Times, New York Newsday,* and *Mirabella*.

ED WETSCHLER, a native New Yorker, is a senior editor at *Diversion* magazine. He claims his rooftop garden is the best in Manhattan.

LYNN YAEGER is the author of a biweekly column in the *Village Voice* on antiques and collectibles and was also a contributor to *The Village Voice Guide to Manhattan's Shopping Neighborhoods*. A resident of New York for more than 20 years, she has written on fashion for *Cosmopolitan, Mademoiselle,* and other publications.

THE BERLITZ
TRAVELLERS GUIDES

THE BERLITZ TRAVELLERS GUIDE TO NEW YORK CITY

Sixth Edition

ALAN TUCKER
General Editor

BERLITZ PUBLISHING COMPANY, INC.
New York, New York

BERLITZ PUBLISHING COMPANY LTD.
Oxford, England

THE BERLITZ TRAVELLERS GUIDE
TO NEW YORK CITY
Sixth Edition

Berlitz Trademark Reg U.S. Patent and Trademark Office
and other countries—Marca Registrada

Published by Berlitz Publishing Company, Inc.
257 Park Avenue South, New York, New York 10010, U.S.A.

Distributed in the United States by
the Macmillan Publishing Group

Distributed elsewhere by Berlitz Publishing Company Ltd.
Berlitz House, Peterley Road, Horspath, Oxford OX4 2TX, England

ISBN 2-8315-1704-4
ISSN 1057-4743

Designed by Beth Tondreau Design
Cover design by Dan Miller Design
Cover photograph by Dennis Hallinan/FPG International
Maps by Mark Stein Studios
Illustrations by Bill Russell
Edited by Stephen Brewer and Amy K. Hughes

Printed in the United States of America
1   3   5   7   9   10   8   6   4   2

THIS GUIDEBOOK

The Berlitz Travellers Guides are designed for experienced travellers in search of exceptional information that will enhance the enjoyment of the trips they take.

Where, for example, are the interesting, out-of-the-way, fun, charming, or romantic places to stay? The hotels described by our expert writers are some of the special places, in all price ranges except for the very lowest—not just the run-of-the-mill, heavily marketed places in advertised airline and travel-wholesaler packages.

We are *highly* selective in our choices of accommodations, concentrating on what our insider contributors think are the most interesting or rewarding places, and why. Readers who want to review exhaustive lists of hotel choices as well, and who feel they need detailed descriptions of each property, can supplement the *Berlitz Travellers Guide* with tourism industry publications or one of the many directory-type guidebooks on the market.

The Berlitz Travellers Guide to New York City highlights the more rewarding parts of the city so that you can quickly and efficiently home in on a good itinerary.

Of course, this guidebook does far more than just help you choose a hotel and plan your trip. *The Berlitz Travellers Guide to New York City* is designed for use *in* New York. Our writers, each of whom is an experienced travel journalist who either lives in or regularly tours the city or surrounding area of the city he or she covers, tell you what you really need to know, what you can't find out so easily on your own. They identify and describe the truly out-of-the-ordinary restaurants, shops, activities, and sights, and tell you the best way to "do" your destination.

Our writers are highly selective. They bring out the significance of the places they *do* cover, capturing the personality and the underlying cultural and historical resonances of a city or region—making clear its special appeal.

The Berlitz Travellers Guide to New York City is full of reliable information. We would like to know if you think we've left out some very special place. Although we make every effort to provide the most current information available about every destination described in this book, it is possible too that changes have occurred before you arrive. If you do have an experience that is contrary to what you were led to expect by our description, we would like to hear from you about it.

A guidebook is no substitute for common sense when you are travelling. Always pack the clothing, footwear, and other items appropriate for the destination, and make the necessary accommodation for such variables as weather and local rules. Of course, once on the scene you should avoid situations that are in your own judgment potentially hazardous, even if they have to do with something mentioned in a guidebook. Half the fun of travelling is exploring, but explore with care.

ALAN TUCKER
General Editor
Berlitz Travellers Guides

Root Publishing Company
350 West Hubbard Street
Suite 440
Chicago, Illinois 60610

CONTENTS

THE
BERLITZ
TRAVELLERS
GUIDE TO
NEW YORK
CITY

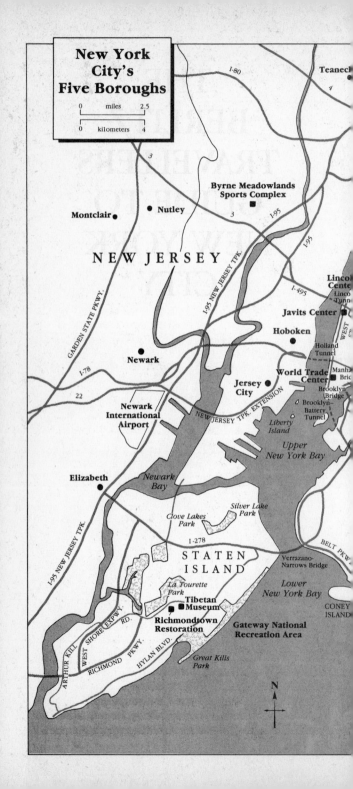

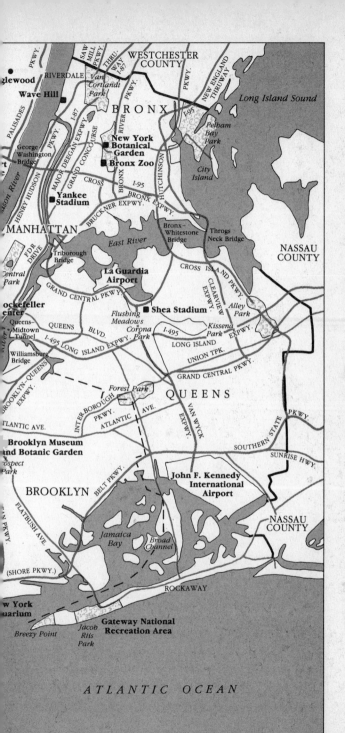

OVERVIEW

By Alan Tucker

Alan Tucker came to Manhattan under cover of darkness in 1964 and has lived on the Upper West Side for all but two of his years here. He is general editor of the Berlitz Travellers Guides and a member of the Society of American Travel Writers and the New York Travel Writers' Association.

We know: New York City is the cultural and creative cynosure of the entire world and still the foremost national and international financial center—the place where the big deals are made in the film industry, the broadcasting industry, in the art and theatrical businesses, in publishing and advertising, in banking and fashion and export-import.

Trends may start elsewhere, but they're not official until they're acknowledged here.

The people who live and work here create the strikingly high level of ambient human energy that fuels all this activity and is also drawn forth by it (the chicken and the egg). Talented folks from all over the country (and the world) choose to live here not just because they want to survive, but because they have something they want to *do*—and they figure this is the place to do it.

As for you, the visitor, you might want to come to see the totalitarian architecture of the World Trade Center, the robber barons' booty in the Metropolitan Museum of Art, the latest Broadway musical extravaganza, and the like. These "major attractions" are interesting, or at the very least diverting. But Niagara Falls is interesting, too, and yet it's not quite parallel to the real lure of New York City.

We think you will probably get the most out of visiting the city if you also look for the less obvious benefits that New Yorkers enjoy—while of course at the same time sidestepping the well-known day-to-day nuisances that living here brings (such as the privilege of paying half your salary in rent, not having your own back yard for growing tomatoes, leaving the office at 8:30 every night, and tolerating ever-spreading piles of uncollected garbage).

What benefits? For example, the restaurants; the neighborhoods; the variety of people (What an understatement! More on that later.) and their conversation; the easy, casual access to jazz, classical music, and other performing arts even outside the Sacred Palaces of Culture; the mania for graphic art and arresting design (everywhere); the shops and artisans and galleries (you name it, and it's on sale here—probably cheaper than it is in Hong Kong, too).

These are the things we want to tell you about in our guidebook. We do want to mention Lincoln Center, the Museum of Modern Art, Macy's, and such, but our hearts really lie in talking about downtown performance lofts, where to have brunch while you read your Sunday *New York Times,* where to buy private-label opera recordings, and how to take an afternoon's stroll in New York City from China to Italy to Bohemia.

To get to the goodies that you want to hear about we have had to cover the city in two dimensions.

One is in terms of *neighborhoods.* The other is by way of the city's *specialties,* such as antiques, dance, food, the literary world, fashion shopping, and so on.

The Neighborhoods

Even **Midtown**, the business center where most visitors huddle and where the great department stores are concentrated, is really a collection of neighborhoods (gamy Clinton, residential Murray Hill, the area around the United Nations, the Garment District around Seventh Avenue in the 30s, etc.). But there's more variety—and more of those special New York experiences we've been talking about—in some of the city's other neighborhoods.

- The **Wall Street area** is full of the history of early New York and it also has the South Street Seaport historical/shopping/dining district and the

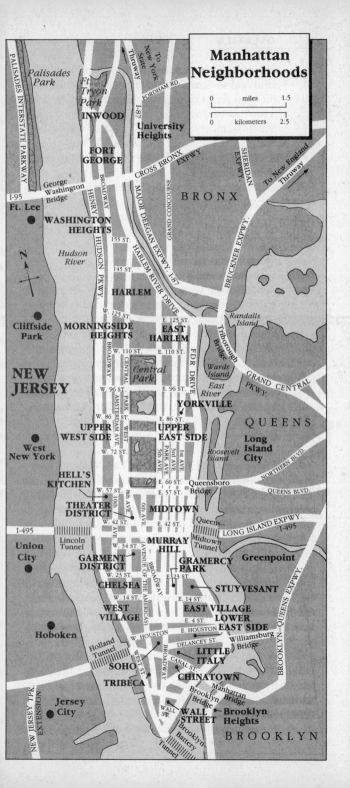

Manhattan Neighborhoods

| 0 | miles | 1.5 |
| 0 | kilometers | 2.5 |

ferry rides to the Statue of Liberty and Ellis Island and to Staten Island (the ferry ride itself is the wonderful experience here; Staten Island has a few interesting historical sites but is best left to Staten Islanders). And you'll want to see the New York Stock Exchange and the World Trade Center (get the view at the top of the south tower, number 2).

- **Chinatown** is one of the largest such enclaves in the world—and it's no living museum, either.
- **TriBeCa** is an area of artists' and arty lawyers' lofts and unusual bars, restaurants, cafés, and clubs.
- **Little Italy** is for eating.
- **SoHo** was once an inexpensive place for artists seeking large work space and is now an expensive but interesting area of galleries, boutiques, restaurants, and bars.
- The **Lower Broadway area** has trendy shops, punk barbershops, Tower Records, roomy if undistinguished restaurants, the Joseph Papp Public Theater, and Cooper Union arts and sciences school—all between Canal and 8th streets. It is a sort of Luxembourg, with Little Italy, Chinatown, and the Lower East Side (or "East Village") on one side and SoHo and Greenwich Village on the other.
- The **Lower East Side** and the **East Village** are perhaps the last remaining bastions of youthful avant-garde artistic and literary activity on Manhattan Island, with attendant clubs and cafés— and lots of street crime and drug sales amid the remnants of an earlier Eastern European immigrant culture.
- **Greenwich Village** has New York University at its heart and is populated by comfortable mid- to upper-level professionals as well as (especially along Christopher Street in the so-called West Village) a concentrated gay community. There are lots of good bars, restaurants, and shops in the Village, but its bohemian days have given over to a sort of *New York Review of Books* gentility— ironically, the Village proper no longer even has a vital literary center, like the old Eighth Street Bookstore.
- **Chelsea**, its main street being along Eighth Ave-

nue above 14th Street, has lots of rough edges, but it does have some of the bohemian elements that the Village has lost. Chelsea also has more than its share of nifty restaurants and clubs and a few leading-edge modern-dance venues, as well as punk rockers, the last especially along West 23rd Street (its northern border) near the famous Chelsea Hotel.

- The **Lower Fifth Avenue** area, also known variously as the Flatiron District, "SoFi" (*S*outh of the *Flati*ron Building), the Ladies' Mile, and the Madison Square area, has trendy restaurants and photographers' lofts on the side streets in the high teens and the 20s up to 23rd Street.

- The **Upper West Side**, north of Midtown and west of **Central Park**, is anchored at the south by Lincoln Center and at the north by Columbia University. Its Columbus Avenue shop and restaurant strip, which has come down a peg or two since its apogee in the early 1980s, still attracts the so-called bridge-and-tunnel people (Manhattan's neighbors on all sides, who must use one or the other to get onto the island). Amsterdam Avenue and Broadway, parallel and to the west of Columbus, are for the Upper West Side's own residents—who are much tighter with their money (they generally have less) and much more inclined toward the shabby genteel than their East Side compatriots. The Upper West Side is home to many actors, musicians, dancers, and writers, for example. Look here for casual jazz clubs and pretty good Chinese restaurants—and some good bookstores.

- **Harlem**, beginning at around 116th Street, may well be one of the most fascinating "neighborhoods" anywhere—not only for the Apollo Theater and other remnants of its Golden Age and for its vitality as the heart of urban black culture in America, but because Harlem has more unspoiled blocks from old New York than any other part of the city. Way up at the northern tip of Manhattan, beyond Harlem, is The Cloisters, the Metropolitan Museum's bastion of Medieval art.

- The **Upper East Side** (east of the park) is the embodiment of gentility that *isn't* shabby: Bankers, brokers, doctors, and lawyers live in apartments along Fifth and Park avenues that cost as much as the Latin American nations owe Chase Manhattan Bank; private schools occupy just about every side street; every other shop on Madison Avenue sells museum-quality art or antiques; and on Third, Second, and First avenues young corporate fodder prowl bars and restaurants with names like Tooties and J. J. Monkerton. In **Yorkville**, along East 86th Street and a little down Second Avenue, there are also vestiges of the earlier German and Eastern European working-class presence. The Metropolitan and other museums lie along Fifth Avenue from the 70s to the 90s and even higher, and—for what it is worth—the Whitney Museum of American Art is over on Madison Avenue at 75th Street.

- **Brooklyn** is a sort of residential alternative to Manhattan for increasing numbers of professionals, but it is the residence of choice for genuine Brooklynites, those of "youse" and "whaddaya dune" and "geddadayear" renown from places such as Bensonhoist (as pronounced) and Bay Ridge (both heavily Italian-American), Canarsie, and Red Hook. Visitors go to Brooklyn for the adventurous Brooklyn Academy of Music (BAM) and the Brooklyn Museum (Egypt!), as well as for great Middle Eastern food on Atlantic Avenue near Brooklyn Heights.

- Largely residential **Queens** has its ethnic areas as well: Greeks in Astoria, Koreans and Chinese in Flushing, and more. But most Manhattanites only go to Queens to get a flight at La Guardia or JFK airports; more's the pity.

- And then there are interesting day-trip destinations from New York City: The Bronx Zoo, the New York Botanical Garden, and Wave Hill (a park on the Hudson River) are refreshing retreats within the city; Franklin Delano Roosevelt's home at **Hyde Park** up on the Hudson; the United States Military Academy at historic **West Point** not far from there; early American farms, homes, and estates in the still-beautiful **Hudson River valley**; the **Hamptons**, at the eastern end of Long Island, an area that was once an artists' colony (Winslow Homer, then Jackson Pollock and Willem de Kooning) and is now a toney summer resort for rich or highly leveraged Manhattanites and lesser beings slipstreaming on them; the **Fire Island** beach communities, closer in on Long Island's south shore, which are reached by ferries; and **Princeton** and **Yale** universities, the former being the more attractive in a movie-set sort of way.

In all these places, particularly in Manhattan neighborhoods, however, what you are primarily looking for, as a visitor in search of the New York Experience, are the *people* and their colorful turns of phrase, as in the "She can't do relationships" or "He gives good phone" or "What am I, chopped liver?" genre of fast talk and one-liners. Although occasionally you'll hear talk of Poincaré or William Blake, most conversations will be on a higher plane: job complaints, money, and the price of cooperative apartments (currently about $250,000 for a nice one-bedroom even on the not-most-desirable Upper West Side, on Riverside Drive or West End Avenue). We've taken considerable care to place you in restaurants, bars, and other venues where you'll hear more of the citizens' patter than you may in the end want to. And places where *you* can try *your* hand at it, too; forget the nonsense about New Yorkers being inaccessible.

We've also conspired to get you into as many different neighborhoods as possible. And different each is, with its own distinct subspecies. What subspecies they are, too! Practitioners of thuggee, with orange spiked hair and chrome studs on their tongues (next year, anyway). Wild-eyed messengers looking like a cross between Don Johnson and Donald Pleasance. Overweight cabdrivers from Baffin Island who speak no known language. A couple wearing jellabas and dancing on stilts. An evil-looking no-neck reading Trollope in the subway. You can stand on any street corner here—at any time of day or night—and see "types" that even the most coke-addled Hollywood director hasn't had the imagination to hallucinate for his stylish made-for-TV melodrama of discontinuity, crime, and urban decay.

These same subspecies, from our civic leaders on down (or up), will amaze and mystify you with their adaptability as well. After all, earlier New Yorkers didn't exactly earn a place in the annals of indomitable patriotic resistance when the British were comfortably ensconced here during the American Revolution. Plenty of money was mysteriously made here during the embargo against Southern cotton during the U.S. Civil War, too. New Yorkers can figure out a way around anything. Now, we do indeed have clear principles; we're just prepared to change them as circumstances dictate.

Any New Yorker will tell you that the city is currently going through a difficult period. Besides the filthy condition of the streets there is also an obvious profusion of beggars, homeless people, and street peddlers. Because of the recession there is also serious unemployment and a noticeable reduction of municipal services. You won't have to be especially perceptive to detect a certain diminution of confidence among New Yorkers these days, and perhaps a parallel aggressive or edgy atmosphere on the streets. But this, too, will pass—and in the meantime you shouldn't allow it to interfere with your enjoyment of the city's unsurpassed and quite intact offerings.

The City's Specialties

Besides by neighborhood, the other way to come to terms with how to "do" the city is by what special interests you yourself have. Here again we've been selective, opting for the most brilliant aspects as against the more mundane. Surely no one will contest that the city's best efforts show in the areas of:

- Museums
- Art
- Architecture
- Photography and filmmaking
- Classical music
- Popular music
- Dance
- Theater
- The literary world and bookstores
- Shopping (for antiques, clothing and accessories, housewares, and any number of unusual things)
- Food

Another kind of specialty—and one on which we lavish quite a bit of space—is what we call "After Hours," meaning after the day's nine-to-five activities are accomplished:

- Dining
- Bars and cafés
- Nightlife and entertainment

We've tried to weed out the humdrum in order to put you *in position* to have a satisfying visit to New York City. We consider our guidebook to be a sort of starter kit. It's up to you to take it from here and begin developing your own New York for yourself. It may take a number of visits, and it will be a different town every time.

USEFUL FACTS
(Unless noted otherwise, telephone numbers are in the 212 area code.)

When to Go
A popular postcard depicts the four seasons in New York, showing the same shot of a gray, treeless street four times. New York actually has four distinct seasons: a hot, humid summer; crisp autumn; cold, sloppy winter; and gentle spring. Unless you enjoy extremes, April, May, September, and October are the best months for a visit, and the weeks between Thanksgiving and New Year's are wintry but very cheerful times in the city. You can expect thunderstorms in the summer, snow and rain in the winter, and showers at other times. For weather information, Tel: 976-1212.

What to Wear
New Yorkers dress well. You will feel out of place wearing jeans, shorts, and other casual clothing at the theater and concerts, in many restaurants, and even on the streets of Midtown during business hours. On the other hand, you will rarely feel overdressed in this city where it is not unusual to find yourself seated next to someone in full evening dress. Women should pack skirts, dresses, or fashionable slacks; men, slacks, sports coats and/or suits, and ties (you may be able to get by with just a jacket in many places). Do not wear expensive-looking jewelry on the street and public transportation; otherwise, you may be a target for thieves.

To equip yourself for the weather, bring: *in winter,* wool clothing, gloves, scarf, raincoat with liner or overcoat, boots or galoshes, umbrella; *in summer,* lightweight cotton clothing; *other seasons,* a sweater and raincoat; *all seasons,* good, sensible walking shoes.

Getting In

The United States requires a passport and visitor's visa or long-term visa of many visitors (Canadians and Japanese are notable exceptions) who are not United States citizens. Check with the United States Embassy or consulate nearest you before you depart. Lines for customs clearance at Kennedy and Newark airports tend to be long; the wait can be up to an hour and even longer at peak arrival times (between 4:00 and 6:00 P.M. for those coming from Europe). The arrival process at Kennedy's International Arrivals building (for most airlines except TWA, British Airways, and others that have their own terminals) appears to run more smoothly since a recent renovation of the customs halls.

Arrival by Air

New York is served by three major airports: La Guardia, in Queens, for shorter domestic flights (does not handle 747s); Kennedy ("JFK"), also in Queens, for domestic and international flights; and Newark, outside Newark, New Jersey, for domestic and some international flights.

Excellent public transportation links the three airports to Manhattan. For information on all the many forms of public and private transportation into Manhattan as well as to the other four boroughs and the surrounding suburbs, Tel: (800) AIR-RIDE, toll free from anywhere in the United States.

By taxi: The half-hour cab ride from La Guardia to Midtown costs about $25; the 45-minute ride from Kennedy about $40; the 45-minute trip from Newark about $50 (for trips to and from Newark, drivers add $10 to the amount registered on the meter). At all airports cabs leave from well-marked stands, manned by dispatchers, outside flight arrival areas. It is illegal for cabs to pick up passengers outside of these areas. Do not be intimidated by the long lines; they move quickly. To partake of the New York custom of "cutting on line" is a sure way of starting a row.

By bus from La Guardia: Carey buses (Tel: 718-632-0500) run every 20 to 30 minutes between 6:45 A.M. and midnight; they leave from posted areas at curbside outside air terminal arrival areas and go to Grand Central Station, at 42nd Street, and Park Avenue in Midtown with connections to Port Authority and several Midtown hotels: the New York Hilton, at Sixth Avenue and 53rd Street; the Sheraton Manhattan, at Seventh Avenue and 51st

Street; the Holiday Inn Crowne Plaza, at Broadway and 48th Street; and the Marriott Marquis, at Broadway and 45th Street; $8.50 to Grand Central and Port Authority, $10 to hotels; allow 45 minutes to one hour.

By bus from Kennedy: Carey buses run every 20 minutes between 6:00 A.M. and midnight from posted areas at curbside outside terminal arrival areas to Grand Central Station and the Port Authority bus terminal in Midtown, with connections to the same hotels listed above; $11 to Grand Central and Port Authority, $12.50 to hotels. Allow one hour to an hour and 15 minutes.

By bus from Newark: Olympia Trails buses (Tel: 964-6233) run every 20 to 30 minutes between 6:45 A.M. weekdays/7:15 A.M. weekends and 8:45 P.M. weekdays/8:15 P.M. Saturdays/10:45 P.M. Sundays and holidays from posted areas outside terminals to the World Trade Center (West Street, next to the Vista Hotel, in the downtown Wall Street area); $7; allow at least 25 minutes. Olympia Trails buses also run every 20 to 30 minutes between 6:15 A.M. and midnight from Newark to Grand Central Station, at 42nd Street and Park Avenue in Midtown; $7; allow 35 to 45 minutes; and from Newark to Pennsylvania Station at 34th Street and Seventh Avenue; $7; allow 25 to 35 minutes. New Jersey Transit buses (Tel: 201-762-5100) run every 15 to 20 minutes between 5:40 A.M. and midnight, with infrequent service in the small hours, from Newark to Port Authority Bus Terminal, at 42nd Street and Eighth Avenue near Times Square; $7 one way, $12 round trip; allow at least 45 minutes.

By boat from La Guardia: Passengers arriving at the Marine Air Terminal on Delta Shuttle flights from Washington and Boston may take the Water Shuttle (Tel: 800-54-FERRY) to Pier 11, on the East River at the foot of Wall Street, and to the foot of East 34th Street, Mondays through Fridays; $25 one way, $45 round trip; allow 25 minutes to 34th Street, 40 minutes to Wall Street. Sailings to both at 7:45 A.M., 8:45 A.M., 9:45 A.M., 10:45 A.M., 3:45 P.M., 4:45 P.M., 5:45 P.M., and (to 34th Street only) 6:45 P.M. (Boats make the return trip from Wall Street at 8:30 A.M., 9:30 A.M., 2:30 P.M., 3:30 P.M., 4:30 P.M., and 5:30 P.M.; from East 34th Street at 7:45 A.M., 8:45 A.M., 9:45 A.M., 10:45 A.M., 2:45 P.M., 3:45 P.M., 4:45 P.M., 5:45 P.M., and 6:45 P.M.)

By train from La Guardia and Kennedy: Carey buses run every half hour from both airports to the Jamaica, Queens, station of the Long Island Railroad (Tel: 718-217-5477); $5; allow half an hour. From the station, trains run about every 5 to 10 minutes to Pennsylvania Station; $5, $3.50 weekends and other off-peak hours; allow 25 minutes. From Jamaica, you may also connect to trains serving Brooklyn and Long Island stations.

By subway from La Guardia: The Q 33 and Q 47 buses connect with the E, F, G, R, and 7 trains at the Roosevelt Avenue/Jackson Heights subway station. Allow one hour for the trip to Midtown.

By subway from Kennedy: The bus to the Long Term Parking Lot connects with the A train at the Howard Beach subway station. Allow an hour and a half for the trip to Midtown.

By helicopter from Kennedy: New York Helicopter (Tel: 800-645-3494) flies from major JFK terminals to the East Side Heliport, 34th Street at the East River in Midtown, roughly every half hour between 2:30 P.M. and 7:30 P.M.; $65; the trip takes just ten minutes; from Midtown, flights operate every half hour between 2:30 P.M. and 7:30 P.M.

Arrival by Train

Amtrak trains arrive at Pennsylvania ("Penn") Station, at 34th Street and Seventh Avenue. For Amtrak information, Tel: 582-6875 or (800) 872-7245. New Jersey Transit trains and those of the Long Island Railroad, serving suburban areas, leave from Penn Station. For New Jersey Transit information, Tel: (201) 762-5100; for Long Island Railroad information, Tel: (718) 217-5477. Metro-North trains, serving Connecticut, Westchester County, and other northern suburbs, leave from Grand Central Station, at 42nd Street and Park Avenue; for information, Tel: 532-4900. Both Pennsylvania and Grand Central stations are well served by buses and subways. At both, taxis can be difficult to procure at rush hours; be patient and steadfast in your efforts. Dispatchers (not always on duty) help speed things along.

Arrival by Bus

Your bus will be one of the 7,500 that each day pull in and out of Port Authority, the world's largest bus terminal, on Eighth Avenue between 40th and 42nd streets. For Greyhound-Trailways information, Tel: 971-6363; for information on New Jersey Transit, the major suburban line serving Port Authority, Tel: (201) 762-5100; for information on other lines, Tel: 564-8484. Some buses also service the Port Authority's terminal at the Manhattan end of the George Washington Bridge, at 178th Street between Fort Washington and Wadsworth avenues, Tel: (201) 346-4000.

Arrival by Sea
The only transatlantic liner that still regularly serves New York is the Cunard Line's *Queen Elizabeth II*. She and the many cruise ships that dock in New York tie up at the Hudson River piers off 12th Avenue in the West 50s. A fleet of taxis meets all ships.

Arrival by Car
If you do insist on bringing a car into Manhattan (*not* a good idea), you'll soon discover the borough really is an island, connected to the rest of the United States by a dozen or so bridges and four tunnels. It can take longer to traverse any of these crossings than it does to fly from New York to Paris on the Concorde. Most tolls are $4.00, and at most bridges and tunnels are imposed only on cars entering Manhattan. The Triborough Bridge is a notable exception, charging $3.50 each way. Once here, park in a garage (many charge as much as $12 an hour) and walk or take public transportation. If you do park on the street, remember that New York enforces an alternate-side-of-the-street-parking law—on alternate mornings it is illegal to park on one side of the street, meaning that at times during the week you may not leave your car in a space for more than one night. (And *never* leave anything in your car.)

Getting Around
A few basic rules to keep in mind when moving around Manhattan:

Avenues run north–south and streets run east–west. Avenues increase in number from east to west—First Avenue is on the East Side and Tenth Avenue is on the West Side. Streets increase in number from south to north, with 4th Street being downtown and 74th being uptown.

Fifth Avenue is the dividing line between East and West; 1 East 50th Street would be just east of Fifth, 1 West 50th just west of Fifth. (South of Washington Square the division is less clear cut, with Broadway serving to divide the streets immediately beneath the square into east and west.)

Most streets are one way, with traffic on even-numbered streets travelling east and traffic on odd-numbered streets

Manhattan Address Locator

To find an avenue address, cancel the last figure in the address number, divide by 2, and add (+) or subtract (−) the key number below. The result is the nearest numbered cross street. Cross-street addresses increase east or west from Fifth Avenue, which runs north to south (see examples on 57th Street below). The cross streets west of Central Park (see West 72nd Street), which increase from Central Park West, are the exception.

Ave. A, B, C, D . . . . . . + 3
1st, 2nd Ave. . . . . + 3
3rd Ave. . . . . + 10
4th Ave. . . . . + 8
5th Ave.
  Up to 200 . . . . + 13
  Up to 400 . . . . + 16
  Up to 600 . . . . + 18
  Up to 775 . . . . + 20
  775 to 1286 . . . . Cancel
    last figure and . . . . − 18
  To 1500 . . . . + 45
  Above 2000 . . . . . + 24
6th Ave. (Ave. of the
  Americas) . . . . − 12
7th Ave. . . . . + 12
8th Ave. . . . . + 10
9th Ave. . . . . + 13
10th Ave. . . . . + 14
Amsterdam Ave. . . . + 60
Broadway (23–192 Sts.)
  . . . . − 30
Columbus Ave. . . . . . + 60
Central Park West . . . . . .
  Divide house no. by 10
  and . . . . + 60
Lexington Ave. . . . . . + 22
Madison Ave. . . . . . . + 26
Park Ave. . . . . + 35
Riverside Dr. . . . . . . Divide
  house no. by 10 and
  add 72 (up to 165th St.)
St. Nicholas Ave. . . . + 110
West End Ave. . . . . . + 60
York Ave. . . . . + 4

travelling west. Traffic flows both ways on major crosstown streets, including Canal, Houston, 14th, 23rd, 34th, 42nd, 57th, 72nd, 79th, 86th, and 96th (the last three are routes across Central Park).

Addresses on north–south streets are not consistently numbered, so 500 Fifth Avenue is actually many blocks north of 500 Second Avenue. Always get a cross street when you ask for an address.

By subway and bus: The $1.25 subway and bus fare is payable with tokens (available at subway stations) or, on buses only, with exact change, no bills. Subway lines frequently used by visitors include the IRT 1 and 9, which make frequent stops on the West Side (many along Broadway and Seventh Avenue), and the IRT 6, which makes frequent stops on the East Side (mostly along Lexington Avenue). Buses run uptown on Tenth, Eighth, Sixth, Madison, Third, and First avenues and downtown on Ninth, Seventh, Fifth, and Second avenues. Some of the major east–west bus routes are 14th, 23rd, 34th, 42nd, 57th, 65th/66th, 79th, 86th, and 96th streets (the last four are the only crosstown streets that traverse Central Park).

Bus and subway maps are available at subway stations and at the office of the New York Convention and Visitors Bureau, on Columbus Circle (59th Street and Broadway and locations throughout the city). For inquiries regarding buses and subways, including routes and schedules (they'll tell you the best route to your destination, for example), call the Transit Authority; Tel: (718) 330-1234.

By taxi: Cabs licensed by the New York City Taxi and Limousine Commission are equipped with lighted signs on their roofs. When the sign is lit, the cab is available to pick up passengers. When the sign is not lit, the cab is occupied. When the sign reads "Off Duty" the driver is supposedly not picking up passengers. Cabs charge $1.50 at the initial drop of the meter arm and $.25 for each subsequent one-fifth of a mile and $.25 for each 75 seconds when the car is not in motion. A $.50 surcharge is imposed for trips commencing after 8:00 P.M. and before 6:00 A.M. A 20 percent tip is customary. If you have a problem with a cabdriver, call the commission's complaint number, 221-TAXI. The driver's photo and license number are clearly posted on the dashboard of every taxi.

Beware of unlicensed cabs that cruise the streets. Often they don't have meters, and you may find yourself at the mercy of a mad driver who doesn't know the difference between the East and West Sides; these cabs are easy to spot—they're usually not yellow and don't have medallions and other official insignia.

By car: A word of advice: Don't. Garage parking runs about $12 an hour. Streets are full of potholes. New York drivers (especially cabbies) are criminally insane or are in some stage of becoming so. What's the point of driving to, say, Macy's, when there's no place to park once you get there? (See also "Arrival by Car," above.)

Sightseeing

Ask a New Yorker what sights to see and you'll probably get at least a hundred answers. Here's our very subjective list of the 11 things you must do and see in New York.

1) Ride the Staten Island Ferry. The views—of lower Manhattan, New York Harbor, Ellis Island, and the Statue of Liberty—are unforgettable. And it costs only 50 cents, round trip. (See our Lower Manhattan and the Harbor section.)

2) For everyone's favorite views of New York, ascend to the top of the World Trade Center (see Lower Manhattan and the Harbor) or the Empire State Building (see Midtown).

3) Visit Little Italy and Chinatown for a taste of more than pizza and steamed dumplings—you'll also get a feel for what immigrant-thronged New York was like a century ago. (See the Chinatown and Little Italy sections in the Downtown chapter.)

4) Walk through Grand Central Station at rush hour. You'll see what the late novelist Isaac Bashevis Singer meant when he described his beloved city in a word: "Rush!" (See Midtown.)

5) Sit in the Channel Gardens at Rockefeller Center. Here's Midtown at its best. (See Midtown.)

6) Have a drink in the lobby bar of the Algonquin Hotel. The bons mots of Dorothy Parker and other literary habitués still cling to the well-worn upholstery. (See our Accommodations and Bars sections.)

7) Take a stroll in Central Park. You'll understand why concrete-bound Manhattanites treasure these 843 acres so. (See the Central Park section.)

8) See a Broadway show (and/or opera, ballet, concert). Sure, the road troupe may be coming to your home town, but the experience just isn't the same. (See our sections on Classical Music, Dance, and the Theater.)

9) Window shop on Madison Avenue between 59th Street and the low 90s. You will never again be so

tempted to spend so much money in so little time. (See our Shopping sections.)

10) Tour the Metropolitan Museum of Art. Best time to go: on a Friday or Saturday evening, when, relatively speaking, you'll have the treasures to yourself. (See Museums.)

11) Last, but certainly not least important, Eat. You have your choice of 12,000-some restaurants. Between meals, shop the city's delis, bakeries, markets, and food emporiums. (See our Dining and Food sections.)

Tours

You may want to take in a packaged tour or two before venturing out on your own. Our choices among the many tours that will help you see New York follow; the Weekend section of the Friday *New York Times* keeps tabs on tours scheduled for the upcoming weekend.

Backstage on Broadway. 228 West 47th Street, Suite 346; Tel: 575-8065. Actors and directors show you their behind-the-scenes domain; $8, $7 students and senior citizens.

Central Park. Walking tours of this delightful urban oasis, courtesy of the Urban Park Rangers (see also our Central Park section). Tel: 427-4040.

Circle Line Sightseeing Tours. Leaves from West 42nd Street and Hudson River, Pier 83; Tel: 563-3200. A three-hour boat cruise around the Manhattan shoreline, all 31 miles of it; runs March 12 through December 24, every 45 minutes between 9:30 A.M. and 4:30 P.M., with a two-hour evening cruise at 7:00 P.M.; $18 adults, $9 children under 12.

Gray Line of New York. 900 Eighth Avenue (between 53rd and 54th streets) and 166 West 46th Street (near Seventh Avenue); Tel: 397-2600. Your choice of 20 specialized tours lasting two to nine hours, from $17.50.

Harlem Spirituals. 1697 Broadway (at 53rd Street); Tel: 757-0425. Tours of Harlem's historic sites also include Baptist gospel services and soul-food meals; from $29 to $65.

Island Helicopter. East River at 34th Street; Tel: 683-4575. Unforgettable aerial tours, from $47 to $119.

Lower East Side Tenement Museum. 97 Orchard Street (between Delancey and Broome streets); Tel: 431-0233. Ingenious walking tours trace New York's heritage: One explores the haunts of the Bowery Boys and other thugs who have terrorized New Yorkers over the centuries, others provide colorful looks at Little Italy, Jewish New York, and Chinatown; $12.

Municipal Art Society Tours. 457 Madison Avenue (between 50th and 51st streets); Tel: 935-3960. Excellent, informed walking tours of New York neighborhoods; from $10 to about $30; the society's free, hour-long tour of Grand Central Station leaves Wednesdays at 12:30 P.M. from beneath the Chemical Bank sign.

Museum of the City of New York. 1220 Fifth Avenue (at 103rd Street); Tel: 534-1672. Walking tours of the city on different themes, such as Walt Whitman's New York; about $15, but prices vary.

NBC Studio Tour. 30 Rockefeller Plaza; Tel: 664-4000. A look at New York as television and radio capital; every day from Memorial Day to Labor Day, Monday through Saturday at other times, every 15 minutes between 9:30 A.M. and 4:30 P.M.; $8; children under six not admitted.

New York Stock Exchange. 20 Broad Street; Tel: 656-5168. A bird's-eye view of the trading floor; open Monday through Friday, 9:20 A.M. to 4:00 P.M.; tickets are distributed from 9:00 A.M. until they run out; free.

92nd Street Y tours. 1395 Lexington Avenue; Tel: 415-5600. Knowledgeable experts lead tours of historic and architecturally interesting neighborhoods around the city; from $12 to $20.

Petrel. A boat tour that leaves from Battery Park at the southern tip of Manhattan; Tel: 825-1976. Sailings across New York Harbor on a 70-foot yawl; daytime and evening sailings from 45 minutes to two hours long, seven days a week, April through October only; from $8 to $20.

United Nations. First Avenue and 46th Street; Tel: 963-7713. Seven-days-a-week, one-hour-long tours leave every half hour from 9:15 A.M. to 4:45 P.M. and include the General Assembly and Secretariat; $6.50 adults, $4.50 students and seniors, $3.50 children; children under five not allowed on tours. For tours in languages other than English, call 963-7539 the day you wish to visit the United Nations.

Taking Photographs

New York is a photographer's paradise: There's no end of subject matter, and—to serve the world's largest concentration of professional photographers—there are many suppliers of film and equipment (see our Photography and Filmmaking chapter). Please observe rules of etiquette: You are not allowed to take photos during most performances, or in many art galleries, churches, synagogues, and other places.

Local Time

New York observes Eastern Standard Time from November through April and Eastern Daylight Time from the end of April through October. The city is three hours ahead of the West Coast, five hours behind London, six hours behind Paris, and 15 hours behind Sydney. For the exact time of day, Tel: 976-1616.

Electric Current

Despite its dissimilarity to the rest of America, New York uses standard North American current: 110 volts, 60 cycles. Many of the better hotels have installed special wiring to accommodate European appliances.

Currency

Major foreign money exchanges in New York include: American Express (150 East 42nd Street, between Lexington and Third avenues), Tel: 687-3700 or 640-2000; Chequepoint (551 Madison Avenue, at 55th Street), Tel: 980-6443; Thomas Cook International (630 Fifth Avenue, between 50th and 51st streets), Tel: 757-6915. All have other outlets throughout the city; call for locations nearest you.

Foreigners using this guidebook will probably find a branch of their major national bank in Manhattan. To name but a few: Bank of Ireland, 640 Fifth Avenue, Tel: 397-1700; Canadian Imperial Bank, 425 Lexington Avenue, Tel: 856-4000; Australia and New Zealand Bank, 120 Wall Street, Tel: 820-9800. Check the Manhattan telephone directory for others.

Most larger shops and restaurants accept credit cards, especially VISA, MasterCard, and American Express. To report lost or stolen credit cards, make balance inquiries, or for other matters, call: American Express, Tel: (800) 528-4800; Discover, Tel: (800) 347-2683; MasterCard, Tel: (800) 826-2181; check with the bank that issues your Diner's Club or VISA card for service numbers. Traveller's checks are also widely accepted, although a surprising number of establishments are reluctant to take them. To report lost or stolen traveller's checks, contact: American Express, Tel: (800) 221-7282; Cook and MasterCard, Tel: (800) 223-7373; or VISA, Tel: (800) 227-6811. Bankcard holders who subscribe to the Cirrus Network (instant cash) will find outlets throughout Manhattan; Tel: (800) 424-7787.

Telephoning

New York is divided into two area codes: 212 for Manhattan, 718 for the Bronx, Brooklyn, Queens, and Staten Island. Subterranean New York is crisscrossed by 20 million miles of telephone wire, and there are almost 6 million telephones in the city. (The most used set is a public phone at Penn Station on the Long Island Railroad concourse; it is used 230 times a day.) There are other public telephones on almost every corner in Manhattan, although when you try to use one you will observe a peculiarly New York phenomenon: They are almost always in use. Many telephones throughout the city (especially those at railway terminals and airports) accept credit cards.

When calling long distance in the United States, you must dial "1" before dialing the area code; to make international calls, dial "011," then the country code, then the city code (omitting the zero in the city code). For operator assistance, dial "0"; for local directory assistance, dial "411"; for directory assistance outside the local area code, dial "1," then the area code of the number you are seeking, then 555-1212; to obtain a toll-free, "800" number, Tel: 1-800-555-1212.

Post Offices

In general, post offices are open from 8:00 A.M. to 6:00 P.M. weekdays, and some from 8:00 A.M. to 1:00 P.M. Saturdays, with many exceptions. The main city post office, on Eighth Avenue at 33rd Street, is open 24 hours a day, seven days a week. Tel: 967-8585 for information, including branch hours. Sample postage: one-ounce letter within the United States, 29 cents; half-ounce letter (airmail) to Europe and Australia, 50 cents; one-ounce letter to Europe and Australia, 95 cents; one-ounce letter to Canada, 45 cents; airmail postcard to Europe and Australia, 40 cents; postcard to Canada, 30 cents.

If you're coming to the Big Apple but don't have an address, you can pick up mail (upon presentation of a passport, driver's license, or other identification) addressed to you care of: General Delivery, General Post Office, 421 Eighth Avenue, New York, NY 10001.

Tipping

As a rule of thumb, tip 15 percent in restaurants (a handy way to determine the tip is to double the 8¼ percent sales tax amount shown on the bill); tip cabdrivers 20 percent of the fare; give $1 to doormen who help you carry packages or procure a cab for you; tip delivery people $1 or $2, more for heavy bundles; leave $1 or $2 a day for helpful chambermaids; give a helpful maître d' $5 or so. You're under no obligation to tip anyone who is rude or decidedly unhelpful.

Business Hours and Holidays

Many shops in New York do not open until 10:00 or 10:30 A.M. and close at 6:00 or 6:30 P.M. There are a great number of exceptions. In neighborhoods outside of Midtown, many businesses open at noon and don't close until 8:00 or 9:00 P.M., so they can cater to residents on their way home from work. (Many New Yorkers don't report to their jobs until 9:30 or 10:00 A.M., often even later, and work until 6:00 or 7:00 P.M., often even later; a nine-to-fiver is the exception here.) Most major department stores are open, in addition to regular daytime hours, on Monday, Thursday, and Friday evenings and on Sunday afternoons. Many Jewish-owned businesses close on Friday afternoons and Saturdays for the Sabbath and open on Sundays.

Most major museums are open Sundays but closed Mondays; notable exceptions are the Museum of Modern Art, which is open Mondays but closed Wednesdays, and The Guggenheim Museum, which is open Mondays but closed Thursdays. Most are open at least one evening a week, usually Tuesdays. The Metropolitan Museum of Art and the Guggenheim Museum have the good grace to keep late hours on Fridays and Saturdays.

Restaurants tend to serve lunch from noon to 2:30 or 3:00 P.M. (1:00 is the most popular time for a lunch date) and dinner from 6:30 or 7:00 to 10:30 and later (Manhattanites eat late, often at 9:00 or later). In the theater district, many restaurants offer special before- and after-theater menus.

Most bars and clubs stay open until 2:00 A.M. and many as late as 4:00, the latest they are allowed to serve liquor. A New York Sunday brunch, a popular meal in the city, rarely begins before noon, as establishments are not allowed to serve liquor on Sundays until then.

Many New York businesses are always open, even on such traditional holidays as Christmas and New Year's Day. However, holidays that are commonly observed in New York include: New Year's Day; Martin Luther King's birthday, January 15, observed the third Monday of the month; Lincoln's birthday, February 12; Washington's birthday, February 22, observed on the closest Monday; St. Patrick's Day, March 17, noted by the presence of hordes of inebriated suburban teenagers who descend upon the city to watch the parade on Fifth Avenue and vomit on city sidewalks; Easter Sunday; the first day of Passover; Memorial Day, May 30, observed on the closest Monday; Fourth of July; Labor Day, September 2, observed on the first Monday of September; the first day of Rosh Hashanah; Yom Kippur; Columbus Day; Veterans Day, November 11; Thanksgiving Day, the fourth Thursday of November; the first day of Hanukkah; Christmas Day.

Street Fairs and Festivals
New York graces its concrete canyons with an inordinate number of parades and street fairs, where you can expect to find booths selling exotic foods and goods. Some of the major ones are: Chinese New Year, Chinatown, January or February (an explosive event); St. Patrick's Day Parade, Fifth Avenue, March 17; Greek Independence Day Parade, Park Avenue, late March; Easter Parade (not an official parade; rather, New Yorkers parade up and down Fifth Avenue in finery and costumes), Easter Sunday.

Ninth Avenue International Festival (meaning *food*), mid-May, Ninth Avenue around the 40s; Amsterdam Avenue Festival, late May, Amsterdam from 77th to 90th streets; Memorial Day Parade, Memorial Day, very late May, from 72nd Street and Broadway to Soldiers and Sailors Monument at 89th Street and Riverside Drive; Feast of St. Anthony, ten days in early June, Sullivan Street, SoHo (a most nonholy mix of games of chance and carnival attractions); Second Avenue Festival, early June, 68th to 96th streets; 52nd Street Fair, mid-June, Park Avenue to Sixth Avenue; Lexington Avenue Festival, late June, 23rd to 34th streets.

Fourth of July, Macy's Fireworks, East River or Hudson River (varies); Third Avenue Summerfest, mid-August, 42nd to 57th streets; Third Avenue Fair, mid-September, 14th to 34th streets; Columbus Avenue Festival, mid-September, 66th to 86th streets; Feast of San Gennaro, ten days in mid-September (like the feast of St. Anthony, but bigger), Mulberry Street in Little Italy.

Columbus Day Parade, on or around October 12, Fifth Avenue; Halloween Parade, October 31, Greenwich Village (very strange costumes); Veterans Day Parade, November 11, Fifth Avenue; Macy's Thanksgiving Day Parade, Thanksgiving Day, fourth Thursday in November, Central Park West from 77th Street to Columbus Circle, Broadway from Columbus Circle to Herald Square.

Sports

New Yorkers are as ardent about sports—spectator and participatory—as they are about other pursuits.

Baseball. The **Mets** play at Shea Stadium, Roosevelt Avenue and 126th Street, Flushing, Queens, reached by the number 7 subway; Tel: (718) 507-8499. The **Yankees** play at Yankee Stadium, West 161st Avenue and River Avenue in the Bronx, reached by the number 4 IRT subway from the East Side of Manhattan, and the CC and D subways from the West Side of Manhattan; Tel: (718) 293-6000.

Basketball. The **Knickerbockers** (the Knicks) play at Madison Square Garden, West 33rd Street and Seventh Avenue, Tel: 465-6741. The **Nets** play at the Byrne Meadowlands Sports Complex, exit 16 off the New Jersey Turnpike, East Rutherford, New Jersey, Tel: (201) 935-3900; can be reached via New Jersey Transit, Tel: (201) 762-5100.

Football. The **Giants** and the **Jets** also play at the Meadowlands (see Basketball, above).

Hockey. The **Rangers** play at Madison Square Garden (see Basketball, above). The **Devils** play at the Meadowlands (see Basketball, above). The **Islanders** play at Nassau Coliseum, Hempstead Turnpike, Uniondale, Long Island, Tel: (516) 794-9300; can be reached via the Long Island Railroad with connections to local transportation, Tel: (718) 217-5477.

Horse racing. **Aqueduct Raceway,** Rockaway Boulevard at 110th Street, Ozone Park, Queens, Tel: (718) 641-4700. **Belmont Raceway,** Hempstead Turnpike and Plainfield Avenue, Elmont, Long Island, Tel: (718) 641-4700; can be reached by the Long Island Railroad, Tel: (718) 217-5477. **Meadowlands Racetrack,** in the Meadowlands (see Basketball, above), Tel: (201) 935-8500.

The easiest way to get some exercise yourself in the city

is to walk, or to join thousands of New Yorkers on their run around the "loop," as the six-mile road following the perimeter of Central Park is known, or on the 1.5-mile path around the reservoir in Central Park. For information on bicycling, ice skating, roller skating, row boating, and playing tennis in the park, see also our Central Park chapter. Participatory sports in the city:

Bicycling. Rentals available at Loeb Boathouse in Central Park, Tel: 861-4137.

Billiards. Amsterdam Billiard Club, 344 Amsterdam Avenue (at West 76th Street), Tel: 496-8180. The **Billiard Club,** 220 West 19th Street (between Seventh and Eighth avenues), Tel: 206-7665.

Bowling. Bowlmor Lanes, 110 University Place (in the Village), Tel: 255-8188.

Handball/Racquetball. 92nd Street YM-YWHA, 1395 Lexington Avenue (on the Upper East Side), Tel: 427-6000.

Horseback Riding. Claremont Riding Academy, 175 West 89th Street (near the four and a half miles of bridle paths in Central Park), Tel: 724-5100.

Ice Skating. Rockefeller Center Skating Rink, Tel: 757-5730; **Sky Rink,** 450 West 33rd Street (near Penn Station), Tel: 695-6555; **Wollman Memorial Rink,** Central Park near the 59th Street entrance, Tel: 517-4800.

Miniature Golf. Wollman Memorial Rink (summer only; see Ice Skating, above).

Roller Skating. Village Skating, 15 Waverly Place (in Greenwich Village), Tel: 677-9690; **Wollman Memorial Rink** (summer only; see Ice Skating, above).

Tennis. The **USTA National Tennis Center** (where the U.S. Open is held), Flushing Meadows, Queens, Tel: (718) 592-8000 (28 outdoor courts, 9 indoor courts available by the hour). For information on tennis courts in Central Park and other city courts, Tel: 280-0205.

The Movies

New Yorkers are movie buffs. To serve their demanding and catholic tastes, first runs, foreign films, and revivals show late into the night at theaters all over town. For popular first runs, show up at least an hour in advance to buy tickets.

Listings run in the daily press, as well as in *New York* magazine, *The New Yorker,* and the *Village Voice.* The Friday *New York Times* carries reviews by Vincent Canby and Janet Maslin. *The New Yorker* runs its famous capsule synopses, and newly appointed critics, among them Terrence Rafferty, are ably holding up the magazine's high standards; in *New York,* David Denby reviews and the listings are extensive. Here are but a few of the major theaters (our categories are not exclusive; a house that usually shows first-runs, for example, may often also show foreign films or revivals):

First-run Houses: Cineplex Odeon Chelsea Cinemas, 260 West 23rd Street, Tel: 691-4744; Murray Hill Cinemas, 160 East 34th Street, Tel: 689-6548; United Artists Criterion Center, Broadway at 44th Street, Tel: 354-0900; Baronet and Coronet, Third Avenue at 59th Street, Tel: 355-1663; Loews 84th Street Sixplex, Broadway at 84th Street, Tel: 877-3600.

Foreign and Art Films: Angelika Film Center, 18 West Houston Street, Tel: 995-2000; Film Forum, 209 West Houston Street, Tel: 727-8110; Carnegie Hall Cinemas, Seventh Avenue between 56th and 57th streets, Tel: 265-2520; Lincoln Plaza, Broadway at 63rd Street, Tel: 757-2280.

Revival Houses: Film Forum 2, 209 West Houston Street, Tel: 727-8110; Theatre 80 St. Mark's, 80 St. Mark's Place, Tel: 254-7400.

Foreign and revival films are also shown regularly at the Joseph Papp Public Theater, 425 Lafayette Street, Tel: 598-7171; the Museum of Modern Art, 11 West 53rd Street, Tel: 708-9500; and the Metropolitan Museum of Art, Fifth Avenue at 82nd Street, Tel: 570-3791. The Film Society of Lincoln Center shows an amazingly varied program of foreign films, revivals, and not-yet-released films at its Walter Reade Theater, and in September and October hosts the New York Film Festival, with dozens of entries from all over the world, at Alice Tully Hall, Broadway at 65th Street, Tel: 875-5610; tickets for the festival sell out well in advance, but you can often buy a returned ticket at the door or from ticket holders who sell extras just outside the theater.

Other Sources of Information

The New York Convention and Visitors Bureau distributes a wealth of information about New York from its central office at Columbus Circle; Tel: 397-8222. The bureau also has information booths at 43rd Street and Broadway, 47th Street and Broadway, and at the World Trade Center, in the south tower mezzanine.

For up-to-date information on theater, art exhibitions,

movies, and other events, consult weekly editions of *The New Yorker, New York* magazine, or the *Village Voice,* as well as daily newspapers, especially the Weekend section of the Friday *New York Times.* A good radio station to tune into while you're in New York is WNYC (AM 830; FM 94), which provides a lively mix of classical music, jazz, and chatter about goings on around town.

Getting Outside the City

New York is surrounded by some of the most pleasant countryside in America (see our Day Trips section), and you don't have to rent a car to see it. The city is served by an extensive network of public transportation. Some numbers of note: Amtrak, Tel: 582-6875 or (800) 872-7245; Metro-North's Hudson, Harlem, New Haven, and other rail lines to Connecticut and other points north of the city, Tel: 532-4900; New Jersey Transit (buses and trains), Tel: (201) 762-5100; Long Island Railroad, Tel: (718) 217-5477; Hampton Jitney (buses to eastern Long Island), Tel: 936-0440; bus service departing from Port Authority terminal at 42nd Street and Eighth Avenue, Tel: 564-8484.

Renting a Car

Most major rental-car agencies have outlets in Manhattan. Like many other goods and services, rental cars cost more in Manhattan than they do elsewhere, and you are likely to get a better rate if you pick up a car at one of the airports. Check with your airline for fly-drive packages. Also remember that many New Yorkers do not own cars, so rental cars are often booked weeks in advance, especially on summer weekends. Some telephone numbers: Alamo, (800) 327-9633 (rents out of Newark Airport only); Avis, (800) 331-1212; Budget, (800) 527-0700; Dollar, (800) 421-6868; Hertz, (800) 654-3131; National, (800) 328-4567; Thrifty, (800) 331-4200 (rents out of La Guardia Airport, only).

—*Stephen Brewer*

BIBLIOGRAPHY

The best single source for books on New York is the **New York Bound Bookshop**, in the lobby of 50 Rockefeller Center.

History and Biography

Biographies are listed alphabetically by subject; other works are arranged alphabetically by author.

JERVIS ANDERSON. *This Was Harlem: A Cultural Portrait, 1900–1950* (1982). Jazz, politics, and the other elements that have made Harlem a bastion of black culture.

PATRICIA BOSWORTH. *Diane Arbus* (1984). An insightful look at the life and times of this native New Yorker best known for her stark photographs of freaks.

LOUIS AUCHINCLOSS, EDITOR. *The Horne and Strong Diaries of Old Manhattan* (1989). The day-to-day journals of early New Yorkers Philip Horne (1780–1851) and George Templeton Strong (1820–1875) provide a personal, fresh view of the city.

THOMAS BENDER. *New York Intellect: A History of Intellectual Life in New York City, from 1750 to the Beginning of Our Time* (1988). A veritable Who's Who that's great reading, too.

STEPHEN BIRMINGHAM. *Life at the Dakota, New York's Most Unusual Address* (1979). A highly readable blend of a hundred years' worth of architecture, social history, and gossip.

STEPHEN GARMEY. *Gramercy Park* (1984). An illustrated history of a New York neighborhood, from the time of Peter Stuyvesant to the present.

GRACE GLUECK AND PAUL GARDNER. *Brooklyn: People and Places, Past and Present* (1992). A loving tribute to this colorful and proud borough.

JOHN STEELE GORDON. *The Scarlet Woman of Wall Street* (1988). Good storytelling about mid-19th-century New York and the Erie Railway wars.

HELEN HANFF. *Apple of My Eye* (1977). The New Yorker who charmed us with her letters to a London book dealer in *84, Charing Cross Road* lovingly evokes her native city.

HELEN HAYES AND ANITA LOOS. *Twice Over Lightly* (1972). A thoroughly charming and sprightly account of how the "first lady of the American stage" and the author of *Gentlemen Prefer Blondes* spent a summer exploring unlikely aspects of New York City.

IRVING HOWE. *World of Our Fathers: The Journey of the East European Jews to America and the Life They Found and Made* (1976). Fascinating chronicle of arrival and assimilation; lavishly illustrated.

ELIA KAZAN. *A Life* (1988). An encyclopedic account of a long career, much of it spent on the New York stage.

ALFRED KAZIN. *New York Jew* (1978). Coming of age in the political and literary circles of mid-century New York.

JEFF KISSELOF. *You Must Remember This* (1989). New York from 1890 through World War II, as recounted by New Yorkers of the time.

JOHN A. KOUWENHOVEN. *The Columbia Historical Portrait of New York* (1972). A social and physical history of New York; richly illustrated and fact filled.

MABEL DODGE LUHAN. *Movers and Shakers* (1936). An eye-witness account of Greenwich Village before World War I.

DAVID MCCULLOUGH. *The Great Bridge* (1972). A thorough and lively account of the construction of the Brooklyn Bridge.

ISAAC METZKER, EDITOR. *A Bintel Brief* (1971). Excerpts from the Jewish daily *Forward* evoke the turn of the century, when New York was the capital of Yiddish America.

ARTHUR MILLER. *Timebends* (1988). An autobiographical journey from Harlem to Brooklyn to the New York stage.

JAN MORRIS. *The Great Port: A Passage through New York* (1969). A chronicle of New York as a hub of transportation.

ROBERT A. CARO. *The Power Broker: Robert Moses and the Fall of New York* (1975). The highly acclaimed biography of the man who built much of the city we see today.

JERRY E. PATTERSON. *The City of New York: A History Illustrated from the Collections of The Museum of the City of New York* (1978). History at its most entertaining and attractive.

A. SCOTT BERG. *Max Perkins, Editor of Genius* (1978) and *Editor to Author: The Letters of Maxwell E. Perkins* (1987). A superb biography and selected letters document the career of New York's most famous editor, the man who published Hemingway, Fitzgerald, Wolfe, and most of the other great American writers of the 20th century.

ANDREW PORTER. *A Musical Season; Music of Three Seasons: 1974–1977; Music of Three More Seasons: 1977–1980; Musical Events, A Chronicle: 1980–1983.* These collected reviews and essays by the music critic of *The New Yorker* give a magnificent overview of the city's recent musical history.

JACOB RIIS. *How the Other Half Lives: Studies among the Tenements of New York* (1890). These sociological studies of poverty in turn-of-the-century New York instigated massive reforms in housing and social programs.

NED ROREM. *The Paris & New York Diaries* (1983). A composer's journal of his New York experiences during the 1950s and 1960s.

RON ROSENBAUM. *Manhattan Passions: True Tales of Power, Wealth, and Excess* (1987). Fascinating portraits of the rich and famous: Malcolm Forbes, Governor Mario Cuomo, gossip columnist Liz Smith, et al.

JOSEPH C. GOULDEN. *Fit to Print: A. M. Rosenthal and His Times* (1988). How the executive director of *The New York Times* rose to power; based on 317 interviews.

JAMES THURBER. *The Years with Ross* (1959). A memoir of Harold Ross, founding editor of *The New Yorker,* to which Thurber contributed several volumes' worth of his sardonic essays and short stories.

STEVEN RUTTENBAUM. *Mansions in the Clouds* (1986). The life of architect Emery Roth (1871–1948) and the evolution of the New York skyscraper apartment house.

PETER SALWEN. *Upper West Side Story: A History and Guide* (1989). Thorough and lively evocation of a New York neighborhood.

LUC SANTE. *Low Life: Lures and Snares of Old New York.* This highly enjoyable chronicle of the city's seamy history makes today's Big Apple look pretty wholesome.

JAMES ATLAS. *Delmore Schwartz: The Life of an American Poet* (1977). A superb portrait of one of the century's finest poets and the New York world in which he lived.

JEAN STEIN. *Edie, An American Biography* (1982). Blue-blooded actress-model/Warhol groupie Edie Sedgwick caught up in the social whirl of 1960s New York.

ARNOLD SHAW. *Fifty-Second Street: The Street of Jazz* (1977). Fifty-second Street during its mid-century heyday as a jazz center.

KATE SIMON. *Fifth Avenue: A Very Special History* (1979). A very readable history of the city's poshest avenue. *Bronx Primitive* (1983) chronicles the writer's beginnings in a less glamorous part of town.

EILEEN SIMPSON. *Poets in Their Youth* (1982). Sympathetic portraits of John Berryman, Robert Lowell, Delmore Schwartz, and their like, poets who lived and worked in New York in the 1940s.

GAY TALESE. *The Kingdom and the Power* (1986). A foray into the workings of *The New York Times*.

JAMES TRAGER. *West of Fifth: The Rise and Fall of Manhattan's West Side* (1984). Social and architectural history of a New York neighborhood. His *Park Avenue: Street of Dreams* (1990) goes beyond the obvious glitter and covers everything from the *barrio* under the El at the north end of the avenue to less-than-posh Fourth Avenue at its lower end.

JEROME TUCCILLE. *Trump* (1985). All you ever wanted to know about New York's biggest ego.

FLORENCE TURNER. *At the Chelsea* (1987). An affectionate history of the shabby but famous 23rd Street hotel, a favorite among New York's literati.

ELLIOT WILLENSKY. *When Brooklyn Was the World: 1920–1957* (1986). Text and photographs evoke Brooklyn in its golden days.

Literature

WOODY ALLEN. *Without Feathers* (1976), *Getting Even* (1977), *Side Effects* (1980). Humor that exposes New York as the hotbed of neurosis and anxiety it really is.

JAMES BALDWIN. *Go Tell It on the Mountain* (1953) and *Just Above My Head* (1979). Both novels are set in the author's native Harlem.

TRUMAN CAPOTE. *Breakfast at Tiffany's* (1958). The Manhattan adventures of stylish, free-spirited Holly Golightly. *Answered Prayers* (unfinished at the author's death in 1984, published posthumously in 1987) is populated by thinly disguised versions of real-life, upper-crust New Yorkers (who aren't at all happy with their portrayals).

BARBARA COHEN, SEYMOUR CHWAST, AND STEVEN HELLER. *New York Observed: Artists and Writers Look at the City* (1987). Selections from 96 writers and 51 artists.

NIK COHN. *The Heart of the World* (1992). Fictive vignettes populated by New York flâneurs are set on and around Broadway as it cuts its swath through the city.

STEPHEN CRANE. *Maggie: A Girl of the Streets* (1893). Realist fiction about life in the slums of lower Manhattan at the end of the last century.

E. L. DOCTOROW. *Ragtime* (1975). New York in the first half of this century, as experienced by a Jewish immigrant, a suburbanite WASP, and a black. *World's Fair* (1986) revolves around a middle-class New York City Jewish family in the 1930s.

JOHN DOS PASSOS. *Manhattan Transfer* (1925). Hundreds of sketches of characters and events in New York between the two world wars.

JACK FINNEY. *Time and Again* (1970). A man shuttles back and forth between the New York of today and of the 1880s, providing an exceptionally detailed and vivid account of the city in the late 19th century.

F. SCOTT FITZGERALD. *The Great Gatsby* (1925). New York before the Great Depression.

FEDERICO GARCIA LORCA. *Poet in New York* (1955). Early alienation poetry from the Spanish surrealist poet and dramatist.

WASHINGTON IRVING. *History of New York from the Beginning of the World to the End of the Dutch Dynasty* (1809). Satirical, fact-filled account of Dutch New York, as presented by the fictional Diedrich Knickerbocker.

HENRY JAMES. *Washington Square* (1881). Greenwich Village in the middle of the last century.

TAMA JANOWITZ. *Slaves of New York* (1986). These slick tales of offbeat New Yorkers do provide a glimpse into contemporary New York—but prove just how vapid contemporary writing about New York can be.

BEL KAUFMAN. *Up the Down Staircase* (1965). Trials and triumphs of a Manhattan schoolteacher.

FRAN LIEBOWITZ. *Metropolitan Life* (1978). Humorous essays on life in the country's largest metropolis.

MARY MCCARTHY. *The Group* (1963). Vassar graduates descend on New York in the 1950s.

JAY MCINERNEY. *Bright Lights, Big City* (1984). Glib, empty novel about glib, empty young New Yorkers, yet it does picture a certain New York. More of the same surfaces in *The Story of My Life* (1988).

BERNARD MALAMUD. *The Tenants* (1971). Anguish of a lonely immigrant in an abandoned New York tenement.

MIKE MARQUESEE AND BILL HARRIS. *New York, An Anthology* (1985). In poetry and prose, how writers feel about New York.

JOSEPH MITCHELL. *Up in the Old Hotel and Other Stories* (1992). These rich stories, written for the *New Yorker* in the 1930s, resound with the language and impressions of gypsies, waterfront workers, and other denizens of a long-lost New York.

HOWARD MOSS, EDITOR. *New York Poems* (1980). Poets inspired by a common subject.

CLIFFORD ODETS. *Awake and Sing* (1935). One of the first plays by the master playwright who shaped the New York stage chronicles the life of a Jewish family in the Bronx.

CONRAD OSBORNE. *O Paradiso* (1988). An outrageous novel of New York's opera crazies.

GRACE PALEY. *Enormous Changes at the Last Minute* (1975). Short stories, many of them set in Greenwich Village.

DOROTHY PARKER. *The Portable Dorothy Parker* (1944). Poems, stories, and reviews by this renowned denizen of the Algonquin Round Table.

JOHN RECHY. *City of Night* (1952). Fictionalized account of New York's homosexual underworld.

HENRY ROTH. *Call It Sleep* (1964). A novel centered on the family life of Jewish immigrants.

DAMON RUNYON. *The Bloodhounds of Broadway and Other Stories* (reprinted, 1981). The author of *Guys and Dolls* explores the Broadway underworld.

J. D. SALINGER. *Catcher in the Rye* (1945). A modern classic in which Holden Caulfield, upper-middle-class son of New York, comes of age.

HUBERT SELBY, JR. *Last Exit to Brooklyn* (1964). A seething portrait of low life in a Brooklyn neighborhood.

BETTY SMITH. *A Tree Grows in Brooklyn* (1943). A sentimental novel about an Irish girl growing up in Brooklyn.

WILLIAM STYRON. *Sophie's Choice* (1976). An evocative tale of a Holocaust survivor in Brooklyn after the war.

CHUCK WACHTEL. *Joe the Engineer* (1983). A novel of working-class life in Queens.

EDWARD LEWIS WALLANT. *The Pawnbroker* (1961). Tribulations of a concentration-camp survivor in Harlem.

NATHANAEL WEST. *Miss Lonelyhearts* (1933). Economic and emotional depression as it affects an advice-to-the-lovelorn columnist in 1930s New York.

EDITH WHARTON. *The Age of Innocence* (1920). Pulitzer Prize–winning novel of upper-class life in late-19th-century New York.

E. B. WHITE. *Essays of E. B. White* (1977). A superb collection of works by this contributor to *The New Yorker,* including "Here Is New York" (1949), perhaps the best lines ever written about the city.

THOMAS WOLFE. *Of Time and the River: A Legend of Man's Hunger in His Youth* (1935). Despairing novel of New York during the Great Depression; sequel to *Look Homeward, Angel.*

TOM WOLFE. *Bonfire of the Vanities* (1987). This highly stylized novel draws on the tumultuous social realities of New York in the 1980s.

HERMAN WOUK. *Marjorie Morningstar* (1955). Social aspirations of a middle-class Jewish family on the Upper West Side.

Architecture and Photography

BERENICE ABBOTT. *New York in the Thirties* (1939). Photographs by this master who made it her business to chronicle the entire city.

ANDREW ALPERN. *New York's Fabulous Luxury Apartments* (1975). Floor plans of grand dwellings in the city's finest buildings.

MARY BLACK. *Old New York in Early Photographs: 196 Prints, 1853–1901, from the Collection of The New-York Historical Society* (1973). The best from the society's collection.

CHRISTIAN BLANCHET AND BERTRAND DARD. *Statue of Liberty: The First Hundred Years* (1985). A rich text (translated from the French) and a treasure trove of historic illustrations, many from European collections; the best book ever on the much-publicized Lady of the Harbor.

BENJAMIN BLOM. *New York: Photographs, 1850–1950* (1982). A fine collection on New York people and buildings.

JOSEPH BYRON. *Photographs of New York Interiors at the Turn of the Century* (1976) and *New York Life at the Turn of the Century in Photographs* (1985). Exquisite photographs from the Byron Collection of the Museum of the City of New York.

BARBARALEE DIAMONSTEIN. *The Landmarks of New York* (1988). Thorough documentation of historic New York, by one of the city's most visible socialites.

LORRAINE B. DIEHL. *The Late, Great Pennsylvania Station* (1985). The construction, decay, and tragic demolition in 1963 of New York's greatest landmark, one of the "few buildings vast enough to hold the sound of time" (Thomas Wolfe).

CARIN DRECHSLER-MARX AND RICHARD F. SHEPARD. *Broadway* (1988). The 293 blocks from the Battery to the Bronx along this famous street are discussed in terms of people, culture, and history.

DAVID DUNLAP. *On Broadway: A Journey Uptown over Time* (1990). A block-by-block, stone-by-stone tour of the architecture that graces the city's main street; a bit esoteric for anyone other than an architecture aficionado.

ANDREAS FEININGER. *New York in the Forties* (1983). One of the greatest photographers of his age takes on a willing subject.

MARGOT GAYLE AND EDMUND V. GILLON, JR. *Cast Iron Architecture in New York* (1974). A photographic record of the style that flourished in New York at the end of the last century.

EDMUND V. GILLON, JR., AND HENRY HOPE REED. *Beaux Arts Architecture in New York: A Photographic Guide* (1988). A luxurious look at some of the city's most stylish buildings.

PAUL GOLDBERGER. *The City Observed* (1979). The architecture critic of *The New York Times* comments on the major buildings of Manhattan.

ADA LOUISE HUXTABLE. *Classic New York: Georgian Gentility to Greek Elegance* (1964). Remarkable observations from the former architecture critic of *The New York Times*.

CHARLES LOCKWOOD. *Bricks and Brownstones* (1972). A thorough history of the New York row house.

DONALD A. MACKAY. *The Building of Manhattan* (1987). Masterful drawings and evocative text show how telephone lines were laid, skyscrapers erected, and Manhattan Island otherwise conquered by a city of builders.

DONALD MARTIN REYNOLDS. *The Architecture of New York City* (1984). History and commentary on 80 major buildings and monuments.

REBECCA REED SHANOR. *The City That Never Was: Two Hundred Years of Fantastic and Fascinating Plans That Might Have Changed the Face of New York City* (1988). A landing strip in Central Park and other schemes that never made it off the drawing board; well written and illustrated.

NATHAN SILVER. *Lost New York* (1967). A heavily illustrated account of New York's lost architectural landscape.

ROBERT A. M. STERN, GREGORY GILMARTIN, AND THOMAS MELLINS. *New York 1900* (1984). Monumental overview of the city's Beaux Arts architecture. Followed by *New York 1930* (1987), focusing on architecture between the wars.

J.-C. SUARES. *Manhattan* (1981). This expensive and arty photo collection is the best of our time.

JOHN TAURANAC. *Essential New York* (1979). Short, incisive writeups on Manhattan's major buildings, parks, and bridges.

JOHN TAURANAC AND CHRISTOPHER LITTLE. *Elegant New York: The Builders and the Buildings, 1895–1915* (1985). Ninety great residential and corporate palaces.

EDWARD B. WATSON AND EDMUND V. GILLON, JR. *New York Then and Now* (1976). Old and new photographs of the same sites show how the city has and hasn't changed.

NORVAL WHITE AND ELLIOT WILLENSKY. *AIA Guide to New York City* (1988). An authoritative, building-by-building guide to New York, sanctioned by the American Institute of Architects; recently and thoroughly revised.

NORVAL WHITE AND ELLIOT WILLENSKY. *New York: A Physical History* (1988). A unique cultural, economic, and technical account of man-made New York.

Unusual Guidebooks

RICHARD ALLEMAN. *The Movie Lover's Guide to New York: The Ultimate Guide to Movie New York* (1988). Movie stars' homes, film locations, and the like; exhaustive.

JUDITH H. BROWNING. *New York City Yesterday and Today: 30 Timeless Walking Adventures* (1990). Detailed forays into almost every corner of the city, with maps, illustrations, and knowledgeable commentary.

JEROME CHARYN. *Metropolis: New York as Myth, Marketplace, and Magical Land* (1986). A tour of Manhattan people, places, and legends.

JUDI CULBERTSON AND TOM RANDALL. *Permanent New Yorkers: A Biographical Guide to the Cemeteries of New York* (1987). New York cemeteries as museums.

SUSAN EDMISTON AND LINDA D. CIRINO. *Literary New York: A History and Guide* (1976). This geographic tour tells who wrote what where.

MARGOT GAYLE AND MICHELE COHEN. *The Art Commission and the Municipal Art Society Guide to Manhattan's Outdoor Sculpture* (1988). Expert commentary.

JOYCE GOLD. *From Windmills to the World Trade Center: A Walking Guide to Lower Manhattan History* (1988). Personal and anecdotal guide to lower Manhattan.

HARMON GOLDSTONE AND MARTHA DALRYMPLE. *History Preserved: A Guide to New York City Landmarks and Historic Districts* (1974). Well-guided tours for history buffs.

JOSEPH LEDERER AND ARLEY BONDARIN. *All Around the Town: A Walking Guide to Outdoor Sculpture in New York City* (1975). Comprehensive and fun.

JAMES D. MCCABE, JR. *New York by Gaslight* (1882). A Southern journalist's guide to the city; now in a reprint.

HENRY MOSCOW. *The Book of New York Firsts: Unusual, Arcane, and Fascinating Facts in the Life of New York City* (1982). The first balloon ascent over Manhattan and other interesting New York facts. Moscow's *The Street Book: An Encyclopedia of Manhattan's Street Names and Their Origins* (1978) provides more fun New York history.

New York City Guide (Reprint, 1982). The original, 1939 WPA guide to New York. Insightful, though dated.

The New York Times World of New York: An Uncommon Guide to the City of Fantasies (1985). Essays by Vincent Canby, Nora Ephron, David Frost, and their famous like; often so clever they miss the point but good reading all the same.

MARY PEACOCK, EDITOR. *Village Voice Guide to Manhattan's Shopping Neighborhoods* (1987). With contributions by this guidebook's shopping maven, Lynn Yaeger.

KATE SIMON. *New York: Places and Pleasures* (1971). The eloquent travel writer directs her innate charm to her home city.

Stubs: The Seating Plan Guide (1989). With plans of theaters, auditoriums, and other public spaces, invaluable help in selecting the perfect seat.

Books about New York for Children

SARAH LOVETT, WITH ILLUSTRATIONS BY SALLY BLACKMORE. *Kidding Around New York City: A Young Person's Guide to the City* (1989). Hundreds of ways to show young sightseers the town.

ELAINE L. KONIGSBURG. *From the Mixed-up Files of Mrs. Basil E. Frankweiler* (1967). A girl and her brother take up temporary residence in the Metropolitan Museum of Art.

LYNN SCHNURNBERGER. *Kids Love New York!: The A–Z Resource Book* (1984). Some 800 suggestions on how to keep the little ones happy in the Big Apple.

GEORGE SELDEN, WITH ILLUSTRATIONS BY FAITH WILLIAMS. *Cricket in Times Square* (1960). A wandering cricket finds bed, board, and friendship at a Times Square newsstand.

HILDEGARDE H. SWIFT AND LYNDE WARD. *The Little Red Lighthouse and the Great Gray Bridge* (1942). New York kids' favorite fable of a landmark that's still here, in the Hudson River at 181st Street.

KAY THOMPSON, WITH ILLUSTRATIONS BY HILARY KNIGHT. *Eloise* (1955). The story of a little girl who lives a charmed life at the Plaza Hotel.

E. B. WHITE. *Stuart Little* (1945). A mouse who sets out to see the world takes in some of the sights of New York City.

Movies

New York has been a favorite film location since the movie camera was invented. *The Movie Lover's Guide to New York,* by Richard Alleman (see "Unusual Guidebooks," above), is your best guide to the Big Apple as movieland. The following films are only a few of the best in which New York steals the show.

Breakfast at Tiffany's (1961). A sophisticated movie version of Truman Capote's classic, with Audrey Hepburn as Holly Golightly.

Easter Parade (1948). Fred Astaire and Judy Garland show how to partake of this annual Fifth Avenue tradition in high style.

East Side, West Side (1949). Typical New Yorkers—chic, savvy, neurotic, selfish—portrayed by Barbara Stanwyck, James Mason, Ava Gardner, Nancy Davis (Reagan), others.

Forty-Second Street (1933). Backstage drama with onstage extravaganzas by Busby Berkeley.

Guys and Dolls (1955). A snappy film version of the Broadway musical, inhabited by those amusing Damon Runyon characters.

Hester Street (1975). A nice Jewish girl from the Old Country (Carol Kane) doesn't like turn-of-the-century New York one bit.

King Kong (1933). The big hairy ape goes to the top of the Empire State Building and he doesn't even use the elevator. (He does a repeat performance at the World Trade Center in a campy 1976 remake.)

Miracle on 34th Street (1947). A highly convincing and charming argument for the validity of the Santa Claus myth.

Moonstruck (1988). They toss stereotypes around like pizza dough, but Cher, Nicholas Cage, and their co-stars do a pretty good job of convincing us that New York is still inhabited by some really decent folks.

My Sister Eileen (1955 musical version, based on the 1938 novel by Ruth McKenney). Two Ohio girls come to Greenwich Village with songs in their hearts. (The real-life Eileen married novelist Nathanael West; the couple was killed in an automobile accident in 1940.)

Next Stop, Greenwich Village (1976). Brooklyn boy explores 1950s bohemia.

On the Town (1949). Gene Kelly and Frank Sinatra dance their way up and down Manhattan.

On the Waterfront (1954). Marlon Brando sweats, scowls, and scrapes on the Jersey docks.

Prisoner of Second Avenue (1975). The city begins to get to Anne Bancroft and Jack Lemmon.

An Unmarried Woman (1978). Upper East Side housewife loses her husband, takes up with a SoHo artist, and moves into an Upper West Side brownstone: What could be more typically New York?

When Harry Met Sally . . . (1989). How do they live so well in Manhattan (the real love object in this romance) and work so little?

Where's Poppa? (1970). Ruth Gordon at her best as a batty Upper West Side Jewish mamma.

The World of Henry Orient (1964). New York as experienced by two wacky adolescents.

Finally, the films of Woody Allen, most of which are really just manifestations of the director's love affair with his native city. Of special note for their indulgence of New York: *Annie Hall* (1977), *Manhattan* (1979), *Broadway Danny Rose* (1984), *Hannah and Her Sisters* (1986), *Radio Days* (1987), *Alice* (1991), and his segment in the otherwise lackluster *New York Stories* (1989).

—*Stephen Brewer*

ACCOMMODATIONS

We organize New York hotels by geographic area and list them generally from most to least expensive in each group. Many of the city's most prestigious hotels are located on the Upper East Side, north of 59th Street, with its art galleries, boutiques, and museums. From Midtown West and the residential Upper West Side (home to a number of pleasant, budget-priced hotels) it's easy to reach Lincoln Center, Broadway theaters, and Carnegie Hall—an important advantage because cabs can be hard to find just before and after performances. Midtown East is convenient for shoppers and business travellers, while the Murray Hill neighborhood, a quieter residential district in the east 30s, offers some of the most appealing accommodations in the moderate range. There are a few hotels downtown near Wall Street and the World Trade Center.

Following the listings by neighborhood, we offer a rundown on the city's growing number of all-suite properties, a listing of the big convention hotels, and a selection of bed-and-breakfast agencies.

For each hotel we give the rates at press time for double room, double occupancy, and, if applicable, for suites as well. Hotel rates can change considerably over a short period of time; always check the rates before making a reservation. All hotels have better rates on weekends, in summer, and during other promotional periods; be sure to ask about special offerings.

Hotels won't include tax when quoting rates, so add it in when figuring costs—a hefty 19¼ percent plus $2 per night for rooms over $100, 14¼ percent plus $2 for hotels under $100.

The telephone area code for Manhattan is 212.

Upper East Side
The ▶ **St. Regis** has emerged from a three-year, $100-million restoration by the Sheraton Corporation, regaining the glamour it evoked when John Jacob Astor opened the original hotel in 1904. Enlarged rooms have 12-foot-high ceilings, chandeliers, marble baths, Louis XV reproduction furniture, and tasteful fabrics in pale muted colors. Every floor offers butler service, there's a luxurious health club, and, rest assured, the wonderful mural by Maxfield

Parrish still adorns the **King Cole Bar**. Such luxury comes at a price, among the highest room rates in New York.

2 East 55th Street (at Fifth Avenue), New York, NY 10022. Tel: 753-4500 or (800) 759-7550; Fax: 787-3447. $350–$450; suites from $550.

The ▶ **Plaza Athénée** does not try to match the grandeur of its Parisian sister but is instead a pampering, intimate sanctuary. In the small, formal lobby, softened by a blue-green pastoral tapestry and pale rugs, guests are seated at an 18th-century desk for check-in, then escorted by a manager to their well-appointed rooms. Duplicates of the trademark gilt clocks of the original hotel await in every room, along with traditional furnishings, fresh flowers, and such niceties as trouser pressers, tie racks, shoe trees, safes, pantries, bathrobes, and humidifiers to combat dry room heat in winter. **La Régence** serves fine French food amid hand-painted panels, ceilings painted with clouds, and chandeliers.

37 East 64th Street (between Madison and Park avenues), New York, NY 10021. Tel: 734-9100 or (800) 447-8800; Fax: 772-0958. $310–$390; suites $590–$2,300 (penthouse).

The ▶ **Pierre** has the air of a luxurious and exclusive private club and provides crackerjack service and welcome privacy. The lobby gleams with Old World elegance. Rooms, many of which are leased on a permanent basis, have been lavishly refurbished, maintaining the Chippendale and Chinoiserie styles. High tea in front of the grand staircase in the **Rotunda** is a daily ritual, and many a business deal has been consummated here over breakfast croissants.

2 East 61st Street (at Fifth Avenue), New York, NY 10021. Tel: 838-8000 or (800) 332-3442; Fax: 940-8109. $225–$400; suites from $600.

The ▶ **Carlyle**'s understated elegance and impeccable service have kept it at the top of the New York list for decades, the choice of presidents and dignitaries. There's a hushed quality to the dimmed lobby with its antiques and tapestries. The spacious rooms are done in fresh florals accented with antiques and greenery—nothing ostentatious, just quiet good taste. Rooms provide all the amenities of one of the world's best hotels, including serving pantries, and the hotel bowed to current fashion recently and installed a well-equipped fitness center. Things are surprisingly lively in the evening, when top pianists play under the colorful murals at **Bemelmans**

Bar—and when Bobby Short holds court at the **Café Carlyle**.

35 East 76th Street (at Madison Avenue), New York, NY 10021. Tel: 744-1600 or (800) 227-5737; Fax: 717-4682. $275–$375; suites from $500.

The ► **Stanhope** is an ornate showplace filled with Louis XVI furnishings and Baccarat chandeliers. Rooms are decorated with reproduction 18th-century armoires, displays of antique porcelain, and antique books. The choice rooms and suites overlook the Metropolitan Museum across the street and Central Park beyond. Staff outnumbers guests here two to one, and the hotel provides convenient limousine transportation to Midtown. The sidewalk café on Fifth Avenue is one of New York's most popular oases.

995 Fifth Avenue (at 81st Street), New York, NY 10028. Tel: 288-5800 or (800) 828-1123; Fax: 517-0088. $235–$350; suites from $295.

The ► **Mayfair Hotel Baglioni**, long known as the Mayfair Regent, has a new Italian affiliation. But it retains the services of manager Dario Mariotti, whose warmth sets the cosmopolitan tone for this small and charming hotel, and attracts a loyal, largely European clientele. The spacious quarters are pretty and tasteful, with such thoughtful comforts as the umbrella hanging in the closet, just in case. Coffered ceilings, wing chairs, and a fireplace make the lobby a place for lingering, and the columned and mirrored lounge has become a favorite setting in the city for business breakfasts and afternoon teas. Guests also have charging privileges at the restaurant off the lobby—the renowned **Le Cirque**.

610 Park Avenue (at 65th Street), New York, NY 10021. Tel: 288-0800 or (800) 223-0542; Fax: 737-0538. $295; suites $355–$490.

At the ► **Westbury** the lobby is understated and the recently redecorated rooms are agreeably fussy, with stripes, flowery chintz, Oriental rugs, and ruffles and plants all around. The combination seems to appeal to the many well-dressed European travellers who keep the hotel well booked. The **Polo Lounge**, with its dark mahogany bar and paisley seats, is popular with the neighborhood crowd as well as with guests. The hotel has recently added a fitness center.

15 East 69th Street (between Fifth and Madison avenues), New York, NY 10021. Tel: 535-2000 or (800) 321-1569; Fax: 535-5058. $265–$295; suites from $400.

There's a bit of show-biz glitz to the ▸ **Regency**, the grand hotel in the Loews chain. The decor is elaborate Regency style with lots of marble, brocade, and mirrors. The **540 Restaurant** has been redone in appealing light colors, and is still the place to transact deals over morning coffee. Guests are welcome to use the fitness center in the lower lobby.

540 Park Avenue (at 61st Street), New York, NY 10021. Tel: 759-4100 or (800) 233-2356; Fax: 826-5674. $175–$295; suites from $350.

The ▸ **Mark**, formerly known as the Madison Avenue, has emerged from an elegant renovation that won an award from the Friends of the Upper East Side Historic District. There's a stylish new lobby, and rooms have a smart, Neoclassical Italian look, done with Piranesi prints, a pale yellow and pearl gray color scheme, and such niceties as Frette sheets and down pillows. The excellent café serves a fine afternoon tea.

25 East 77th Street (at Madison Avenue), New York, NY 10021. Tel: 744-4300 or (800) THE-MARK; Fax: 744-2749. $265–$275; suites from $525.

The ▸ **Barbizon**, once a residence hotel where such well-bred young ladies as Grace Kelly were properly chaperoned when they arrived in New York, has been stylishly renovated, and the pastel contemporary rooms, while small, are the best value in the neighborhood. The tower suites with terraces and city views appeal to many celebrities.

140 East 63rd Street (at Lexington Avenue), New York, NY 10021. Tel: 838-5700 or (800) 223-1020; Fax: 888-4271. $99–$175; suites from $295.

The turn-of-the-century ▸ **Hotel Wales** is the closest thing to a small European hotel in New York. The old marble staircase, fine woodwork, and the fireplaces have survived a $5 million renovation, but bathrooms and furnishings are new. The residential Carnegie Hill neighborhood, though inconvenient for Midtown, is quiet and close to the Upper East Side museums. Complimentary Continental breakfast and afternoon tea are served in the second-floor Pied Piper Room, which is decorated with antique children's-book illustrations. Guests also have the choice of two restaurants, including **Sarabeth's Kitchen**, a longtime neighborhood favorite.

1295 Madison Avenue (at 92nd Street), New York, NY 10128. Tel: 876-6000 or (800) 428-5252; Fax: 860-7000. $150–$170; suites from $195.

Midtown East

The skyscraper that I. M. Pei designed for the new ▶ **Four Seasons New York** is already being called a landmark. When you enter the limestone-columned lobby with its 33-foot-high ceiling—the atmosphere and dimensions of an ancient monument—you'll see why. With superior service and amenities and exquisitely lovely modernist furnishings, the hotel, which opened in spring 1993, promises an exciting and comfortable stay—and a refreshing change from all those Old World hotel rooms we've become accustomed to.

57 East 57th Street (between Madison and Park avenues), New York, NY 10022. Tel: 758-5700 or (800) 487-FSNY; Fax: 758-5711. $325–$450; suites $525–$3,000.

The opulent and romantic ▶ **Box Tree Hotel** is a 15-room inn that occupies two city brownstones and reflects the flamboyant and luxurious tastes of owner Augustin Paege. Each room and suite has a different theme, previewed by the hand-painted trompe l'oeil panel on the door. Decor swings wildly from Oriental to Louis XVI to English Gothic to 1930s Paris. All rooms have working marble fireplaces. The tab here is softened considerably by a $100 daily credit in the intimate and expensive Box Tree restaurant.

250 East 49th Street (between Second and Third avenues), New York, NY 10017. Tel: 758-8320; Fax: 308-3899. $290–$320.

The ▶ **New York Palace** incorporates the opulent public rooms of the restored 1881 Villard Houses. Afternoon tea in the **Gold Room** is a perfect way to see the treasures, including the sweeping staircase, grand ballroom, exquisite carving, and Stanford White interiors inspired by the Palazzo della Cancelleria in Rome. The pale, oversize rooms of the 55-story hotel beyond are formally Baroque.

455 Madison Avenue (at 50th Street), New York, NY 10022. Tel: 888-7000 or (800) 221-4982; Fax: 872-7272. $195–$275; suites from $395.

Architect Kevin Roche won a prize for the superb, soaring ▶ **United Nations Plaza Park Hyatt Hotel**, where luxurious guest rooms begin on the 28th floor and big windows provide the best East River views in town, particularly from the recently renovated 27th-floor pool and health club (there's also a tennis court on the 39th floor). Marble, chrome, and mirrors reflecting Japanese floral arrangements mark the lobby, where a harpist offers soothing music in the afternoon. When the UN is in session, ambassadors, diplomats, and such dignitaries as the secretary of state may be in residence. The hotel provides a quick Continental breakfast for busy guests in the Wickery, a bower off the lobby, and limousine service to Wall Street and Midtown by day, the Theater District at night. The **Ambassador Grill** has a pleasant ambience, and its prices are moderate.

One United Nations Plaza (44th Street and First Avenue), New York, NY 10017. Tel: 355-3400 or (800) 233-1234; Fax: 702-5051. $260–$280; suites from $350.

The ▶ **Waldorf-Astoria**, the first bastion of New York elegance, is now a busy Hilton property, but there is still cachet to the handsome Art Deco lobby. The giant clock executed for the Chicago World's Fair of 1893 is a carry-over from the original hotel (which gave way to the Empire State Building). Most rooms are big and very nicely done in French Provincial style. Tucked away from the crowd with its own entrance, the more expensive and exclusive ▶ **Waldorf Towers** has recently undergone a refurbishing that restored many of the original architectural details. The flower-adorned piano played nightly in the Peacock Alley cocktail lounge belonged to Cole Porter when he was a Towers resident. For those who like the variety of restaurants and services of a large hotel, this one remains special.

301 Park Avenue (between 49th and 50th streets), New York, NY 10022. Tel: 355-3000 or (800) HILTONS; Fax: 872-7272. $175–$330; suites from $325.

The ▶ **Inter-Continental New York** is the old Barclay, revived by the distinguished international chain. The brass birdcage and Tiffany ceiling in the lobby and the air of genteel refinement remain intact. The spacious rooms have been tastefully redecorated with traditional furnishings, and a brand-new, state-of-the-art health club has taken over the third floor.

111 East 48th Street (between Lexington and Park avenues), New York, NY 10017. Tel: 755-5900 or (800) 327-0200; Fax: 644-0079. $220–$280; suites from $350.

The ▶ **Roger Smith**, once basic business quarters, is now an intimate hideaway in the busy Grand Central neighborhood. The lobby glows with vibrant paintings and sleek brass sculptures, and no two rooms are alike. Complimentary Continental breakfast is served on the mezzanine, and dinner in Lily's Restaurant, off the lobby.

501 Lexington Avenue (at 47th Street), New York, NY 10017. Tel: 755-1400 or (800) 445-0277; Fax: 319-9130; $125–$180; suites from $175.

At the ▶ **Elysée**, new owners have added a pleasant breakfast room and library but retained the marble-top tables, carved desks, and ornate headboards that give each guest room a different look and homey appeal. Some rooms have kitchenettes and terraces, and all have sleek marble baths. Downstairs, the murals in the **Monkey Bar** will be preserved—including the Hirschfeld caricatures that depict Tallulah Bankhead, Joe DiMaggio, the Gish sisters, Tennessee Williams, and other former residents of the hotel.

60 East 54th Street (between Madison and Park avenues), New York, NY 10022. Tel: 753-1066 or (800) 535-9733; Fax: 980-9278. $145–$165; suites from $350.

The ▶ **Helmsley Middletowne Hotel** suits those who prefer a small, quiet hotel. The tiny marble lobby is stylish; rooms, while not large, are well appointed, tasteful, and cheerful, with comfortable sitting areas, and sinks and refrigerators. Complimentary morning coffee is served in the lobby. A good buy in this convenient neighborhood.

148 East 48th Street (between Third and Lexington avenues), New York, NY 10017. Tel: 755-3000 or (800) 221-4982; Fax: 832-0261. $99–$155; suites from $175.

If it weren't for the tour groups that clog the lobby, the ▶ **Doral Inn** would be the top choice for a reasonably priced Midtown hotel with modern, well-decorated rooms. For those willing to put up with possible waits at the desk, however, there are rewards, such as a fitness center on the fourth floor with saunas and three squash courts, a 24-hour coffee shop, a bar and restaurant, and a convenient, money-saving, do-it-yourself laundry room.

541 Lexington Avenue (at 49th Street), New York, NY 10022. Tel: 755-1200 or (800) 223-DORAL; Fax: 319-8344. $145–$160; suites from $225.

The family-owned ▶ **Beverly** is among the best values in the lineup of hotels near the Waldorf-Astoria. There are quiet, comfortable, good-size rooms here, as well as suites with kitchens. The lobby is warm and unpretentious, and there are a restaurant, cocktail lounge, and coffee shop on the premises.

125 East 50th Street (at Lexington Avenue), New York, NY 10022. Tel: 753-2700 or (800) 223-0945; Fax: 759-7300. $149–$169; suites from $180.

▶ **Journey's End Hotel**, the first New York property opened by the Canadian chain, is modern, spanking fresh, and spotless. Room furnishings are upscale motel, but baths are big and the location just off Fifth Avenue is excellent. Each room has a convertible sofa bed; children stay in parents' rooms free.

3 East 40th Street (between Fifth and Madison avenues), New York, NY 10016. Tel: 447-1500 or (800) 668-4200; Fax: 213-0972. $141.88.

The small ▶ **Pickwick Arms**—known to thousands of New Yorkers who first stayed here when they came to the city from the small towns of America—is well located in a nice part of east Midtown and has recently been refurbished. The pleasant lobby is done in pale hues, and the modest but comfortable rooms are well equipped. Even the spacious studios cost less than most standard doubles in this area, and for travellers on tight budgets there are some rooms without baths (shared facilities are down the hall). The hotel has a coffee shop, a Spanish restaurant, and a rooftop garden.

230 East 51st Street (between Third and Second avenues), New York, NY 10022. Tel: 355-0300 or (800) PICKWIK; Fax: 755-5029. $85–$99.50.

Midtown West

The New York ▶ **Peninsula** occupies the 1905 Beaux Arts landmark building that used to be the Gotham Hotel. The noted Peninsula group of Hong Kong has added trademark touches such as page boys dressed in white and a proper English tea in the Gotham lounge. A double staircase sweeps from the lobby toward the guest rooms, which have custom cherry furnishings and Art Nouveau accessories. Some baths have six-foot whirlpool tubs and bidets. Fifth Avenue views from higher floors are striking, but the best are from the rooftop-level fitness center, spa, and pool overlooking Manhattan. The 23rd-floor **Pen-Top Bar** has an open terrace in summer that is the perfect place for a drink on a balmy night.

700 Fifth Avenue (at 55th Street), New York, NY 10019. Tel: 247-2200 or (800) 262-9467; Fax: 903-3949. $295–$395; suites from $495.

The ▶ **Essex House** has been restored to its Art Deco heritage and to the top ranks of New York lodgings after a multimillion-dollar makeover by the Nikko hotel group of Japan. The lobby, with black marble columns with original brass details, overlooks Central Park across the street. As in many New York hotels, rooms seem on the small side, but many face the park and there is no faulting the good taste of the decor. No two rooms are alike, and all are done in rich colors and traditional English stripes and florals. Amenities include a health club, business center, and three restaurants, including Japanese food at BenKay and French fare at **Les Célébrités**—which has been getting good reviews.

160 Central Park South, New York, NY 10019. Tel: 247-0300 or (800) NIKKOUS; Fax: 315-1839. $265–$345; suites from $450.

The former Parc Fifty-One has new Italian owners, the Starhotels group, who have christened it ▶ **Michelangelo**. No drastic changes are planned, however, for this sophisticated hotel just off Broadway. The two-story, pink-marble lobby is wonderfully removed from the bustle of the neighborhood. There are no look-alike rooms here; decor runs from French Provincial to Art Deco to black-and-white Modern. Continental breakfast is served on the balcony over the lobby, and Harry Cipriani's restaurant **Bellini** is just off the lobby. Among the many amenities are beepers available at the front desk so guests needn't miss important calls during the theater.

152 West 51st Street (at Seventh Avenue), New York, NY 10019. Tel: 765-1900 or (800) 237-0990; Fax: 541-6604. $240–$375; suites from $400.

The look of the ▶ **Royalton** is somewhere between a 21st-century luxury ocean liner and the Orient Express. The playful hotel incorporates the favorite travel experiences of the men who created it, Ian Schrager and the late Steve Rubell, formerly of Studio 54. Designer Philippe Starck's tapered columns, curved lines, and sweeps of mahogany and granite make for a stunning modern lobby. The lobby café, 44, buzzes with editorial types at lunch, and the small round bar, 44 **Round**, is equally busy after working hours. Walking the narrow dark-blue corridors is like making your way toward a slick train compartment. Rooms are efficient affairs, with built-in seating and storage and a big bed tucked in like a captain's bunk. Love it or hate it, you have to admit there's nothing else like the Royalton.

44 West 44th Street (between Fifth and Sixth avenues), New York, NY 10036. Tel: 869-4400 or (800) 635-9013; Fax: 869-8965. $180–$380; suites from $335.

The ▶ **Plaza**, still New York's grand hotel, has the best

location in town, at the foot of Central Park on the most European of the city's plazas. Since Donald Trump acquired this national historic landmark in 1989, major restoration has returned the Plaza to its original turn-of-the-century glitter. In the public rooms and corridors this means acres of burgundy carpeting, gold leaf, frescoed ceilings, custom-made tapestries, and Belgian crystal chandeliers. Guest rooms have been redone in high Victorian style. Wisely, Mr. Trump elected to refurbish rather than remodel such longtime favorite meeting places as the **Palm Court**, the Oyster Bar, and the **Oak Bar**.

786 Fifth Avenue (at 59th Street), New York, NY 10019. Tel: 759-3000 or (800) 228-3000; Fax: 546-5324. $235–$355; suites from $650.

The ▶ **Ritz Carlton** is a clubby enclave that has recently undergone a $20 million remodeling to lend guest rooms a look of European elegance. The rooms aren't large compared to others in this price category, but the Central Park views from the front rooms are breathtaking; settle for a quiet back room and the rates go down considerably. The **Jockey Club** restaurant, a meld of antique pine and leather, has an inviting and busy bar ably commandeered by Norman Bukofzer, the longtime bartender.

112 Central Park South (at Sixth Avenue), New York, NY 10019. Tel: 757-1900 or (800) 241-3333; Fax: 757-9620. $230–$380; suites from $450.

For ▶ **Le Parker Meridien** the French chain has chosen showy elegance rather than Gallic charm, with a pink-columned, two-story entry arcade setting the tone. Rooms have recently been renovated with striped wallpapers, contemporary Biedemeier-style furnishings, and marble baths. The glass-enclosed 42nd-floor pool and the outside sun deck and running track have soaring city views. For indoor exercise, the basement health club has a weight room, squash and racquetball courts, whirlpool, sauna, and aerobics classes.

119 West 56th Street (between Sixth and Seventh avenues), New York, NY 10019. Tel: 245-5000 or (800) 543-4300; Fax: 307-1776. $225–$275; suites from $275.

The front of the new ▶ **Holiday Inn Crowne Plaza**, the flagship of the chain's luxury division, is festooned with neon, as befits its Broadway location. Rooms have expansive views of Times Square or the Hudson River; the top club floors have a spacious private lounge serving breakfast and cocktails with a view. There is a choice of three dining rooms, and the big, well-equipped health club has the largest hotel pool in the city. This is not your typical Holiday Inn.

1605 Broadway (at 49th Street), New York, NY 10019. Tel: 977-4000 or (800) 243-6969; Fax: 333-7393. $210–$245; suites from $250.

The ▶ **Dorset** gives off a dignified, quiet Old English air in its gracious paneled lobby and muraled dining room. Rooms are large and attractively furnished and have convenient serving pantries. The hotel is overdue for some refurbishing but is a good buy in this neighborhood.

30 West 54th Street (between Fifth and Sixth avenues), New York, NY 10019. Tel: 247-7300 or (800) 227-2348; Fax: 581-0153. $195–$255; suites from $350.

Dorothy Parker, Alexander Woollcott, and their fabled Round Table of the 1920s are gone from the ▶ **Algonquin**, but conversation still hums in the **Rose Room**, and authors, publishers, actors, producers, and people watchers gather in the paneled lobby sitting room–cum–cocktail lounge, summoning the waiter with the traditional brass bell on each table. The Algonquin is where *The New Yorker* magazine was born (it is still found in every room), where Lerner and Loewe wrote *My Fair Lady,* where Angela Lansbury lived when she starred in *Mame.* The guest list also includes such names as Mordecai Richler, Eudora Welty, and Maya Angelou. A recent refurbishing has added new furniture and fabrics but has carefully kept the determinedly old-fashioned look. Bathrooms, while upgraded, are still not state of the art, but what the rooms lack in modern amenities they make up for in coziness, warmth, and the palpable feeling of tradition.

59 West 44th Street (between Fifth and Sixth avenues), New York, NY 10036. Tel: 840-6800 or (800) 548-0345; Fax: 944-1419. $150–$195; suites from $300.

The young and the hip will love ▶ **Paramount**, part of the Morgans Hotel Group. Here, designer Philippe Starck (see the Royalton, above) turned his imagination to lower-priced whimsy, smack in the heart of the Theater District. Expect the unexpected—headboards are giant-size old-master paintings; chairs resemble sculptures. Starck's multilevel lobby is smashing, with a stone staircase that seems to float its way upward. Children have their own playroom, and adults elbow for room at the bar at **Whiskey**, one of the hottest watering holes in town. Dean & DeLuca, the ever-so-chic SoHo food shop, runs the Parisian-style charcuterie off the lobby, with delicious snacks and takeout meals for guests. Rooms here are tiny, but most guests don't seem to care.

235 West 46th Street (between Broadway and Eighth Avenue), New York, NY 10036. Tel: 764-5520 or (800) 225-7474; Fax: 354-5237. $150–$205; suites from $330.

The ▶ **Salisbury**, near Carnegie Hall, offers a good central location, a quiet and pleasant lobby, and spacious if undistinguished rooms. Most rooms also include serving pantries, making this a good place for families.

123 West 57th Street (between Sixth and Seventh avenues), New York, NY 10019. Tel: 246-1300 or (800) 257-1111; Fax: 754-5638. $135–$155; suites $155.

The spacious old-fashioned rooms at the ▶ **Wyndham** are among New York's best buys, personally decorated by the resident owners, who put their money into paintings and charm rather than room service or fancy new plumbing. (Everything works—it just isn't state of the art.) The deep red lobby–sitting room is as cozy as a home parlor, and you ring the bell for admittance as in a home. The hotel is a favorite of visiting performers; Jessica Tandy and Hume Cronyn keep a permanent apartment here. Reserve well in advance.

42 West 58th Street (between Fifth and Sixth avenues), New York, NY 10019. Tel: 753-3500. $130–$140; suites from $175.

After a sparkling renovation, the dowdy old ▶ **Edison** has become one of the best budget places to stay in the theater district. The lobby is now restored to its original 1931 Art Deco splendor, complete with murals, etched brass trim, and fanciful fixtures. Rooms are freshly decorated in pleasing floral fabrics, and baths have been nicely modernized. A coffee shop, bar, and restaurant are on the premises.

228 West 47th Street (between Broadway and Eighth Avenue), New York, NY 10036. Tel: 840-5000 or (800) 637-7070; Fax: 719-9541. $90–$99; suites from $125.

A golden cherub guards the door of the ▶ **Herald Square Hotel**, a newly renovated building that was the original home of *Life* magazine. Classic early *Life* covers by famous illustrators decorate hallways and rooms. Bedspread fabrics are attractive, bathrooms sparkle, and there are such niceties as remote-controlled television and a well-tended rose garden under lights at the bottom of an airshaft. The location, convenient for shopping or for the Javits Center by day, is all but deserted late at night, but at these rates, you can afford to take a cab home from dinner.

19 West 31st Street (between Broadway and Fifth Avenue), New York, NY 10001. Tel: 279-4017 or (800) 727-1888; Fax: 643-9208. $55–$75.

Indian restaurateur Sant Chatwal, owner of New York's Bombay Palace restaurant, has gathered seven hotels, all older properties now in various stages of renovation, under the ▶ **Chatwal Inns** umbrella. While some rooms are small and furnishings simple, everything is fresh, bathrooms are new, and the values are excellent, particularly the junior suites, which are ideal for families. Several locations provide self-serve Continental breakfast. The hotels are managed by a number of chains, but reservations can be made through Chatwal Inns, Tel: (800) 826-4667. Recommended addresses include:

▶ **Best Western Woodward**, 210 West 55th Street, New York, NY 10019. Tel: 247-2000 or (800) 336-4110; Fax: 581-2248. $120; suites from $155.

▶ **Best Western President Hotel**, 234 West 48th Street, New York, NY 10036. Tel: 246-8800; Fax: 974-3922. $99–$119; suites from $135.

▶ **Quality Inn–Midtown**, 157 West 47th Street, New York, NY 10036. Tel: 768-3700; Fax: 768-3403. $99–$130; suites from $175.

▶ **Chatwal Inn on 45th Street**, 132 West 45th Street, New York, NY 10036. Tel: 921-7600; Fax: 719-0171. $95–$125; suites from $105.

Upper West Side

The ▶ **Mayflower**, on Central Park and an aria away from Lincoln Center, has an Old World look in its painting-lined lobby. Rooms are comfortable but beginning to show their age. Of course, with a park view you may never notice, and there's often interesting artistic company in the **Conservatory Café**.

15 Central Park West (at 61st Street), New York, NY 10023. Tel: 265-0060 or (800) 223-4164; Fax: 265-5098. $160–$180; suites from $235.

With a top-to-bottom renovation complete, the ▶ **Radisson Empire** has moved out of the budget category but still remains a solid value, especially on weekends, when special rates are offered. Befitting the hotel's location directly across from Lincoln Center, its lobby now displays shadow boxes of scenes from operas. The three-story lobby is baronial, replete with mahogany paneling, a carved antique mantel, and a lavish Oriental rug. Rooms are in attractive florals, and besides TV and VCR each boasts a

Nakamichi stereo, tape deck, and CD player. The spiffy **Empire Grill** has a well-priced pre-theater menu.

44 West 63rd Street (at Broadway), New York, NY 10023. Tel: 265-7400 or (800) 333-3333; Fax: 765-6125. $135–$200; suites from $250.

The ▶ **Beacon**, a former residential hotel next to the well-known theater of the same name (a frequent venue for popular music performers), recently opened its doors to overnight guests. There is a smart, black-and-white lobby, and the comfortable, newly decorated rooms have all the standard hotel comforts as well as kitchenettes— which can be nicely stocked at Zabar's, Fairway, and the other Upper West Side food stores nearby.

2130 Broadway (between 74th and 75th streets), New York, NY 10023. Tel: 787-1100 or (800) 572-4969; Fax: 724-0839. $99–$110; suites from $140.

The ▶ **Milburn**, another refurbished old Upper West Side residential hotel, offers overnight guests spacious studios and two-room suites, all with kitchenettes. The lobby has a pleasant Old World look, and the rooms, while a bit spare, have modern bathrooms and comfortable eating areas. There's also a laundromat in the building.

242 West 76th Street (between Broadway and West End Avenue), New York, NY 10023. Tel: 362-1006 or (800) 833-9622; Fax: 721-5476. $89–$110; suites from $130.

The ▶ **Excelsior Hotel** is a favorite with long-time visitors to New York who like its quiet location on the Upper West Side, a pleasant walk across the park from the Metropolitan Museum of Art. Rooms, many with views of the park-like grounds of the American Museum of Natural History, are comfortable, though faded.

45 West 81st Street (between Columbus Avenue and Central Park West), New York, NY 10024. Tel: 362-9200 or (800) 368-4575; Fax: 721-2994. $75; suites $99.

Another of the budget-priced hotels in this lively neigh-borhood, the ▶ **Broadway American** has a modernistic lobby and trendy Art Deco furnishings in black (with a tiny whimsical print of the Statue of Liberty embedded in each headboard). Bathrooms are new, and each room comes with a refrigerator and TV. Those on severe bud-gets can opt for sharing the ample baths down the hall.

2178 Broadway (at 77th Street), New York, NY 10024. Tel: 362-1100; Fax: 787-9521. $65–$89.

Finally, good news for backpackers and the budget-conscious is New York's first ▶ **American Youth Hostel**, in a renovated century-old landmark building on the upper Upper West Side. As in most hostels, rooms accommodate four to eight people in bunk beds, and guests use communal bathrooms. At press time rates were $22 for AYH members, $25 for nonmembers. Some family rooms are available at slightly higher rates. Members' kitchens and dining rooms and coin-operated laundry machines are also available, and there is an outdoor garden.

891 Amsterdam Avenue (between 103rd and 104th streets), New York, NY 10025. Tel: 932-2300; Fax: 932-2574. $22–$25.

Murray Hill

An old brick façade and flower boxes filled with geraniums and trailing vines make it clear that the ▶ **Sheraton Park Avenue** (the old Sheraton Russell) is not the usual chain hotel. Inside, the paneled lobby is decorated with needlepoint upholstery and a library of leather-bound books. The rooms upstairs have Chippendale-style furniture, with soft florals, long drapes, and Old New York prints on the walls. Many have fireplaces (nonworking). Bookshelves and banquettes make the bar—the setting for the scene in *The Verdict* in which Paul Newman punches out Charlotte Rampling—a cozy place for a fast lunch or to hear jazz at night. Guests are also welcome at the monthly lunch meeting of the Park Avenue Literary Club.

45 Park Avenue (at 37th Street), New York, NY 10016. Tel: 685-7676 or (800) 325-3535; Fax: 889-3193. $235–$245; suites from $300.

Even the tieless doorman looks like a rock star at ▶ **Morgans**, the first hot property created by Ian Schrager and the late Steve Rubell (see also the Royalton and Paramount). No hotel clichés here—not even a sign out front. French designer Andrée Putnam's black-and-white minimalist world is clean, uncluttered Modern, from the optical-illusion cube carpeting in the lobby to the gray-and-white pinstripes on the beds and the stainless steel sinks in the bath. Furniture in the smallish rooms is functional—padded window seats lift to make room for suitcases and clutter, coffee tables have casters to roll where they are wanted—and all rooms come with a refrigerator and a stereo.

237 Madison Avenue (at 38th Street), New York, NY 10016. Tel: 686-0300 or (800) 334-3408; Fax: 779-8352. $205–$235; suites from $275.

The chic ▶ **Doral Park Avenue**, a small hotel with big-time ways, is treasured by those who have discovered it. The round entryway sets the Neoclassical mood, with frescoes, columns, and ornate grillwork. The newly decorated rooms follow the same motif. Many have sweeping views of Park Avenue. Willing room-service personnel here will provide anything from breakfast in bed to a VCR to an exercise bicycle. Energetic guests are welcome at the Doral Health Club in the more expensive ▶ **Doral Tuscany** around the corner. The Saturnia Restaurant has health-conscious menus adapted from Doral's noted Saturnia Spa in Miami, Florida, and there's a sidewalk café out front.

70 Park Avenue (at 38th Street), New York, NY 10016. Tel: 687-7050 or (800) 22-DORAL; Fax: 949-5924. $205–$225; suites from $350.

▶ **Doral Court**, one of three sister properties in leafy Murray Hill, is another pleasant choice. The good-size rooms are fresh and pretty, with entry foyers, king-size beds, and 25-inch televisions. Each bath has a dressing alcove with a vanity and a refrigerator. Four choice digs on the 15th floor have terraces with views of the Chrysler Building and the New York skyline. And the Courtyard Café downstairs, in a greenhouse setting, has a hidden garden with a gurgling waterfall.

130 East 39th Street (at Lexington Avenue), New York, NY 10016. Tel: 685-1100 or (800) 22-DORAL; Fax: 889-0287. $165–$195; suites from $210.

An option for budget-watchers in Murray Hill is the reincarnation of the old Seville Hotel, now known as the ▶ **Carlton**. Behind the Beaux Arts façade everything has been spruced up, including lobby, room decor, and bathroom fixtures. While not lavish, the hotel is cheerful and attractive, and with such amenities as a concierge, room service, and valet service, it is a good buy in its category.

22 East 29th Street (at Madison Avenue), New York, NY 10016. Tel: 532-4100 or (800) 542-1502; Fax: 889-8683. $129–$159; suites from $225.

The ▶ **Roger Williams** offers a convenient, quiet location and a nice extra—a kitchenette in every room. Furnishings are undistinguished and plumbing is old, but beds are decent, and at these rates the place is a real find.

28 East 31st Street (between Madison and Park avenues), New York, NY 10016. Tel: 684-7500 or (800) 637-9773; Fax: 576-4343. $60–$75; suites $95.

Downtown and Chelsea

Lower Manhattan's brand-new luxury hotel, the ▶ **Millenium**, is a sleek black column rising 58 stories between the World Trade Center and St. Paul's churchyard. Views from the upper floors are sensational; the spelling of the hotel's name is not. The decor is elegant, contemporary simplicity, from the rosewood and granite lobby to guest rooms done in ultramodern teak and curly maple furnishings, with high-tech lighting and sophisticated black-marble baths. The 561 guest rooms are dispersed 10 or 12 per floor, giving an air of intimacy unusual in such a big hotel. The fifth-floor health club and pool area overlook the green churchyard next door, and there are a business center, two restaurants, and an attractive bar. Rooms are a bit small for the price; best choices are the suites—but they don't come cheap.

55 Church Street (at Fulton Street, just east of the World Trade Center), New York, NY 10007. Tel: 693-2001, (800) 752-0014, or (800) 835-2220; Fax: 517-2316. $149–$325; suites from $195.

Furnishings in the 507 rooms at the ▶ **Marriott Financial Center** are of standard hotel ilk. But the Hudson River views definitely are not, and the hotel offers an indoor pool as well as a health club. Rates are in the upper-moderate range for business travellers during the week but are budget-priced on weekends, allowing visitors in New York for pleasure to sample the growing diversions of the lower Manhattan area.

85 West Street (south of the World Trade Center), New York, NY 10006. Tel: 385-4900 or (800) 228-9290; Fax: 227-8136. $235–$245; suites from $450.

The ▶ **Holiday Inn Downtown**, the first large hotel to open in Chinatown, is disappointing, but convenient if you have business in the area or want to explore this vibrant section of old New York. Artificial flowers flank the escalator to the second-floor lobby, where things look a little more promising, thanks to some nice Asian accessories. But the guest rooms are small and unimaginative.

138 Lafayette Street (at the corner of Howard Street), New York, NY 10013. Tel: 966-8898 or (800) 282-3933; Fax: 966-3933. $125–$195; suites from $155.

The ▶ **Washington Square**, the only hotel in the heart of Greenwich Village, is being transformed into an elegant albeit modest hostelry. The entry, with iron grillwork, marble, plants, and prints, is inviting. Narrow hallways are brightened by Mexican tiles and sponge-painted walls.

Rooms are very small but pleasant, and there's a new restaurant and a fitness center on the way. (Refurbishing is still underway upstairs, so be sure to ask for a renovated room.)

103 Waverly Place (just northwest of Washington Square), New York, NY 10011. Tel: 777-9515 or (800) 222-0418; Fax: 979-8373. $95–$115.

The façade of the ▶ Chelsea Hotel, a historic landmark and literary shrine, bears plaques in memory of Dylan Thomas, Thomas Wolfe, O. Henry, Arthur Miller, Brendan Behan, Mark Twain, and other assorted geniuses who lived and worked here. More recently the residents have included Virgil Thomson, Sid Vicious, and artists who hope someone will know their names someday, which may tell something about the condition of the place. Rooms are big, cheap, and reasonably clean, but are desperately in need of refurbishing; many have kitchens. The lobby is filled with art both Op and odd and an equally diverse assortment of arty people. The neighborhood is similarly funky—but similarly interesting.

222 West 23rd Street (between Seventh and Eighth avenues), New York, NY 10011. Tel. and Fax: 243-3700. $85–$145; suites from $175.

(For another option in lower Manhattan, see also the New York Vista, in the Convention Hotels section, below.)

Suite Hotels

Many hotels in New York now specialize in suites, though they may also have rooms as well. With double the space of a hotel room, plus cooking facilities, a suite in each of the following is a good value in its price category. (We give the rates for suites here; room rates will be lower.)

The ▶ Lowell, one of the city's smallest and most unusual lodgings, offers along with doubles and singles 48 luxurious suites with fireplaces, libraries, full kitchens, marble baths, and a sophisticated mix of French, Art Deco, and Oriental decor. Breakfast, Sunday brunch, and tea are served in the lacy Pembroke Room, which seats just 35 and might have been lifted from a fine European hotel. The staff outnumbers the guests.

28 East 63rd Street (between Madison and Park avenues), New York, NY 10021. Tel: 838-1400 or (800) 221-4444; Fax: 319-4230. $320 and up.

The new 54-story ▶ Rihga Royal Hotel avoids a big, impersonal feeling by virtue of its serene lobby and having just 6 to 13 rooms per floor. The 500 luxury rooms are set up as one- or two-bedroom suites with sitting and sleeping areas separated by mirrored French doors. Each has a bar with ice maker in the entry hall and such touches as fresh flowers and plants. The attractive furnishings are classic in design with a slight Art Deco feel. Bathrooms are peach marble. Evenings, there's live entertainment in the **Halcyon** bar-restaurant off the lobby.

151 West 54th Street (between Sixth and Seventh avenues), New York, NY 10019. Tel: 307-5000 or (800) 937-5454; Fax: 765-6530. $260 and up.

There's no sign outside to tell you that the ▶ **Lombardy** is not just another posh New York apartment building. In fact, the studios and apartments are privately owned and are rented out hotel-style by absentee owners. This means that furnishings vary according to owners' tastes, but all units are spacious, and the rates are good for the neighborhood. Guests can also enjoy full hotel service, including room service.

111 East 56th Street (between Lexington and Park avenues), New York, NY 10022. Tel: 753-8600 or (800) 223-5254; Fax: 754-5683. $170 and up.

The ▶ **Kimberly** was built as a condominium and is now an all-suite hotel with all the comforts of home, including a terrace with most one-bedroom apartments. The furnishings have an impersonal feel, but there's plenty of space, even in the studio suites, and 24-hour concierge service in the very tasteful lobby.

145 East 50th Street (between Lexington and Third avenues), New York, NY 10022. Tel: 755-0400 or (800) 877-2232; Fax: 486-6915. $175–$265.

Befitting its location above the Palace Theater on Broadway, the ▶ **Embassy Suites** is a dramatic hotel. The slim 43-story tower has a smashing skylit lobby and Art Deco furnishings throughout. Each two-room suite comes with a pullout sofa bed, two TV sets, a wet bar, refrigerator, microwave, and coffee maker. Guests are treated to a full breakfast, a two-hour nightly cocktail reception, and use of an exercise room—extras that make the rates a solid value. Children under 12 stay free, and they can hang out in the hotel's Cool Kat Kids Club while their parents go off to play.

Corner of 47th Street and Seventh Avenue; send mail to 1568 Broadway, New York, NY 10036. Tel: 719-1600 or (800) EMBASSY; Fax: 921-5212. $179–$355.

The ▶ **Beekman Tower** belongs to the Manhattan East

Suite Hotels group, which has nine properties in the city, most offering roomy accommodations for less than the price of a luxury hotel room. This one has a convenient location, great views, and a lovely Old World lobby with a handsome Persian rug and brass chandelier. The recently refurbished room furnishings are traditional and the service is caring. The Zephyr Grill offers Continental fare, and the **Top of the Tower** cocktail lounge on the 26th floor is dazzling at night, with superb views of the East River and the Midtown Manhattan office towers.

Three Mitchell Place (off First Avenue at 49th Street), New York, NY 10017. Tel: 355-7300 or (800) 637-8483; Fax: 753-9366. $215–$395.

The ► **Shelburne Murray Hill** is another attractive Manhattan East Suite Hotel, with Persian rugs, chandeliers, and antiques in the lobby, room furnishings a shade above some of the other properties, and an in-house health club. Lunch and dinner are served in the Secret Harbor Bistro.

303 Lexington Avenue (at East 37th Street), New York, NY 10016. Tel: 689-5200 or (800) 637-8483; Fax: 779-7068. $205–$395.

Other ► **Manhattan East** properties are listed below. There is a toll-free number for all hotels in the chain; Tel: (800) 637-8483.

The ► **Surrey**, 20 East 76th Street, New York, NY 10021. Tel: 288-3700; Fax: 628-1549. $205–$580.

► **Plaza Fifty**, 155 East 50th Street, New York, NY 10022. Tel: 751-5710; Fax: 753-1468. $185–$475.

► **Dumont Plaza**, 150 East 34th Street, New York, NY 10016. Tel: 481-7600; Fax: 889-8856. $185–$415.

► **Lyden Gardens**, 215 East 64th Street, New York, NY 10021. Tel: 355-1230; Fax: 758-7858. $190–$235.

► **Lyden House**, 320 East 53rd Street, New York, NY 10022. Tel: 888-6070; Fax: 935-7690. $180–$220.

► **Eastgate Tower**, 222 East 39th Street, New York, NY 10016. Tel: 687-8000; Fax: 490-2634. $175–$390.

► **Southgate Tower Suites**, 371 Seventh Avenue (at 31st Street), New York, NY 10001. Tel: 563-1800; Fax: 643-8028. $174–$210.

Convention Hotels

New York's largest hotel properties (800 to 1,800 rooms) are first-class and, while busy, can provide any needed amenity. The Vista's location near Wall Street may appeal to some travellers. Most rates are in the luxury category.

▶ **New York Vista**, 3 World Trade Center, New York, NY 10048. Tel: 938-9100 or (800) HILTONS; Fax: 321-2107. $240–$305; suites from $450.

▶ **Grand Hyatt**, Park Avenue at Grand Central Terminal (42nd Street), New York, NY 10017. Tel: 883-1234 or (800) 233-1234; Fax: 697-3772. $220–$245; suites from $350.

▶ **New York Hilton and Towers at Rockefeller Center**, 1335 Sixth Avenue (at 53rd Street), New York, NY 10019. Tel: 586-7000 or (800) HILTONS; Fax: 315-1374. $179–$244; suites from $375.

▶ **New York Marriott Marquis**, 1535 Broadway (at 45th Street), New York, NY 10036. Tel: 398-1900 or (800) 228-9290; Fax: 704-8930. $179–$260; suites from $425.

▶ **Sheraton New York Hotel and Towers**, 811 Seventh Avenue (at 53rd Street), New York, NY 10019. Tel: 581-1000 or (800) 223-6550; Fax: 315-4265. $139–$209; suites from $550.

▶ **Ramada Hotel**, 401 Seventh Avenue (between 32nd and 33rd streets), New York, NY 10001. Tel: 736-5000 or (800) 223-8585; Fax: 502-8798. $119–$160; suites from $260.

New York Bed and Breakfast

The most encouraging development for travellers on limited budgets is the blooming of bed-and-breakfast lodgings in city apartments. Many of them are in some of New York's best neighborhoods, where resident hosts have decided to make use of extra space to help with the heady rent bills. Some of these rooms are short on privacy, but all tend to be strong on friendliness. Some registries offer unhosted apartments as well. Rates are usually $60 to $90 nightly for a double in a hosted apartment, including breakfast, and are frequently lower for longer stays. Unhosted apartments usually begin at about $90. The following registries have a number of listings around the city:

▶ **Aaah! Bed & Breakfast #1, Ltd.**, P.O. Box 200, New York, NY 10108. Tel: 246-4000.

▶ **Abode Bed and Breakfast, Ltd.**, P.O. Box 20022, New York, NY 10028. Tel: 472-2000.

▶ **At Home in New York**, P.O. Box 407, New York, NY 10185. Tel: 956-3125 or 265-8539; Fax: 247-3294.

▶ **Bed & Breakfast (& Books)** (specializes in hosts in the arts), 35 West 92nd Street (Attn: Judith Goldberg), Apt. 2C, New York, NY 10025. Tel: 865-8740.

▶ **Bed & Breakfast Network of New York,** 134 West 32nd Street, Suite 602, New York, NY 10001. Tel: 645-8134.

▶ **City Lights Bed & Breakfast, Ltd.,** P.O. Box 20355, Cherokee Station, New York, NY 10028. Tel: 737-7049; Fax: 535-2755.

▶ **New World Bed and Breakfast, Ltd.,** 150 Fifth Avenue, Suite 711, New York, NY 10011. Tel: 675-5600 or (800) 443-3800; Fax: 675-6366.

▶ **Urban Ventures, Inc.,** P.O. Box 426, Planetarium Station, New York, NY 10024. Tel: 594-5650; Fax: 947-9320.

—Eleanor Berman

NEIGHBOR-HOODS

LOWER MANHATTAN AND THE HARBOR

By Amy K. Hughes with Dwight V. Gast

Amy K. Hughes, a New York freelance writer and editor specializing in art, nature, and travel, has edited several guides in the Berlitz Travellers series. Dwight V. Gast has written for numerous publications.

The southern end of Manhattan is where the city began: Henry Hudson landed here, the Dutch settled here, and Peter Stuyvesant "bought" the island from native Indians here. The harbor attracted trade (which boomed in the 19th century with the opening of the Erie Canal), and the New York Stock Exchange had its earliest incarnation here in 1792. George Washington's presidential inauguration took place here, the Statue of Liberty became the symbol of America here, and millions of immigrants entered the New World here. History, harbor, commerce, government, and hordes of people converge on this triangular plot of land, much of which has been built up on landfill. Manhattan's newest real estate, its oldest buildings, its richest corporations, and its civic powers are all jumbled together, providing wild contrasts and jolting juxtapositions and some of the most exciting sights in all of New York City.

We start with Manhattan's southernmost tip, the Battery, with its harborside promenade from which are launched the ferries to Liberty, Ellis, and Staten islands. We then go

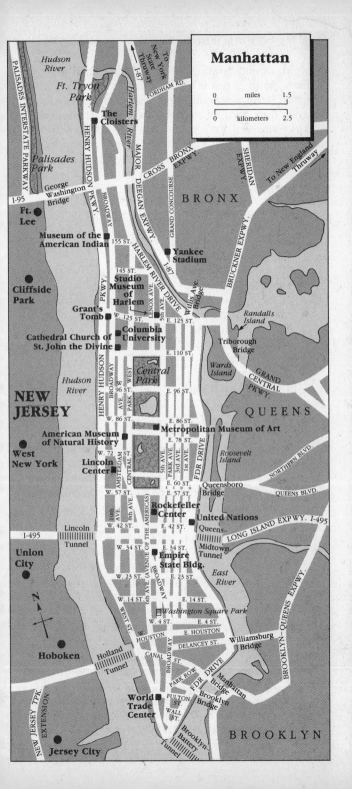

Manhattan

| 0 | miles | 1.5 |
| 0 | kilometers | 2.5 |

Hudson River
Ft. Tryon Park
PALISADES INTERSTATE PARKWAY
To New York State Thruway
I-87
FORDHAM RD.
The Cloisters
HENRY HUDSON PKWY.
Harlem River
MAJOR DEEGAN EXPWY.
CROSS BRONX EXPWY.
SHERIDAN EXPWY.
Palisades Park
BROADWAY
GRAND CONCOURSE
BRONX
To New England Thruway
George Washington Bridge
I-95
Ft. Lee
BRUCKNER EXPWY.
Museum of the American Indian
155 ST.
HARLEM RIVER DRIVE
I-87
Yankee Stadium
WILLIS AVE.
Wills Ave. Bridge
Cliffside Park
145 ST.
Studio Museum of Harlem
LENOX AVE.
5th AVE.
Randalls Island
Grant's Tomb
W. 125 ST.
E. 125 ST.
Cathedral Church of St. John the Divine
Columbia University
Triborough Bridge
Wards Island
HENRY HUDSON PKWY
BROADWAY
WEST
E. 110 ST.
GRAND CENTRAL PKWY.
Hudson River
Central Park
W. 96 ST.
E. 96 ST.
NEW JERSEY
AVE.
PARK
W. 86 ST.
E. 86 ST.
QUEENS
Metropolitan Museum of Art
American Museum of Natural History
E. 78 ST.
FDR DRIVE
Roosevelt Island
West New York
AMSTERDAM
CENTRAL
W. 72 ST.
Lincoln Center
5th AVE.
PARK AVE.
3rd AVE.
1st AVE.
NORTHERN BLVD.
W. 60 ST.
E. 60 ST.
W. 57 ST.
E. 57 ST.
Queensboro Bridge
QUEENS BLVD.
10th AVE.
5th AVE. (AVENUE OF THE AMERICAS)
Rockefeller Center
United Nations
I-495
Lincoln Tunnel
W. 42 ST.
E. 42 ST.
Queens-
LONG ISLAND EXPWY. I-495
Union City
W. 34 ST.
E. 34 ST.
Midtown Tunnel
Empire State Bldg.
W. 23 ST.
E. 23 ST.
East River
BROADWAY
W. 14 ST.
E. 14 ST.
N
WEST ST.
5th AVE.
Washington Square Park
W. 4 ST.
E. 4 ST.
E. HOUSTON
Hoboken
HOUSTON
DELANCEY ST.
Williamsburg Bridge
Holland Tunnel
CANAL ST.
BROADWAY
PARK ROW
FDR DRIVE
BROOKLYN–QUEENS EXPWY.
NEW JERSEY TPK. EXTENSION
World Trade Center
FULTON ST.
Manhattan Bridge
Brooklyn Bridge
WALL ST.
Jersey City
Brooklyn–Battery Tunnel
BROOKLYN

inland, around Bowling Green and on up historic Pearl Street. North of that is the Financial District, dominated by Wall Street. The South Street Seaport, on the East River, is our next stop, followed by the World Trade Center, World Financial Center, and Battery Park City on the opposite shoreline. Last, we cover Civic Center, including City Hall, with a foray onto the Brooklyn Bridge.

MAJOR INTEREST

The Statue of Liberty
Ellis Island
Harbor views from Battery Park
The Staten Island Ferry
The Financial District
South Street Seaport
200-mile panorama from the top of the World
    Trade Center
The World Financial Center
Battery Park City's Esplanade
Civic Center
City Hall
The Brooklyn Bridge

The Battery

"The Bronx is up and the Battery's down" is how New York's geography ("up" meaning to the north and "down" to the south) was succinctly described in the Comden-Green-Bernstein musical *On the Town*. At the downtown tip of Manhattan, the Battery is as far down as you can go. It takes its name from the battery of cannon that protected Manhattan at what was once the island's tip, coinciding with the current Battery Place. The cannon were aimed directly at the area now occupied by Battery Park, which has been built up over the years with landfill.

BATTERY PARK

At Battery Park's entrance on Battery Place, the Netherlands Memorial Monument briefly recounts the history of the settlement of Manhattan, in English and Dutch. A long mall then leads to **Castle Clinton National Monument**, which once stood on a parcel of land some 300 feet offshore (since joined to the rest of the island with landfill). Although it was built for the defense of Manhattan (it was begun in 1807 as West Battery to provide protection against the British), the circular sandstone fort is more fondly remembered as a monument to New York entrepreneurship. In 1824 it reopened as Castle Garden, where in 1850 P. T. Barnum made a fortune staging a concert by Jenny Lind, a singer whom he promoted as the "Swedish Nightingale." He drummed up even more publicity (and ticket sales) by planting anonymous letters in the papers claiming she was vastly overrated, selling out the house of 6,000 at the then-exorbitant fee of three dollars for the cheapest seat. The facilities were subsequently used as the Immigrant Landing Depot (1855 to 1890) and remodeled by the prestigious and prolific architectural firm of McKim, Mead & White as the New York Aquarium (1896 to 1941).

Now restored, Castle Clinton is a tourist center, housing an exhibit on the castle's various incarnations, a bookstore/information booth, and a kiosk selling tickets for the boat to the Statue of Liberty and Ellis Island. But there's not much reason to linger. Pass through it to reach the **Admiral George Dewey Promenade**, offering spectacular views of the harbor spread out before you. Facing out toward the bay you can see Brooklyn Heights to the east and **Governors Island** to the west of that, the first island inhabited by the Dutch. Its fort, Castle William, was built in 1811 to defend the harbor in conjunction with Castle Clinton. Now occupied by the United States Coast Guard, Governors Island is open once a year in summer to the general public; Tel: 668-7000. Visitors are ferried over from Battery Park and can explore different commands on the island and board Coast Guard cutters. Bring a lunch. To the south and southeast are Staten Island, Liberty Island, and Ellis Island, all of which you can visit by boat. Immediately to the west is the 1886 landmark **Pier A**, with its picturesque clock tower facing the Battery. The building is scheduled to be restored beginning in the fall of 1993 and converted into a restaurant complex and a state-run harbor tourism center. Beyond Pier A are the shores of New Jersey.

Now turn around to take in the dramatic vista of the skyscrapers of lower Manhattan. The **East Coast War Memorial**, set against this stunning backdrop, consists of a giant bronze American eagle by Albino Manca surrounded by eight granite slabs (engraved with the names of World War II casualties) rising sharply like the towers behind them. Take a few more minutes to stroll in this breezy and agreeable park. The salt air, the busy harbor, the street

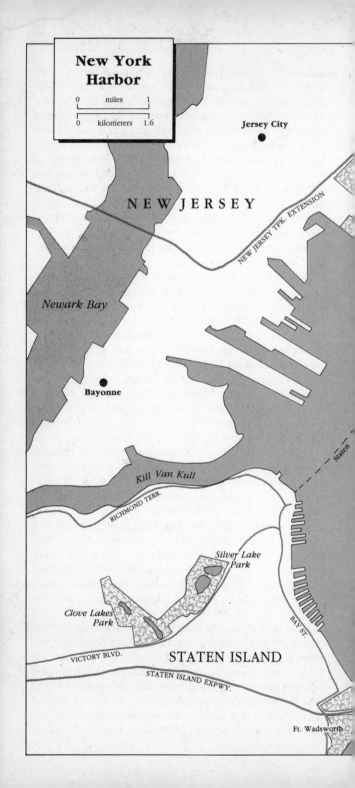

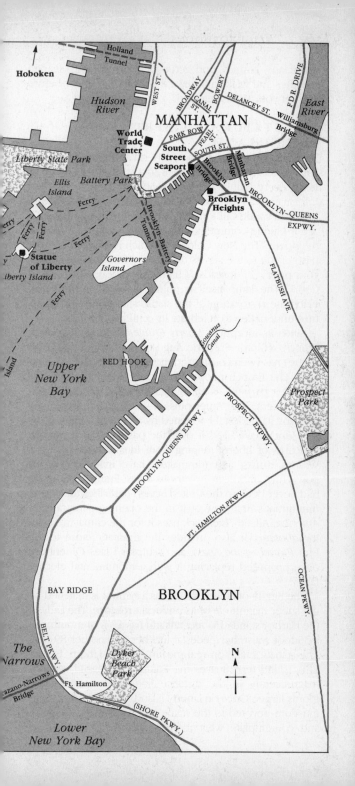

musicians, comics, and acrobats, the pleasantly shaded benches and walkways make this a place to linger before you set your sights seaward.

THE STATUE OF LIBERTY AND ELLIS ISLAND

Tickets for the excursion to Liberty and Ellis islands are sold at Castle Clinton from 8:30 A.M. to 4:30 P.M. Boats leave every half hour, from 9:30 A.M. to 4:30 P.M. (For information about ferry schedules, Tel: 269-5755.) Emerging from Castle Clinton, facing the Statue of Liberty, you'll see a plaque commemorating Emma Lazarus, author of the poem "The New Colossus," which is engraved on the base of the statue across the water. "Give me your tired, your poor . . . ," it reads, "I lift my lamp beside the golden door!" The lamp itself is golden as well, owing to an elaborate restoration of the statue and its support structure undertaken to celebrate its centennial in 1986.

Since its inception, *Liberty Enlightening the World* (as French sculptor Frédéric Auguste Bartholdi entitled his statue) has been considered more a symbol than a sculpture. The French people, who paid for the statue, supported it partially as an implicit criticism of the French government. The Americans, who almost begrudgingly paid for its pedestal (designed by architect Richard Morris Hunt), have used it over the past century to invoke concepts of liberty ranging from idealistic to mawkish. Writers, artists, and filmmakers have made use of its powerful symbolism in various ways: Franz Kafka (who had never been to the United States) describes the classic immigrant's first view of it in the opening paragraph of *Amerika,* Alfred Hitchcock uses it for the climactic scene in *Saboteur* (it also provides the dramatic close to the film *Planet of the Apes*), and sculptor Claes Oldenburg once proposed replacing it with a monumental electric fan.

The Statue of Liberty's force as a symbol is matched by the sheer magnitude of its physical presence. The Lady in the Harbor stands 151 feet tall and has a 3-foot mouth and a 35-foot waist; her pedestal lifts her up another 89 feet. The statistics take on real meaning as the Liberty Island/Ellis Island ferry leaves the Battery: Manhattan recedes magnificently in the distance and the massive statue looms larger. Once on Liberty Island, you can visit a small museum devoted to the statue and its history at its base and contemplate what it once meant to the huddled masses. Then, at the base of the statue, you can join the line for the elevator to an observation deck in the statue's crown. Expect a considerable wait in summer and on weekends.

Return to the boat to continue your journey to **Ellis Island**, the primary point of entry for immigrants to the United States from 1892 to 1924, closed to the public in 1954. Its cavernous main building was recently (and, at a price tag of $150 million, expensively) restored to its 1918–1924 appearance and in 1990 reopened as the **Ellis Island Immigration Museum**. Exhibits of immigrants' personal belongings, documents, and processing paraphernalia recount the story of the American immigrant, but it is the site itself that conjures up the past here, where so many of our ancestors made their entry to the United States. The names of some of them are commemorated on the American Immigrant Wall of Honor; immigrants, or their descendants, can have their names placed there by donating at least $100 to the museum.

THE STATEN ISLAND FERRY

Many New Yorkers have never been to the Statue of Liberty, but thousands board the Staten Island Ferry just for the ride. The ferry terminal, at the east end of the Battery Park promenade, was recently gutted by fire, and for the time being boats leave from the nearby U.S. Coast Guard slip. A new terminal, which will have a monumental lighted clock to greet Manhattan-bound ferries, is being designed by Venturi, Scott Brown & Associates and Frederic Schwartz.

The ferry leaves on the hour and the half-hour; the one on the half-hour is an older boat, with picturesque wooden seats. Primarily used by commuters from Staten Island, at 50¢ for a round-trip fare the ferry also provides a very enjoyable pauper's boat tour of Upper New York Bay (25 minutes each way), passing near Governors Island and Liberty Island and offering spectacular views of lower Manhattan and its bridges. Edna St. Vincent Millay wrote about one such trip in her poem "Recuerdo":

> We were very tired, we were very merry,
> We had gone back and forth all night on the ferry.
> We hailed "Good morrow, mother!" to a shawl-
>   covered head,
> And bought a morning paper, which neither of us
>   read;

And she wept, "God bless you!" for the apples and
    pears,
And we gave her all our money but our subway
    fares.

STATE STREET TO BOWLING GREEN

Off the northeastern corner of Battery Park is minuscule
Peter Minuit Plaza, a bedraggled place not of interest in
and of itself. Its flag pole, however, has a plaque commemorating the first group of Jews to arrive in this country, a Spanish and Portuguese contingent that came from
Brazil in 1654 and founded the Shearith Israel Congregation. (The cemeteries of this group, farther uptown in
Chinatown and Greenwich Village, are far more interesting reminders than the plaque.)

The curved brick building with the two-story colonnade across State Street (at number 8, between Pearl and
Whitehall streets) is the Federal-style former James Watson house, built in 1800, the last of many such mansions
that lined State Street. The building is now the **Shrine of
Saint Mother Elizabeth Ann Seton** (1774–1821), the first
American-born saint, who converted from Episcopalian-
ism to Catholicism and founded the first order of nuns, as
well as several Catholic parochial schools, in the United
States. You can get a glimpse of the interior by stepping
into the peaceful, white-painted chapel inside.

17 State Street

Another religious structure, the beloved Seamen's Church
Institute, once stood on a site just to the north (the site was
also the birthplace of Herman Melville) but was demolished in 1986 to make way for the glass-and-aluminum
skyscraper at 17 State Street. The loss of Seamen's Church
caught many by surprise, as preservationists had been
especially watchful in New York after the demolition of
Pennsylvania Station in 1963, an act of stupidity and brutality that brought about the formation of the New York City
Landmarks Preservation Commission.

Seventeen State Street has redeemed itself somewhat
by providing housing for **New York Unearthed**, the city's
archaeological museum (the entrance is around the back
of the Seton shrine, in a structure separate from the 17
State Street main building). Pass through the pleasant
cobblestoned plaza, with plenty of shaded wood-and-cast-
iron benches, for a quick look at finds from some of the
city's digs: crockery, dolls, gemstones, Native American

artifacts, coins, buttons, and one set of false teeth. The ten-minute video presentation, which takes place in an elevator cab and pretends to take you on a futuristic journey, is somewhat patronizing, and definitely not for claustrophobics. Returning to State Street, you can't help but notice the receptionist's desk at 17 State Street: The desk, phone, chair, and accessories are all clear Plexiglas, and the receptionist looks as if she's perched in midair. The scene is an amusing contrast with the cobblestone floors that continue from the plaza into the lobby.

The Custom House

Farther north on State Street, at Battery Place, is the former **United States Custom House**, built in 1907 to the designs of Cass Gilbert, and one of the city's finest examples of the ornate style that American architects learned from the Académie des Beaux-Arts in Paris. Customs operations moved to the World Trade Center in 1973, and this building is finally undergoing a top-to-bottom cleaning and renovation for its new role as the George Gustav Heye Center of the **National Museum of the American Indian**, part of the Smithsonian Institution (scheduled to open in fall 1994). The choice of the customhouse to display that particular collection is not without irony, given the submissive posture of the native behind the allegorical statue of America at the building's entrance. The sculptures, *The Four Continents,* by Daniel Chester French, represent telling turn-of-the-century American attitudes. *Asia* and *Africa* sit at the most removed extremes (*Africa* is actually asleep), *Europe* is surrounded by icons of education, and *America* looks progressively forward with her own torch of liberty and enlightenment, accompanied by Labor turning the wheel of progress. On the cornice are 12 statues representing commercial powers from history, past and present (*Germany* was renamed *Belgium* during World War I). A more recent vision of commerce is provided by the Reginald Marsh murals of nautical themes in the oval rotunda indoors on the second floor.

Bowling Green

Just north of the customhouse is **Bowling Green**, the city's first park, leased at a fee of one peppercorn a year in 1733. Originally part of the Dutch cattle market, it became a green for the sport of bowling and later contained a statue of King George III that was melted down for bullets after the Declaration of Independence was read publicly on July 9, 1776. The exuberant patriots also tore off the crowns that once topped the iron fence erected around the park in 1771, but the rest of the fence remains and has been declared a city landmark. On the northern end of the park the sculpture *Charging Bull,* by Arturo DiModica, optimistically faces Wall Street. Before departing the area, have a look at the Bowling Green subway station (Lexington Avenue line). Clean, spacious, and bright with glazed red-orange tile, it is among the most pleasant stations you'll see in New York's massive system.

Two impressive buildings around Bowling Green are reminders of this area's former importance as the center of the city's shipping industry. One Broadway (at the corner of Battery Place) is the United States Lines–Panama Pacific Lines Building, built in 1884. Its site was once the tip of Manhattan, where the original Dutch Fort Amsterdam, the headquarters of George Washington and then of British admiral Richard Howe, once stood. The immense Renaissance-style structure to the north at 25 Broadway was designed by Benjamin Wistar Morris and built in 1921 for the Cunard line. Its lavish lobby is now occupied by the United States Postal Service, which has preserved the ornate interior with its intricate (though badly illuminated) ceilings and frescoes. The building with the curved façade across the street (at 26 Broadway) is the former headquarters of the Standard Oil Company. It, too, has a fine lobby, and is topped with a structure shaped like an oil lamp.

PEARL STREET

Round Bowling Green and head east down Whitehall Street to Pearl Street, named for the mother-of-pearl with which it used to be paved. This narrow old thoroughfare once ran along the East River shoreline and still manages to retain much of its colonial-era atmosphere, despite the presence of massive office towers all around it.

Fraunces Tavern, at 54 Pearl Street (at Broad Street), is a 1907 reconstruction of a tavern where George Washington bade farewell to his troops. Inside are displays of memorabilia from the Revolution and a restaurant serving food that some claim dates from the same period—but having a drink here is a harmless way of paying homage to history. This entire block of 18th- and 19th-century row houses is a historic district, a fact that explains the rustic-style signs and interiors in the fast-food shops within them. The plaza across Pearl Street at 85 Broad Street is a pleasant place for an alfresco lunch. Below the plaza's pavement under glass are a cistern and the underground foundations of **Governor Lovelace's Tavern**, which stood from 1670 to 1706 and served briefly as city hall.

A block east is the New York Veterans' Memorial in **Vietnam Veterans Plaza** (55 Water Street), a translucent wall of glass block engraved with letters from Vietnam soldiers and other writings. It is especially effective at dusk, when interior illumination gives the memorial an eerie glow. At the 55 Water Street building to the north there is another plaza, accessible by escalator, with fine views across the East River.

Head west along Coenties Slip for two blocks to look down **Stone Street**, the city's first paved street (hence its name), cobbled in 1658. Although now lined with 19th-century buildings, the street retains the irregular pattern of the warren of narrow lanes that crisscrossed lower Manhattan when it was called New Amsterdam.

The Financial District

Some of the most expensive land in the world lies in the area of lower Manhattan known as the Financial District. Traditionally this district encompasses the area around Wall Street and Exchange Place, but is sometimes taken to mean the World Trade and World Financial centers as well (which we treat separately). The Financial District, like London's City, is hardly residential at all. The vast majority of its population consists of dayworkers for large corporations. In his 1853 short story "Bartleby, the Scrivener" Herman Melville described a Wall Street "which of week-days hums with industry and life, at nightfall echoes with sheer vacancy, and all through Sunday is forlorn." That aspect still holds true. And despite the enormous social changes that have occurred in the city over the last several decades, this area seems to have resisted sociocultural change as well. It's a masculine place, where power smells like cigars and martinis, and all the secretaries are women.

What *has* changed are the buildings owned by the banking and other institutions that give the Financial District its name. Many corporations have built their headquarters here, and the corporate emphasis on edifying edifices makes architecture one of the great pleasures of

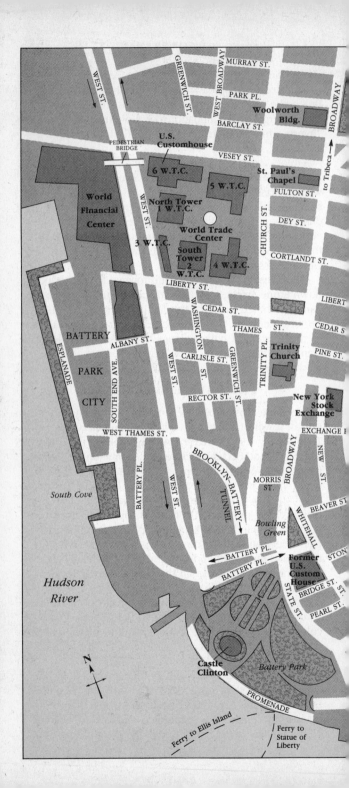

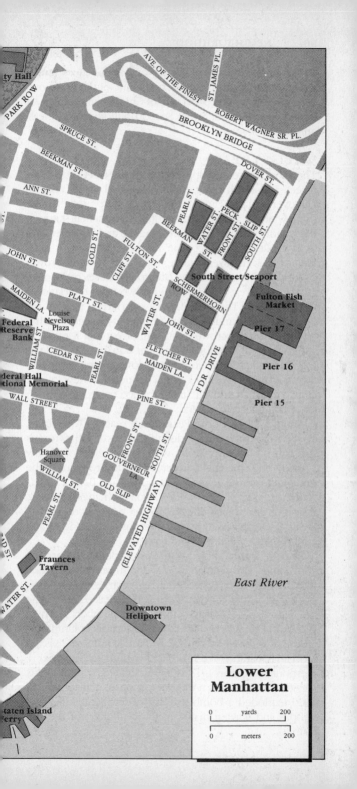

a visit to the area. But don't worry about neck strain: Down-to-earth attractions such as some of the finest outdoor public sculpture this side of Chicago and the salt air of the nearby South Street Seaport will keep you pleasantly level-headed.

WALL STREET

The most impressive approach to Wall Street is via Pearl Street. Just north of Coenties Slip, Pearl Street reaches **Hanover Square**. Though the square is commercial, the mellow stone and the innocuous monumental statue in the middle make it easy to imagine the area's former days as a residential district. The Italian palazzo–style India House, at 1 Hanover Square, made of the same brownstone so associated with the later town houses on Manhattan's Upper West Side, was originally built as the Hanover Bank in 1851. The building houses **Harry's at Hanover Square**, a meat-and-potatoes restaurant that gets such a serious drinking crowd from Wall Street that it might as well be called "Harry's at Hangover Square." Before leaving Hanover Square, look west down narrow Hanover Street from Pearl Street for a wonderful view of the ornate tower of 40 Wall Street, framed perfectly between two plain concrete towers.

Another block north, Pearl Street reaches Wall Street. To the west you'll see the definitive view of Wall Street as the canyon of Manhattan, with the steeple of Trinity Church, once the tallest structure in the city, rising at the end. At the convergence of Pearl, Wall, and Beaver streets is the wonderful New York Cocoa Exchange building, now housing a sprawling espresso bar and restaurant, **Dean & DeLuca Wall Street**, offering the best food and refreshments you'll find in the area.

As you amble down Wall Street, dodging hurrying young men and women (many of whom really do look like the bejeweled Staten Island secretaries with big hair portrayed in the movie *Working Girl*), take note of the old Merchants Exchange building at number 55 (now Citibank). Its tiers of Ionic and Corinthian columns encase an impressively classical interior. At number 23 is the Morgan Guaranty Trust Company, built by financier J. Pierpont Morgan in 1913 as an understated symbol of his wealth. The symbolism was not lost on anarchists, who in 1920 exploded a bomb in front of the bank, killing 33 people and leaving marks in the building that are still visible.

What to do next is a toss-up. Across Broad Street is the New York Stock Exchange; across Wall Street is **Federal Hall National Memorial**, whose staircase is a good place to sit and watch the action at this busy intersection. The rotunda inside provides some relief from the summer heat. A Doric temple built of Westchester marble, the memorial stands on the site of the first English City Hall, later Federal Hall, where George Washington took his oath of office in 1789 (a bronze statue by John Quincy Adams Ward commemorates the event). The present building dates from 1842 and houses the **Museum of American Constitutional Government**, with exhibits related to George Washington and other aspects of American history. Free lunchtime concerts are sometimes given in the rotunda; Tel: 866-2086.

The **New York Stock Exchange** was born in 1792 when 24 brokers met beneath a buttonwood tree at the corner of Wall and William streets. It is now housed in a Roman temple on Broad and Wall streets, above whose Corinthian columns is a pediment depicting *Integrity Protecting the Works of Man*. For a look at the trading floor, go to the visitors' entrance at 20 Broad Street, where free tickets are distributed weekdays between 9:00 A.M. and 3:45 P.M. (or until they run out). Displays and recorded narration explain the mysterious chaotic activity spread out below you in what seems a disorganized, entangled mess.

Down at the head of Wall Street, at Broadway, is the 1846 **Trinity Church**, the third such Episcopal church on the site. Its Gothic Revival complex with its well-maintained cemetery is an architectural oasis in this part of Manhattan. It has also long been a spiritual oasis: "And in this yard stenogs, bundle boys, scrubwomen, sit on the tombstones, and walk on the grass of graves," wrote Carl Sandburg in his poem "Trinity Peace," "speaking of war and weather, of babies, wages and love." People still pass time in the churchyard, enjoying the solitude or visiting the graves of Alexander Hamilton and Robert Fulton. In summer there are sometimes concerts here during the lunch hour. Inside the church is a fine museum with exhibits about the intertwined histories of the church and the city. The cast-iron lamppost in front of the church, dating from 1896, is one of some 30 such "bishop's crooks" that remain on the city streets.

Across the street from Trinity Church, at 100 Broadway, is the Bank of Tokyo, an 1895 Beaux Arts building restored and adapted for use as a modern bank in 1975. The contrast of old and new extends to the building's art: outdoors are Greek-inspired statues above Ionic columns, indoors an aluminum sculpture by Isamu Noguchi.

The **Equitable Building**, up the block at 120 Broadway, literally brought zoning laws into existence in New York City. Its massive bulk caused such a commotion when it was built in 1915 that the following year the nation's first law was passed requiring that buildings be stepped back at certain levels in order to admit light to the street, thus forming the "zoning envelope," or legal limit to building proportions, that has since shaped so many of the city's skyscrapers.

The architectural firm of Skidmore, Owings & Merrill designed the Marine Midland Bank, just to the north, at 140 Broadway, which has a black steel-and-glass façade that plays nicely off the ornamentation of the nearby buildings reflected in it. The spacious plaza in front of the building, with its huge sculpture, *The Red Cube,* by Noguchi, is a welcoming public space, not least for the fact that during the work week an inordinate number of food vendors gathers here. It is certainly more inviting than 1 Liberty Plaza, across Broadway, another Skidmore, Owings & Merrill creation, this one a cynical concession to the newest zoning law, which requires public open space as a trade-off for more floor space. In this context even J. Seward Johnson Jr.'s cleverly sited bronze sculpture *Double Check,* a banker seemingly going about his business in the plaza, becomes symbolically indifferent to his surroundings.

Turning eastward down Liberty Street you'll see the charming façade of the Beaux Arts New York State Chamber of Commerce building, at 65 Liberty Street, now subjected to the indignity of selling discount women's clothing. Down the street is Chase Manhattan Plaza, another open space, this one decorated with a sunken garden by Noguchi and the *Group of Four Trees* sculpture by Jean Dubuffet. The plaza is dominated by the glass-and-aluminum Chase Manhattan Bank building, built by the ubiquitous Skidmore, Owings & Merrill.

Across the street, at 33 Liberty Street, is the **Federal Reserve Bank of New York,** an enormous limestone building inspired by Florentine Renaissance palazzi that goes on and on and on for an entire block. The building stores one-quarter of the official monetary gold of 80 countries— more than Fort Knox. These billions of dollars of gold bars never leave the building, which serves as a sort of monumental counting house with the bars moving from one nation's pile to another in the balance of trade. The gold can be seen during free one-hour tours. To reserve, Tel: 720-6130 at least one week in advance; tickets will be mailed to you for the next available date.

At William Street, Liberty Street merges with Maiden Lane, named for the young girls who did the family washing in a brook that once flowed along the site. A small park at the intersection called **Louise Nevelson Plaza** has seven brown constructions (called *Shadows and Flags*) by the sculptor, who until her death in 1988 had a home and studio in downtown Manhattan and was an active figure in the city's cultural life.

South Street Seaport

Continue east down Maiden Lane to Water Street, where you can sit at the counter facing out the window at **Au Bon Pain** (southwest corner) and have homemade soup with a croissant sandwich. Just down Water Street, between Maiden Lane and Pine Street, is a building designed by I. M. Pei (formerly at 88 Pine Street, now called 1 Wall Street Plaza), where a waterfall provides a relaxing backdrop and a sculpture by Yu Yu Yang reflects passersby in a mirrored disk. A couple of blocks north, the delightful public space at 127 John Street is full of brightly colored metal furniture and neon-lit canvas canopies. In case you miss the point, a lobby plaque announces with characteristic Gotham candor, "This building was designed to create an atmosphere of pleasure, humor and excitement for people." At the corner of Water and Fulton streets is a small lighthouse that marks the entrance to South Street Seaport, a historical/commercial district bound roughly by John Street on the south, Water Street on the west, Peck Slip on the north, and the East River.

New York's busiest port district during the 19th century, the area fell into disuse over the intervening years, except for the ever-thriving Fulton Fish Market and a few pleasantly seedy seafood restaurants. Over the past couple of decades the area has been undergoing renovation as a pedestrian mall by the Rouse Company, which was responsible for similar projects at Faneuil Hall in Boston and Harbor Place in Baltimore. Rouse's Pier 17 Pavilion and Fulton Market Building are food-and-shopping malls full of shops, bars, and restaurants with contrived names that attract hordes of tourists and beer-guzzling traders from the Financial District. The area is best avoided on Friday evenings and weekends in summer, when it is overrun with the masses.

THE SOUTH STREET SEAPORT MUSEUM

The Seaport Museum controls most of the authentically historical sights here, although many of these have been considerably sanitized and would be unrecognizable to the sailors and old salts that drank, caroused, and flopped here in the 19th century. Nonetheless, the mix of blatant commerce and cleaned-up history works pretty well: It doesn't feel like the real thing, but it's a fun, safe, and engaging place.

Not the typical exhibits-behind-glass museum, the Seaport Museum comprises buildings, streets, shops, galleries, and eight ships. Many of these sights are free, but others are accessible only if you buy a museum ticket. The ticket gets you into two galleries, a children's center, and three ships, and entitles you to join a walking tour.

Buy your museum ticket at the booth on Pier 16, or go to the **Seaport Museum Visitors' Center**, housed in **Schermerhorn Row** (2–18 Fulton Street, between Front and South streets), an original group of warehouses and counting houses built in 1811 by Peter Schermerhorn. With their red-brick walls (inside and out) and sharply sloping roofs, these buildings give an idea of what much of the area was like until just a few decades ago.

Water Street between Fulton and Beekman streets houses a number of the museum's buildings, including the **Museum Gallery**, with changing exhibits about New York City history; **Bowne & Co., Stationers**, a 19th-century working print shop that still takes orders and sells stationery; the **Melville Library**, a repository of city and maritime history, open by appointment only (Tel: 669-9437); and the museum's shops.

The museum's other main exhibition space, the **Norway Galleries**, is in the A. A. Low Building, which is on the block of John Street that is back to back with Schermerhorn Row. Originally the counting house of a merchant in the China trade, it now features maritime displays from the museum's excellent collection, which was given a substantial boost when it acquired 2,000 items from the Seamen's Bank for Savings in 1990. The museum's **children's center** (hands-on exhibits, workshops) and **Boat Building Shop** flank the Norway Galleries on either side.

On the Piers

The wide, low, brick building just across South Street from this part of the seaport area houses the **Fulton Fish Market**, which supplies the most authentic Old New York energy at the seaport—and is a perfect place for insomniacs, as the boisterous transactions are in full swing by 4:00 A.M. (Tours, given on the first and third Thursdays of the month at 6:00 A.M., may be reserved by calling 669-9416.)

Pier 17, directly behind the market, is occupied by Rouse's enormous altar to consumption, the Pier 17 Pavilion. Along Piers 16 and 15, to the south, are the museum's ships, three of which can be boarded with the museum ticket: the four-masted *Peking,* the second-largest sailing ship in the world; the lightship *Ambrose,* whose beacon once guided ships in the harbor; and the three-masted *Wavertree.* Other ships can be boarded for a fee. The 100-year-old schooner *Pioneer* takes two-hour sails in the harbor as far as the Narrows, where Brooklyn and Staten Island almost meet; reservations suggested, Tel: 669-9417. The **Seaport Line** offers cruises aboard a 19th-century paddle wheeler (the *Andrew Fletcher*) and steamer (the *DeWitt Clinton*). Both take in the sights of lower Manhattan as well as the Statue of Liberty and Ellis Island. Cocktail cruises are offered, too; Tel: 669-9405 for schedules. The seaport hosts many special events throughout the year, including concerts on the pier (Tel: 669-9424, for information), as well as an outdoor greenmarket on Front Street Wednesdays and Saturdays from June to December.

Shopping and Dining

When it comes to shopping and eating at the seaport there's almost an embarrassment of riches ... well, riches might be too strong a word for the restaurants here. The third floor of Pier 17 is crammed with fast-food joints, although there are a couple of restaurants here—the casual **Liberty Café** (seafood, pasta, and pizza baked in a wood-fired oven), which has an outdoor terrace, and the more formal **Harbour Lights** (steak and seafood cooked in various Continental preparations)—that have fabulous views of the lower Manhattan skyline and the Brooklyn Bridge, respectively, if middling food.

At the southeastern corner of South and Fulton streets are a trio of old reliables. **Sloppy Louie's** and **Sweet's** both serve reasonably good, unfancy seafood. Sweet's has the added distinction of being the seaport's oldest restaurant (established 1842), but unlike its nearby competitor is closed weekends. Between the two is **North Star Pub**, whose well-stocked line of imported beers, ales, and single-malt scotches is certainly a draw, and the food— fish and chips, shepherd's pie—is not bad either.

Two other decent restaurants in the seaport proper are the old-fashioned **Roeblings Bar & Grill**, in the Fulton Market Building, a hangout for workers from the nearby Civic Center; and **Café Fledermaus** (in 1 Seaport Plaza, the building that occupies the block just west of the Schermerhorn Row block), serving a nice light lunch of salads and sandwiches—topped off with rich Viennese pastries.

Perhaps the best meals around here can be had at the **Bridge Café**, which is north of the seaport, farther north than many of the tourists and Wall Street traders dare to go. Simply follow Water Street up to number 279, at Dover Street. The turn-of-the-19th-century building is the last wood-frame edifice in the area: a fine old backdrop for good, imaginative seafood, chicken, and meat dishes. Just up Dover Street is the more casual **Jeremy's Ale House** (254 Front Street, at Dover Street), featuring fried seafood and sandwiches.

Shops at the seaport range from that breed of annoyingly silly theme shop (cat knickknacks, or heart-shaped objects, or all-purple items) that seem to thrive in fancy malls to run-of-the-mill mall shops (Footlocker, the Limited) to fine, upstanding, if ubiquitous clothing and gift shops: Abercrombie & Fitch for men; Ann Taylor for stylish but tradition-minded women (great shoe department, though); Banana Republic, the Gap, Benetton, and J. Crew for well-made casual weekend clothes. The **Nature Company**, an appealing gift shop on Schermerhorn Row with lots of animal-theme toys and puzzles and the like, has seminars and workshops for kids.

Seamen's Church Institute

Just up Water Street from the seaport's hub, between Beekman Street and Peck Slip, is the Seamen's Church Institute, the new headquarters for this worthy 158-year-old organization, founded to aid mariners. The two-story lobby, with fine East River views and several maritime displays, and the cool, quiet chapel are open to visitors.

WEST TO BROADWAY

Fulton Street leads from South Street Seaport a few blocks west to Nassau Street, a creepy pedestrian mall that attempts to make low-end chain stores look quaint.

At Fulton Street and Broadway the steeple rising against a background formed by the towers of the World Trade Center belongs to the oldest building in Manhattan, **St. Paul's Chapel**, designed by Thomas McBean in 1766. George Washington worshiped in the elegant Georgian interior (his pew is still here) with its pink and aqua walls, white trim, and chandeliers. Don't enter St. Paul's by the main Broadway door, which brings you in behind the altar. To get a proper impression, go around back through the lovely green churchyard with its many 18th-century gravestones to the rear door. St. Paul's often hosts classical music concerts; Tel: 602-0768 for information.

From St. Paul's churchyard you may notice the sleek black ▶ **Millenium**, lower Manhattan's newest luxury hotel, rising to the southeast (at Fulton and Church streets); see the Accommodations section for details.

The World Trade Center and West to the River

WORLD TRADE CENTER

Dominating lower Manhattan (and most of the New York metropolitan area, for that matter) are Minoru Yamasaki's twin towers of the World Trade Center, two 110-story buildings rising like the prongs of a colossally unaligned tuning fork from the depths of Manhattan. The scale and monotony of the buildings are, in fact, completely out of tune with the romantic skyscrapers that surround it. If record-breaking height was the goal, the buildings lose on that scale as well, as their altitude was soon surpassed by the Sears Tower in Chicago. Though there are attempts to humanize the seven-building complex (sprawling westward from the base of Church Street) with works of art such as tapestries and sculptures, the scale of the buildings is too overpowering to allow the works to stand on their own.

In February 1993 a bomb exploded in a subterranean level of the World Trade Center—the most obvious act of terrorism ever leveled against a target in the United States. Above ground the visible structural damage was most evident in the New York Vista Hotel, which remained closed until the fall of 1993. The towers received smoke and operating-systems damage, but reopened within months, with the exception of Windows on the

World, which remained closed through summer 1993. The bomb blast took the center's maintenance, physical-plant, and security staffs by surprise. In response, they have reconsidered evacuation procedures, safety guidelines, and emergency communications, and the physical plant, with attendant ventilation systems and power supplies, is being overhauled. All in all, the towers are probably safer now than they have ever been, and if you ascribe to the logic of the John Irving character Garp, there may be no safer place (lightning never strikes twice).

Tobin Plaza

Enter the World Trade Center from Church Street (a block south of St. Paul's, at Dey Street) into the five-acre Austin J. Tobin Plaza, which is dominated by a fountain topped by a large bronze sphere by Fritz Koenig that looks, unhappily, like the head of a space alien. Surrounding the plaza are the WTC's seven buildings: the twin towers (number one to the north, two to the south), three office buildings, the Vista Hotel, and the U.S. Customhouse. Within the buildings are mainly marketing, advertising, finance, international trade, and governmental offices.

The plaza, a vast concrete platform, is in line with the overall scale of the World Trade Center, whose unfriendly interior spaces are cavernous and institutional and strangely seedy. Nonetheless, the view from here straight up the towers is impressive and dizzying. An awesome sight at any time, they seem to soar especially high at night, when the plaza is empty and you get the feeling you are the only person out south of Chambers Street. Some of the stunts pulled here—such as tightrope artist Phillip Petit's high-wire walk between the towers and mountaineer George Willig's climb up the outside—seem foolhardy indeed from this vantage point. Even window washers don't risk these heights: The towers' miles of glass are cleaned by machines that glide up and down on steel tracks.

Sculptures on the plaza include a stabile by Alexander Calder (in front of 7 World Trade Center), a black-granite piece by Masayuki Nagara (at the plaza's main entrance), and *Ideogram,* by James Rosati (between the towers). On Tuesdays and Thursdays one of city's lively Greenmarkets takes over the plaza. In the summer the plaza hosts free lunchtime, and occasional evening, concerts (ranging from pop and rock to jazz, opera, and an assortment of international music), dance, and stand-up comedy as well as special events such as puppet shows and crafts fairs. Pick up a schedule in one of the towers or call 435-4170.

The Twin Towers

You'll want to go into Two World Trade Center (the south tower) first, which you'll enter from the plaza on the mezzanine level. The huge crowd you see huddled together on the left is waiting to be hurled into the sky on a one-minute elevator ride to the 107th-floor Observation Deck. Before you buy your ticket, squeeze past the crowd until you can see the sign that posts the visibility. On the very best days you can see up to 55 miles in every direction. So if the visibility is only a few miles you'd best come back another day, although you'd be surprised at the number of people who stick it out on the worst days, remaining in line even after the sign reads "zero visibility." Beyond the line you'll see the **TKTS booth**, which sells cut-price tickets for Broadway and Off Broadway shows on the day of performance. The line here is much shorter than the one at its counterpart in Times Square.

But for tickets to the Observation Deck you have to hustle around to the right, past the New York City Visitors Bureau information center (staffed by exceedingly friendly and helpful people who love their city), to the ticket booth in the opposite corner. When you finally get to the glassed-in Observation Deck on the 107th floor, you'll find yourself standing 1,310 feet high, with miles of New York and New Jersey spread out before you in every direction. Landmarks are outlined and labeled on the window glass, so you can line them up in your sight and identify them. Weather permitting, you can take the escalators up another 67 feet to an open rooftop promenade above the 110th floor. If it's too windy, however, you'll have to content yourself with the views, souvenirs, and snack food on 107.

Once you've returned to earth, you can take the escalator from the tower's mezzanine down to the enormous mall that connects all the center's buildings. There are lots of middle-of-the-road mall shops here, as well as restaurants, the best of which is probably the **Market Bar and Grill**, a steak and seafood type place with a fancy dining room as well as a more casual bar area. **Sbarro** has quick Italian dishes and pizza, and the **Big Kitchen** has a self-serve salad and entrées bar. All the restaurants are in the northeastern corner of the complex. Big-name banks (several of which have handy automatic-teller machines) and entrances to the A, E, N, R, 1, and 9 subways as well as to New Jersey Path trains also anchor the mall.

Head into One World Trade Center to get to the center's famous 107th-floor restaurants and bars (but call before making a special trip; they remained closed after the bomb explosion through summer 1993). **Windows on the World** is a brunch spot popular with New Yorkers hosting out-of-town guests (reserve well in advance; Tel: 938-1111). **Cellar in the Sky** is just what is sounds like: no windows. But its seven-course meal, with wine, is far superior to Windows's less inspired fare (same telephone number as Windows). If you'd rather just have a drink and appetizers with those soaring views, pop up to the **Hors d'Oeuvrerie** or **City Lights Bar**, both of which require jacket and tie for men (and do not allow jeans).

THE WORLD FINANCIAL CENTER AND BATTERY PARK CITY

A recent aesthetic and commercial challenge to the World Trade Center has been the jazzy World Financial Center, just to the east, housing the world headquarters of such heavy firms as American Express, Merrill Lynch, and Dow Jones. Designed by Cesar Pelli and Associates, the World Financial Center consists of four 34- to 51-story towers clad in granite and reflective glass and topped with geometrically shaped copper roofs, visible along the entire length of Sixth Avenue. It comprises some of the most exciting new public spaces to open in New York in years, including the city's first plaza on the Hudson River. The only (minor) complaint one might have about the complex is that it's somewhat sterile and soulless. New York City isn't supposed to be this clean and well behaved. But after several days touring Manhattan's cluttered and dirty streets, most people find it a welcome antidote.

The most impressive entrance to the World Financial Center is from the World Trade Center, via the pedestrian bridge on the mezzanine (plaza) level of the U.S. Customhouse (another pedestrian bridge lies to the south at Liberty Street). This brings you directly into the Winter Garden, a barrel-shaped glass palace with 90-foot-high palm trees that looks out onto the Hudson River. The Winter Garden is the site of free concerts during the lunch hour and after work; Tel: 945-0505 for information.

Dozens of shops, restaurants, and cafés are scattered throughout the center to cater to those who work here. Northeast of the Winter Garden is the Courtyard, a glass-covered European-style plaza flanked by café-style bars and restaurants. The shops are many notches above those at the World Trade Center: Barneys New York, Ann Taylor, Mark Cross, Bally of Switzerland, Rizzoli International Bookstore, and St. Moritz Chocolatier, among many others. The restaurants are better, too. The formal **Hudson River Club** features such traditional dishes as rabbit pot-pie and venison, with intimate river views; Tel: 786-1500. **Le Pactole** serves classical French dishes in a pretty, airy setting just off the Winter Garden; Tel: 945-9444. **Edward Moran Bar & Grill** has an extremely pleasant outdoor café in summer.

The Esplanade

Head out the Winter Garden doors to the Esplanade, a lovely outdoor promenade right on the Hudson River that stretches south the length of Battery Park City, a residential complex built on landfill constructed from the dirt and rubble that was dug up when the World Trade Center was built. There are several pretty green parks south along the Esplanade, and the views of the comings and goings along the mighty Hudson as well as the Statue of Liberty and Ellis Island are magnificent. The park's sculptures include Ned Smyth's *Upper Room,* at Albany Street, a playful outdoor environment made of concrete embedded with glass, stone, and mosaic; and Richard Artschwager's *Living Room,* gigantic stone, wood, and iron furniture, a little farther south, at West Thames Street. Landscape architect Susan Child and sculptor Mary Miss have created an intricate landscape around **South Cove** (stretching south from Third Place), which is lit at nightfall with cobalt-blue lanterns. The wooden promenade extending over the water is one of the finest spots in the city for an evening picnic. New plans for a park at the very tip of Battery Park City have been developed and are expected to go ahead. Scheduled to open in 1996, the new park will have harbor views as its main feature, with inviting broad stairways, a foot bridge, and viewing platforms to accommodate crowds of lingerers.

The Battery Park City residential buildings along the way run the gamut from clumsy apartment blocks to cheerful town houses to graceful towers.

NORTH OF THE WORLD FINANCIAL CENTER

To the north the Esplanade becomes a part of the much less populated **Hudson River Park**, which has what may be one of the best playgrounds in New York City, with sections for kids of various ages, from middle years down to pre-toddler. The park's waterfall spilling onto the lily pond is an exceptionally peaceful place, far from traffic and crowds. At the northern tip of the Esplanade, known as **North Park**, is a sculptural environment by Tom Otterness involving 100 fanciful bronze figures.

Vesey Street leads out of the World Financial Center's northern edge. One block to the west you'll encounter 140 West Street, the entrance to the New York Telephone Building, a 1926 skyscraper by Voorhees, Gmelin & Walker, complete with Art Deco detailing on the façade and in the lobby. Its Vesey Street side has a sheltered arcade. At 20 Vesey Street is the former New York Evening Post Building, a soaring Art Nouveau structure topped with statues by John Gutzon Borglum, the sculptor of Mount Rushmore.

Civic Center

Many of the city's government agencies and buildings are clustered east of Broadway and north of Fulton Street. From the World Financial Center, continue east on Vesey Street to Broadway. Veering off to the northeast is **Park Row**, known as Newspaper Row at the turn of the century because of the newspaper offices that once lined the street, a fact commemorated by a statue of printer Benjamin Franklin at the intersection. (Park Row, which runs northeast behind the Municipal Building and on up to the southern edge of Chinatown, is now lined with discount electronics stores.)

A block north, on the northwest corner of Broadway and Barclay Street, is everyone's favorite skyscraper, the **Woolworth Building**. Designed by Cass Gilbert with heavy Gothic detailing and incredible mosaic ceilings in the lobby, it was nicknamed "The Cathedral of Commerce" when it opened in 1913. It bore the distinction of being the world's tallest building until the Chrysler Building went up in 1930. Frank Woolworth, of the discount store chain, paid for his building entirely in cash, an act depicted along with other amusing scenes in bas-reliefs in the ornate three-story lobby.

CITY HALL PARK

Across from the Woolworth Building is City Hall Park, the southern end of the few blocks where the city's civic buildings are scattered. Decorated with statues of patriot Nathan Hale and newspaper mogul Horace Greeley, the park has as its real centerpiece **City Hall**, a remarkably small and genteel building for such a large and noisy metropolis. When it was built—between 1802 and 1811— it was faced in marble on the south side and cheaper brownstone on the north side, the side then facing away from the city. Though the city continued to pinch pennies as tightly as ever, in 1959 it loosened up enough to replace the entire façade with limestone. Walk into the elegant and palatial lobby and up to the second-floor columned rotunda to get to the restored Governor's Room, which serves as a museum and portrait gallery (weekdays only).

North of City Hall is the old New York County Courthouse, a Victorian building now familiarly called **Tweed Courthouse**, after William Marcy "Boss" Tweed, the corrupt New York City official who made off with some $10 million of the $14 million budgeted for its construction. The building is now undergoing a long-term renovation project and is encased in scaffolding. Its WPA murals are being cleaned, but when the work is finished they'll be accessible to the public weekdays.

THE BROOKLYN BRIDGE

Opposite the east side of City Hall Park is the Manhattan-side pedestrian entrance to the Brooklyn Bridge (of late rather hard to distinguish amid the rubble of road construction; just look for the sign warning pedestrians to watch for bicycles—and take heed). Immortalized in poetry by Walt Whitman and Hart Crane, captured on canvas by Joseph Stella, and gloriously illuminated by the Grucci family's fireworks during its centennial celebration in 1983, the bridge's practical significance was perhaps best described by architecture historian James Marston Fitch: "The nineteenth century saw three great developments in structural theory: the enclosure of great areas in the Crystal Palace, the spanning of great voids in the Brooklyn Bridge, and the reaching of great heights in the Eiffel Tower."

A series of tragedies befell its designers, John A. and Washington Roebling. John died of gangrene following a crushed foot he incurred while taking measurements for the bridge, and his son, Washington, developed the bends from taking pressurized caissons underwater to work on the foundations. After the loss of many men, the bridge was completed in 1883. It is composed of two Gothic-style granite towers, from which the world's first steel span is suspended from four huge cables and a vast network of wires.

The walk across, on a boardwalk that runs down the middle of the bridge, elevated above the traffic, is one of those things you must do in New York City. Whether in bright daylight, at sunset, or after nightfall, it will be splendid.

Elizabeth Bishop's poem "Invitation to Miss Marianne Moore" describes one such circumstance:

> From Brooklyn, over the Brooklyn Bridge, on this
>   fine morning,
> please come flying.
> In a cloud of fiery pale chemicals,
> please come flying,
> to the rapid rolling of thousands of small blue
>   drums
> descending out of the mackerel sky
> over the glittering grandstand of harbor-water,
> please come flying.

NORTH OF CITY HALL PARK

Across the street from City Hall Park, on the northeast corner of Broadway and Chambers Street, is a remnant from the area's newspaper publishing days—the outdoor clock that marks the building that once housed the offices of the *New York Sun*. (The Italian palazzo–style building, originally built for the A. T. Stewart Department Store, began a trend for Italianate commercial buildings in the city.) To the south of Chambers Street, at 270 Broadway, is **Ellen's**, where local politicos gather for breakfast and lunch (even Mayor Dinkins is inclined to drop in from time to time). There are also two lobbies worth looking into on Chambers Street: Number 51 (between Broadway and Elk Street) is the Emigrant Savings Bank Building, with its stately banking facilities on the first floor; number 31 is the **Surrogate's Court** or Hall of Records, an ornately façaded Beaux Arts building (the sculpture, by Philip Martiny, represents *New York in Its Infancy* and *New York in Revolutionary Times*) with a theatrical foyer to match.

A block and a half north of Chambers Street, by way of

Elk Street and Republican Alley (but at a site not open to the public), archaeologists have uncovered the **African Burial Grounds**, an early cemetery for blacks that appears in documentation as early as 1755 as the Negros Burial Ground. At that time blacks couldn't become members of the city's churches, and their graveyard was outside the city limits. A 34-story federal office building slated to occupy the site had been delayed while the cemetery was properly explored and documented. Unfortunately, as many as 20 graves were destroyed by construction work, and another six were plundered by grave robbers. Nonetheless, more than 400 burials have been uncovered. The developers of the building may install a permanent exhibit on the burial ground in the lobby. The burial ground and the surrounding area encompassing City Hall Park north to Foley Square was designated an official landmark in 1993 as the African Burial Grounds and the Commons Historic District.

Across Centre Street from Tweed Courthouse, and astride Chambers Street, is the **Municipal Building**, another Beaux Arts skyscraper, designed by McKim, Mead & White. Built in 1914 to house city offices, it has become too small for the job, but many of the city's functions remain there—including the Marriage License Bureau (unmarried couples—heterosexual and homosexual alike—may also register here now as partners). Many a couple can be seen ceremoniously leaving the building beneath its central arch (at present closed for repair), through which Chambers Street once flowed. In typical Beaux Arts fashion, the building is adorned with statuary. Adolph Alexander Weinman's gilded *Civic Fame* graces the top of the building.

Through the arch, a pedestrian mall leads to three-acre Police Plaza, one of Manhattan's largest public spaces, dominated by an aptly arresting Cor-Ten steel sculpture by Bernard Rosenthal called *Five in One*. The Police Headquarters building is the large red-brick structure toward the river. Like many of the nearby modern buildings, it was designed by Gruzen & Partners in the 1970s as part of a redevelopment program for this part of the city. The Neo-Georgian church in the plaza is **St. Andrew's** (pleasantly dark and woody within), which adds a comforting touch to its large-scale surroundings, as do the food vendors' booths set up here during the warmer months.

FOLEY SQUARE

Go west from St. Andrew's to Foley Square, a low-lying area that was once the site of the Collect Pond, the city's reservoir during its early years. Two large Greek temples that stand on the east side of the square, on either side of Pearl Street, suffer from the need of a grand thoroughfare to set them off. The **United States Courthouse** (the one on the south side of Pearl Street) is topped with that golden pyramid you've been catching glimpses of from all over lower Manhattan—you can't see it from here, however, only from afar. The building was designed by Cass Gilbert, who was responsible for the Woolworth Building, and his son, Cass Junior. The main lobby is a welcoming spot for a rest or a snack. The temple on the north side of Pearl Street is the **New York County Courthouse** (Manhattan Supreme Court), whose façade belies the building's hexagonal shape, designed by Guy Lowell. Venture inside to see the fantastical zodiac depicted in the rotunda pavement.

The site of the intersection of Baxter, Pearl, and Worth streets, just northeast of Foley Square, was the most dangerous slum in the city in the mid-19th century. Known as Five Points, it was the center for such street gangs as the Dead Rabbits, the Shirt Tails, and the Plug Uglies. An archaeological dig here has unearthed remains of the slum at the site upon which a new 27-story federal courthouse is being erected.

People in the area lived in the kind of squalor recounted by Jacob Riis in *How the Other Half Lives:* "The family's condition was most deplorable. The man, his wife, and three small children shivering in one room through the roof of which the pitiless winds of winter whistled. The room was almost barren of furniture; the parents slept on the floor, the elder children in boxes, and the baby swung in an old shawl attached to the rafters by cords by way of a hammock. The father, a seaman, had been obliged to give up that calling because he was in consumption, and was unable to provide either bread or fire for his little ones."

Riis's documentation changed public attitudes toward social injustice, and the construction of the Foley Square courthouse complex, beginning in the 1920s, transformed the slum dwellers' former domain into a display of the justice system.

NORTH OF FOLEY SQUARE

At 60 Lafayette Street (between Leonard and Franklin streets) is the Family Court Building, a black granite mass that seems somewhat alien to its function. A steel sculpture by Ray Gussow, *Three Forms,* stands in front of the building. Farther up the street is the side entrance to the Civil and Municipal Court Building, a plain façade enlivened by Joseph Kiselewski's bas-relief *Justice.* (William Zorach's bas-relief *Law* is at the main entrance at 111 Centre Street.) Across White Street at 87 Lafayette is a fanciful building housing a community center for nearby Chinatown. Though it looks like a French château, it was originally a fire station.

Returning downtown on Centre Street: At number 100 is the notorious, towering Art Deco prison known as **The Tombs.** The name was originally given to an Egyptian-style prison that once stood across Centre Street, though the menacing appearance of the present structure has equally deadly connotations. Architecture critic Paul Goldberger has described its front door as "one of the most brilliantly contrived, if evil, stage sets in the City of New York." Officially called the New York Criminal Courts Building, it hosts courtroom proceedings in a system so overloaded that some take place at its special night court, a fascinating and free spectacle—especially if it's not compulsory.

DOWNTOWN

By Lenore Malen and Edward Hernstadt
with Dwight V. Gast

Lenore Malen, a New York artist and the executive editor of the Art Journal, *is a long-time resident of SoHo. Edward Hernstadt, a former contributor to* The Berlitz Travellers Guide to France, *lives downtown.*

New Yorkers refer to the generous section of Manhattan that extends north from City Hall to 14th Street as "downtown." Here the visitor to New York can experience most vividly the intermingling of old and new, immi-

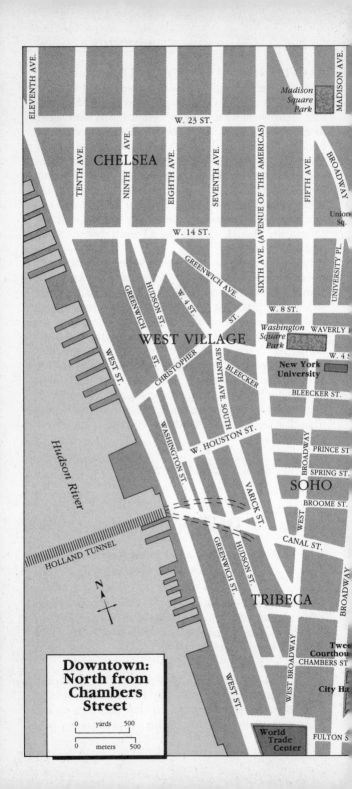

Downtown:
North from
Chambers
Street

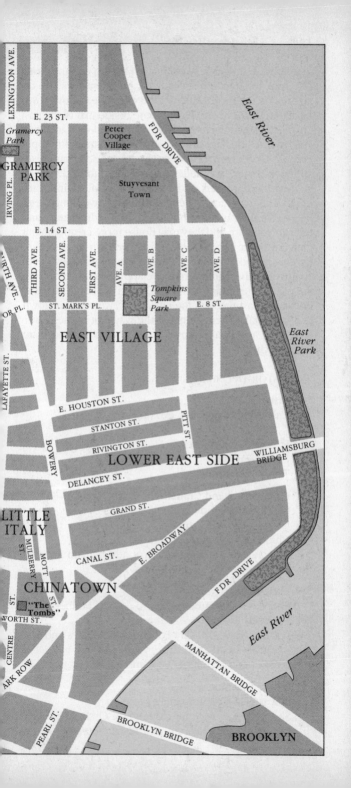

grant and avant-garde, wealth and poverty, and the vastly different architectural styles that typify New York. This is an area on the move. Much of the west side of downtown has been restored and has become residential in the past 20 years as manufacturers have moved out of Manhattan, and its east side has seen major shifts in immigrant populations. Downtown boasts every conceivable variety of antiques dealer, bookseller, art gallery, club, and café, as well as food markets and restaurants of all ethnic varieties. The downtown neighborhoods have long been known for their unconventionality, their individuality, and their informality, and they may house more creative talent than any other part of New York. Downtown residents are fiercely proud of the area, often claiming that they never venture north of 14th Street. We approach the area from the south, beginning in TriBeCa and working our way north and east through the ethnic enclaves of Chinatown and Little Italy. Then we go all the way east to the Lower East Side, and finally move west to SoHo and north to Greenwich Village.

MAJOR INTEREST

TriBeCa
Cast-iron architecture evoking old, industrial
    New York
Federal town houses
Duane Park
Trendy restaurants

Canal Street and Chinatown
Outdoor fish and vegetable markets
Narrow, crowded streets
Chinese shops and restaurants
Old and new architecture around Chatham Square
Chinese New Year celebrations

Little Italy
Shops and restaurants on and around Mulberry
    Street
Former New York City Police Headquarters and St.
    Patrick's Old Cathedral
Feast of San Gennaro (September)

Lower East Side
Lower East Side Tenement Museum
Shopping for discount clothing on Orchard Street
Old World delicatessens and restaurants

Old synagogues and other historic buildings, many
  around East Broadway
The Bowery

SoHo
Cast-iron architecture
Art galleries
Dean & DeLuca and other chic shops
The trendy scene
New Museum of Contemporary Art and Guggen-
  heim Museum SoHo
Fanelli and other hangouts

Greenwich Village
Washington Square and surrounding houses

West Village
Twisting, tree-lined streets
Christopher Street
Jefferson Market area

East Village
Astor Place and Cooper Union
St. Mark's Place
On and around Second Avenue

TRIBECA

Until the early 1970s the area now known as TriBeCa
(*Tri*angle *Be*low *Ca*nal, commonly defined by Chambers
Street to the south, Canal Street to the north, Broadway
to the east, and West Street on the Hudson River to the
west) was a bustling commercial district with a seemingly endless number of small factories lining narrow
cobblestoned streets. Most of TriBeCa's textile factories
and printing shops are now closed, and the buildings
have been transformed into residential lofts. The cast-
iron façades of many of them—which are bolted to a
supporting masonry structure and are considered one of
New York's great contributions to 19th-century commercial architecture—scrupulously copy elaborate Renaissance stone design. (The only remaining cast-iron façade
attributed to James Bogardus, inventor of cast-iron architecture, can be found in TriBeCa, at 85 Leonard Street,
built 1860–1861.)

Shabby in some parts, TriBeCa still retains much of the
character of its brusque industrial heritage and carries on

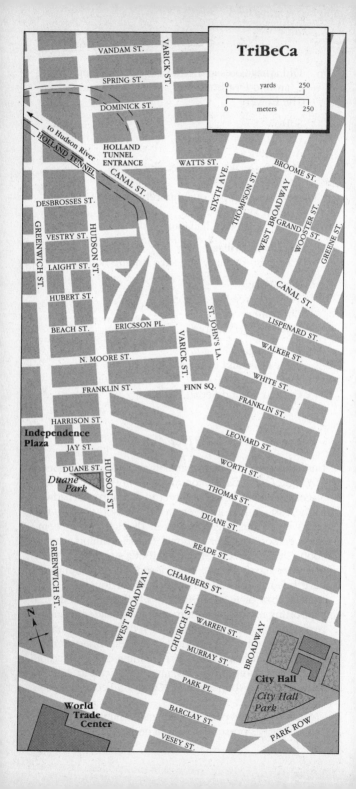

an ongoing romance with that past. Set off from the rest of residential Manhattan, it has long been attracting adventurous New Yorkers in search of space, relative quiet, cobblestoned streets, and perhaps anonymity. Such celebrities as Robert De Niro and David Letterman have made their homes in TriBeCa. Isabella Rossellini, Cyndi Lauper, David Byrne, and Laurie Anderson have lived in one single, star-studded building.

The boulevardier will quickly notice that TriBeCa is not really one neighborhood. Rather, like so much of New York, it is an amalgam of smaller districts.

AROUND DUANE PARK

The best-restored areas of TriBeCa can be found near the river, around Greenwich and Hudson streets, both of which run north–south. The block on Harrison Street between Greenwich and Hudson streets consists entirely of restored, two-story, 18th-century Federal town houses, giving a suggestion of what the neighborhood looked like 200 years ago. The **New York Mercantile Exchange**, at 6 Harrison Street (on the corner of Hudson Street), is a Victorian pile, a brick edifice with a mansard-type tower and rose window, rare indeed for New York City. (The exchange abandoned the building for sterile but more efficient headquarters in the World Trade Center in 1977.) **Bazzini**, just one block south at 339 Greenwich Street (at the corner of Jay Street), is another taste of old New York, a dried-fruits and nuts factory and retail store that has been in the same family and in the same location (with its original loading dock) since 1886.

The **Western Union Building**, just south of Harrison Street at 60 Hudson Street, is one of TriBeCa's stunning architectural landmarks. The façade of the Art Deco building is patterned in 19 tones of reddish brick.

Duane Park, one block farther south on Hudson Street, is a pleasant urban oasis that was once lined with Federal houses, now with loft buildings. The park was in the center of the hubbub of Washington Market, New York City's food market until the early 1970s. The market now occupies faraway Hunt's Point in the Bronx, and the old market buildings have been replaced with a dispiriting high-rise apartment complex called Independence Plaza. There are still a few butter-and-egg wholesalers in the vicinity, and if you are here on a Wednesday or Saturday during the warmer months, you can pay homage to the past by doing some shopping in the outdoor green-market in Independence Plaza.

ALONG BROADWAY

The busiest section of TriBeCa is its stretch along Broadway three blocks east of Duane Park along Duane Street. Two blocks north of Duane Street, at Broadway and Worth Street, is the windowless, 28-story monolith called the **AT & T Long Lines Building**, actually a giant chunk of electronic equipment clad in pink granite. Directly across the street—an example of New York's amazing juxtapositions of scale—is the one-story **Merchants Club**, built in 1871 when TriBeCa was the commercial hub of the city, if not the country.

The **Clocktower**, at 346 Broadway (two blocks north, at Franklin Street), is an exhibition space operated by the Institute of Art and Urban Resources occupying the 13th floor of the clock tower that the architectural firm of McKim, Mead & White designed for this building, the headquarters, at the turn of the century, of the New York Life Insurance Company. A view from the terrace, where giant eagle sculptures stand watch over TriBeCa as its unofficial culture vultures, gives you a glimpse north of a stretch of lower Broadway as far as the spire of Grace Church at East 10th Street in Greenwich Village.

WEST BROADWAY

Most of TriBeCa's cultural institutions line West Broadway, two blocks to the west of the real Broadway and a good route to follow as you head north to SoHo or to Canal Street, where you can turn east toward Chinatown. The **Hal Bromm Gallery**, one of the deans of the art galleries that have quartered themselves in TriBeCa in recent years, is at number 90 (near Duane Street). **Ceres**, at 584 Broadway, is a feminist gallery. **Artists Space**, at 223 West Broadway (near Franklin Street), was founded in 1973 and has given exhibitions to thousands of young artists. **Franklin Furnace** is an equally innovative exhibition center at 112 Franklin Street.

EATING IN TRIBECA

The ever-popular **Odeon**, 145 West Broadway (at Thomas Street), is no longer New York's trendiest restaurant. That distinction is currently enjoyed by the American bistro **TriBeCa Grill**, 375 Greenwich Street (at Franklin Street), owned partly by Robert De Niro. TriBeCa, in fact, houses a number of New York's better restaurants; others are the American **Riverrun Café** (176 Franklin Street); the French restaurants **Bouley** (165 Duane Street), **Chanterelle** (2 Harrison Street), and **Montrachet** (239 West Broadway); the Italian **Barocco** (301 Church Street); and **Duane Park Café** (157 Duane Street).

—Lenore Malen

CANAL STREET AND CHINATOWN

On its way north West Broadway soon comes to Canal Street, named for a 40-foot-wide canal dug on the site in 1805 to drain the waters of the Collect Pond (then New York's reservoir) into the Hudson River and paved over in the 1820s. Until recently, Canal Street around West Broadway was home to office-furniture and hardware stores that carried every imaginable kind of industrial part and catered to the factories and businesses nearby. As businesses have left the area, though, Canal Street has succumbed to a more transient clientele. As you walk east on Canal Street from West Broadway, you'll pass a number of establishments specializing in car stereos; each store has obliterated its Federal-style façade, and each blares music in competition with the other. In the midst of the din at 308 Canal Street (between West Broadway and Mercer Street) you'll find the five-story **Pearl Paint Company**, arguably the best-stocked and best-priced art-supply store in the East. Just up the street, at 336 Canal Street, is a newly established avant-garde performance space and gallery, **The Cultural Space**, home to the First World performance theater.

Chinatown

The traditional boundaries of Chinatown proper are Baxter Street on the west, the Bowery to the east, Canal Street to the north, and Worth Street to the south, but recently the district has begun to spread north into Little Italy and east into the Lower East Side. You'll know you're in Chinatown when the signs become predominantly Chinese, and you see many structures, including phone booths, topped with pagodas. Stalls selling exotic vegetables and practically every kind of seafood—from live frogs and terrapin to horseshoe crabs—overflow onto the sidewalk in all seasons. This is the only place in town

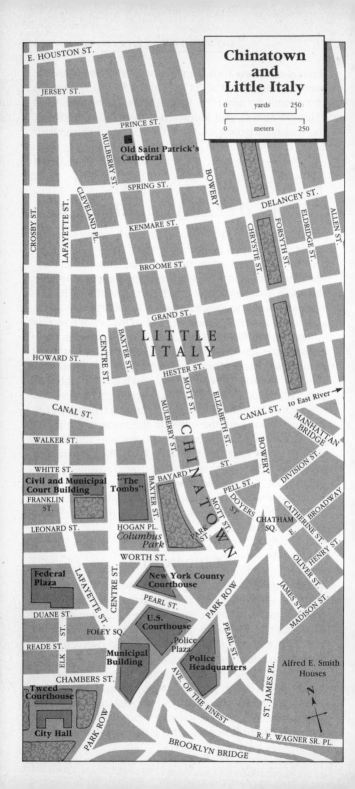

Chinatown and Little Italy

0   yards   250

0   meters   250

E. HOUSTON ST.

JERSEY ST.

PRINCE ST.

MULBERRY ST.

Old Saint Patrick's Cathedral

SPRING ST.

BOWERY

DELANCEY ST.

CLEVELAND PL.

KENMARE ST.

CHRYSTIE ST.

FORSYTH ST.

ELDRIDGE ST.

ALLEN ST.

CROSBY ST.

LAFAYETTE ST.

BROOME ST.

GRAND ST.

CENTRE ST.

BAXTER ST.

L I T T L E
I T A L Y

HOWARD ST.

HESTER ST.

MOTT ST.

ELIZABETH ST.

CANAL ST.

CANAL ST.   to East River →

MANHATTAN BRIDGE

WALKER ST.

MULBERRY ST.

C H I N A T O W N

ST.

BOWERY

DIVISION ST.

WHITE ST.

BAYARD ST.

PELL ST.

DOYERS ST.

CATHERINE ST.

BROADWAY

Civil and Municipal Court Building

"The Tombs"

BAXTER ST.

MOTT ST.

CHATHAM SQ.

FRANKLIN ST.

PARK ST.

E.

HENRY ST.

LEONARD ST.

HOGAN PL.
Columbus Park

WORTH ST.

OLIVER ST.

JAMES ST.

MADISON ST.

Federal Plaza

New York County Courthouse

PARK ROW

LAFAYETTE ST.

CENTRE ST.

PEARL ST.

DUANE ST.

U.S. Courthouse

ST. JAMES PL.

ELK ST.

FOLEY SQ.

Police Plaza

PEARL ST.

READE ST.

Municipal Building

Police Headquarters

Alfred E. Smith Houses

CHAMBERS ST.

AVE. OF THE FINEST

Tweed Courthouse

City Hall

PARK ROW

BROOKLYN BRIDGE

R. F. WAGNER SR. PL.

N

you can buy chrysanthemum tea or jibble grass jelly on a street corner.

A vast number of Chinatown's residents, many of whom are illegal immigrants from Shanghai, Hong Kong, and, recently, Vietnam, speak no English, live in squalor, and work in textile sweatshops not much different from those decried at the end of the 19th century. Gone are the opium dens that during the Jazz Age made the expression "going to Chinatown to kick the gong around" synonymous with getting high, but the Chinese street gangs still make drug trafficking one of Chinatown's problems. Despite the poverty evident in Chinatown's densely overcrowded warren of narrow streets, there is enormous energy here, evidenced by thousands of thriving small businesses and dozens of banks fueled by investments coming from soon-to-be communist Hong Kong.

A number of large stores on Canal Street cater to the half a million or so New Yorkers of Chinese extraction, most of whom live in the outer boroughs and the suburbs. The sprawling department store **Pearl River** (277 Canal Street, near Broadway; and a branch at 200 Grand Street, between Mott and Mulberry streets) has an enticing selection of exotic Chinese dry goods under its roof. **Kam Man**, at 200 Canal Street (between Mott and Mulberry streets), offers the area's widest selection of Chinese food, cooking utensils, and unusual herbal remedies.

MOTT STREET

Chinatown's main drag is Mott Street, where a dragon and other revelers parade during the Chinese New Year festival, which falls in January or February. (For a noiseless taste of the scene off-season, have a look at the mural *Wall of Respect for the Working People of Chinatown* on the Bowery at Hester Street.) Mott Street is the place to wander freely, to stop in at practically any restaurant for an inexpensive and excellent meal (tradition dictates ordering several dishes per table and sharing) or at a coffee shop for such snacks as pork buns and custard tarts with tea or coffee routinely served with real cream. You'll also find Chinese bookstores; a Buddhist temple (number 64, at the same site for 80 years); curio shops; and the bizarre **Chinatown Fair** (number 8), a sideshow-type emporium where amusements include a live chicken that dances, wax displays of Chinese food, and the dragon that winds through the streets during the New Year's festivities. The side streets offer further diversions.

CHATHAM SQUARE

If you follow Canal Street to the Bowery and walk south for a couple of blocks you will come to Chatham Square, an area surrounded by architecturally distinguished modern apartment buildings such as Chatham Towers (170 and 180 Park Row) and Chatham Green (185 Park Row). The most imposing structure on the square is the towering apartment house known as **Confucius Plaza**, with its bronze statue of the sage by Tiu Shih. The Chatham Square area's architectural distinction is over a hundred years old, however. The Chatham Square Branch of the New York Public Library, at 33 East Broadway, was designed by McKim, Mead & White in 1903; the Mariners' Temple Church, at 12 Oliver Street, was built in 1842; St. James Roman Catholic Church, at 32 St. James Place, in 1837; the Chinatown Mission, at 48 Henry Street, in 1830; the William Clark House (a fine Federal-style structure), at 51 Market Street, in 1824; the Sea and Land Church (now the First Chinatown Presbyterian Community Affairs Corporation), at 61 Henry Street, in 1819; 6 Bowery (the site of the former Olliffe's Pharmacy, the oldest drug store in America), in 1803; and a Federal-style house, at 18 Bowery, in 1785. On the south side of the square is the area's—in fact, Manhattan's—earliest extant artifact: the **First Shearith Israel Graveyard**, the original burying ground for the city's Spanish and Portuguese Jewish community, dating from 1683.

DIM SUM IN CHINATOWN

Each weekend New Yorkers flock to Chinatown's 300 or 400 restaurants to sample cuisine from varying regions of China. On Sundays (usually from noon to 4:00 P.M.) it is a Cantonese custom to dine on *dim sum* (Cantonese for snack), small plates of delicate steamed or fried dumplings and other morsels. The best-known place for this fare is the Hong Kong–style **Silver Palace**, just south of Canal Street at 50 Bowery. (For more on Chinatown's restaurants, see our Dining chapter.)

—*Lenore Malen*

LITTLE ITALY

Little Italy lies just to the north of Chinatown, strung out along Mulberry Street above Canal Street. Most of the descendants of the neighborhood's original Italian residents long ago left for Brooklyn and the suburbs, and in recent years Chinese investors have been actively buying real estate here. Three blocks north of Canal Street, at the intersection of Broome and Mulberry streets, you can now find a number of wholesale Chinese food suppliers, and on weekday mornings trucks congregate from a 100-mile radius to collect exotic supplies for their Chinese restaurants. In the afternoon when all is quiet Little Italy regains its Italian character.

The copper dome you see looming to the west above Little Italy is the top of the former New York City Police Headquarters (the entrance is at 240 Centre Street), a Renaissance-style palazzo topped with a Baroque-type cupola that has recently been converted to luxury condominiums.

MULBERRY STREET

The Italian character is most pronounced—almost theatrically so—along Mulberry Street north of Canal Street. The street is lined with Italian restaurants (many of which move tables out on the sidewalk in warmer weather), shops selling Italian food and other goods, and black limousines parked in front of brick-faced "social clubs" solemnly guarded by elegantly coiffed young men in tight clothing. Rarely do *Godfather*-style gun wars break out, although in 1972 a member of the Colombo crime family allegedly shot rival Joey Gallo at Umberto's Clam House (there are bullet holes in the building to prove it). The everyday street scene you are likely to encounter is fairly low-key.

The intersection of Mulberry and Grand streets is the heart of Little Italy, where you'll find a variety of restaurants, cafés, and excellent neighborhood food stores, including a trio on Grand Street: **Italian Food Center** (number 186), **Alleva** (number 188), and **Piemonte** (number 190). If they were located in any other part of town, these stores would be called gourmet shops, but here they are part of the remaining Italian residents' daily marketing routine.

Most of Little Italy's restaurants serve a heavy cuisine mutated from southern Italian immigrant cooking. The neighborhood is not, as a rule, the place for gourmet dining. (See the Italian section of our Dining chapter for the best choices in Little Italy.) **Ferrara Café** (195 Grand Street) draws a large late-evening crowd for dessert and espresso after dinner elsewhere in Little Italy and Chinatown; **Caffè Roma** (385 Broome Street), a little farther north, off Mulberry, is more intimate.

The Feast of San Gennaro

This boisterous feast marks the best or worst time to visit Little Italy, depending on your point of view. The street fair is named after the patron saint of Naples (whose blood, kept in a reliquary in his home city, is said to turn to liquid on his feast day), reflecting the neighborhood's southern Italian origins. During the ten days around September 19 on which the festivities take place, amid the Baroque swirls of arches made of light bulbs and the batteries of Port-a-Potties set up especially for the occasion, thousands of people descend upon Mulberry Street determined to have a good time. Old-time residents recall the days when the feast used to be celebrated by dancing in the street to the strains of a small orchestra. Now the revelers commemorate it by drinking beer, eating greasy versions of Italian (and, increasingly, Latin American and Asian) food on sale in stands along the street, and playing games of skill or chance in other booths. San Gennaro himself smiles on it all, his image decorated with dollar bills and paraded around the streets on September 19, then displayed through the end of the feast in a special grandstand constructed for the purpose.

MOTT STREET

Mott Street (with its marvelous views of the Empire State Building neatly framed by the street's tenements) is a block east of Mulberry Street. Mott is becoming increasingly Chinese on this stretch above Canal Street, but still has some of the most typically Italian institutions in the area. At 116 Mott Street is **Fretta Bros.** butcher shop, which sells a variety of domestic and foreign Italian sausages, as does **DiPalo Fine Foods**, at 206 Grand Street (on the corner of Mott Street), along with homemade and imported Italian cheeses. Farther uptown, **Caruso's Fruit Exchange**, at 152 Mott Street, is a remnant of the pushcart days, and **Parisi Bakery**, at 196 Mott Street, sells loaves of fresh bread, with which it also makes delicious sandwiches.

The pride of Little Italy is **St. Patrick's Old Cathedral**, at 260–264 Mott Street. The site of the original 1809 Roman Catholic cathedral of New York, the present church was gutted by a fire in 1866 and restored in 1868, only to have the archdiocese move to the uptown (and current) St.

Patrick's in 1879. The church and its adjacent walled cemetery (among others, Pierre Toussaint, the first black American candidate for sainthood, is buried here) are well maintained and add a dignified air to the neighbor-hood. While here take a look at the outdoor portrait mural by Chuck Close on the west wall of 26 Prince Street.

—Lenore Malen

THE LOWER EAST SIDE

So rich in energy and street culture was the Lower East Side during the first half of the 20th century that the composer Irving Berlin, who moved here from Russia as a boy, once said that "everybody ought to have a Lower East Side in their life." In those days the entire Lower East Side had the feeling of an open-air market, with pushcarts lining the streets and peddlers selling goods to thousands of immigrants who spilled out from the tenements. The Yiddish culture that the Eastern Euro-pean Jewish refugees brought to the Lower East Side has all but disappeared; taking its place nowadays are the cultures of Spanish-speaking and Chinese immigrants. Today most outsiders—meaning anyone not from this area of tenements and housing projects wedged be-tween Houston Street to the north, Grand Street to the south, the Bowery to the west, and the East River to the east—see it only through their windshields on their way to and from the East River Drive.

Artifacts of this area's once-thriving Jewish culture—including synagogues, delicatessens, restaurants, and dis-count clothing stores—do remain, and they attract Jewish and Gentile visitors alike.

ORCHARD STREET
A good place to begin a tour of the neighborhood is the **Lower East Side Tenement Museum**, at 97 Orchard Street (just south of Delancey Street). With gallery displays of old furnishings, historic photographs, and other remind-ers of the area's rich past, as well as excellent walking tours, the museum endeavors to tell the story of the Jews and other immigrant groups, including freed slaves, who settled here. For information on the walking tours, Tel: 431-0233.

From the museum you may want to set off on your own

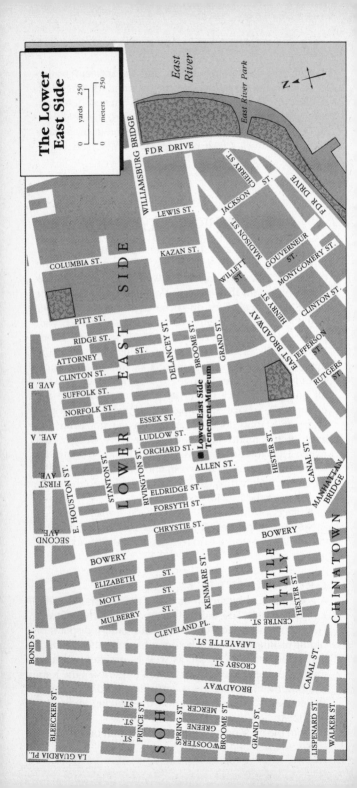

to partake of the staples for which the neighborhood is justly famous: discount clothing and other dry goods, and Jewish cuisine. For the former, you need only continue north up Orchard Street from the museum (toward Houston Street). For years Orchard Street was *the* place in New York to buy designer clothing at deep discounts—even ten years ago women from the Upper East Side would flock here to shop. As discount clothing has become more widely available elsewhere, the street seems a pale imitation of its boisterous, frenzied former self, but there are still finds, and bargains, to be had.

AROUND EAST HOUSTON STREET

You'll know you've reached East Houston (pronounced HOUSE-ton) Street when you see the cars and limousines double-parked in front of **Katz's**, a cavernous delicatessen at number 205 (just east of Orchard Street) that is a true haven for meat eaters. Signs from the World War II era still dangle from the ceiling: "Send a salami to your boy in the army."

The same street also has a number of other food shops (Ben's Cheese Shop and Moishe's Bakery at number 181, Russ and Daughters delicatessen at number 179, and Yonah Schimmel's Knishes Bakery at number 137). For the grandest bouffe of all, make your way south again, this time on decrepit Chrystie Street (several blocks west of Orchard Street) for a meal (it may be your last) at the not-so-cheap **Sammy's Rumanian Restaurant**, at number 157 (just south of Rivington Street). Each table comes equipped with, in addition to the usual salt and pepper, a jar of rendered chicken fat (*schmaltz*) as a cholesterol-laden condiment; a bottle of seltzer water (the owners call it "Jewish Perrier 1936"), a container of milk, and a bottle of chocolate syrup for making your own egg cream, the quintessential Lower East Side comestible. You'll note that it contains no egg and no cream.

Your next stop might be **Schapiro's House of Kosher and Sacramental Wines**, the only winery in the city, several blocks east of Sammy's, at 126 Rivington Street (between Essex and Norfolk streets). Tours and samples of the syrupy stuff are available on Sundays; for information, Tel: 674-4404. **Economy Candy**, just to the west, at 108 Rivington Street, sells what may well be the best marzipan and halvah in town.

AROUND DELANCEY STREET

A south turn on Essex Street brings you to more of New York's most cherished culinary institutions. At Delancey Street begins the two-block-long **Essex Street Market**, an indoor food market catering to the neighborhood's Chinese, Hispanic, and Jewish residents. You can buy the Lower East Side's most distinguished contribution to American gastronomy, pickles, from outdoor barrels at **Essex Street Pickles**, sandwiched between electronics stores at 35 Essex Street. This is probably the only remaining outdoor pickle shop in New York City; there used to be dozens.

Two of New York's most cherished restaurants, as famous for their meatless cuisine (blintzes and borscht are standard fare) as they are for their rude waiters, remain: **Ratner's**, just east of Essex Street at 138 Delancey Street, and **Grand Dairy Restaurant**, just west of Essex Street at 341 Grand Street. In the unlikely event you feel like dessert after a meal in either, you can savor coffee and ruggelah on old-fashioned, bare Formica tables at **Gertal's**, just west of Essex Street at 53 Hester Street. There is also still a thriving upholstery and bed-linen district nearby, on and around Grand Street between Forsyth and Eldridge streets, a vestige of the old bed-linen market that flourished here in the early part of the century when Romanians poured into the neighborhood.

AROUND EAST BROADWAY

Several architectural remnants of the area's Jewish history are on East Broadway. At number 175 is the building where the *Forward,* the Jewish newspaper, was originally published. Down the street, at 197 East Broadway, is the Educational Alliance, an organization founded by wealthy uptown Jews in 1883 to assist recent Jewish immigrants. Across the street, at 192 East Broadway, is the Seward Park Branch of the New York Public Library, where Leon Trotsky is rumored to have studied when he was in town. A block south and two blocks east is the **Henry Street Settlement**, a still-functioning community-service organization that served as the prototype for such programs around the country.

The **Bialystoker Synagogue**, at 7–13 Bialystoker Place, just south of East Broadway, was originally a Methodist Episcopal church built in 1826 and is one of the area's best-preserved synagogues. The first of the Lower East

Side's numerous synagogues built for use as such (and still the most impressive) was **Congregation K'hal Adath Jeshurun**, at 12–16 Eldridge Street, between Forsyth and Hester streets. An eclectic blend of Moorish, Gothic, and Romanesque architectural elements, it contrasts greatly with the surrounding tenements. Though it, too, is in a sad state of repair, it is slowly being restored to its former glory.

THE BOWERY

Once the road that led to Peter Stuyvesant's farm, or *bouwerie,* the Bowery is probably known most for the derelicts who have inhabited its streets and its flophouses for more than a century. This decidedly shabby avenue forms the western border of the Lower East Side, running from just south of Canal Street to just north of Houston Street, where it becomes Fourth Avenue. It has a certain élan even in its squalor, however: The Bowery was where songwriter Stephen Foster died destitute in 1864 and was called by Stephen Crane, whose 1893 novel *Maggie: A Girl of the Streets,* was set here, "the only interesting street in New York." He sketched the scene there: "Long streamers of garments fluttered from fire escapes. In all unhandy places there were buckets, brooms, rags and bottles. In the street infants played or fought with other infants or sat stupidly in the way of vehicles. Formidable women, with uncombed hair and disordered dress, gossiped while leaning on railings, or screamed in frantic quarrels. Withered persons, in curious postures of submission to something, sat smoking pipes in obscure corners. A thousand odors of cooking food came forth to the street. The building quivered and creaked from the weight of humanity stamping about in its bowels."

The Bowery was New York's theater and music-hall district in the mid-19th century and achieved renewed vitality after Crane's day when the Third Avenue elevated train brought people to its popular entertainments: John Sloan and other early-20th-century artists depicted the era in numerous prints and drawings. The theaters are gone, but the area retains a certain amount of architectural fantasy in the palatial **Bowery Savings Bank** (130 Bowery, at the corner of Grand Street) by McKim, Mead & White, dating from 1894, and the 1910 Beaux Arts approach to the **Manhattan Bridge** (at the Bowery's intersection with Canal Street at the edge of Chinatown), with its monumental sculpture representing *The Spirit of Commerce, The Spirit of Industry,* and, of all things, *Buffalo Hunt.*

The Bowery is still considered by some New Yorkers to be the city's skid row, but a walk along the avenue from Canal Street north to Houston Street will reveal many recent changes. The vagrants, most of them alcoholics, who lined the street and slept in its flophouses are by and large gone, and the tenement buildings are being restored. The Bowery's close proximity to SoHo and Greenwich Village and its relatively cheap rents have spawned a number of new avant-garde galleries, performance spaces, and clubs. The **Knitting Factory**, just off the Bowery at 47 East Houston Street, a bar and experimental music and performance space, and **La Mama La Galleria**, just off the Bowery at 6 East 1st Street, which exhibits avant-garde artists, are relatively new additions to the neighborhood. The legendary club **CBGB**, at 315 Bowery (at Bleecker Street), has been a fixture for years and is still a good place to see new bands. **Liz Christy's Bowery-Garden**, at the northeast corner of Bowery and Houston Street, was planted in 1973 on a rubble-filled lot and now, in spring and summer, is a near-mirage of pathways, exotic water lilies, peonies, and rare flowering trees. At the **Irreplaceable Artifacts Garden Annex**, just across the street, you can find pricey but interesting fragments of classical statuary (reproductions) and garden furniture.

An entire district of shops selling lighting fixtures thrives on the Bowery between Grand and Broome streets, and farther north on the Bowery around Houston Street there is a restaurant-supply district. A stop at **Moisha's Luncheonette**, 237 Grand Street, a classic New York diner that serves up what may be the best rice pudding in the world, is a mandatory stop for anyone venturing near the Bowery.

—*Lenore Malen*

SOHO

Walking through the chic streets of SoHo today, you might find it hard to believe that only a quarter-century ago this area was a thriving manufacturing and textile district where thousands of workers crowded the streets, loading and unloading bales of dry goods from dawn to nightfall. Decades ago city planners coined the name that is now so famous in the art world for this 43-block area, the *So*uth *Ho*uston district, or SoHo for short. SoHo indeed lies south of Houston Street (a reminder: pronounced HOUSE-ton), and north of Canal Street, west of Lafayette Street, and east of Sixth Avenue. From TriBeCa, you can reach SoHo simply by following West Broadway north. From the Bowery or Little Italy, follow Prince Street west across Lafayette Street.

SoHo has emerged over the past 20 years, a time of explosive growth in the art, real-estate, and stock markets, as the hub of the art world, that "industrious and rather devout society," as one writer dubbed it. By the mid-1980s at least 4,500 artists, curators, critics, and gallery owners claimed to live in SoHo. Many of them were pioneers who moved to the area in the 1960s and 1970s when there was only raw space in large manufacturing buildings to be had, with no bathrooms, no kitchens, no buzzers on the front doors (artists dropped keys on strings from their windows when visitors arrived). Rents were minuscule and entire floors of buildings could be bought for relative pennies. These early residents were celebrated by Tom Wolfe, who wrote in *In Our Time,* "Oh, to be young and come to New York and move into your first loft, and look at the world with eyes that light up even the rotting fire-escape railings, even the buckling pressed-tin squares on the ceiling, even the sheet-metal shower stall with its belly dents and rusting seams." Today, SoHo real estate is among the most expensive in New York. Capitalizing on the cachet of an artists' neighborhood, many chic boutiques, restaurants, and antiques shops were drawn to SoHo, followed by many well-heeled residents.

If for no other reason, SoHo is worth a visit just on the merits of its architecture—it has the greatest concentration of cast-iron-faced buildings (brick or masonry buildings with elaborate, prefabricated cast-iron façades bolted onto their frames) in the world. Most of these structures were built between 1860 and 1890 as factories and warehouses. The SoHo Cast-Iron Historic District, bounded by West Broadway and Houston, Crosby, and Canal streets, was created in 1973 to preserve these architectural treasures. All streets in the district are now being resurfaced with paving stones and granite curbs. If you look down as you walk around SoHo you may find yourself treading on worn-down stone sidewalks, some of which date to the Civil War period.

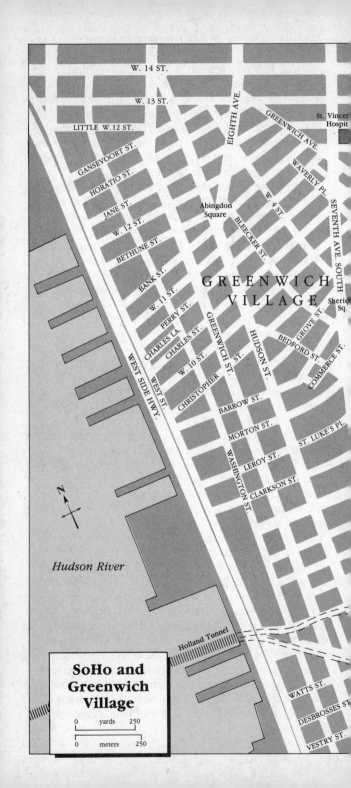

SoHo and Greenwich Village

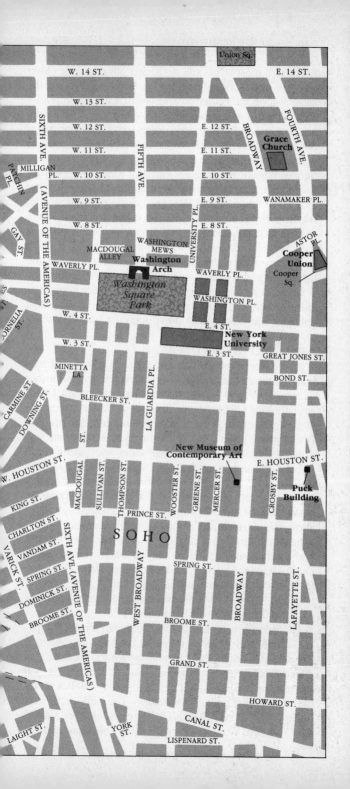

Though most artists can no longer afford to live either in SoHo or to show in its galleries, SoHo has become the most important center in the world for contemporary art—galleries and, more recently, editorial offices of the art magazines have moved here—and its boundaries have spread every which way from West Broadway, still its main drag. Even in these days of a soft market, art-world figures engage in a regular ritual of looking at the new shows on Saturdays (the serious SoHo galleries are closed on Sundays and Mondays) during the art season, which extends roughly from Labor Day through Memorial Day. Gallery hopping has become a social event as well, and Saturday, when SoHo is most crowded, is also a good time to see the latest fashions being worn in the galleries, on the streets, or in watering holes.

If you'd prefer to avoid the scene on Saturdays, the galleries are open Tuesdays through Fridays as well. Most galleries and other shops don't open until around noon.

AROUND BROADWAY

A good place to begin a tour of SoHo is at the neighborhood's eastern fringe on Lafayette Street, where a number of antiques shops have blossomed in recent years. **Urban Archaeology** (285 Lafayette Street, near Prince Street) is a huge store selling pricey but intriguing castoffs of demolished buildings and their furnishings. **Lost City Arts**, just down the block at 275 Lafayette Street, specializes in old street signs and other New York memorabilia. The **Puck Building** (295 Lafayette, on the corner of Houston Street) is the former headquarters of the satirical magazine *Puck*—hence the two statues of the Shakespearean imp above the entrance and at the building's northeast corner. (The irreverent *Spy* magazine is now quartered here.) You might also want to check out whatever temporary exhibit happens to be up at **Lieutenant Joseph Petrosino Park**, a sculpture park two blocks south at Kenmare and Lafayette streets. Then follow Prince Street two blocks west to LoBro, or Lower Broadway.

In the past few years, Broadway has given serious competition to West Broadway (note that the latter is a separate street four blocks west of Broadway) for the area's largest concentration of institutions. **Dean & DeLuca**, at 560 Broadway (at Prince Street), is a food shop that is a veritable museum of culinary delicacies. The building is also occupied by such prestigious galleries as Salvatore Ala and Max Protetch. This stretch of Broadway also has some of the area's most important buildings. Across the street, at 561 Broadway, is one façade of the L-shaped **Singer Building** (the other façade is on Prince Street) by Ernest Flagg. Toward the south is the **Haughwout Building**, at 488 Broadway—a handsome Palladian adaptation well known for its Otis elevator, the first passenger lift in the world when it was installed in 1857. At 478 Broadway is another important cast-iron beauty, the **Roosevelt Building**, designed by Richard Morris Hunt in 1874.

Broadway Galleries and Museums

SoHo's largest proliferation of galleries under one roof is currently at 568 Broadway, where you may want to stop into John Gibson, Curt Marcus, **Granary Books**, **Crown Point Press**, or a new annex to the **Leo Castelli Gallery** for representative examples of what the art world is looking at. Two bank branches, Marine Midland, in this block, and Chase Manhattan, one block north across Houston Street, mount changing exhibitions of local artists. You will find galleries all along this stretch of Broadway, usually on the upper floors of loft buildings.

The **New Museum of Contemporary Art** (583 Broadway, between Prince and Houston streets) is a noncommercial institution that mounts exhibitions by artists of all types from all over the world. In brand-new quarters, the **Alternative Museum**, right across the street at 594 Broadway, shows similar, out-of-the-mainstream contemporary art. The **Guggenheim Museum** opened a SoHo branch on the same block this past summer, at 575 Broadway. The loft-like space rotates works from the museum's vast collections of mainly 20th-century art. For a complete and current listing of the city's gallery shows, pick up a copy of *Art Now Gallery Guide,* available at most dealers' front desks.

PRINCE STREET

To continue into the heart of SoHo, head west off Broadway on Prince Street. **Fanelli**, at the corner of Prince and Mercer streets, has existed since SoHo was known only as the Eighth Ward in the 19th century, serving workers from the nearby warehouses. It is still the only serious drinking bar in SoHo, though its ownership has changed and the stains on its clientele's clothing are less likely to be from motor oil than from extra-virgin olive oil. There's a string of nice galleries down the block, among them **Annina Nosei** (100 Prince Street) and **David Beitzel** (102 Prince Street, second floor). The **Edward Thorp Gallery**, above the post office at number 103, is one of the nicest spaces in SoHo, with a lovely skylight illuminating the art. The **Museum of Holography**, around the corner and south on Mercer Street at number 11, shows crowd-pleasing displays of three-dimensional laser photography.

A mural by Richard Haas adorns the corner of Prince and Greene streets; it is a painting of the building's cast-iron façade on the brick wall of its east side and incorporates real windows. Important **Greene Street** galleries include Metro Pictures (number 150, between Prince and Houston streets); Pace, Sperone Westwater, and John Weber (all at number 142, on the same block as Metro); Barbara Gladstone (number 99, between Prince and Spring streets); and 300 Gallery and M13 (numbers 89 and 72, respectively, both between Spring and Broome streets). Among Greene Street's cast-iron masterpieces are the buildings at numbers 72–76 and 28–30, both dating from the early 1870s. SoHo's newest gallery building is a former bakery at 130 Prince Street (on the corner of Greene Street). The colorful Postmodern façade is entirely appropriate to one of its tenants, the **Louver Gallery, New York**, the East Coast branch of the well-known Los Angeles gallery.

Wooster Street, parallel to and one block west of Greene Street, also has a number of art galleries and spaces. The Paula Cooper Gallery, the first to move to SoHo in the 1960s (number 155, between Prince and Houston streets), still shows many of the same minimalist artists from that era. The **Dia Art Foundation** displays a very urban phenomenon just down the street at number 141: Earthworks artist Walter De Maria has filled an entire room with dirt. The **Drawing Center** (number 35, between Broome and Grand streets) is the only institution in the United States that specializes in drawings (frequent exhibitions). The **Performing Garage**, next door (number 33), is one of New York's longest-established experimental theaters.

WEST BROADWAY

Prince Street next runs into West Broadway, considered the main street of SoHo. **Rizzoli Bookstore** (454 West Broadway, between Prince and Houston streets), with its Postmodern façade and staff to match, specializes in international art books and international periodicals and is a great place for browsing while listening to music on its excellent sound system. (Four other SoHo bookstores specialize in art: **Spring Street Books**, now at 169 Spring Street, near West Broadway; **Printed Matter**, at 77 Wooster Street; **Jaap Rietman**, the oldest and most extensive, at 134 Spring Street; and **SoHo Books**, down the street from Rizzoli at 351 West Broadway.) The Mary Boone gallery, at 417 West Broadway (between Prince and Spring streets), more than most galleries often functions as a chic toll booth from an artist's studio to a major collection. The building just a few steps up (and across) the street at 420 West Broadway has housed so many well-known galleries—currently Leo Castelli, 49th Parallel, Germans Van Eck, Marilyn Pearl, and Sonnabend—that its entrance has become a rendezvous for friends and tours meeting in SoHo.

SPRING AND BROOME STREETS

Spring and Broome streets are better known for sights other than art galleries. The outstanding piece of architecture on Spring Street is the 1870 cast-iron building at number 101 (near Mercer Street), which has a façade pierced with ample expanses of glass. The **New York City Fire Museum**, at 278 Spring Street (way west between Hudson and Varick streets), has the most comprehensive collection of fire-fighting equipment in the country. Broome Street between West Broadway and Greene Street is an architectural field day: Number 484 is an 1890 Romanesque-style brick building; numbers 478 (1873), 475 (1873), 461 (1871), and 455 (1873) are all cast-iron buildings.

THE SOUTH VILLAGE

At the west end of Prince Street is a long-standing residential area sometimes known as the South Village, incorporating Thompson, Sullivan, and MacDougal streets, all of which continue north across Houston Street into Greenwich Village. A stroll in this intimate little enclave will bring you down to earth after your time among the lofty trendsetters. Nearly all of the numerous tiny shops here are staffed by their owners, and they sell anything from one-of-a-kind old toys to Art Deco furniture, ceramics, Tibetan hats, and heirloom clothing. Over the past several years, many of the neighborhood's old social clubs, including the one favored by jailed crime boss John Gotti, have closed, sometimes giving way to art galleries and French bistros.

The area retains quaint shops, such as the **Vesuvio Bakery**, at 160 Prince Street, that have served the area residents, predominantly Italian, for decades. The neighborhood's Portuguese population has quietly increased recently, though. The parish church, dedicated to Saint Anthony of Padua, holds an Italian street fair on Sullivan in June but celebrates mass in Portuguese (coincidentally, Saint Anthony was born in Lisbon). The otherwise nondescript M & O Market, at 124 Thompson Street, is one of the few places in town where you can purchase authentic Portuguese fish, cheese, sausages, olives, olive oil, and mineral water, discreetly mixed in with more ordinary items.

The last sights SoHo reveals are those of early New York: There are a pleasant Federal–Greek Revival house at 203 Prince Street and Federal houses on residential Charlton, King, and Vandam streets—now given landmark status—west of Sixth Avenue.

EATING AND HANGING OUT IN SOHO

SoHo habitués are likely to stop in at the **Cupping Room** (359 West Broadway, near Broome Street) for coffee or tea; or the **Manhattan Brewing Company** (40 Thompson Street) for beer. Chic sustenance is provided by the Euro-industrial–style coffee bar **Dean & DeLuca**, at 120 Prince Street, or you might want a sample from the extensive wine list of the **SoHo Kitchen** (at 103 Greene Street), perhaps accompanied by an inexpensive hamburger at the bar. **I Tre Merli** (463 West Broadway) is a cavernous, high-tech Italian restaurant serving palatable food or sparkling *prosecco* wine for a quick pick-me-up. The **Broome Street Bar** (363 West Broadway), one of the original SoHo hangouts, is a good place for an inexpensive hamburger. The **Ear Inn** is a funky café-restaurant within sight of the Hudson River, at 326 Spring Street.

—*Lenore Malen*

GREENWICH VILLAGE

The first thing to know about Greenwich Village is that it is not a single neighborhood, but a collection of distinct yet equally eclectic communities radiating from their geographic (and perhaps spiritual) center, Washington

Square Park. We begin our coverage of the Village at Washington Square, then wander through the West Village. We then go east, crossing Broadway and Lafayette Street to the East Village.

There is not one defining area or mentality or resident; you can find everyone and everything on earth within the confines of the Village. Hippolyte Havel, an anarchist and sometimes obnoxious headwaiter whom Emma Goldman brought to the Village with her from Europe at the turn of the century, once said, "Greenwich Village has no boundaries. It's a state of mind." The world is a vastly better place for actually having the Village to provide a sanctuary in which various states of mind have been able to roam, play, and make their homes.

Historically, the Village has always been a haven for the wealthy, like John Jacob Astor; and the powerful, like Boss Tweed and the Tammany Hall gang; and the marginal, like the pantheon of writers, artists, and radicals who have lived here. Immigrant communities of French, Italian, Irish, and Eastern Europeans have also settled in various sections of the Village, enhancing the essential heterogeneity of the area. The heady mix of personalities and cultures led John Reed, one of the Village's most compelling heroes, to boast that "within a block of my house was all the adventure in the world; within a mile every foreign country."

In general, though, Washington Square and the West Village have become respectable and prosperous as a solid bourgeoisie has supplanted the bohemians who gave the Village its racy élan. Today artistes and dropouts are much more likely to take up residence in the scruffier East Village, which the noted nonconformist Quentin Crisp, current East Village resident and author of *The Naked Civil Servant,* calls the "district where the new ideas of America are born." But even here, you're as likely to share the sidewalks with straight folks with office jobs as you are with nonconformists.

People-watching is a New York art form, and it is in the Village that this art has reached its zenith. Spend an afternoon wandering the streets, or drinking in the crowds from the vantages of such sidewalk spots as 7A (7th Street and Avenue A), Time Café (Lafayette at Great Jones Street), Caffè Borgia (MacDougal and Bleecker streets), or the White Horse Tavern (567 Hudson Street) and you will likely see every form of life known to civilization. The Village is the stage of New York, and therefore the country.

But the energy and theatrical variety with which the Village is historically and romantically linked is today most obvious when its denizens take to the streets during two parades. The Village Halloween parade is a vast, phantasmagoric collaboration of local talent and imagination that marches, skates, struts, and runs up Sixth Avenue from Houston Street to 23rd Street "clothed" in an array of outrageous costumes, and has become the occasion of a citywide party. Gay Pride Day takes place in late June to commemorate the infamous Stonewall Riot, which exploded on June 28, 1969, when police brutally raided the Stonewall Bar on Christopher Street and its gay customers fought back, sparking a night-long confrontation. Like avenging angels, Dykes on Bikes leads the annual Gay Pride Day Parade down Fifth Avenue and across Christopher Street, where the parade culminates in an all-night celebration of sexual orientation.

The Village began, as far as we know, in its western precincts as the Indian town of Sapokanican. When Dutch farmer Yellis Mandeville moved upscale in the late 1600s from Brooklyn to the lush pastures of the West Village (near where one used to find the Mineshaft, one of the most renowned hard-core 1970s–1980s gay bars), he brought with him the name of the Brooklyn village that bordered his former estate, Greenwyck. A sleepy grouping of farms and country estates throughout the 1700s, Greenwich Village first leaped in popularity during the 1822 yellow-fever epidemic, when city folk of New York fled two miles upstate to the healthier climate of this quaint village. The weirdly crisscrossing streets of the West Village follow the patterns of old Indian paths, creeks, and farm borders that became thoroughfares as the town grew. In 1818, early Village activists (primarily farmers seeking to sell their land to developers) fought against the Common Council's proposed grid plan for Manhattan, which would have sliced through the existing land plots, and won an exemption for Greenwich Village streets west of Sixth Avenue. The only building affected by the refusal to succumb to the new layout, ironically, was the very structure in which the engineer John Randel, Jr., conceived the grid, then and now a grocery on the corner of Bleecker and Christopher streets: In 1828 the building lost 20 feet to ease traffic at that intersection. The brick wall marks the side that is surgically shortened.

Washington Square Park Area

In the early years of New York, Washington Square Park was a cemetery. A potters' field took up what is now the south half of the square, while a burial ground established by early German immigrants occupied the north half, the division mirroring the wealth of the neighborhoods above and below the park. Until 1819 the sturdy branches of the still-standing elm tree (claimed to be the oldest in New York) in the northwest corner served as a fulcrum from which to hang wrongdoers—and the hangman lived in a shack on the present site of the New York University Catholic Center. The dead gave way to the living in 1828, when the square was created.

The **Washington Arch**, in the square, marks the top of the park and the beginning of Fifth Avenue. It was designed by McKim, Mead & White in 1892 to replace a wooden arch erected on the spot in 1889 for the centenary of George Washington's presidential inauguration. The massive, though hollow, monument incorporates the statue *Washington in Peace,* by Alexander Stirling Calder, on the east pier of the arch; and *Washington in War,* by Herman MacNeil, on the west pier. In the 1917 Washington Square Rebellion, the artist Marcel Duchamp and five other Village residents climbed to the top of the arch and declared the independence of Greenwich Village (their "Declaration" consisted only of the word "whereas" declaimed again and again). They conspired, got drunk, and left; mission accomplished. To this day, scheming and drinking, as well as Frisbee playing, jogging, drug dealing, roller skating, begging, sleeping, and just plain hanging around are the major activities in the park.

AROUND THE SQUARE

The elegant town houses fronting Washington Square North are considered to be the finest examples of the Greek Revival style in America, and they provided the setting for Henry James's novel *Washington Square* (though the actual house where his grandmother lived was torn down in 1950 to make way for the cumbersome 2 Fifth Avenue apartment building). Over the years, John Dos Passos, Edward Hopper, Edmund Wilson, and other famous New Yorkers have been fortunate enough to live in the houses, known as **The Row**. Although James never even visited his grandmother's house, he was intimately familiar with the neighborhood, having been born at 21

Washington Place, a historic building acquired by New York University and home to its Grey Art Gallery. Richard Wright and Willa Cather both lived farther along Washington Place, at number 82, at different times.

Behind The Row to the east of Fifth Avenue lies the small-scale, tree-lined **Washington Mews**, once stables to The Row and now housing New York University faculty; to the west of Fifth Avenue is the gorgeously out of place **MacDougal Alley**—even the mixed-up street numbers are from another time.

Judson Memorial Church, on the square's south side, is an 1892 Romanesque church by McKim, Mead & White, with stained glass by John La Farge and a relief by Herbert Adams executing a design by Augustus Saint-Gaudens. The church has long been a center of political and artistic activism. In the 1960s and 1970s it housed the Judson Dance Theater, where such seminal figures in the dance world as Trisha Brown, Simone Forte, Yvonne Rainer, and Twyla Tharp gave performances early in their careers.

Social firebrands John Reed and Lincoln Steffens (whose *The Shame of the Cities* was an early attack on corrupt city government) lived at 42 Washington Square South, now the site of the NYU Law School. Stephen Crane and another early social critic, Frank Norris, lived and wrote in the so-called House of Genius at 61 Washington Square South, which is now part of the NYU student center.

As is apparent, NYU is the area's dominant landlord and developer. The university's relationship with the community has improved since its foundation in 1833, when use of prison labor to cut stone at bargain rates for the first building led to the Stonecutter's Riot.

At 70 Washington Square South you discover a prominent New York University building that the *AIA Guide to New York City* cuttingly dubs one of the Redskins: the hulking red-granite Elmer Holmes Bobst Library, designed by Philip Johnson. (The other two "Redksins," from the same quarry, are the André and Bella Meyer Physics Hall, at 707 Broadway, and Tisch Hall, at 40 West 4th Street.) Equally hulking buildings in the area are the I. M. Pei apartment blocks collectively known as **Washington Square Village**, at 100–110 Bleecker Street and 505 La Guardia Place (a northern extension of SoHo's West Broadway). The buildings' scale is somewhat softened by the Picasso sculpture *Portrait of Sylvette* in the central plaza. A plaque on the northwest corner of Washington

Place and Greene Street commemorates the nightmarish Triangle Shirtwaist Fire of 1911, in which 146 women perished horribly when a blaze broke out in the **Asch Building**, still standing at 29 Washington Place. Some were forced to jump in flames from the upper floors because the sweat-shop owners had locked the fire stairs to prevent the women from wasting time on breaks.

As you leave the area, head south on **MacDougal Street**, which was once the moral center of the beatnik world. Most evocative perhaps is **Caffè Reggio**, at 119 MacDougal (near 3rd Street), open since 1927, its walls covered with paintings and discolored from decades of smoke and steam from its espresso machine. Farther down the street, at the corner of Bleecker Street, **Caffè Borgia** (once The Scene, a beatnik centerpiece) and **Le Figaro Café** sit opposite each other like funky Village versions of Paris's Café Flore and Les Deux Magots, while at 81 MacDougal Street is **Caffè Dante**, decorated with scenes of Florence. Any one of these places makes a pleasant spot for an afternoon of people-watching or for capping off a night's entertainment at, say, the historic **Provincetown Playhouse** (133 MacDougal Street), in the confines of which Village resident Eugene O'Neill had a number of plays produced and Bette Davis broke into show business. The original playhouse was started in a stable that has since been plowed under the NYU law school. The **Bitter End** and **Village Gate** are still important venues on the entertainment strip of Bleecker Street, east of MacDougal, while the **Sullivan Street Playhouse** (181 Sullivan) still houses the indestructible production *The Fantasticks,* running since 1960.

NORTH OF WASHINGTON SQUARE PARK

The quiet streets north of Washington Square Park encompass the Village's most placid and least dramatic section, though its almost pastoral tree-lined aspects and lovely 19th-century façades make for a pleasant walk. Even this area's commercial avenue, University Place, is sedate and refined, lined with staid old apartment houses whose ground floors are occupied by antiques shops and unexciting but comfortable neighborhood restaurants.

As you walk north from Washington Square on Fifth Avenue, first dash across West 8th Street, where at number 8, Gertrude Vanderbilt Whitney founded the Whitney Museum (now housed in far less charming quarters at

75th Street and Madison Avenue); next door at the corner of Fifth Avenue, John Taylor Johnston's backyard collection of artifacts and paintings gathered in Europe became the founding collection of the Metropolitan Museum of Art. The long-since-demolished house at Fifth Avenue and 9th Street of Henry Brevoort, whose name has been seized by the developers of the huge, ugly apartment house a block south, was the first of a great many fashionable mansions along Fifth Avenue in 1834.

Wander a few steps west of the avenue on West 10th Street, which, like West 9th, 11th, and 12th streets between Sixth Avenue and University Place, is a neatly combed version of the twisting streets found in the West Village, where you will discover some more literary associations—Mark Twain lived briefly at number 14 and Sinclair Lewis at number 7. Two people who probably were not friends also resided on West 10th Street: Emily Post at number 12 and the artist Marcel Duchamp at number 28. On the northwest corner of Fifth Avenue and West 10th Street is the 1840 Church of the Ascension, which contains stained-glass windows and John La Farge's masterpiece, an altar mural, as well as a marble altar relief by Augustus Saint-Gaudens. At 47 Fifth Avenue, between 11th and 12th streets, is the **Salmagundi Club**, the oldest artists' club in America, founded in 1870 in this 1853 mansion (the avenue was once lined with such residences). Among its members were John La Farge, Louis Comfort Tiffany, and Stanford White, and it still sponsors exhibitions, worth attending more for a look at the building's Victorian interior than its members' art. The best place in the area to enjoy art for art's sake is the **Forbes Magazine Galleries**, at 60 Fifth Avenue, famous for the Fabergé eggs collected by the late publisher Malcolm Forbes. The American Communist Party long had its headquarters nearby, at 50 East 13th Street, and the proximity undoubtedly influenced Forbes's choice of address.

Stroll west down 12th Street to the **New School for Social Research**, founded in 1919 as an educational institution for adults, and typically denigrated by Tom Wolfe as the "School for Utility Cultures." Its graduate school, at 65 Fifth Avenue, enjoys a reputation for excellence in the academic world, particularly in the social sciences (Hannah Arendt and other exiled European intellectuals taught at the graduate school and at the college, as have Aaron Copland, Thomas Hart Benton, Berenice Abbott, and other Village locals), but its adult education division is better known among New Yorkers, who take courses for edification in an unusual variety of subjects ranging from basket weaving to Byzantine history (often merely as a pretext for meeting other adults) in its evening division. The school's building at 66 West 12th Street houses the 600-square-foot mural *The Coming Together of the Races,* painted by Mexican artist José Clemente Orozco in 1931.

Cut back through the school's pleasant sculpture garden and out the 11th Street exit, where at 72–76 West 11th Street lies the **Second Shearith Israel Cemetery**, a peaceful triangular plot (it was twice its present size until 11th Street was expanded in 1830) used by the congregation of the city's Spanish and Portuguese synagogue from 1805 to 1829. Finally, stop for a moment at the oddly shaped building at 18 West 11th Street, whose flaring façade came to be when the house was rebuilt after a 1970 explosion killed two members of the radical group the Weathermen.

The West Village

The area west of Sixth Avenue between Houston and 14th streets has the greatest concentration of the atmosphere and architecture associated with the Village. Start at tiny **Minetta Street**, which runs northeast from the corner of Bleecker Street and Sixth Avenue. This minute slice of history was the heart of New York's first black ghetto from the early to mid-1800s. In the latter part of the century French immigrants took it over and later, when Frenchtown had become an early Village tourist site, they gave way to newly arrived Italian immigrants. The **Minetta Lane Theater**, at number 18, offers some of the best Off-Broadway productions in town.

Nearby, at West 4th Street and Sixth Avenue, Eugene O'Neill spent many of his early, completely drunken days in the Golden Swan, a pleasant little tavern hated by its neighbors and known to its habitués as the "Hell Hole." Sadly, this icon, which was the model for the bar in O'Neill's *The Iceman Cometh,* was torn down in 1928 when the IND subway line was built. To facilitate the construction, Sixth Avenue was cut through buildings fronting the angled cross streets, and left in its wake the historical rubble of those 19th-century structures and the several odd little plazas that dot the west side of Sixth Avenue from King Street to Minetta Street. Fortunately, the chapel that since 1932 has housed the **Little Red**

Schoolhouse at 196 Bleecker Street, one of the city's most progressive private schools, was left untouched.

For a quick taste of Greenwich Village's Italian community, cross Sixth Avenue and run up and down Bleecker Street, starting from the parish church of Our Lady of Pompeii (which holds a street festival each July), at the intersection of Carmine Street; there are baked goods at Rocco's (number 243), Bleecker Street Pastry (245), and A. Zito Bakery (259); Faicco's Pork Store (260), Zampognaro (262), and Ottomanelli & Sons (285) are mouth-watering shrines to the art of the Italian-American grocery.

Take Leroy Street (which has a pleasing array of residential architecture) across Bedford and Seventh Avenue South to **St. Luke's Place**, a stunning row of brownstone houses dating from the 1850s. Mayor Jimmy Walker lived at number 6, which accounts for the lanterns at the entrance, an old New York custom for indicating the mayor's residence. Theodore Dreiser, at number 16, and Sherwood Anderson, at number 12, were neighbors of the corrupt but dandy mayor. St. Luke's leads to Hudson Street, where just south of number 487 is the **Church of St. Luke-in-the-Fields** (with a pleasant walled garden), which stood on the river's edge when it was built in 1821, before one of many landfills extended the island. Its first warden, Clement Clarke Moore, penned "'Twas the Night Before Christmas." Number 487, the first in a series of Federal houses, was once the residence of Bret Harte, whose tales of life in California mining camps earned him a literary reputation in the United States and Great Britain in the late 19th century. The **White Horse Tavern**, a few blocks north at number 567, was the site of Dylan Thomas's last and fatal encounter with whiskey.

ON AND AROUND BEDFORD STREET

Head south to Christopher Street and loop east for a block to Bedford Street for a leisurely stroll around the West Village's most characteristic residential streets, where many of the houses date from the early 1800s. The ramshackle structure at 102 Bedford Street has a characteristically Greenwich Village history: Originally a town house built in 1830, it reopened in its present elaborate state in 1926, christened "Twin Peaks," and was soon inhabited by a bohemian mix of artists, writers, and actors. The largest remaining wood frame house in the Village stands at the corner of Bedford and Grove streets. Grove Court, at 12 Grove Street, was originally built by the corner grocer to import more customers to his block. It was on the wall of this courtyard that the doomed artist in O. Henry's short story "The Last Leaf" painted the leaf that wouldn't fall. The Whittemore Mansion, at number 45, was once the home of the poet Hart Crane, who wrote part of his classic epic "The Bridge" in a second-floor room in the house.

Back on Bedford Street, number 86 is the secret back-door exit from **Chumley's**, a still lively bar that was once a rollicking speakeasy entered through a courtyard passage, at 58 Barrow Street. The Bedford Street door was employed for hasty retreats when government agents arrived. (The bar still does not announce its presence with a sign.) Dust jackets of the publications by modern American writers who have haunted Chumley's—just about everyone from Hemingway to Faulkner to Kerouac to Mailer—still adorn the faded, smoke-stained walls. What is probably the Village's oldest house is at 77 Bedford Street, built in 1799; and 75½ Bedford is the narrowest residence in the city (9½ feet wide), but once housed one of the Village's most expansive residents, the poet Edna St. Vincent Millay (given her middle name from another Village institution, St. Vincent's Hospital). If you are interested in historical residences, turn right on Commerce Street, where Washington Irving lived at number 11 and Aaron Burr at number 17. The **Cherry Lane Theater**, at number 38 (opposite a pair of lovely, early-1800s houses at numbers 39 and 41), is another of the Village's best Off Broadway theaters.

From the Cherry Lane, wander across Barrow Street and head west several blocks to West Street and up a short block to the foot of Christopher Street.

CHRISTOPHER STREET

Originally a lane running to a pleasant little cove on the Hudson River, Christopher Street has been one of the West Village's main arteries since the 1790s, when the area's first major market informally opened there. The town of Greenwich was compelled to build market stalls in 1812, soon doubling the width of the street between West and Washington streets to handle the traffic of goods and people. The former Federal Archives on Washington Street, the largest building in the Village, now teeming with apartments, stands on the site of the old market. The state prison that once stood a block north of the market inspired the term "up the river," which remains meaningful to contemporary New Yorkers because of the prison's move well and truly up the river to Sing Sing in Ossining, New York, in 1829.

Today Christopher Street is considered to be the center of the New York gay community. Now departed, the Stonewall, at 51 Christopher Street at Sheridan Square, was the scene of the 1969 riot that energized a generation of gay men. Though the Gay and Lesbian Community Center is north of the area, at 208 West 13th Street, there are a number of establishments in the immediate vicinity that cater to a homosexual clientele. The stretch of Christopher Street just off Seventh Avenue is now the home of the **Oscar Wilde Memorial Bookshop**, at number 15. **Pandora's Box** (70 Grove Street) and **Henrietta Hudson** (438 Hudson Street) are lesbian bars; **Marie's Crisis Café** (59 Grove Street) is where men gather to sing show tunes in Thomas Paine's former home (the name of the establishment is a reference to *The Crisis,* one of the patriot's publications); and **The Monster** (80 Grove) offers drag cabaret and video. Rougher bars are found closer to the waterfront at the west end of Christopher Street. The community is also home to many straight residents, and subject to the visitors who come for Off Broadway theater at the **Lucille Lortel** (121 Christopher Street), and for shopping at such specialty shops as Li-Lac Chocolates, at 120 Christopher Street, McNulty's Tea & Coffee provisioners, at 109 Christopher Street, and the Pleasure Chest, at 156 Seventh Avenue South, which sells sexual equipment for all persuasions, or to participate in *Tony n' Tina's Wedding,* a free-form marriage and reception performance piece encouraging audience participation (the bride's father may complain to you about the cost of the food or the number of the groom's relatives) that takes place seven times a week at St. John's Church, 81 Christopher Street. (For tickets, call Ticketcentral; Tel: 279-4200.)

SHERIDAN SQUARE AND JEFFERSON MARKET

Sheridan Square, at Christopher Street and Seventh Avenue, is actually an intersection of six streets, created in 1914 when the IRT subway line was slashed through the cockeyed Village streets. In return for bowing to the city's rigid grid plan south of Greenwich Avenue (at least in respect to the Seventh Avenue north–south artery), the Village was blessed with the city's first zoning ordinances restricting certain areas to residential use.

During the 1920s antic New Yorkers flocked to Sheri-

dan Square's many "Goofy Clubs," such as the Pirates Den
at present-day number 10, which featured every possible
pirate prop a fertile imagination could conceive and a
willing hand could strap on—pistols, boots, earrings,
parrots, cutlasses, eyepatches—the works. The Greenwich Village Inn (now the Circle Repertory Theater) became in 1919 the site of the first Prohibition arrest in New
York, and shortly thereafter one of the city's leading
speakeasies. At 1 Sheridan Square, Billie Holiday opened
in 1938 as the first headliner at Café Society, an interracial
jazz supper club that was the class of the city for a
generation. Today the **Ridiculous Theatrical Company**
resides in the hallowed basement space.

Continuing east a block you arrive at the triangle-
shaped Northern Dispensary, which was built in 1831 and
once dispensed medicine to Edgar Allan Poe; it is known
as the building with one side on two streets (the junction
of Grove and Christopher streets) and two sides on one
street (Waverly Place). The Northern Dispensary closed as
a health facility for low-income patients and is now a
nursing home for AIDS sufferers. Follow Waverly Place
east to Gay Street, which, though it intersects Christopher
Street, was so called as far back as 1827, long before the
word got its present-day homosexual connotation. A
ghetto until the 1920s, the street, whose name originally
connoted frivolity, was immortalized for that quality at
number 14, where Ruth McKenney wrote *My Sister Eileen,*
the definitive tale (later made into a musical and two
films) about the time-honored tradition of Midwesterners
moving to New York City.

At the other end of Gay Street, follow Christopher
Street east to Greenwich Avenue (Note: Greenwich *Street,*
way to the west, is a different entity.) The three-sided plot
bounded by Greenwich Avenue, West 10th Street, and
Sixth Avenue is dominated by the towering Victorian
Gothic building at 425 Sixth Avenue. Originally a courthouse, designed by Frederick Clarke Withers and Calvert
Vaux (one of the architects of Central Park) in 1876, it is
now the last remnant of a complex that included a
women's jail, firehouse, and market on the adjacent property, now a bright spot of landscaping. Thanks to a 1967
conversion by Giorgio Cavaglieri, the building houses the
Jefferson Market branch of the New York Public Library.
Some of the neighborhood's most gentrified marketing
takes place across the avenue at Balducci's, 424 Sixth
Avenue, or up the block at Jefferson Market, 455 Sixth

Avenue. At number 414 is **C. O. Bigelow Chemists**. Opened in 1838, it is New York's oldest continuously operating pharmacy, although the famous counter at which Truman Capote, Mel Brooks, and others once lunched is gone. Wander back up Sixth Avenue to West 10th Street to see two more narrow Village streets: **Patchin Place**, off West 10th Street before Sixth Avenue, and Milligan Place, to the left on Sixth Avenue. The novelist Djuna Barnes and the poet e. e. cummings were longtime neighbors on Patchin Place; in their later years, cummings had a morning ritual of standing beneath Barnes's windows and shouting, "Djuna, are you dead yet?" John Reed lived here for those of the last four years of his life when he wasn't in Russia, where he died in 1920 and was interred near the Kremlin Wall.

THE GREENWICH AVENUE AREA

From here, stroll up Greenwich Avenue, which has been a well-trod thoroughfare since its origin as an Indian footpath. The building that once stood at number 91 housed the offices of *The Masses,* a radical monthly founded in 1911 to make trouble for those in power. The paper survived for eight brave years on unpaid articles from the likes of Upton Sinclair (whose *The Jungle* gutted the Chicago slaughteryards), Sherwood Anderson, Carl Sandburg, and, of course, John Reed, until it was shut down under the Espionage Act for protesting America's impending involvement in World War I.

About face and then head west across lovely tree-lined Bank Street, past apartment buildings that over the years have been inhabited by John Lennon (number 105), Lauren Bacall (number 75), John Dos Passos (number 11), and Willa Cather (number 5). The huge building at 463 West Street (between Bank and Bethune streets) is now the **Westbeth**, a co-op providing apartments and studio space for artists and performers. Western Electric put up the huge structure, however, and it was here Alexander Graham Bell made the first coast-to-coast phone call, and where, between 1922 and 1930, Bell Laboratory scientists invented commercial radio, public address systems, spoken sound for movies (talkies), color television, and stereophonic radio. Washington Street north takes you through the meat-packing district, also a cruising spot for gay men and transvestite hookers, to the Gansevoort Meat Market, on the spot where Fort Gansevoort was erected in 1811 to protect New Yorkers from a British invasion during the War of 1812.

EAST OF WASHINGTON SQUARE

Broadway

Broadway cuts a north–south swath east of Washington Square Park, making for a neighborhood between the square and the East Village that really resembles neither, a sort of *entre-deux-villages*. From the early 1800s until the 1870s this stretch of Broadway was home to some of New York's most opulent mansions, ritziest hotels, and finest emporiums. Today, relics of that wealth are interspersed with turn-of-the-century warehouses-turned-lofts and tenement buildings, and the street is a teenage mall rebel's dream, crammed with street vendors and hordes of youth coming and going from such establishments as **Tower Records**, at number 692.

One elegant survivor of Broadway's sweeter days is **Grace Church**, on the east side of Broadway between 10th and 12th streets. Its 1845 construction brought Gothic architecture to the city's houses of worship, and was the first design by James Renwick, Jr., who later designed St. Patrick's Cathedral. Nearby, Alexander Graham Bell in 1877 made the first interborough (and public) telephone call from the now-departed St. Denis Hotel (at 11th Street) to Brooklyn via wires strung over the then-unopened Brooklyn Bridge.

Lafayette Street

Lafayette Street was home to some of the mid-19th century's highest flyers, the Astor, Vanderbilt, and Delano families, who all had town houses on what was at the time the most fashionable address in New York, then called Lafayette Place. John Jacob Astor put his imprimatur on the area in 1832 with the **Colonnade**, a series of nine very expensive connected houses (of which only four, at numbers 428–434, remain) with massive (and now sadly decrepit) Corinthian columns. The **Joseph Papp Public Theater**, across the street, was originally the Astor Library, the city's first free library and the result of a bequest encouraged by Washington Irving. Slated for destruction in the 1960s, it was saved as a landmark and converted to theater spaces by Giorgio Cavaglieri in 1966, after which Joseph Papp moved his New York Shakespeare Festival into its newly restored halls. The theater was recently renamed for Papp after his death in 1991. Farther along, across the street from the theater, is 376–380 Lafayette Street, an 1888 warehouse building designed by Henry J. Hardenbergh, architect of the Plaza Hotel and the Dakota Apartments; the ground floor houses the ultra-chic Time Café. Cross Lafayette Street and continue back uptown to the northeast corner of East 4th Street, where, at 399 Lafayette, there is another noteworthy warehouse, the De Vinne Press Building, designed by Babb, Cook & Willard in 1885. Down East 4th Street, at number 29, is another remnant of the area's fashionable days, the **Old Merchant's House**, a fascinating and fully restored Greek Revival residence dating from 1832 that is open for afternoon tours (closed Fridays and Saturdays).

The East Village

Like SoHo, the East Village, which stretches from Fourth Avenue all the way east to the East River, is a name created by canny real-estate agents hoping to cash in on the cachet of the Village. The success of this venture has been limited in Alphabet City (Avenues A through D, way to the east) by persistent poverty, a profitable drug trade, sprawling villages of homeless camps, and blocks of burnt-out and abandoned buildings. Some blocks have flourished, however, carving out an oasis of beauty in an otherwise difficult area. The section of the East Village from Avenue A to Third Avenue and running from Houston to 14th Street has fared better, and the influx of suits and folks willing to pay what longtime residents considered outrageous rents has lowered the happiness quotient of some of the artists, writers, dropouts, mystics, and punks who have long made this part of town home.

In the 19th century parts of the East Village were pleasant residential areas. Tompkins Square, created in 1834, once had the appearance, almost, of an English park. The area has gone from high culture to counterculture, and its principal street, St. Mark's Place, is the main drag of the city's not insubstantial residual punk population, and is charged by the fashion and music scenes that director Susan Seidelman so deftly caught in her film *Desperately Seeking Susan*. The seeds of the 1960s grass-roots movement have sprouted somewhat scraggly results in the East Village, evidenced by the proliferation of lively mosaics by street artist Jim Powers that decorate sidewalks and lampposts throughout the neighborhood like punked-out

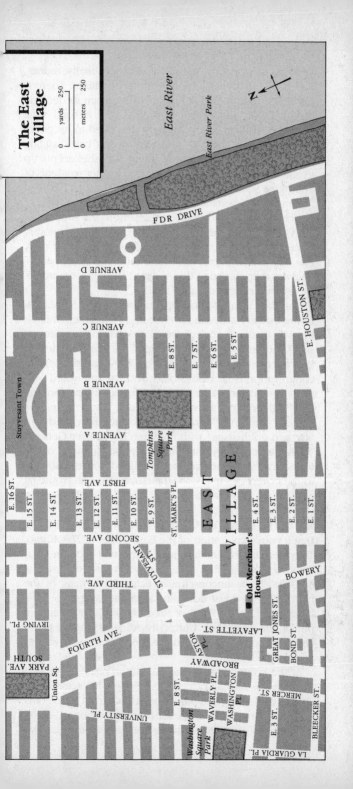

versions of works by Antoni Gaudí, social-realist murals, and public gardens along its eastern perimeter. There is not much reason to visit Alphabet City, given its decrepitude, danger, and dearth of architecture beyond what longtime resident Allen Ginsberg described in his poem "Waking in New York" as "tenement streets' brick sagging cornices" and the spontaneous temporary shelters put up in abandoned lots by the now-evicted former residents of **Tompkins Square Park**, which occupies the area between 7th and 10th streets and Avenues A and B. Hundreds of police moved in and emptied the park in the summer of 1991, destroying the increasingly permanent temporary homes of the hundreds of homeless men and women. The city used the excuse of renovating the ailing park— and was then forced to do so—so at least the community can enjoy a renewed public facility.

The East Village's most historic building is **St. Mark's-in-the-Bowery** at Second Avenue and 10th Street. Built on the site of the chapel of Dutch Governor Peter Stuyvesant's former estate (he is buried in the cemetery next to the church), the church dates from 1799. Its Episcopalian congregation is far from stodgy, and has sponsored progressive and innovative programs of poetry, performing arts, and political activisim for years. Houdini, Isadora Duncan, and Andy Warhol all performed here, and Sam Shepard got his start with the church's Theater Genesis. To the west is Stuyvesant Street, a remaining tract of the former carriage lane that once extended from the Bowery to the governor's mansion (the Stuyvesant-Fish House, at number 21, dates from 1803).

ASTOR PLACE AND ST. MARK'S PLACE

Begin your exploration of the East Village at *The Alamo,* Tony Bernard Rosenthal's huge black steel cube on Astor Place, a popular East Village rendezvous. Its shape is consciously or unconsciously echoed by many of the hairdos created just down the street at Astor Place Hair Designers (2 Astor Place, at Broadway), where the line of punks and New York University students waiting to be cheaply shorn and shaped has been known to extend around the block.

At the corner of Lafayette Street and Astor Place, step through the morass of vendors selling what seem to be articles of clothing and other goods lifted from refuse bins (although one visitor to the area recently reported seeing the contents of a suitcase stolen from his car less than five minutes earlier spread out on the sidewalk) to the Cooper Union Foundation building, the centerpiece of **Cooper Union for the Advancement of Science and Art**. Founded in 1859 by industrialist Peter Cooper, it was the first coed, nonpartisan college in the country. Tuition at this major center for art, architecture, and engineering is still free. Susan B. Anthony, Henry Ward Beecher, Mark Twain, and Abraham Lincoln each rallied the crowds in its Great Hall, a tradition that continues with the weekly meetings there of the AIDS activist group ACT-UP. The 1859 brownstone exterior of Cooper Union masks a total reconstruction that gave the building a high-tech interior in 1975 and revealed that in constructing the country's first steel-frame building, Cooper used his own rails. On the south side of the building is an 1894 bronze statue of the school's founder by former student Augustus Saint-Gaudens, with a base by Stanford White.

Continue across Third Avenue and along to **St. Mark's Place** for a strong dose of street theater. Boisterous punks, shops, and restaurants characterize St. Mark's Place, which has the appearance of unusual width because most of its buildings were built farther back from the street than those on other streets in the city. To get a taste of the variety of the neighborhood's activities, take a look at the bulletin board of the recently enlarged **St. Mark's Bookshop**, at 12 St. Mark's Place. At 23 St. Mark's Place is a community center (which can get pretty roisterous) that was the onetime home of Andy Warhol's exploding Plastic Inevitable, where Lou Reed and the Velvet Underground was the house band; W. H. Auden was a longtime resident of the house at number 77.

ON AND AROUND SECOND AVENUE

Pop up north a few blocks to the former **Yiddish Art Theater**, at Second Avenue and 12th Street. Now a modern, semi-art-house multiplex cinema, it was lovingly restored to a portion of its former glory, and those lucky enough to see a film in the upstairs theater can loll beneath the gorgeous original domed ceiling. Emma ("the Red") Goldman lived for a while with her lover Hippolyte Havel a block north, at 208 (formerly 210) East 13th Street. For decades the **Tenth Street Turkish Baths**, just east of Second Avenue at 268 East 10th Street, has provided a respite from the harsh realities of New York life and is one of the last such places of its kind.

As you head back downtown, an excursion across East

7th Street reveals Allen Ginsberg's 1950s residence at 206 Second Avenue, where Jack Kerouac and William Burroughs were frequent, and troublesome, visitors. The **Kiev**, 117 Second Avenue (at 7th Street), is the best-known of the neighborhood's Eastern European restaurants, serving a weird and youthful clientele who live in tenements built to house immigrants a century ago. Bill Graham's mythical and glorious **Fillmore East**, at 105 Second Avenue, was New York's center for righteous rock until 1971, while George and Ira Gershwin, musical giants of another stripe, grew up at number 91.

Two of the Village's most important theaters are based on East 4th Street: the **La MaMa Experimental Theater**, at number 74A, which has been at the forefront of avant-garde drama since the mid-1960s; and the **WOW** (Women's One World), at number 59, which, as you might imagine, focuses exclusively on women's issues. East 3rd Street is the site of Manhattan's **Marble Cemeteries**, 18th-century graveyards housing some of the city's most famous dead in two stretches between First Avenue and the Bowery.

Any tour of the East Village is properly concluded at **CBGB** (which stands for "Country, Blue Grass, and Blues"; the little-used continuation of the name, OMFUG, is an acronym for "Other Music for Uplifting Gourmandizers"), still the head-banging, slam-dancing heart of New York's punk music scene, at the Bowery and Bleecker Street. The knots of arguably deranged-looking folks (and piles of empty beer cans) out front have not changed too much since the club's patrons crowded in to see The Ramones, Talking Heads, Blondie, and Patti Smith—except that they are now mellower.

—*Edward Hernstadt*

14TH STREET TO 34TH STREET

By Lenore Malen with Dwight V. Gast

T he gridlike streets that lie between Greenwich Village and Midtown can not compete with Wall Street for its heady atmosphere of wheeling and dealing, with the Village for its prettiness and artiness, with Midtown for glamour, or with the Upper West and Upper East sides for residential atmosphere. Instead, this is a place to experience real, everyday, sometimes gritty, New York life. Photographers' studios, advertising agencies, and publishing houses have taken over the loftlike spaces that even 50 years ago housed light industry, some remnants of which remain. Gone are the department stores that once graced Broadway between 14th and 34th streets (known as "Ladies' Mile") and Sixth Avenue in the 20s ("Fashion Row"), but the grand structures they once occupied remain, now given over to printing shops, office space, and apartments. The area has its charms—some of the city's most distinctive public spaces are here, Union and Madison squares, for instance, as is the city's only private greensward, Gramercy Park, which also happens to be the center of one of the city's nicest residential quarters.

We begin our coverage just north of Greenwich Village in the area around Union Square. We then move north and farther east to Gramercy Park, then west through the Madison Square area to Chelsea.

MAJOR INTEREST

Union Square Area
The renovated square and its greenmarket
Strand bookshop

Gramercy Park Area
Irving Place
The park and its surrounding buildings
Theodore Roosevelt birthplace

Madison Square Area
The square and surrounding buildings, including
    the Flatiron Building
Ladies' Mile on Broadway
Trendy bars and restaurants
Fashion Row along Sixth Avenue
The Flower and Garment districts

Chelsea
Chelsea Hotel
Chelsea Historic District and General Theological
    Seminary

The Union Square Area

This appealing, animated square is just north of Greenwich Village, lying between 14th and 17th streets, with Broadway to its west and Park Avenue South to its east. Originally named Union Place after its role in uniting Bloomingdale Road (now Broadway) and Bowery Road (Fourth Avenue), Union Square was a residential square with its own private park in the mid-19th century, much as Gramercy Park is today (see below). The center of New York's theater district in the 1850s, the Union Square area was, by the late 19th century, the very heart of New York's most fashionable retail and residential districts. By the 20th century, however, fashionable New York had moved farther uptown and for years the Union Square area has been down at its heels.

In recent years, the allure of large spaces and lower rents has drawn many publishing houses and advertising agencies away from Midtown to the area around Union Square, especially to newly renovated loft buildings near the square on Broadway and Park Avenue South. With the influx has come any number of new businesses, including restaurants that are usually abuzz with the latest media gossip. (See our Dining and Bars chapters for the best dining and drinking choices in the area.) Among the current favorites are the noisy, ever-crowded **Union Square Café** (a pleasant place to lunch or dine alone at the bar), just off the square, at 21 East 16th Street, and the no longer super trendy but still sumptuous **Gotham Bar and Grill**, south of the square, at 12 East 12th Street. One of New York's oldest neighborhood bars, the creaky **Old Town**, is at 45 East 18th Street (between Park Avenue South and Broadway).

Despite this new glitz, there's still a funky, removed-from-the-mainstream air to the area. The well-stocked shelves of **Revolution Books** are just a few steps off the square at 13 East 16th Street. Until a decade ago, the streets just south of Union Square, especially Broadway and University Place, housed many antiquarian and used-book sellers. Fortunately, the best among these shops continues to thrive: the **Strand**, a wonderful, extensively stocked bargain-filled place at Broadway and 12th Street.

UNION SQUARE

In the early years of this century, this once glamorous park was the rallying point for political and labor disputes. In the Great Depression orators addressed crowds numbering in the thousands; a labor demonstration in 1930 was attended by 35,000 people. The park's most famous rally was the 1927 protest against the execution of anarchists Sacco and Vanzetti.

For much of the 20th century Union Square was also home to flourishing budget department stores, the best known of which was Klein's. (Fourteenth Street, which runs along the south side of the Square, is still lined with discount shops serving Hispanics, many of whom travel for miles to shop here.) Come Saturday morning, middle-class New Yorkers would descend on the square to shop, then lunch afterward at Horn & Hardart's Automat on 14th Street. By the 1970s, however, the square had fallen on hard times, becoming a nest of drug dealers, and the stores closed their doors. The square was redesigned in 1985 as part of a gentrification project that included the building of the Zeckendorf Towers apartment complex, topped with grandiose pyramids, just to the east. The complex now blocks the view from the square of one of New York's famous landmarks, the clock tower of Consolidated Edison power company, a block east at 14th Street and Irving Place, but that's a relatively small price to pay for regaining a lively urban space: Union Square has made a complete turnaround. On Mondays, Wednesdays, Fridays, and Saturdays, New York's largest **greenmarket** takes place here. New Yorkers, many pushing infants in strollers, come to finger the radicchio, sample the goat cheese, and generally exchange pleasantries instead of the usual business cards. Trendy restaurants gave the area the finishing touches of gentrification, leading to the opening of even more meteoric establishments throughout the general area.

Union Square is blessed with an unusual amount of statuary within the park. Henry Kirke Brown's 1856 *George Washington* is the city's first monumental bronze; the same sculptor's *Lincoln* is also here; Frédéric Auguste Bartholdi, who created the Statue of Liberty, was given another chance to honor his native France with his *Lafayette*. Karl Adolf Donndorf designed the square's elaborate drinking fountain, and Anthony de Francisci did bas-reliefs for the base of the Independence Flagstaff. The glass and steel structure at the southern end of the square is an entrance to the New York City subway system; Union Square is a major hub (and was the site of one of the system's worst crashes ever, in 1991).

The Gramercy Park Area

Fourteenth Street, a busy, somewhat unattractive thoroughfare south of Union Square, has some interesting historical sites. At the turn of the century Mack Sennett, Mary Pickford, and D. W. Griffith invented the film industry in the now long vanished Biograph Film Co. Studio, just off Broadway at 11 East 14th Street. Many folks in the business dined at Lüchow's (between Third and Fourth avenues), one of the city's great show-business restaurants for a century (until it moved to Midtown in 1982 and closed shortly thereafter). The eatery's husk is still there and may yet be revived. To explore New York's most gentrified park and its environs, follow 14th Street a block east to Irving Place. Have a look at the enormous mural above the entrance to the **Palladium**, at 126 East 14th Street; the club was New York's trendiest disco many seasons back, and though it's no longer "hot," it still draws a crowd. The mural, by Hank Pressing and Jeff Green, contains an image of Pallas Athena pulling aside a curtain to reveal a rock concert. If not exactly social realism, it is at least a sort of social reality.

IRVING PLACE

Irving Place is named for Washington Irving, the author of "The Legend of Sleepy Hollow" and other American classics. A plaque on a brick house up the way at number 40 identifies it as the author's home, though it's unlikely he ever entered the house as anything other than a visitor. The writer William Sydney Porter, who went by the pen name O. Henry, was a true habitué of Irving Place at the turn of the century. **Pete's Tavern**, at 18th Street, claims to be the place where O. Henry wrote his most famous short story, "The Gift of the Magi." Pete's, a cozy, dark place, is one of the oldest bars in New York. To survive Prohibition the management opened a flower shop in front and ran a speakeasy in the rear, complete with a convenient getaway door onto 18th Street.

In an area crowded with warehouses and tall commercial buildings to the west and rather sterile 1960s apartment buildings to the east, Irving Place and the streets immediately surrounding Gramercy Park are a sea of tranquility, recapturing the neighborhood as it was in the 19th century: a place of genteel respectability. As you walk north on Irving Place, cast a sidelong glance east

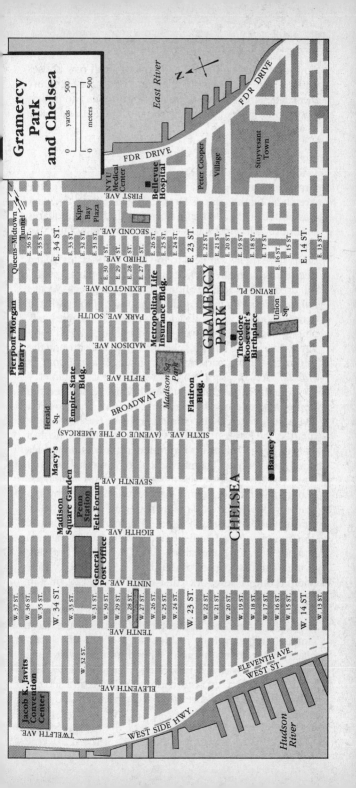

down 19th Street, a tree-lined lane of small row houses and converted stables. In the early part of the century these side streets were populated by artisans and tradespeople, but today are among the most prized real estate in Manhattan.

GRAMERCY PARK

Gramercy Park begins at East 20th Street, known in the stretch along the park as Gramercy Park South. The park was built in 1831 and bears a certain similarity to squares in London, a fact that status-conscious residents of the area often point to with pride. The park is private (area residents have their own keys to the stately iron gates), but a peer through the iron fence quickly reveals what a peaceful urban oasis it is. Children play near Gregg Wyatt's *Fantasy Fountain* in the southeast corner of the park, the water spouting from dancing giraffes as nannies talk among themselves on well-shaded benches. You'll soon get a sense of the square's charms as you walk around the perimeter of the park. Another statue, *Edwin Booth as Hamlet,* faces the actor's former residence, at 16 Gramercy Park South. The architect Stanford White remodeled the house, a simple brownstone built in 1845, and gave it a lavish, Italian Renaissance façade in 1888. The house now quarters the Players, a club that Booth (brother of Lincoln's assassin, John Wilkes Booth) founded for actors. Besides Booth and White, Thomas Nast and Winston Churchill have counted themselves among the club's members. (Churchill's mother, Jennie Jerome, was born nearby in a mansion that once stood on the southeast corner of Madison Avenue and East 26th Street.) The mansion at number 15 Gramercy Park South, remodeled by Calvert Vaux, is another club, the National Arts Club. The elegant building at the southeast corner of the park at 34 Gramercy Park South is one of New York's first apartment houses, built in 1883.

If you leave the square and walk two blocks west on East 20th Street, you can enter the world of the most famous Gramercy Park resident area of all—the birthplace and boyhood **home of Theodore Roosevelt**, now owned by the National Park Service, at number 28. The home is actually a reconstruction, an architect and decorator's understated interpretation of "Speak softly and carry a big stick."

LITTLE INDIA

The Indian restaurants and shops on a stretch of Lexington Avenue just north of Gramercy Park between 23rd and 28th streets have aptly given this stretch of the avenue the name Little India. You'll know you are approaching Little India when the New York air becomes heady with the scent of exotic spices. Of the ever-changing roster of places to eat on the street, one of the oldest and most respected is **Annapurna**, where a mural of a sunset over the swaying palms of an Indian beach will transport even the most harried editor or copywriter working in the surrounding publishing houses and ad agencies to Nirvana.

THE FAR EAST 20S

Another nearby and recently preserved architectural remnant recalls a side of New York social history quite different from that of Gramercy Park: the **Asser Levy Bathhouse**, six blocks east of Gramercy Park on 23rd Street between First Avenue and FDR Drive. The ornate building, modeled on the baths of ancient Rome, opened in 1906 to provide free bathing facilities to the residents of the area's bathless tenements, and is now part of a public swimming-pool complex. Blocks of the cramped, airless tenement structures were razed in the late 1940s to make way for the seemingly endless and soulless rows of brick apartment houses that begin at 23rd Street and stretch south to 14th Street between First Avenue and the F.D.R. Drive. Actually, these buildings and their pleasantly landscaped grounds make up two of the city's most successful public housing ventures, **Peter Cooper Village** and the adjoining **Stuyvesant Town**. The 50,000 middle-income New Yorkers who live in the large (relatively, for New York) one- to three-bedroom apartments pay some of the most reasonable rents in town, and the waiting list is years long.

The Madison Square Area

The next area to explore is just north and east of Gramercy Park, around Madison Square, at the intersection of Broadway and Fifth Avenue between East 23rd and East 26th streets. From Gramercy Park, walk a couple of blocks west to Broadway, which cuts a northwest swath up to Madison Square. You may want to linger and take in the architecture on this stretch of Broadway, which in the late 19th century was known as **Ladies' Mile**, because so many department and dry-goods stores lined the corridor from 14th to 34th Street. Though these retail concerns have long since closed or moved on to more fashionable precincts, the grand buildings that housed them still stand. Numbers 881–887 Broadway (at 19th Street), designed by Griffith Thomas, housed the Arnold Constable Dry Goods Store in 1869 (extensions were made in 1873 and 1877); a block north is 900 Broadway, an 1887 loft building by McKim, Mead & White; 901 Broadway was the Lord & Taylor Dry Goods Store in 1870; and a block west, at 153–157 Fifth Avenue, is the first headquarters of Charles Scribner's Sons publishing company, built in 1894 by Ernest Flagg.

Until the beginning of this century Madison Square was the center of one of New York's most fashionable districts, surrounded by elegant hotels and private homes. The famed Flatiron Building, facing the square from a triangular plot formed as Broadway crosses Fifth Avenue at 23rd Street, brought business to what was to become a solidly commercial district of giftware and toy manufacturers, as well as professional photographers. Recently, publishing companies and advertising agencies have been moving into this area too, and the photographers whose flashes have brightened big lofts are being driven farther west to less expensive studio space in Chelsea as many buildings are being converted to apartments.

MADISON SQUARE

Like Union Square to the south, Madison Square has also been refurbished recently, and it, too, has its own nearby clock tower (the Metropolitan Life Insurance Company headquarters). While today the most startling sight a visitor is likely to encounter is that of office workers in states of partial undress lunching in the park, New Yorkers of the late 19th century were treated to a rare spectacle indeed: the long arm of the Statue of Liberty, placed here as an early (and unsuccessful) ploy to raise funds for the statue's erection in New York Harbor after it had been exhibited in the Philadelphia Centennial Exposition in 1876.

The square's best-known structure was the original Madison Square Garden designed for the northeast corner of East 26th Street and Madison Avenue by the illustrious architect Stanford White. Demolished in 1925, the Garden was also the scene of White's demise: He was shot dead in 1906 in its Roof Garden Theater by Harry K. Thaw, the jealous husband of one of White's former mistresses, Eve-lyn Nesbit. (The story was the subject of the film *The Girl in the Red Velvet Swing*.) One architectural treasure still stands on the square: the Appellate Division of the New York State Supreme Court, at the northeast corner of 25th Street and Madison Avenue. A small Palladian palace dating to 1900, it is a decorator's extravaganza, covered with idealized statuary depicting historical personages and lofty themes and outfitted with an ornate interior. A new Holocaust Memorial faces the square from the south side of the court building.

Dr. Norman Vincent Peale, author of *The Power of Positive Thinking*, was pastor at the Marble Collegiate Church, an 1854 Gothic-Revival-style edifice on Fifth Avenue at the northwest corner of West 29th Street. The Gothic-style Church of the Transfiguration is around the corner, at 1 East 29th Street. Built from 1849 to 1856, with later additions, in 1870 it was the site of the burial rites for an actor named George Holland, after a nearby church refused to perform them and referred the funeral party to a "little church around the corner." Since then it has been known as the **Little Church Around the Corner** and is a favorite spot for actors. It contains a stained-glass window by John La Farge depicting Edwin Booth as Hamlet and sponsors a small acting company. Around the corner from the Transfiguration, up at 120 Madison Avenue, is McKim, Mead & White's 1907 Colony Club, now the home of the American Academy of Dramatic Arts.

THE FLATIRON BUILDING AND LOWER FIFTH AVENUE

Immortalized in the photographs of Edward Steichen, the Flatiron Building is one of Chicago architect Daniel H. Burnham's masterpieces. When completed, it was the tallest building in the world and had an observation platform on top. Its triangular shape gave the building its name (it was originally called the Fuller Building), but to some it also suggests the prow of a ship and indeed does create a sense of movement. The shape also creates an unusual flurry of air currents, and in the building's first years men used to gather to watch the billowing skirts of 23rd Street's female shoppers blown about, giving rise to the expression "23 skiddoo!" which constables used in order to shoo gapers from the area.

Real-estate developers trying to attract business to the surrounding blocks have dubbed the area to the south "SoFi" (*So*uth of the *Flati*ron). Fortunately, the term has not entered the New York lexicon, but businesses and their largely youthful followings have been moving into the area nonetheless. The stretch of Fifth Avenue running south of the Flatiron Building into the teens is now a hip version of Fifth Avenue in Midtown, with Giorgio Armani and other designers showing their wares in strikingly chic and expensive shops.

Many shoppers here, though, forgo fashion for the loftier pursuits at the longstanding **Barnes & Noble** bookstores that face one another from opposite sides of Fifth Avenue at 18th Street. The store at 105 Fifth Avenue stocks a huge selection of current fiction and nonfiction, and has a section crammed with medical and academic text books. The sales annex across the street at 128 Fifth Avenue sells current and out-of-print books at deep, deep discounts.

The side streets off Fifth Avenue are an eclectic mix of the area's old and new elements. Dusty camera stores have serviced the area's many photographers for years (see our Photography and Filmmaking section), and the lights of new restaurants and clubs burn late into the night on dark, otherwise deserted streets inhabited largely by light industry (many printing houses are here) and wholesalers.

FASHION ROW

To continue your exploration of this stretch of Manhattan, now head west across 23rd Street from Madison Square toward Chelsea. Aficionados of cast-iron buildings should take some time to explore Sixth Avenue between West 23rd and West 18th streets, lined with the cast-iron skeletons of the palatial department stores that flourished in the area in the late 19th century. Sixth Avenue was so devoted to shopping that it was known as Fashion Row.

Begin a tour of Fashion Row at 32–36 West 23rd Street, the site of the 1878 Stern's Dry Goods Store. At 695–709 Sixth Avenue is what was originally the 1889 Erlich Brothers Emporium; 675 was the 1900 Adams Dry Goods Store (the third and final cemetery of the Spanish and Portuguese synagogue, used between 1829 and 1851, is just around the corner, at 98–110 West 21st Street); the former 1875 Hugh O'Neill Dry Goods Store, recently refurbished and optimistically renting floor space, is at 655–671 Sixth Avenue (across the street, at 47 West 20th Street, is the 1846 church of the Holy Communion by Richard Upjohn, preserved for better or worse as the

Limelight discotheque); 621–625 Sixth Avenue was, from the building's beginning in 1877 until 1906, the site of the B. Altman department store; and the building at 616–632 Sixth Avenue, dating to 1895, housed the Siegel-Cooper Dry Goods Store.

On weekends there's a flea market on the east side of Sixth Avenue between 24th and 26th streets. The northern part of the area is now dubbed the **Flower District**, given over to wholesale florists (some can be coaxed into selling retail) on Sixth Avenue around West 28th Street. Their flowers and potted trees fill the sidewalks, turning the concrete jungle into a lush, green one and creating some of the most pleasant few blocks in the city. Garment manufacturing—one of New York's largest industries—is centered slightly to the north on Seventh Avenue in the 30s: the **Garment District**. Seventh Avenue, in fact, has been dubbed Fashion Avenue on the street signs between 26th and 28th streets, where the **Fashion Institute of Technology**, a school for those interested in the clothing industry as a profession, is located.

Chelsea

Chelsea lies roughly between 14th and 30th streets from Seventh Avenue to the Hudson River. Named for the estate of Captain Thomas Clarke (which covered most of the area when the district was laid out in 1750), Chelsea is today an area of brownstones, tenements, and large apartment houses—a busy, unglamorous city neighborhood that is not without its distinctive landmarks.

Chelsea's most famous resident of the past may well be Clarke's scholarly grandson, Clement Clarke Moore, the author of the *Compendious Lexicon of the Hebrew Language* but better remembered for the Christmas poem *A Visit from St. Nicholas* (" 'Twas the night before Christmas . . . "). Moore grew up in the now-demolished family mansion on Eighth Avenue and West 23rd Street. The Hudson River Railroad brought warehouses to Eleventh Avenue in the 1850s, and New York's first elevated railroad brought crowds to a flourishing theater district here in the 1870s. Artists and writers moved in when the theaters moved to Times Square (the old theaters and warehouses were briefly recycled as movie studios), and creative residents—including rock musicians—still add a touch of character to the area.

AROUND THE CHELSEA HOTEL

Chelsea's most famous structure is the Chelsea Hotel, 222 West 23rd Street, midway between Seventh and Eighth avenues. Architecturally, the place is a wonder, a Victorian Gothic brick pile complete with gables, dormers, and ornate cast-iron balconies. One of the city's first cooperative apartment buildings when it was built in 1884, the Chelsea earned its fame for the roster of celebrity artists who took up residence when it became a hotel in 1905— from Mark Twain, O. Henry, Edgar Lee Masters, Thomas Wolfe, and Dylan Thomas to Virgil Thomson, Janis Joplin, and Sid Vicious. (Vicious, who hacked his girlfriend, Nancy Spungen, to death in one of the hotel's funky rooms, was the subject of the Alex Cox film *Sid and Nancy,* part of which was shot in the Chelsea.) Masters wrote a poem about his beloved hostelry, "The Chelsea Hotel": "Who will remember that Mark Twain used to stroll / In the gorgeous dining room, that Princesses / Poets and celebrated actresses / Lived here and made its soul."

Actually, plenty of New Yorkers and non–New Yorkers alike seem to have no problem remembering the Chelsea's romantic and illustrious past (it's one of the city's favorite landmarks), and should you have any trouble doing so, plaques on the façade will enlighten you. The pleasant eclecticism of the hotel's architectural style still extends to its guest roster; after inspecting its façade, take a look at the lobby to see its grand staircase and perhaps some of the regulars.

For more of a taste of neighborhood history, from the hotel walk down Eighth Avenue to West 20th Street, the heart of the **Chelsea Historic District,** a quiet area filled with late-19th-century residences ranging from town houses to large apartment buildings. The **General Theological Seminary** is a conglomeration of 19th-century buildings that from the 1820s and 1830s went up on land donated by Clement Clarke Moore, on the north side of West 20th Street between Ninth and Tenth avenues. The entrance, at 175 Ninth Avenue, leads to a pleasant oasis of well-kept grounds. Note the row houses on the south side of West 20th Street: Numbers 406 to 418, known as Cushman Row, date from 1840; the Greek Revival houses at numbers 446 to 450 date from 1855.

Chelsea's later development is reflected a few blocks away at Tenth Avenue and West 23rd Street, where the entire north side of the block is taken up by a vast apartment complex called London Terrace, built in 1930. The **Empire Diner**, at 210 Tenth Avenue, at the corner of 22nd Street, is a 24-hour Art Deco–style eating establishment that gets a glassy-eyed crowd (increasingly of the *Saturday Night Fever* variety) from the nearby clubs during the wee hours.

BARNEY'S AND THE CHELSEA THEATERS

Most New Yorkers go to Chelsea for a specific purpose, to shop or see innovative dance, for instance. New York's largest concentration of high-line retail clothing is at **Barney's** (Seventh Avenue and West 17th Street). A walk through this attractive emporium is a little like a stroll past the ultra-fashionable shops on the boulevard St.-Germain in Paris. It's okay to gasp at the prices; even the good-looking models and celebrities who shop here regularly do. Barney's is opening an Upper East Side branch this year.

Dance concerts are held at the **Joyce Theater** (175 Eighth Avenue, at 19th Street) and the **Bessie Schönberg Theater** (219 West 19th Street, west of Seventh Avenue); theater is performed at the **Hudson Guild Theatre** (441 West 26th Street, between Ninth and Tenth avenues) and the **WPA Theatre** (519 West 23rd Street, at Tenth Avenue). Several interesting bars and restaurants—such as the Italian **Chelsea Trattoria**—cluster around the Joyce Theater on Eighth Avenue.

MIDTOWN

By Ed Wetschler

Ed Wetschler, a native New Yorker, is a senior editor at Diversion *magazine.*

New York City, and maybe the whole world, would be duller without Greenwich Village, dowdier without the Upper East Side, and blander without Chinatown—but if most people had to choose just one taste of the Big Apple, they would happily pick Midtown. Strictly speaking, this

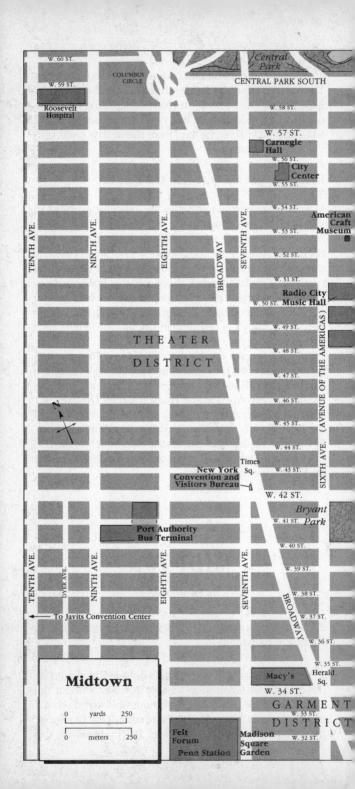

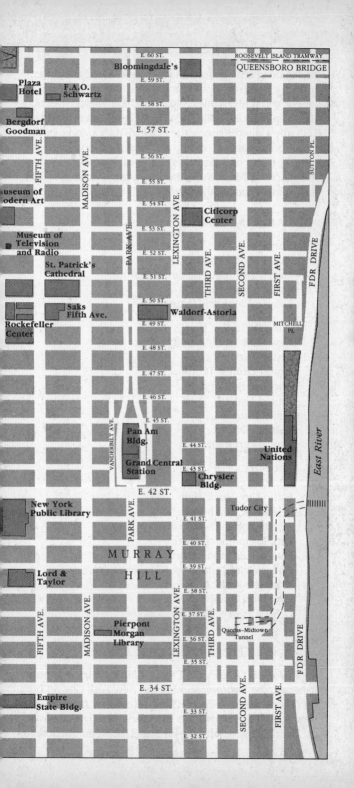

rectangle reaching from 34th Street to 59th Street (Central Park South) is not the middle of town at all. But it is where you'll find Times Square and the Theater District, the Empire State Building, Rockefeller Center, Carnegie Hall, the United Nations, the original Macy's, some of the best restaurants on earth, and almost everything else people think of when they think of New York. So go ahead, call it "Midtown"; others have gone so far as to call it the Crossroads of the World.

MAJOR INTEREST

The 30s
Herald Square area
Macy's and other department stores
Empire State Building
Pierpont Morgan Library

The 40s
New York Public Library
Bryant Park
Grand Central Terminal
Chrysler Building
United Nations
Times Square
Theater District
Bars and restaurants

The 50s
Rockefeller Center
Radio City Music Hall
St. Patrick's Cathedral
St. Bartholomew's Church
Park Avenue architecture
Museum of Modern Art
Galleries and shops on 57th Street
Carnegie Hall
The Plaza Hotel
Central Park South's restaurants

Herald Square Area

Poor Horace Greeley. "Go west," said Greeley, the publisher of *The Tribune,* so what did New York City do but erect a statue of him on 32nd Street that faces *north.* Worse yet, they named the little park directly in front of the statue, just north of 34th Street between Broadway and Sixth Avenue, **Herald Square**. Understand, *The Herald* was Greeley's competitor. And for a final indignity, almost everyone now calls the whole intersection "Herald Square," despite the fact that the proper name of the little park south of 34th Street is **Greeley Square**. No wonder the bronze giant looks so glum.

Relief may be on the way: The city may soon reroute traffic away from Greeley and Herald squares—and give Horace Greeley's statue a more prominent position. But that would happen in 1995 at the earliest. Until then, "Give my regards to Broadway, Remember me to Herald Square," as James Cagney put it in *Yankee Doodle Dandy*. But first, with a nod to Greeley, go west. Directly across the avenue from Greeley Square is a building whose flashing lights belong in Reno. Once the home of Gimbel's department store, archenemy of Macy's until it folded in the 1980s, it has been completely redesigned and renamed the **A & S Plaza**, an 80-store complex anchored by a gigantic A & S department store. Its overall impression is that of a mall in the hinterlands: Glass elevators swoop up a nine-story atrium highlighted by pink and chrome balconies. On the second floor you can sit on park benches while a man plays 1940s tunes on a baby grand. On the top floor are clean restrooms, a visitors' center, and cute eateries with patio tables and chairs. People are even polite.

Just a step to the north is "The World's Largest Department Store," **Macy's** flagship, reaching from Broadway/Sixth Avenue to Seventh Avenue between 34th and 35th streets. If you've forgotten to dab on your morning perfume or cologne, the salespeople on the first floor will gladly spritz you. The modern escalator on the Broadway side of the store, which opened in 1902, yields to a wooden one at the third floor, and by the fifth-floor landing, with its old French doors, you've travelled back to a gentler time. Best buys in Macy's are linens, during the frequent white sales. The most tempting department is Macy's Cellar, the foods and kitchenware center in the basement. But what you're most likely to purchase are men's accessories, handsomely displayed on the Seventh Avenue half of the main floor.

Exit at Seventh Avenue and glance at **Madison Square Garden** and **Pennsylvania Station**, two blocks to the south, just to assure yourself that they aren't worth visiting (unless the Bulls or Suns are in town). Even Amtrak admits that the destruction in 1963 of the *real* Penn

Station, which once provided a splendid welcome to the city, was a colossal mistake. Rumor has it that Amtrak now wants to relocate the terminal to the General Post Office building, an imposing Parthenon-like temple directly behind plastic Penn Station.

I. M. Pei's **Jacob K. Javits Convention Center**, a four-block-long glass palace looking over the Hudson River at 655 West 34th Street, is a far more interesting modern structure than Penn Station. But go there only if the boat or car show (in January and April, respectively) is in town; otherwise, this place is so far west, you'll feel as if you've wandered off to no-man's-land.

Walking eastward on 34th Street is not scintillating, but if you pause for a look to the north and the south from the west side of Sixth Avenue (and ignore a few street-level signs on the 12-story buildings that stretch up and down the avenue), you can enjoy an unspoiled view of New York as it looked before World War I. The only thing missing is the Model T Fords.

Empire State Building and
North to 40th Street

It's hard to appreciate the **Empire State Building** when you're walking alongside it on 34th Street between Sixth and Fifth avenues. Constructed in just 19 months, the Empire State is a relatively sedate (albeit towering) member of the Art Deco generation of skyscrapers built in the late 1920s and the 1930s. Art Deco was the marriage (menage, really) of Egyptian and pre-Columbian motifs with Cubism and futuristic streamlining, among other things. It's the kind of decor you see in every Fred and Ginger movie, not to mention odd sci-fi films like *Things to Come*. False columns on the exterior of the Empire State Building top out at the fourth floor with geometric palm fronds akin to those painted on mummy coffins. Inside the lobby, molded, streamlined metal walkways seem to offer passage to the utopia that designers thought technology would soon create. That was 1931, and alas, were they ever wrong.

The Empire State Building's 1,250-foot-high observatory is not quite as high as that of the World Trade Center, and its visitors' facilities are hardly state-of-the-art. But the Empire State's observatory is open till midnight, and it can be mightily romantic. And whereas the World Trade

Center plunks you on the stern of the ship that is Manhattan, the Empire State Building invites you to stand in the pilothouse and captain the ship. During the summer, an actor in a King Kong suit wanders the premises, welcoming visitors to his favorite climbing post.

E. L. Doctorow fans know the **Pierpont Morgan Library**, to the northeast, at 36th Street and Madison Avenue, from the siege scene in *Ragtime* (another James Cagney movie). Designed in 1906 by McKim, Mead & White (that's Stanford White, also trashed in *Ragtime*), this Neo-Renaissance jewel has some of the most beautiful carved and painted wood ceilings in North America, as well as rich red, blue, and gold illustrations from medieval bibles; travelling art exhibitions; and handwritten letters, music, and even cartoons from the likes of Bach, Mozart, Einstein, and Gilbert and Sullivan.

Returning to Fifth Avenue and heading north you'll find **Lord & Taylor** department store on the corner of 38th Street. Long an exponent of American (that is, country club) style, Lord & Taylor serves the well-born working woman with such necessities as a calculator with faux-pearl buttons ($19.99).

From the east side of Fifth Avenue at 40th Street you'll see how the compact but stately **Republic National Bank**, built as the Knox Hat Building on the southwest corner in 1901–1902, now cowers below a mammoth glass accordion of an edifice. A typical Midtown mismatch—it's so wrong, it's right.

New York Public Library Area

Don't visit this neighborhood if you don't like superlatives; these blocks have more than their share. The **New York Public Library**, for a start, is one of America's grandest man-made sights. Sprawling along Fifth Avenue between 40th and 42nd streets, it emulates 19th-century French government buildings that emulated Roman temples. Beyond a terrace dotted with café tables, Corinthian columns and statues of Truth (male) and Beauty (female, and nude to boot) frame three doors that lead to a marble lobby. Proceed inside to see the carved wooden ceiling in the exhibit hall just behind the lobby, as well as the library's marble stairways, Gilbert Stuart's paintings of George Washington in Room 316, the dramatic murals in the McGraw Rotunda, and the woody, masculine Main Reading Room. This place makes you want to read.

Bryant Park, behind the library, has been completely redesigned in recent years (the job took twice as long as the erection of the Empire State Building). Bryant Park now looks like a miniature of Paris's Tuileries, and it is *the* place for young executives to unwind at lunchtime on a summer's day. So if your idea of a good time is eating lunch amongst accountants with their shirts off, buy a sandwich in the park or croissants and pizzas (all kinds imaginable and otherwise) on the northern corners of 42nd Street and Sixth Avenue, and join in.

New York's best-kept secret is the kiosk in the northwestern corner of the park, the **Bryant Park Ticket Booth**. Not only does it offer 50 percent discounts to first-rate dance and music events, but you can call ahead to see what's available (Tel: 382-2323). Moreover, there's never a line, since almost no one takes advantage of this facility.

Looking north toward 43rd Street and Sixth Avenue, you'll see a green sign with flashing numbers that indicate how fast the national debt is growing: At last count, your family owed close to $60,000. You could either pay it off or take the kids to dinner at Lutece. On the north side of that corner (1133 Sixth Avenue) is the Midtown branch of the **International Center of Photography**, which is as underutilized as the tickets kiosk in Bryant Park. This three-level Bauhaus-style gallery gives photographs the space they need to look spectacular; subjects run the gamut from India to stand-up comedians.

The south side of 42nd Street leading back toward Fifth Avenue is chockablock with crafts stands. Peruvian sweaters, Indian jewelry, and hand-painted tee-shirts for kids typify the mad mix that is New York City—and they make far, far better gifts than Statue of Liberty paperweights. While you're browsing, take a look at the W. R. Grace Building across the street: Its ski-slope design produces delightfully askew reflections of its architecturally straight-arrow neighbors.

Grand Central Terminal Area

East of Fifth Avenue the crafts stalls are replaced by tables with bad greeting cards, outdated maps, and forgettable books. But do check out the vintage comic books and baseball cards—addictive stuff, as the dozens of office workers who were supposed to have returned from lunch 15 minutes ago will attest. Also on the shopping front, Madison Avenue between 42nd and 46th streets boasts a full house of stores purveying traditionally styled men's clothing, including **Worth and Worth** (at 43rd Street), **Brooks Brothers** (at 44th Street), and **Paul Stuart** (at 45th Street). First-rate fly-fishing gear and sporting clothes are sold at **Orvis**, on the southeast corner of Madison and 45th Street.

Back on 42nd Street (the south side) heading east, the colonnaded southern façade of Grand Central Terminal and the elevated section of Park Avenue that nearly strangles it come into view (so does another weird reflection, as the black glass of the Grand Hyatt Hotel seems to break up the turn-of-the-century terminal into a Cubist painting). Beyond the Hyatt looms the **Chrysler Building** (405 Lexington Avenue), the world's tallest skyscraper in 1930—only to be bested by the Empire State Building less than a year later. But height is no matter: This is the cream of Art Deco. Its summit, protected by Cubist gargoyles and sheathed in molded steel curves, looks like a giant 1920s radio floating 1,000 feet in the sky. Inside, considerable care has gone into the red marble walls and the elevator doors of inlaid wood, yet the Chrysler's lobby seems strangely small and cramped. It's on the outside, as viewed from afar, that this landmark flaunts its brash high spirits.

Such optimism is countered by the presence of homeless people as you approach **Grand Central Terminal**. Unlike some of the squatters in the Port Authority Bus Terminal, fortunately, these denizens of the Grand Central area are more to be pitied than feared. Even without the homeless, there is nothing particularly grand about the main entrance to Grand Central Terminal, which is on Vanderbilt Avenue. Nor is the station's function very grand any more, now that only commuter lines stop here. But step inside. Suddenly, you're on a balcony overlooking a stunningly large room—125 feet high and 375 feet long—with lofty marble walls, huge clocks, and an intriguing (if inaccurate) star-map ceiling. Get a railing seat at the café on the balcony, nurse a cappuccino, and enjoy this mighty space. It's especially entertaining at rush hour, when thousands of Gordon Geckos hell-bent on suburbia cut across the **Grand Concourse** in different directions, miraculously not colliding. At some point you, too, will want to descend the Grand Staircase and join the floor show. It's glorious just to *walk* in this big a room.

From the concourse you can go downstairs to the famous **Grand Central Oyster Bar** in the basement if you like eating fresh seafood in a place that looks like a cross between a medieval crypt and a white-tiled men's room. Or you can take an escalator from the concourse up into the what is now the MetLife Building. Pan Am built this skyscraper above the terminal in 1963, a blasphemy for which New Yorkers never forgave the airline. But the building does have one virtue: Just beyond the top of the escalator, a bit to the right, is a fabulous magazine shop. Name your obsession, be it music, gardening, wine, or worse, and you'll find that this store stocks dozens of publications on that topic that you never even knew existed.

For an indoor picnic, visit the glass-walled sculpture garden on the ground floor of the **Philip Morris Building**, on the southwest corner of Park Avenue and 42nd Street, across from Grand Central. You can buy a power sandwich (e.g., prosciutto rather than American ham) at the shop and enjoy it at a table under a bona-fide tree. Free tours of the Grand Central Terminal area start from in front of Philip Morris headquarters every Friday at 12:30 P.M. These tours are so witty and eye-opening that many locals take them—repeatedly.

Comedian Alan King, comparing Manhattan to a film studio's back lot, has said, "The excitement of New York City is that you turn the corner and it's an entirely different set." This is true, but on East 42nd Street you don't even have to turn the corner. The **Home Savings Bank of America** (at number 110), which opened in 1923, has a somber stone exterior and an arched entryway that evoke monuments from the late Roman Empire. Inside, the vast room with carved ceilings and marble columns seems right out of some D. W. Griffith epic. But right next door the scene changes from Lillian Gish to Carole Lombard at the **Chanin Building** (number 122), completed just a few years after the bank. By 1928 Art Deco was the rage, and it shows: Notice the patterned metal exterior, the period lettering of "CHANIN" by the door, the vaguely Cubist friezes of muscle men in the alcove, and the brass birds throwing sun rays across the elevators.

United Nations Area

You will wait in vain for Clark Kent, if not Superman, to dash out of the **News Building** (220 East 42nd Street, between Third and Second avenues), which stood in for

The Daily Planet in the Christopher Reeve movies. This is a blocky, overrated structure, but check out the huge globe in the lobby and the compass marks on the floor—reminders that what is considered "east" and "west" in Manhattan does not agree with what the rest of the world knows as east and west. There are beautiful brass weather instruments in the lobby, too; the one that measures wind direction is indispensable if you plan to go sailing on 42nd Street.

Continuing east on 42nd Street, once you cross Second Avenue, the Midtown swarm of Brooks Brothers suits begins to yield to saris, turbans, burnooses, and African robes. The United Nations can't be far.

Foundations of all stripes have set up shop near the UN. The **Ford Foundation** looms on the north side of 42nd Street. It's as humid as a jungle inside the 11-story atrium (open to the public), which may be why the jungle that's planted there—like something out of a dream Henri Rousseau might have had, only indoors and in Midtown—is so lush. Farther eastward normal New York life (an oxymoron?) continues to recede. At the tops of stairways on both sides of 42nd Street between Second and First avenues are little parks with shady trees, well-kept plantings, benches, and Tudor apartment houses, an area known as **Tudor City**. It's so *quiet;* sit down, and you may not get up again for hours.

THE UNITED NATIONS

Emerge from beneath the overpass that crosses 42nd Street at First Avenue and suddenly the United Nations' **Secretariat Building** comes into view. Shaped like a glass-walled tablet that teeters 39 stories high, it was radical in 1950, and it still is. At its foot sit the **Dag Hammarskjold Library**, the Conference Building, and the General Assembly, a nearly 400-foot-long sloping structure with concave sides—all on an 18-acre chunk of real estate donated by John D. Rockefeller in 1946.

Hour-long guided tours in English leave about every 30 minutes from 9:15 A.M. to 4:45 P.M. daily from the visitors' entrance near 46th Street. When you enter the visitors' center lobby, note exactly where the big Foucault pendulum is meeting the circle in the floor over which it swings; one hour later, its position will have changed, thus providing evidence that the world is still rotating. You'll also see a moon rock and a replica of the first

Sputnik at this starting point for the tours. For most visitors, the most awesome sight on the tour is the **General Assembly Hall**, with its seating for more than 2,000 participants and visitors, the embracing wood backdrop behind the podium, the labeled seating areas for almost 200 nations, and those earphones that offer translations into six languages.

Beyond the tour, visit the United Nations Gift Shop and Post Office; the stamps are lovely. Spectator seating at UN meetings is often available at the visitors' entrance, too. Finally, the **United Nations Delegates Dining Room** is great for people-watching, but call ahead, because it's increasingly hard to get into (Tel: 963-7625). For an alternative, have a drink at the **Top of the Tower** in the Beekman Tower Hotel, on First Avenue and 49th Street: Seated amid the international crowd and the ever-so New York Art Deco details, you begin to get the feeling that any minute Demi Moore might saunter in with the Sultan of Brunei.

THE EAST 40S

If your internationalist cravings are not yet sated, visit **Japan House**, at 333 East 47th Street (between First and Second avenues). Not only are its visual and performing-arts shows first-rate, but the Japanese-designed building, with its black-slate walls and its terrace and pool gardens, is one of a kind. Heading back to the Grand Central area, you'll find vest-pocket parks sprinkled along 44th Street east of Third Avenue and on 43rd Street between Third and Lexington. The take-out **salad bar** at 136 East 43rd Street has cold salads, broiled meats, Chinese stir-fried dishes, Italian pasta, Greek feta cheese . . . smorgasbord heaven.

Times Square

When the character played by Fred Astaire in *Bandwagon* revisits 42nd Street after a long stay in Hollywood, he's stunned to see that some theaters in which he once performed are no more. And that was 1951!

The area continued to decline over the succeeding decades, as the strip between Seventh and Eighth avenues was taken over by porn houses and X-rated everythings. But Astaire—and we—should not kid ourselves. New York's famed theater district has always had its share of offstage characters, and people knew that 60 years ago when the musical *Forty-second Street* first hit the stage:

> Come and meet those dancing feet
> On the Avenue I'm taking you to,
> Forty-Second Street. . . .
> Sexy ladies from the Eighties, who are indiscreet.
> They're side by side,
> They're glorified.
> Where the underworld can meet the elite,
> Naughty, bawdy, gawdy, sporty,
> Forty-Second Street.

Broadway merges with Seventh Avenue at 46th Street before it resumes its grid-busting, southeastward crawl at 43rd Street. Just south of 43rd, in the crotch formed by the crossing of the avenues, is where *The New York Times* erected its offices in 1904—ergo, Times Square. Concurrently, the theater district was moving northward from the older Herald Square area; a subway station opened on Times Square; and huge billboards followed, with enough neon lights to illuminate the dark side of the moon—ergo, the Theater District, the Crossroads of the World, the Great White Way, and any other cliché that comes to mind.

Almost all those clichés were, and still are, true. Only the name, Times Square, may be outdated, since the newspaper has moved on to West 43rd Street. In place of the old Times tower stands a nondescript building covered with so many electronic ads and news flashes that if you watch it while driving south you're almost guaranteed to rear-end the car in front of you.

And that's just one reason hoofing it is safer than driving in this district. Thanks to an infusion of police and other security measures, Times Square's much-vaunted crime rate has plummeted. Robberies dropped substantially, and crime on 42nd Street has been cut in half. It looks as if the authorities have finally taken to heart Nathan Detroit's oddball insight from *Guys and Dolls:* "The streets are covered with tourists and I do not want you molested."

THE THEATER DISTRICT
And we do not want to see you lost. Or confused. So start any excursion to Times Square with a stop at the visitors' center at the northwest corner of 42nd Street and Seventh

Avenue. This new facility has information on *everything*. It often has discount coupons to various events and eateries and such, too.

The much-touted Times Square redevelopment program has just been put on hold, but only after half the occupants on 42nd Street between Seventh and Eighth avenues were evicted. Just the same, take a stroll along the south side of the street, even if you're not quite up for a showing of *Debbie Does North America*. In 1900 Oscar Hammerstein *père* built the first of West 42nd Street's theaters, the Republic, at number 207. Its name was eventually changed to the Victory Theatre, and its offerings changed even more drastically, but the building is still there. Peering above and behind its marquee, as well as others on that side of the street, you'll see colonnades, faux Greek bas-reliefs, and other Neoclassical features from an age that saw 42nd Street as an elegant address. At least six of these historic theaters, including the Victory, are to be spared the wrecking ball and restored to their turn-of-the-century grandeur—but right now, the New Amsterdam Theater (214 West 42nd Street) is the only one where work has actually begun.

The Theater District has been on a roll in recent years. The 1991–1992 season was a record one at the box offices, and 1992–1993 was even better. Shows like *The Who's Tommy* and *Guys and Dolls* helped receipts soar past $325 million, and attendance almost hit the eight million mark.

Most Broadway shows are not actually on Broadway, but on side streets in the mid-40s. Since almost everyone who comes to town tries to see as many shows as possible, thousands of Texans and Italians and such end up waiting in line at the discount **TKTS** booth on Duffy Square (the divider-like park north of the Broadway/Seventh Avenue crossing), which is fine if it's exactly 71 degrees and sunny, but there are two alternatives. First, if you're visiting downtown, you'll find that the TKTS booth at Two World Trade Center is less crowded. Second, an outfit called **Hit Show Club** offers coupons with which you can buy discount tickets for productions in advance—without standing in line. The company distributes some of its coupons through visitors' centers, restaurants, and other outlets, but you can also call to find out what's available and pick up whatever you want at Hit Show Club's headquarters, at 630 Ninth Avenue (eighth floor), between 44th and 45th streets; Tel: 581-4211.

OFF BROADWAY'S THEATER ROW

A Chorus Line, The Little Shop of Horrors, Forever Plaid, Driving Miss Daisy—these shows all started out in Off Broadway theaters, and some never left those friendly circumstances. Off Broadway continues to sprout hits in more intimate theaters with lower-priced tickets than those of Broadway theaters, and the Midtown heart of Off Broadway is 42nd Street between Ninth and Tenth avenues, a modest stroll from the Duffy Square TKTS booth. Walking there along West 42nd Street you'll pass **Kaufman's Army & Navy** at number 319. Those are real cannon out front, and this store is one of New York's last purveyors of genuine military pants, caps, camping gear, khaki underwear ... you get the idea. (If it's raining, you can walk from Eighth to Ninth Avenue without getting wet by passing through the Port Authority Bus Terminal.)

Cross Ninth Avenue and all remaining traces of 42nd Street–Port Authority scruffiness vanish. There's a modern brick apartment complex on the north side of the street that houses many actors and other artists. On the south is **Theater Row**, a string of sparkling, low-rise playhouses built in the late 1970s in place of massage parlors and flophouses. Interspersed with the theaters are such restaurants as **Chez Josephine** (number 414), owned by none other than Josephine Baker's adopted son, and the reasonably priced **West Bank Café** (number 407), actually a cabaret/bar/restaurant, as well as several Thai restaurants and an ambitious trompe l'oeil painting that should be called *Art Deco Meets Caesar.* To the north, **Zen Palate** (663 Ninth Avenue, at 46th Street) is among the best vegetarian restaurants in town. Finally, there are few better Big Apple souvenirs than the spices, olive-oil soap, and fresh-roasted coffee beans sold at **Ninth Avenue International Foods**, at 543 Ninth Avenue, between 40th and 41st streets.

THEATER DISTRICT HANGOUTS

Actors, writers, and other perpetrators of theater have made the ▶ **Algonquin Hotel**, at 59 West 44th Street (between Fifth and Sixth avenues), a home away from home ever since Manhattan's sharpest wits sat down at a round table here in the 1920s. The Algonquin's parlor-like lobby has always been a cozy place to sink into an armchair and nurse a pre-theater glass of *fino* sherry, or better yet, two or three sherries. Just be aware that the improperly attired gentleman may be obliged to don the headwaiter's spare sports jacket, and that jacket is not a thing that will land you on any "best dressed" list.

Doormen in black futuristic fascist gear guard the postmodern **Royalton Hotel**, right across the street at 44 West 44th Street. Inside, the nearly bare walls in the restaurant/lounge and the furniture covered with what seems to be sheets give the impression that someone has died, and the house is being sold. But lots of publishing heavies hang out here; the Royalton is *hot*. Also cold.

A good place to recuperate between bouts at the TKTS line is at the Broadway Lounge on the eighth floor of the ▶ **Marriott Marquis**, at 1535 Broadway (at 45th Street). The **View**, a restaurant that spins around the bar at the dizzying speed of one revolution every 90 minutes, has neither the best food in town nor the highest lookout, but there's an old saying in New York City: location, location, location.

Sardi's and Joe Allen have been theater crowd hangouts since Yul Brynner was passing for the king of Siam. Located at 234 West 44th Street (between Broadway and Eighth Avenue), **Sardi's** is a throwback to the 1950s, but in the best sense: dark wood walls hung with caricatures of stars, white tablecloths, and a somewhat pricey menu that still makes room for a (very good) ten-dollar burger. **Joe Allen**, at 326 West 46th Street (between Eighth and Ninth avenues), attracts more certified actors these days, which means it's less formal, not to mention less pricey. **Orso** (322 West 46th Street), owned by the same outfit, specializes in boutique pizzas and pastas, and is even hotter than its older brother. Also popular with the theater crowd is **Sam's** (263 West 45th Street), a brick-wall place with unpretentious food and the funniest hosts in town.

Other choices: The upstairs room at **Cabaña Carioca** (123 West 45th Street, between Broadway and Sixth Avenue) serves gigantic platters of Brazilian fare at impossibly low prices. **Ollie's Noodle Shop and Grille** (190 West 44th Street, between Times Square and Eighth Avenue) is a no-frills eatery that's popular with New Yorkers for its first-rate Chinese fish, dumpling, and noodle dishes. For Continental and soul food in a Southern antiques-store setting, **Jezebel** (630 Ninth Avenue, at 45th Street) is, as the name suggests, a gas. There's a piano player every night after 9:00 P.M. **Les Pyrénées** (251 West 51st Street, between Broadway and Eighth Avenue) offers traditional French dishes, and damn the nouvelle crowd. Carmine's (200 West 44th Street, between Broadway and Eighth Avenue) is a blast if you have a party of six or more—and reservations. Three restaurants along West 51st Street between Sixth and Seventh avenues offer top-notch dining: **Cité** at number 120, **Palio** at number 151, and **Le Bernardin** at number 155. Cité is easily the most affordable of the lot. Palio boasts the bonus of a colorful mural by Sandro Chia over the bar that might be called *Crimson Centaur at Framer's Shop*.

Recent years have seen the return of social dancing to the Broadway scene. **Red Blazer Too** (349 West 46th Street, between Eighth and Ninth avenues) has undistinguished food and a dance floor that's a tad small, but the place is affordable, unpretentious, and cheerful, and its swing bands are so upbeat, it's hard *not* to dance. Of the more romantic supper clubs, **Laura Belle** (120 West 43rd Street, between Sixth Avenue and Broadway) plays Benny Goodman–era tapes during dinner, only to jar diners at 10:30 P.M. with a sudden blast of disco music. The **Supper Club** (240 West 47th Street, between Broadway and Eighth Avenue) has stars-in-your-eyes ambience, a fine big band, and (behold!) a creative, enticing menu. It feels the way a nightclub is supposed to feel. Finally, if you simply want to dance, **Roseland** (239 West 52nd Street, west of Broadway) is still the classic. Its bands are top-rung, the people who go there regularly put on a veritable show, and the well-waxed floor is big enough to accommodate the most sweeping, graceful peabody. As for bonafide, post-disco nightlife, **Club USA** (218 West 47th Street, west of Seventh Avenue) is *the* place. Can such a club remain hot for more than a year or two? Your call.

Caroline's Comedy Club (1626 Broadway, between 49th and 50th streets), a recent addition to the Great White Way, is the slickest venue for stand-up comics in New York City. Of course, today's scene has yet to produce a Mort Sahl—that is, someone who will satirize big issues rather than sex and parents—so the crowd tends to be fairly young and unsophisticated. That said, Caroline's does hire the biggest names in town. Tel: 757-4100.

At 49th and Broadway is **Colony Record & Radio Center**, which does not have the lowest prices in Manhattan, but if there's an album you want that's distributed by some obscure European or garage-band label, Colony can find it. Just east of Broadway on **West 48th Street** is a string of musical instrument stores, including **Sam Ash** and **Manny's**, that offer the best selection and prices you'll find anywhere.

For something completely different, the lobby in the **Equitable Center** (Seventh Avenue and 51st Street) displays paintings so monumental that they overwhelm the gallery off to one side. Enter this building and you'll be astonished by the sheer size of Roy Lichtenstein's *Mural with Blue Brushstroke,* the largest painting this king of pop has ever made. Thomas Hart Benton's *America Today,* a mural that inspired many other murals of the Depression era, depicts heroic, hard-working Americans toiling at the docks, farms, and mines. This moving homage to the working class was and is pro-labor rather than pro-capital; it's amazing that it ended up in an insurance company's headquarters.

Rockefeller Center Area

The 19-building complex between 48th and 51st streets and Fifth and Sixth avenues is the manifestation of John D. Rockefeller's power and drive to build his own city within the city—during the Great Depression, no less. The buildings and the hundreds of artworks, commissioned to illustrate man's inexorable progress, are relentlessly, even humorlessly optimistic. Rockefeller Center is vintage Art Deco, futuristic fantasies and all.

A nearly nude Atlas stands directly across the avenue from St. Patrick's Cathedral, flaunting a neo-Cubist body, a sphere with zodiac signs, and an all-around pagan attitude. John D., it must be said, was no Roman Catholic.

Opposite Saks Fifth Avenue, between 49th and 50th streets, the promenade leading westward into Rockefeller Center between the British Empire Building and La Maison Française is called the Channel Gardens (get it?). Listen to the accents of people around you while you're admiring the ever-changing display of flowers and foliage. This is the United Nations all over again, but without diplomatic immunity. Not only do the Channel Gardens inspire friendliness in all comers; they also manage to attract young couples with the cutest, happiest little children in the world.

Some force will eventually draw you to the Lower Plaza in the center of the project. An ice-skating rink from October to April, the plaza is the site of two outdoor restaurants in the warm months. A gilded Prometheus, giver of fire to mankind (and, no doubt, a figure with whom John D. identified), guards the proceedings. Just behind Prometheus is where that famous Christmas tree of Rockefellerian proportions is installed every winter. Regardless of the season, both locals and out-of-towners spend staggering numbers of hours just staring over the Lower Plaza railing.

Just beyond the Lower Plaza rises **30 Rockefeller Plaza** (the former RCA Building, now called the GE Building), at 70 stories, the tallest skyscraper in the complex. The frieze of Wisdom, over the entrance, is an object lesson in Art Deco, with its parallel-ray beard, strong but simplified body, and grandiosity at the expense of warmth. Inside, the Goliath-size figures in the *American Progress* mural further cow us mere mortals, but it's a fascinating piece nonetheless—a monumental paean to the construction industry. (Yes, that's Rockefeller Center in the background of this mythical scene.)

When the **Rainbow Room** first opened atop 30 Rockefeller Plaza in 1934, its generous round dance floor, fine dining, top-notch bands, and utterly romantic ambience quickly made it *the* quintessential supper club. And when it reopened a few years ago after a dark spell, it immediately regained that stature. If you can get reservations, and if you can afford the tab, this is the best place on earth to celebrate an occasion. Tel: 632-5100.

The most beloved part of the Rockefeller Center cluster is **Radio City Music Hall** (corner of Sixth Avenue and 50th Street), a 6,000-seat theater with massive murals, a sunset design over the stage that's first cousin to the top of the Chrysler Building, a gloriously spacious downstairs lounge, and an organ that's so big it's been named the Mighty Wurlitzer. Oh, yes, and the Rockettes. Forget your pride and see a show here, or at least take the one-hour, seven-dollar tour, which leaves every half hour from Radio City's 1260 Sixth Avenue entrance.

Finally, note that you can roam, and even shop, for blocks in any direction in the basement-level concourse under Rockefeller Center—a godsend when it's raining. You can even get over to the buildings on the other side of Sixth Avenue via the concourse. When you come up to street level, have a look up and down the west side of Sixth Avenue. At lunchtime, the plazas that front the office buildings fill up with enough young office workers to sink an aircraft carrier. But more to the point, this seemingly endless line of unadorned, rectangular skyscrapers offers a quick course in glass-box architecture run amok.

THE EAST 50S

St. Patrick's Cathedral, the largest Roman Catholic cathedral in the United States, stretches eastward from Fifth Avenue to Madison Avenue, between 50th and 51st streets. This 1879 creation is unabashedly Gothic; massive stone columns that look like clusters of narrow columns run the length of the nave, whose ribbed ceiling seems to reach more than halfway to heaven. The cathedral is somewhat austere, lacking the surfeit of statuary, historic and otherwise, that you might expect. St. Patrick's does have a beautiful rose window, best seen from the south transept, but it is this cathedral's vast scale, rather than its details, that impresses and even humbles the casual visitor.

Arrogant hunk that he is, Atlas glares at God's house from across Fifth Avenue, while aromas of perfume waft across 50th Street from **Saks Fifth Avenue**. Farther to the south, good buys on gold, silver, and diamonds attract visitors to the 47th Street **Diamond District**. (The Orthodox Jews who conduct this trade make deals among themselves right out on the street by a simple shake of the hand, a rare practice in this day and age.) To the north of the cathedral, at Fifth Avenue and 52nd Street, are Cartier and Piaget—more jewelry. On Madison Avenue, immediately behind St. Patrick's, the 1880s palazzo-style brownstones that used to house the Chancery of the Archdiocese now form a glittery entryway to the ▶ **New York Palace Hotel**. In short, it's not easy fighting for the renunciation of materialism in Gotham City.

PARK AVENUE

One block farther to the east, on Park Avenue between 50th and 51st streets, is **St. Bartholomew's**, an Episcopal church that was designed to look French Romanesque but could pass for Eastern Orthodox. The domed roof glitters with what seem to be white and gold mosaics, while the carved porticoes over the three doors appear to have been transported, like the Cloisters in northern Manhattan, from Europe. (They are, in fact, from an earlier church, but one that was built in New York in 1902.) The stained glass inside this handsome building is stunning, but best of all is the organ, with great pipes everywhere. Tiptoe in on a Saturday afternoon and, if you're lucky, no one else will be there except the organist, practicing for Sunday's services and raising a deep and mighty noise that fills the marrow of your bones.

Look to the south (on your left) as you leave St. Bart's, and you'll see the **Helmsley Building**, a late Beaux Arts beauty planted squarely in the path of Park Avenue (which swerves around it). Towering behind and above the 1929 edifice is that ubiquitous MetLife, née Pan Am, Building.

By contrast, the recently restored ▶ **Waldorf-Astoria** (301 Park Avenue, between 49th and 50th streets) looks even better than ever. Step inside for a look at an old-style New York lobby; then have a drink at the piano bar where presidents and royalty have bent the elbow. If your appetite and credit line are boundless, come back for Sunday brunch, among the best in New York City.

One more architectural detail: Although the **Lever House** (390 Park Avenue, between 53rd and 54th streets) was erected after the UN Secretariat Building was begun, it is this edifice that inspired that string of glass boxes on Sixth Avenue opposite Rockefeller Center. Thus, it is one of the most celebrated buildings in town, at least in some architectural circles, but you are forgiven if you feel yourself unmoved.

Instead, you're hungry, right? On Third Avenue, between 53rd and 54th streets, is an edifice known as the "Lipstick Building" (just look up if you don't know why). The **Lipstick Café**, on the ground floor, is a fine place for well-prepared snacks and light meals. **Vong's**, the French/Thai restaurant at 200 East 54th Street (at Third Avenue), has loud acoustics and sky-high prices—and some of the most delicious dishes in town.

THE WEST 50S

People have been known to stay forever in the **Museum of Television & Radio** (25 West 52nd Street, between Fifth and Sixth avenues). Housed in a handsome building that opened in 1991, this is no place for a casual drop-in. Step into one of the comfortable screening rooms where people are watching *Saturday Night Live* episodes from the 1970s or an old Frank Sinatra special—you might end up sitting there for hours. In other rooms people can choose their own favorites and watch them on any of 96 semiprivate screens. When have you last seen Steve Allen, Roy Rogers, or Edward R. Murrow? And, if you *really* "like to watch" (as Peter Sellers put it in *Being There*), **El Morocco Nightclub** offers "exotic" revues at 307 East 54th

Street (between Second and First avenues). But even so, Steve Allen is a hard act to follow.

The **"21" Club,** in a brownstone just next door (21 West 52nd Street), is a fine place for lunch or dinner in an upscale masculine setting. In recent years the landmark has been dragged into the 20th century: The menu has been updated and paintings of yachts and such have replaced the stuffed animal heads that used to eye your roast beef.

CBS chairman William S. Paley, the force behind the creation of the Museum of Television & Radio, also created **Paley Park,** on 53rd Street just east of Fifth Avenue. A tiny oasis with trees and an artificial waterfall, this is one of the most pleasant spots in Midtown to just sit and/or have a picnic.

St. Thomas Church (Episcopal), on the northwest corner of 53rd Street and Fifth Avenue, has quintessentially Gothic images of saints around its entrance and a sign that welcomes visitors to "Pray for peace with Our Lady of Fifth Avenue." The 80-foot-high carved stone piece behind the altar was designed, in part, by Lee Lawrie, an Art Deco master whose work is all over Rockefeller Center, but it is true to the Gothic spirit of the church: Its saints are almost arrows, pointing and even rising toward heaven.

Some contemporary artists have accused the **Museum of Modern Art** (just steps to the east at 11 West 53rd Street) of being too conservative, but the flip side is that MoMA's collection will remind the stodgiest museumgoer that he does, after all, love modern art. A gleaming escalator invites you to the second floor, where Cézanne's *Bathers,* Rousseau's *Sleeping Gypsy,* van Gogh's *Starry Night,* Monet's *Water Lilies,* and so many other master works are, each in its way, simply perfect. On other floors there are photographs, paintings by Andrew Wyeth and Edward Hopper and Salvador Dali, furniture you'll want to steal, that Milton Glaser poster of Bob Dylan with Gorgon's hair, a gorgeous little helicopter, and more. There's a choice of cafeterias, a terrific film program, and an outdoor sculpture garden with both comfortable seats and great art. And finally, there is enough genuinely avant-garde work—abstract, Conceptual, Postmodern, and contemporary—to enthrall those who already know that they like 20th-century art.

Across the street, at 40 West 53rd Street, is the **Ameri-**

can Craft Museum, the best of its sort in the nation. Some
MoMA partisans would argue, however, that since textiles,
pottery, furniture, and such generally exist because of
their functions, they can never be as satisfying to just look
at as fine art, which is unfettered by function.

TAKASHIMAYA AND THE DONALD

There is nothing in America like Takashimaya, the new
Japanese department store at 693 Fifth Avenue that seems
more like a museum than a hard-sell, time-is-money business. You enter an elegant three-story atrium that has an
art gallery, a smattering of bonsai trees and portable moss
gardens, and a sales staff who, despite being a bunch of
round-eyes, are unfailingly courteous. Fashions and accessories are all upstairs, but meanwhile, the very walls of
this establishment seem to say, *relax, you are our honored guest.*

If good taste and exquisitely good manners bore you,
of course, you can always head north one block to Trump
Tower, that upwardly striving black glass high-rise on the
east side of Fifth Avenue at 56th Street. Just inside, polished brass display cases, piped-in sounds of Vivaldi's
Four Seasons, and people with shopping bags that say
"Cartier" and "Galeries Lafayette" hint that The Donald
has finally done something with tasteful restraint. But a
few feet farther on, you catch sight of an artificial waterfall
tumbling over a cliff of marble squares: This is elegance
as defined by Atlantic City casinos. By this point, moreover, the music is too loud—way too loud. It should be
said that there are fine rest rooms on the bottom level,
where you can also buy license plates at Eastern International that say "TRUMP"—but why would you?

Visitors may walk through the New York branch of the
Parisian department store Galeries Lafayette, which opens
into Trump Tower on the left, right into the atrium of the
IBM Building (590 Madison Avenue). This is one of the
most inviting atriums in the city. Café tables and chairs,
colorful flowers, lofty bamboo trees, free concerts at 12:30
P.M. on Wednesdays—it's all a delight. By contrast, the
public spaces in the Sony (formerly AT & T) Building, right
across 56th Street, are so dark and dank that they're slated
for a redesign. But the place isn't all bad. Look at the
pediment atop the Madison Avenue side of this Philip
Johnson edifice and you'll see why locals call it the Chippendale Building.

Fifty-Seventh Street Area

At the risk of mangling an old joke, let it be said that the three words you will never hear on 57th Street are "Attention Kmart Shoppers." This is one of the premier stretches of galleries and boutiques on God's green earth. Many of the galleries around here offer a free pamphlet called *Art Now Gallery Guide,* and you should grab one; not only does it tell you what's currently on display, but it alerts you to establishments that don't have ground-floor showrooms.

EAST 57TH STREET

Pace operates several galleries at 32 East 57th Street (between Madison and Park avenues). **Pace Master Prints and Drawings**, on the tenth floor, displays works by Rembrandt, Picasso, and other immortals, while the second-floor gallery is well worth a stop if you want to see what Julian Schnabel, the most commercially successful artist of our day, is up to. The prices on the paintings are out of sight, not surprisingly, but climb the spiral staircase to the third floor, where Schnabel prints such as *Gothic Run Riot* can be had for, oh, just $10,000.

Having decided to pass on the Schnabel for now, drop into the lobby lounge at the brand new ▶ **Four Seasons Hotel** (57 East 57th Street). This place was designed by I. M. Pei to give every other luxury hotel in town a run for the money. But if you step into the lounge for a drink, don't look for chintz or that comfy men's club look that characterizes so many other luxury hotels. The vast, airy space is rather austere for New York; you might feel as if you're having a drink in a monument.

Back on street level, Victoria's Secret (34 East 57th Street) sells products almost guaranteed to liven up your stay in the big city, but by and large, this block just east of Madison Avenue is handbag country: Ghurka, Prado, Celine, and, of course, Louis Vuitton. West of Madison Avenue, 57th Street is a showplace for accoutrements beyond handbags, but unlike the trendier emporiums on Madison Avenue in the 60s, these shops display clothing with classic, enduring style. Laura Ashley, Hermès, Burberry, and Ann Taylor are here, as is Chanel, at (what else?) number 5.

57TH STREET AND FIFTH AVENUE

Still more classics hug the corners of Fifth Avenue: On the southwest corner, the Crown Building sports a gold-emblazoned summit that can be seen from outside Chanel. On the northwest corner is **Bergdorf Goodman**, the ultimate upscale department store. (Note that the men's department is now across the street at 745 Fifth Avenue.) **Tiffany** holds down the southeast corner, as well stocked as always, albeit surprisingly noisy. Just to the south, down Fifth Avenue, you'll find Fendi, Henri Bendel (at number 714; well worth a walk-through), Godiva Chocolates, Fortunoff, Gucci, and other world-famous shops. To the north is F.A.O. Schwarz (767 Fifth Avenue, at 58th Street), which is to most kids' stores what the Rainbow Room is to a bar and grill.

WEST 57TH STREET

Back on 57th Street, the building behind that big red sculpture of a "9" may spark déjà vu; it's a doppelgänger of 42nd Street's W. R. Grace Building. A very unlikely store on this posh block between Fifth and Sixth avenues is **Curaçao Export, Ltd.**, on the fourth floor of 20 West 57th Street. It has somehow been discovered by European tourists, who fill shopping bags there with Levi's jeans, Ray Ban sunglasses, and other prestigious Yankee products. Beyond that, at 31 West 57th Street, **Rizzoli**'s cast-iron storefront, marble door frame, carved ceiling, and handsome wooden shelves remind us of how fine bookstores looked before malls and chains turned them into mere supermarkets.

For a meatless refueling stop, visit the **Great American Health Bar**, 35 West 57th Street. One block to the south, at 1377 Sixth Avenue, **Ellen's Stardust Diner** pipes in hits from the 1950s and 1960s, with food to match; it's ideal for culture shock if you're grabbing a bite prior to an evening at nearby Carnegie Hall. Just west of Sixth Avenue on 57th Street, the New York Deli (formerly a Horn & Hardart automat, but let's not tax the tear ducts) has a Hellmann's Mayonnaise plaque on its door, which is a bad omen indeed—rather like hanging a Heinz Ketchup sign at the entrance to a French restaurant. Visit the **Carnegie Delicatessen and Restaurant** instead, at 854 Seventh Avenue, between 54th and 55th streets.

The official entrance to the ▶ **Parker Meridien** is on 56th Street (between Sixth and Seventh avenues), but you may enter or even just cut through the block via the door at 118 West 57th Street. There used to be chairs in the passageway, but when homeless people started to claim them, the hotel packed the chairs away. At last sighting, the Buildings Department ordered the Parker Meridien to return the chairs to their place, but no doubt they will remain at loggerheads over this issue.

On the subject of loggerheads, Bruce Willis, Sylvester Stallone, and Arnold Schwarzenegger own **Planet Hollywood**, down the block at 140 West 57th Street. The handprints in concrete on the exterior belong to celebrities who run the gamut from Cher to Joanne Woodward, but the real wonder is how Dudley Moore's got so high. Inside (if you can get inside—the lines are formidable) you may sit below the head used in *Creature from the Black Lagoon,* or even the sweaty leather jacket Kevin Costner wore in *Robin Hood.* In all, this is the Hollywood answer to the **Hard Rock Café**, which happens to be a couple of blocks down at 221 West 57th Street; it's the place with the rear end of a wide-finned Cadillac serving as a canopy.

Dustin Hoffman visited the **Russian Tea Room** (number 150) in drag for one scene in *Tootsie,* but you're more likely to spot the world's finest musicians dressed as themselves, which isn't bad. An etched-glass revolving door, red banquettes with polished brass trim, shiny brass samovars, chandeliers with Christmas tree decorations, and even the tunics on the waiters make this 65-year-old restaurant a visual delight. This is the place to splurge on frozen vodka and caviar.

Next door, that expansive beige building with five porticoes is, of course, **Carnegie Hall**. For opening-night podium duties the hall brought Tchaikovsky over from Russia; that was in 1891, and since then, anyone who is anyone has appeared here. When Red Skelton received an ovation in this sacred space, he said, "If I had known it would be like this, I would have studied the violin." Most experts agree that recent renovations have slightly diminished the richness of Carnegie Hall's acoustics, but this big cream-colored room with burgundy seats is still the premier place to hear music in these United States.

And the premier place to watch baseball? Why, Yankee Stadium, the House that Ruth Built. But if you don't have time for a trip to the Bronx, visit **Clubhouse Source** (110 East 59th Street, between Lexington and Third avenues), which is Yankee paraphernalia heaven. Yeah, you can get Mets and Chicago Bulls items there, too.

CENTRAL PARK SOUTH

A tour of Central Park South properly begins at Fifth
Avenue. Get into the spirit by beginning with a pit stop at
Harry Cipriani's (781 Fifth Avenue, at 59th Street) for a
Bellini—that is, the peach-nectar-with-Spumante drink
made famous in Harry's Bar, Venice. But limit yourself to
one, for it may not be the last drink you have in the
course of the next few blocks.

On the other (west) side of Fifth Avenue, where 59th
Street becomes known as Central Park South, the ▶ **Plaza
Hotel** faces Central Park, to its north, and **Grand Army
Plaza**, with its grandiose Pulitzer Fountain, to the east. Its
being set apart is appropriate, for the Plaza, like the
Waldorf-Astoria, is that rare hostelry whose very name
conjures up images of Old World elegance. Fear struck
New York when the Trumps got hold of the 1907 landmark in 1988, but fortunately the ensuing renovations
were worthy of the place. Have tea in the **Palm Court**, a
pre–World War I indoor café with white marble columns
and a first-rate piano/violin duo. Or enjoy pre-theater
dinner at the **Edwardian Room** or the swank **Oak Bar**;
management will arrange for a car to get you to your
show in time.

Heading west from the Plaza, cross over to the north
side of Central Park South. Not only does this allow you to
view the upper-floor details of the Plaza, but it gives you a
close-up look at the park and the inevitable queue of
horse-drawn hansom cabs. New York's carriage-horse
business has long been a bone of contention among
surrey owners, animal-rights supporters, anal compul-
sives, and the city government. Things reached a nadir
during Ed Koch's mayoralty, when carriage drivers were
obliged to fit their horses with giant diapers.

Mickey Mantle's Restaurant and Sports Bar (42 Central
Park South) is not the only jock-owned eatery in New
York City, it is merely the best. Nine television monitors
beam a variety of sporting events, the walls are festooned
with valuable memorabilia from baseball history, the
food (*tender* steaks, real mashed potatoes) is simple but
right, and big-name athletes really do eat here—all the
time. And yes, that includes the Mick.

You could get a meal at **Rumpelmeyer's** (50 Central
Park South), too, but what this teddy-bear-filled eatery is
really known for is desserts. The strawberries Romanoff
and hot-fudge sundaes here are downright immoral, and
that's not bad. **Les Célébrités**, in the Nikko Essex House

Hotel (160 Central Park South), offers yet a different sort of dining experience; it is that rare establishment that has a gimmick—paintings by TV and movie stars—*and* excellent cuisine. There are no gimmicks at **San Domenico** (240 Central Park South), just very expensive Northern Italian fare.

The only truly interesting building façade on Central Park South beyond the Plaza, the **Gainsborough Studios** (number 222), sports a statue of Thomas Gainsborough (of course) over its door, full-windowed artists' studios that you'd expect to find in Greenwich Village rather than Midtown, and colorful mosaics. The Gainsborough was built in 1906, and, to be sure, few painters would be able to afford a flat there these days, but its list of residents does include at least one artist of another sort: Candice Bergen. And people in the neighborhood will tell you that she's a lovely person, in spite of her having single-handedly inspired the breakdown of the American family.

THE UPPER WEST SIDE

By Stephen Brewer

Stephen Brewer, the editorial consultant for this guide-book, has lived on the Upper West Side for many years.

You have probably read and heard of the Upper West Side many, many times. Theodore Dreiser's Sister Carrie lived here, in a fifth-floor flat on Amsterdam Avenue. J. D. Salinger's fictional Glass family occupied a roomy apartment on Riverside Drive, not far from the Central Park West home of the Morningstars, that parvenu clan of Herman Wouk's *Marjorie Morningstar.* The tough denizens of *West Side Story* walked the same streets that you will if you choose to travel just north of Midtown to see this neighborhood, and you certainly should.

One reason to go to the Upper West Side is, of course, to see its major attractions, the Lincoln Center for the Performing Arts and the American Museum of Natural History foremost among them. The neighborhood's location is in itself appealing. These 200-some blocks occupy a narrow strip of land between the Hudson River on the west and Central Park on the east, running from Columbus Circle north to Columbia University, at around 116th Street. This means that an Upper West Sider who steps out for a bit of air can stroll along the shores of the river that the writer Thomas Wolfe found so comforting ("like long pipes and old tobacco"), walk across the neighborhood to sit for a while on a bench in Central Park, the most successful of all urban greenswards, and be back in the apartment in less than an hour.

You may also want to go to the Upper West Side to see for yourself traces of the reputation it has won over the years for harboring New Yorkers of artistic temperaments. Edgar Allan Poe wrote much of *The Raven* on West 84th Street. Two houses on the block bear plaques marking the site where the poor man allegedly lived; the correct address is 206.

The neighborhood still attracts many writers, musicians, dancers, and actors, and an Upper West Sider who returns home from a night at the theater on the M 104 bus may have the pleasure of sitting next to one of the performers he has just seen on stage. (The M 104 begins at the United Nations on the East Side, crosses 42nd Street to Times Square, then proceeds north along Eighth Avenue and Broadway; if you are staying in Midtown, it is an excellent way to reach any of the sights on the Upper West Side.) If you walk the streets of the Upper West Side any time during a weekday, you will find yourself, on crowded sidewalks, in the company of many relatively prosperous-looking men and women. They *do* work, just on schedules and at occupations (in the cast of a soap opera, for example) unlike those of most people elsewhere in the country.

In fact, the real reason to go to the Upper West Side is not to take in famous sights or partake of artistic traditions. Rather, even a brief walk here will give you the chance to see a quintessential New York neighborhood, a place where New Yorkers eat and sleep and go about their daily business, however eccentric that may be compared to quotidian activities elsewhere. The mainstays of the neighborhood have always been the bourgeoisie. As soon as the Upper West Side began to develop, which was not until the late 19th century, the prosperous middle classes fled from the cramped downtown neighborhoods

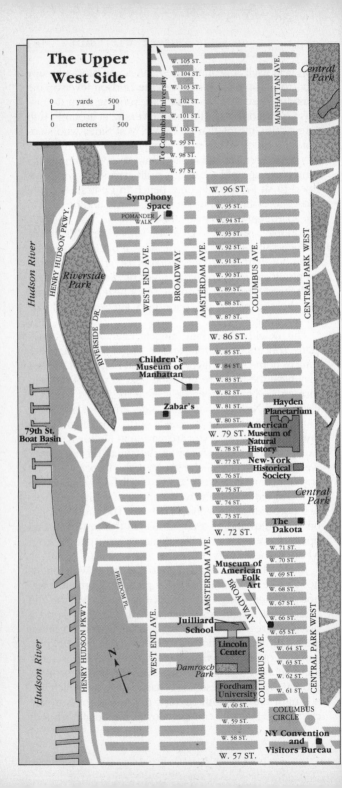

The Upper West Side

| 0 | yards | 500 |
| 0 | meters | 500 |

To Columbia University

W. 105 ST.
W. 104 ST.
W. 103 ST.
W. 102 ST.
W. 101 ST.
W. 100 ST.
W. 99 ST.
W. 98 ST.
W. 97 ST.

Central Park

MANHATTAN AVE.

W. 96 ST.
W. 95 ST.
W. 94 ST.
W. 93 ST.
W. 92 ST.
W. 91 ST.
W. 90 ST.
W. 89 ST.
W. 88 ST.
W. 87 ST.

Symphony Space
POMANDER WALK

WEST END AVE.
Broadway
AMSTERDAM AVE.
COLUMBUS AVE.
CENTRAL PARK WEST

Hudson River

HENRY HUDSON PKWY.

Riverside Park

RIVERSIDE DR.

W. 86 ST.
W. 85 ST.
W. 84 ST.
W. 83 ST.
W. 82 ST.
W. 81 ST.
W. 80 ST.

Children's Museum of Manhattan

Zabar's

Hayden Planetarium

American Museum of Natural History

W. 79 ST.
W. 78 ST.
W. 77 ST.
W. 76 ST.
W. 75 ST.
W. 74 ST.
W. 73 ST.

79th St. Boat Basin

New-York Historical Society

Central Park

The Dakota

W. 72 ST.
W. 71 ST.
W. 70 ST.
W. 69 ST.
W. 68 ST.
W. 67 ST.
W. 66 ST.
W. 65 ST.
W. 64 ST.
W. 63 ST.
W. 62 ST.
W. 61 ST.

FREEDOM PL.

AMSTERDAM AVE.

BROADWAY

Museum of American Folk Art

Juilliard School

Lincoln Center

COLUMBUS AVE.

CENTRAL PARK WEST

Damrosch Park

Fordham University

N

WEST END AVE.

HENRY HUDSON PKWY.

Hudson River

W. 60 ST.
W. 59 ST.
W. 58 ST.
W. 57 ST.

COLUMBUS CIRCLE

NY Convention and Visitors Bureau

to take up residence in what are still some of the city's most commodious apartment houses and in brownstones.

Harlem, beginning at the northern boundaries of the Upper West Side, was also developed to house the white bourgeoisie but was destined for a more distinctive role in American culture: For almost a century it has been the heart of black culture. This rich heritage is in evidence at the Apollo Theater, in fine museums, and on block after block of brownstones and row houses, such as those in Hamilton Heights, that look much as they did when the neighborhood was a garden suburb. The other side of Harlem—neglect, public-housing projects (some successful and others soulless and frightening), and poverty— are much in evidence, too. But don't let these realities deter you from seeing one of the most important places in American culture and a vital part of New York.

MAJOR INTEREST

Upper West Side
Lincoln Center for the Performing Arts
Zabar's and other food shops on Broadway
The Dakota and other grand apartment houses
Central Park West
American Museum of Natural History
Columbus Avenue shopping and street life
Riverside Drive and Park and the Hudson River
Columbia University and neighborhood
Cathedral Church of St. John the Divine

Harlem
Jazz and gospel tours
The Apollo Theater and 125th Street
Museums
Strivers' Row
City University
Hamilton Heights
Morris-Jumel Mansion
Audubon Terrace and Trinity Cemetery
Harlem River Houses

The Cloisters

Columbus Circle and
Lincoln Center

If you walk north from Midtown, you will approach the
Upper West Side from its southern boundary, **Columbus
Circle**. This vast, open space could have the monumental
presence of, say, the Place de la Concorde—that is, were
it not almost always full of a rush of traffic roaring around
a tiny statue of the explorer perched atop an 80-foot
pedestal. Pedestrians keep to the circle's periphery, first
past the white marble pseudo-Islamic mosque at the
southern tip of the intersection that has inspired jokes
about Persian brothels since A & P heir Huntington Hartford put it up as a gallery of modern art in 1965. The
building's saving grace is its current tenants, the **New
York Convention and Visitors Bureau**, which distributes
pamphlets and maps of the city from its ground-floor
office, and the city's Department of Cultural Affairs.

As you make your way around the circle in a counter-
clockwise direction, you will pass the extravagant, white
marble *Maine* Memorial, which commemorates the incident that sparked the Spanish-American War in 1898 and
marks one of the main entrances to Central Park. You will
then come to the foot of an utterly banal office tower
once known by the name of the corporation that built it
in 1970, Gulf & Western. The edifice is now the property
of Paramount Communications, and its only mark of distinction is a pronounced tilt to the east, suggesting that it
might one day have the good grace to topple out of sight.

From here begin the walk north on Broadway. As you
leave the circle, you will see on your left the old New
York Coliseum, an ugly, functional structure that became
dysfunctional when the five million-some conventioneers
that New York hosts every year moved their shows to the
new Jacob K. Javits Convention Center in Midtown near
the Hudson. No sooner had the city announced plans to
demolish the hall than New Yorkers, who had never paid
any attention to it before, began to protest, fearful that the
two snazzy skyscrapers that are to go up in its place will
cast mile-long shadows over the southwestern corner of
Central Park. Some variation of these buildings will undoubtedly go up, but the protest gives you a good idea of
just how protective New Yorkers have become of their
land and the air above it, even when the space in question
is as unremarkable as Columbus Circle.

LINCOLN CENTER

Follow Broadway north for several blocks to the Lincoln
Center for the Performing Arts. New Yorkers have been
taking pot shots at the pedestrian appearance of this 12-
acre complex since it opened in 1962. (You can see the
neighborhood that once stood in its place in the film *West
Side Story;* it was shot in the deserted streets and buildings of the slum that the center replaced, just before the
wreckers moved in.) To fuss about the appearance of
Lincoln Center is to miss the point. The world's most
accomplished performing artists grace its theaters, which
surround a large marble plaza that despite its cold formality is made friendlier by its large fountain and in the
summer by an outdoor café and bar. The best time to take
a seat on the rim of the fountain is 10:30 P.M. or so, when
the performances end and the audiences spill out onto
the plaza, looking much happier than New Yorkers usually do en masse. The mood becomes even more festive
on weekend evenings in the summer, when a band plays
and New Yorkers, whether they are attending a performance in one of the halls or not, come here to dance
under the stars late into the night.

Perched atop one of the buildings across Broadway is
one of New York's favorite unheralded landmarks, a working model of the Statue of Liberty. When the designs for
Lincoln Center were being laid, there was a movement
afoot to tear down this and other surrounding buildings
to extend the plaza all the way to Central Park—a dream
that soon faded in the face of the realities of Manhattan
real estate.

Anyone who comes to New York for even a short stay
should try to buy a ticket and step off the plaza into one of
the surrounding halls. **Avery Fisher Hall**, on the north
side of the plaza, was originally called Philharmonic Hall.
But when the esteemed New York Philharmonic moved
into its new quarters and sounded its first notes, the
acoustics were so bad that the audience made a beeline
for the doors. The symphony made a plea to electronics
czar Avery Fisher, and the hall was lined with oak paneling. As a result, Mr. Fisher is immortalized in one of the
world's favorite venues for classical music, and the rest of
us are treated to some of the best acoustics to be found
anywhere.

The **Metropolitan Opera House** occupies center stage
at the far western end of the plaza. This hall, home to the
Metropolitan Opera Company and the American Ballet

Theatre, wins the prize for showmanship even before the curtain goes up. From the six-story height of its glass-fronted lobby hang two murals by Marc Chagall—they are visible even from a bus passing by on Broadway, except in the morning when they are shrouded to protect them from the sun. Inside, the theatrics begin when the huge crystal chandeliers float into the ceiling just before curtain time so they won't interfere with the sight lines, which are unobstructed from all but a dozen or so seats. The **New York State Theater**, where the New York City Opera and the New York City Ballet perform, occupies the south side of the plaza. The theater is the property of the state, and when the governor comes to the city he often throws official parties in the foyer and on the second-floor loggia.

The rest of Lincoln Center stretches to the north and west behind the Metropolitan Opera House. The **Vivian Beaumont Theater**, which stages plays and musicals, shares a building with a branch of the New York Public Library, the **Library and Museum of Performing Arts**. Among the treasures of this amazing collection of sheet music and books on the performing arts are some 12,000 recordings that New Yorkers can borrow; the library also mounts changing exhibits on the performing arts. Just beyond the reflecting pool outside, with a Henry Moore sculpture rising from its midst, is the esteemed **Juilliard School**, whose well-trained graduates often return to perform on Lincoln Center's stages. **Alice Tully Hall**, the Lincoln Center Chamber Music Society's main venue, and the **Walter Reade Theater**, operated by the Film Society of Lincoln Center and the best place in the city to see repertory films, occupy the Juilliard complex. Excellent tours, taking in the stages and labyrinthine costume storage rooms of the center's halls, leave frequently from the Metropolitan Opera House; Tel: 582-3512.

Around Lincoln Center

Any number of establishments in the Lincoln Center neighborhood stay open well into the early hours to serve theatergoers late suppers—weather permitting, often at tables outdoors on the broad sidewalks along Broadway. The most perennially popular of all seems to be the **Saloon**, across Broadway from Lincoln Center at 64th Street. Two of the city's largest music stores are also nearby, staying open late to catch concertgoers when the strains of the music they have just heard are still running through their heads: **Tower**, at 66th Street and Broadway, and **HMV**, competition at 72nd Street and Broadway.

Across Broadway from Lincoln Center, Columbus Avenue begins its northward run (more on the avenue later in this chapter). The **Museum of American Folk Art**, with its noted collection of paintings, textiles, furniture, and decorative arts, is at the foot of Columbus, just north of 65th Street. A gift shop, selling an eclectic collection of antique and contemporary Americana, adjoins.

The **Hotel des Artistes** is just up the avenue and around the corner at number 1 West 67th Street. This fine building has been popular with creative New Yorkers since the earliest days of this century. Its double-height apartments were built to accommodate painters, but it has been years since anyone but the very rich has been able to afford them. Isadora Duncan, Norman Rockwell, Rudolph Valentino, and Noel Coward have called the des Artistes home, but it was the debauched Harry Crosby who gave the place its racy élan. One evening in 1929 this nephew of J. P. Morgan and founder of the Paris-based avant-garde Black Sun Press locked the door to an apartment here, made love to and then shot his lovely mistress, and put the gun to his own head. You can enter these portals and partake of a meal or a drink at the attractive **Café des Artistes** on the ground floor. One of the café's famous neighbors is the equally popular **Tavern on the Green**, set just inside Central Park at 67th Street. Festooned with Christmas lights and decorated in an eclectic style, the place makes even regulars feel like tourists out for a night on the big town; it's a good place to stop in for a drink, though, especially in the summer when the garden is open. Many of the buildings here in the West 60s house television studios of local stations and national networks. ABC has just moved into its sleek new semicircular headquarters between 66th and 67th streets.

72nd Street and North

If you continue north from Lincoln Center on Broadway you will soon come to its busy intersection with 72nd Street, where just 100 years ago stood the homestead of Jacob Harsen. His farm was then one of many on the Upper West Side. Less than 200 years ago Washington Irving described vast tracts of this area as "a sweet rural valley ... enlivened here and there by a delectable little Dutch cottage."

Could you have stood here a hundred years ago on a Sunday, you would have witnessed an extraordinary sight. By the thousands, New Yorkers of the day used to drive their carriages and ride their bicycles—only just invented—north from Grand Circle (now Columbus Circle) up the Boulevard (now Broadway), across 72nd Street to Riverside Drive, and follow it north to roadhouses along the Hudson River. "After dark Riverside Drive seemed alive with fireflies, so numerous were the varicolored lamps flashing under the trees," wrote one observer of the day trippers returning home.

Seventy-second Street's few remaining kosher restaurants and butchers have long served the neighborhood's large Jewish population. One of the most notable of these is the **Eclair**, between Broadway and Columbus Avenue, a pleasant restaurant and pastry shop that is still a gathering spot for European Jews who came to New York half a century ago.

At the less gracious end of café society, **Gray's Papaya**, a gaudy stand-up counter on the southeast corner of the 72nd Street and Broadway intersection, two dollars will get you two of New York's best frankfurters ("better than filet mignon," their motto claims) and a fruit drink, and will also bring you closer than you may want to be to some very seedy clients. Many of them are habitués of **Verdi Square** across the street. This tiny patch of greenery has long been known as Needle Park, in part because of its triangular shape but more so because of the lively drug trade that goes on beneath a statue of composer Giuseppe Verdi, put up by New York's Italian citizenry in 1906. At the center of the intersection of Broadway, 72nd Street, and Amsterdam Avenue you will see a brick kiosk, the entrance to the subway that, when it opened in 1904, finally brought civilization to the Upper West Side.

New Yorkers had already begun to take up residence in huge new apartment houses on Broadway in the decade or so before the arrival of the subway. One of these, the Dorilton, at 71st Street, opened to an onslaught of sour reviews, the most dire of them claiming "the sight of it makes strong men swear and weak women shrink afrightened"; New Yorkers have survived a full century of the building's ornate Beaux Arts presence. When the **Ansonia** opened at 73rd and Broadway in 1901, it sported two swimming pools, a lobby fountain populated by seals, and a roof garden where a bear roamed freely. These trappings, as well as its turrets, gargoyles, and apartments of as

many as 18 rooms, have wooed some of New York's most
flamboyant citizens over the years, including Theodore
Dreiser, Florenz Ziegfeld, and Babe Ruth. The West Side is
graciously endowed with such fine old buildings, impart-
ing to the neighborhood the aura of a bourgeois quarter of
a European capital.

UP BROADWAY

In fact, the broad, cosmopolitan sidewalks that proceed
north up Broadway may create for romantic souls (with a
gift for shutting out the hubbub) the feeling that they
have found themselves in a *beau quartier* of Paris. Like
residents in European cities, New Yorkers tend to shun
supermarkets—some in Manhattan maintain shoddy standards of cleanliness and service that would send Betty
Crocker into a swoon—in favor of specialty shops such as
the many on this stretch of Broadway. **Fairway**, 2127
Broadway, at 74th Street, is a pleasure; even if New York's
largest selection of greens and fruits isn't high on your
New York shopping list, the cheeses, breads, coffees, and
other specialty foods sold here may well be. The store
serves some 30,000 customers a week, many of whom
stop in every day on their shopping rounds. Just up
Broadway at 75th Street is **Citarella's**, a fishmonger that is
as noted for its piscine window displays as it is for its
exquisite selection of fresh fish. If you can't accommodate
a red snapper ripening in a corner of your hotel room,
you can partake of shellfish at Citarella's stand-up clam
bar.

La Caridad, at 78th and Broadway, is the best of a
breed of Cuban-Chinese restaurants unique to New
York. These places are run by Chinese who immigrated
to Cuba, then fled to New York after Castro's takeover; La
Caridad was once a favorite hangout of taxi drivers but is
now packed with affluent young newcomers to the
neighborhood. The large white apartment house across
78th Street is the Apthorp, one of New York's best addresses, occupying an entire block and built around a
luxuriously quiet courtyard.

The Upper West Side's, and New York's, most famous
food store is **Zabar's**, north on Broadway at 80th Street.
The store's 160 employees sell 10,000 pounds of coffee,
10 tons of cheese, and 1,000 pounds of salmon a week—
as well as Cuisinarts, microwave ovens, pots and pans,
even tea towels, for total sales of $25 million a year. Most
notable, Zabar's charges the lowest prices in New York for

nearly every item it stocks, be it a vacuum cleaner or a loaf of bread.

There is still much else to see on the Upper West Side, and you would do well to fortify yourself with coffee and pastry in Zabar's busy little coffee room. After that you might continue to pursue the neighborhood's two passions, food and books. For yet another sample of the former, walk across 80th Street to **H & H Bagels**, the city's largest manufacturer—70,000 a day—of this New York staple. **Shakespeare & Company** bookstore, north of Zabar's on Broadway at the corner of 81st Street, has only slightly less character than its Paris namesake and is very well stocked. **Gryphon**, just across Broadway, has a very fine, rather dusty collection of secondhand books (and an annex at 246 West 80th Street). These smaller shops have recently been eclipsed by **Barnes & Noble**, a massive, glitzy emporium on Broadway between 82nd and 83rd streets that is crowded day and night.

CENTRAL PARK WEST

The Dakota, New York's first great apartment house, is at the corner of 72nd Street and Central Park West. When Edward Clark, heir to the Singer sewing machine fortune, put up this yellow-brick building in 1881, it was so far removed from urban Manhattan that his detractors said it may as well have been in the Dakota Territory, giving the house its now very famous name. The well-to-do were then still wary of apartments, considering it vulgar to share halls and recently invented elevators with strangers. Accordingly, Clark fashioned the Dakota in the style of a château, even surrounding it with a moat. So convincing was the effect that the Russian composer Tchaikovsky, visiting music publisher Gustav Schirmer here, thought that his host owned the entire house and that Central Park was his alone. The Dakota has also been home to such other musically inclined tenants as Theodore Steinway, the piano manufacturer, and, more recently, Leonard Bernstein and John Lennon, who was shot to death outside its gates in 1980.

You can pay tribute to the musician across the street in **Strawberry Fields**, an acre of Central Park that Yoko Ono had landscaped in her husband's memory. This is a very pleasant place to enjoy the park, walking beneath the arbor that leads off 72nd Street or wandering down to one of the gazebos alongside the rowing lake. If you come here at night you will notice a curious phenomenon: New Yorkers do not enter the park after dark (except in large groups of half a million or so to attend concerts on the Great Lawn), even in the hottest days of summer. They are heeding the advice of Ogden Nash, who warns anyone who finds himself in the park after dark to "hurry, hurry to the zoo, and creep into the tiger's lair, frankly you'll be safer there."

From the Dakota walk north on Central Park West, a handsome avenue whose commodious apartment houses facing the park went up in the 1930s to house, among others, well-to-do Jewish families who had arrived on the Lower East Side from Europe only a generation before.

THE WEST SIDE MUSEUMS

At 77th Street and Central Park West you will come to the **New-York Historical Society**, a quiet, stodgy institution-cum-museum with rich collections of Tiffany glass and portraits, and a fine library. The society is under a dark financial cloud and is hobbling precariously, and temporarily, on emergency state funds.

The **American Museum of Natural History**, just across 77th Street, is a wonderful if rather musty collection of bones, gems, and other items—some 37 million in all—relating to natural history. The Hope diamond is here, as is the largest meteorite ever recovered. Anyone who grew up in New York counts among his or her happiest school days those field trips here, parading past dioramas of African scenes and dark rooms lined with mummies to the top-floor galleries where the dinosaurs rear their reptilian heads beneath the skylights. The museum has expanded haphazardly and somewhat confusedly since it opened in 1877, so you may want to stop at the information desk at the main entrance and join one of the excellent tours. The Hayden Planetarium is adjacent, just to the north.

The **Children's Museum of Manhattan**, west on 83rd Street between Amsterdam Avenue and Broadway, pales in comparison with these grander institutions on Central Park West, but is popular with its young visitors, who can see themselves on TV, make animated cartoons, and learn about science and the arts at the many changing exhibitions.

COLUMBUS AVENUE

If you leave the Museum of Natural History by the 77th Street exit you will be just a few steps away from Columbus Avenue. On the evening before and in the early morning hours of every Thanksgiving, Macy's uses this stretch of 77th Street as a staging ground for its parade, blowing up the huge balloon figures that will float down Central Park West and then Broadway to the department store in Herald Square. Many Upper West Siders stand here through the night, watching the familiar figures take shape. Year round on Sundays the schoolyard at 77th Street and Columbus is taken over by a much-patronized outdoor market selling fresh produce, clothing, antiques, and other goods.

Columbus Avenue from Lincoln Center to 86th Street is almost always crowded with the well-dressed patrons of its shops and restaurants. Stroll up the avenue of a summer's evening and, falling in step with the well-turned-out neighborhood boulevardiers, you will feel you have stumbled upon an elaborate mating ritual. Until recently, though, Columbus was decidedly middle class. The elevated subway, the "El," rushed above it, and the stores below did a lively business supplying the apartment houses of Central Park West. Of all these long-gone shops, the best remembered is Hellman's delicatessen, whose homemade mayonnaise has achieved fame far beyond the Upper West Side. The avenue now belongs to suburbanites in for a day's or evening's jaunt and to the well-reared, well-educated young New Yorkers who pay as much as $2,000 a month in rent for a few rooms in a brownstone that their grandparents could have rented in its entirety for $100.

Seeing so many well-heeled young people crowd into the neighborhood's bars and restaurants on weekend evenings, it is hard not to be cynical. These pampered youth bring to mind what Dorothy Parker, who grew up in this neighborhood, said when half a century ago she was asked to comment on the attendees of a Yale prom: "If all those sweet young things were laid end to end . . . I would not be at all surprised." Keep in mind, though, that young professionals like those who now inhabit so much of the Upper West Side have always formed a sizable portion of Manhattan's population. Keep in mind, too, that the difference between the haves and have nots is shockingly distinct in New York. Within blocks of this affluent strip are sordid tenements housing welfare families, and it is impossible to walk these streets without seeing, and often being approached by, at least a few of the city's estimated 75,000 homeless citizens.

COLUMBUS AVENUE SHOPS AND CAFES

The shops on Columbus Avenue and elsewhere on the Upper West Side are more or less of two types: those that have been serving a loyal neighborhood clientele for years and the trendy new places that tend to go out of business almost as soon as they open. With exceptions, the best shopping is to be had at those that have been here for a decade or more. On 71st Street, just east of Columbus Avenue, is **Café La Fortuna**, a pleasant little coffeehouse where you will be encouraged to linger over your cappuccino and Italian pastry. With its cookbooks and mail-order gourmet food business, the **Silver Palate** has cornered a nationwide reputation—from its tiny headquarters on the west side of Columbus at 73rd Street. Freshly made breads and the shop's own specialty mustards and vinegars are packed high to the ceiling. **Maxilla & Mandible**, across the avenue just north of 81st Street, takes advantage of its proximity to the natural history museum to stock a gruesomely fascinating collection of bones and taxidermic specimens.

The natty building across the avenue is the Endicott, an expensive cooperative apartment house that typifies the renovation that has reshaped so much of the Upper West Side in recent years. Before its conversion, the Endicott was a hotel of dubious distinction, losing on the average a guest a month to homicide. In an irony typical of this neighborhood, **Endicott Bookseller**, one of the smart shops on the ground floor, is a gathering spot of local literati. There is still a hotel nearby, the modest though pleasant ▶ **Excelsior**, overlooking the museum on 81st Street between Columbus and Central Park West. A large double room here still costs $75, and slightly more will put you in a suite with a kitchenette (see our Accommodations section).

AMSTERDAM AVENUE

Amsterdam, one block to the west, is the last of the Upper West Side avenues to be "discovered." The *bodegas,* secondhand furniture shops, and shoe-repair shops here are quickly giving way to hair salons and bars with names like the Raccoon Lodge and Caddy Shack that are usually packed with sloppily inebriated college students. New shops and restaurants take the edge off what was once fairly harsh terrain, yet the avenue has not yet been gentrified to the point of homogeneity.

For New York's best smoked fish, walk up Amsterdam to **Barney Greengrass the Sturgeon King**, a deli and restaurant at number 541, just north of 86th Street. The Greengrass family counts among its past and present clientele the likes of Franklin D. Roosevelt, Groucho Marx, and Woody Allen.

WEST END AVENUE AND RIVERSIDE DRIVE

Walking west from Broadway anywhere above 72nd Street, you will first cross **West End Avenue**, a street of tall, handsome apartment buildings that seems more typical of a residential quarter of Paris, Vienna, or old Berlin than of New York. What makes West End Avenue unusual is the absence of shops and the uniformity of its architecture. (Oddly enough, when the West Side was being laid out in the late 19th century, Broadway was to have been the residential street, serviced by businesses on West End.) Most of these solidly middle-class buildings went up in the 1930s. In New York, leases are often passed from generation to generation, and many of these apartments are still occupied by the original tenants or their children and grandchildren. In recent years many of the buildings here and elsewhere on the Upper West Side have become cooperatives, and a comfortable two-bedroom apartment selling for less than $300,000 is a bargain. The same size apartment rents for $2,500 a month or more.

If you follow West End as far north as 94th Street, you will find one of the West Side's hidden treasures: **Pomander Walk**, a row of little town houses that look for all the world like cottages in a British village. Indeed, the walk, built in the 1920s, was modeled on stage sets from a then-popular British play of the same name. Suitably, these tiny rooms have been home to Humphrey Bogart, the Gish sisters, and many other actors.

Riverside Drive, one block to the west of West End Avenue, curves gently above the banks of the Hudson, which flows a hearty stone's-throw away on the far side of narrow Riverside Park and the busy West Side Highway. New Yorkers once built mansions along Riverside Drive, still a lovely, exclusively residential, noncommercial avenue. None was more exquisite than the 75-room French château, complete with private chapel, that steel tycoon Charles Schwab built at Riverside Drive and 74th Street in 1906. Alas, in an uncharacteristic show of modesty, the city fathers decided not to buy the palace and make it the official mayor's residence, and the house came down to make way for an apartment building in the 1940s.

There are still a few survivors from the old days, though, including a dilapidated mansion at the corner of 89th Street and a whole block of fine French town houses between 105th and 106th streets. For the most part, the apartment buildings that have replaced the private homes are very pleasant places to live.

RIVERSIDE PARK

Riverside Park, like Central Park, was laid out by Frederick Law Olmsted and Calvert Vaux in the 1870s. The park occupies a long, narrow, shady shelf of shoreline running all the way from 72nd Street to 153rd Street. Wide promenades cut through the park most of the way up, affording soulful views of the silvery Hudson to one side and the forested embankment and man-made cliffs of Riverside Drive apartment houses to the other. Given its isolation next to the river and below the drive, you should confine your daylight exploration to well-trodden footpaths and at night venture no farther north than the Soldiers and Sailors Monument, perched above the park on the drive at 89th Street.

A good place to see both park and river is the **79th Street Boat Basin** (just follow 79th Street all the way west). This shabby little marina is home to the few New Yorkers who live on houseboats, and the grassy slope stretching up from the broad, noble river is as peaceful a place as any in New York for a picnic.

Columbia University and Its Neighborhood

Many residents of the Upper West Side went to school here, at Columbia University. You can walk to the campus, a straight shot up Broadway to 114th Street, or you can board the M 104 bus anywhere along Broadway.

Columbia bows to its Ivy League status with a large green quadrangle, but this is a decidedly urban, overbuilt campus that is squeezed between Broadway and, to the east, Morningside Park. The university's major real-estate holding is not here but in Midtown—Columbia owns the land upon which Rockefeller Center was built. Columbia is the anchor of a sizable intellectual community. **Barnard College**, long considered to be one of the finest women's colleges in the country, is on the west side of Broadway between 116th and 120th streets, on land where George Washington fought the battle of Harlem Heights in his unsuccessful attempt to take Manhattan from the British. The **Union Theological Seminary**, between 120th and 122nd streets west of Broadway, is a major center of liberal Protestant thought. The red-brick Victorian buildings of Columbia's **Teacher's College** are directly across Broadway, and the **Jewish Theological Seminary** is at the northeast corner of 122nd Street and Broadway. The light that burns in its tower at the corner commemorates the victims of the Holocaust. All of these institutions welcome visitors.

Like most universities, Columbia is surrounded by some good bookstores and inexpensive restaurants. Of the former, the best is **Barnard Book Forum**, just across Broadway from the main entrance to the campus and especially strong in history, philosophy, and literature, as well as books published by the Columbia University Press.

The students' favorite eateries are next to one another on Amsterdam Avenue between 110th and 111th streets. The **V & T Pizzeria** serves a pie that alone justifies a trip this far north. The **Hungarian Pastry Shop** allows its patrons to sit and read, downing strong coffee and rich poppy-seed rolls, as long as they wish. For a Columbia student, or for that matter any Upper West Sider, a Saturday night often begins at one of the Chinese restaurants on Broadway around 96th Street and the blocks just to the north. These places change names and hands so frequently that it is almost impossible to keep up with them.

THE CATHEDRAL AND OTHER MONUMENTS

At 112th Street and Amsterdam is the **Cathedral Church of St. John the Divine**, which will be the world's largest cathedral if it is ever completed. The monstrous Episcopal edifice has been so long in the making, since 1892, that no one would recognize the site if it weren't buzzing with stone carvers. (Replicas of the gargoyles they make are for sale in the cathedral shop.) Not all of the carvings here are of saints and sinners; many are of such contemporary subjects as the Manhattan skyline and Nelson Mandela. The neighborhood's two other monuments are west, on Riverside Drive, which retains its grandeur up here and, with varying degrees of genteel shabbiness, all the way up to its terminus at about 165th Street. **Grant's Tomb** is at Riverside and 122nd Street, where the former president, who retired to New York four years before he died in 1885, lies next to his wife in a pompous marble mausoleum. The even colder, more imposing structure next door is **Riverside Church**, built by John D. Rockefeller, Jr., in the 1920s.

Harlem

Officially, Harlem runs from 116th Street north to 168th Street, from the Hudson River on the west to the Harlem River (dividing Manhattan from the Bronx) on the east. But to most New Yorkers, Harlem's geographic boundaries aren't nearly as important as its cultural significance. This old neighborhood (one of the best preserved in Manhattan) was developed in the late 19th century to house, like the rest of the Upper West Side, the white middle class, but was soon settled by the city's growing black population. It is still the heart of black culture in New York and arguably in America. Duke Ellington, Count Basie, Billie Holiday, and many of the other famous black entertainers of the 20th century lived in Harlem. Many of them got their starts here, playing to whites-only audiences at the Cotton Club (still operating, in new guise, at 666 West 125th Street, west of Broadway) and at the Apollo Theater, also on 125th Street, between Seventh and Eighth avenues, which in Harlem take the names Adam Clayton Powell Jr. Boulevard and Frederick Douglass Boulevard, respectively.

Marcus Garvey founded his Back to Africa movement in Harlem in the 1920s. (A hilly park on Fifth Avenue between 120th and 124th streets is named after him.) Civil-rights leader Malcolm X was assassinated in 1965 at the Audubon Ballroom, at 166th Street and Broadway. (The city-owned building, once an ornate movie theater, is now the center of a controversy; the city wants to tear it down and preservationists and neighborhood leaders want to restore it.) Adam Clayton Powell, Jr., preacher, civil-rights leader, and U.S. congressman, preached at the Abyssinian Baptist Church, 132 West 138th Street, be-

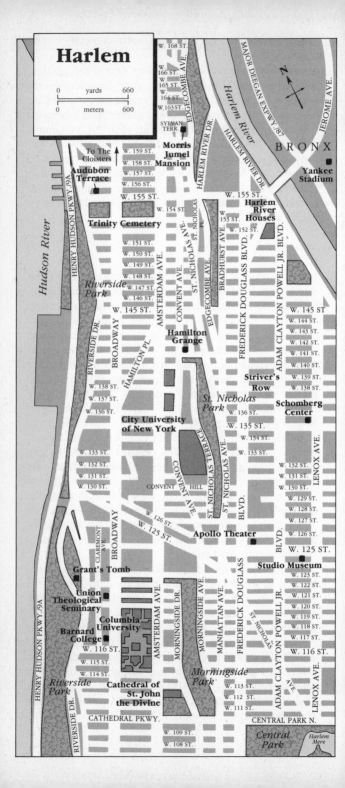

tween Seventh and Lenox avenues. (The church now has a room filled with memorabilia from Powell's political career.)

For all its reputation as a nest of crime and its all-too-real signs of poverty and urban despair, Harlem today still offers much to see and appreciate—its museums, well-preserved buildings and districts, some of the most successful public housing in the country, and a renaissance of sorts, as a growing black middle-class presence renovates homes and shops that just ten years ago seemed to be lost forever. Unfortunately, the area's reputation for danger is to a degree warranted. Walkers should confine their excursions to busier avenues. You can best reach some of the places we describe here briefly on the M 1, M 4, and M 5 buses, which begin in Midtown and run uptown to Harlem along Madison Avenue.

You can book a tour with **Harlem Spirituals**, 1697 Broadway, Tel: 757-0425, with visits to historic sights as well as excursions to Sunday morning church services, jazz evenings, and soul-food dinners; from $29. **Gray Line**, 900 Eighth Avenue (between 53rd and 54th streets), Tel: 397-2600, conducts a tour of historic Harlem and a Gospel tour to many of the area's ubiquitous churches; both $31.

THE 125TH STREET AREA

The commercial center of Harlem is 125th Street, especially the stretch around Lenox Avenue (Sixth Avenue). With limited city funds and seemingly inexhaustible neighborhood interest, the street is improving. The Adam Clayton Powell Jr. State Office Building, an eyesore of a skyscraper at Adam Clayton Powell Jr. Boulevard, has brought jobs and activity to the area. Two bastions of black culture are just down the street. The **Studio Museum of Harlem**, at 144 West 125th Street, shows changing exhibitions of works by black artists and a permanent collection with works by Romare Bearden and others (see also our Museums section). The **Apollo Theater**, at 253 West 125th Street, opened in 1913 and has welcomed the likes of Charlie Parker, Dizzie Gillespie, Aretha Franklin, and many other black entertainers. After a much-heralded renovation, the old theater reopened briefly as a jazz club in 1980 but has since been converted to a television studio.

Ten blocks north up Lenox Avenue, at 135th Street, the **Schomburg Center for Research in Black Culture** (a branch of the New York Public Library system) houses the world's most extensive collection of materials relating to blacks. Holdings include 75,000 books and 50,000 prints and photographs. Harlem's most popular restaurant (gauging by the number of New Yorkers from elsewhere in the city who come here to eat the Southern cooking), **Sylvia's**, is nearby on Lenox Avenue between 126th and 127th streets (see also our Dining section).

THE ST. NICHOLAS HISTORIC DISTRICT

Some of Harlem's finest houses are in the St. Nicholas Historic District, on 138th and 139th streets between Frederick Douglass Boulevard and Adam Clayton Powell Jr. Boulevard. These neo-Georgian town houses (those on 139th street are of yellow brick, those on 138th street are red brick) have long attracted upper-middle-class black families (Eubie Blake lived here), giving the two streets the sobriquet **Strivers' Row**.

City University of New York occupies fine old buildings and some modern extensions between West 130th and 135th streets, between Convent Avenue and the hilly terrain of St. Nicholas Park (roughly a block west of Lenox Avenue). Founded in 1847, the university was once free to any student who could pass the entrance exams. In the early years of this century City College (as it was then known) educated legions of intellectually ambitious immigrants, and continues to offer relatively inexpensive tuition to New Yorkers who could not afford to attend another school (students recently staged a protest in response to tuition increases that now bring the tuition to about $2,500 a year). The attractive, neo-Gothic campus, most of it built in the 19th century, incorporates the castlelike Croton Gatehouse at 135th Street and Convent Avenue. Once an important part of the 1880s Croton aqueduct system that channeled 250 million gallons of water a day to the city from Westchester County, the gatehouse has been rendered obsolete by massive new water tunnels. It remains unused but is still a glorious reminder of old New York, as is much of the other architecture in Harlem.

HAMILTON HEIGHTS TO AUDUBON TERRACE

The **Hamilton Heights Historic District** begins north of the campus at 140th Street. **Hamilton Grange**, where Alexander Hamilton, the first U.S. secretary of state and author of the *Federalist Papers,* lived when he was shot to death in a duel with Aaron Burr in 1804, is on Convent Avenue between 141st and 142nd streets. Now in the hands of the National Park Service, the grange is open for tours Wednesdays through Sundays, from 9:00 A.M. to 5:00 P.M.; admission is free. The real attraction here, though, is the architecture to be found on street after street of finely preserved brownstones, home to prosperous blacks who have the privilege of living in one of the loveliest areas in New York.

The hilly terrain to the north, between St. Nicholas and Edgecombe avenues from 143rd to 155th streets, is known as **Sugar Hill**, because the black bourgeoisie have long lived the "sweet life" in the area's grand apartment houses and brownstones. As you continue north along Edgecombe Avenue you come to small, hilltop Roger Morris Park and one of the city's greatest architectural treasures: the **Morris-Jumel Mansion**. Relatively unscathed by the centuries and now undergoing careful renovation, the house was built in 1765 as a country retreat for British colonel Roger Morris and is still surrounded by lush gardens. It served as temporary headquarters for George Washington during his campaign to take Manhattan during the Revolutionary War and was the longtime residence of Madame Elizabeth Jumel, friend of Napoleon, second wife of Aaron Burr, and the adulterous participant in some of 19th-century New York's most talked-about scandals. The house is open Tuesdays through Sundays from 10:00 A.M. to 4:00 P.M.; the entrance fee is $3. **Sylvan Terrace**, a cobblestoned alley comprising Manhattan's largest collection of wooden houses, is across Jumel Terrace from the mansion, between West 160th and 162nd streets.

One of Harlem's other great architectural achievements lies to the west, on Broadway at 155th Street. **Audubon Terrace** (officially known as the Washington Heights Museum Group) is a pleasant cluster of Beaux Arts buildings on land that was once part of the riverside estate of artist and ornithologist John James Audubon. The terrace now houses a delightfully eclectic mix of exhibitions: the **Museum of the American Indian**, a comprehensive collection of Native American artifacts (scheduled to move to lower Manhattan in fall 1994); the **Hispanic Society of America**, whose collection includes paintings by Goya, Velázquez, and El Greco that are the envy of many a larger museum; the **American Numismatic Society**, the world's largest collection of coins; and the **American Academy of Arts and Letters**, which has changing exhibits of American art. (See also our Museums section.)

Trinity Cemetery, covering rolling, tree-shaded terrain between Broadway and Riverside Drive from 153rd to 155th streets, is the final resting place of some of New York's most famous citizens of the past, among them John Jacob Astor and his family, the aforementioned Madame Jumel, and Clement Clarke Moore, who wrote "A Visit from St. Nicholas." Trinity Church in the Wall Street area (see our Lower Manhattan section) established the cemetery in 1846, when it outgrew its tiny, historic churchyard but had no room to expand. Like so many other places in Harlem, the church of the Intercession, across Broadway at 155th Street, is another reminder that all of Manhattan is not concrete; on a grassy knoll, with bell tower and vicarage, the church looks like the peaceful center of a prosperous parish in the English countryside.

Across Harlem, the **Harlem River Houses** bring you back to this century and urban realities. Built in 1937 between 151st and 153rd streets along the Harlem River Drive, the light, airy low-rise buildings are clustered around landscaped courtyards and along the river. (The Harlem River separates Manhattan from the Bronx and, in effect, Upstate New York.) They house 575 families and should provide a model for public housing everywhere. Harlem may well be able to preserve its rich cultural and architectural heritage and also continue to meet contemporary needs with projects like this one.

The Cloisters and
Northern Manhattan

If you travel still farther north, to the tip of Manhattan, your reward will be **The Cloisters**. You can reach the museum on the M 4 Madison Avenue bus, which will afford you a good look at Harlem and at Washington Heights, a middle-class Jewish and Hispanic neighborhood whose lower rents have in recent years attracted young, creatively inclined New Yorkers of the type who once settled in Greenwich Village and on the Upper West Side. A faster route is the A train, on the Eighth Avenue subway line.

The Cloisters is a collection of five Medieval European cloisters, a 12th-century chapter house, and other substantial treasures collected piecemeal in the early years of this century by George Bernard, a sculptor and architecture enthusiast. Mr. Bernard often had to pry discarded pillars and stones away from European homeowners who were using them as garden ornaments. He managed to reassemble the lot upon his return to New York and sold it to John D. Rockefeller, Jr. The multimillionaire in turn presented the artifacts and a building to house them to the Metropolitan Museum of Art.

The Cloisters, whose magnificent collections include the Unicorn Tapestries, is now handsomely planted with herb gardens and flowers, making it very easy for you to imagine you are in Europe and not in Manhattan—which will, nonetheless, lure you back after a pleasant afternoon here.

CENTRAL PARK

By Mitchell Nauffts

Mitchell Nauffts is a freelance writer based in Manhattan.

For apartment dwellers living on or near it, Manhattan's Central Park is the world's biggest back yard, an ideal spot for a birthday party, an after-school catch, or an impromptu picnic. For music lovers it's a vast open-air arena where opera, rap, and everything in between is presented free of charge. For bird-watchers and amateur horticulturists it's a remarkable oasis of species diversity in the midst of Manhattan's concrete-and-glass canyons. And for everyone else who calls New York home it's simply "the park," an endlessly varied and diversion-filled landscape where the *Sturm und Drang* of the country's most densely populated city takes a backseat to less pressing concerns. Indeed, the 120-year-old park is such an integral part of the New York experience that for many New Yorkers life without it would be unimaginable. Out-of-towners seem to agree: After the Statue of Liberty and the United Nations, Central Park tallies more visitors than any other attraction in the city.

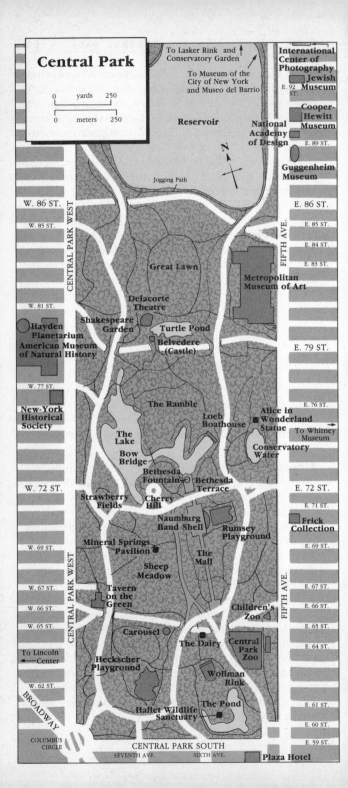

MAJOR INTEREST

The Children's District
Central Park Zoo
Wollman Rink
The Dairy (visitors' center)
The Carousel

Mid-Park
Tavern on the Green and the Sheep Meadow
The Mall and Concert Ground
Bethesda Terrace
Strawberry Fields
The Ramble
The Lake: restaurants and rowboating
Conservatory Water (the model-boat pond)
The Obelisk
Shakespeare-in-the-Park
Belvedere Castle

The Upper Park
The Reservoir
The Pool and Cascade
The Meer
Conservatory Garden

The need for such a public space was evident to at least one civic-minded New Yorker as early as the 1840s. Though much of Manhattan north of 59th Street was still rugged, largely unpopulated terrain, the poet William Cullen Bryant, then editor of the *New York Evening Post,* sensed that industrialization and booming population growth would eventually bury the island under block after block of right-angled buildings—a state of affairs even then on its way to being realized. Already the largest city in the country, with a population approaching half a million, New York crowded its immigrant poor into squalid tenements south of 14th Street, where they suffered from the worst disease mortality and highest crime rates in the Western world. Bryant's call for a large municipal park where impoverished city dwellers could escape the noise, crime, and overcrowding that characterized their lives appealed to the city's elite, who saw it as a way to defuse the social consequences of continued industrialization, and soon captured the public imagination as well.

In 1853, following a decade of debate, the city's board of aldermen approved a site that extended from what is now 59th Street north to 106th Street and from Fifth Avenue west to Eighth Avenue. After more than two years of deliberations and assessments the land was purchased for the unheard-of sum of $5,069,693. Shortly thereafter, a second disbursement was approved for the purchase of a hard-to-develop parcel of land that extended from 106th Street to the beginning of the Harlem plain at 110th Street. The perimeters of the park—five times longer than it was wide—were set.

Scattered over the site of the future park were ramshackle camps where squatters eked out an existence raising pigs and goats, boiling bones, and making moonshine. In addition, almost 140 acres of the 843-acre total were taken up by the receiving reservoirs of the Croton Aqueduct system (which had only recently begun to deliver a crystal-clear supply of water to the growing city). The smaller of the two reservoirs was nothing more than a huge rectangular box (since filled in to create the Great Lawn); the larger—today called simply the Reservoir—almost cut the site in half.

The clearing of the park began in earnest in April 1857. By the end of the year more than 2,000 men were at work removing squatters' shacks, draining bogs, and hauling away rubble and debris. Supervising this rough-hewn army of laborers was a frail-looking Connecticut Yankee by the name of Frederick Law Olmsted, who soon became intimately acquainted with the site's rolling contours, granite outcroppings, and trickling streams. After the park commissioners announced a design competition with a $2,000 first prize in October 1857, Olmsted was persuaded to enter the competition by a diminutive English-born architect named Calvert Vaux. Collaborating in their spare moments throughout the winter of 1857–1858, the two men were rewarded come spring when the park commissioners chose their design over more than 30 other entries; Olmsted was named the park's architect-in-chief, Vaux his assistant.

The "Greensward Plan," as Olmsted and Vaux called their winning design, is essentially what you see when you enter the park today. Like the other entries in the competition, it had to meet certain requirements put forth by the commissioners, among them a parade ground of 20 to 40 acres; a prospect tower; a winter skating ground; a principal fountain; and at least four east–west crossings, without which the commissioners feared the commercial life of the city eventually would be choked. It was Olmsted and

Vaux's treatment of this last requirement that seems to have secured them the first-place prize. The Greensward Plan called for four transverse crossings—at 65th Street, 79th Street, 85th Street, and 97th Street—to be sunk below ground level, an elegant solution that hid them from view and muffled the clatter of horse-drawn carriages. (These transverses would be the first traffic underpasses in America.)

Much of the ultimate success of the Greensward Plan was due to Olmsted's conviction that every "bit of work done on the Park should be done for the single purpose of making the visitor feel as if he had got far away from the town"—a tall order, indeed, when the long and narrow configuration of the site meant that the "town" was never more than a quarter mile away. To foster this illusion, Olmsted favored screens of tall trees planted along ridge lines and the park's perimeter walls as a means of blocking out "the artificial wall" of the city's buildings.

Illusion was also behind Vaux's design for Belvedere Castle (the prospect tower required by the commissioners). When viewed from a distance, its less-than-full-scale dimensions make it appear farther away than it really is. Olmsted and Vaux employed similar principles in designing the Lake, weaving its contours around existing rock features in order to conceal its actual limits. The 32 miles of footpaths in the park are the product of the same sensibility: Instead of speeding the visitor from one point to the next, they wind and wander, encouraging harried city dwellers to dally and enjoy the park's many pastoral delights.

The money and labor expended to create these ingenious effects was staggering. Twenty thousand pounds of gunpowder were used to dislodge stubborn bedrock. Nearly five million cubic yards of stone and topsoil—enough to cover every one of the park's acres to a depth of four feet—were hauled into or out of the park. More than four million trees, shrubs, and vines (accounting for 334 species, most of them exotics) were planted. Olmsted, in poor health and under constant pressure to keep costs down, submitted his resignation on five different occasions (twice in conjunction with Vaux). And yet by 1873, the year construction was completed and Nature allowed to take over, the two men had managed to translate their vision into stunning reality.

Over the years, successive city administrations—particularly those in which the controversial Robert Moses served as parks commissioner—have tried to accommodate the park's various constituencies while doing their best not to trample the spirit of Olmsted and Vaux's original design. Still, as the more contemplative pursuits of the 19th century have given way to the mania for sports that typifies our own age, the personality of the park has changed. Today, for better or worse, Central Park boasts more playgrounds (22), ballfields (25), tennis courts (30), and man-made skating rinks (2) than Olmsted and Vaux could have imagined. At the same time, much of what was special about the Greensward Plan, though tattered in places and overgrown in others, remains. Beyond the rushing traffic and hordes of people, the dusty ballfields and litter, the park, like an old-fashioned magic show, is a series of illusions and surprises.

The Central Park visitors see today is a far cry from what they would have encountered 15 years ago. Back then, decades of neglect and abuse had left the park a dirty and depressing place, its architectural gems graffiti-covered and in disrepair. The slide was stemmed and then reversed in the late 1970s and early 1980s by a succession of energetic city parks commissioners and the efforts of the **Central Park Conservancy**, a private group committed to the restoration of the park. The Conservancy has raised more than $70 million in its 12 years of existence, and today contributes fully half of the New York City Parks Department's $10 million annual operating budget. This additional funding has enabled the Parks Department to restore and maintain lawns, prune trees, plant shrubs, rebuild bridges, remove graffiti, and offer a full range of children's programs and educational exhibits. More important, the park is once again a place where New Yorkers of all ages and every stripe come to play, promenade, and relax.

SETTING OFF ON A TOUR

It is unfortunate that many first-time visitors to Central Park enter it with trepidation. It's also understandable—on those infrequent occasions when violent crimes are committed in the park the media have a field day. But by taking some commonsense precautions—confining your wanderings to well-worn paths and daylight hours, and keeping an eye on your bicycle, for example—you shouldn't have any problems. If you do, there are call boxes located throughout the park that will put you in immediate contact with the dispatcher for both the Park Enforcement Patrol and the New York City Police Department's Central Park precinct house, located in the center of the park on the 85th Street transverse.

If you get lost, simply look for a lamppost. Affixed to most is a metal tag bearing a number. The first two digits signify the number of the nearest cross street ("66" means you're near 66th Street), while the last two indicate what side of the park you're on: even numbers for the East Side, odd numbers for the West Side.

If you'd prefer to begin your explorations with some guidance, an excellent source of information is the **Central Park Information and Visitor Center** (Tel: 794-6564), located in the center of the park just south of the 65th Street transverse in the building known as the Dairy. In addition to the latest on tours and the many different park programs, the visitors' center offers changing historical exhibits, a seven-minute video on the history of the park, a small selection of park-related books and gifts, and a colorful pocket map that's handsome enough to frame. (Closed Mondays.)

The **Urban Park Rangers** offer a changing schedule of weekend walks to various parts of the park. Departure points and times can be obtained by calling 427-4040, or by dropping by the rangers' headquarters in the North Meadow building, north of the 97th Street transverse in the center of the park.

Another option (from April 28 to the last week in October) is the Central Park Conservancy's new **trolley** tour, a one-and-a-half-hour trip aboard a quaint, red-painted bus that takes in major points of interest in the southern half of the park. The trolley leaves from Grand Army Plaza (Fifth Avenue at 60th Street) every weekday at 10:30 A.M., 1:00 P.M., and 3:00 P.M. The cost is $14 for adults, $12 for seniors, and $7 for children. For information and/or reservations, Tel: 360-2727, or stop by the Conservancy's information kiosk at Fifth Avenue and 60th Street.

THE CHILDREN'S DISTRICT: SOUTH OF 65TH STREET

As work on Central Park progressed during the 1860s the most fashionable addresses in Manhattan were concentrated along lower Fifth Avenue between Washington and Madison squares, two miles to the south. Then, as now, the most popular gateway to the park was the one closest to the burgeoning city, the so-called Scholars' Gate—one of 22 named gates providing access to the park—at Central Park South (59th Street) and Fifth Avenue. Today the hansom cabs lined up in the vicinity of Grand Army Plaza are a reminder of the those bygone days, even if their fares aren't (plan on spending $34, before tip, for a half-hour tour of the park and an additional $10 for every 15 minutes thereafter; longer tours start at $54).

Scholars' Gate funnels park visitors into the Children's District—so named by Olmsted and Vaux.because, as the section of Central Park closest to the growing city, it was easily accessible to parents and their children. Comprising everything south of the 65th Street transverse, it was designed with amusements crowded together so that youngsters could be led easily from one activity to the next. While time and changing attitudes have somewhat tarnished Olmsted and Vaux's original intent, there are any number of surprises and one restored jewel awaiting the visitor in this section.

The Pond and Wildlife Sanctuary

To begin your exploration of the Children's District, follow the path along the southern shore of the **Pond**, once a swamp and today a horseshoe-shaped body of stagnant water that attracts a surprising variety of birdlife, including the occasional black-crowned night heron and great white egret. Circling the Pond's far end, you'll pass the Promontory, a four-acre chunk of land that was left relatively untouched in the original Greensward Plan. Fenced off and declared a bird sanctuary in 1934, and renamed the **Hallet Wildlife Sanctuary** in 1986, it has more or less reverted to its natural state and is a favorite haunt of rabbits, raccoons, muskrats, and woodchucks as well as many species of birds.

Perched on a large outcrop of Manhattan schist just west of the sanctuary is a rustic structure known as the **Cop Cot**, which means "little house on the crest of a hill" in Scots dialect—a description perhaps closer to the spirit than the reality of the restored structure here (the original Cop Cot was razed in the 1930s). The sweeping views the site once provided have long been blocked by the park's dense canopy of trees, and these days the structure seems to be more popular with the homeless than with New Yorkers looking to escape the hustle and bustle of the city.

Heading north from the Cop Cot, continue around the wildlife sanctuary to the arched span of **Gapstow Bridge**, one of the most frequently photographed and painted features in Central Park. Ignoring for the moment Wollman Rink to your left, turn right where the path forks and follow it through Inscope Arch to the zoo.

Central Park Zoo

The delightful Central Park Zoo, one of the great success stories of the park's ongoing restoration, is located directly behind the **Arsenal**, the Neo-Gothic building housing the park's administrative offices at 64th Street and Fifth Avenue. The original Central Park Zoo, little more than a collection of animals in cages, had fallen into such a sorry state by the late 1920s that keepers carried guns in the event the rusted bars gave way. After a complete renovation, the zoo reopened to great fanfare in 1934. But this version, too, became obsolete, a casualty of changing notions about the humane treatment of captive animals. Now administered by the New York Zoological Society, which also administers the Bronx Zoo and the New York Aquarium, the new Central Park Zoo displays its animals in naturalistic settings that re-create the animals' native habitats, from the polar regions (penguins and puffins, harbor seals, and Arctic foxes) to the rain forest (free-flying birds, caimans, exotic plants). In place of lions and tigers moping about cramped cages visitors are treated to sea lions, snow monkeys, and back-stroking polar bears—named Gus, Ida, Lily, and Germany—that actually look healthy and happy in their environments.

Sea-lion feedings, always a festive occasion, are at 11:30 A.M., 2:00 P.M., and 4:00 P.M. The zoo also has a gallery featuring changing exhibits of wildlife art and photography, a wildlife education center, a gift shop, and a fast-food café with an outdoor patio. The zoo is open daily, and at $2.50 for adults and 50¢ for children under 12 (free for children under 3), it's one of the great entertainment values in the city.

Before leaving the zoo area be sure to take a peek at the charming **Delacorte Clock**, located above the arch at the northeast corner of the complex. The musical clock was a gift to the city from the philanthropist George Delacorte, who in the course of his long life (he died in 1991 at the age of 97) also gave New Yorkers the Alice in Wonderland statue at the north end of Conservatory Water and the open-air theater at the southwest corner of the Great Lawn, among other bequests. It's well worth the wait until the quarter-hour to see the revolving clock's bronze animal musicians spinning to the chimes. Just a few steps to the north is the **Children's Zoo**, a conglomeration of colorful cartoony structures (the Noah's Ark is a particular favorite), closed until further notice for renovation.

Wollman Rink

From the zoo it's a short walk back across East Drive to the rock-and-roll ambience of Wollman Rink, one of two man-made skating rinks in the park. Disparaged by many as an unsightly blemish on Olmsted and Vaux's carefully conceived design, the rink nevertheless remains one of the most popular gathering spots in Central Park. And with ice skating surfaces in the city at a premium, Wollman is usually a madhouse during the winter months. (Lasker Rink, less expensive and usually less crowded, is located in the northern end of the park between 106th and 107th streets.)

With the arrival of warm weather Wollman Rink is converted into a roller rink and miniature golf course. A skating session costs $6 for adults and $3 for children under 13; a round of miniature golf costs the same. Ice-skate, roller-skate, and Rollerblade rentals are available on the premises, as are a variety of snacks and soft drinks. The rink is open daily from 10:00 A.M.; Tel: 517-4800 for closing times and upcoming special events.

North to the Dairy and the Carousel

From Wollman Rink a footpath heads north past outcrops of Manhattan's famous bedrock to the octagonal **Chess & Checkers House** (on your left), which occupies the site of the former Kinderberg, an ornate rustic shelter where tired parents could rest while their offspring wore themselves out. The present building was erected on the site in 1952, and a smaller version of the original pergola was added in 1985. There are 24 concrete game boards outside and ten tables inside; playing pieces can be picked up at the Dairy, just up the hill to the right, free of charge (have an up-to-date photo ID handy).

Designed by Vaux and opened to the public in 1870, the **Dairy** was for many years exactly that: a dairy-cum–milk bar where parents could bring their children for a glass of fresh milk. Cows were pastured out front on the sweep of meadow that ran down to the northern loop of the Pond (since paved over for Wollman Rink). Today the Dairy houses the very helpful Central Park Visitor and Information Center (see above).

The ever-popular **Carousel**, due west of the Dairy on the far side of Center Drive (Playmates Arch funnels pedestrian traffic under the roadway), the fourth carousel to grace the site, was brought to the park from Coney Island after the third one was destroyed by fire in 1950. Built by Stein and Goldstein of Brooklyn in 1908, the carousel boasts 58 beautifully carved steeds that race to old-fashioned hurdy-gurdy music from 10:30 A.M. to 5:00 P.M. daily (weather permitting); a ride costs 90¢.

Heckscher Playground to Columbus Circle

From the Carousel follow the footpath south past the 17-acre Heckscher complex, which in Olmsted and Vaux's original design was a grassy meadow set aside for the use of youngsters. As baseball's popularity soared in the last decades of the 19th century, however, the **Ballfield** was besieged by adult males in thrall to the new national pastime. The five permanent ballfields were constructed in 1927, and the playground facilities followed during Robert Moses's tenure as city parks commissioner. The snack stand on the northern edge of the complex replaces an earlier structure by Calvert Vaux (demolished in 1969) and features an elegant tile frieze by William Braham and Brenda Bertin. **Umpire Rock**, the imposing outcrop on the western side of the complex, is the perfect spot from which to survey the nonstop action below.

If you've had enough exploring for the day, you can exit the park at **Columbus Circle**, a major stop on all the West Side subway lines; just follow the footpath heading south over Pinebank Arch—designed, as most of the park's architectural features were, by Calvert Vaux—and then west through Greyshot Arch. The large marble monument at the southwestern entrance to the park honors the 260 sailors and soldiers who were killed in the 1898 explosion of the battleship *Maine*.

MID-PARK: 65TH STREET
TO THE RESERVOIR

From the Ballfield it's a short walk north on West Drive past the 65th Street transverse to **Tavern on the Green**, one of the city's best-known landmarks. (It can also be reached from the Upper West Side at 67th Street.) Designed by Jacob Wrey Mould, and considered to be one of the finest examples of Victorian-style cottage architecture in the country, the structure, minus its more recent additions, originally was the sheepfold for a flock of Southdown sheep that grazed on the nearby green (known as the Sheep Meadow). In one of his first acts as parks commissioner, Robert Moses got rid of the sheep—many of which were malformed as a result of decades of inbreeding—and converted their domicile into a restaurant. Today Tavern on the Green is one of the city's busiest restaurants and one of its glitziest catering facilities. If your budget allows for only one expensive dinner, have it someplace else (see the Dining chapter); if, on the other hand, a drink in a quaintly exotic setting is all you have in mind, the outdoor terrace here is as pretty a spot as New York has to offer.

The Sheep Meadow

The Sheep Meadow is located on the east side of West Drive, which is mobbed on weekends with Lycra-clad Rollerbladers and whizzing dervishes on state-of-the-art racing bikes. Not too many years ago this glorious carpet of grass was a dusty, glass-littered wasteland. Thanks in part to funds provided by the Central Park Conservancy, as well as to new park policies that relocated large-scale extravaganzas to the Great Lawn and ensured the grass was picked clean of litter every night, the Sheep Meadow today is the most popular sunbathing spot in the city. On a typical spring or summer day, with thousands of New Yorkers in various states of dishabille (can they all be unemployed actors?), the scene here falls somewhere between a Frankie-and-Annette beach party and a Grateful Dead concert. Because radios and most sports are banned in this area, however, it's all surprisingly civilized.

The gravel path skirting the northern perimeter of the Sheep Meadow takes you past the park's **bowling greens** and **croquet lawns**, where practitioners of those oh-so-refined pursuits compete against each other with murderous precision. Just beyond the lawns is the **Mineral Springs Pavilion**, where in the park's early days more than two dozen varieties of mineral water were dispensed to a thirsty public from an ornate cast-iron structure; today a brick concession stand offers a less exotic assortment of snacks and refreshments. If you stay on the path for another 50 yards or so, you will end up on a stretch of glass-smooth asphalt that seems to have been airlifted into the park from southern California. Jammed from early afternoon to sundown with roller skaters and Rollerbladers, skateboarders and volleyball players, this is New York's hip-hopping answer to Venice Beach.

The Mall and Concert Ground

A short stroll to the east are the Mall and adjacent Concert Ground, one of the few areas of Central Park where Olmsted and Vaux allowed formality to encroach on their design. A long north–south axis lined by a quadruple row of elm trees (Central Park's magnificent elm trees comprise one of the largest remaining stands in the country), the **Mall** was one of the first elements of the Greensward Plan to be completed and was a hit from the start. As one writer describes it, every afternoon between four and five o'clock the quarter-mile promenade hosted a parade of carriages filled with the city's notables, and in time became "a dominant incubator of courtship and marriage" and "one of the very few public places to which a young man might take a girl unchaperoned." Given the Mall's lively past, the stillness that envelops it these days can leave the visitor with a strange, almost elegiac feeling; on sunny days a soft light filters through the trees, bringing to mind the interior space of a great cathedral, while on rainy days the clip-clop of horses trudging past on Center Drive can give even sober-minded skeptics pause.

Heading north from the Mall, you approach the **Concert Ground**, which has recently emerged from a badly needed renovation with banks of carved wooden benches and pretty flower beds. In the early days of the park, appreciative summertime crowds were entertained twice weekly here from a wrought-iron bandstand designed in the same ornate style as the Mineral Springs Pavilion. Across the way, the **Wisteria Pergola** offered keen-sighted music lovers seats in the shade. During the 1920s, with the bandstand in disrepair, a retired merchant named Elkan Naumberg donated the funds for a Neoclassical band shell, which was soon built on the eastern edge of the grounds. Over the next three decades the Naumberg Bandshell became one of the more recognizable landmarks in the city, as large crowds gathered a couple of times a week to dance under the stars in front of its half-dome. Once again, however, time and changing fashions undermined the best of intentions, and an ongoing debate over whether or not the band shell should be demolished rages on.

From June through August a younger crowd of music lovers and performing-arts aficionados congregate at nearby **Rumsey Playfield** (just east of the Concert Ground and easily accessible from the Upper East Side by way of 72nd Street), where the acclaimed **SummerStage** series presents an eclectic lineup of musical ensembles, dance troupes, and literary notables in an open-air setting that brings out the best in performer and audience alike. Past lineups have featured the likes of Max Roach, Tito Puente, Los Lobos, John Cage, the Neville Brothers, Bali's Topeng Clowns, the Erick Hawkins Dance Company, Ken Kesey, Oscar Hijuelos, and Paule Marshall. Show times vary, but most shows are free; Tel: 360-CPSS.

Bethesda Terrace

The large, formal space known as Bethesda Terrace, due north of the Mall and Concert Ground on the north side of the 72nd Street transverse, fronts on the **Lake** and is the centerpiece of Central Park. It was here that Olmsted and Vaux sited the only piece of sculpture originally commissioned for the park—Emma Stebbins's winged *Angel of the Waters,* which commemorates the opening in 1842 of the Croton Aqueduct, sole source of the city's drinking water for almost a century. Jacob Wrey Mould, the architect of the Sheepfold (now Tavern on the Green), created the overall design of the terrace as well as of the barrel-vaulted arcade that passes under the transverse road. He also contributed the delicate sandstone carvings that grace the balustrades on either side of the double set of stairs leading down to the terrace.

Olmsted, Vaux, and Mould succeeded brilliantly here: For sheer beauty and aesthetic harmony, Bethesda Terrace is a public space without equal in New York City. If you're lucky enough to happen upon the terrace on one of the first warm spring days, you'll see what an exceedingly pleasant place it is. The Lake laps gently against the terrace steps, while rowboats glide by.

As part of a recent renovation of Bethesda Terrace, 24 terra-cotta panels—which were called for in Mould's original design but were canceled as a result of the financial panic of 1873—have been set into niches in the arcade that passes under the road. If park administrators have their way, the panels will soon be joined by refurbished tiles that once decorated the arcade's barrel vault but were removed in 1983 when it was discovered that runoff from the road surface above was corroding them. To protect the valuable tiles against vandalism, park administrators want to erect wrought-iron gates at either end of the arcade that can be closed and locked after sundown; advocates for the homeless, who use the arcade as a refuge from the elements, are opposed to the idea. The conflict between those who want to maintain

Central Park as a pristine retreat and those who feel it belongs to the people, however desperate their straits, is as old as the park itself: In the 1850s, impoverished squatters had to be forcibly evicted from the future park before work on it could begin, and later during the Depression a Hooverville sprouted up in the drained receiving reservoir that eventually became the Great Lawn.

At this point, visitors who wish to continue their exploration of the park have a choice of options: They can head west in the direction of Cherry Hill, Strawberry Fields, and, just beyond the park's perimeter wall, the Dakota apartment building; they can cross Bow Bridge to the far side of the Lake and the free-form maze known as the Ramble; or they can head northeast in the direction of the Boathouse and Conservatory Water, also known as the model-boat pond.

Cherry Hill and Strawberry Fields

Cherry Hill, the leafy knoll due west of the terrace—you can follow a curving path from Bethesda Terrace or take the short road that heads up the hill from the transverse road—is frequently bypassed by visitors in a hurry to see Strawberry Fields and the Dakota. It's a shame, because the concourse and fountain atop the knoll, though neither as large nor as elaborate as the Bethesda complex, are nonetheless elegant examples of Olmsted and Vaux's unfailing good taste. Here, as elsewhere in the park, the architect-in-chief and his trusted assistant seamlessly combined a utilitarian function with naturalistic effects: Although Cherry Hill was used as a carriage turnaround and watering trough during the park's equestrian heyday, it was designed with unobstructed views of the artful arrangement of trees, grass, and water below.

At the bottom of the hill, beyond a narrow finger of the Lake, a scowling Daniel Webster looks down from his perch at the legions of joggers, bicyclists, and pedestrians who make this the busiest intersection in the park. A path on the other side of West Drive leads up a short hill to the gentle landscape of **Strawberry Fields**. Although official tallies aren't kept, this carefully tended tear-shaped patch of greenery seems to have become the most visited spot in Central Park. Its upkeep is underwritten by Yoko Ono in memory of her husband, former Beatle John Lennon, whose adoring fans are frequently seen paying their respects at the *Imagine* mosaic, located just inside the perimeter wall at 72nd Street. Ono and the couple's son still live just across Central Park West in the fine old apartment building known as the Dakota, in front of which a mentally disturbed fan gunned Lennon down in the autumn of 1980.

Bow Bridge to the Ramble

The second route from Bethesda Terrace heads west along the shore of the Lake, which Olmsted and Vaux created by rerouting a creek. The graceful span of **Bow Bridge**, one of the seven cast-iron bridges designed for the park by Calvert Vaux, arches across the narrowest point of the 22½-acre body of water, which here seems to meander out of sight, merely hinting at its farthest extent. The 38-acre **Ramble**, which stretches northward from the Lake to Belvedere Castle, was the first section of Central Park to be completed, and was an instant hit with harried New Yorkers. Today the Ramble is one of the last places on Manhattan island where the sounds of bird song and trickling water prevail; you can almost forget you're standing in the middle of one of the world's most densely populated cities. It is an exhilarating, not to mention peculiar, sensation. The Ramble's miles of footpaths seem to twist and turn at random (thus its name), and there is usually a scenic surprise waiting around the next bend. But because it's a bit more isolated and less trafficked than other areas of the lower park, visitors are encouraged to explore it with a friend. If you get lost, just remember that any path heading downhill eventually ends up back at the Lake.

Loeb Boathouse to Conservatory Water

The third route from Bethesda Terrace swings around the eastern end of the Lake to the **Loeb Boathouse**, a busy meeting place with boat- and bike-rental concessions and a restaurant and snack bar. (Located at 74th Street and East Drive, the boathouse is easily reached by car, and has a parking lot.)

Spending an hour rowboating on the Lake is one of those quintessential New York experiences that most New Yorkers never get around to doing. Of course, when they finally do they say things like, "Why haven't I done this before?" Don't make the same mistake. From early spring to late fall, the boat concession is open daily from 10:00 A.M. (9:00 A.M. on weekends). The price is $10 for the first hour, and $2 for each additional quarter-hour; you'll be asked for a $20 refundable deposit.

After plying the waters, you might want to stop at the **Boathouse Café** for a drink on the deck-style patio overlooking the Lake. There is also a restaurant here specializing in pricey Northern Italian cuisine served on a pretty terrace with views of Bethesda Terrace across the Lake. For those swept away by the romantic setting, the café's very own Venetian gondola is available in the evenings, by reservation only, at $35 per half hour; Tel: 517-CAFE.

Head east from the boathouse through Trefoil Arch to reach **Conservatory Water**, better known to New Yorkers as the model-boat pond, the formal, rink-size pool situated just inside the Fifth Avenue wall at 74th Street. Visitors will discover some of the most beautiful tree specimens in the park on the grounds surrounding the pond as well as a pleasant sit-down café (weather permitting) and a small refreshment stand at its southern end. Starting in late March and running through Thanksgiving, Conservatory Water is also the scene of a model-boat regatta almost every Saturday morning. Most boats have radio-controlled booms and are put through their paces by skippers standing at the edge of the pond with remote-control devices in hand; a handful of the bigger boats are "free sail." These adult toys, which can cost as much as $1,200, are stored in the Kerbs Memorial Boathouse on the eastern edge of the pond; boathouse hours vary, but when it's open the public is welcome to step inside and take a peek. For information about racing schedules or how to become a member of the Central Park Model Yacht Club, you can call the commodore, Madeline Tucker, at 874-0656.

Of the 50-odd pieces of artwork in the park, the most popular is probably José de Creeft's **Alice in Wonderland**, situated on a raised platform at the northern end of Conservatory Water. Donated by the philanthropist George T. Delacorte, the sculpture of Alice usually wears a coat of scrambling children. Almost as popular is George Lober's bronze of a kindly looking **Hans Christian Andersen** and friend (opposite the boathouse on the far side of the pond). On Saturday mornings during the warm-weather months the Andersen statute is also the backdrop for a very popular storytelling hour.

Around the Metropolitan Museum

The vast Metropolitan Museum of Art, with its main entrance on Fifth Avenue, sprawls over 14 acres of the park between 80th and 84th streets (see the Upper East Side and Museums sections for a description of its treasures), and at certain hours can be entered via its new parkside **Petrie Sculpture Court**—an experience that induces a totally different sensation from entering via the grand staircase and Great Hall on the Fifth Avenue side.

Sooner or later most visitors to New York discover that the Met has an ancient Egyptian temple under glass, yet comparatively few people know that the oldest man-made object in the park is situated just a stone's throw from the back of the museum on the west side of East Drive. The 3,500-year-old obelisk, known as **Cleopatra's Needle** (though that famous Egyptian queen had nothing to do with its creation), was first erected in ancient Heliopolis during the reign of Pharaoh Thutmose III and commemorates his deeds as well as those of his predecessors, Ramses II and Osarkon I. The most remarkable thing about the 224-ton granite monument, however, is that it has been moved not once, but twice: by the Romans to Alexandria in 12 B.C., and again by the city of New York (using a giant sling and cannon balls) in 1880. (The monument's twin, a gift of the Egyptian government to Great Britain, now stands in London, on the Thames, near the House of Lords.) Sadly, the deterioration of the hieroglyphics that once covered all four sides of the obelisk is attributable almost solely to New York's humid climate and air pollution.

The Great Lawn Area

If the Mall and Bethesda Terrace are symbols of a Victorian gentility that has disappeared from the public life of the city, the dusty expanse of the **Great Lawn**, due west of the obelisk, is emblematic of the wonderful energy and cultural diversity that have become the hallmarks of New York. Originally the site of a rectangular reservoir, the Great Lawn was established in the early years of the Robert Moses era after a Hooverville sprouted up in the drained reservoir basin. Half a century later it's where New Yorkers of every age and stripe gather to play softball, soccer, flag football, and anything else they can dream up. During the summer months, the Great Lawn is also the site of concerts by the New York Philharmonic and Metropolitan Opera—always festive (and free) occasions attended by tens of thousands of New Yorkers toting blankets, picnic hampers, and coolers. Metropolitan Opera performances usually are spaced over three weeks in

June; Tel: 362-6000. Philharmonic concerts are staged during the month of August after Shakespeare-in-the-Park (see below) has run its course; Tel: 875-5709.

Tucked away off the southwest corner of the Great Lawn, adjacent to the Turtle Pond (also known as Belvedere Lake, another Robert Moses creation), is the **Delacorte Theater**, where **Shakespeare-in-the-Park** has been staged every summer for 33 years. The productions (two a season, each running a month) usually feature a well-known actor from the film or television world. Part of the Shakespeare-in-the-Park experience is the ritual that ensures the equitable distribution of tickets to each performance. Tickets (which are free) are distributed at 6:15 the evening of the performance, but lines begin to form several hours before that. Patrons in line are given numbered slips and may request a second numbered slip for a companion not present. Only patrons actually present at 6:15 will receive a ticket in exchange for a numbered slip. For further information, visit the box office at the theater or call 861-PAPP. The theater is easily reached by way of the West 81st Street entrance to the park.

If you make it this far, be sure to reward yourself by climbing the stairs to the Gothic Revival–style **Belvedere Castle**. On the way you'll pass the **Shakespeare Garden**, featuring plants and flowers mentioned in the Bard's plays and, after decades of neglect, now entrusted to a professional gardening staff. The castle, another Calvert Vaux creation, sits atop Vista Rock, the second-highest point in the park. (Summit Rock, the highest point, is just inside the perimeter wall at 83rd Street and Central Park West.) Views from the castle's loggia give the visitor a sense of just how avidly the sprawling metropolis embraces the park. The castle is also home to the **Central Park Learning Center**, which is operated by the Central Park Conservancy and has the same hours as the Dairy; Tel: 772-0210 for information on its learning-center and workshop programs.

THE UPPER PARK: THE RESERVOIR TO 110TH STREET

The raised bed of the **Reservoir**, located due north of the Great Lawn and 85th Street transverse, occupies almost one-eighth of the park's 843 acres and is all but impossible to miss. For years now the mile-and-a-half cinder path skirting the Reservoir's shoreline has been famous in road-running circles as the busiest jogging track in the world. From sunrise to sunset 365 days a year, legions of New Yorkers, including Dustin Hoffman in the film *Marathon Man,* lap the track. Lately, however, the intriguing possibility that the Reservoir might become something more than just a body of water to run around has been raised due to the impending completion of New York City's third water tunnel. When the tunnel is finished, the Reservoir will no longer be needed as a water-holding body, at which point the Bureau of Water Supply will turn it over to the Parks Department. The Parks Department will then have to decide whether to leave it as is or convert it into something else—say a boating lake or (dare we dream?) a public swimming hole complete with sandy beach. Only time will tell, but whatever the outcome New Yorkers are sure to be arguing about it over cocktails and in movie lines for years to come.

The 26 clay **tennis courts** and four all-weather courts between the Reservoir and the 97th Street transverse are also among the busiest in the world. They are open (and crowded) seven days a week, 7:00 A.M. to 8:00 P.M. (or dusk, whichever comes first), from April 1 to the onset of bad weather (usually November). Anyone can pick up a same-day pass ($5), good for one hour of play, at the Tennis House, although you'll want to call ahead to check on court availability before you change into your sneakers; Tel: 280-0205. Season passes are available at the Arsenal (see above) for $50. Rental lockers, equipment, and snacks and refreshments are also available on the premises.

The northern third of the park, stretching from the 97th Street transverse to 110th Street, is both wilder and less heavily trafficked than its other sections, facts that discourage most visitors from exploring it further. This is understandable perhaps, but a shame nonetheless. There are many features of interest here, including the gentle landscape surrounding the **Pool,** just inside the perimeter wall at West 101st Street, and the adjacent **Cascade,** whose gurgling flow of water was recently restored with funds provided by the Central Park Conservancy.

Having reversed the deterioration in much of the lower park, the Conservancy is now concentrating its efforts on the upper park. As of this writing **Lasker Rink,** located in the center of the park at 106th Street, and the 11-acre body of water known as the **Meer,** which is tucked into the park's far northeastern corner between 106th and 110th streets, are also undergoing extensive face-lifts.

In addition to a more natural shoreline and new wetland plantings, the Meer will soon be graced by the **Charles A. Dana Discovery Center**, the first new structure to rise in the park since the Children's Zoo opened in 1960. Designed by the firm of Buttrick, White & Burtis in a Neo-Victorian style reminiscent of the Dairy, the center will house rotating natural-history exhibits downstairs and laboratories and classrooms upstairs. It may be joined, in a few years, by a separate restaurant/catering facility—part of a master plan aimed at generating increased traffic to and interest in this neglected portion of the park.

If the restoration of the beautiful **Conservatory Garden** (again spearheaded by the Conservancy) is any indication of what to expect, New Yorkers and visitors alike have much to look forward to. Located just inside the wrought-iron Vanderbilt Gate at 105th Street and Fifth Avenue, Central Park's only formal gardens began life as one of two nurseries created by Olmsted and Ignaz Anton Pilat, his head gardener, for the propagation of trees and shrubs that were later transplanted to various areas of the park. A complex of huge glass greenhouses replaced the original nurseries in 1899 and became one of the more popular attractions in the park over the next three decades. However, rising maintenance costs and the master-builder mentality of Robert Moses doomed the structures in 1934. The present gardens were dedicated in 1937 and restored with the aid of outside funds from 1982 to 1984.

Today, whether splashed with the vivid colors of spring tulips or cloaked in the brilliant foliage of autumn, the arbors and walkways are a favorite backdrop for concerts, weddings, and a variety of special events. The gardens are open to the public daily from 8:00 A.M. to dusk. Free tours and concerts are offered in the summer months; information regarding them is posted inside the front gate.

SERVICES AND FACILITIES

Tours and Information
Central Park Conservancy Trolley, Tel: 360-2727
Central Park Learning Center, Tel: 772-0210
Central Park Information and Visitor Center, Tel: 794-6564
Urban Park Rangers, Tel: 427-4040

Recreation
Boathouse Café gondola reservations, Tel: 517-CAFE
Carousel, Tel: 879-0244

Central Park Model Yacht Club, Tel: 874-0656
Central Park Zoo, Tel: 439-6500
Lasker Pool and Rink, Tel: 722-9781
Loeb Boathouse, Tel: 517-4723
Loeb Boathouse bike rentals, Tel: 861-4137
Tennis courts, Tel: 280-0205
Wollman Rink, Tel: 517-4800

Performing Arts
Metropolitan Opera, Tel: 362-6000
New York Philharmonic, Tel: 875-5709
Shakespeare-in-the-Park, Tel: 861-PAPP
SummerStage, Tel: 360-CPSS

Refreshments
The popular restaurant Tavern on the Green occupies a converted sheepfold just inside the park at West 67th Street. The Boathouse Café is on the lake at 74th Street and East Drive. Other refreshment concessions are located at the Mineral Springs Pavilion, just north of the Sheep Meadow, and near Conservatory Water, just inside the Fifth Avenue wall at 74th Street.

Restrooms
Heckscher Puppet House, 62nd Street
Mineral Springs Pavilion, 69th Street (seasonal)
Bethesda Terrace, 72nd Street (seasonal)
Loeb Boathouse, 74th Street (seasonal)
Delacorte Theater, 80th Street
Conservatory Garden, 103rd–106th streets

Books
Eugene Kinkead's *Central Park: The Birth, Decline and Renewal of a National Treasure,* a wonderful paean to an extraordinary place, is probably the single best book on Central Park. Also good is *The Central Park Book,* by Elizabeth Barlow Rogers, a former parks commissioner and founding director of the Central Park Task Force (the forerunner of the Central Park Conservancy).

THE UPPER EAST SIDE

By Patricia Lynden

Patricia Lynden writes for a wide variety of publications. She is a senior editor of Longevity *magazine.*

This is the fabled silk-stocking district of New York. Even some hardened New Yorkers from other neighborhoods speak of the Upper East Side in reverential tones, as if every denizen were, in the words of F. Scott Fitzgerald, "different from you and me." Yes, indeed, the neighborhood is rich, one of the wealthiest in the world. Yes, it is home to some of the most famous people in the world. And yes, its streets are full of limousines, white-gloved doormen, uniformed nannies, and women in haute couture. But this is New York City, and the Upper East Side (roughly the area east of Fifth Avenue and Central Park from 60th to 96th streets) is as full of contrast and diversity as the city's other neighborhoods—even as it retains its manicured, stuffy veneer.

Some of Manhattan's loveliest residential areas are here. But as you wander along quiet, tree-shaded blocks past beautifully kept single-family town houses you'll also notice less-glitzy buildings that are home to the many solidly middle-class—well, upper-middle-class—New Yorkers who live on the Upper East Side because parts of it are more affordable than many people think. Also down to earth is the Irish bar that seems to be right around every corner—one of those vestiges of a bygone era before designer water was invented and whiskey was thought to be, if not good for you, at least not bad for you—where just about everyone in the neighborhood goes to drink. That's New York.

To the celebrities who live up here, the Upper East Side is just "the neighborhood," and many of these people can be spotted on their daily rounds. New Yorkers, of course, consider it uncool to gape or ask for autographs, although sometimes their jaded façades fall apart when they find themselves face to face with a celebrity idol. Not long ago, an Upper East Side woman stopped at a neighborhood ice-cream parlor for a cone. As she was paying she noticed actor Paul Newman standing next to her.

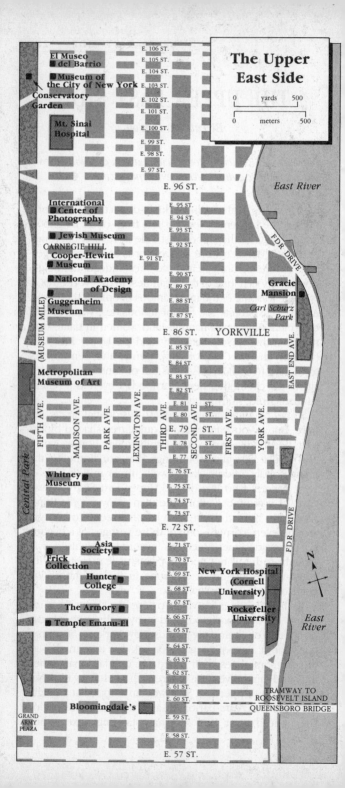

Flustered, she accepted her change, put it into her handbag, and turned to leave. Suddenly Newman spoke to her: "Ma'am," he said, "You just put your ice-cream cone into your purse."

The mayor lives here, too, way over by the East River in a handsome late-18th-century house that now provides a glimpse of a peaceful, pastoral New York that is for the most part long gone. The neighborhood just south of the mayoral mansion, Yorkville, is an old German enclave with a few *wurst* shops still remaining. The opposite side of the district is anchored by Museum Mile—a stretch of Fifth Avenue with no fewer than nine important museums. In between runs Madison Avenue, an impacted concentration of the world's most fashionable couture houses and pedigreed antiques and antiquities shops and art galleries. Other streets offer glimpses of unfathomable wealth, reassurances of middle-class solidity, and plenty of everyday neighborhood life to put it all in perspective.

MAJOR INTEREST

Fifth Avenue
Clubs and mansions
Temple Emanu-El
Frick Collection
East 70th Street residential architecture

Museum Mile
Metropolitan Museum of Art
Guggenheim Museum
Cooper-Hewitt Museum
Jewish Museum
International Center of Photography
Museum of the City of New York
Museo del Barrio

Carnegie Hill
Millionaires' Row mansions and town houses
View down Park Avenue

Yorkville
Old German neighborhood
Henderson Place Historic District
Gracie Mansion
Carl Schurz Park
Church of the Holy Trinity

Madison Avenue
Antiques shops, boutiques, and art galleries
Whitney Museum of American Art
Asia Society

As you move north of Midtown on the East Side, you'll notice that the streets are less crowded and both the air and the energy level thin out—especially on summer weekends, when the entire population of the Upper East Side seems to flee the city for seaside or country retreats.

You might get your last gasp of Midtown's frenzy at **Bloomingdale's** (Lexington Avenue at 59th Street). This is one of the world's great department stores, offering goods at prices ranging from bargain to the positively stellar. Bloomingdale's is *always* busy, so don't go when you're feeling pressed for time.

After Bloomingdale's, you might want to pay a visit to **Serendipity**, an eccentric restaurant at 225 East 60th Street (between Third and Second avenues) that draws adults and children in equal numbers. You can eat real food here—foot-long hot dogs and tea-room fare—but the big draw is "frozen hot chocolate," an extraordinarily delicious concoction that is just that, served in a huge bowl.

Fifth Avenue

A stroll up Fifth Avenue from **Grand Army Plaza** at the 59th Street end of Central Park is a good way to begin your exploration of the Upper East Side. While every one of the avenues that form the north–south part of the district's grid has its own distinct character, somehow Fifth Avenue feels more like the Upper East Side than the others. Perhaps it's because it was built in an era when the rich wanted everyone to know they were rich. The limestone architecture of the apartment houses and few remaining mansions along the avenue is extravagantly ornate. The quiet, well-dressed pedestrian traffic and the old trees and inlaid stone sidewalks (the stones brought over as ballast in ships arriving from Europe) on the Central Park side of the avenue provide foils for the important-looking architecture lining the east side. The park saves Fifth Avenue from the stolid, somewhat forbidding dullness of Park Avenue, the other frankly rich residential avenue of the Upper East Side.

Fifth Avenue in the 60s is the land of elegant private clubs. Nonmembers can't get past the lobbies of these establishments, but the exteriors are architecturally distinguished, and they're interesting for the bit of history they reveal. The **Metropolitan Club**, just a few steps off Fifth Avenue at 1 East 60th Street, was built in 1893 by the great architect Stanford White and financed by J. P. Morgan, then a pushy parvenu, after he was denied entrance into the elite Union Club (several blocks northeast, at Park Avenue and 69th Street). White also designed the **Harmonie Club**, on the same block (4 East 60th Street), in 1906 for the wealthy German-Jewish community whose members were barred from both clubs. The **Knickerbocker Club**, on Fifth Avenue at 62nd Street, is an "old boys'" club founded in the early part of the century for gentlemen who wanted a place where they could get away from their families, smoke cigars, snore into their newspapers, and talk business over dinner. The very grand, cold-looking building at 65th Street and Fifth Avenue is **Temple Emanu-El**, the world's largest Reform synagogue—and the most fashionable temple in town.

70TH STREET

The beautifully tended mansion surrounded by gardens at Fifth Avenue and 70th Street was once the home of Henry Clay Frick, the robber baron who headed Carnegie Steel Corporation. It now houses the **Frick Collection**: European paintings, antiques, and bibelots displayed pretty much the way they were when the industrialist and his family lived here. The house, built in 1914, and the collection are wonderful, and the lovely courtyard is as peaceful a place as you'll find anywhere in the city.

Take a detour off Fifth Avenue here to stroll east along 70th Street all the way over to Lexington Avenue. Many New Yorkers consider this the most beautiful stretch of residential blocks in Manhattan, particularly the block between Park and Lexington avenues. There you'll find one of the most charming architectural mixes of brownstones and mansions on a beautifully kept tree-lined street that feels intimate and a world removed from the noisy avenues at either end.

MUSEUM MILE

Return to Fifth Avenue and continue north until you arrive at 82nd Street and the **Metropolitan Museum of Art**, set on the edge of Central Park and the first of nine museums on the stretch of Fifth Avenue (from here north to 104th Street) known as Museum Mile. The accommodating staff at the Met's circular desk just inside the main entrance will provide the maps and information you need to get a grasp of this huge institution. While the Egyptian and European galleries are mandatory viewing, even a brief tour should include at least some of the museum's lesser known, but no less extraordinary, collections. Among them: the stunning Englehardt Court of American sculpture; the Iris B. and Gerald Cantor Roof Garden, open May to November, for more sculpture and terrific views of Central Park; and the Japanese galleries, especially the late Isamu Noguchi's glorious *Fountain*. The clamorous restaurant/bar at the museum's south end, off the Great Hall, is best visited in the relative quiet between meals. The Met's shop, with reproductions of pieces in the collections, jewelry, books, note cards, and other items, is probably the best museum shop in the world. The very English **Stanhope Hotel**, just across Fifth Avenue, serves an excellent high tea (no tea bags here). If the weather is fair, sit outside; the theater of fashion on the street is marvelous.

The eight other museums of Museum Mile are spread out along the east side of Fifth Avenue to the north. The **Yivo Institute for Jewish Research** (1048 Fifth Avenue, at 86th Street) is housed in one of the avenue's most exquisite mansions, with Ionic pilasters, balustrades, rosettes, and bull's-eye windows. The museum is devoted to the history of Eastern European Jews. Frank Lloyd Wright's circular **Solomon R. Guggenheim Museum** (number 1071, between 88th and 89th streets) is one of the city's most distinctive buildings, newly renovated. A new annex has been added, and some parts of the original building that had been used for offices have been converted to exhibition space—most notably a small rotunda that makes a charming setting for small paintings and sculpture. The Guggenheim's collection focuses on 20th-century European and American art.

A block north, between 89th and 90th streets, is the **National Academy of Design** (number 1083), a respected museum devoted to the conservative, academic style in American painting and sculpture. At 90th Street stands the Episcopal **Church of the Heavenly Rest**, a Gothic-style church with a tiny side chapel.

This part of the Upper East Side has been called Carnegie Hill since 1901 (see below for more on this neighborhood), when steel magnate Andrew Carnegie built a 64-room mansion at the corner of Fifth Avenue and 91st

Street. It is now the **Cooper-Hewitt Museum**, the Smithsonian Institution's museum of design. Exhibits from the museum's own excellent collection of decorative arts, as well as travelling exhibitions, change regularly. The museum's enormous, ornate rooms are fascinating for their glimpse into the way America's robber barons lived, and they do make wonderful galleries.

Directly across the street is the Convent of the Sacred Heart (1 East 91st), a neo-Italian palazzo, now the most social of Manhattan's Catholic girls' schools. (This area contains a number of the city's private schools, most on the side streets.) Just up Fifth Avenue is the **Jewish Museum** (number 1109, at 92nd Street), which has a permanent collection of Judaica and runs temporary exhibits. The museum's French Renaissance–style mansion reopened in spring 1993 after an extensive renovation and expansion. In addition to more space, the museum now has a chic café serving delicious, light fare.

The **International Center of Photography** (number 1130, between 94th and 95th streets) is a zippy museum that shows constantly changing exhibitions of portrait and "art" photography as well as photojournalism. If you've got children with you, the **Museum of the City of New York** (number 1130, between 103rd and 104th streets) is a pleasantly musty old place that is very hospitable to them. It houses art, costumes, dolls, and other relics from old New York. A big draw for kids is the room containing a mock-up of the old Dutch fort at the tip of Manhattan. The museum sponsors marvelous Sunday walking tours of different parts of the city; Tel: 534-1672.

El Museo del Barrio (number 1230, between 104th and 105th streets) has made a point of not establishing ties with the other museums on the "mile." Rather, it looks north to Spanish Harlem and has tried to be a real community museum for Manhattan's Latin population. It has an excellent collection of religious artifacts, and displays artwork of Puerto Rican and Latin American artists. The Three Kings Day festival, on January 6, when the Latino community celebrates Christmas, recreates the journey of the Magi with local school children and live camels and donkeys. It's wonderful. (But you'll have to wait till 1994 to see it; the museum is closed for renovation until early that year.)

Right across Fifth Avenue from the Museum of the City of New York is a relatively untrod oasis in Central Park, the **Conservatory Garden**. This lovely public garden has been brought back from ruin in the last few years, and is a fine place to rest, wander, and unwind.

Carnegie Hill

Carnegie Hill stretches from about 86th to 96th Street, from Fifth to Park Avenue, but sometimes reaches over as far as Lexington and Third avenues, as indicated by some shop and building names. Until Andrew Carnegie built his mansion here in 1901, the socially acceptable place to live was south of 59th Street. His bold step set off a trend, and before long several mansions sprang up along a section of upper Fifth Avenue, facing Central Park. The Astors, the Vanderbilts, and other wealthy families began migrating northward, and upper Fifth Avenue soon became known as **Millionaires' Row**. The growth of Madison Avenue and the side streets between Madison and Fifth followed. Today, Carnegie Hill continues to be one of the most quietly rich neighborhoods in the world.

The best way to get a feel for the area is to wander aimlessly. Most of the mansions and lavish town houses (many now small museums or consulates) line Fifth Avenue or are tucked away on side streets, especially in the lower 90s between Fifth and Madison avenues. Two 19th-century wood-frame, clapboard houses at 120 and 122 East 92nd Street (between Lexington and Park avenues) are a complete surprise amid all the surrounding brick and concrete.

PARK AVENUE

Over on Park Avenue at 92nd Street, there's a Louise Nevelson sculpture called *Night Presence,* a 22-foot-high steel work donated to the city by the artist in 1972. A block north is the headquarters of the Synod of Bishops of the Russian Orthodox Church Outside of Russia, which in the late 1920s was the home of banker George F. Baker, who had a private railroad car that stopped directly beneath the building (the railway tracks for Grand Central Terminal run under Park Avenue here). It's not open to the public, but you can look in at a garden courtyard that leads to a ballroom that Baker added to the original 1918 structure. The **92nd Street Y**, a block east of Park Avenue at Lexington Avenue, is one of New York's great cultural institutions, with an excellent and diverse program of dance and music performances, readings, and lectures. Step inside for a schedule.

From Carnegie Hill you can look down Park Avenue to what used to be the New York Central Building (now the Helmsley Building), between 45th and 46th streets, with the Pan Am Building looming over it. In contrast to the present-day vista, before the turn of the 20th century Park Avenue was not a coveted address. The railroads ran aboveground and were lined with rather humble dwellings and unattractive factories. Beginning in 1872 the tracks were moved below street level as far north as 56th Street. It was not until after the completion of Grand Central Terminal in 1913, however, that the tracks were hidden below the street as far north as 96th Street. By the 1920s the avenue had become very desirable real estate, and that roaring era saw one luxury residential building after another go up. But if the decade was madcap, these folks were the stuffy bores you never read about in history books. Just look at this street: It has none of the sidewalk life you see in the rest of the city. Park Avenue's residents have secured for themselves the distinction of getting all public buses and commercial trucks banned from their thoroughfare. Although the philanthropist Mary Lasker paid to have flowers planted down the middle of the street and replanted seasonally, somehow the display just doesn't help. Architecturally, and from the standpoint of city life, Park Avenue is stodgy, dignified, and boring, boring, boring.

So, as you cross Park Avenue, look to the left and look to the right so you can say you've seen it, and keep moving east, in the direction of Yorkville.

Yorkville

Yorkville, historically an old middle-class German neighborhood, begins abruptly at Lexington Avenue, once the demarcation line between the rich East Side (to the west) and the poor East Side (to the east). The main shopping area of Yorkville is today a tacky hodge-podge of shops of many nationalities on and around 86th Street. The region east of "Lex," as locals call Lexington Avenue, has come up economically, if not architecturally, in the last 20 years. Developers have had a field day here, throwing up huge numbers of tall, characterless apartment buildings for young singles and professionals. The area's remaining German shops and restaurants are mostly clustered on the south side of 86th Street between Third and Second avenues. **Kleine Konditorei**, at number 234, serves traditional German fare and has a bakery in front. The **Ideal** restaurant, at number 238, serves the world's second-best potato pancakes. (They rank only "second best" because a German regular and connoisseur has pronounced them the finest he's ever had outside of his grandmother's Stuttgart kitchen.) The extremely reasonably priced restaurant is a long, narrow, very clean but run-down place that caters to working-class neighborhood old-timers. **Elk Candy**, number 240, specializes in marzipan, and is worth a visit if only to meet Squeaky, the shop's ancient cat. **Schaller & Weber**, at 1654 Second Avenue, just south of 86th Street, is New York's most famous German butcher shop, with a true New York sense of salesmanship—they will mail sausages anywhere in the world.

To the east on 86th Street (past York Avenue on the north side of the street) is **Henderson Place Historic District**, a charming group of 24 (once 32, until a developer got them) small, Queen Anne–style houses built in 1882 for people of moderate means. Although they're only 16 feet wide and 40 feet deep, these houses are no longer for people of such means: They sell for around $900,000 apiece (although given their charm and location, and the fact that smaller apartments on Park Avenue sell for $1 million or many times that, by New York City standards they're a good deal).

GRACIE MANSION AREA

At East End Avenue (the next block to the east), look across the street and just north. That big, gracious, wooden house—the one with the police cars out front— is **Gracie Mansion**, where the mayor lives. Built in 1799 by Archibald Gracie, a wealthy merchant, when this part of Manhattan was a rural area far north of the city, it is one of the few and best-preserved houses of the Federal period in Manhattan. The Gracies were a social couple and entertained some of the most distinguished people of their day, among them Alexander Hamilton, Washington Irving, Louis Philippe (who became king of France), John Quincy Adams, James Fenimore Cooper, and the marquis de Lafayette. The city bought the house in 1887, restored it, and filled it with 19th-century furnishings. It became the mayor's official residence in 1942 during the administration of Fiorello La Guardia. You can visit it on Wednesdays, but you must have a reservation; Tel: 570-4751.

Gracie Mansion is surrounded by **Carl Schurz Park**, a

lovely stretch of green along the East River, affording spectacular views of the Triborough Bridge and of the shipping traffic that goes along this deep-water channel. It's a great place to relax.

The nearly 100-year-old **Church of the Holy Trinity**, around the corner on 88th Street between First and Second avenues, may well be the most beautiful church in New York, a French Gothic–style extravaganza with gargoyles, flying buttresses, and arches. It is also much admired by music-loving New Yorkers for its outstanding winter classical music concerts; Tel: 289-4100 for schedules of musical events.

Madison Avenue

For anyone who likes to shop, Madison Avenue from 60th to 96th Street may well be the most exciting stretch of pavement in the world. You won't find a better place to window shop (be sure to look up, because many fine shops and art galleries occupy upper floors). Ralph Lauren, St. Laurent, Armani, and Kenzo (you get the picture) all have shops on this avenue, as do many fine antiques and antiquities dealers (see the Shopping chapter for details). World-famous art and antiques auction houses to the east of Madison deal in everything from foreign castles to antique watches to priceless paintings to the clothes and jewels of deceased movie stars. The fine-arts auctioneer **Christie's** is at 502 Park Avenue (at 59th Street); Tel: 546-1000 for information. Sotheby Parke Bernet, known as **Sotheby's**, the American branch of the world's oldest firm of arts auctioneers, is up toward Yorkville, at 1334 York Avenue (at 72nd Street); Tel: 606-7000. This is the auction house that sold most of Andy Warhol's estate, and van Gogh's *Irises* for $53.9 million.

The **Whitney Museum of American Art**, housed in a modern concrete building on Madison Avenue between 75th and 76th streets, exhibits American art of this century. Alexander Calder's mobile group *Circus,* permanently installed just inside the entrance, may well be the most popular piece of art in New York. East of Madison, at Park Avenue and 70th Street, is the **Asia Society** (725 Park Avenue), founded under the guidance of John D. Rockefeller III, who wanted to increase American awareness of Asian culture. The society goes a good way toward achieving this goal with its fine collection of Asian ceramics and sculpture, an ambitious film and lecture program, and a good bookstore. Back on Madison Avenue is the ▶ **Carlyle Hotel** (35 East 76th Street), a favorite retreat of presidents and dignitaries. Crooner Bobby Short still holds court in the evenings—as he has for 25 years.

By the time Madison Avenue reaches the 90s (you're now back in Carnegie Hill) its stores become quirkier and more neighborly. Just for an example: The **Corner Bookstore**, at 93rd Street, holds an annual party for the neighborhood dogs. **Sarabeth's Kitchen**, at 92nd Street, is famous for the proprietress's (there really is a Sarabeth) jams and marmalade, and baked goods on sale in the front. Her preserves, which come gift wrapped, make nice, authentic New York souvenirs to take home. On these blocks, too, is the city's strip of kids' shops where dresses for two-year-olds cost $300 and more. As we said, Carnegie Hill is very rich indeed.

BROOKLYN

By Randall Short

Randall Short is a columnist for the New York Observer. *He reports regularly on literature and the arts for* The New York Times, New York Newsday, *and* Mirabella.

When the sun is shining and the wind is right," says a character in Richard Condon's *Prizzi's Honor,* "there ain't no place like Brooklyn!" If Manhattan is flash and glitter, Brooklyn (perhaps recalling its origins as Dutch-colonized farmland in the 1600s) is the gentler side of urban living in New York. Manhattanites used to disdainfully regard Brooklyn as little more than a working-class bedroom community across the river: The very mention of the borough's name by native sons like Phil Silvers and Danny Kaye was enough to guarantee a laugh in Hollywood films of the 1940s. In recent years, however, that attitude has given way to a vigorous sense of local pride perceptible even to the casual visitor. The borough owes much of its character to close-knit neighborhoods, a diverse ethnic mix—West Indians, Hasidic Jews, Norwegians, Russians, and Middle

Easterners barely begin to exhaust the list—and a superbly preserved heritage of 19th-century architecture.

Older Brooklynites still joke about a time when "fine dining" meant one thing: chow mein and egg rolls in one of the borough's numerous Chinese restaurants. In the 1930s and 1940s these were a Canarsie kid's usual introduction to foods more exotic than bagels or corned beef. At that time the borough was home to working-class Irish, Italian, and Jewish families, whose distinctive accents and don't-try-to-bullshit-me attitudes still characterize the Brooklynite. Now, however, Brooklyn offers variety in dining comparable to that in Manhattan—often at significantly lower prices—and its row houses are being snatched up by Manhattanites for a relative song, compared to prices across the East River.

Brooklyn lies to the east and south of Manhattan, connected to it by three bridges (the Brooklyn, Williamsburg, and Manhattan), one car tunnel (the Brooklyn-Battery), and a network of subways. Prior to its annexation into New York City in 1898 ("the Big Mistake," as Brooklyn-born journalist Pete Hamill called it), the borough's 78.5 square miles formed a separate city composed of six principal towns and numerous small independent villages. Much of the area still has a strong regional feel; inhabitants consider themselves Bay Ridgers or Williamsburgers or Park Slopers first, Brooklynites second, and the neighborhoods bear strong witness to several successive waves of immigrant history.

The following suggestions represent a largely arbitrary, and admittedly nonexhaustive, plan for a first-time visitor to Brooklyn whose aim is to get a representative taste of the borough. "Only the dead know Brooklyn," wrote Thomas Wolfe—a reference not to bad gangster jokes but to the fact that even an entire lifetime seemed too short to sample more than a little of its sheer, dizzying diversity. But here we restrict ourselves to major highlights—no disrespect implied or intended to Bay Ridge, Sheepshead Bay, Sunset Park or their fellows, any one of which is worth a day trip of its own.

MAJOR INTEREST

Brooklyn Bridge
Brooklyn Heights' Promenade view of Manhattan
    skyline and Brownstone Belt
Atlantic Avenue's Middle Eastern community

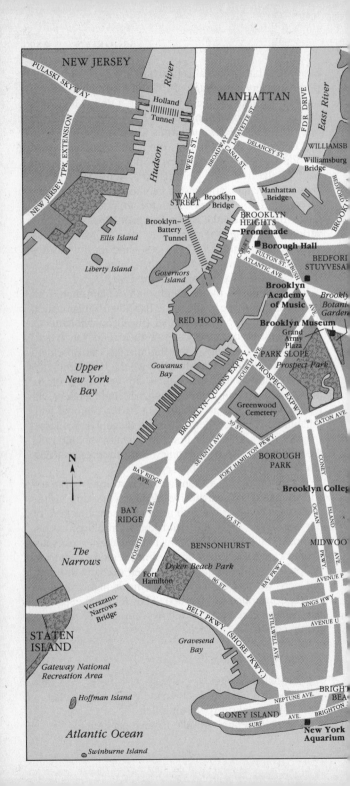

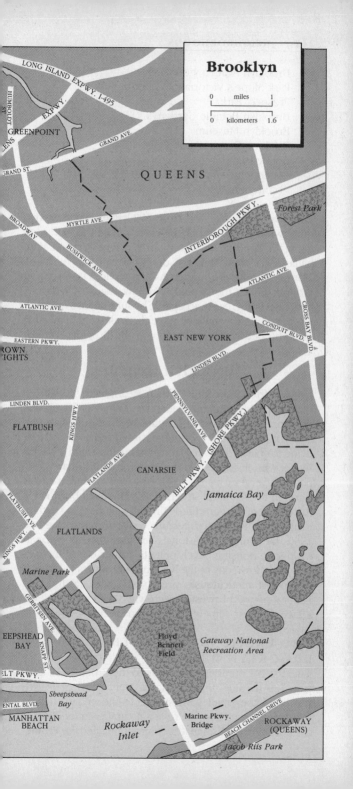

Brooklyn Academy of Music
Park Slope's Victorian architecture
Prospect Park
Brooklyn Botanic Garden
Brooklyn Museum
Brighton Beach's Little Odessa
Coney Island
Greenpoint's old European immigrant
    communities

Cabdrivers will take you from Manhattan into Brooklyn quite willingly, but it may be more difficult to hail a cab going the opposite direction—drivers tend to prefer Manhattan's crowded Midtown district for pickup business. However, there are numerous car services to ferry you around (check the Brooklyn Yellow Pages). Of course, Brooklyn is also easily accessible by subway. Or—an alternative solution—you can make the trek from Manhattan over the pedestrian walkway atop the Brooklyn Bridge.

Brooklyn Heights

In the early 19th century, when steam-ferry service between Brooklyn and Manhattan was begun, the riverbank neighborhood **Brooklyn Heights** became America's first suburb. Then as now it was an oasis of genteel *rus in urbe* living for harried lower Manhattan businessmen. Thomas Wolfe, who lived here in the 1930s, is said to have composed several of his books during long midnight strolls through its tree-lined streets. Today the neighborhood is the center of the gentrified "Brownstone Belt," a swath of magnificent urban architecture rediscovered in the late 1950s by young professionals resisting the call of Levittown-style housing developments farther out of the city.

A walk down any of the surrounding streets will reveal dozens of meticulously preserved Greek Revival and Federal-period brownstones crowned with gargoyles, oriel windows, and finely detailed ornament.

THE PROMENADE AND THE BROOKLYN BRIDGE

Take the IRT number 2 or 3 train to the Brooklyn Heights stop (20 minutes from Midtown Manhattan), walk two blocks to the small park square at the end of nearby Montague Street, and you're at a natural point of entry to the borough, the Esplanade, commonly called the **Prome-**

nade, a pleasant bench- and tree-lined walkway built by legendary city commissioner Robert Moses. (You may remember Judy Holliday waltzing on its edge with Dean Martin to "Just in Time" in *Bells Are Ringing*.) Fronting the East River and lower Manhattan, it offers an unparalleled view of the harbor, the Financial District, and the borough's best-known symbol, the **Brooklyn Bridge**, the 1883 dedication of which opened Brooklyn to large-scale industrial and residential development. Built by the immigrant German father-and-son team of John and Washington Roebling, pioneers in the engineering and construction of modern suspension bridges, it was at the time the largest such structure in the world. If you find yourself interested in a closer look at the bridge, a walk to the end of the Promenade and down a sharply sloping hill will bring you to its foundations. Their high, vaulted stone chambers were restored for the bridge's centennial in 1983 and now serve as an art gallery–performance space.

The nearby **River Café** (1 Water Street; reservations essential, Tel: 718-722-5200), a favored after-work hangout for the Wall Street set, offers pleasantly elegant (and expensive) waterside dining from a French-style menu featuring American classics. The view of the Wall Street area across the East River is unforgettable, especially at night.

WALKING THROUGH BROOKLYN HEIGHTS

A convenient route through the Heights is to start south on Hicks Street near the northern end of the Promenade and make side excursions, as the whim takes you, on Middagh, Pierrepont, Montague, Henry, Strawberry, Joralemon, and Warren streets.

If, on the other hand, you should find your interest in Brooklyn taking a more methodical turn, tour the **Brooklyn Historical Society** (128 Pierrepont Street). The society spent several years refurbishing its handsome, mansionlike premises and adding a new museum gallery and has recently reopened its doors to the public. Besides acting as custodian for a large collection of papers and artifacts relating to the borough's history, it offers a wide variety of tours, educational programs, and lectures. Many of these are held in a lecture hall where Mark Twain and Rudyard Kipling, among others, entertained 19th-century audiences with tales of their travels abroad.

In the 1800s Brooklyn acquired the nickname "Borough of Churches" for the number and distinction (both architectural and clerical) of its ecclesiastical institutions. Several of the most prominent still stand in central Brooklyn Heights, just around the corner from the historical society. **St. Ann's and the Holy Trinity**, an Episcopal parish church at Clinton and Montague streets possessing the first stained-glass windows made in the United States, hosts a popular arts series (Tel: 718-834-8794) emphasizing Off Off Broadway–type (*"waaay* off Broadway," as the locals like to put it) drama, music, and performance art. From the pulpit of nearby **Plymouth Church**, at Orange and Hicks streets—formerly known as "the Grand Central Terminal of the Underground Railroad"—the clergyman and abolitionist Henry Ward Beecher preached against "the peculiar institution" and harbored large numbers of fugitive slaves seeking sanctuary in the North.

SHOPPING AND DINING IN BROOKLYN HEIGHTS

Montague Street, the Heights' main shopping thoroughfare, is filled with bookstores, clothing boutiques, art galleries, and lots of convivial, moderately priced places for a bite and a swallow. The bars at **Peter Hilary's Bar and Grill** (number 174), **Slade's** (number 107), and **Montague Street Saloon** (number 122) draw a young professional crowd from the nearby downtown City Hall and court districts. If you're in the mood for game, **Henry's End** (44 Henry Street, four blocks down from Montague Street) regularly features such catches as pheasant, quail, bear, buffalo, and reindeer; a 52-selection beer list is available to help wash them down. And, after a few anxious months spent in the shadow of the wrecker's ball a few years ago, the classic wood- and mirror-paneled 1870s salon of **Gage & Tollner** (372 Fulton Street, in the nearby downtown shopping district; Tel: 718-875-5181) has been rescued by restaurateur Peter Aschkenasy and restored to its full gastronomic glory. "Brooklyn's Landmark Restaurant," as it bills itself, now offers both its hallowed seafood specialties (try the clam bellies) and Virginia-style dishes (Smithfield ham, homemade breads and preserves) by the renowned Southern chef Edna Lewis.

Atlantic Avenue

From the shopping district, a walk of two or three blocks will bring you to the center of New York's—and

America's—largest Arab community. Atlantic Avenue is lined with shops and restaurants, many of which are operated by and cater to the recent wave of Middle Easterners who have relocated in Brooklyn. An antiques district with dozens of small independent stores has also sprung up here to service the growing crowd of new home buyers. It offers prices substantially lower than those in Manhattan. After you've loaded up on porcelain and sconces, try the kebabs, curries, and couscous at **Tripoli** (156 Atlantic Avenue), one of the area's more elegantly appointed Arab restaurants. Slightly more modest, but just as good, is **Adnan** (129 Atlantic Avenue).

BROOKLYN ACADEMY OF MUSIC

Avant-garde performance is alive and flourishing just off the intersection of Atlantic and Flatbush avenues, a brief stroll eastward from the Atlantic Avenue restaurant district, at the **Brooklyn Academy of Music** (20 minutes from Midtown Manhattan on the D train to the Atlantic Avenue station; box office, Tel: 718-636-4100), America's oldest continuously operating performing arts center. Harvey Lichtenstein, its flamboyant impresario, likes to emphasize that in the early years of the century Brooklyn, with more than 40 playhouses, was a major theatrical center rivaling Manhattan's Broadway. Times may have changed a bit since then, but BAM, as it's commonly known (which, in addition to its programs, provides advice and administrative help for the dozens of smaller producers currently working in the borough), is firmly pledged to a revival of that legacy. Operating out of a superb 1908 opera house, it offers New York's largest ongoing concentration of experimental dance, music, and theater. The fall Next Wave festival regularly premieres new work by the likes of Pina Bausch, Philip Glass, Peter Sellars, and Robert Wilson. Around the corner, BAM's **Majestic Theater,** a turn-of-the-century variety stage, has been renovated in the Postmodern manner by director Peter Brook, who, along with Ingmar Bergman, makes his American creative home here. (For more on shows at BAM, see our Classical Music, Dance, and Theater chapters.)

Park Slope

From BAM, Flatbush Avenue runs southeast through a renovated commercial district into Park Slope (five minutes away by bus or subway), a magnificent enclave of late

Victorian homes developed in the 1880s for Brooklyn's prosperous English and German upper middle classes. The houses' satisfying combination of sober practicality and fancifulness (elaborately carved stone detailing, delicate cast-iron filigree, decorative castings) today seems more modern—certainly more popular—than ever.

Park Slope's focal point is the center of old Brooklyn, **Grand Army Plaza** (40 minutes from Midtown Manhattan on the number 2 or 3 West Side IRT train to the Grand Army Plaza station; 20 minutes on the D train to the Seventh Avenue station), a European-style traffic circle with a memorial arch built in 1892 to honor Brooklyn's Union Army war dead. The group of statues at its summit, featuring Columbia (the pre–Uncle Sam symbol of America) at the center of a victory quadriga, are by the prominent 19th-century American sculptor Frederick MacMonnies; relief panels of Abraham Lincoln over the inner entrance doorways by Thomas Eakins are the only public Eakins sculptures in New York City. In June the plaza is the site of the Welcome Back to Brooklyn festival, a gala homecoming party attended by famous and not-so-famous Brooklynites from all over. By 1995 it will be the western starting point of the **Brooklyn–Queens Greenway**, a pedestrian strip of grass, trees, and shrubs now under construction that will connect 13 parks across the length of the two boroughs.

Walk from the plaza down the wide, pleasant spaces of Eighth Avenue and its side streets (Carroll, Garfield, Montgomery Place) for a look at the comfortable gentility of the 19th-century good life; then skip over for drinks on **Seventh Avenue**, the main shopping drag, at **Rex Café** (222 Seventh Avenue), an old Irish bar with a new Caribbean flair. **Cousin John's Café**, with two Seventh Avenue locations, makes its own pastry and fresh ice cream on the premises. Over on Fifth Avenue, a little farther down, the kitchen of **Aunt Suzie's** (number 247, between Carroll and Garfield streets) turns out inexpensive trattoria fare in a homey atmosphere.

AROUND PROSPECT PARK

Three of the borough's proudest attractions (Prospect Park, the Brooklyn Botanic Garden, and the Brooklyn Museum) are within a few minutes' stroll of one another. **Prospect Park**, a pastoral, 526-acre expanse of trees, grass, and water (its Long Meadow offers the largest green vista unbroken by buildings in New York City), is the masterpiece of urban designers Frederick Law Olmsted and Calvert Vaux, who also created Manhattan's Central Park. Unlike Central Park, whose more formally sculpted garden spaces and numerous transverse roads engage it in a sort of dialogue with the surrounding urban bustle, Prospect Park was explicitly conceived as an enclosed, forested space that would provide as dramatic a contrast as possible with the urban grid. Its stunningly beautiful, undulant landscape, alternating lengths of open meadow with lakes and brooks running through stands of the oaks and sycamores that originally covered most of Brooklyn, is as close as one gets to sylvan wilderness in this city. Begun in 1866, much of the park was built on land from the estate of city father Edwin Litchfield, whose palatial Italianate villa is now the park's headquarters.

Contemporary Brooklynites of every stripe now come from all over to picnic, ice-skate, play ball, and enjoy concerts in the band shell, site of the popular Celebrate Brooklyn summer festival. Across from the band shell is **Raintree's** (142 Prospect Park West), a restaurant in a converted drugstore with tile floors and stained-glass windows that open onto the park. A couple of blocks down, **Aunt Sonia's** (1123 Eighth Avenue), named for the neighboring Ansonia Clock Factory, serves classic American dishes with a piquant twist in an intimate, friendly atmosphere.

The Botanic Garden
Dismayed by the intrusion of not entirely appropriate buildings (such as the Metropolitan Museum) into their design for Central Park, Olmsted and Vaux didn't make the same mistake twice: They insisted that the Prospect Park commissioners set aside a tract of land separate from the park proper to accommodate subsequent developments. That explains why you have to take a few steps across Flatbush Avenue to reach the **Brooklyn Botanic Garden** (1000 Washington Avenue; Tel: 718-622-4433). With a design reminiscent of an English estate and grounds, this assemblage includes a Japanese scholar's garden, a cherry esplanade that bears great clouds of soft pink blossoms in the spring, the Cranford Rose Garden (third largest in the United States), and the new Steinhardt Conservatory of tropical and desert plants.

The Brooklyn Museum
Take the number 2 or 3 subway line to the Eastern Parkway station for the garden and the **Brooklyn Museum** (200

Eastern Parkway). The museum's stately Beaux Arts building is undergoing expansion these days. Its collection of Egyptian art is the most comprehensive outside of Cairo and London; the Chinese and African galleries are also strong, and the always intriguing Grand Lobby, featuring works by contemporary artists, is frequently the first venue for shows that go on to attract national attention. After you've taken them in, the **New Prospect Café** (393 Flatbush Avenue), a comfortable, wood-and-mirror-paneled bistro just a few minutes' stroll down Flatbush Avenue, on the outskirts of Park Slope, is convenient for a light lunch or supper.

Brighton Beach

If you're in the mood for a longer trip, 40 minutes on the D train from Midtown Manhattan (20 minutes from Park Slope) will land you in Brighton Beach, just up the boardwalk from Coney Island and until the last decade best known as a fertile breeding ground for Jewish-American comedians and humorists (Moss Hart, Neil Simon, Woody Allen). It's now familiarly known as Little Odessa for the massive numbers of Russian nationals who relocated to this seaside neighborhood when Soviet emigration restrictions eased in the early 1970s. On **Brighton Beach Avenue**, the area's commercial center, bookstores (a recent big seller: Gorbachev's *Perestroika*), restaurants (caviar, *shashlik*), and omnipresent balalaika music attest to its status as America's largest Russian community.

Check out the Saturday crowds shopping for smoked fish and garlicky sausage at **M & I International Foods** (number 249); then cross the street for a lunch accompanied by vigorous Slavic renditions of American pop tunes at **Primorski** (number 282b). (You've never heard Elvis till you've heard him in Ukrainian.) Fifteen dollars here will bring more food than one human being can reasonably consume; Russians, explains the owner, "like good value for their money." **Café Zodiac** (number 309) offers slightly lighter fare in the same vein, but dinner visitors to the **National Restaurant** (number 273) should be prepared to do things in a big way: For $25 you get dinner, drinks, dancing, a nightclub show, and the chance to participate in the most passionate audience singalongs this side of Kiev. You might want to plan a walk in the salty air of the boardwalk along the beach first in order to whet your appetite.

Coney Island

A ten-minute stroll from the Brighton area along the same beachfront (45 minutes on the D train from Midtown Manhattan, 25 minutes from Park Slope) will put you in the center of this authentic American landmark. Lawrence Ferlinghetti named one of the first volumes of Beat poetry for it; Maksim Gorki, who visited it in the early days of the Soviet Union, came away with a phantasmagorical vision of American urban intensity; it's the birthplace of the hot dog. It's Coney Island, of course, and since the 1840s—first by railroad, later, and more democratically, by subway—this first and best known of American seaside parks has enabled stressed-out New Yorkers to leave behind the hot summer city for a few hours of sun, sand, and surf.

Creative types have long flocked here for inspiration; a frequent early 19th-century visitor was Brooklyn poet Walt Whitman, who composed many of his poems to the companionable roaring of the surf. These days you might well catch sight of *New York Review of Books* caricaturist David Levine painting, as he has for 30 years, the families who come to the beach to play, talk, swim, and eat. Coney Island, he has said, is for him what North Africa was for Delacroix.

Frankness, though, compels an admission that the resort is not in the best state of repair these days. The carousels, roller coasters, and fantasy rides that made its Luna and Steeplechase parks famous at the turn of the century (Steeplechase's Ferris wheel, visible 38 miles out to sea, was often the first piece of America sighted by European immigrants) were allowed to decay in the 1960s, when amusement parks everywhere suffered a decline in popularity. The good news, however, is that a private developer has recently signed an agreement with the city to restore the concessions to their full former glory.

In the meantime, you can take in the **New York Aquarium** (Boardwalk and West 8th Street), rent a fishing pole and catch dinner from one of the city-operated piers, grab a bench on the boardwalk and watch the world go by, or simply enjoy the waves. As might be expected, there are quite a number of good, inexpensive seafood restaurants in the neighborhood, but no serious eater would consider visiting Coney Island without paying his respects to **Nathan's Famous**, the mecca of tube-steak—all right, all right, hot dog—lovers. Many older New Yorkers can still recall heading for a day at "Coney" in the 1920s with four nickels in their pockets: two for the subway ride there and back, two for a pair of Nathan's mustard-and-sauerkraut *spe-cialités de la maison*. Nathan's continues to feed thousands of visitors a day at Surf and Stillwell avenues—garish, yellow-green, and eternal.

Greenpoint

In 1862, the ironclad *Monitor* emerged from the Continental Ironworks in Greenpoint to fight for the Union against the Confederate *Merrimac*. Edging neighboring Queens at the northernmost point of the borough, this area was responsible for the the international reputation as an industrial center that Brooklyn wielded by the 1890s. Its numerous factories and plants specialized in cast-iron manufacture, pottery, printing, and petroleum. Although all of those enterprises have long since departed, the neighborhood is still populated by the descendants of the Polish, Italian, and Irish immigrants who came over to work in them. The Polish community has recently expanded to include a large number of Solidarity activists who left the homeland when martial law was imposed in 1981. Many of the community's activities are centered around St. Stanislaus Kostka Church (607 Humboldt Street), where a brass plaque commemorates the 1969 visit of Polish Cardinal Karol Wojtyla before he became Pope John Paul II.

If you go to Greenpoint (a ten-minute trip from lower Manhattan on the M or J subway to the Marcy or Lorimer stations), try the Polish pastries at the **White Eagle Bakery** (600 Humboldt Street). **Bamonte's** (32 Withers Street) and **Crisci** (593 Lorimer Street) are landmark Italian restaurants, each boasting several generations of family ownership.

Williamsburg

There's no real debate about this area's most exceptional dining experience: **Peter Luger** (178 Broadway; Tel: 718-387-7400), under the shadow of the elevated train in neighboring Williamsburg, is by itself worth the trip—from anywhere. This Teutonic *keller*, with worn wooden floors and an atmosphere redolent of more than a century's worth of beer, tobacco, and red meat, serves the finest steaks in New York City, aged to perfection in the restaurant's own warehouse and served in classic German-American style by waiters in high, white, starched aprons. The way there via subway (D or N lines from Midtown) is slightly inconvenient, so take a cab; there's not a driver in greater New York who doesn't make the trip regularly.

Williamsburg sprawls a bit too much for concise sightseeing, which may deter the casual tourist, but will be of slight importance to those visiting for more spiritual reasons: It's home to the largest concentration of Orthodox and Hasidic Jews outside Israel, whose unvarying black-and-white garb is the rule rather than the exception on these streets.

QUEENS

By Barry Lewis

Barry Lewis, an architectural historian, has created tour programs and produced lecture series for New York City's 92nd Street Y. He has also written articles on the city's architectural history for many publications and was a contributing writer to the Municipal Art Society's Juror's Guide to Lower Manhattan. *He lives in the borough of Queens.*

Queens: To residents of Manhattan it's New York's Midwest, the Archie Bunkerville where dwell the cabdrivers, the firemen, the secretaries, and the plumbers of New York City. Built up before and after World War II, Queens was considered, in the 1950s and 1960s, the "suburbia" to Manhattan's "city." But things change—New York always does—and this borough of nearly two million has changed with it.

Queens is New York's London. It doesn't look like London, but it acts like it. Its dozens of small towns and small cities are, like London's boroughs, instinctively independent and terribly insular. If nuclear testing were planned for Flushing, the people in Jackson Heights—two "towns" away—would be relieved that it had nothing to do with them. Each neighborhood is different in class,

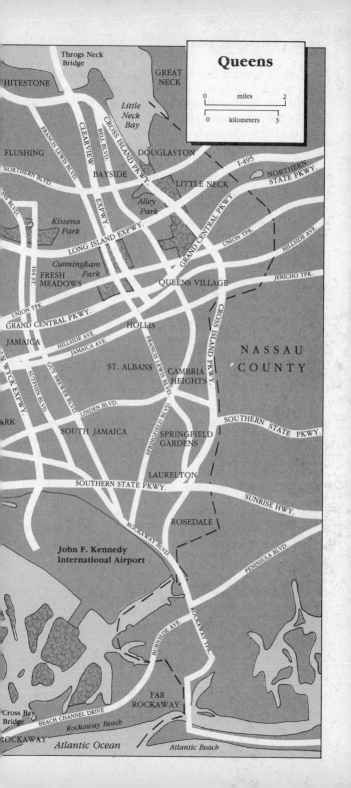

in ethnic texture, and even in architectural scale. From the Brooklyn-style row houses of Ridgewood to the Upstate New York, small-town atmosphere of College Point, from the modernistic factories of increasingly artsy Long Island City to the bustling, Hong Kong–like downtown of Flushing, Queens is a mosaic of real-life New York.

Today Queens is New York's melting pot, serving the city as the Lower East Side once did. But here the number of people is far larger, their origins more exotic, and their lifestyles more prosperous than those of their 19th-century predecessors along Manhattan's Rivington, Mac-Dougal, and Mott streets. Queens has one of the densest ethnic mixes in the world, counting among its residents Greeks, Latins, Middle Easterners, West Indians, and Russian Jews, as well as denizens from the entire arc of eastern and southern Asia. It stands to reason, then, that almost any kind of ethnic foodstuff, cooking gadgetry, and restaurant can be found here. The atmosphere in these shops and restaurants is home-style—home, that is, to a Greek, an Indian, or an Argentine. Restaurants are not glitterized with Postmodern decor; they just have plain cloths on the tables and simple pictures on the walls. They are not written up; you simply have to know about them. The food, however, is excellent, cheap, and abundant.

For those who can spare only an afternoon to cross the East River and visit Queens, a walk around Astoria's Greek enclave at Ditmars Boulevard and 31st Street or a visit to the Noguchi Museum and Socrates Sculpture Park and nearby Broadway in Long Island City might give you a taste of this other-side-of-the-world quality. Similarly, Jackson Heights's Latin American district along 82nd Street and Roosevelt Avenue or downtown Flushing's Little Asia along Main and Union streets can give you a quick take on this other New York perspective.

MAJOR INTEREST

Garden-city planning
The Seven Sisters neighborhoods
Forest Hills' Russian enclave
Latin American and Indian quarters in Jackson
    Heights
Queens Museum of Art
New York Hall of Science
Corona Avenue's Italian enclave
Flushing's Little Asia

Long Island City's Socrates Sculpture Park
Isamu Noguchi Garden Museum
American Museum of the Moving Image
Greek community in Astoria

Queens, first settled in the 17th century, was annexed to
New York in 1898 and achieved full throttle with the
opening of the Queensboro (59th Street) Bridge and the
Long Island Railroad (LIRR)/Pennsylvania Station complex, both around 1910. In the next 30 years Queens
boomed. The city had arrived, but it was a verdant city,
where architects and developers often tried to thread
gardens and greenbelts around their apartment buildings
and private homes. Some neighborhoods were built up
in the repetitive patterns of Archie Bunker–type developments. Others, however, such as Astoria in the northwest
or the older sections of Rego Park in the center of the
borough, were built with the kind of garden-style apartments and row houses that give much of Queens a leafi-
ness absent in over-bricked Manhattan.

A word about the Queens street system: There appears
to be a "system," but there really isn't. After Queens
merged with the rest of New York City in 1898, city hall
imposed a Manhattan-style grid on the new borough. Old
street names were replaced by numbers, with, theoretically, 1st Street at the East River end and 250th Street at
the eastern end (Nassau County), and First Avenue along
the northern Long Island Sound shoreline and 150th
Avenue at the southern end near what is now Kennedy
Airport. But the old patchwork of separate street systems
resisted easy codification. The result is a crazy quilt of
numbers pretending to be organized. An address such as
83-10 125th Street means, in theory, that the building is
on 125th Street near 83rd Avenue, but usually that's only
the beginning of your quest, because the system doesn't
always work so neatly. The best advice is to call ahead to
the address you plan to visit and get explicit directions.
When you get there, you can then set out to explore the
surrounding neighborhood.

The Seven Sisters

Scattered among the patchwork of towns and developments that covers Queens is a group of planned neighborhoods known as the Seven Sisters. These seven indepen-
dently developed communities—Richmond Hill, Kew

Gardens, Forest Hills Gardens, Jackson Heights, Sunny-side Gardens, Fresh Meadows, and Douglaston—brought garden-city ideals to the often crass New York real-estate scene of the late 19th and early 20th century. Sports facilities, parkland, and community clubhouses were built for homeowners and apartment dwellers, giving residents "rest and recuperation" from the frenzy, noise, and dehumanizing congestion of modern industrial life. Here we cover three of the Sisters that cluster together in south-central Queens and can be toured on a single visit. Several of the other Sisters are covered farther below.

RICHMOND HILL

The Seven Sisters began with Richmond Hill (from Man-hattan take the E or F subway line to Union Turnpike, Kew Gardens, and the Q 10 bus to Hillside Avenue), an 1880s speculative development. Shingle-style "Meet Me in St. Louis" Victorians fan out from a village center and town common clustered around the intersections of Hill-side, Jamaica, and Myrtle avenues and Lefferts Boulevard. Some of the best houses stand north of Myrtle Avenue between 112th and 115th streets; a few blocks farther on Myrtle is the 538-acre, densely wooded **Forest Park**.

Richmond Hill's 1890s town center is nostalgic, if slightly run-down. The tiny common became, in 1905, the campus for one of the libraries that industrialist Andrew Carnegie built throughout the East toward the end of the last century (at Lefferts Boulevard and Hillside Avenue). Inside, in one wing of the library, is a 1937 WPA mural by Philip Evergood depicting, in exuberant 1930s optimism, *The Story of Richmond Hill.* For a meal, there is the **Triangle Hofbrau**, at 117-13 Jamaica Avenue, at Myrtle Avenue, a long-standing German restaurant—Mae West frequented it when she lived nearby, and it was one of Babe Ruth's favorites—whose premises were originally an 1860s way station on the Jamaica Turnpike (now Ja-maica Avenue). For just a hamburger, across the street at 117-33 Myrtle Avenue is the **Junction Diner**—streamlined inside, 1980s remodeling outside. This is a *real* diner, not one of the cleverly packaged mock-ups so popular these days.

KEW GARDENS

Just to the north, on the other side of Forest Park, is Kew Gardens, developed in the 1910s as a neo-Tudor "village" centered around the railroad station at Lefferts Boulevard and Austin Street. (From Manhattan take the LIRR Main line to Kew Gardens, or the E or F subway line to Union Turnpike; from Richmond Hill simply return on the Q 10 bus.) Its eclectic mixture of apartments and row houses, and especially its variety of private homes that range from modest to mansion, are carefully sited to fit respectfully into the rolling, hilly landscape. The neo-Tudor and neo-Colonial buildings lie in the shade of 80-year-old pin oaks that line the streets.

FOREST HILLS GARDENS

Adjacent and to the west of Kew Gardens is the most famous of the Sisters, Forest Hills Gardens, a superb example of garden-city planning. (From Manhattan take the LIRR to Forest Hills, or the E or F line to Continental Avenue, Forest Hills, and walk south; from Kew Gardens take the E or F back two stops toward Manhattan.) Lushly landscaped by Frederick Law Olmsted, Jr (son of the designer of Central Park), the "Gardens" includes housing of all types, from apartment towers to mansions to experimental poured-concrete row houses made friendlier with neo-Tudor detailing. Station Square, the 1912 "town center" by architect Grosvenor Atterbury that clusters around the LIRR station, is a fine example of urban design. As much Expressionistic as it is Medieval Revival, it evinces character and a sense of place without ever being cloying or cute.

While visiting the neighborhood you might want to try the varied and freshly made Mexican dishes at **Sgt. Garcia's**, 70-09 Austin Street (upstairs), in the bustling shopping district near the railroad station.

Forest Hills and Jamaica

Two neighborhoods near the cluster of Forest Hills Gardens, Kew Gardens, and Richmond Hill, one to the east and one to the west, aptly illustrate that Queens is not just a homogeneous suburb. Forest Hills is home to Russians and Eastern Europeans, while Jamaica and its neighbors have long attracted middle- and upper-class blacks.

FOREST HILLS

Forest Hills is about 20 blocks northwest of Forest Hills Gardens. (Take the R train from Manhattan to the 63rd Drive, Rego Park station; walk east from the station.) Russian Jews have established a small colony on 108th

Street north of 65th Avenue, far from the better-known settlement in Brighton Beach, Brooklyn. A Russian deli, **Misha & Monya's**, at 64-46 108th Street (at 65th Avenue), sells such delicious staples as freshly made sour cream, dried fish, pickles, and pirogi. A block north, at 64th Road, **Carmel Middle Eastern Grocery** (64-27 108th Street) serves the local population of Sephardic Jews, specializing in freshly made hummus, *babaganouj,* olives, pickles, and Middle Eastern grains and spices.

JAMAICA

Downtown Jamaica, along Jamaica Avenue from Parsons Boulevard to 169th Street (take the F subway line from Manhattan or Forest Hills to the Parsons Boulevard stop, or the R from Manhattan to Continental Avenue), is now, like many other old downtowns, struggling to revive itself. If you find yourself here, in the borough's historic county seat, stop in to see the **Tabernacle of Prayer** (165-11 Jamaica Avenue, at Merrick Boulevard). Formerly the Loew's Valencia, a grand, atmospheric 1929 movie palace in the Spanish Baroque style, it's been remade with a new color scheme into an evangelical church, where everyone is welcome for Sunday services. A few blocks west is the **Jamaica Arts Center** (161-04 Jamaica Avenue, at Union Hall Street), a cultural center and art gallery housed in the small but flamboyant City Register Building, built soon after the 1898 annexation.

This area of Queens is blighted by the poverty belt of South Jamaica that runs south of downtown Jamaica along Sutphin and Guy R. Brewer boulevards. But South Jamaica's plight too often blinds us to the handsome solidity of the black middle-class communities nearby. The row-house-lined streets of **Cambria Heights** and the eclectic mansions of **St. Albans** (both east of Jamaica) were early suburban areas opened to upscale blacks coming out of Manhattan's Harlem and Brooklyn's Bedford-Stuyvesant area. St. Albans in particular had, in the 1950s, a stellar residents' list that included Roy Campanella, James Brown, and Count Basie.

The Roosevelt Avenue Corridor

Roosevelt Avenue, one of Queens's major thoroughfares, stretches from Sunnyside, in the northwestern part of the borough, to Flushing, in north-central Queens. The avenue is served by the IRT number 7 train from Manhattan's Times Square or Grand Central Station. The train rises aboveground (indeed, above street level) in Queens, and so is known as "the El," short for "elevated train." Our tour along the number 7 route takes in two more of the Seven Sister neighborhoods, Sunnyside and Jackson Heights, the second of which is a vibrant Latin American community; the old World's Fair site at Flushing Meadows Corona Park, now a museum and sports center; and ends at downtown Flushing, familiarly known as Little Asia.

SUNNYSIDE GARDENS

Sunnyside Gardens (take the number 7 to 46th Street and walk north) was a utopian experiment of the 1920s designed by the gifted team of Clarence Stein and Henry Wright. It was built as a model housing complex, including verdant commons within the blocks and a still extant community park that is the only private park in the city besides Manhattan's Gramercy Park. The Midtown Manhattan skyline now rises picturesquely in the background. The neighborhood was home for many years to the late urban critic and *New Yorker* columnist Lewis Mumford and was once known as the "Nursery of Greenwich Village" for the number of former Village artists who moved there to raise their families. For information about the neighborhood, contact the Sunnyside Foundation, Tel: (718) 392-9139.

JACKSON HEIGHTS

Several stops farther east on the number 7 train (descend at 82nd Street and walk north) is Jackson Heights, a mainly Latin American neighborhood centered on 82nd Street at 37th Avenue. Jackson Heights was built in the 1910s and 1920s with blocks of apartment houses of imaginative historic-revival designs, threaded with greenbelts. Many of these apartments boast three or four exposures, floor-through plans, and separate service and bedroom wings.

Jackson Heights offers a marvelous opportunity for a culinary tour; bring your Spanish phrase book with you. Two wonderful Colombian restaurants not far from the El are **Tierras Colombianas** (82-18 Roosevelt Avenue, east of 82nd Street) and **La Pequeña Columbia** (83-27 Roosevelt Avenue, one block farther east). On Baxter Avenue, at number 80-32, south of Roosevelt Avenue and 84th Street, is **La Fusta**, an Argentine restaurant specializing in *parrillada,* Latin American–style barbecue. Under the El on Roosevelt are several Latin nightclubs and elegant restaurants. Farther east (take the number 7 line to the Junction Boulevard station) is an expatriate Cuban restaurant, **Rincon Criollo**, at 40-09 Junction Boulevard, just south of the El.

On the western side of Jackson Heights (the 74th Street/Broadway stop on the number 7, or Roosevelt Avenue/Jackson Heights stop on the E, F, and R trains) is one of New York's many Indian communities: 74th Street, north of Roosevelt Avenue, is a veritable Sari Alley, and it and the surrounding area are filled with Indian sari shops, restaurants, and grocery stores.

FLUSHING MEADOWS CORONA PARK

Flushing Meadows Corona Park was once the dusty "valley of ashes" described in F. Scott Fitzgerald's *The Great Gatsby.* Subsequently, it hosted two world's fairs, and is now the site of two major sports arenas and a pair of terrific museums. Exit the number 7 train at the Willets Point/Shea Stadium stop. There you'll see brightly painted **Shea Stadium**, home of the New York Mets baseball team. Just to its south is the **National Tennis Center**, site of the U.S. Open championships. Just south of the tennis center (walk toward the 1964 World's Fair Unisphere), housed in the New York City pavilion of the 1939 World's Fair, is the **Queens Museum of Art**, which is in the midst of a large-scale renovation project that is bringing back much of the building's 1939 glamour (the museum will remain open during the construction, although certain sections will close). Besides excellent art and photography shows, the museum has the **New York Panorama**, a scale model of the entire city of New York, including every building and street within the five boroughs (the panorama is closed for renovation until 1994).

On Flushing Meadows's western edge, about a five-minute walk from the Queens Museum over the Grand Central Expressway bridge, is the **New York Hall of Science** (47-01 111th Street, at 48th Avenue), a tremendously popular hands-on experience of applied science and high technology housed in a reinforced concrete "amoeba" originally built for the 1964 World's Fair. (If you're visiting just the Hall of Science, you can take the number 7 line to the 111th Street station and walk south eight blocks to 48th Avenue.)

CORONA

Getting hungry? From the Hall of Science walk south on 111th Street (that's a left on exiting the hall) three blocks to 51st Avenue and turn right one block to 108th Street (only in Queens is 108th one block from 111th). There, where Corona Avenue intersects 108th and 51st, is Joseph Lisa Memorial Square, the heart of an Italian neighborhood. On the square the **Lemon Ice King of Corona** (52-02 108th Street) still makes New York's best Italian ices in an endless variety of flavors. The **Parkside Restaurant** (107-01 Corona Avenue, on the 51st Avenue side of the square) serves Italian cuisine in a posh style that attracts people from all over the city. For more modest, but excellent, dining try the nearby **Army's Italian Cuisine** (50-01 108th Street, at 51st Avenue). For cappuccino and pastry there is **Baldi's Italian Pastry Shop** (108-15 Corona Avenue, at 53rd Avenue).

Corona's small-town atmosphere seems to have suited one notable American: It was the longtime home of jazz great Louis Armstrong, whose house is now a national historic site and archives (34-56 107th Street; Tel: 718-478-8274). Nearby, though long closed and picked clean of debris, was Louis Comfort Tiffany's studio (96-18 43rd Avenue), where many a Tiffany lamp and Favrile glass vase were fabricated.

FLUSHING

Downtown Flushing's Little Asia is concentrated on Main Street from Sanford Avenue to Northern Boulevard, and on side streets, including Union Street, parallel to and east of Main Street. When you exit the number 7 train at the end of the line, at Main Street and Roosevelt Avenue, you will be right in the heart of the business district—and it will be clear to you why this train is nicknamed "The Orient Express." The intense small shops, billboards in foot-high Oriental letters, and mixture of Korean, Chinese, Indian, and Japanese residents will make you feel that you have just flown across the China Sea.

Asian restaurants and food shops dot Flushing's streets. **Cho Sun Ok** (136-73 Roosevelt Avenue, upstairs, one block east of the subway terminal) is a Korean restaurant specializing in hibachi-based barbecue. **Nippon Daido USA** is a Japanese supermarket (with an attached Dosanko fast-food restaurant) at 137-80 Northern Boulevard, at Union Street. Several excellent Chinese and Korean supermarkets line Main Street near Sanford and Maple avenues (about three blocks south of the subway), and Indian grocers and delis cluster on Main Street another block farther south.

Nearby, to the east of Main Street, a Hindu temple built by Indian craftsmen flown over from the subcontinent sits among the surrounding Victorian houses. Home to the **Hindu Temple Society of North America** (45-57 Bowne Street, at Holly Avenue; Tel: 718-460-8484), the temple has a richly decorated interior of shrines and Hindu gods and goddesses, and has a welcome mat out for strangers (call for hours and directions).

Northeastern Queens

The list of ethnic neighborhoods and their specialty stores could go on and on. Yet Queens is also beginning to attract the kinds of cultural institutions that people will go out of their way to visit. Several of these are found directly across the East River from Manhattan, in Long Island City. And just to the north of these is Astoria, New York's old movie-making town, now an exciting Greek community.

LONG ISLAND CITY

Housed in a fortresslike 19th-century school, **P.S. 1** (46-01 21st Street, at Jackson Avenue; Tel: 718-784-2084) is a combination of art gallery, artists' working lofts, and some-time performance space that pioneered Long Island City's role as a new center for the "downtown" art scene. The number 7 line's Court House Square/45th Road station (three stops from Grand Central) and the E and F's 23rd Street/Ely Avenue station (one stop from Citicorp Center) are only a few blocks away.

Farther north, along Long Island City's industrial river-front, is the **Socrates Sculpture Park** (31-29 Vernon Boulevard, at Broadway and the East River), where large-scale modern sculpture can be seen against the spectacular backdrop of the Manhattan skyline. (Take the N train from Manhattan to the Broadway station; from P.S. 1 take the number 7 one stop to Queensboro Plaza, then transfer to the N and continue north; it's an eight-block walk west to the riverfront and Socrates.) The park is open daily during the summer, but only on weekends in the winter.

Just two blocks south of the Socrates along the river-front, at 33rd Road, is the **Isamu Noguchi Garden Museum** (32-37 Vernon Boulevard; Tel: 718-204-7088), housed in the late sculptor's former studio. Open only Wednesdays and Saturdays, the museum displays the artist's works in a redesigned industrial loft of almost monastic simplicity, and in an austerely beautiful garden. The museum's shop sells lamps and other Noguchi designs. From the riverfront you can cross a bridge over the East River to Roosevelt Island, from which you can take the tram to Manhattan.

ASTORIA

Queens was America's first Hollywood. During the days of the silents and the early talkies, before producers discovered Los Angeles, Astoria Movie Studios was one of the principal centers of the movie industry. Today that studio, renamed **Kaufman Astoria Studios**, is thriving again. Queens was also the first Beverly Hills. The stars of stage and screen (and jazz, too)—including Charlie Chaplin, Al Jolson, Will Rogers, Billie Holiday, Bix Beiderbecke, and the immortal Louis Armstrong—settled in from Corona to Forest Hills to Bayside, some to lead quiet lives away from Manhattan's din and others to lead the North Shore Long Island lifestyle that would soon move to "West Egg" and be immortalized in *The Great Gatsby.*

The **American Museum of the Moving Image** (at 36-01 35th Avenue, at 36th Street), a new addition to Kaufman/ Astoria, has itself become a box-office smash, giving visitors a multimedia understanding of TV, video, and film production. The museum, which also hosts screenings in its theaters, is four blocks from the R train's Steinway Street station—that's three stops from Bloomingdale's in Manhattan. You can also get there from Long Island City's Noguchi Museum or Socrates Park: Walk back east on Broadway, five blocks past the El to 36th Street, and turn right, or south, two blocks to 35th Avenue to reach the Moving Image. It's a "schlepp," as New Yorkers say, but the sights and aromas of Astoria's Broadway might make the walk less taxing than you think.

Astoria's Greek community is clustered along 31st Street, beneath the elevated N line (the "El," which runs from Bloomingdale's in Manhattan). Once German, then Italian, now one of the largest concentrations of Greeks outside of the home country, Astoria has conveniently concentrated its major attractions at the N line's terminus, Ditmars Boulevard. Greek coffee and pastry shops (and Italian pastry shops as well), Greek-language newsstands, and a Greek-language movie house serve the local population. **Tony's Ristorante** (33-12 Ditmars Boulevard, two blocks east of 31st Street), **Lefkos Pirgos Bakery** (at 31st Street and 23rd Avenue, one block south of Ditmars), and **Europa Delicacies** (22-42 31st Street, under the El just south of Ditmars) are just the appetizers to a culinary feast. Broadway, near the El station, is another frenzy of food shops: **Roumely Taverna** (33-04 Broadway, east of the El) and **Karyatis Restaurant** (35-03 Broadway, two blocks east of Roumely's) are two excellent restaurants in that stretch.

DAY TRIPS FROM MANHATTAN

By Eleanor Berman with Stephen Brewer and Amy K. Hughes

Eleanor Berman is a widely published travel writer. Her guide Away for the Weekend: New York *has been a regional bestseller since 1982. She has contributed to all the major metropolitan daily newspapers, as well as to such national magazines as* House Beautiful, Modern Bride, Caribbean Travel and Life, *and* Physicians' Travel and Meeting Guide.

Visitors caught up in the Manhattan maelstrom may wonder, How does anybody live here? Here's the secret: New Yorkers get away—often. Greenery, scenery, history, prime beaches, ivy-clad campuses, and even early American charm are only a day's trip away. Here are some of the escapes the natives favor.

MAJOR INTEREST

New York City
Bronx Zoo
New York Botanical Garden
Wave Hill mansion and grounds

New York State
Philipsburg Manor's early Dutch farm grounds
Washington Irving's retreat, Sunnyside

Van Cortlandt Manor colonial house
Union Church of Pocantico Hills
Franklin D. Roosevelt National Historic Site at
    Hyde Park
United States Military Academy at West Point
Donald M. Kendall Sculpture Gardens
Storm King Art Center and Sculpture Park
New Paltz, in mountainous Upstate
The Hamptons, beaches and resort towns
Fire Island beach communities

Connecticut
Yale University
Litchfield, historic New England town

New Jersey
Princeton University and the historic town
Spring Lake, on the Jersey Shore

Pennsylvania
Doylestown, in Bucks County

New York City

THE BRONX ZOO

The New York Zoological Society has replaced nearly all of its cages with spectacular natural habitats—re-creations of Asian steppes, Himalayan highlands, and African plains— for its 4,000-some animals. Black leopards, white-cheeked gibbons, crocodiles, and other creatures live in Jungle World, separated from people and one another only by ravines, streams, and cliffs; visitors walk through the World of Birds while the multicolored inhabitants soar free above them. You get the idea—it's all as natural as a zoo can be.

To reach the zoo (and the New York Botanical Garden; see below) by car from Manhattan's East Side, take FDR Drive to the Triborough Bridge and then the Bruckner Expressway east to the Bronx River Parkway northbound. From the exit marked Bronx Zoo, turn left to the Bronx-dale parking field. From the West Side, take the West Side Highway/Henry Hudson Parkway north to the Cross Bronx Expressway east to the Bronx River Parkway; at the Bronx Zoo exit turn into the Bronxdale parking lot. The botanical garden is directly opposite, across Fordham Road. Call the zoo or the garden for alternative means of transportation.

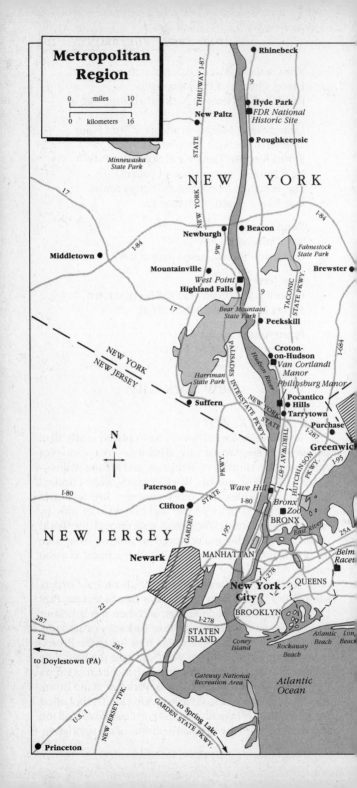

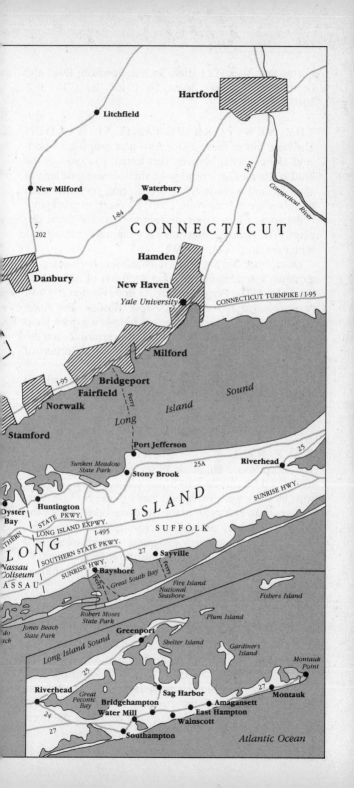

The New York Zoological Society, Fordham Road and Bronx River Parkway, Bronx, NY 10460. Tel: (718) 367-1010.

THE NEW YORK BOTANICAL GARDEN

The best part of these 250 acres—part unspoiled woodland along a winding river, part formal gardens—is the Enid A. Haupt Conservatory, 11 shimmering pavilions of glass around a courtyard and reflecting pools. Beneath the glass are a leafy palm court, a desert, tropical-plant collections, a fern forest, and showy seasonal floral displays. (The Haupt Conservatory is temporarily closed; it is scheduled to reopen in 1995.)

Outdoors there are a perennial garden, herb and rock gardens, a conifer garden, and a garden of native New York plants. The Peggy Rockefeller Rose Garden is a lush two acres planted with 2,700 rose bushes. The stone museum building on the grounds houses a garden shop that sells horticultural items, an orchid terrarium, and the Harriet Barnes Pratt Library, an excellent collection of literature on horticulture.

New York Botanical Garden, Southern Boulevard and 200th Street, Bronx, NY 10458. (See the Bronx Zoo, above, for directions; enter on Southern Boulevard.) Tel: (718) 817-8705.

WAVE HILL

Theodore Roosevelt, Mark Twain, and Arturo Toscanini have lived on this 28-acre Bronx estate, now a city park, with its lawn, woodlands, and views of the Hudson. New Yorkers from every part of the city come here to enjoy the quiet and beauty as well as chamber-music concerts, outdoor dance and music programs, and organized bird and nature walks. The estate is next to **Riverdale Park**, 97 wooded acres with walking trails paralleling the Hudson River.

Wave Hill is a short drive from Manhattan by car. From the East Side take the Major Deegan Expressway northbound. Exit at the Henry Hudson Parkway and take the first right to the Henry Hudson *southbound*. Take the 254th Street exit, turn left at the stop sign, left again at the light, right at 249th Street to Wave Hill. From the West Side take the West Side Highway/Henry Hudson Parkway northbound. Get off the parkway at the 246th–250th Street exit; continue north to 252nd, go left at the overpass, left again, and right at 249th Street.

Metro-North trains stop at the nearby Riverdale Station at 254th Street (Tel: 212-532-4900), Liberty Lines express buses go within walking distance (Tel: 718-652-8400), and Mosholu Limousine Service offers transport from Manhattan (Tel: 212-543-6900). Wave Hill, 249th Street and Independence Avenue, Bronx, NY 10471. Tel: (718) 549-3200.

New York State

ALONG THE HUDSON

Historic Hudson Valley

Much of the early history of New York State was forged in the great manor houses due north of Manhattan along the Hudson River. Historic Hudson Valley, a nonprofit corporation, was formed more than 35 years ago to preserve some of the most important properties:

Philipsburg Manor in North Tarrytown was the domain of a Dutchman who came to the New World in the early 1650s as Peter Stuyvesant's carpenter and amassed his own fortune through the clipper trade and a good marriage. The manor's mill, where tenant farmers brought grain to be ground, bagged, and shipped, has been restored to approximate its appearance during its most prosperous period, 1720 to 1750. The garden is planted only with 18th-century species, and the cows, sheep, and chickens roaming the farm have been "back-bred" to reproduce the breeds of an earlier day. The simple stone farmhouse with its whitewashed walls contains samples of rustic early New York furniture and Dutch Delft ceramics.

Sunnyside, in nearby Tarrytown, is the quaint Victorian cottage and gardens of author Washington Irving. The estate, which he appropriately called his "snuggery," contains Irving's furniture, possessions, and library.

Van Cortlandt Manor, north of Sunnyside, in Croton-on-Hudson, was the home of a Dutchman, Oloff Stevense Van Cortlandt, who arrived in New Amsterdam in 1638 and sired a prominent family that included a mayor of New York City and a lieutenant governor of the state. The house has been restored to the elegant period between 1790 and 1814. Most of its fine furnishings were made in New York and belonged to the Van Cortlandts, who remained in residence here until 1945. The gardens are planted with herbs, flowers, and vegetables typically grown in this country prior to 1814.

The **Union Church of Pocantico Hills**, in North Tarry-town, is the worshiping place of the Rockefeller family, whose estate is nearby. Marc Chagall made the windows; their blues, greens, and golds fill the small sanctuary with beautiful light. The small circular rose window over the altar is Henri Matisse's final work. Visiting hours are limited, so phone Historic Hudson Valley for information (see below) before you plan a trip.

All of the above Westchester properties are off Route 9 on the east side of the Hudson and can be reached by taking the New York State Thruway (Route 87) to exit 9, Tarrytown; follow Route 9 south 1 mile to Sunnyside, north 2 miles to Philipsburg, north another 9 miles to Van Cort-landt Manor. To reach the Union Church, go east on Route 448 from Route 9 in North Tarrytown. Signs mark the turnoffs clearly. To see all the sites, a car is necessary. Historic Hudson is now offering day trips by ferry to some of the sites. Ferries leave from the ferry terminal at 38th Street in Manhattan; for information, Tel: (800) 53-FERRY.

Historic Hudson Valley, 150 White Plains Road, Tarry-town, NY 10591. Tel: (914) 631-8200.

Franklin D. Roosevelt National Historic Site

Officially called Springwood, usually referred to as **Hyde Park**, the house and grounds of this former president's estate have an uncanny, lived-in quality, reinforced by the presence in various rooms of Eleanor's knitting and Franklin's collection of ship models and his elegant Ford Phaeton convertible with hand controls.

The museum of the Franklin D. Roosevelt Library, in the main house, contains a series of photos and displays commemorating the life of the only man elected for four presidential terms, who guided the nation out of its worst depression and through its most perilous war. The library also houses Roosevelt's study (where he gave some of his famous radio fireside chats) and his presidential desk.

Franklin and Eleanor are buried in the rose garden beside the house. Eleanor never felt at home at Hyde Park, where Sara Roosevelt, Franklin's mother, reigned. She built a small retreat on the estate two miles away from the main house in 1926. It was often her weekend escape, and it was in this unpretentious pine-paneled house, **Val-Kill**, that she lived from 1945 until her death in 1962.

Hyde Park is a two-hour drive from New York City. Follow the New York State Thruway (Route 87) to exit 18

(New Paltz); go east on Route 299 for 5 miles and then right on Route 9W south to the Mid-Hudson Bridge. Cross the bridge and follow signs for Route 9 north to Hyde Park.

Franklin D. Roosevelt National Historic Site, Route 9, Hyde Park, NY. Tel: (914) 229-9115.

You can eat very well nearby at the **Culinary Institute of America**, on Route 9 in Hyde Park, the nation's top training ground for chefs. Formal French fare is served in the Escoffier Room, regional American favorites are the specialty at the American Bounty, and a healthful, low-calorie menu is served at St. Andrew's Café, where guests receive a printout of the nutritional content of their meal. All serve both lunch and dinner. Reservations are essential; phone far ahead for weekends. Tel: (914) 471-6608.

The Hudson Valley merits an overnight stay—to see the foliage, pick apples, hike in the mountains, or explore the other great estates along the river: Montgomery Place, Clermont, Mills Mansion, and Olana north of Hyde Park, and the Vanderbilt Mansion and Boscobel to the south. A good guide to the area is *The Hudson River Valley: A History & Guide* by Tim Mulligan. There are pleasant overnight accommodations at the ▶ **Beekman Arms**, a stagecoach inn dating back to 1700, 10 miles north of Hyde Park on Route 9 in Rhinebeck (Tel: 914-876-7077).

The United States Military Academy

Standing on a crest on the west bank of the Hudson River, the gray stone buildings and vast grounds of the United States Military Academy at **West Point** are intended to impress, as they indeed do. You'll want to see the Cadet Chapel, with the largest church organ in the world (18,000 pipes); the gracious 19th-century homes of the superintendent and the commandant; and the parade ground known as the Plain, where Ulysses S. Grant, Robert E. Lee, Thomas J. "Stonewall" Jackson, Douglas MacArthur, Dwight Eisenhower, and astronauts Buzz Aldrin, Frank Borman, and Michael Collins have marched. Dress parades, with cadets in full regalia, are held on the Plain on football weekends in autumn and at various times throughout the year (phone the academy for current schedules). **Fort Putnam** is the original 1778 garrison constructed under the supervision of General George Washington.

The **visitors' center** outside Thayer Gate in Highland Falls supplies all the information needed for a visit.

Guided bus tours are available for a fee. The **West Point Museum** in Olmsted Hall, just outside the gate, houses one of the largest collections devoted to military history in the Western Hemisphere. A one-and-a-half-hour Hudson Highlands river cruise runs from May to October (Tel: 914-446-7171 for reservations). While you are at West Point the ▶ **Thayer Hotel** on campus is the best place for meals; Tel: (914) 446-4731.

West Point is 50 miles from New York City. By car, take the George Washington Bridge to the Palisades Interstate Parkway northbound, to Bear Mountain Circle, then Route 9W north, following signs to Highland Falls and West Point.

United States Military Academy, West Point, NY 10996. Tel: (914) 938-2638.

ELSEWHERE NORTH OF THE CITY

Donald M. Kendall Sculpture Gardens

Some 112 acres of formally landscaped grounds at the Pepsi corporate headquarters, in Purchase, New York, serve as an outdoor gallery for 40 works by a virtual Who's Who of 20th-century artists—Calder, Dubuffet, Rodin, Miró, and Moore among them. The grounds are open to the public daily, year round, free of charge. On the campus of the State University of New York at Purchase, across the street, the **Neuberger Museum** exhibits American and primitive art.

To reach the sculpture gardens, take Route 87 (the Deegan Expressway) north to exit 4, then the Cross County Parkway eastbound. Exit onto the Hutchinson River Parkway northbound, continue to exit 28, go north on Lincoln Avenue, turn right at the end of Lincoln onto Anderson Hill Road. Depending on traffic, allow 45 minutes to an hour for the 35-mile trip from Manhattan.

PepsiCo, Inc., Anderson Hill Road, Purchase, NY 10577. Tel: (914) 253-2000.

The Storm King Art Center and Sculpture Park

Mountain peaks are a dramatic backdrop for 130 post-1945 sculptures, many of them massive in size, set on 400 acres of woodland and open lawns.

Take the George Washington Bridge outbound to the Palisades Parkway to the New York State Thruway (Route 87). At exit 16 (Harriman) turn north on Route 32, continuing for 10 miles, and follow signs to the center, about

55 miles from Manhattan. Storm King is open from April to November.

Storm King Art Center, Old Pleasant Hill Road, Mountainville, NY 10953. Tel: (914) 534-3190.

New Paltz

This small village west of the Hudson at the foot of the Shawangunk Ridge of the Catskills was settled in 1678 by French Huguenots. Today New Paltz is a mix of rock climbers, academics (from the state university campus here), and old-time locals, with an artistic bent and a counterculture undercurrent. Shops tend to the solitary-sports (**Rock and Snow**, in the shopping center just south of the intersection of North Chestnut and Main streets, is the place to find equipment and information for a jaunt into the mountains) and tie-dyed-clothing variety, while restaurants are mainly vegetarian and/or ethnic or beer-and-burger college hangouts. **Fred Hansen's Antiques**, on North Chestnut Street, is a barn of a place crammed with European furniture, justly famous for its clocks (the repair of which is Hansen's specialty), armoires, and low prices. Just across the street and up the hill is the **Wildflower Café** (corner of North Front and Church streets), where you can sit in the outdoor garden and sip cappuccino made with fresh-ground coffee or have a beer and a bowl of vegetarian chili. Stone Houses Road, next to Fred Hansen's, leads to **Huguenot Street**, lined with six of the original Huguenot stone houses, built in the 17th and 18th centuries. The Huguenot Historical Society, in Deyo Hall (Tel: 914-255-1660, Wednesdays through Sundays), gives tours of the furnished and well-kept houses and the reconstructed old church, to which parishioners were once summoned by the blowing of a giant conch shell.

The mountains high above New Paltz are worth an excursion as well—indeed, are the reason many come here. There are trails, waterfalls, and swimming holes in heavily wooded **Minnewaska State Park** (drive west out of town on Main Street for 6 miles, take a right at Route 44/55, and continue up the mountain until you reach the park entrance, on the left). If you drive under the cliffs on a crisp fall day you will see hundreds of neon-clad rock climbers clinging to the cliff face.

Twelve hundred feet above the valley sits the last of the Catskills' great resort hotels, the ▶ **Mohonk Mountain House** (drive west out of town on Main Street, take the first right after the bridge onto Springtown Road, and follow the signs). The hotel's lake and acres of grounds and trails are breathtaking, and the view from its tower takes in five states. Tel: (914) 255-1000.

To get to New Paltz, simply take the New York State Thruway (Route 87) north, crossing over the Hudson on the curving Tappan Zee Bridge at Tarrytown, and continuing north until the New Paltz exit. Then turn left onto Route 299, and drive past the strip of fast-food joints and shopping centers into the village proper, about 90 miles north of New York City.

New Paltz Chamber of Commerce, 257½ Main Street, New Paltz, NY 12561. Tel: (914) 255-0243.

—*Amy K. Hughes*

Long Island

THE HAMPTONS

This chain of half a dozen towns—Southampton, East Hampton, Bridgehampton, Water Mill, Amagansett, and Sag Harbor—on the South Fork at the eastern end of Long Island is summer and weekend home to all sorts of New Yorkers: socialites, artists, writers, publishing executives, and prominent faces from the arts and entertainment worlds, and just ordinary folks seeking seaside relief from the city. The miles of magnificent, unspoiled, dune-backed white-sand beaches are among the finest in the East. The most popular are **Main Beach** in East Hampton and **Atlantic Avenue Beach** in Amagansett, both favored by the many young, single New Yorkers who share summer homes in the area.

The beaches themselves are free, but beach-parking permits are necessary if you go by car. Each village imposes its own rules and regulations. In Southampton, you may purchase a daily permit at the beaches (call the Parks and Recreation Department, Hampton Road, for information; Tel: 516-283-6000). East Hampton Village oversees five local ocean beaches. You can pick up permits for all five at Main Beach Village Hall, Main Street; Tel: (516) 324-4150. The rest of the beaches are under the umbrella of the Town of East Hampton; permits are available at the beaches or at Town Hall, Pantigo Road, East Hampton; Tel: (516) 324-4142. Permits are expensive for short visits, but many lodgings make parking permits available to their guests; it pays to ask before you reserve.

Inland from the beaches, the Hamptons are 300-year-old towns with windmills, village greens, and clapboard homes. The Studio, on East Hampton's picturesque green, was the home of watercolorist Thomas Moran, and two doors down, at 217 Main Street, is the Summer White House of President John Tyler. The town's wind-powered Hook Mill—rising above the ancient stones in the nearby Hook Mill Burying Ground—is still operating.

Gordon's, on Main Street in Amagansett (the village just east of East Hampton), is a longtime favorite dining spot, as is the **1770 House**, 143 Main Street, East Hampton. There are two branches of Manhattan's pricey **Palm** steak house in East Hampton, at the **Huntting Inn**, 94 Main Street, and **The Hedges**, 74 James Lane. The Italian fare at **Sapore di Mare**, Route 27 and Wainscott Road, Wainscott (just west of East Hampton), is considered the best in the area. For the best lobster, drive to the very end of the island and join the waiting line at **Gosman's Dock** at Montauk harbor.

If you choose to stay overnight, East Hampton's ► **1770 House** (see above; Tel: 516-324-1770) and ► **Centennial House**, 13 Woods Lane (Tel: 516-324-9414) are among the most appealing lodgings, along with the ► **Mill Garth Country Inn** (Tel: 516-267-3757), cottages in a garden, on Windmill Lane in Amagansett.

Southampton is 96 miles from Manhattan—but it feels like 296 in Friday-night traffic in summer. Drive *only* at nonpeak hours. Take the Long Island Expressway to exit 70, go right for 3 miles to Sunrise Highway (Route 27), then follow that east. Long Island Railroad has frequent service from Manhattan (Tel: 718-217-5477), as does the Hampton Jitney bus (Tel: 212-936-0440).

Southampton Chamber of Commerce, 76 Main Street, Southampton, NY 11968. Tel: (516) 283-0402. East Hampton Chamber of Commerce, 4 Main Street, East Hampton, NY 11937. Tel: (516) 324-0362.

FIRE ISLAND

This narrow strip of land, about 32 miles long and never more than half a mile wide, lies just off the center of the south shore of Long Island. It has garnered a considerable and deserved reputation for hedonism over the years. There are gay, lesbian, and heterosexual singles scenes as well as many quiet communities where the atmosphere is not quite so sexually charged. There are also miles of wide beaches on the ocean side of the island, dunes and scrub forests, and a friendly, relaxed atmosphere. Keep in mind what's not here, too: no cars, and few hotels, restaurants, and, unfortunately for those without shares (a bed in a beach house shared by other, usually young weekenders), no public facilities. You can, though, settle for **Robert Moses State Park**, a wide beach at the far western edge of the island. You can drive to the park (the rest of the island is accessible only by ferry) and from its easternmost beaches walk to the first, but not the best, of Fire Island's communities, Kismet.

Robert Moses Park is about 50 miles from Manhattan. Follow the Southern State Parkway to the exit for the Robert Moses Causeway. Villages on Fire Island are accessible only by ferries that leave from the Long Island towns of Bay Shore and Sayville. Both can be reached by the Long Island Railroad (Tel: 718-217-5477). From Bay Shore, you then board one of the boats operated by Fire Island Ferries (Tel: 516-665-3600); from Sayville, one of the boats operated by Sayville Ferries (Tel: 516-589-0810). Depending upon where you are going, the crossing usually takes from 20 minutes to half an hour.

—*Stephen Brewer*

Connecticut

YALE UNIVERSITY

Founded by ten clergymen in 1701 and named for an Englishman who saved the fledgling school from bankruptcy, Yale educated Nathan Hale, Noah Webster, Eli Whitney, and William Howard Taft, as well as a roster of contemporary leaders that includes George Bush. History aside, Yale's museums alone are worth the trip to New Haven.

The misty sea- and landscapes of Constable and Turner, the bawdy London of Hogarth, and the portraits of Gainsborough and Reynolds hang in the **Yale Center for British Art** (1080 Chapel Street), the 1977 gift of philanthropist Paul Mellon. The modernistic building designed by Louis Kahn shows off the center's paintings with natural radiance from skylights. The **Yale University Art Gallery** (1111 Chapel Street) is the nation's oldest college art museum, with eclectic exhibits that span the continents and the centuries. The museum's collection of musical instruments is world renowned, numbering some 850 antique and historical pieces from the 16th to 19th centuries. The **Beinecke Library** has its own displays of rarities, including a Gutenberg Bible, original Audubon bird prints, and Medieval manuscripts.

Free guided tours of the campus leave twice daily on weekdays, once on Saturdays and Sundays, from the information office at Phelps Gate, 344 College Street, off the New Haven Green. If you prefer, you can wander on your own, armed with the office's walking-tour map. The green is one of nine squares laid out in 1638 in America's first planned city. Among its three notable churches, the 1812 Center Church is considered a Georgian masterpiece.

Theater lovers might wish to catch one of the excellent productions at the **Yale Repertory Company** or New Haven's **Long Wharf Theater**, an outstanding regional company where many Broadway hits have been born.

Wooster Street is famous for its Italian restaurants; the pizza at **Sally's** and **Pepe's** is legendary in Connecticut—come early or late to avoid the lines.

New Haven is a 1-hour-and-45-minute train ride from New York via Amtrak or Metro-North; take a cab or buses A, J, or U from the station to the campus. By car, follow Route 95 (the Connecticut Turnpike) north to exit 47. For information call the Visitors and Convention Bureau; Tel: (203) 432-2300.

LITCHFIELD

Many of the homes around the village green of this archetypal New England town can be seen easily on foot because they are concentrated on two long blocks, North and South streets, radiating from the green. Little restoration has been necessary; many of Litchfield's homes have been continuously occupied—some by their original families—since they were built 200 years ago.

Most of the houses are still privately owned, open to visitors only on Open House Day, once a year in the summer (call for the date). But you can always visit the house on South Street where Tapping Reeve opened the nation's first law school, with his brother-in-law Aaron Burr as his first pupil. Among the school's alumni were three Supreme Court justices, 26 senators, some 90 congressmen, two vice presidents, and 14 governors. Farther down the street is the 1736 home where Ethan Allen, Revolutionary War leader of the fabled Green Mountain Boys, is believed to have been born. Also on South Street is a white clapboard house, circa 1775, that was the home of Oliver Wolcott, Sr., a signer of the Declaration of Independence who became governor of Connecticut. And there is the obligatory structure boasting "George Washington Slept Here"—in this case the former Elisha Sheldon Tavern. The Reverend Lyman Beecher first preached against the evils of intemperance in the Litchfield village meetinghouse. His son, abolitionist Henry Ward Beecher, and his daughter, Harriet Beecher Stowe, were born in the 1787 parsonage next to the church.

The **Litchfield Historical Society Museum**, also on South Street, has recently opened after a renovation; its displays of locally made furniture include the tall case clocks for which Litchfield was once famous.

Toll Gate Hill Inn, on Route 202, a 1700s Colonial building, is the appropriately historic spot for a meal or lodging (Tel: 800-445-3903 or 203-567-4545). And, while it is strictly 20th century, gardeners won't want to miss Litchfield's **White Flower Farm**, on Route 63 south, nationally known for its 1,200 varieties of unusual perennials.

Litchfield is 85 miles from New York. Take the New York State Thruway (Route 87) north to Route 287 east to Route 684 north, then Route 84 east into Connecticut. At Danbury pick up Route 7 north and at New Milford follow Route 202 into Litchfield.

Litchfield Hills Travel Council, P.O. Box 1776, Marble Dale, CT 06777. Tel: (203) 868-2214.

New Jersey

PRINCETON

The shaded lanes of this historic town are lined with outstanding Colonial and Federal buildings. Add the beautiful, ivy-clad campus of its eponymous university and you can understand Princeton's charm. The place to begin is where Princeton University began—at **Nassau Hall**. The building, one of the largest in Colonial America, housed the entire college for nearly 50 years beginning in 1756, and served as home to the Continental Congress for six months in 1783. Whig and Clio halls, twin buildings just south of Nassau Hall, resemble Greek temples and once housed the rival societies where two 18th-century students, James Madison and Aaron Burr, honed their debating skills (the two groups merged in 1929). Princeton's University Chapel has glorious stained-glass windows, oak pews, and a 16th-century pulpit from France. It took 100 men a year to carve the choir and clergy stalls, made of wood from Sherwood Forest of Robin Hood fame. Firestone Library, next to the chapel, has changing exhibitions.

The strikingly modern **Princeton University Art Museum** houses Chinese paintings, prints, and drawings, and other collections that range from African ritual masks to paintings by Cézanne and van Gogh. The Picasso sculpture just outside is part of the outstanding outdoor collection that covers the campus and includes dozens of works by such masters as Louise Nevelson, Henry Moore, Alexander Calder, and Jacques Lipchitz.

You can join a free, one-hour guided tour of the campus at Maclean House, just inside the main gate off Nassau Street, the town's main street. For information on other historic sites in and around town, stop for a guide at Bainbridge House, the headquarters of the Princeton Historical Society on Nassau Street. Among sights worth seeing are Rockingham, George Washington's onetime headquarters; Morven, the former official residence of the governor of New Jersey; the Stony Brook (Quaker) Meeting House; and the homes of Woodrow Wilson (the Woodrow Wilson School of Public and International Affairs is at Princeton), Albert Einstein, and Aaron Burr. There are dozens of fine historic homes to be viewed on Nassau Street and its side streets Alexander, Mercer, and Stockton. Nearby, to the west (though a fairly long walk), are the attractive Neo-Gothic Graduate School and, beyond that, the world-famous **Institute for Advanced Studies**.

Le Plumet Royal in the Peacock Inn, 20 Bayard Lane, and **Lahiere's**, 5 Witherspoon Street, are Princeton's best restaurants. The **Omni Nassau Inn** in Palmer Square is newer than it looks but is pleasant and convenient for lunch (accommodations reservations, Tel: 800-862-7728 or 609-921-7500).

New Jersey Transit (Tel: 201-762-5100) runs frequent trains to Princeton from Penn Station, with a change at Princeton Junction. The trip takes an hour and the center of the university is a three-minute stroll from the station. Bus service is available via Suburban Transit (Tel: 212-868-7367) from the Port Authority Bus Terminal to the center of town.

To reach Princeton by car, take the New Jersey Turnpike south to exit 9, then Route 18 north to Route 1 (Trenton exit). Drive approximately 15 miles on Route 1 south to the Princeton–Hightstown Road exit, and go right on Route 571. At the third traffic light make a left onto Nassau; this puts you right in the middle of Princeton.

Princeton Chamber of Commerce, P.O. Box 431 (20 Nassau Street), Princeton, NJ 08542. Tel: (609) 921-7676.

SPRING LAKE

A turn-of-the-century boardwalk and shady avenues lined with gingerbread-trimmed hotels and gracious Victorian homes with canopied porches are the stage sets for an old-fashioned day by the sea. The spring-fed lake that gave Spring Lake, on the New Jersey shore, its name is in a sylvan park in the heart of this pretty village, once known as the Irish Riviera because so many wealthy Irish families summered here.

Spring Lake's ▶ **Normandy Inn** (Tel: 908-449-7172) and ▶ **Ashling Cottage** (Tel: 908-449-3553) are small, charming Victorian homes turned bed-and-breakfast inns. Take your meals at the **Beach House** at the Warren (Tel: 908-449-9646), the **Breakers** (Tel: 908-449-7700), and other big hotels.

Spring Lake is about 65 miles from Manhattan. Follow the New Jersey Turnpike south to the Garden State Parkway. Take exit 98, then Route 34 south to the traffic circle, and Route 524 east into town.

Greater Spring Lake Chamber of Commerce, P.O. Box 694, Spring Lake, NJ 07762. Tel: (908) 449-0577.

Pennsylvania

DOYLESTOWN, BUCKS COUNTY

Archaeologist Henry Chapman Mercer was so intrigued with the work of the old Pennsylvania German tile makers that in the 1890s he apprenticed himself to a master. Mercer tiles can be seen today in the casino at Monte Carlo and the Gardner Museum in Boston. Mercer's **Moravian Pottery and Tile Works** factory is now a museum but still turns out tiles according to his patterns. His collection of 25,000 early American tools is on view nearby at the **Mercer Museum**, which has an interior spiral design that is said to have inspired Frank Lloyd Wright's design for New York's Guggenheim Museum. Most intriguing of all is Mercer's home, **Fonthill**, a concrete fantasy of columns, balconies, beams, towers, and winding staircases, with tiles everywhere. The three attractions are known collectively as the Mercer Mile. The nearby **James A. Michener Art Center**, housed in a former 1800s jail, has exhibits of contemporary art and crafts, a sculpture garden, and a schedule of performing arts. It was funded by Michener, Doylestown's best-known native son. Don't confine your wanderings to Doylestown, though: The Bucks County countryside is beautiful, especially along the Delaware River.

Two good bed-and-breakfast inns in Doylestown are ► **Highland Farms**, the former Oscar Hammerstein estate (Tel: 215-340-1354), and the ► **Inn at Fordhook Farm**, once the estate of seed king David Burpee (Tel: 215-345-1766).

To get to Doylestown, take the New Jersey Turnpike south to exit 10, then go north on Route 287 for 15 miles and stay left for another exit 10, Route 22. Drive west for about 3½ miles and turn right at the sign marked Flemington-Princeton. This is Route 202, which leads across the Delaware River to Doylestown, about 85 miles from Manhattan.

The Mercer Mile, Doylestown, PA 18901. Fonthill, East Court Street; Tel: (215) 348-9461. Mercer Museum, Pine Street; Tel: (215) 345-0210. Moravian Pottery and Tile Works, 130 Swamp Road; Tel: (215) 345-6722. James A. Michener Art Center, 138 South Pine Street; Tel: (215) 340-9800.

THE CITY'S SPECIALTIES

MUSEUMS

By Amy K. Hughes

One of the first things you will notice when you are exploring the city's museums is that while they are attended by visitors they are also full of New Yorkers, and it's because of this sophisticated, hard-nosed clientele that New York's museums are among the best in the world. From the largest, stuffiest, wealthiest institution to the smallest and quirkiest, each has its own appeal.

Most major museums in New York are open on weekends and closed on Mondays, but some close on Sundays or Tuesdays as well, to make a "weekend" of it; exceptions to these general rules are noted. Many stay open late one or two evenings a week, also noted. Like everything else in New York, the hours of museums are subject to change, as are the addresses and phone numbers (and there are the inevitable closures for renovation). With New York City's recent budget problems, many museums have had to greatly reduce their hours or stagger the hours of certain exhibits, and a few are threatened with closure. We recommend you telephone a museum before setting aside time or going out of your way to visit it.

All museums listed are in Manhattan (telephone area code 212) unless otherwise indicated.

A late-18th-century carriage house quarters the **Abigail Adams Smith Museum**, with music room, dining room, kitchen, bedrooms, and sitting rooms decorated in period furnishings. 421 East 61st Street, between First and York avenues. Tel: 838-6878. Open Mondays; closed weekends in winter, Saturdays in summer.

The **Alternative Museum** shows contemporary political and sociopolitical art that you won't find in the uptown museums. It also puts on solo, mid-career shows for artists out of the traditional mainstream. 594 Broadway, between Houston and Prince streets. Tel: 966-4444. Closed mid-August through September.

If you equate crafts with summer camp, the sophisticated ceramics, glass, textiles, woodwork, metalwork, and basketry by craftspeople of today and yesterday on display at the **American Craft Museum** will change your outlook forever. 40 West 53rd Street, between Fifth and Sixth avenues. Tel: 956-6047. Open late Tuesdays.

The **American Museum of the Moving Image** is dedicated to demonstrating, displaying, portraying, explaining, analyzing, and celebrating television, video, and film—in an exciting, exhilarating arena. 35th Avenue at 36th Street, Astoria, Queens. (From Manhattan take the R train to the Steinway Street station.) Tel: (718) 784-0077.

Most native New Yorkers share Holden Caulfield's memory of tramping through the **American Museum of Natural History** on a school field trip. The kids are still here, marveling at the massive dinosaur skeletons and the giant whale hanging from the ceiling. The exhibits include dioramas with animals from around the world, a spectacular mineral and gem collection, a giant-screen movie theater, and the Hayden Planetarium, which brings the universe down to earth. The new Hall of Human Biology, featuring dioramas of our prehistoric ancestors, comprises some of the most provocative exhibits in this venerable institution. The museum's world-famous dinosaur exhibits are undergoing an extensive renovation (completion in 1997, or so), but there will always be dinosaurs on view, including the new Barosaurus display in the Theodore Roosevelt Rotunda (second floor). Central Park West at 79th Street. Tel: 769-5100. Open every day; open late Fridays and Saturdays.

The **Asia Society**'s special exhibitions, programs, films, and lectures focus on the art, culture, and history of the East. The society's permanent holdings include the John D. Rockefeller collection of Oriental arts. 725 Park Avenue, at 70th Street. Tel: 288-6400.

Intriguing displays of local artists, themes, and history as well as exciting travelling exhibitions (such as the programs related to the Metropolitan Museum's recent Mexico exhibition) can be found at the **Bronx Museum of the Arts**. 1040 Grand Concourse, at 165th Street, Bronx. (From Manhattan take the Sixth Avenue express D train to the 167th Street/Grand Concourse station, one stop past Yankee Stadium.) Tel: (718) 681-6000.

Everyone with kids should spend a day among the bright, colorful hands-on exhibits at the **Brooklyn Children's Museum**. Natural history, science, and technology are brought to life in an environment that inspires and ignites young imaginations. 145 Brooklyn Avenue, at St. Mark's Street. (Call for directions.) Tel: (718) 735-4400.

You'll find all the wonders of Brooklyn—Coney Island, the Dodgers, Brooklyn Bridge, even "The Honeymooners"—documented and exhibited in the recently refurbished **Brooklyn Historical Society**. The 1881 Queen Anne–style building is one of the city's most treasured pieces of architecture. 128 Pierrepont Street, Brooklyn Heights. (Take the 2, 3, 4, or 5 IRT train to Borough Hall or the R or M BMT train to Court Street.) Tel: (718) 624-0890.

A world-famous collection of Egyptian art, Colonial American furnishings, Oriental prints, and European paintings (and everything and anything in between) can be found at the superb **Brooklyn Museum**, which of late is gaining a reputation for showing anti-establishment artists. Be sure to check out one of the best, most affordable museum shops in New York. 200 Eastern Parkway, near Washington Avenue. (Easily reached from Manhattan via the number 2 or 3 IRT subway lines, Eastern Parkway station.) Tel: (718) 638-5000.

The **Children's Museum of the Arts** is designed to turn kids into art lovers when they're young (12 months to 10 years), before they get the idea that art is dull and museums stupefying. Exhibits are hands-on and interactive. 72 Spring Street, between Broadway and Lafayette. Tel: 941-9198.

When the **Children's Museum of Manhattan** was in its planning stages it engaged a special advisory committee whose members ranged in age from 5 to 14. Its original exhibitions destroyed in a fire, the museum now has changing exhibitions (an environmental installation with a rain-forest construction and exhibits on garbage, for example) with hands-on activities geared to different age groups. At the media center kids can operate a television camera or pretend to be a newscaster. 212 West 83rd

Street, between Broadway and Amsterdam Avenue. Tel: 721-1223. Open Mondays, closed Tuesdays.

The Gothic **Cloisters**, an outpost of the Metropolitan Museum of Art, evokes the Middle Ages. The treasures and artworks are augmented by the monastic setting, the herb garden, and the view of the Hudson and the Palisades. West 190th Street and Fort Washington Avenue in Fort Tryon Park, at the northern tip of Manhattan. (From Midtown, take either the A subway line to 190th Street and walk through the park or take the M 4 Madison Avenue bus directly to the Cloisters.) Tel: 923-3700.

In Andrew Carnegie's 64-room mansion, the **Cooper-Hewitt Museum**, an affiliate of the Smithsonian Institution, displays superb collections of wallpapers, drawings, prints, glass, porcelain, textiles, embroidery, lace, woodwork, metalwork, and anything else that falls into the categories of design and decorative arts, both the old and the new. 2 East 91st Street, at Fifth Avenue. Tel: 860-6898. Open late Tuesdays.

The restored registry building that houses the **Ellis Island Immigration Museum** was the site of many a European immigrant's first, and often frightening, encounter with American bureaucracy. This long-awaited museum, with its authentic setting, oral histories, and it-happened-here realism, promises to tell the true story of the American immigrant. Ferries depart from Battery Park at the tip of Manhattan (Tel: 269-5755) and Liberty State Park, New Jersey (Tel: 201-435-9499). Ferries from Battery Park stop at the Statue of Liberty first. The ferries from New Jersey go to the Statue of Liberty after Ellis Island.

The stone on which George Washington stood during his presidential inauguration is one of the displays at **Federal Hall National Memorial**, a museum devoted to New York's and America's early days. 26 Wall Street, at Nassau Street. Tel: 264-8711. Closed weekends. Free.

The Fabergé eggs are the stars of the **Forbes Magazine Galleries**, which also house 500 toy boats, 12,000 toy soldiers, and a fine collection of master paintings. 62 Fifth Avenue, at 12th Street. Tel: 206-5548. Groups only on Thursdays. Free.

The exhibits on the second floor of **Fraunces Tavern**—in the room where George Washington took leave of his fellow officers after the Revolution—document the culture and history of New York City in its colonial days. 54 Pearl Street, at Broad Street, at the southern tip of Manhattan. Tel: 425-1778.

The **Frick Collection** of old-master paintings, sculptures, furnishings, and decorative arts could not be shown to better advantage—in what was once Henry Clay Frick's home. The garden is an oasis of peace in the bustling city. 1 East 70th Street, at Fifth Avenue. Tel: 288-0700.

The **Solomon R. Guggenheim Museum**, which reopened in 1992 after an extensive renovation and restructuring, is probably more famous for its spiraling Frank Lloyd Wright building than it is for its extensive modern-art collections. The main rotunda, with sparkling new skylights, and a smaller rotunda that had long been used for offices provide a stunning and graceful backdrop for Picassos, Kandinskys, and Giacomettis that seem like old familiar friends. A new annex provides additional gallery space and airy views of Fifth Avenue and Central Park. The venerable food sellers Dean & DeLuca operate the museum's enlarged café, which sports Wright's stainless-steel porthole windows. 1071 Fifth Avenue, at 88th Street. Tel: 423-3500. Closed Thursdays. Open late every day.

The brand-new **Guggenheim Museum SoHo**, a series of all-white loft-like galleries, will feature changing exhibitions from the Guggenheim Foundation's collection. 575 Broadway, at Prince Street. Tel: 423-3500. Closed Tuesdays, open Mondays; open until 10:00 P.M. Thursday through Saturday.

Spanish and Portuguese paintings (by Goya, Velázquez, and El Greco), sculptures, artifacts, and mosaics from Roman times to the 20th century are in the fine collection at the **Hispanic Society of America**. Audubon Terrace, Broadway at 155th Street. Tel: 926-2234.

Past and present photographers and photojournalists are represented in one-person and theme shows at the **International Center of Photography**. 1130 Fifth Avenue, at 94th Street. Tel: 860-1777. There is also a branch at 1133 Sixth Avenue, at 43rd Street. Tel: 768-4682. Both branches open late Tuesdays.

Aboard the **Intrepid Sea-Air-Space Museum** (housed on a decommissioned aircraft carrier), military history is conveyed through exhibits, films, authentic aircraft, and the carrier itself. Hudson River, Pier 86, West 46th Street. Tel: 245-2533. Open every day in summer.

The permanent collections of art, artifacts, and treasures at the **Jewish Museum** are augmented by changing exhibitions that highlight different aspects of Jewish life and culture. The museum reopened in 1993 after a renovation of the original landmark building and the construction of an addition that doubled exhibition space. The museum's new Café Weissman serves delicious New American fare. 1109 Fifth Avenue, at 92nd Street. Tel: 423-3200.

The **Liberty Science Center** is a brand-new participatory science museum designed to get kids interested in the workings of our world. Laser shows, an insect zoo with live tarantulas and giant hissing cockroaches, a pitch-black tunnel maze, a real ambulance, and a huge expanding and contracting geodesic globe are among the exhibits. Liberty State Park, 251 Phillip Street, Jersey City, New Jersey; Tel: (201) 200-1000. Ferries to Liberty State Park leave from Manhattan's Midtown Ferry Terminal (38th Street and 12th Avenue) and the Hoboken Ferry Terminal (North End Avenue, off Vesey Street behind the World Financial Center in lower Manhattan); for ferry information, Tel: (800) 533-3779. To reach the museum by public transportation take the PATH train from Manhattan to Grove Street in Jersey City, then get the Central Avenue Bus Company express bus to the museum. By car take the Holland Tunnel to the New Jersey Turnpike; take the Turnpike Extension to exit 14B, turn left onto Burma Road, which becomes Phillip Street, and follow it to the museum.

In addition to its galleries featuring historical exhibits, the **Lower East Side Tenement Museum**, housed in an 1853 tenement building, sponsors walking tours of the area highlighting the experiences of different groups, including Jews, Italians, Chinese, and freed slaves. The museum plans one day to open tenement rooms with furnishings representative of different ethnic groups. 97 Orchard Street, between Broome and Delancey streets. Tel: 431-0233.

As soon as you enter the Great Hall at the **Metropolitan Museum of Art** you know you are in New York's biggest and best. Wander through such sections as the Egyptian Temple of Dendur, the American Wing, and the Blumenthal Patio and you'll feel as if you've been transported around the world and through time. Paintings by masters old and new, sculptures from ancient Greece and Rome to modern times, the Costume Institute, the primitive-art collection, and famous collections of the arts of Egypt and the Middle East are just a few of the best-known attractions. Due to funding cuts, the museum has staggered hours in some of its galleries; if you are going to see a specific collection, call first to find out its hours. Fifth Avenue at 82nd Street. Tel: 535-7710. Open late Fridays and Saturdays.

El Museo del Barrio displays paintings, sculpture, photographs, and films by contemporary artists of Puerto Rican and Central and South American heritage, as well as historical and cultural artifacts. 1230 Fifth Avenue, at 104th Street. Tel: 831-7272. Closed for renovation until early 1994.

The **Museum for African Art** brings the traditional arts of Africa's myriad cultures to New York, with changing exhibitions, films, and lectures. The museum's new location, in SoHo, features a flowing, colorful series of galleries designed by Maya Lin. 593 Broadway, between Houston and Prince streets. Tel: 966-1313.

Quilts, weather vanes, tin toys, decoys, and furniture are some of the things you might find at the **Museum of American Folk Art**, most with a quirky twist that characterizes this type of work. 2 Lincoln Square, Columbus Avenue at 66th Street. Tel: 595-9533.

You can find out anything you want to know about New York City at the **Museum of the City of New York**. Recent exhibitions have focused on Walt Whitman and the history of Broadway theater. The museum's Sunday walking tours of different neighborhoods are among the best in town. 1220 Fifth Avenue, at 103rd Street. Tel: 534-1672.

Since its opening in 1929, the **Museum of Modern Art** (MoMA) has been a major force in promoting the arts of this century and the end of the last, when modern art was born. All the important movements of modern art and design are represented here, be they photos, paintings, sculptures, furniture, or household appliances. 11 West 53rd Street, between Fifth and Sixth avenues. Tel: 708-9480. Open Mondays, closed Wednesdays, open late Thursdays.

Radio and television buffs shouldn't miss the **Museum of Television & Radio**, where they can listen to old broadcasts, watch old TV shows or commercials, and look up favorite scripts. 25 West 52nd Street, between Fifth and Sixth avenues. Tel: 621-6800. Open late Thursdays and Fridays.

Samuel F. B. Morse and Rembrandt Peale were among the founders of the **National Academy of Design**, which houses an impressive collection of paintings, drawings, and sculptures, many of them from Renaissance times. 1083 Fifth Avenue, at 89th Street. Tel: 369-4880. Open late Fridays.

The displays of clothing, artifacts, sculpture, jewelry, and masks at the **National Museum of the American Indian** are designed to further the understanding of the cultures of native peoples of the Americas. Through fall 1994 the collection remains at Audubon Terrace, Broadway at 155th Street. Tel: 283-2497. Part of the collection will be relocated to the Smithsonian's new National Museum of the American Indian in Washington, D.C., by the end of the decade. The New York branch of the museum (renamed the George Gustav Heye Center of the National Museum of the American Indian) will move to the old U.S. Custom House (renamed the Alexander Hamilton Custom House), on State Street in lower Manhattan, across from Bowling Green; due to open in fall 1994.

For a glimpse at art that is perhaps too avant-garde for the more buttoned-down galleries and museums, stop in at the **New Museum of Contemporary Art**. 583 Broadway, between Prince and Houston streets, in SoHo. Tel: 219-1355. Open late Saturdays.

What better place to learn about the history of firefighting than in the old firehouse that quarters the **New York City Fire Museum**, featuring old engines and equipment and exhibits on the city's great fires. 278 Spring Street, between Hudson and Varick streets. Tel: 691-1303.

The **New York Hall of Science**, on the site of the world's fairs of 1939 and 1964, houses a fascinating assemblage of hands-on space, technological, and science exhibits. Flushing Meadows Corona Park, 47-01 111th Street, at 48th Avenue, Queens. (From Manhattan, take the number 7 subway line to 111th Street in Queens, and walk five blocks south to 48th Avenue.) Tel: (718) 699-0005.

Learn what's made New York tick for 350 years at the **New-York Historical Society**, a repository of furnishings, prints, fine art, artifacts, and documents pertaining to New York and early America. Nearing bankruptcy in 1993, the society was forced to close temporarily. At present the reference library is open several days a week; the galleries are expected to reopen in 1995. In the meantime the society will be sponsoring exhibits in other parts of the city (call for information). 170 Central Park West, at 77th Street. Tel: 873-3400.

You won't find gladiators' breastplates or emperors' goblets at **New York Unearthed**, the city's archaeological museum, but the displays of dishes, tools, and household objects found at local excavation sites are just as intriguing, as they recall the past of our city's ordinary folk. 17 State Street; entrance in courtyard. Tel: 363-9372. Open Mondays, closed Sundays. Free.

For a glimpse into the 1830s, don't miss the **Old Merchant's House**, which contains the original furnishings, mementos, and clothing of the family that lived there. 29 East 4th Street. Tel: 777-1089. Call for special and seasonal events. Closed Fridays and Saturdays.

The **Pierpont Morgan Library** affords a stunning backdrop for inspired temporary shows and the superb permanent collections, which include old-master drawings, Medieval and Renaissance artworks, and valuable manuscripts. A major expansion program completed in 1991 doubled the museum's space and opened a glass-enclosed garden court and the neighboring Morgan House. 29 East 36th Street, at Madison Avenue. Tel: 685-0610.

A giant scale model of the five boroughs of New York featuring every building is the most popular display at the **Queens Museum of Art**, housed in the New York City pavilion from the 1939 World's Fair, but the changing exhibits of works by contemporary artists are also fine. The museum is in the midst of a major expansion and renovation that will return the building to its 1939 architecture (due to be completed in 1994). The first phase of the work opened up a large gallery space with two-story-high windows that look out on the Unisphere. The scale model of the city, however, is under renovation and won't be on view until 1994. Flushing Meadows Corona Park. (From Manhattan, take the number 7 subway line to the Shea Stadium stop; walk ten minutes through the park toward the Unisphere.) Tel: (718) 592-5555.

The Staten Island Historical Society's **Richmondtown Restoration** is a series of historic buildings—school, grocer, general store—that have been restored and furnished to particular periods in the area's history. 441 Clarke Avenue, at Arthur Kill Road. (Call for directions.) Tel: (718) 351-1611. Hours vary seasonally.

Sideshows by the Seashore crams the heyday of old Coney Island under its roof: old rides, funhouse mirrors, signs and other memorabilia, and a freak show—complete with the Bearded Lady and the Human Blockhead. Boardwalk at West 12th Street, Coney Island. Tel: (718) 372-5159.

Tall ships, galleries, hands-on children's exhibits, and a summer concert series are all part of the bustling **South Street Seaport Museum and Marketplace**, which endeavors to keep the spirit of the area's early 18th-century heyday alive. The "museum" is not in a single building but encompasses sights and activities in the area. Visitors' center on Fulton Street between Front and South streets. Tel: 669-9400. Open every day.

The **Studio Museum in Harlem** is a showcase for contemporary black artists (of Africa, the Caribbean, and the Americas); its permanent collections and special exhibitions are among the finest and most thought-provoking in the city. 144 West 125th Street, between Lenox and Seventh avenues. (Take the West Side IRT 2 or 3 train to the 125th Street station.) Tel: 864-4500.

The **Theodore Roosevelt Birthplace** is a re-creation of the childhood home of the New York City police commissioner who became president. 28 East 20th Street, between Park Avenue South and Broadway. Tel: 260-1616.

A reconstruction of a Tibetan temple, gardens, and a lotus pool, and a remarkable collection of Tibetan and Buddhist art are some of the attractions of the Jacques Marchais Center of Tibetan Art, better known as the **Tibetan Museum**. Besides students and lovers of Orientalia, its visitors include Buddhist monks from a New Jersey monastery. 338 Lighthouse Avenue, Staten Island. Tel: (718) 987-3478. Call for directions and winter hours.

The history and the traditional arts and crafts of Ukraine are on display at the **Ukrainian Museum**, devoted to keeping that culture alive in the American melting pot. 203 Second Avenue, between 12th and 13th streets. Tel: 228-0110.

For an impressive overview of the most influential American artists of this century—from Edward Hopper to Georgia O'Keeffe to Andy Warhol—visit the **Whitney Museum of American Art**. 945 Madison Avenue, at 75th Street. Tel: 570-3676. Open late Thursdays.

A branch gallery, the **Whitney Museum of American Art at Philip Morris** (120 Park Avenue, at 42nd Street), features special exhibitions. Tel: 878-2550. Closed weekends, open late Thursdays.

ART

By Eleanor Heartney

Eleanor Heartney is a writer and critic specializing in contemporary art. She is a regular contributor to Artnews, Art in America, *and the* New Art Examiner.

New York City is haunted by the ghosts of art worlds past. You can stroll around Union Square and nod to the spirits of Isabel Bishop and Reginald Marsh as they toss off rapid sketches of the inhabitants of a quieter America between the wars. Then, heading south along University Place, you pass near the sites of legendary watering holes where Jackson Pollock, Willem de Kooning, Philip Guston, and their cronies tipped their bottles in the raucous hours between their solitary labors. A detour along Washington Square takes you past the Judson Memorial Church, which during the 1960s served as a stage for happenings, experimental dance and theater productions, and environmental installations by such avant-gardists as Red Grooms, Allan Kaprow, Allen Ginsberg, and Yvonne Rainer. Of course, the most obvious places to partake of New York's rich artistic heritage are the city's many art museums, covered in the neighborhood sections and the Museums chapter.

However, to penetrate the heart of *today's* art world, you must continue south from the Village across Houston Street to SoHo, that once shabby warehouse district that now boasts what is undoubtedly the richest concentration of artists, artworks, and art talk in the world. There are, by conservative estimate, roughly 500 art galleries in New York City, more than half of which are in SoHo, and perhaps as many as 90,000 artists living in the city and its immediate environs. Such sheer numbers, at once the cause and effect of the burgeoning art market, have re-created the art world in ways that would have seemed unimaginable even 15 years ago. As art, money, and hype mix here in a sometimes unwholesome stew, bohemia today wears a distinctly modern face, and though black remains the sartorial color of choice, the notion of starving in garrets or repulsing the bourgeoisie is definitely passé.

It's possible to chart the ebb and flow of the national economy by following the migration of galleries and art spaces across downtown New York. The entrepreneurial spirit of the early 1980s took root in the tiny storefronts of the East Village, where ambitious young artist-dealers opened galleries in what were essentially their living rooms. Those who made good moved several years later to the poshly appointed, so-called shopping-mall gallery buildings on Broadway at the edge of SoHo, in which the galleries clustered one atop the other in stacks. Come the 1990s and economic recession, many galleries have been downscaling and moving to less expensive quarters along Broome and Grand streets. At the same time, the surplus of real estate has proved a boon for a new generation of independent curators and dealers who are able to strike deals with tenant-hungry landlords for use of partially refinished warehouse spaces. These new spaces have become showcases for sprawling, eclectic exhibitions of work by known and unknown artists. With their deliberate rejection of 1980s-style elegance, they embody the funky, streetwise energy that seems to be the hallmark of the embattled 1990s.

THE GALLERY AS SHOWCASE

Ensconced in clean white exhibition spaces and equipped with an open-door policy, a revolving schedule of exhibitions, and a quasi-educational function, many galleries today attempt to duplicate the museum experience. Yet, unlike museums, they support themselves through the sale of work. This lends them a slightly schizophrenic character, a fact brought forcefully home recently when the New York Department of Cultural Affairs decreed that galleries, like all other retail businesses, must display an up-to-date price list of all items on view. Some galleries quietly complied, others protested vigorously that too much emphasis on commerce would detract from aesthetic contemplation—and a few evaded the regulation entirely by preselling entire shows.

The price-list furor dramatizes the complicated role galleries play in the contemporary art world. Commercial galleries today are the primary mechanism through which artists emerge into the art mainstream (due in part to the decline of the alternative space; see below). Hence a gallery exhibition is far more than a display of wares for sale; it is a crucial milestone in an artist's career, a way to enter the art dialogue, to get reviewed, to be considered for museum exhibitions. Therefore, it is important for everyone involved that the exhibition be open to the general public and be seen by a larger audience than that composed of potential buyers.

At the same time, however, the gallery is a place of sale. Typically, each gallery represents a "stable" of artists, whose works are available for viewing and sale at all times in the back room. Most galleries support themselves as much or more through the back room as through sales of exhibited work. In theory, at least, this allows them to present work that may be risky and potentially unsalable out front.

DOING THE GALLERIES

Given the number of galleries and the varieties of art currently on display, "doing" the galleries in New York can seem a somewhat daunting task. Once an activity that might fill a pleasant afternoon, gallery going now threatens to overwhelm the unselective visitor. In order to survive a day of gallery hopping, begin with a definite plan of attack. The indispensable tool is the *Art Now Gallery Guide,* a monthly listing of the exhibitions currently on view in more than 500 galleries and museums around the city. The *Gallery Guide* is available from the listed galleries (though toward the end of the month copies tend to become very scarce) and at some bookstores. The guide divides the city into areas, and each section is accompanied by a small map.

Because they benefit from spillover traffic, galleries tend to cluster together. The greatest concentrations exist in **SoHo**, of course, where you can expect to find the work of the most hotly debated new artists and styles. The galleries on **57th Street**, with several lively exceptions, focus on artists of more solidly established reputations. And those on the Upper East Side along **Madison Avenue**, in elegant brownstones, present art of historical and contemporary importance with a quiet decorum that contrasts strikingly with the downtown scene's noisy self-promotion.

The first-time visitor wanting to get the flavor of New York art could do worse than focus on the various multi-gallery buildings, such as those at: 420 West Broadway, 130 Prince Street, and 560, 568, and 578 Broadway in SoHo; and 41 East 57th Street, 50 West 57th Street, and 724 Fifth Avenue in the 57th Street area. Those with more time or specific interests will want to venture as well to the more dispersed galleries listed in the *Gallery Guide*.

Though distinctions have begun to blur somewhat, the old division between haughty uptown and hip downtown remains largely in force.

What follows are a few thumbnail sketches of some notable galleries in the three major art zones. While the vast majority of galleries in New York feature contemporary art or a mix of contemporary and modern (late 19th and 20th century) art, there are also a number of dealers listed here who specialize in historical work. We have made no effort to be comprehensive (an impossible task anyway), so this selection should be taken as a mere starting point for gallery exploration.

SoHo Galleries

As much a tourist attraction in her own right as she is a purveyor of art, **Mary Boone** (417 West Broadway, between Prince and Spring streets) almost single-handedly redefined the gallery business in the 1980s. Her talent for showmanship and marketing has helped her bend with the shifting winds of the art market. Her current stable (which includes feminists Sherrie Levine and Barbara Kruger; Tim Rollins and his youthful, Bronx-based collaborators, the Kids of Survival; German star Sigmar Polke; and abstract painters Gary Stephan and Brice Marden) reflects the multiple interests that make up today's art world. Tel: 431-1818.

By contrast, the grand old man of the New York art scene is **Leo Castelli**, who made his reputation in the early 1960s with his unwavering support of then-brash newcomers such as Andy Warhol, Roy Lichtenstein, and Jasper Johns. The work of these artists, as well as such younger artists as Joseph Kosuth, Robert Therrien, and Edward Ruscha, can be seen at Castelli's three locations in SoHo: 420 West Broadway (between Prince and Spring streets), Tel: 431-5160; 578 Broadway (between Houston and Prince streets), Tel: 431-6279; and 65 Thompson Street (between Spring and Broome streets), Tel: 219-2219.

Irreverent newcomers devoted to unorthodox formats and political and social themes are the fare at the deliberately low-key **American Fine Arts** (22 Wooster Street, between Grand and Canal streets). Here you can see the work of such installation artists as Peter Fend, Mark Dion, and Jessica Stockholder. Tel: 941-0401.

The place to find the "old" austere Conceptual and Minimal art is **John Weber Gallery** (142 Greene Street, between Houston and Prince streets), whose stable includes such venerable names as Sol LeWitt, Alice Aycock, and Robert Smithson, as well as younger artists with a compatible outlook. Tel: 966-6115.

Ronald Feldman Fine Arts (31 Mercer Street, between Grand and Canal streets), one of the more independent and idiosyncratic galleries in town, offers artists as different as the elegantly restrained Conceptualist Arakawa, the boisterous Russian expatriates Komar and Melamid, and the self-appointed nouveau Andy Warhol, Mark Kostabi. Tel: 226-3232.

A cryptic, cerebral, ironic aesthetic is to be found at **Metro Pictures** (150 Greene Street, at Houston Street). Home of the so-called Pictures Generation, whose politically attuned media explorations offered a counterpoint to Neoexpressionism in the early 1980s, Metro has matured with its artists, who include such internationally known figures as Cindy Sherman, Mike Kelley, Robert Longo, and Martin Kippenberger. Tel: 925-8335.

Max Protetch (560 Broadway, at Prince Street) celebrates the marriage of art and architecture, offering architectural drawings and models as well as quasi-functional and architecturally inspired sculpture by such artists as Siah Armajani, Alan Sonfist, and Betty Woodman. Tel: 966-5454.

The **Holly Solomon Gallery** (172 Mercer Street, at Houston Street) shows a roster of artists that includes Nicholas Africano, William Wegman, and Izhar Patkin in a sun-drenched, two-tiered space. Tel: 941-5777.

And finally, the spirit of the 1990s is perhaps best embodied by some of the newest SoHo showcases. **Threadwaxing Space** (476 Broadway, between Broome and Grand streets) seems to occupy a niche between the old-style commercial gallery and the alternative space. Located in a sprawling warehouse once devoted to the industry enshrined in its name, it has no stable of artists but instead exhibits experimental works and theme shows, many of which are organized by invited curators. It maintains as well a schedule of performances, readings, and multimedia events. Tel: 966-9520.

57th Street Galleries

With a venerable history behind it (its proprietor was linked to the discovery of Pop Art in the 1960s), **Sidney**

Janis Gallery (110 West 57th Street, between Sixth and Seventh avenues) is noted for the museum quality of its exhibitions of the art of such historical figures as Alberto Giacometti, Piet Mondrian, and Josef Albers, as well as more recent masters like George Segal, Duane Michals, and Tom Wesselmann. Tel: 586-0110.

Many uptown galleries focus on modern masters and historically important artists from the early 20th century to the present. Works by artists ranging from Pablo Picasso and Henri Matisse to Willem de Kooning, Robert Rauschenberg, Henry Moore, and Jackson Pollock can be seen at **Barbara Mathes** (41 East 57th Street, between Park and Madison avenues). Tel: 752-5135.

New work by the major figures of the color-field school is frequently the fare at **André Emmerich Gallery** (41 East 57th Street, at Madison Avenue), whose stable boasts, among others, Jules Olitski, Lawrence Poons, Kenneth Noland, Helen Frankenthaler, and Sam Francis. Tel: 752-0124.

A wide-ranging and international group of artists is showcased within a series of elegant, spacious rooms at **Marlborough Gallery** (40 West 57th Street, between Fifth and Sixth avenues). The gallery's stable ranges from pop artist Red Grooms to the late British expressionist Francis Bacon to Scottish fabulist Steven Campbell. Tel: 541-4900.

The focus at **Marian Goodman Gallery** (24 West 57th Street, between Fifth and Sixth avenues) is on the European avant-garde, with an emphasis on *arte povera,* Conceptualism, and large-scale sculpture projects. This is the place to see the work of such international stars as Tony Cragg, Rebecca Horn, and Anselm Kiefer, as well as European artists (such as Lothar Baumgarten, Thomas Struth, and Giuseppe Penone) who are better known outside the United States than they are here. Tel: 977-7160.

Galerie St. Etienne (24 West 57th Street, between Fifth and Sixth avenues) specializes in an odd mix: Austrian and German Expressionist painters from the turn of the century alongside contemporary and 19th-century American folk art. This gallery, operating in New York for 50 years, was the first to introduce an American audience to such artists as Gustav Klimt, Paula Modersohn-Becker, and Grandma Moses. Tel: 245-6734.

Uptown Galleries

M. Knoedler & Co. (19 East 70th Street, between Fifth and Madison avenues), one of the oldest and most elegant galleries in New York (founded in 1846), is home to a distinguished stable of artists that includes such illustrious names as Frank Stella, Nancy Graves, and Richard Diebenkorn, as well as historical figures such as Adolph Gottlieb, David Smith, and Alexander Calder. Tel: 794-0550.

In elegant, spacious surroundings, **Gagosian Gallery** (980 Madison Avenue, north of 76th Street) offers shows whose quality and presentation rival those of the Museum of Modern Art. Here is the place to see museum-quality exhibitions of work by such renowned modern masters as Jackson Pollock and Yves Klein, as well more recent luminaries such as David Salle, Cy Twombly, and Brice Marden. Tel: 744-2313.

Hirschl & Adler (21 East 70th Street, between Fifth and Madison avenues; Tel: 535-8810) concentrates on historical material, including American folk art, from the 18th century through the early 20th century. In SoHo, **Hirschl & Adler Modern** (420 West Broadway, between Prince and Spring streets; Tel: 966-5331) focuses on 20th-century modernists and contemporary artists.

Colnaghi USA Ltd. (21 East 67th Street, between Fifth and Madison avenues) is the American branch of a London gallery that was founded in 1760. The New York gallery specializes in old-master drawings, prints, and paintings and English watercolors ranging from the 14th century to the early 20th century. The gallery has two large exhibition spaces and annually offers two or three exhibitions of drawings and prints from its own stock. It sometimes draws on outside loans for its two painting shows a year on scholarly themes. Tel: 772-2266.

Wildenstein & Co. (19 East 64th Street, between Fifth and Madison avenues) also has an impressive pedigree. Founded in Paris in 1875 and established in New York in 1902, it offers a broad scope of historical work ranging from the 12th century to the early 20th century and specializes in such areas as 18th-century French art, French Impressionism, and Postimpressionism. Its two or three exhibitions a year are often of museum quality and may include works by artists of the stature of Goya, Rembrandt, Monet, and Manet. Tel: 879-0500.

ALTERNATIVE SPACES AND UNORTHODOX INSTITUTIONS

During much of the 1970s the art market seemed to be running on empty. In response artists began to organize their own not-for-profit, cooperatively run exhibition spaces to provide commercially unviable and emerging artists with a means of exposure. Many of the most prominent artists today were first presented to the art world under the auspices of the alternative space, as these institutions came to be known. With the resurgence of the art market in the early 1980s, commercial galleries began to reassert their role as taste makers and talent scouts. The alternative movement faded but it did not die. Ironically, the current recession and its deleterious effect on the once booming art market have given alternative spaces a new lease on life. While financially strapped galleries are often unwilling or unable to take on risky art, there has been an explosion of interest in artists who work in such decidedly noncommercial formats as performance, installation, and political art. These artists have begun turning again to alternative institutions for support and exhibition opportunities.

But as alternative spaces have become more visible, they have also become more embattled. Their frequent focus on provocative and politically or socially sensitive art sets them at odds with the conservative mood of the larger society, while their reliance at least in part on grants from federal and state governments has made them vulnerable to the current zeal for budget trimming and urge to censor. As a result, a number of the institutions listed below have been embroiled in controversies over funding and content, but are toughing it out, as they have done since the 1970s. Alternative spaces remain the most likely places to find the most unvarnished sampling of contemporary art.

The newest member of the alternative community is **Exit Art/The First World** (548 Broadway, between Prince and Spring streets). The huge, 17,000-square-foot space houses a café and an art department store that sells inexpensive works by contemporary artists. Two exhibition areas house theme shows and the works of individual artists. Shows tend to have a social or political edge and mix established and just-emerging artists. Tel: 966-7445.

Artists Space (223 West Broadway, between Franklin and White streets, in TriBeCa) is one of the most respected alternative spaces, both for the innovative quality of its exhibitions and for the intelligence of its choices. Some of the artists who received their first exposure in its modest galleries include such contemporary heavyweights as Laurie Anderson, Jonathan Borofsky, Robert Longo, David Salle, and Cindy Sherman. Artists Space achieved notoriety in 1990 when an exhibition dealing with the victims of AIDS was singled out for explicit criticism by John Frohnmayer, then head of the National Endowment for the Arts. Many of its exhibitions are issue-oriented, and it has long focused as well on such noncommercial forms as video art and installation. Artists Space also maintains a computerized slide registry that outside curators, dealers, and critics may peruse to locate artists who do not necessarily have a gallery affiliation. Tel: 226-3970.

P.S. 1 and the **Clocktower** are two outposts of the same organization, the Institute for Art and Urban Resources. P.S. 1 is located in a rambling red-brick schoolhouse at 46-01 21st Street, in Long Island City, Queens (Tel: 718-784-2084), while the Clocktower occupies the top two floors in the old courthouse building, including the rather spectacular clock tower itself, at 108 Leonard Street, between Broadway and Lafayette Street, in lower Manhattan (Tel: 233-1096).

Both locations offer a schedule of provocative special exhibitions, but their most innovative feature is the studio program. Each year a number of local, national, and international artists are awarded working space in the P.S. 1 and Clocktower buildings. Visitors to the studios may catch glimpses of artists at work, and during the three or four openings a year, when resident artists transform their small cubicles into exhibition spaces, curious passersby have the opportunity to talk to the artists about their work. Given the diversity of artists, it is possible on these occasions to view a dizzying variety of work, ranging from traditional painting and sculpture to video works, environmental installations, and multimedia performance art set side by side in jolting juxtaposition. Not to be missed as well at P.S. 1 is James Turrell's *Meeting,* a permanent site installation consisting of a sitting room whose ceiling is open to the sky, making this one of the most serene, contemplative spots in the city. (To get to P.S. 1 take the number 7 subway line from Times Square or Grand Central Station to the 45th Road/Courthouse Square exit, or take the E or F line to the 23rd Street/Ely Avenue exit.) Both institutions close summers.

The **Dia Center for the Arts,** founded in 1976, reflects the expansive ambitions of the art of that era. Dedicated to the encouragement of projects that "cannot obtain sponsorship or support from other public or private sources because of their nature or scale," Dia has exhibited a commitment to long-term installation and environmental projects in New York and elsewhere in the United States. In SoHo Dia has maintained two works by Walter De Maria since 1977: *The New York Earth Room* (literally that, a room filled with earth), at 141 Wooster Street, between Prince and Houston streets, and *The Broken Kilometer* (a magical gallery space where the floor is lined with a kilometer's-worth of metal pipe), at 393 West Broadway, between Spring and Broome streets. In 1987 Dia opened a huge new exhibition space on the far West Side (548 West 22nd Street, between 10th and 11th avenues) that will present a series of year-long exhibitions of specially commissioned works by important contemporary artists. Dia is unique among New York's not-for-profit art institutions both for the high-profile nature of the participating artists (recent exhibitions have involved such artists as Joseph Beuys, Blinky Palermo, Robert Ryman, Jenny Holzer, and Tim Rollins and K.O.S.) and the generous financing it provides for its contributors' projects. For all Dia locations, Tel: 431-9232.

The **New Museum of Contemporary Art** (583 Broadway, between Houston and Prince streets) is in a category all its own—not exactly an alternative space, but not a traditional museum either. Founded in 1970 by former Whitney Museum curator Marcia Tucker, the New Museum was originally run in a spirit of radical egalitarianism. Eventually the idea of paying all employees the same rate and rotating jobs proved impractical, but the institution's resistance to orthodoxy remains strong. Shows tend to be conceptual, political, or for one reason or another on the fringes of the mainstream. (It is also one of the few museums in New York that makes a concerted effort to incorporate works by regional artists in its group shows.)

The offerings at the New Museum tend to be a mixed bag; the museum can be excessively leery of popular themes or artists. Nevertheless, the New Museum remains a remarkable and admirable experiment. Tel: 219-1355.

Other not-for-profit spaces worth a visit are **White Columns**, 154 Christopher Street, between Greenwich and Washington streets (Tel: 924-4212), **55 Mercer**, named for its address, between Broome and Grand streets (Tel: 226-8513), the **Storefront for Art and Architecture**, 97

Kenmare Street, between Lafayette and Mulberry streets (Tel: 431-5795), and the **Alternative Museum**, 594 Broadway, between Houston and Prince streets (Tel: 966-4444).

BUYING PRINTS, PHOTOGRAPHS, AND DRAWINGS

Buying a work of art is not always a simple proposition. Some of the tonier galleries, maintaining that they have a responsibility to place their artists in only the most important, most visible collections, practically require an audition before they will part with a work of art. Other dealers, especially those specializing in non-superstars, younger or emerging artists, or in specialty items such as prints, photographs, drawings, or old-master works, are more than willing to steer potential collectors through the art labyrinth. A listing of reputable dealers, which includes information on their areas of specialization, can be obtained by writing or calling the Art Dealers Association, 575 Madison Avenue, New York, NY 10022; Tel: 940-8590.

Other important sources of information for a novice art collector are the major art magazines: *Art in America, Artnews, Arts,* and *Artforum,* which publish reviews of recent exhibitions and articles on important contemporary artists and trends. The Friday edition of *The New York Times* and the weekly *Village Voice* may be even more helpful, because they contain reviews of shows currently on view.

Despite what you may have heard about skyrocketing art prices, quality works of art are still available at reasonable prices. Good values abound within some of the less visible specialty markets. Photography, for instance, remains undervalued, and striking works by both young and established photographers can be found at some of the New York galleries that focus exclusively on this medium, among them: **Laurence Miller Gallery** (138 Spring Street, between Greene and Wooster streets; Tel: 226-1220), and **Pace/MacGill Gallery** (32 East 57th Street, between Madison and Park avenues; Tel: 759-7999). (See the Photography and Filmmaking chapter for more on purchasing and viewing photographs.)

Prints can also be a bargain. A number of important contemporary-print workshops have outlets in New York, where you can find innovative works by well-known and emerging artists priced from $500 on up. Among the most interesting are **Pelavin Editions** (13 Jay Street, between Hudson and Greenwich streets; Tel: 925-9424); **Crown Point Press** (568 Broadway, at Prince Street; Tel: 226-5476); **Quartet Editions** (568 Broadway, between Houston and Prince streets; Tel: 219-2819); and **Petersburg Press** (380 Lafayette Street, between East 4th and Great Jones streets; Tel: 420-0890). Call first, as some of these outlets are open by appointment only.

Old-master and vintage-print galleries are also a source of bargains. At the high end are such outlets as **Pace Prints** (32 East 57th Street, third floor, between Park and Madison avenues; Tel: 421-3237), which, along with its contemporary and modern division, operates an old-master gallery featuring works by such artists as Rembrandt and Giambattista Piranesi. At the other end of the spectrum are operations selling anonymous historical works that originally appeared as book illustrations, calendars, or mass-market graphics. Worth exploring in this vein are **Illustration House** (96 Spring Street, between Broadway and Mercer Street; Tel: 966-9444), featuring original illustrations dating from 1860 to 1960 and including everything from *New Yorker* cartoons to original Norman Rockwell prints; **Old Print Shop** (150 Lexington Avenue, between 29th and 30th streets; Tel: 683-3950), which focuses on original American prints from the 17th century to about 1950 and covers the range from Audubon etchings to sporting prints; and **Stubbs Books and Prints** (153 East 70th Street; Tel: 772-3120), dealing in inexpensive decorative prints ranging from botanical illustrations to architectural graphics to animal prints.

You may be interested in some of the more eccentric specialties. The **Circle Gallery of Animation Art** (205 Front Street, between Fulton and Beekman streets; Tel: 732-5625), for instance, offers one of the most comprehensive selections of animation art in the country. Here you can find hand-painted original works used for the creation of your favorite Disney or Hanna Barbera film, as well as cartoons by Jules Feiffer, Gahan Wilson, and Arnold Roth. The **Margo Feiden Galleries** (699 Madison Avenue, between 62nd and 63rd streets; Tel: 677-5330) is the exclusive outlet for the work of long-standing *New York Times* illustrator-caricaturist Al Hirschfeld. Hirschfeld etchings start as low as $350, while his original works may reach $15,000. **Granary Books Inc.** (568 Broadway, between Houston and Prince streets; Tel: 226-5462) fea-

tures limited-edition books by contemporary artists that
are artworks in themselves and are made under the artist's sole directorship. These unusual works range in
price from $20 to $30,000.

ART AUCTIONS

For those who like a little adventure with their art hunting, New York is probably the best city in the world in
which to purchase art at auction. Prices are not always
lower than those attainable at the galleries, but the astute
collector can find some bargains. Contemporary-art auctions are held twice a year, in November and May. The
evening sales are for the heavy hitters, but the daytime
sales focus on younger artists with shorter track records
and on smaller works. Also of interest to the novice
collector are the weekend previews held before the major auctions, at which the works to be auctioned can be
viewed. N.B.: At most auction houses, buyers pay a service
fee that amounts to 15 percent of the sales price, or 10
percent if the price is $50,000 or higher.

The two major auction houses are **Sotheby's** (1334 York
Avenue, at 72nd Street; Tel: 606-7000 or 606-7245) and
Christie's (502 Park Avenue, at 59th Street; Tel: 546-1000 or
371-5438). Neck and neck in competition for the best
offerings, Sotheby's and Christie's are practically indistinguishable in the range and quality of their art lots. A distant
third is **Phillips** (406 East 79th Street, between First and
York avenues; Tel: 570-4830).

In order to participate in the auctions you will want to
subscribe to the catalogs for the sales that interest you
(contemporary, modern, prints, etc.). The catalogs, distributed before every sale, cost about $20 each and contain
pictures of the works to be auctioned and the high and
low estimates of the sale price, along with information
about the work's ownership history. Generally there is
also an unstated reserve price below which the seller will
not go.

One interesting development of recent years is the
tendency for collectors and dealers to use the auction as
the testing ground for the prices of works by younger
artists. When a work by someone like Julian Schnabel or
David Salle goes at auction for as much as or more than
the gallery price, this confirms the validity of those prices.
Thus, astute collectors follow the auctions closely to
gauge the ups and downs of major reputations.

A final bit of advice: A lot of ink has been spilled in

recent years about art as investment, but for most collectors the old advice is still the best—buy only the works you truly love. Then, whether their value rises or falls, you will still be a winner.

HANGING OUT

The best experience of the art-world-as-theater is to be obtained at gallery openings. Ostensibly, the purpose of these receptions is to inaugurate a new exhibition, but they are actually opportunities to see and to be seen, to network, to party. Once the gallery begins to fill up with artists, collectors, and well-wishers, the art becomes invisible anyway, so anyone seriously interested in viewing the exhibition is advised to return another day.

On any given night through the art season (which lasts from September to June or July) there are likely to be multiple openings, so that a determined opening aficionado can take in quite a variety of different scenes. Times and dates of openings are listed in the back of the *Gallery Guide* or can be obtained from the galleries.

One note: Most galleries long ago abandoned the practice of serving food at openings, and most offer only inferior wine. Plan instead to stop off afterward at such SoHo art hangouts as **Fanelli** (at Prince and Mercer streets) or the **Spring Street Bar** (at Spring Street and West Broadway), where post-opening crowds gather.

ART AND CRAFT SUPPLIES

AIN Plastics (300 Park Avenue South, between 22nd and 23rd streets; Tel: 473-2100), and **Industrial Plastic** (309 Canal Street, at Mercer Street; Tel: 226-2010), specialize in plastics, acrylic, acetate, buterate, and so forth.

Arthur Brown (2 West 46th Street, just off Fifth Avenue) carries materials of interest to designers and art directors. Tel: 575-5555.

Charrette (215 Lexington Avenue, at 33rd Street) offers a variety of fine-art and commercial materials, with a particularly good selection of architectural and drafting supplies. Tel: 683-8822.

CK & L Surplus Store (307 Canal Street, between Broadway and Mercer Street) carries metal screening, wire, and the like. Tel: 966-1745.

David Davis Fine Arts Materials (435 Hudson Street, between Morton and Leroy streets) is revered among artists for its informed help, selection of imported materials, and overall quality. Tel: 229-1550.

Jam Envelope and Paper (621 Sixth Avenue, at 19th Street, and other Manhattan locations) is a wholesale outlet specializing in paper; sells retail, too. Tel: 255-4593.

New York Central Art Supply (62 Third Avenue, at 11th Street) carries an excellent selection of papers as well as a full line of art supplies. Tel: 473-7705.

Pearl Paint (308 Canal Street, between West Broadway and Mercer streets) is moderately priced and has a fairly comprehensive inventory for the fine artist. Pearl also carries hardware and supplies for designers and crafts-people. Tel: 431-7932.

Utrecht (111 Fourth Avenue, between 11th and 12th streets) is popular among fine artists. It carries its own line of paints, which are relatively inexpensive but not as high in quality as the name brands. Tel: 777-5353.

See the Bookstores section in the chapter on Literary New York for shops that specialize in **art books** and old prints.

ARCHITECTURE

By Barry Lewis

New York is a great maw for architecture. Throughout its existence it has built itself up as a city, played out history in that city, and then ripped it out a generation later only to replace it with yet another. Some downtown lots have been redeveloped five times since 1800. In Europe, buildings stand for centuries; in New York, a lifetime for a building might be only 30 years.

And yet, peruse certain neighborhoods and it would seem as if time has stood still: the brownstone-lined streets of Chelsea, the Greek Revivals of Greenwich Village, the 19th-century row houses of the East 50s hard by the soaring towers of Midtown. Ghostly department stores of the Victorian Ladies' Mile still line Broadway above Union Square, and Federal row houses still stand among the industrial buildings of SoHo. So much of New York is surprisingly old; so much of it can be harshly new.

New York's buildings are eclectic beyond imagination. The city, with its well-deserved reputation of trying to mimic the airs of European aristocracy, is often unfavorably compared to Chicago and California, where a fresh American originality was encouraged. New York, though, has been no slouch in forging its own original style and flair. Witness the streets around Union Square, where a modern commercial style was hammered out in turn-of-the-century loft buildings; or the Upper West Side, where from the 1880s to the 1930s new forms for urban residences were developed in row houses and apartment houses; or the Grand Central Terminal area, where in the 1920s the image of the skyscraper was indelibly etched in the world's imagination.

New York, being completely American, is the product of private speculators, some of whom have demanded architectural quality, most of whom have demanded the cheapest product. This has resulted in a good deal of banality and some extraordinary exceptions, but the sum total is quite impressive. The city's buildings, like its people, are numerous, jammed together, and at times they rise to dizzying heights to make an estimable silhouette—especially from afar. That's why some of the best views of Manhattan are from "offshore" looking back: from atop the Jersey Palisades in Weehawken's Hamilton Park, along the Brooklyn Heights promenade, or from the Socrates Sculpture Park on Long Island City's East River shore. But walking the city's streets and seeing it in detail is rewarding as well. The new, the old, and the older are layered along the same block. New York may seem to be a chaotic jumble of buildings, but actually there is an order, a sequence, and a logic. Like any archaeologist, you only need to know the "key" in order to understand the hieroglyphics.

THE ROW HOUSE

The Federal Style

Back in the 1810s New York was a town clustered hard by the Battery and extending no farther than the brand-new City Hall in City Hall Park (between Broadway and Park Row). The city's merchants were fast making their town America's busiest port and most populous metropolis. Earning their money from the sailboats lining the East River docks—parts of today's **South Street Seaport** are all that remain—they lived in handsome town houses along lower Broadway and along Greenwich Street near the verdant Hudson River shoreline, where they could stroll in evening promenades and "take the air." These houses, built in the Federal style, with fanlights in their entrances, brick and marble-trimmed fronts, and delicate interiors, represented a simplified, "Yankee" version of England's richly ornamented, brilliantly colored late Georgian or Adam style. Although hundreds of these town houses were built for the newly prosperous lawyers, merchants, and bankers, all that remains intact is a relative handful, among which the most elegant is the **James Watson House** (1793–1806; John McComb, Jr.), at 8 State Street, opposite Battery Park, now part of a Roman Catholic shrine to Elizabeth Ann Seton, the first American saint.

As the city grew, the wealthy residential district pushed northward to Canal Street and, by the 1820s, beyond. Federal row houses scattered among the circa 1900 tenements and factories of Chinatown, Little Italy, and SoHo attest to those areas' former roles as the Upper East Side of a bygone era.

Greek Revival

The Erie Canal, opened in 1825, put New York over the top. First the canal and then the railroads funneled America's—and the world's—raw produce and goods through New York's harbor. In the 1830s the city began an explosion of growth that, until the financial troubles of the 1970s, seemed to be without end. By 1835 the city had reached and engulfed the rural town of Greenwich Village, and the emerging Greek Revival style would embellish the new precincts of Washington Square and lower Fifth Avenue. Especially distinctive are the houses of West 10th Street between Fifth and Sixth avenues and **The Row** on Washington Square North (numbers 1–13 and 21–26; 1831; Martin Thompson, architect), which, though slightly altered, evoke the stiff-backed restraint of antebellum society.

Though larger and more monumental than the Federal houses, the Greek Revivals followed the same basic elevation and plan. The configuration of the New York row house had been essentially set by 1800. The stoop had already appeared, a New York phenomenon dictated by the lack of back alleys (New York developers balked at cutting alleyways through expensive real estate). No back door meant deliveries, garbage, and honored guests all had to pass through the front. The stoop allowed for an "upstairs-downstairs" double entry, with service personnel entering the ground-floor servants' quarters and guests entering the first-floor parlor and dining room.

These monumental exterior staircases were actually a poor solution to the problem of a double front entry, dictating clumsy exteriors and a cramped interior layout. But rich New Yorkers loved them as their descendants would love Cadillacs; a house with a stoop indicated that the family within had finally arrived. Designers of the day, from James Renwick (architect of St. Patrick's Cathedral) to Olmsted and Vaux (creators of Central Park), railed against the crowded interiors that a stoop dictated, but New Yorkers turned a deaf ear. They would not give up their stoops until the later, more sophisticated generation of the early 1900s was persuaded by the likes of Stanford White and Edith Wharton to adopt the more graceful, street-level-entry town-house designs of London and Paris.

The Italianate: Brownstones

Around 1845 a war of styles broke out, as the Greek Revival was challenged by the newer Neo-Gothic and Italianate. Within five years the dust had settled and the Italianate had won. It was obvious that New Yorkers, preferring the Renaissance palazzo look, identified themselves with the Medici and Sforze rather than medieval prelates or ancient Athenians. But the New York palazzo was of brownstone (a material native to Connecticut and New Jersey, not Tuscany), and the streets were soon lined with what Edith Wharton disparagingly called a "chocolate sauce." Thousands of these new town houses were built along the streets of Chelsea, Longacre Square (now Times Square), Turtle Bay, and Murray Hill. So many brownstone-fronted houses went up in New York, Brooklyn, and the Jersey towns atop the Palisades that to this day New Yorkers habitually call any old row house—of whatever material or style—a "brownstone."

Behind the brownstone façades a revolution in domestic technology was unfolding. Modern water systems, sewers, and gas lines meant indoor bathrooms, gas-fed globes to replace dripping candles, modern kitchens with stoves, hot and cold running water, and "refrigerators" (they were actually iceboxes), and, thanks to cheap coal from Pennsylvania, central heating systems. The "modern" house had arrived. By the 1860s the average New York bourgeois could boast of a high-tech domesticity, smugly knowing that the great palaces of Europe still remained cold and unplumbed. It's no wonder that the people of those times thought theirs was truly the "Century of Progress."

Some of the city's merchants, preferring quiet and a more sylvan setting, began constructing villas and town houses on the bluffs of **Brooklyn Heights**, directly opposite Manhattan's southern tip. Horsecar lines laid out in the 1840s and 1850s led to the development of brownstone-lined streets in still more Brooklyn neighborhoods, such as **Fort Greene**, **Boerum Hill**, **Cobble Hill**, and **Carroll Gardens**. These districts, after having gone through cycles of prosperity, decline, and then revival, today comprise Brooklyn's much admired "Brownstone Belt."

Because land was cheaper in Brooklyn than it was in Manhattan, brownstones there were wider, roomier, and more verdantly sited. A middle-class family could get more for its money and live better in Brooklyn, provided the breadwinner was willing to brave the rigors of the East River ferries. Brooklyn Heights eventually became home to some of the city's wealthiest merchants, and remains today one of New York's finest residential districts, and its waterfront **Promenade**, built in the 1950s, one of the best vantage points for a spectacular view of the downtown Manhattan skyline. The completion of the Brooklyn Bridge in 1883 opened up such late-Victorian neighborhoods as **Park Slope**, **Clinton Hill**, and **Crown Heights**.

The Neo-Grec to the Eclectic Styles

After the Civil War the French mansard style, with all its nouveau-riche flamboyance, became popular, though often all New Yorkers did was take a prewar brownstone and stick a mansard on top of it. Instead of the Italianate, the new rage was a mechanistically rendered Neoclassicism, called the Neo-Grec, reflecting the growing Victorian interest in an honest, machine-age style. These Neo-Grec, mansard-roofed brownstones lined the streets of the Upper East Side. Thoroughly middle class—the rich then lived on Fifth Avenue in the 50s—the neighborhoods' breadwinners commuted down to Wall Street on the new elevated railroads.

In the 1880s brownstone fell out of favor and Eclectic styles ranging from the Queen Anne to the Neo-Romanesque became popular. It was the age of Richardson, Sullivan, and Furness; their intuitive genius for the simple rendering of materials is reflected in the glorious palette of stone, brick, tile, and terra-cotta that New York architects used for this new generation of city houses. Streets from the West 70s to the West 130s, just then being developed, were alive with brilliant coloration and texture. The Eclectics were also interested in new interior layouts (it wasn't easy squeezing a home into a narrow row-house plot), and they introduced bay windows, interlocking balconies, terraces, and towers to make the rooms inside both more interesting and more open. There are superb examples of this era's accomplishments on West 76th Street off Riverside Drive and around the corner on West End Avenue.

Following the construction of elevated railroad lines (the legendary "Els"), developers built communities farther uptown in Harlem and Hamilton Heights that could rival in Eclectic elegance Boston's Back Bay or Philadelphia's Rittenhouse Square. **Strivers' Row** (1891), on West 138th and 139th streets between Seventh and Eighth avenues, includes work by McKim, Mead & White and Bruce Price. The Victorian vistas of Lenox Avenue between West 119th and 124th streets and the adjoining **Mount Morris Park Historic District** are almost nonurban in their domestic scale and their kaleidoscopic richness of texture, color, and material. Walking south on three-block-long **Hamilton Terrace**, between West 144th and 141st streets, you will notice that the bays, oriels, and gables of the houses and of City College of New York's 1903 neo-Gothic **Shepard Hall**, rising on a bluff in the distance, present a vista that is surprisingly European.

With the construction of the Brooklyn Bridge and a system of feeder "El" train lines, Brooklyn expanded eastward and southward in the 1880s and 1890s, creating new haut bourgeois precincts that rivaled in their Eclectic beauty and originality anything put up in Manhattan. Park Slope, west of Prospect Park, especially from 3rd Street to Berkeley Place between Prospect Park West and Seventh Avenue, is one of the New York area's finest Victorian districts. Similarly, the streets of Clinton Hill (next to Pratt Institute) are handsomely embellished, especially Clinton Avenue (between DeKalb and Willoughby avenues), which is still lined with the fin-de-siècle mansions built for the Pratt family, a clan that settled in Brooklyn after making millions in oil. There (at number 241), the 1893 **Charles Pratt House** by William Tubby, now serving as the residence of the Roman Catholic bishop of Brooklyn, stands solidly and spartanly in Richardsonian Romanesque splendor.

Nearby **Bedford-Stuyvesant** includes several sections of well-tended late-Victorian town houses of rich variety and texture. Neo-Grecs, Queen Annes, and Neo-Romanesques line the streets around Grant Square (Bedford Avenue around Bergen, Pacific, and Dean streets) and north of Fulton Street (Fulton to Hancock streets, Nostrand to Throop avenues), and fill out the **Stuyvesant Heights Historic District**, along Stuyvesant Avenue between Chauncey and Macon streets.

Of all the thousands of row houses built since the 1830s, two are open to the public as house museums. One is the 1832 **Old Merchant's House**, at 29 East 4th Street (between Bowery and Lafayette), a late Federal gem, and the other is the **Theodore Roosevelt Birthplace**, 28 East 20th Street (between Broadway and Park Avenue South), a Neo-Gothic brownstone from 1848 (rebuilt in 1923). Go first to the Old Merchant's House (open Sundays only) and notice its spare Yankee simplicity, then visit Roosevelt's boyhood home to see firsthand the growing Victorian penchant for decoration and embellishment.

Beaux Arts and Neoclassical

By 1900 the price of Manhattan real estate had made row-house living prohibitive for the middle class. Between 1900 and 1930, the last major era of the Manhattan town house, these houses went up almost exclusively in the new wealthy precincts of the Upper East Side. The rich had been displaced by the growth of Midtown, so they moved north of 59th Street, where they built Beaux Arts–style town houses and freestanding Fifth Avenue mansions reflecting the Neoclassicism of Italy, France, England, and colonial America. Of the town-house-lined side streets, East 79th Street off Fifth Avenue is an excellent example. As for the mansions, few are left, and almost all have been recycled for other uses. Among the earliest and the best are the **Villard Houses** (1883; McKim, Mead & White), at Madison Avenue and 50th Street, a group of six houses expertly arranged to give the look of a Renaissance palazzo. (How different they are from the provincial brownstones of the 1850s!) The gem of the group was Villard's own house, today the south wing of the New York Palace Hotel. The clarity, simplicity, and sophistication of the interior, which is now well restored, was 20 years ahead of its time. Other grand mansions still extant are the French 18th-century-style Duke mansion (1912; Horace Trumbauer; Fifth Avenue at 78th Street), now the **New**

York University Institute of Fine Arts; the Loire Valley–style Warburg mansion (1908; C. P. H. Gilbert; Fifth Avenue at 92nd Street), now the **Jewish Museum**; and two Neo-Georgian houses, also on Fifth Avenue, that are today the homes of the **Cooper-Hewitt Museum** (Andrew Carnegie's home, with its interior beautifully restored; 1902; Babb, Cook & Willard), at 91st Street; and the **International Center of Photography** (Willard Straight's house; 1914; Delano & Aldrich), at 94th Street.

Built to last forever, many of the Upper East Side mansions were demolished within a few decades. In typical New York fashion they were removed by the 1930s to make way for a new city, one of office buildings and elegant department stores south of 59th Street and elegant apartment houses north of it.

THE APARTMENT HOUSE

Middle-class Americans of the 19th century insisted, as did the English, on living in private homes. Tenements were fine for the immigrant poor (tenements first appeared before the Civil War in ethnic slums such as the Irish Five Points, now Chinatown, and the German Bowery district, now the Lower East Side), but the middle class would not adopt the Continental style of apartment-house living until they had to. By 1900, they had to. Real-estate prices made town houses a luxury commodity, and the New York bourgeoisie began moving into new "apartment-hotels."

Belle Epoque

The luxury apartment house first appeared en masse on the Upper West Side and in Harlem, the two New York districts most associated with the solid middle class. The famous **Dakota** (Henry J. Hardenbergh), at Central Park West and 72nd Street, opening in 1883, was a bit ahead of its time. By the 1900s the city's first subway line, the IRT, linked upper Broadway with Wall Street—and the apartment-house boom was on. The **Ansonia** (1904; Graves & DuBoy; 2109 Broadway, at 73rd Street), the **Apthorp** (1908; Clinton & Russell; Broadway between 78th and 79th streets), and the **Belleclaire** (1903; Emery Roth; Broadway at 77th Street, southwest corner) were typical of the new breed. The Ansonia especially, with its blowsy Neo-Baroque style, reminds us of a Parisian extravagance of the Belle Epoque. But the New York version was far taller and contained more high-tech gadgetry than any Parisian apartment house.

These new high-rise residences were state-of-the-art palaces with garages (equipped with outlets for electric cars), underground shopping centers, and health clubs. Elevators, built-in refrigerators, pneumatic mail-delivery systems, and miles of piping and wiring for gas, electricity, water, and heat made these new luxury apartment houses the equivalent of oceangoing steamships anchored to the New York streets. To assuage the "shame" of living in a ten-room flat, these early apartment houses offered hotel-like amenities, including maid service, room service, elegant in-house restaurants, and rooftop gardens and pavilions for private soirees.

The super rich, too, finally capitulated to apartment-house living, but they insisted on doing so in their own aristocratic manner. McKim, Mead & White's elegantly proportioned building at **998 Fifth Avenue** (1910; 81st Street, northeast corner) set the pattern. Rejecting the West Side's middle-class flamboyance, the East Siders preferred the subtlety and simplicity of a Renaissance palazzo. This restrained academicism took hold, and when New York went apartment-house wild after World War I, when Park Avenue on the Upper East Side, Fifth Avenue opposite Central Park, and West End Avenue on the Upper West Side were rebuilt to the new scale, it was flat-topped, porticoed Neoclassicism that prevailed.

Art Deco

In the 1930s the new Moderne, or Art Deco, style emerged. It was especially popular in the new apartment towers of Central Park West, such as the **Century** (1931; the Chanin Co.), at 62nd Street, the **Majestic** (1930; the Chanin Co.), at 72nd Street, the **San Remo** (1930; Emery Roth), between 74th and 75th streets, and the **Beresford** (1929; Emery Roth), at 81st Street—though the last two are a mixture of Moderne and Mannerist. The new skyscraper-style apartment houses emphasized wraparound corner windows (only possible in a steel-cage building), spacious foyer-plan interior layouts, and soaring towers housing magnificent apartments with four exposures—literally "mansions in the sky"—making that era seem, by today's standards, the golden age of the New York apartment house.

Uptown in the Bronx, the **Grand Concourse**, an Art Deco Champs-Elysées, was built by developers in the years between the depression and World War II. From East 161st Street to Fordham Road, a distance of about two and a half miles, the Grand Concourse was lined with mid-rise apartment houses in a Deco style that more often looked like a Yankee cousin to South Miami Beach than like the suavely elegant and luxurious apartment towers of Central Park West. These buildings were filled by Jews, Italians, and Irish moving up from the Manhattan ghettos into the middle class. The excellence of their construction, their exuberant design, and the layouts of the apartments helped keep the concourse intact through the difficult days of the 1970s, when so much of the adjoining neighborhood was abandoned.

Postmodern Design

After World War II apartment house design was reduced to simple brick boxes, but inside, the layouts continued to be spacious. Beginning in the 1960s, however, apartments and their rooms began to shrink, and materials seemed to "shrink" as well. Today's elaborate Postmodern decor, concierges' desks, and in-house health clubs cannot hide the fact that the apartments themselves, considering the price, are often pale shadows of their magnificent Beaux Arts and Art Deco predecessors.

THE GARDEN SUBURB

For New Yorkers who wanted a more *rus in urbe* environment that was accessible to downtown and Midtown Manhattan, a number of planned neighborhoods were built in the outer reaches of the Bronx, Brooklyn, and Queens. These planned communities were rooted in the English garden suburb movement of the 19th and early 20th centuries, based on the notion that people who work all day in the noise, congestion, pollution, and tumult of the city center require rest and recuperation when they go home at night. Nature can give us that needed sense of peace, sports and recreation will alleviate our stress, and a strong sense of community will combat the modern malaise of social anomie. **Riverdale**, in the Bronx, and **Prospect Park South**, in Brooklyn (where *Sophie's Choice* was filmed), both of which developed in the early 20th century, were models of this kind of thinking, but the highest concentration of these civilized prototypes of urban life can be found in Queens. Seven planned neighborhoods were built between 1910 and 1950 (though the earliest, Richmond Hill, dates back to the 1880s). The so-called Seven Sisters include: **Richmond Hill, Kew Gardens, Forest Hills Gardens, Douglaston, Jackson Heights, Sunnyside Gardens**, and **Fresh Meadows**.

The most famous of them, Forest Hills Gardens, lying south of Queens Boulevard and 71st Avenue, was the product of a dynamic team: Mrs. Russell (Olivia) Sage served as patron, Grosvenor Atterbury as architect, and Frederick Law Olmsted, Jr. (the son of Central Park's co-designer), as landscape architect. Directly influenced by London's Hampstead Garden suburb of the early 1900s, Forest Hills's urban center, Station Square, is more reminiscent of Dutch or German Expressionism than Tudor Revival England, with picturesque medieval revival apartment towers, arcaded shops, pedestrian bridges over the street, and a landmark clock tower. Atterbury's churches are equally original, especially the Gothic Revival **Church in the Gardens** from 1912, at Ascan Avenue and Greenway North, and the Gaudi-esque **Christian Science Church** on Greenway North facing the commons.

Experimental building systems were used to bring down costs in constructing Forest Hills Gardens. A cluster of poured-concrete houses facing Hawthorne Park off Burns Street, which Atterbury designed in 1919, is analogous to the experimental work done in California by architect Irving Gill.

The **Community House**, built in 1921, served as the center of social and cultural life, with its Georgian Revival ballroom, tiled pool, and auditorium/gymnasium. Nearby were the wooded hills of Forest Park, with tennis courts, a golf course, and equestrian trails. Yet all this was within walking distance of shops ("the village" as locals call the retail district) and the Long Island Railroad, which can bring residents to Midtown Manhattan's Pennsylvania Station in 15 minutes.

Residential units in Forest Hills Gardens include apartment houses, row houses, two-family houses, and free-standing mansions, allowing for a mix of economic classes. The apartment towers here, as in Kew Gardens, Jackson Heights, and Sunnyside Gardens, were Eclectically designed for individual character and, unlike the book-ended apartment houses of Manhattan and the Bronx, were surrounded by greenbelts of flowering trees and shrubs and interlaced with interior gardens. Foyer-plan layouts, cross ventilation, and three or four exposures were available in *all* apartments, not just the precious few one might find in a Manhattan tower. Standing in a Jackson Heights or Forest Hills Gardens apartment, surrounded by trees, flowers, greenery, and sky, one easily begins to understand the 18th-century English admiration for country-house life from whence our concept of the garden suburb originates.

It's ironic that 70 years after the construction of Forest Hills Gardens these very principles of urban design are being touted once again among progressive urban planners. The husband-wife team of Elizabeth Plater-Zyberk and Andres Duany has been designing planned communities in Florida and Maryland that are being hailed as the antidote to the traffic-choked, car-bound woes of late-20th-century America. Yet both these developments are obvious offspring of the Anglo-American Seven Sisters of the borough of Queens.

DEPARTMENT STORES AND COMMERCIAL BUILDINGS

Traditionally, New York's downtown (Wall Street) was where the money was made and Midtown—the city's retail, theater, and café district—was where the money was spent. Downtown remained stationary, though growing taller every generation, but Midtown followed the northward expansion of the luxury class that frequented it and moved constantly farther uptown.

Lower Manhattan

In the 1840s Midtown settled at Broadway near City Hall Park, producing America's first department store, **A. T. Stewart's** (Snook & Trench), which rose at Chambers Street and Broadway (northeast corner) in 1845 and is still standing. (It is now called the Sun Building after a newspaper tenant of later years; being city owned, it is in terrible condition.) Stewart's was not only a new phenomenon in retailing, it also brought the Italianate style to New York, sparking a fashion in architecture that would sweep the city during the next two decades.

SoHo's Cast-Iron District

By the 1850s Midtown had moved to what is today called SoHo, with Tiffany's at 550 Broadway (now altered) and Lord & Taylor (now demolished) at Grand Street. Cast-iron construction, a modern modular system for erecting buildings (much like a kid's erector set) became all the rage, and so many cast-iron department stores in the guise of Venetian palazzi rose along Broadway that New Yorkers dubbed that thoroughfare "the Grand Canal." The Venetian Renaissance style's open, well-fenestrated arcading allowed architects to exploit cast iron's possibilities, creating Victorian "glass boxes" framed in Neoclassical packaging. The 1857 **Haughwout Store** (J. P. Gaynor) still stands at Broadway and Broome Street (northeast corner). Its cast-iron framing was originally a glistening white painted with faux marble veining to give the illusion of antiquity. (Inside, the building was the first in New York to be equipped with a passenger elevator.) It mattered little to New Yorkers that their "palazzi"—bigger and glassier than anything in Renaissance Venice—would have been impossible to build before the age of iron.

Ladies' Mile and Fashion Row

After the Civil War Midtown jumped north to the Ladies' Mile and Fashion Row: Broadway and Sixth Avenue from 14th Street to 23rd Street. Grand department stores in the French Second Empire style, with cast-iron framing and iron-crested mansard roofs, lined Union and Madison squares and Sixth Avenue from 18th Street to 23rd Street. Many still stand, like so many ghosts from a vanished past, and several have recently been refurbished as office buildings and apartment houses. The new money of the infamous Gilded Age, an era expertly captured in Jack Finney's novel *Time and Again,* had a chance to display itself strolling fashionable 14th and 23rd streets. The department stores were generally built with skylit interior atriums, open-cage elevators, and acres of glass windows and skylights, making each store a veritable Crystal Palace. Tiffany's moved to Union Square West and 15th Street (now severely altered to house a labor union) in 1869; Arnold Constable (1869; Griffith Thomas) opened at Broadway and 19th Street (southwest corner), and serves today as the home of ABC Carpets (across the street ABC also occupies the old 1881 W & J Sloane store); and Lord & Taylor (1869; James Giles) settled in at Broadway and 20th Street, part of which (the altered part) is now occupied by Saint Laurie Clothiers. The opening of Lord & Taylor prompted Teddy Roosevelt, Sr.—whose brood, including the future president, lived just down the block—to exclaim that the neighborhood was changing, and it was time to move. That they did in 1873, to the new address of note, West 57th Street.

Beaux Arts: North from 34th Street

By 1910 Midtown had moved again, this time to Fifth Avenue north of 34th Street. B. Altman & Co. (Trowbridge & Livingston) opened in 1906 at 34th Street, where the building still stands, though the venerable department store has closed its doors. Acknowledging the Beaux Arts fashions of the day, Benjamin Altman wrapped his 11-story steel-cage department store in the elegant detailing of a Renaissance palazzo (a far more sophisticated version than A. T. Stewart's back in 1845), and the other great shopping emporia followed suit. In the same year Tiffany's moved into McKim, Mead & White's glass palazzo at the southeast corner of 37th Street (it's now the Reverend Moon's printing plant); **Lord & Taylor** (Starrett & Van Vleck) opened at 39th Street in 1914; **Arnold Constable** moved to 40th Street (now the Mid-Manhattan Library); and **Saks Fifth Avenue**'s "palazzo" (Starrett & Van Vleck) capped the trend when it opened in 1924 at its current location—way uptown!—between 49th and 50th streets. By this time a distinct middle-class shopping district had blossomed at Herald Square (Macy's opened there in 1902), and the theater district had followed its own path up Broadway, settling down around 42nd Street and Times Square in the 1900s.

Up to 57th Street

Midtown shifted slightly again—to 57th Street—in the 1930s and 1940s. **Bergdorf Goodman** (Buchman & Kahn) moved into its streamlined headquarters on 57th Street in 1928. **Tiffany's** (Cross & Cross), moving again, built a Classical-Moderne "safe" for its jewels at 727 Fifth Avenue in 1940. This time, however, the central business district was moving northward as well, and for the first time in the city's history corporate skyscrapers joined the department stores and retailers to share Midtown's streets.

The Beaux Arts–embellished Heckscher Building (Warren & Wetmore; now the **Crown Building**, recently restored and spotlit) opened at Fifth Avenue and 57th Street, southwest corner, in 1922, and ten years later Rockefeller Center rose opposite Saks Fifth Avenue and St. Patrick's Cathedral. Midtown, continuing to shift, had always been moving up the island's spine. In 1910 people assumed that by the 1950s, Midtown would probably reach 125th Street—but it never happened. Midtown New York, having moved northward for more than 100 years, finally stopped at the southern gates to Central Park.

PUBLIC BUILDINGS

New York's unrelenting grid gives few public buildings a chance to shine—no vistas or grand boulevards here. But many structures do shine: **City Hall** (1802–1811; Mangin & McComb), in City Hall Park (between Broadway and Park Row), is still one of America's most impressive city halls, even though it was plagued by extended deadlines and cost overruns, proving that certain civic practices have a deep-rooted tradition. When New York entered its great age of civic design, the Beaux Arts era between 1890 and 1930, its architects produced a few buildings whose qualities of planning and design we had not seen before and may never see again. The 1898 consolidation of New York created a five-borough city of four million people that demanded new public facilities. The New York architectural establishment rose to the occasion by producing buildings of extraordinarily skillful planning and outstanding civic presence. This new generation of professional, Beaux Arts–trained American architects married the sublimity of European Neoclassicism with the pragmatism of the Yankee mind. The result was great Neoclassical palaces fine-tuned to become machines for modern life, criticized by a later, so-called Modern generation for stylistic irrelevancy. In today's Postmodern era we have put aside those prejudices to appreciate once more the masterworks of that earlier generation.

The **American Museum of Natural History** and the **Metropolitan Museum of Art** (both begun in the 1870s), on opposite sides of Central Park, received new Beaux Arts fronts, though in these instances the Neoclassical faces, though skillfully done, masked decades of willy-nilly additions. There were, however, four public buildings built from scratch that became instant landmarks for all times. In typical American fashion, indicative of how we build our cities, three of these four "public" buildings were in fact built by private corporations.

United States Custom House

The former United States Custom House (1907; Cass Gilbert), in lower Manhattan on Bowling Green, is the only true public building of the group. Reminiscent in its palatial guise of the deep-rooted traditions of Western architecture, behind its Beaux Arts façade it is a paradigm of skillful functionalist planning. Separation of freight and people was achieved by giving cars and trucks a street-level basement entrance in back and pedestrians a first-floor monumentalized entry in front. The statue-flanked Neo-Baroque grand entrance (Daniel Chester French did the *Four Continents*—and are they kitsch!) made New

Yorkers understand instantly where the customhouse was and where they should enter. The grand stair leads, in the Neoclassical tradition of an architectural promenade, to the nerve center of the building, a skylit rotunda where the customs officials waited for the business at hand. In 1937 Reginald Marsh, under the auspices of the Work Projects Administration, embellished the ceiling of the rotunda with gritty scenes of New York Harbor showing its piers bustling with passengers and freight. In 1973 the United States Customs Service moved to the World Trade Center (where, thanks to the Modern idiom, you can't even find the customhouse, and if you do, you can't figure out how to get in), and the 1907 customhouse came close to being demolished. Saved after a preservation battle, it will become the new home of the Museum of the American Indian in fall 1994.

New York Public Library

The New York Public Library (1902–1911; Carrère & Hastings) rose on Fifth Avenue between 40th and 42nd streets in the same decade as the U.S. Custom House. Though it is usually compared unfavorably to its inspiration, the Boston Public Library (1890; McKim, Mead & White), people often forget that Boston's library, though aesthetically richer and more sophisticated, is a building that never worked. The New York Public Library, on the other hand, was designed by librarians with the help of architects (an unusual shift in architects' priorities) and is as superbly functional today as it ever was—and is undergoing a badly needed restoration program (by Davis, Brody & Associates with Giorgio Cavaglieri).

The library's practical layout, ingenious use of natural light, and its deft mixture of specialized libraries and the more modern stack system (via a 1911 pneumatic-tube system that is still state-of-the-art today) make it a working machine for everything from scholarly research to casual reading. Its varied rooms, as they come out from under the restoration wraps, are a marvelous synthesis of sensibility and function. Its newly restored (1987) Bartos Forum, originally the circulating library, skylit and metal-framed, is a gem of Beaux Arts–influenced machine-age design. The main entrance plaza, facing Fifth Avenue, is one of the city's great public spaces, its steps and flanking terraces a constantly shifting scene of street theater and schmoozing. Its exhibitions in the reopened Gottesman Hall are usually first rate, and the daily tours by trained docents worth attending. No city can call itself civilized without a great library at its heart, and New York's, after years of sad neglect, is again becoming the vibrant core it once was and should always be.

Grand Central Terminal

Grand Central Terminal (1902–1913; Reed & Stem, Warren & Wetmore) is another of the city's great successes. Replacing an earlier terminal on the same site, the present GCT is actually a city-within-a-city, accommodating trains, subways, taxis, automobiles, and pedestrians. The steel-framed Beaux Arts building sits atop a double-deck underground railroad yard that stretches from Lexington to Madison Avenue, from 42nd to 50th Street. As Park Avenue developed in the 1920s and 1930s, every building on the avenue up to 50th Street, from the terminal to the Waldorf-Astoria, was positioned on the roof of that yard, one of our earliest examples of "air rights" development. An iron-framed highway, built in 1904 and one of the nation's first, carries Park Avenue traffic around the building, and underground "streets" link the terminal to more than half a dozen skyscrapers and two major hotels.

The terminal itself is an ingenious interlocking of specialized spaces, lit by a system of skylights and interior windows that fully exploit its steel frame. Its monumental concourse is one of the city's great plazas, a roofed piazza San Marco, serving the dashing commuter and the casual pedestrian alike. The Municipal Art Society (Tel: 935-3960) conducts tours of the terminal every Wednesday at 12:30 P.M. Few complexes today combine with such skill the efficient and the humane. It is truly one of the nation's great architectural works.

McKim, Mead & White's Pennsylvania Station

The same could have been said of its sister railroad complex, the original Pennsylvania Station, McKim, Mead & White's 1910 architectural wonder at Seventh and Eighth avenues, 32nd to 34th Street. They modeled its concourse in front on the Baths of Caracalla and built its train platforms in back in a totally functionalist idiom of exposed iron and glass. No one could accuse these architects of using historical styles for lack of imagination. As in the three other public buildings we've mentioned, the station's designers used history where they felt its symbolism was appropriate, and utilized modernity where the building program demanded it. But that Penn Station is gone, buried under the cracker-box skyscrapers and garish arena of Madison Square Garden. The station's demolition in 1960–1963 so infuriated the New York public that it led to the establishment of the New York City Landmarks Commission, given authority to prevent that kind of vandalism from ever happening again.

Brooklyn Museum

Across the East River, Brooklyn was building its own civic monuments. In 1897 the firm of McKim, Mead & White was hired to design the new home of the Brooklyn Museum on Eastern Parkway, just east of Prospect Park. The annexation of Brooklyn to New York in 1898 drained the project of patronage, and only a sixth of the original plan was completed. Then, in the 1930s, in a misguided attempt to modernize, the grand stair in front was removed and a new entrance carved at street level into the original basement. But in the 1980s a new expansion plan was adopted under the aegis of architects James Stewart Polshek and the Japanese wunderkind Arata Isozaki. Money was largely secured before the economic crisis of the 1990s set in, and parts of the plan have already been realized. In 1991 the museum opened the Isozaki-designed Iris and B. Gerald Cantor Auditorium, considered one of the finest new facilities of that kind in the New York area.

The Postmodern Era

Of the comparatively recent additions to New York's public architecture, few are as dramatic as Frank Lloyd Wright's **Solomon R. Guggenheim Museum**, at Fifth Avenue and 88th Street, completed in 1959 and reopened in 1992 after a major restoration. The great tradition of public architecture might be revived in the Postmodern era, but that remains to be seen. Fans of high-tech will be interested in the **Jacob K. Javits Convention Center** (1987; I. M. Pei's James I. Freed; the Hudson River at 37th Street), whose steel-and-glass superstructure has given New York City its own Crystal Palace. But the great public buildings of the Beaux Arts period have yet to be surpassed—or even equaled—in their skillful integration of function, beauty, and humane concern for the private citizen. That kind of architectural largesse may, in fact, be a lost art.

THE SKYSCRAPER

The skyscraper, invented in Chicago in 1885, arrived in New York in 1890. The first New York skyscraper, at 50 Broadway, lasted fewer than 30 years, when, characteristically for New York, it was torn down to make way for a bigger building. In the ensuing generations Chicago and New York vied with each other for superlatives of height. The Chicago style often won the acclaim of critics for its no-nonsense, flat-topped rationality; New York came in a poor second, criticized for its costumy historicism and "vulgar" flamboyance. But if the scholars preferred Chicago, the public preferred New York, and a new generation of critics is beginning to swing around to give New York its due.

New York's first steel-cage buildings popped up downtown in the Financial District and in the wholesale belt from Canal Street to 34th Street. Using a Neoclassical formula, the New York architects artificially divided their buildings' façades into a base-shaft-capital arrangement that draws its inspiration from the parts of a classical column—even though steel-cage construction is modular and uniform from bottom to top. The critics charged "façade-ism" and "artifice," but on closer look we find that the New York architects were not such dummies.

The tripartite formula allowed for a decorative base at the sidewalk level where pedestrians can relate to it (no one ever looks above the third floor—except on a walking tour); an austere midsection to keep the decorativeness in check; and a fanciful top that announced the building's presence in the city's skyline. The romantic top, later so despised by the Moderns, often served parenthetically as a "billboard" for the corporation located within. Chrysler's spire, Bankers Trust's ziggurat (at Wall and Nassau streets), and Standard Oil's oil lamp (22 Broadway, seen best from New York Harbor) were the best advertisements a company could buy.

In the Wall Street area the designs were largely Neoclassical, because prestige and "image" were so important to financial institutions. The narrow streets, soaring towers, masonry street walls, and the recurring Beaux Arts formula encouraging decoration disciplined by a rhythmical order created streetscapes not seen anywhere else in the world. Midtown, with its broad avenues and river-to-river streets opening up views in all directions, does not compare. Downtown New York is its own special place. Typical is lower Broadway, where Bowling Green, framed by the 1907 customhouse, and the Beaux Arts–era skyscrapers create one of the city's finest vistas.

Turn of the Century to World War I

Around 1900 a satellite office district emerged uptown in the Madison Square area (23rd Street and Fifth Avenue). After part of the old Ladies' Mile was ripped out, the new construction produced two of New York's more notable skyscrapers, the **Flatiron Building** (1902; Daniel Burnham; Fifth Avenue at 23rd Street) and the **Metropolitan Life Tower** (1909; Napoleon Le Brun & Sons; Madison Avenue at 24th Street).

In the wholesale district, east and west of Broadway from Canal Street to 34th Street, the buildings were more anonymous but no less interesting. Perhaps feeling less restrained, the architects gave the façades of their loft buildings eclectic treatments that melded (Louis) Sullivanesque modernity with Beaux Arts formality. Brick, stone, iron, glass, and terra-cotta were used to create high-rise tapestries of incredible originality. Blocks to notice include East 12th and 13th streets between Broadway and University Place. Down in SoHo, the so-called **Little Singer Building** (1904; Ernest Flagg; 561 Broadway) and the **New Era Building** (1893; Alfred Zucker; 495 Broadway) both give Chicago stiff competition in the game of high-rise aesthetics.

As buildings grew to astronomical heights it became obvious that their massiveness would have to be pruned back—if only to allow light and air to penetrate the streets below. Ernest Flagg's magnificent Singer Building (1908; Broadway and Liberty Street; now demolished!) pointed toward a solution with its narrow, ornamented tower rising from a stubby base, but it was the **Woolworth Building** (1913; Cass Gilbert; Broadway at Barclay Street and Park Place) that gave the basic formula to the next generation of skyscraper designers. Its secular Neo-Gothicism made the building's unprecedented 795 feet soar into the clouds. Its multiuse base included shops, a luxury restaurant, a health club (still in operation), and a direct link with the new BMT subway line, making it more a "city" than just a building. Its two-story-high mosaic-tiled lobby served as grand entrance and interior "court" (a must-see; the Woolworth personnel are very hospitable), giving access to all the building's multiple functions. The world's tallest building until 1930, it still remains today—thanks to the Woolworth

Company's vigilance—one of the finest skyscrapers of its day and a template for all times.

The 1920s through the Depression: Art Deco

In 1916 New York adopted America's first zoning code, requiring setbacks and narrow towers, and the Woolworth Building was its prototype. In the unparalleled building boom of the 1920s the city's skyline was reshaped largely in the Woolworth image. The great Art Deco skyscrapers of the 1920s were built mostly in Midtown on the "new Wall Street" (as the area around Grand Central was then called). Skyscrapers such as the **Chanin Building** (1929; Sloan & Robertson; Lexington Avenue at 42nd Street, southwest corner), the **Chrysler Building** (1930; William Van Alen; Lexington Avenue at 42nd Street, northeast corner), and the **Empire State Building** (1931; Shreve, Lamb & Harmon; Fifth Avenue at 34th Street, southwest corner) gave the world its definitive image of what a skyscraper should look like. No Chicago skyscraper ever captured so intensely the public's imagination as these did. (The Empire State Building's window frames are being repainted their original color—tomato red—returning the building to its 1931 appearance.)

They borrowed their silhouettes from the American skyscraper gothic, their details from the German Expressionists, and their nomenclature from the French Exposition des Arts Décoratifs of 1925. Traditional materials such as marble and stone were mixed with new materials like stainless steel and Monel Metal, so that references to both the past and the future were interwound. The Chrysler Building, with its Art Deco marble lobby, elevators paneled with inlaid wood, and stainless steel tower, is the epitome of its time. Its top was planned to be brilliantly lit (finally achieved in 1985), as in Fritz Lang's Expressionistic film *Metropolis*.

Downtown Art Deco skyscrapers were pinstriped and bankerish, though one of the finest, the Irving Trust Co. (now the **Bank of New York**), at 1 Wall Street (1932; Voorhees, Gmelin & Walker), houses a brilliant red and gold mosaic banking hall, now used as an office but accessible to the public. Uptown the Deco buildings were more colorful, both outside as well as inside, whether serving as a corporate headquarters—like the **Fred F. French Building** (1927; Fred F. French Co.; Fifth Avenue at 45th Street, northeast corner)—or as commercial loft space, such as **Two Park Avenue** (1927; at 32nd Street), Ely Jacques Kahn's confection of Vienna Secessionist color and form.

Even Brooklyn was getting into the skyscraper act. In 1929 the **Williamsburgh Savings Bank** put up its new 512-foot-high headquarters (Halsey, McCormick & Helmer) at Flatbush Avenue and Hanson Place, in the low-rise eastern fringe of downtown Brooklyn. The bank hoped to pull development in its direction (a similar ploy was being used in Manhattan by the contemporary Empire State Building), but the depression intervened. Today, the Postmodern towers of the **Metrotech** office complex have given a new skyline to the heart of downtown Brooklyn, but the bank's tower, with its four-faced 27-foot-wide clock, is still visible in its isolated splendor for 30 miles around.

The boom went bust as we all know, but the depression era produced one of the finest skyscraper complexes the world has ever seen. Pushing the Midtown office district farther north to around 50th Street between Fifth and Sixth avenues, **Rockefeller Center** (1931–1938; the Associated Architects) put slab towers atop low-rise bases (for more light and air both in the building and on the street) and tied its buildings together with a vast underground shopping center. The center gave the public an unprecedented pedestrian promenade and sunken plaza (used for ice-skating in the winter), direct access to the new IND Sixth Avenue subway, and provided for underground truck deliveries (below the skating rink), making its streets more civilized to negotiate.

Its two music halls (one is now gone) and cinema (the Guild, at 50th Street) provided entertainment, while sculpture, art works, and museums (the museums are also gone now) provided culture. Raymond Hood, the project's chief architect, melded Le Corbusier's insistence on light, airy slabs with the German Expressionists' insistence on symbolism. The result was a then-unique type of "city" that was friendly and familiar, light-filled and open in spite of its gargantuan scale. Yet it gives us "character" as few Modern buildings ever do: The newly spotlit **GE Building** (which to New Yorkers will forever be known by its original name, the RCA Building), the center's visual focus, anchors the city as Medieval cathedrals once anchored old European cities. Many complexes have tried to emulate Rockefeller Center, but few have achieved its balance of size, scale, and civility.

Post–World War II Design

After World War II the Modern "glass box" school came into vogue. Skidmore, Owings & Merrill's Gordon Bunshaft shocked New York with his **Manufacturers Hanover Trust** glass bank (1954) at Fifth Avenue and 43rd Street (southwest corner) and the floating glass slabs of **Lever House** (1952) at Park Avenue and 53rd Street (northwest corner). Here was an urban world of shimmering glass, light, air, and sun. Glass skins began to be wrapped around old-fashioned setback silhouettes.

Mies van der Rohe and Philip Johnson's **Seagram Building** (1958; Park Avenue at 53rd Street, southeast corner) changed the shape of the skyscraper radically and created the template for a generation. Mies's brilliant rendering of bronze, glass, and marble expressed perfectly that generation's search for a new functionalist, machine-age style. The building's pristine glass tower, set in a podium-style plaza, was reproduced superficially by the thousands in cities across the country. In New York itself the Seagram's imagery permeated everything as Midtown pushed up Park, Third, and Sixth avenues, and as downtown expanded from Water Street to the World Trade Center.

The Seagram is perfection both as a piece of sculpture and as an aesthetic statement. But its popularity among developers did not stem from its refined proportioning. Rather, because the building is actually fatter and more complicated than it first appears to be, the Seagram gave them a sleek corporate image while allowing them to stuff a good deal of office space behind the glass façade. Its pristine lobby had no room for messy retail tenants, and the tower-in-a-plaza siting was the perfect expression of the Suburban Decade's dislike of anything remotely urban.

The Seagram is a work of art, but what turned out to be a prototype for mass production was itself, ironically, not truly capable of being mass produced. Most of the building's features—from its bronze mini I-beams, used as decorative mullions, to its bronze-tinted glass windows and special interior lighting (which gives the Seagram at night a totally different effect)—were custom designed and custom made. This classic image of a machine-made product was in fact a custom-made arts-and-crafts artifact costing twice as much as other buildings. Knocked off cheaply, it lost the genius that made its minimalism work. When repeated on a large scale the Miesian city was lifeless, boring, and scaleless, giving 1960s cityscapes an almost fatal case of visual anomie.

Postmodern Construction

Midtown. Everything the Seagram eschewed has come back in the Postmodern 1980s. Decoration, romantic silhouettes, flamboyant tops, intensely active plazas all are now *de rigueur*. One of the first of the Postmodern towers, the **Citicorp Center** (1977; Hugh Stubbins; Lexington Avenue at 53rd Street), is still one of the best, creating a truly urbane interior court that has consistently attracted the public. Others of note are the **Sony Building** (née the AT & T Building), by Philip Johnson (1979; Madison Avenue at 55th Street, northwest corner), known for its Chippendale top (which is probably the building's best part), the **IBM Building**, next door (1983; Edward Larrabee Barnes; Madison Avenue at 57th Street, southwest corner), with its own quite popular glassed-in court, and **Trump Tower** (1979; Swanke Hayden Connell; Fifth Avenue at 56th Street, northeast corner), whose opulent, marble-swathed, vertical shopping center is a fitting altar to New York's worship of the loud and the flashy. Three blocks east, at **135 East 57th Street** (Lexington Avenue, northwest corner), the architectural firm of Kohn Pederson Fox has recently completed a new concave office tower with a pergola entranceway and the adjoining Place des Antiquaires, a building whose only tenants are antiques dealers (125 East 57th). The entire complex, with its lavish use of rich marbles and High Renaissance detailing, is the quintessential expression of the firm's Postmodern Neoclassicism, carefully tuned to the scale of today's corporate Medici.

Times Square. In the Times Square area, a half dozen or so new skyscrapers are being completed, the result of City Hall's efforts, through tax breaks, to steer development away from the overbuilt East Side. Addresses west of Sixth Avenue, long considered to be rather déclassé for corporate purposes, may actually rival those on Park and Fifth avenues in prestige by the end of the century.

Among this new crop of buildings several grab attention, if only because their bulk and illuminated tops demand it. The building at **1585 Broadway** (Gwathmey Siegel & Associates; west side, between 47th and 48th streets) has a handsome block-through lobby and a truncated pyramid at top. Most New Yorkers can't yet place this new sight when looking at the nighttime skyline.

Locals have dubbed **750 Seventh Avenue** (Kevin Roche John Dinkeloo Associates; west side, between 49th and 50th streets) the "finger building" because of its picturesque roofline. **Two Times Square** (a basically nonsense address created for the purposes of prestige), designed by Mayers & Schiff Associates, caps the north end of Times Square, on West 47th Street between Broadway and Seventh Avenue, forever altering what was once one of the world's most famous vistas.

By City Hall fiat, all of these new buildings on Broadway and on Seventh Avenue between 43rd and 50th streets must have provision for neon signs on their lower floors to preserve the electric gaudiness for which the area is famous. The soft economy has kept advertisers from buying into these plans, and though the buildings' first ten floors have been configured to accommodate neon, few signs have actually appeared. The result is, we are looking at not-quite-completed designs in Times Square, even though the buildings are open and filled with tenants.

Downtown. **Battery Park City** (BPC), in lower Manhattan on the Hudson River shore, gives us in one fell swoop all the Postmodern standards on a single stage. Cesar Pelli's **World Financial Center** has mosaic-domed lobbies, a shop-lined walkway system, and the glass-enclosed, café-filled **Winter Garden**, which give us the commercial side, while BPC's new residential districts, with their traditional city streets and apartment buildings reminiscent of prewar designs, show us Postmodernism on the domestic front. The open-space planning and landscaping here is the most imaginative in years, and includes a new version of Gramercy Park as well as waterfront esplanades and parks designed with a refreshing sensibility.

Brooklyn. Such bulk might not be too noticeable in densely packed Manhattan, but in the low-rise outer boroughs it can lead to the creation of architectural Godzillas. The **Morgan Stanley Building** (1988; Haines Lundberg Waehler) at Pierrepont Street and Cadman Plaza West was redesigned because of pressure from the adjoining Brooklyn Heights Historic District. The result is a bit like Roseanne Arnold masquerading as Nancy Reagan, but at least the "neo-Georgian" exterior serves as a polite backdrop to the historic homes nearby, and the mansard top creates a new, picturesque silhouette on the Brooklyn Heights skyline as seen from the piers of Manhattan's South Street Seaport.

Queens. Long Island City, in Queens, now has its own white-collar Gargantua. The **Citicorp Building at Court Square** (1989; Skidmore, Owings & Merrill) rises 50 stories from the surrounding low-rise industrial and residential district. The tallest building between Hartford and Philadelphia (with the notable exception of Manhattan), it is bound to dominate the skyline of the East River's "other bank" for decades to come. Sited directly across the river from Citicorp's more elegantly designed headquarters at Lexington Avenue and 53rd Street in Manhattan, this green giant fills the vista when you look east down Manhattan's 53rd Street, visually drawing Midtown Manhattan across the Queensboro Bridge. Though Skidmore, Owings & Merrill tried to give the tower a crisp, Postmodern sophistication, you have to wonder whether buildings so obviously out of scale with their surroundings can ever be made to work architecturally.

Future Prospects. Though it is too early to tell, the Postmodern style is probably the beginning of a new Eclectic era, when romantic silhouettes, decoration of whatever kind, intense urban activity, and design sources from both the past and the future will predominate. But Postmodern decor cannot mask the changing facts of city life. Manhattan's enormous real-estate costs (even in the midst of financially tough times) mean gargantuan towers, whether commercial or residential. Every one of Manhattan's desirable residential sections is being glutted with apartment houses of unprecedented size.

In the service economy of the postindustrial world, our buildings are being built for computers more than for people. Though Midtown office buildings might be slender and notched to give each member of their corps of corporate executives a corner office, most skyscrapers are now built on a massive scale to give the computerized back-offices and trading floors the immense amount of room they need. Large floors mean fat buildings: Though the World Financial Center's towers average 40-odd stories, each contains at least the square footage of the 102-story Empire State Building.

Whither goes Manhattan? Nobody knows. Looking back over the previous 20-year period, we can with hindsight see that no one could have predicted the changes that would take place five years down the road from any particular time. Who knows when we'll see the next masterpiece—or the next abysmal flop. Whenever it is, you can be sure it won't be long in coming.

MUSEUMS AND BOOKSTORES
FOR ARCHITECTURE

Museum of Modern Art (11 West 53rd Street, between Fifth and Sixth avenues). Galleries and occasional exhibitions on, of course, Modern-movement architects. Don't miss the gallery highlighting modern consumer products. Excellent bookstore and other shops. For museum information, Tel: 708-9480; shops, Tel: 708-9700.

Metropolitan Museum of Art (Fifth Avenue at 82nd Street). Period rooms include French 18th-century salons, an American Neo-Gothic library, and a Frank Lloyd Wright living room. The bookstore has a good selection of titles on architecture. Tel: 879-5500 for all services.

Cooper-Hewitt Museum (Fifth Avenue at 91st Street). The Smithsonian's decorative arts branch, which often has architectural exhibitions. Its building is a major exhibit in itself: the 1901 mansion built for Andrew Carnegie. Check the bookstore's inventory. For museum information, Tel: 860-6898; shop, Tel: 860-6878.

The **Urban Center** (457 Madison Avenue, at 51st Street). Located in the north wing of the 1883 Villard Houses, with the rest of the complex now functioning as the New York Palace Hotel. Often has small exhibits on architectural and city-planning topics, especially relating to New York and/or historic preservation. **Urban Center Books,** located in the Urban Center, is *the* New York bookstore for architecture, city planning, and urban design. Tel: 935-3592.

Rizzoli Bookstore. The main store (31 West 57th Street, between Fifth and Sixth avenues) is as handsome as the books it sells. Its design section features lush volumes on art and architecture. Tel: 759-2424. There are also branches at 454 West Broadway, in SoHo (Tel: 674-1616), and in the new World Financial Center, in lower Manhattan (Tel: 385-1400).

GALLERIES

Max Protetch (560 Broadway, at Prince Street). Devotes one of its galleries full time to architectural exhibits and has original architectural drawings for sale. Tel: 966-5454.

The **Drawing Center** (35 Wooster Street, between Broome and Grand streets). This nonprofit gallery occasionally has smashing shows of architectural drawings. Tel: 219-2166.

Storefront for Art & Architecture (97 Kenmare Street, near Lafayette Street). Offbeat, interesting architectural shows. Tel: 431-5795.

For up-to-the-minute schedules of gallery and museum shows of architectural interest, see the listings in *Blueprint* magazine, a British publication that covers the New York scene, or *Metropolis* magazine, published locally, devoted to architecture, urban design, and the decorative arts. Both are available at Urban Center Books and Rizzoli Bookstore.

ARCHITECTURE BY NEIGHBORHOOD
The following structures and neighborhoods, listed by area, are among the best of New York's architectural treasures and are representative of the many architectural styles that have shaped the city. This listing is by no means exhaustive, however. See our Neighborhoods sections for other sights of architectural interest. In parentheses following each entry you'll find the section of this chapter in which each building or neighborhood is described.

South of Canal Street
A. T. Stewart's/The Sun Building (*Department Stores and Commercial Buildings*)
Battery Park City (*The Skyscraper*)
City Hall (*Public Buildings*)
Irving Trust Co./Bank of New York (*The Skyscraper*)
James Watson House (*The Row House*)
South Street Seaport (*The Row House*)
U.S. Custom House (*Public Buildings*)
Woolworth Building (*The Skyscraper*)
World Financial Center (*The Skyscraper*)

From Canal Street to 34th Street
Flatiron Building (*The Skyscraper*)
Haughwout Store (*Department Stores and Commercial Buildings*)
Jacob K. Javits Convention Center (*Public Buildings*)
Ladies' Mile and Fashion Row (*Department Stores and Commercial Buildings*)
Little Singer Building (*The Skyscraper*)
Metropolitan Life Tower (*The Skyscraper*)
New Era Building (*The Skyscraper*)
Old Merchant's House (*The Row House*)
The Row (Washington Square North) (*The Row House*)
Theodore Roosevelt Birthplace (*The Row House*)
Two Park Avenue (*The Skyscraper*)

Midtown

Arnold Constable (*Department Stores and Commercial Buildings*)

Sony Building (*The Skyscraper*)

Bergdorf Goodman (*Department Stores and Commercial Buildings*)

Chanin Building (*The Skyscraper*)

Chrysler Building (*The Skyscraper*)

Citicorp Center (*The Skyscraper*)

Crown Building (*Department Stores and Commercial Buildings*)

Empire State Building (*The Skyscraper*)

1585 Broadway (*The Skyscraper*)

Fred F. French Building (*The Skyscraper*)

GE Building (*The Skyscraper*)

Grand Central Terminal (*Public Buildings*)

IBM Building (*The Skyscraper*)

Lever House (*The Skyscraper*)

Lord & Taylor (*Department Stores and Commercial Buildings*)

Manufacturers Hanover Trust (*The Skyscraper*)

New York Public Library (*Public Buildings*)

135 East 57th Street (*The Skyscraper*)

Rockefeller Center (*The Skyscraper*)

Saks Fifth Avenue (*Department Stores and Commercial Buildings*)

Seagram Building (*The Skyscraper*)

750 Seventh Avenue (*The Skyscraper*)

Tiffany's (*Department Stores and Commercial Buildings*)

Trump Tower (*The Skyscraper*)

Two Times Square (*The Skyscraper*)

Villard Houses (*The Row House*)

Upper West Side and Harlem

American Museum of Natural History (*Public Buildings*)

The Ansonia (*The Apartment House*)

The Apthorp (*The Apartment House*)

The Belleclaire (*The Apartment House*)

The Beresford (*The Apartment House*)

The Century (*The Apartment House*)

The Dakota (*The Apartment House*)

Hamilton Terrace (*The Row House*)

The Majestic (*The Apartment House*)

Mount Morris Park Historic District (*The Row House*)

The San Remo (*The Apartment House*)

Shepard Hall (*The Row House*)

Strivers' Row (*The Row House*)
West 76th Street off Riverside Drive, town houses (*The Row House*)

Upper East Side
Cooper-Hewitt Museum (*The Row House*)
East 79th Street off Fifth Avenue, houses (*The Row House*)
International Center of Photography (*The Row House*)
Jewish Museum (*The Row House*)
Metropolitan Museum of Art (*Public Buildings*)
New York University Institute of Fine Arts (*The Row House*)
998 Fifth Avenue (*The Apartment House*)
Solomon R. Guggenheim Museum (*Public Buildings*)

Brooklyn
Bedford-Stuyvesant brownstones (*The Row House*)
Boerum Hill (*The Row House*)
Brooklyn Heights (*The Row House*)
Brooklyn Museum (*Public Buildings*)
Carroll Gardens (*The Row House*)
Charles Pratt House (*The Row House*)
Clinton Hill (*The Row House*)
Cobble Hill (*The Row House*)
Crown Heights (*The Row House*)
Metrotech Center (*The Skyscraper*)
Morgan Stanley Building (*The Skyscraper*)
Park Slope (*The Row House*)
Prospect Park South planned community (*The Garden Suburb*)
Stuyvesant Heights Historic District (*The Row House*)
Williamsburgh Savings Bank (*The Skyscraper*)

The Bronx
The Grand Concourse (*The Apartment House*)
Riverdale (*The Garden Suburb*)

Queens
Citicorp Building at Court Square (*The Skyscraper*)
Forest Hills Gardens (*The Garden Suburb*)
Fresh Meadows (*The Garden Suburb*)
Kew Gardens (*The Garden Suburb*)
Sunnyside Gardens (*The Garden Suburb*)

PHOTOGRAPHY AND FILMMAKING

By Steve Ettlinger

Steve Ettlinger is an independent book producer with several award-winning photo books to his credit. He is also a freelance picture editor and was formerly associate picture editor at GEO *magazine. His most recent photo-book project is* Vietnam: The Land We Never Knew, *by Geoffrey Clifford.*

Visual artists of all stripes from all over the world make pilgrimages to New York City to do business, and thousands of others work, study, and live here. The main draw to the city for professional photographers is the concentration of major advertising agencies, magazines, and publishing companies. An editorial photographer from out of town may spend a week here, making appointments to see as many as six editors in a day at such publications as *Time, Life, Newsweek, Vogue, GQ,* and the like. He or she may stop in to see any of the major photo agencies that have their headquarters in New York: Magnum, Gamma-Liaison, Contact, Woodfin Camp, Comstock, Freelance Photographers Guild, Photo Researchers, Associated Press, Bettmann Archives, and so on. The attendant organizations and associations are also here.

Filmmakers also find plenty of reason to come here. The first Westerns were shot in New Jersey, and Queens was the original American movie capital. These days movie and television productions bring New York almost $3 billion yearly in gross revenue, and a major studio, the **Kaufman Astoria Studios**, is located in Queens. (Not open to the public.) Its clients past and present range from D. W. Griffith to Woody Allen. The city even has a one-stop department devoted to assisting filmmakers with obtaining permits to film in the city (a practice that tends to block already crowded sidewalks and streets): the Mayor's Office of Film, Theatre and Broadcasting, at 254 West 54th Street. The office issues permits overnight and arranges for the police film unit to coordinate traffic and control bystanders during chase or fire scenes. It also keeps lists on hand of locales, such as a penthouse apartment overlooking rooftops that give an unblemished 1930s feeling, and the one place in Manhattan where you can walk directly into a river (under the George Washington Bridge).

While most people link Hollywood with the origins of filmmaking, it all started back East, and New York, in fact, claims as many movie landmarks as Los Angeles. This is in part because Thomas A. Edison invented the whole idea in nearby West Orange, New Jersey. His laboratory and home are now a national park most definitely worth a pilgrimage; Tel: (201) 736-1515.

In order to find out what's happening in the business, photographers can turn to a local monthly of some renown, *Photo District News*. (Filmmakers must rely on the national paper *Variety*.) *PDN* is sold for five dollars at various labs and photo stores and may be picked up at the publication's offices (1515 Broadway, between 44th and 45th streets). The classified ads are of help to anyone in need of freelance assistants, a studio to rent, equipment to buy, or any other photographic needs.

THE PHOTO DISTRICT

There is not one main street or neighborhood for filmmakers, though groups of them are found in SoHo, TriBeCa, and the East Village, and a concentration of services is found near the television studios in the West 40s, 50s, and 60s. However, photographers have definitely developed something akin to their own neighborhood, known as the Photo District, anchored by the venerable Flatiron Building at Fifth Avenue and 23rd Street. Among the city's first skyscrapers, it was the location of a 1905 movie featuring the wind blowing women's skirts up in a revealing way. This windy locale gave birth to the phrase "23 skiddoo." Warren Beatty found it a perfect 1902 setting for Diane Keaton's New York City arrival in the film *Reds*. Although there are no official borders, the consensus is that the Photo District extends from 23rd Street south to 14th Street and from Park Avenue South west to Sixth Avenue.

The area has been home to advertising and fashion photographers for years because of its many commercial loft buildings and low rents. Recently, following the usual pattern of gentrification, rents and purchase prices have skyrocketed, forcing new photographers to look elsewhere for living or studio space, while professional-oriented stores and labs, on the other hand, have moved in. In fact, the equipment-rental business (everything from cameras to entire studios) is growing rapidly in the area, which is good news for a visiting photographer. Some of the upward pressure on rents has been generated by the arrival of major advertising agencies and publishers, who have taken over large loft buildings in the district after total renovations.

Photographers themselves are not as much in evidence in the streets of the Photo District as are the businesses that serve them. Beyond the obvious labs and stat houses (the more established ones occupy entire buildings and have reception areas buzzing with messengers, assistants, and students—all displaying the latest in street fashion) are more traditional businesses that have adapted to serve their photographic neighbors. Antiques stores have signs in the windows proclaiming that their goods are available as rental props, and a plethora of gourmet stores cater photo shoots.

PHOTOGRAPHY, FILM, AND BROADCAST MUSEUMS

It is fitting that New York City would have a major museum devoted solely to photography: the **International Center of Photography** (ICP; 1130 Fifth Avenue, at 94th Street; and a Midtown branch at 1133 Sixth Avenue, at 43rd Street). Between the two locations ICP hosts about 20 major shows each year, accompanied by crowded and jolly opening celebrations (be sure to ask when the next one is). Photographers tend to work alone and look forward to socializing, and the editors and agents seem to have been colleagues since whenever they started in the business, so the openings smack of cameraderie. ICP offers a full program of courses, workshops, and lectures, all of which are open to the public, and each branch has a comprehensive bookshop. Uptown, Tel: 860-1777; Midtown, 768-4680.

Two other New York museums, the **Museum of Modern Art** (11 West 53rd Street) and the **Metropolitan Museum of Art** (Fifth Avenue at 82nd Street), have excellent photographic exhibitions. Every photographer should see MoMA's permanent collection, one of the world's most important. The MoMA bookstore's selection supplements the experience.

Filmdom has its own museum in New York City: the **American Museum of the Moving Image**, located within the Kaufman/Astoria studio complex (35th Avenue and

36th Street) in the Astoria section of Queens. This unusual museum is a wonderful blend of education and entertainment and contains a small theater, a large screening room, and special and permanent exhibits on both the art and the business of movie and TV-show making. Tel: (718) 784-0077. (See the Queens Neighborhood section for directions.) The **Museum of Television & Radio** (25 West 52nd Street, between Fifth and Sixth avenues) is geared to television, but you can request televised films from the vast archives and view them in one of the many screening booths. There are frequent lectures and seminars with writers, actors, directors, and producers. Tel: 621-6600.

PHOTOGRAPHY AND FILM BOOKSTORES
(See also the bookstore listings in our Literary New York section).

The **Drama Bookshop** (723 Seventh Avenue, at 48th Street) and the **Gotham Book Mart** (41 West 47th Street, between Fifth and Sixth avenues) go beyond film into theatrical work. **Applause Theatre and Cinema Books** (211 West 71st Street, between Broadway and West End Avenue) is an excellent place to find elusive screenplays. Mainline art bookstores such as **Rizzoli** (main store at 31 West 57th Street, between Fifth and Sixth avenues; branches at 454 West Broadway, between Houston and Prince streets, and 200 Vesey Street, in the World Financial Center) have good selections of photographic books, but the best is probably the **New York University Bookstore** (18 Washington Place, between Washington Square East and Greene Street), which supports all the courses in film theory and the like at NYU's famous film school. Tel: 998-4678.

A Photographers Place (133 Mercer Street, south of Prince Street) has a huge selection of books encompassing damaged bargains and old classics and will also search out a rare title for you on request. There is a mail-order catalog as well. Some antique paraphernalia is displayed in the shop along with occasional shows. Tel: 431-9358. Another good standby in SoHo is **Jaap Rietman** (134 Spring Street, second floor, between Wooster and Greene streets); Tel: 966-7044.

The main **ICP** bookstore (94th Street and Fifth Avenue) has one of the city's most complete selections of contemporary work as well as related texts and technical books. The Midtown store (1133 Sixth Avenue, at 43rd Street), is more limited. Both feature photographer appearances from time to time, although at any time uptown you may find the photographer of the very book you are perusing browsing next to you—so it's a good idea to keep your criticisms to yourself.

Both the Met and MoMA have photo books for sale, but MoMA's selection is broader. Surprise bargains as well as regular discounts are found at both **Barnes & Noble** bookstores across the avenue from each other at Fifth Avenue and 18th Street, as well as at the nearby venerable secondhand store **Strand** (828 Broadway, at 12th Street; Tel: 473-1452). A newer store, **Untitled II**, across from New York University (680 Broadway, at 3rd Street), has a growing reputation among serious photo-book collectors. Tel: 982-1145.

PHOTOGRAPHY AND FILM EQUIPMENT AND SERVICES

While there are no guides to New York City for photography buffs, there is something that is sort of a photographers' Rolodex in book form, listing every conceivable potential supplier of goods or services to photographers: *Professional Photo Source*. It is available at a number of photography-industry vendors in the Photo District for $15.95, or by phone or mail order from Photo Source, 36 West 20th Street, New York, NY 10011; Tel: 675-1093. There are 350 headings, ranging from acrylic ice to walkie-talkies and including various categories of cameras, such as "collectible" and "panoramic." The ads in *Photo District News* are also a decent guide (the articles are useful as well).

Cameras and Equipment

A concentration of large department-store-type camera stores developed in the early postwar period around Macy's, and some are still there. However, bargains are hard to find, and little advice is forthcoming. The better stores, concentrated in the Photo District, include the ultimate bargain places as well as those that may not offer the best prices but make up for that considerably with personal advice, equipment loans, and excellent service. In those you will be rubbing shoulders with a professional crowd. A good number of places are open seven days a week; some close on Saturdays but open on Sundays; and many stay open weeknights until quite late, some until midnight. Most advertise in *PDN* or are listed in *Professional Photo Source*. They attract an international clientele.

For the quintessential New York purchasing experience, two places stand out. **Gould Trading** (7 East 17th Street, eighth floor, just off Fifth Avenue) is found at the end of a long, dark corridor in a very dingy building. If they don't have what you want, with a little cajoling they'll find it for you through their network of dealer friends. (They are especially good with used Nikon equipment.) They'll also pay cash for your own equipment. Bargaining is a way of life here. The selection of new photo books and videotapes on photography is very large, and Gould also makes excellent, inexpensive 35-mm duplicate slides and sells film in bulk at a terrific discount. Similar in atmosphere is **Adorama** (42 West 18th Street, between Fifth and Sixth avenues), with old gadgets piled side by side with the latest Zeiss attachments. At both places it helps to have a good idea of what you want before entering, as neither has a display area for perusal. They are more like bars where you belly up and order. Tel: 243-2306 for Gould; 741-0052 for Adorama.

The **Lens & Repro Equipment Corporation** (33 West 17th Street, between Fifth and Sixth avenues) is noted for its large selection of new and used large-format cameras, including a Japanese brand made of ebony and a house brand. Amazingly, they also have a selection of the rare handmade Deardorfs. Tel: 675-1900. **Ken Hansen Photographic** (920 Broadway, at 21st Street), is more or less the Leica king, though he has a full range of other equipment and a huge lighting equipment display as well. But Hansen prides himself more on the personal-service angle of the business (he publishes the names of his salespeople in his ads) and has many telephone lines so clients can call ahead and make appointments so they don't have to wait. Tel: 777-5900.

Hasselblad maniacs will find therapy at **Gil Ghitelman Cameras** (166 Fifth Avenue, near 22nd Street), especially if they are looking for trades; Tel: 924-3020. **Olden Camera** (1265 Broadway, between 31st and 32nd streets) is favored by students, which keeps the place lively in a pleasant way, and carries a wide range of lines, including used equipment. Tel: 725-1234.

Processing Labs

Every photographer has his favorite laboratory, but for quick service of all kinds the larger labs do an excellent job. **K & L** (222 East 44th Street, between Third and Second avenues, in a building that houses services for the video and film industries as well; Tel: 661-5600), **Ken Lieberman** (118 West 22nd Street, between Sixth and Seventh avenues; Tel: 633-0500), and **Duggal Color Projects** (9 West 20th Street, off Fifth Avenue, Tel: 924-7777; and 560 Broadway, corner of Spring Street, Tel: 941-7000) will do virtually anything you can think of, any way you want it. Duggal has an entire building on 20th Street and is something like the hub of the Photo District. The outfit is owned by an Indian who has helped many of his countrymen immigrate, and they have in turn left Duggal to start their own smaller custom labs, including Baboo, L & I, and Tony (acronym for "To New York," the only English its founder knew when he came here). They are all very aggressive marketers, operating 24 hours a day, and anxious to please.

Rentals

Photographics Unlimited Dial-a-Darkroom (17 West 17th Street, just off Fifth Avenue) rents equipment and darkrooms, both color and black-and-white. Tel: 255-9678.

Professionals in the Photo District rent equipment at: **Ken Hansen** (920 Broadway, at 21st Street; especially good for lighting; Tel: 777-5900); **Lens & Repro** (33 West 17th Street, between Fifth and Sixth avenues; Tel: 675-1900); **Calumet New York** (11 West 20th Street, between Fifth and Sixth avenues; Tel: 989-8500); **Foto-Care** (170 Fifth Avenue, seventh floor, at 22nd Street; Tel: 741-2990); and **Profoto** (128 West 31st Street, between Sixth and Seventh avenues; Tel: 564-6171), which is actually a branch of a store in Hamburg, Germany.

Probably the most amusing place to visit is the **Set Shop** (37 East 18th Street, between Broadway and Park Avenue South). This outfit has one of the biggest and most cluttered bulletin boards, a direct line on the doings of the district, to be seen anywhere—and a superb display of foam-rubber rocks, plastic ice cubes, and rubber fish that fill out its line of props. They have a complete catalog, too, which includes backgrounds, building supplies, studio equipment, and all kinds of gadgets undoubtedly useful in all the visual and theatrical arts. Tel: 979-9790. The **Camera Mart, Inc.** (456 West 55th Street, between Ninth and Tenth avenues), rents any movie- or video-related items you may need, whether for the usual use or as a prop. Tel: 757-6977.

Repairs

For years the pros have gone to **Professional Camera Repair Service** (37 West 47th Street, ninth floor, between Fifth and Sixth avenues; Tel: 382-0550), established in 1946, which can also build customized cameras. **Photo Tech Repair Service** (110 East 13th Street, between Third and Fourth avenues; Tel: 673-8400) specializes in repairing modern, electronic models.

SHOPPING FOR PHOTOGRAPHY IN GALLERIES

New York City supports a wonderful range of galleries that show photography on a more or less regular basis, and you can easily buy pictures from day one of the medium to the absolute cutting edge. Many of the leading painting galleries show the latest "in" photographers, generally those with connections in the fashion or advertising world, and these would be featured in the standard gallery listings (see the Art section). Galleries are usually open Mondays to Saturdays from 10:00 or 11:00 A.M. to 5:00 or 6:00 P.M.

Collectors who are interested in experimental work of both early-20th-century and contemporary photographers from both sides of the Atlantic and Latin America should visit the **Julie Saul Gallery** (155 Spring Street, at West Broadway). They are credited among dealers as having some of the most exciting work in the city in their space, though not in a style that attracts mainstream media attention. (One show, for example, featured portraits of Jean Cocteau.) Tel: 431-0747.

Mid-century American work in the tradition of the Farm Security Administration and the Esso Collection can be seen at **Howard Greenberg Gallery** (120 Wooster Street, between Prince and Spring streets). Modern for them means Robert Frank. Tel: 334-0010.

No doubt the gallery the farthest off the beaten track belongs to dealer Alan Klotz, who holds a very personal European-style salon in his Upper West Side apartment. His **Photocollect Gallery** (740 West End Avenue, between 96th and 97th streets) features vintage 19th- and early-20th-century quality work, ranging from $200 to $200,000. Although he maintains regular gallery hours, a phone call is recommended in case he has just dashed off to make a new acquisition; Tel: 222-7381. A close second to Photocollect in terms of being small and personal is the **Union**

Square Gallery (118 East 17th Street, east of Union Square), which is photographer Todd Weinstein's studio. On Fridays and Saturdays he packs all his gear into his office, hangs some terrific work, and sets up a table with wine and cheese. Tel: 777-8393.

More expensive work of living and dead greats, such as Brassaï, can usually be found in the main art gallery area at the **Marlborough Gallery** (40 West 57th Street, between Fifth and Sixth avenues). Tel: 541-4900. Such stars as Irving Penn are often exhibited at the **Pace/MacGill Gallery** (32 East 57th Street, ninth floor, between Madison and Park avenues), as are well-known painter-photographers. Tel: 759-7999.

The **Witkin Gallery** (415 West Broadway, near Spring Street) is probably the most prominent of the commercial galleries featuring work by the best contemporary photographers. Openings are well attended by noted critics, writers, and, of course, photographers. The gallery also sells a good selection of photo books. Tel: 925-5510. **Ledel** (168 Mercer Street, just south of Houston Street) is another gallery showing consistently good work. Tel: 966-7659.

The major New York auction houses organize among themselves to present a series of auctions of photographic work for one week in late October or early November, and again in April or May. The Friday and Sunday editions of *The New York Times* are the best places to see what is being offered. The venerable houses of **Christie's** (502 Park Avenue, at 59th Street; Tel: 546-1000 or 371-5438) and **Sotheby's** (1334 York Avenue, at 72nd Street; Tel: 606-7000 or 606-7245) usually have the largest number of items, but often **Phillips** (406 East 79th Street; Tel: 570-4830) and **Swann** (104 East 25th Street; Tel: 254-4710) have excellent items for sale. Sales at all of these places are usually confined to three-hour sessions, and their expensive catalogs are very well produced.

PHOTOGRAPHERS' HANGOUTS

For some reason there are not any famous, traditional photographers' hangouts in the Photo District, though if anything comes close it would be the **Old Town Bar** (45 East 18th Street, between Park Avenue South and Broadway), a resolutely dark, dingy, and inexpensive place that has vociferously resisted any attempts at gentrification. The owner has gone so far as to post signs in his dirty window that say the premises are not for sale to any well-dressed developers. The Old Town is one of the few spots that most photographers and assistants can afford. Nearby there are some elegant restaurants that cater to visiting art directors or celebrated photographers, but this clientele is apparently quite fickle, as the hot spots rise up in glory and go out of business in a flash with astounding regularity. Only one place has tried a definite photo orientation complete with ongoing displays of photography: **Portfolio Restaurant and Gallery** (4 West 19th Street, west of Fifth Avenue). The real action in the district, though, is in the labs and photo stores concentrated around West 19th and 20th streets.

PLACES TO SEE FILM
Film buffs need not look far in New York to find satisfaction: There are dozens of theaters and institutions showing absolutely every kind of film made, from the most experimental avant-garde to the most cherished classics. Listings and reviews are easily found in daily and weekly publications such as the *Village Voice* (new issues on Wednesdays), *New York* magazine, *The New Yorker,* and *The New York Times* (you'll find the film reviews in the Friday and Sunday editions). For information on film showings, see "The Movies" heading in the Useful Facts section at the front of this book.

One of the best places to see a wide range of classics, including a good number of silent films, is the **Museum of Modern Art**, which has a regular film program (Tel: 708-9490 for the daily features). Through MoMA's Film Study Center, the archive and film library is open to qualified students and scholars who write in advance for an appointment in a private screening room: MoMA, Film Study Center, 11 West 53rd Street, New York, NY 10019; Tel: 708-9614.

The New York Public Library shows and circulates films, mostly from the comprehensive **Donnell Library** Media Center (across the street from MoMA, at 20 West 53rd Street). The Donnell is one of the more relaxed and yet complete branches of the city's extensive public library system, excellent for someone in need of a convenient Midtown office for a few hours; Tel: 621-0609. The **Performing Arts Library** at Lincoln Center (111 Amsterdam Avenue) does not circulate films but has an amazing collection of clippings, periodicals, memorabilia of all kinds, posters, and books on cinema. The reference service at the library's Billy Rose Theater Collection is a

particular boon to film scholars, with extensively cata-
logued holdings of film memorabilia from which you can
call up items; Tel: 870-1639. Lincoln Center's **Walter
Reade Theater** (on 65th Street between Broadway and
Amsterdam) runs a frequently changing program of classic and little-seen films in a stunning new facility; Tel: 875-
5600.

Each September and October there are two film festivals of note: the **New York Film Festival**, at Lincoln
Center (for information, Tel: 875-5610), and the **Independent Feature Film Market**, which also includes workshops and is oriented toward low-budget films,
including documentaries (Tel: 243-7777). The Film Society of Lincoln Center also produces the **New Directors/
New Films** series every spring, with and at MoMA; Tel:
875-5610. Well-known pros often participate in workshops at **New York Women in Film and Television**; Tel:
679-0870. The New York University filmmaking, video,
and broadcasting studies department at the School of
Continuing Education, 26 Washington Place, offers weekend workshops as well; Tel: 998-7140.

CLASSICAL MUSIC

By Matthew Gurewitsch

*Matthew Gurewitsch has written about music, theater,
film, and dance for* The New York Times, *the* Atlantic,
Mirabella, *and other publications around the world.*

Since the late 1980s a wild spirit has haunted New York
in the person of a gaunt, scruffy pianist with unsmiling
eyes who turns up (usually after dark, lately under the
scaffolding by the Paramount Communications Building
on the east side of Broadway a few blocks south of
Lincoln Center) to bang out selections of his own devis-
ing on a lidless concert grand mounted on casters.
Heard through the din of the street his works might be
mistaken for those of Liszt or Chopin. A tin can—he
does not deign to pass it—stands at the ready for collections. In years past, he would drag his instrument to
work of an evening through the pre-theater gridlock and

drag it uptown after midnight—scenes unmatched for urban surrealism. Of late, he seems to travel less, but he is still around. Making a living at music in this city takes nerve, resolve, and invention. The roving pianist, known as Mee, belongs to the army of the city's homeless, and after hours, his piano is the roof over his head. When he plays, he seems a heraldic device come to life.

Close to curtain time every day of the week, in buses and subways and on street corners, you encounter musicians en route to their jobs: men of all ages, lacking only bow ties to complete their evening dress, negotiating luggage in the telltale shapes of cellos and horns or carrying discreet attaché cases; women in long black dresses and sneakers wrestling harps or swinging violin cases. A glance at their datebooks would confirm that, like Mee, they have to cobble together the existence that suits them. Artistic and economic necessities require it, even of the musicians with the greatest job security.

Thus, many principal players with the New York Philharmonic, with multiple-season contracts running 12 months a year, double as faculty at the Juilliard School, across 65th Street from the Philharmonic's Avery Fisher Hall. Regular players in such busy Manhattan-based ensembles as the self-conducting chamber orchestra Orpheus and the Orchestra of St. Luke's freelance regularly, in accord with their private interests, in groups dedicated to early or contemporary music. Some switch-hit as soloists or establish trios or quartets. The studious-looking international crowd of children, adolescents, and young adults who disappear into Juilliard each morning are headed for careers checkered in just this fashion. The most precocious among them are already on the circuit.

CONCERT HALLS AND VENUES

Lincoln Center for the Performing Arts

Lincoln Center (occupying several blocks between 62nd and 66th streets and Amsterdam and Columbus avenues) boasts the city's highest concentration of stages for music. At the center's epicenter is a fountain: a black marble ring enclosing vertical jets of water whose play, in its abstract fashion, is as ecstatic as the Baroque cascades of Rome. But in the summer it, too, is sometimes covered to double as a platform. Around the fountain spreads a rectangular plaza, bounded on three sides by grandly scaled houses for opera, dance, and concerts: **New York State**

Theater (2,737 seats) on the south, with its soothing gleam, shared by the New York City Opera and the New York City Ballet; the plush, crystal-studded **Metropolitan Opera House** (3,718 seats) on the west; and **Avery Fisher Hall** (2,738 seats) on the north, articulated like the inside of a cream-colored accordion, home to the New York Philharmonic. Add to these the open-air band shell of **Damrosch Park**, at the southwestern corner of Lincoln Center; **Alice Tully Hall** (1,096 seats), to the north of Avery Fisher, built for the Lincoln Center Chamber Music Society; and impromptu outdoor spaces devised for free summer events—and it is hard to imagine that you would ever need to look elsewhere for musical enjoyment.

And to an extent, that is now true. Time was when the New York music scene was divided neatly into "uptown" and "downtown." Uptown meant little beyond mainstream classics from the Continent, a canon closed, after several (some would say) largely wasted decades, when Richard Strauss finished his "Four Last Songs" and laid down his pen. Downtown meant the esoteric John Cage, pixieish guru for the few, heard in cellars, lofts, and assorted holes-in-the-wall; then it meant the minimalists from Terry Riley through Steve Reich and Philip Glass, who after a quiet start have entranced multitudes. Since have come fast-rising children of the tape age, from A (Anderson, Laurie) to M (Monk, Meredith) to Z (Zorn, John).

In the late 1960s downtown found its temple across the East River, at the Brooklyn Academy of Music, whose success has been so phenomenal as to create demand for its artists where else but uptown? And Lincoln Center has come through, scheduling special events and even whole series (like the summertime "Serious Fun!") designed not to hurt a bit. For general information, Tel: 875-5400.

Juilliard School

Although guidebooks for travellers usually don't mention it, the Juilliard School, a constituent of Lincoln Center, is well worth the musical visitor's attention. What with recitals by students and faculty, concerts by student orchestras (often with students or illustrious recent graduates as soloists), master classes, and fully staged productions of operas both familiar and rare, the school offers more than 300 performances a year. Quality, as you might expect, varies; at best, it is superb. Prices, as you might also expect, are low (often, admission is free). And the Juilliard

Theater, though obscurely situated, is Manhattan's only opera house built on a human scale. (It seats 933 comfortably and with good sight lines.) For information, consult the billboards by the bus stop on the west side of Broadway between 65th and 66th streets or call the concert office; Tel: 769-7406.

Carnegie Hall

Carnegie Hall, a short walk away from Lincoln Center (at 57th Street and Seventh Avenue), cannot compete for sheer quantity of programming, but after all, how many concerts can you attend at once? And it is still the incomparable prestige address. Since its construction in 1891, it has ranked not only as the nation's premier concert hall but as the concert hall's Platonic ideal. (You've heard the story: A man stops a man with a violin case on a New York street corner. "How do I get to Carnegie Hall?" asks the first. "Practice!" comes the reply. The joke works for no other hall.)

In 1986 the main hall (2,784 seats) was sumptuously refurbished, and so was the smaller space upstairs then known as Carnegie Recital Hall and since rechristened **Weill Recital Hall** (268 seats). The public heard many assurances beforehand that the fabled warm acoustics, traditionally equaled only by the Amsterdam Concertgebouw, Boston's Symphony Hall, and the Vienna Musikvereinssaal, would be preserved intact. At the reopening, it was instantly apparent that the sound had changed—few listeners thought for the better.

Most agree that the hall has become brighter, colder, more space-age, more aggressive. Some have wondered whether the impression originates in what amounts to an optical illusion: Now that all the dowdy gray drapes and tacky screens have been removed from the stage area (and now that the palette has gone to ivory, rose, and gold, and the ushers have been outfitted by Ralph Lauren), Carnegie Hall certainly *looks* brighter, in a Postmodern-retro way. Nevertheless, experiments with acoustic panels, foam, and other fine tuning are bound to continue for years—and so is the bickering among the experts. Meanwhile, a time-honored flaw in the hall remains: The rumble of the subway is still plainly audible.

Since the departure of the New York Philharmonic to Lincoln Center in 1962, Carnegie Hall has had no resident orchestra. However, the symphonies of Boston, Philadelphia, and other major American cities provide continuity with their regular seasons there. In addition, the hall produces and presents dozens of series with leading international artists. On dates when the hall does not have plans of its own, it is available for rental, which will explain the presence of a decidedly second- or third-tier attraction from time to time. The monthly schedule, available at the box office, is color-coded to distinguish the rentals from Carnegie Hall's own offerings, which can give the critical concertgoer a useful signal when confronted with unfamiliar names. Book especially warily at Carnegie's smaller Weill Hall, a venue much favored for once-in-a-lifetime vanity recitals. But here, too, Carnegie Hall as an institution grows more ambitious with each passing season. Tel: 247-7800.

Brooklyn Academy of Music

The Brooklyn Academy of Music (at 30 Lafayette Avenue, near the intersection of Atlantic and Flatbush avenues in Brooklyn), better known as BAM, has already been cited in passing for its role in legitimizing downtown music. In the process, it has turned itself into something very like the Alternative Lincoln Center, housing under a single roof the festive Opera House (2,085 seats), a well-proportioned playhouse (1,011 seats), and a black box, reconfigurable any which way, called the **Lepercq Space** (seating 350 to 550). In addition, BAM has refurbished the **Majestic Theater** (875 seats), a dilapidated former vaudeville house at 651 Fulton Street (a couple of blocks closer to Manhattan), enshrining its very disrepair.

All of BAM's auditoriums serve many muses, notably those of music and dance. The **Next Wave Festival**, held each autumn, juxtaposes ground-breaking American work with adventurous work from abroad. Thanks to the festival's enduring success, BAM is associated above all with the commercially viable avant-garde.

All the BAM theaters are easily accessible by subway. From Manhattan, take the Broadway express lines (numbers 2 or 3) or the less circuitous Lexington Avenue express (numbers 4 or 5) to Nevins Street for the Majestic; ride one stop farther, to Atlantic Avenue, for BAM proper. The Q, R, B, and N trains will also get you to BAM (though not to the Majestic) from Manhattan; the stop to look for on those lines is Pacific Street. Another convenient option is the BAM Bus, which departs from the Summit Hotel, Lexington Avenue and 51st Street, one hour before curtain time at the Opera House or the

Majestic. On the way back the bus makes several stops, the first in Greenwich Village, the last on Broadway at 72nd Street. For BAM information, Tel: (718) 636-4100.

Intimate Venues

So far, the talk has mostly been of the big venues. For more intimate material—solo recitals or chamber music—there are many smaller spaces, too, frequented faithfully by all but the hugest box-office stars. You would not expect to encounter Jessye Norman or Dietrich Fischer-Dieskau at the **92nd Street Y** (1395 Lexington Avenue), for instance, but Elly Ameling and Hermann Prey are regulars. Tel: 415-5440.

The **Metropolitan Museum of Art** (Fifth Avenue at 82nd Street), for its part, has long presented in its **Grace Rainey Rogers Auditorium** such internationally acclaimed artists as the Guarneri String Quartet, the Beaux Arts Trio, and Les Arts Florissants. Tel: 570-3949. If you enjoy music in beautiful surroundings, you should know that the Metropolitan also offers performances in its Medieval Sculpture Hall, the Temple of Dendur, the Velez Blanco Patio, and elsewhere—as well as at the Funtedueña Chapel at the **Cloisters**, its bastion of Medieval art surrounded by rambling Fort Tryon Park at the northern tip of Manhattan. Often the performances at the Cloisters coincide with church holidays; they almost always have a deliberately archaic cast. (To get to the Cloisters take the uptown-bound A train to 190th Street and Overlook Terrace, exit by elevator, and walk through the park; or hop onto the M 4 bus marked "Fort Tryon Park, The Cloisters." The bus comes up from lower Manhattan via Madison Avenue, but it is a waste of several hours to take it from points downtown or Midtown.) For concert information, Tel: 923-3700.

The **Frick Collection** (1 East 70th Street), some ten blocks down Fifth Avenue from the Metropolitan Museum, retains its character of a connoisseur's private mansion and boasts—apart from a glorious assemblage of paintings—a fine music room, where late-afternoon concerts are held once or twice a month. Important performers appear here with minimal fanfare. No advance notices are published in the newspapers, but the concerts are broadcast on WNYC radio, and the audience is often extremely distinguished. Tickets are free with admission to the museum. The procedure for obtaining them is, however, Byzantine to the point of impossibility. To get in, queue up a half hour or so before the concert and hope for the best. Your patience is likely to be rewarded; there are always no-shows. Tel: 288-0700.

The **Museum of Modern Art** has adapted the Cloisters' example in its own way, offering free summer concerts of small-scale 20th-century works amid the Nadelmans, Maillols, Picassos, and Oldenburgs in the outdoor sculpture garden (enter directly from West 54th Street between Fifth and Sixth avenues). Splendid artists appear here in imaginative programs. Alas, this is Midtown, and the urban racket intrudes. Tel: 708-9480. Ambient noise is a problem in **Central Park**, too, where the New York Philharmonic and the Metropolitan Opera—heavily amplified—play beneath the stars and the airplanes and the mosquitos to the picnicking multitudes on various midsummer nights. Tel: 360-2777.

LISTINGS AND TICKETS

The Arts & Leisure section of the Sunday *New York Times* is indispensable for long-range planning, but for a visitor the weekly magazines and newspapers provide more helpful calendars. The best-organized listings are in *New York* magazine (see the Cue listings section). In the various departments of the "Goings on about Town" section each week, *The New Yorker* prefaces calendar information with a polished, very short essay on some event of special note and proceeds to give just the facts (but often not enough of them) about a reasonable selection of smaller events and all the majors.

Each day the **Bryant Park Ticket Booth** (42nd Street, behind the New York Public Library) sells half-price tickets for music and dance events taking place that evening. The very hottest attractions will not be represented, but many first-rate ones often are. Call 382-2323 to find out what is on offer—and what the booth's hours are; they vary from day to day.

Apart from this booth, ticketing is mostly decentralized. All the leading institutions and most marginal ones will take ticket reservations over the phone and charge them to the standard credit cards. Such sales are final. When ordering by phone, it is usually impossible to find out exact seat locations (you are generally promised "best available" within the price range). Fussy patrons are advised to go to the box office, *Stubs* in hand. Available at magazine stands in the Broadway Theater District, *Stubs* contains seating plans for all but the smallest of the city's theaters and concert halls. These same plans are usually posted at theaters and concert halls also, but are sometimes too far from the box office to be of any use.

SHOPPING FOR MUSICAL INSTRUMENTS

Not surprisingly, the prime shopping area for musical instruments is within a few blocks' radius of Carnegie Hall.

Pianos and Keyboards

The **Steinway & Sons** piano showroom (109 West 57th Street, between Sixth and Seventh avenues) is an institution still redolent of old-time grandeur and occasionally the venue of toney private recitals. Tel: 332-0100. For secondhand pianos look to **Beethoven Pianos**, with a shop on the Upper East Side (1645 First Avenue, near 85th Street; Tel: 288-2099) and a lovely tinned-ceiling showroom in the Bronx (contact the shop for an appointment). Everything from Steinway grands to spinets to uprights suitable for a child's practice session is available and dependable. **Dietrich Pianos**, in a charming old-fashioned shop (211 West 58th Street, between Broadway and Seventh Avenue), specializes in restored grand pianos of particular beauty and superior sound. Tel: 245-1234. Dietrich's **Museum of the American Piano** is next door.

For the keyboardist of the future the obvious stop is the **Yamaha** showroom (10 East 38th Street, between Fifth and Madison avenues). Apart from conventional concert-quality grands, Yamaha has acoustic pianos with brains that allow you to correct mistakes, transpose, speed up, or slow down your live performance, and then to play it back (cleaned up) with no hands. Other Yamahas produce sound electronically, so that, if the occasion requires, you alone, in headphones, can hear what you are up to. The top-of-the-line synthesizers are virtual symphony orchestras in a console, awaiting their New Age Beethoven. Tel: 686-8996.

String Instruments

Jacques Français (250 West 54th Street, 11th floor, between Eighth Avenue and Broadway) is the acknowledged specialist in rare string instruments. Amatis, Guarneris, and Stradivarii probably pass through here as frequently as anywhere else in the world. Tel: 586-2607. Half a dozen or so violin shops reside on the eighth floor of Français's building, which has come to be called the **Violin Building**. Some of these shops make their own instruments and also repair, recondition, and sell used and antique violins. Convenient to Lincoln Center, the **International Music Service** (133 West 69th Street, near Broadway) specializes in harps. Tel: 874-3360.

Brass, Woodwind, and Band Instruments

Rod Baltimore Music Co., Ltd. (174 West 48th Street, between Sixth and Seventh avenues), specializes in the sale and repair/restoration of woodwind and brass instruments. Tel: 575-1508. Musical-instrument stores, most of which lean toward band instruments, abound on **West 48th Street**, between Sixth and Seventh avenues. The many branches of **Sam Ash** strung along the street specialize in guitars and drums (number 160; Tel: 719-2625 for guitars, 719-2661 for drums), violins (number 163; Tel: 719-2299), and electronic and digital equipment (number 155; Tel: 719-2299).

SHOPPING FOR SHEET MUSIC

Classical musicians shopping for scores head for **Joseph Patelson Music House, Ltd.** (160 West 56th Street, across from Carnegie Hall's stage door). The shop also stocks the city's best selection of books on classical music and musicians, and an interesting array of recordings. Another exclusive feature: The latest concert reviews from *The New York Times* (the only ones in town that matter) are pasted into a loose-leaf album by the door. Tel: 757-5587. The **Music Exchange**, in the Professional Musicians Building (151 West 46th Street, 10th floor, between Sixth and Seventh avenues), appears to have every musical score imaginable, from classical to jazz to show tunes to military music. Tel: 354-5858. **Frank Music** (250 West 54th Street, third floor, between Broadway and Eighth Avenue) has probably the best range of classical selections in the city (carrying many works by composers that Patelson shuns), but as you must give your request at the counter, you've got to know pretty much what you want before entering. Tel: 582-1999.

Classical Vocal Reprints is a New York–based mailorder operation specializing in classical vocal pieces, especially rare selections. P.O. Box 20263, New York, NY 10023-1484; Tel: 517-8114. If you are after sheet music for show tunes, go to **Colony Records Center** (1619 Broadway, at 49th Street), where the bossy sales help can probably set you up with whatever you want—even private tapes of musicals never commercially recorded. Tel: 265-2050.

SHOPPING FOR RECORDINGS

Compact Discs and New Recordings

Compact discs are significantly cheaper in the United States than anywhere else, so it is not uncommon to see visitors from abroad loading up on them by the armful. For the latest classical releases (often issued here several months later than in Europe) the most reliable source is the **J & R Classical Outlet** (33 Park Row, near City Hall). It is the store you can count on to order sufficient stock. Tel: 349-0062. **HMV** is thriving at two locations: 86th Street and Lexington Avenue for East Side shoppers, and 72nd Street and Broadway for the West Side crowd. Still, *the* name in this game is **Tower**, also at two locations: 1961 Broadway (at 66th Street), just north of Lincoln Center, Tel: 799-2500; and 692 Broadway (at 4th Street), in the Village, Tel: 505-1500. The downtown location has a more knowledgeable sales staff and a larger selection, though to find what you want you may have to check both stores. For music lovers still interested in vinyl, an attraction at the downtown Tower is the sales annex (4th and Lafayette streets), where conventional LPs, cassettes, and now CDs are available at rock-bottom prices.

Records: New and Vintage

The LPs at **Gryphon Records** (251 West 72nd Street, second floor, between Broadway and West End Avenue) are often pricey, with good reason: They are collector's items. The pleasantly Dickensian emporium specializes in "Proudly Archival Sound." For anyone with a tolerance for a recently obsolete technology and an appreciation for historic performance, Gryphon is a gold mine. Tel: 874-1588. So is **G & A Rare Records Ltd.** (139 West 72nd Street, second floor, between Amsterdam and Columbus avenues), which is a little sprucer to look at and charges similarly outlandish prices. Still, if they have what you've always been looking for. . . . Tel: 877-5020. Another stop for the serious collector of out-of-print records is the **Academy Book Store** (10 West 18th Street, between Fifth and Sixth avenues)—dusty, cramped, and full of surprises. Tel: 242-4848. **Footlight Records** (113 East 12th Street, between Third and Fourth avenues) specializes in hard-to-find Broadway albums, movie sound tracks, big band music, jazz, country, and rock 'n' roll. Tel: 533-1572. For rare rock, drop in at **Midnight Records** (263 West 23rd Street, between Seventh and Eighth avenues). Tel: 675-2768.

A word of caution: Examine all secondhand merchandise critically. While it is possible to find copies of fairly commonplace material in mint condition, many rarer items are much the worse for wear. If you want to hunt further, consult the Yellow Pages of the Manhattan telephone directory under the heading "Records-Phonograph-Retail." Phone before travelling out of your way. Used-record shops are forever going out of business, as anyone who wants to sell used discs quickly discovers.

DANCE

By Joanna Ney

Joanna Ney is a freelance writer specializing in dance. She was formerly dance critic for East Side Express *and* Other Stages *and has contributed to* The New York Times, Cosmopolitan, Cue, *and* V. *Currently she reviews dance for WBAI radio.*

In the economically hard-pressed 1990s, New York's once-undisputed claim to be "dance capital of the world" is tenuous at best. Still, dance remains a viable force in New York, and you can see a performance of interest practically any time of the year. After all, despite these fiscally hard times for the arts, New Yorkers remain remarkably knowledgeable and passionate about dance, be it classical ballet or improvisational performance art.

PLACES TO SEE DANCE

Apart from the formal dance events you can see at the following venues, you can also experience New York's dance wave in many outdoor performances that take place all over the city in the summer. For basic information on all dance events, check the listings in *The New York Times,* the *Village Voice,* or *The New Yorker.*

Lincoln Center

At the heart of New York's dance scene is the Lincoln Center complex (between 62nd and 66th streets and Columbus and Amsterdam avenues), which includes the New York State Theater, the official home of New York City Ballet, and the Metropolitan Opera House, which plays host to American Ballet Theatre as well as to a variety of other major companies from around the world.

The neighborhood around Lincoln Center is packed with restaurants, cafés, boutiques, and much frenetic activity. Strolling up Broadway from Columbus Circle to 79th Street, you can see famous dancers and ballet students making their daily rounds. Ballet dancers are easy to spot, walking briskly in ballet's proverbial first position, carrying the indispensable dance bags that contain the tools of their trade. Their favorite hangout is the plaza fountain at Lincoln Center, which takes on a movie-set glitter when illuminated at night.

New York City Ballet (NYCB), the creation of Lincoln Kirstein and George Balanchine, is now in the hands of Peter Martins, who has adopted Balanchine's favored title, "ballet master in chief." Balanchine preferred that term to the more currently in-vogue "artistic director," saying that if it was good enough for Marius Petipa, it was good enough for him.

Since Balanchine's death the company has had its ups and downs, but even with the dearth of important new choreographers, the dancing at NYCB continues to be outstanding, particularly at the principal level, with the exuberant Darci Kistler and the dazzling Kyra Nichols emerging as two of the company's treasures. The repertory includes ballets by Balanchine, Jerome Robbins, and Peter Martins, with Martins providing several new ballets each season. Martins's streamlined, two-act version of the Petipa classic *Sleeping Beauty,* with scenic designs by David Mitchell, debuted in 1991 and has become the critical and popular success of the company's spring season. This production combines the beauty and pageantry of the original Petipa choreography with the speed and energy for which this company is known. The Diamond Project, Martins's high-profile workshop designed to develop and nurture new choreographers, is also staged in the spring.

NYCB also has its own professional school, the **School of American Ballet** (SAB), which gives dance lovers an opportunity to witness dancers in the making when it presents its annual spring workshop on the stage of the Juilliard School. SAB is headquartered in Lincoln Center's new Rose building on Amsterdam Avenue and 65th Street.

NYCB performs from November through February and from late April through the end of June, with December reserved for the perennial favorite, *The Nutcracker.* Although the company has many faithful subscribers, some tickets are usually available the day of performance, unless it happens to be a company premiere or a dancer's debut in a particular role. Even when a performance is sold out, balletomanes know that if they wait outside the theater before curtain time someone is likely to sell them a ticket. For information, Tel: 870-5570; reservations, Tel: 307-4100.

Across the plaza, the imposing Metropolitan Opera House, with its gigantic Chagall murals and red and gold trappings, is the home of **American Ballet Theatre** (ABT), which, following the resignation of Mikhail Baryshnikov as the company's artistic director, was taken over by codirectors Jane Hermann and Oliver Smith. (Hermann has since resigned.) The board of directors has yet to appoint a new artistic director.

Under Baryshnikov's leadership ABT was said to have become "Balanchinized," losing its star power but gaining an overall sheen and precision in its ensemble dancing. Former director Hermann responded to the public's appetite for "personalities" by spotlighting individual guest artists of the ilk of Sylvie Guillem of the Royal Ballet, and brought back such former ABT stars as Fernando Bujones and Laurent Hilaire in guest appearances. In addition to guest artists, ABT boasts an accomplished array of principal dancers, notably Susan Jaffe and Julio Bocca. Fortunately, despite the problems with the artistic leadership, the level of dancing by soloists and principals remains high.

The company's repertory is eclectic, with ballets by a wide variety of choreographers, from Anthony Tudor to Agnes de Mille to Frederick Ashton. In the 1991–1992 season, ABT pioneered new stagings of *Don Quixote* and *Raymonda Act III,* as well as a new production of *Coppélia.* ABT also has its own full-length *Sleeping Beauty,* staged by Kenneth MacMillan.

When ABT is touring, the Met has no shortage of other illustrious guests. Internationally renowned ballet companies that appear include the Paris Opéra Ballet, Denmark's Royal Ballet, Germany's Stuttgart, and the Bolshoi and Kirov. The Kirov, in addition to maintaining its great classical repertory, has added the formerly "forbidden" Balanchine works to its programs. The company is also graced by some great talents, among them the exotic Altnai Asylmuratova, who has impressed Western critics with her grace and musicality. For ABT information, Tel: 477-3030; for the box office, Tel: 362-6000.

City Center
The Moorish-style City Center (131 West 55th Street, between Sixth and Seventh avenues) is another major showcase for both ballet and modern dance. At various times of the year you can catch the spirited **Joffrey Ballet**, still under the artistic leadership of Gerald Arpino, who returned to the company after resigning in a bitter battle with the board of directors; the **Alvin Ailey Company**, with its unique blend of modern, jazz, and blues arising out of the black experience; the **Dance Theater of Harlem** (led by NYCB alumnus Arthur Mitchell), known for its special ability to combine Neoclassicism with a strong dramatic flair, but which of late is faced with economic hardships due to lack of funding (after a temporary disbandment, DTH performed a successful season at the Brooklyn Academy of Music); and the twin masters of modern dance, **Paul Taylor** and **Merce Cunningham**, without whom no New York dance season would be complete. City Center is one of the most popular and reasonably priced theaters in the city and is, deservedly, a favorite with dancegoers. For City Center information, Tel: 581-7907.

Joyce Theater
A unique addition to the dance scene is the 11-year-old Joyce Theater (Eighth Avenue and 18th Street), housed in an old movie house in the heart of the Chelsea neighborhood. The redesigned and refurbished theater is unique in that it was designed by dancers exclusively for year-round use by small- and medium-sized companies. If the Joyce can be said to have a resident company, it is the **Eliot Feld Ballet**. In fact, Feld was one of the facility's design consultants. As a place to see dance, the Joyce is ideal, and no other hall welcomes a greater diversity of established choreographers (such as Feld) and provocative originals (such as Molissa Fenley), in such an agreeably intimate and comfortable setting. One of the pluses of the Joyce experience is the number of wonderful

restaurants, both modest and chic, from nouvelle to ethnic, virtually on its doorstep. The Joyce season runs from
September to May; single performance tickets are often
available. For Joyce Theater information, Tel: 691-9740;
for tickets call Joyce Charge, Tel: 242-0800.

Small Dance Venues and Companies

Nearby is the **Dance Theater Workshop** (219 West 19th
Street, between Seventh and Eighth avenues), a haven for
experimental dance. Up a narrow flight of stairs is the
Bessie Schönberg Theater, a small, informal space with
bleacherlike seating. Devotees don't mind the slight discomfort: DTW is known as a leading pioneer of new
dance in the country. The theater is accompanied by an
attractive gallery that presents solo art and photo exhibits.
Like other small enterprises, DTW faces fiscal difficulties,
including a possible move due to rent increases. For
information, Tel: 691-6500.

The area between Park Avenue South and Broadway
(very roughly between 30th and 14th streets) is fast becoming the new center for dance schools and dance companies. Peridance, Erick Hawkins, the Feld Ballet, and the
administrative offices of American Ballet Theatre are all
located in this area.

Another space that showcases "downtown" or avant-
garde dance is **P.S. 122** (150 First Avenue, at 9th Street), a
former school building converted into a community arts
center. Seating is on folding chairs on rickety wooden
risers; the audience is young and fashionably artsy.

The 200-year-old **St. Mark's-Church-in-the-Bowery** (131
East 10th Street, at Second Avenue) offers new dance in
its renovated main sanctuary as part of its Danspace Project. This is one of the most beautiful and satisfying performing spaces for dancers and audiences alike. Tel: 674-
8112.

The **Kitchen** (512 West 19th Street, west of Tenth Avenue) is a no-frills utilitarian space and offers a wide
variety of dance, theater, and video pieces for the highly
adventurous.

The **Mark Morris Dance Group** (with headquarter offices at 225 Lafayette Street) is a contemporary dance
company headed by Morris, a young and hugely talented
choreographer from Seattle who was formerly the director of the Monnaie Theatre in Brussels. Morris's company
appears in New York in various venues and tours as part
of the White Oak Project, assembled by Mikhail Barysh-

nikov to showcase Morris's work. Whether setting his eclectic dances to the music of Handel, as in his striking *L'Allegro* and *Il Penseroso* (inspired by Milton), or to music by Bob Wills and His Texas Playboys, as in the jovial *Going Away Party,* Morris is creating his own distinctive brand of American theatrical dance. Tel: 219-3660.

Brooklyn Academy of Music

The Brooklyn Academy of Music (30 Lafayette Avenue, near the intersection of Flatbush and Atlantic avenues, Brooklyn), or BAM, as it is affectionately called, is on the agenda of every committed dancegoer. The main building has three theaters—the Opera House, the Carey Playhouse, and the smaller Lepercq Space. BAM's Majestic Theater is less than two blocks away, at 651 Fulton Street. The turn-of-the-century Opera House is a spacious, beautifully appointed theater on whose stage appear some of the most exciting innovators in dance, performance art, and contemporary music. BAM's Next Wave series is now an established annual event. This is where you'll see the theater pieces of Martha Clark and Mark Morris and hear the work of Philip Glass, Steve Reich, and other minimalists. Like many other arts organizations, BAM has suffered from the current bout of federal and state funding cuts but will undoubtedly persevere.

BAM can be reached via the IRT number 2 or 3 subway on the West Side or the 4 or 5 on the East Side, as well as the Q, B, R, and N on the BMT line. The BAM stop for the IRT trains is Atlantic Avenue; for the BMT, Pacific Street. The BAM Manhattan Express Bus (available for events taking place at the Opera House and the Majestic Theater) leaves Manhattan one hour prior to curtain time from the Summit Hotel, at 51st Street and Lexington Avenue. On return, it makes stops in the West Village, Midtown on the East Side, and the Upper West Side. For BAM information and reservations, Tel: (718) 636-4100.

BAM has a concession area in the lobby where you can stave off hunger pangs with a hot or cold sandwich or salad and a cup of coffee or a soft drink. There is also a full bar. For something more leisurely try **Gage & Tollner** (372 Fulton Street, a 15-minute walk from BAM, but a somewhat dangerous excursion after dark—take a cab). This old New York establishment has served some of the best steaks, chops, and seafood in town since 1879, and with the addition of 78-year-old chef Edna Lewis, also offers a prix-fixe menu with a southern flavor—gumbo,

Cajun shrimp, monkfish, and the like. The dark wood paneling and colored glass lighting fixtures provide an authentic traditional flavor; Tel: (718) 875-5181 (closed Sundays in summer). **Junior's**, an informal, family-style restaurant a few blocks west of BAM (386 Flatbush Avenue) is known for its roast beef and brisket of beef and is justly famous countrywide for its cheesecake; Tel: (718) 852-5257. The attractive **New Prospect Café** (393 Flatbush Avenue, at Eighth Avenue) specializes in holistic nouvelle cuisine and serves fresh produce and excellent desserts. Reservations necessary for parties of three or more; Tel: (718) 638-2148.

DANCE APPAREL AND EQUIPMENT

Capezio (177 MacDougal Street, off 8th Street) is definitely the one-stop place to get outfitted for a dance studio or gym. Its dance-shoe department on the second floor carries a full line of ballet, aerobic, character, and tap shoes. The adjoining Dance Body Shop stocks every conceivable item you will need for a dance, exercise, or aerobics class. Styles range from traditional to the latest in spandex and decorated dancewear. The shop also carries other clothing, accessories, and jewelry. There are other Capezio stores under separate ownership in Manhattan: one at Steps Dance Studio (2121 Broadway, at 74th Street), and a big main branch in Midtown (1650 Broadway, second floor, at 51st Street), with a more hectic pace than the others.

Freed of London (922 Seventh Avenue, at 58th Street) specializes in footwear of fine and durable leather. In addition to superior-quality soft ballet slippers and pointe shoes, the shop also carries leotards, tights, and accessories. There are no bargains here, but the service is efficient and courteous.

On Stage (197 Madison Avenue, between 34th and 35th streets) is a small dance-apparel store nestled between the tall buildings of Madison Avenue. This shop specializes in a full line of dancewear and carries all the major brands as well as the biggest selection of Lycra and cotton leotards and tights in the city. Everything a dancer needs for class—dance bags, leg warmers, headbands, socks, and sports bras—is available here. The store also carries ballet, jazz, and tap shoes. Other pluses: The personnel are knowledgeable about correct fit and know their merchandise; the dressing room is well lit and ample for try-ons; leotards are arranged on hangers by color, so you can see at a glance what is in stock. Price range is in the medium to high category, but if you happen to find something in your size in the "sale basket" you've got yourself a real bargain.

Paragon Sporting Goods (867 Broadway, at 18th Street) also has a section devoted to dancewear. Traditional styles are limited, and the emphasis is on the aerobic and jazzy types. You'll find the top sports lines—Avia and Nike—and a full line of Baryshnikov dancewear, including spandex tights and sweat pants. Another line, Marika, offers basically the same merchandise at lower prices.

Taffy's (1776 Broadway, second floor, at 57th Street) is probably the most congenial and best-run dance-apparel shop in town. Geared primarily to the professional dancer and serious dance student, Taffy's stocks leotards, unitards, and tights for men, women, and children in all major brands; cotton, acrylic, and wool leg warmers; vinyl sweat pants and shorts; dance dresses; shoes (pointe, jazz, ballroom, and character); and a good selection of dance videos, records, and tapes. If the item you want is not in stock, Taffy's is happy to order it. Watch for the annual storewide sale in February or March. Discounts are available for students upon presentation of a school identification card.

DANCE MEMORABILIA AND COLLECTIBLES

The **Ballet Shop** (1887 Broadway, at 63rd Street, just around the corner from Lincoln Center) is a one-of-a-kind establishment owned by Norman Crider, a former champion baton twirler and collector. For the past 20 years the shop has been on this site and managed by the knowledgeable Tobias Leibovitz and his assistant, Joe Marshall, a former ice skater. There is nothing these two don't know about *la danse*. Here you'll find rare prints and lithographs from the Romantic era on, as well as out-of-print books, signed photographs, statuary dating back to the pre-1840 period of ballet, class records for ballet, modern, jazz, and tap, a large video selection ranging from technique to documentary performances, as well as more mundane fare, such as tee-shirts and dance-related gift items. If you've been looking for an original signed Chagall sketch, a rare original Leon Bakst ballet design, or a 19th-century bronze statuette of Fanny Elssler, the Ballet Shop is likely to have it.

The **Performing Arts Shop**, underground at Lincoln

Center, has a more limited and popular selection of items related to dance, such as tee-shirts, ceramic mugs, and books, records, and cassettes. Opera and music items are highlighted.

THE THEATER

By David Berreby

David Berreby is a member of the Outer Critics Circle and the American Theater Critics Association. He reviews theater for the New York Law Journal *and his work has appeared in the* New York Times, *the* Village Voice, Ms., Reader's Digest *and other publications.*

One late-summer afternoon in Midtown Manhattan, a film crew was carefully choreographing an attractive couple, a mounted policeman, a Walkman-toting dancer in pink pants, a hot-dog cart with its distinctive umbrella, great clouds of smoke from a dry-ice device, and, in the center of it all, a gleaming red Ferrari. A happy crowd watched the crew shoot take after take in the glow of theater marquees and immense neon signs, ignoring the honk and roar of passing traffic. Meanwhile, across the street, a posse of young break dancers gyrated to the beat of a powerful portable radio while, a couple of blocks up, a rival group danced to a live drummer. A block up from *them,* a duo played show tunes on a bongo and a steel drum. The whole honking, drumming, banging, yelling chaos seemed to harmonize into a single purposeful scene, over which hovered the electronic headlines of the Times Tower (from which the ball drops at New Year's) and a perpetually wheeling flock of irritated pigeons.

This is Times Square, where Seventh Avenue and Broadway meet to form the Crossroads of the World, as it was known in the 1920s. In many ways, the square and the blocks of the West 40s immediately adjacent still form the heart of New York. And, not coincidentally, the neighborhood is also the heart of New York's **Theater District**.

You need only a few minutes here to see how New

York's essence is bound up with the theater. It's a fact of geography (the world's greatest concentration of theaters is here, just off Broadway in the center of the center of town). It's a fact of economics (drama is a major industry and tourist attraction). But more important, it's a fact of the spirit. Like the theater, New York City is high class yet not entirely respectable, artistic yet crass, insular yet eager for attention and approval from outsiders. Perhaps that's why when the city works, it acts like a well-choreographed show.

Of course, the Broadway Theater District has its lowdown, sleazy, and menacing blocks, where drugs and sex are sold (especially at its southern boundary, 42nd Street, and at Eighth Avenue). And it's also true that the cost of putting on a Broadway show nowadays is so immense that "Broadway" to many people stands for safe dull plays and homogenized international musicals imported from London. Lately, though, with the film industry in recession, more stars and more shows have graced Broadway, and it has regained some of its cachet. In any event, this part of town remains the repository of the city's theatrical tradition, where you can have cheesecake at Lindy's (on Broadway near 45th Street)—a strictly Disney version of the original haunt of show biz, bootleggers, and wise guys immortalized by Damon Runyon—get in a gawk at Sardi's (234 West 44th Street), where opening-night parties are still held, and contemplate the Brill Building farther up on Broadway, where Kern and Gershwin once toiled.

GETTING TICKETS

If you've arrived in New York without a show in mind, you can find listings for all major productions in *The New Yorker* or in *New York* magazine, both sold at newsstands. Shows are listed as "Broadway," "Off Broadway," and "Off Off Broadway"; knowing these categories can give you a good idea of what to expect.

"**Broadway**" is not really a geographic term—most Broadway theaters aren't on Broadway. Broadway is a type of contract, covering a big house, providing big salaries, and generally portending high ticket prices and a certain sumptuousness of staging that visitors expect from one of the city's premier tourist attractions. "**Off Broadway**" contracts cover the kind of smaller productions that sprang up 25 years ago in reaction to Broadway's expense and conventionality. These days, though,

Off Broadway itself is part of the mainstream. (Many Off Broadway shows are offered at discount ticket booths.) Still, it's free of the immense financial pressures of Broadway, and it's less expensive (with a top ticket price of about $40). Off Broadway in turn engendered "**Off Off Broadway**"—smaller, more experimental, more daring (in theory), and cheaper still. Many small Off Off Broadway shows are actually "showcases," in which the actors aren't paid at all but play because it's a chance to do something professional and (you never know) the show might get discovered. Such plays may run only on weekends in a church basement and charge you a mere $10, but they can be excellent theater and they give you a chance to get off the beaten path.

Times Square, not surprisingly, is a good place to start hunting for a show to see, even if you've decided to skip the astonishingly high costs of Broadway, where the highest ticket price is now $100. Many non-Broadway theaters are in the neighborhood, and it's easy to reach others from this central location. Directly adjacent to the Broadway area, for instance, is one of the city's happier urban renewal efforts, **Theater Row**. It's a long block of Off Broadway theaters and restaurants stretching from Ninth Avenue to Tenth Avenue on 42nd Street. Here you can usually find something worth seeing—and a good meal at any number of new restaurants that cater to the theater crowds. (It's also the site of the Manhattan Plaza Garage, which offers among the lowest parking rates in the area. Manhattan Plaza itself consists of two apartment towers that provide subsidized housing to people in performing-arts unions.)

If you want to be sure of seeing one specific show on one exact date, you can always reserve with a ticket agent: **Golden and LeBlang** (1501 Broadway, Tel: 944-8910), for example; or **Hickey's** (251 West 45th Street, Tel: 586-2980). If you're staying in the area, your hotel can put you in touch with a ticket agency, too. The agencies' nominal fees are set by law. You can also line up at the theater to buy last-minute cancellations (be early, though, because the cancellation line for a hit show will start to grow at least two hours before curtain time).

Discount Tickets

The best way to cut your ticket expenses is to go to one of the booths where the Theatre Development Fund sells seats for Broadway and Off Broadway shows. For 18 years these tickets were invariably half price, plus a two-dollar service charge. This past winter, however, TDF bowed to the wishes of producers and began offering tickets for the more popular shows at a 25 percent discount. Whether the discount is a half or a quarter off, the catch is you have to take what's available the same day you buy your ticket. There are three such booths in the city, each marked with a big **TKTS** sign (it's pronounced "tickets," as in "I'll meet you on the tickets line"). The largest is right in Times Square, at Broadway and 47th Street. It opens at 3:00 P.M. and doesn't close until just before curtain time, 8:00 P.M. (It's within sprinting distance of a number of theaters, and hence is still selling at three minutes to the hour.) On Wednesdays and Saturdays, when there are matinee performances at 2:00 P.M., the booths open at 10:00 A.M., close at curtain time, and reopen an hour later for the evening shows. On Sundays they open at noon. Any show that isn't a sold-out hit will turn up on the TKTS listing of available shows. Naturally, you'll have a better chance (and a much shorter wait) if you go on a Tuesday or Wednesday rather than a Friday or Saturday, and the earlier you turn up, the better. (On Mondays, most theaters are "dark"—closed— so if you go then you'll have little to select from.) Count on waiting in line 30 minutes or so if you come midweek before people escape from their offices; it'll take longer if you arrive at, say, 6:30 P.M., or if you come on a weekend.

Unless the weather is bad, the Times Square TKTS line is not an unpleasant place to wait—you've got a perfect perch for watching Times Square go by. You'll likely be approached by hawkers trying to interest you in less-than-sellout shows. Often, they'll offer you a "two-fer"—a ticket-like slip that allows you to purchase two tickets for the price of one. You can then leave the TKTS line and go directly to the theater box office. (Two-fers are also widely available in stores, hotels, and at offices of the New York Convention and Visitors Bureau on Columbus Circle.) Naturally, the more popular a show, the less likely it is that you'll find two-fers for it.

If you hate to wait, the lines are generally shorter at the other TKTS booths: One is in the financial district at 2 World Trade Center (the south tower). This TKTS counter is the only one where it's possible to buy full-price tickets as well as discounted ones. You can also buy matinee tickets here the day before a performance. The third booth is in Brooklyn Heights at the foot of Montague Street in front of the state court building. It opens at 11:00

A.M. **Ticketmaster**, the nation-wide computerized ticket service, now offers discount seats to select shows from a booth in a store at 38 Park Row, across the street from City Hall Park. But beware: Ticketmaster's surcharges—$5 per ticket plus a $2.50 handling fee—can quickly add up. Tel: 307-4100. If you're planning your trip well in advance, you have time for another strategy: joining the **Hit Show Club**, an organization that offers its members discount tickets to most of the top Broadway shows, and distributes discount vouchers around the city. To join, send a stamped, self-addressed envelope to Hit Show Club, 630 Ninth Avenue, New York, NY 10036; Tel: 581-4211.

If the show you're dying to see is sold out until next Christmas, you might consider forgoing a seat. Most Broadway houses sell standing room for a fraction of the usual ticket price; inquire at the box office.

THEATER COMPANIES
Throughout the city, a number of Off and Off Off Broadway productions are sponsored by long-standing theatrical institutions with records of offering high-quality, interesting work. Perhaps the foremost of these is the **New York Shakespeare Festival**, founded and run for more than three decades by the late Joseph Papp. In the 1960s Papp successfully overcame objections and won permission to stage free plays every summer in Central Park. Summer visitors can still enjoy free Shakespeare at the **Delacorte Theater** in the park—but be warned: If the show's a hit, you should arrive in the late morning and spend the afternoon picnicking under the trees on the ticket line, which wraps around the Great Lawn (near 81st Street), until the 6:00 P.M. ticket distribution. Tel: 861-7277 for information.

These days most of the lively, often controversial productions offered by Papp's heirs are to be seen indoors, at the **Joseph Papp Public Theater** (425 Lafayette Street, near 8th Street and Astor Place). The huge building is a converted library that houses legitimate theaters, a movie house, a café, and a bookstore. Many new works, classics, and a complete Shakespeare cycle are in the works. For information, Tel: 598-7100. Appropriately enough for a combative, controversial theater, nearby Astor Place is where, in 1849, a different theatrical *contretemps*—the fight between supporters of the American tragedian Edwin Forrest and fans of English actor William Macready—led to as many as 30 deaths in the infamous Astor Place Riot. (New York theatergoers have always been passionately opinionated.)

Not far from Papp's empire is one of the most venerable avant-garde theater groups in the world, the **La MaMa Experimental Theater Company** (74A East 4th Street, between Third and Second avenues). Founder Ellen Stewart's ideal is to create a genuine world theatrical community, and so La MaMa's offerings have ranged from Andrei Serban's stunning reinterpretation of the Trojan War to Eskimo drama performed by Eskimos (Stewart would have had pygmy dancers come, too, but the government of Zaire refused). Governmental budget cuts and the recession have rendered the company's future precarious, but so far Stewart has managed to hold out. For information, Tel: 475-7710.

Another bastion of innovation is the **Brooklyn Academy of Music** (30 Lafayette Avenue, near the intersection of Atlantic and Flatbush avenues, Brooklyn), where Ingmar Bergman, Peter Brook, Robert Wilson, Peter Sellars, and Laurie Anderson, among others, have presented their work. BAM, as it's known, has been many an experimentalist's ticket into the mainstream. It's the place to go to see work the year before everyone else learns about it. (See the Classical Music or Dance chapter for directions, or call BAM; Tel: 718-636-4100.)

Several other companies are worth seeking out. The **Circle Repertory Theater** (99 Seventh Avenue South, on Sheridan Square in Greenwich Village) was long the home company of Lanford Wilson and has presented many fine new American plays; Tel: 505-6010. The **Roundabout Theatre Company** (1530 Broadway, between 44th and 45th streets) sticks staidly to classics and revivals, and does them well; Tel: 719-9393. The **Jean Cocteau Repertory** (330 Bowery) likes to stage neglected works in its tiny theater on the city's traditional skid row; Tel: 677-0060. Performance art meets theater at the **Performing Garage** (33 Wooster Street, between Broome and Grand streets in SoHo); Tel: 966-9796. **Mabou Mines** is an experimental troupe with a commitment to language as well as image. Headquartered at P.S. 122, a former public school (150 First Avenue, at 9th Street), they perform elsewhere, and their work is worth hunting down in the listings; Tel: 473-0559. And finally, when you get fed up with the wonder of it all, go see **Forbidden Broadway**, a hilarious, constantly updated spoof of the theater scene and of the latest hits. After five years in a cabaret, it's now lodged at the Theater East (211 East 60th Street, between Third and Second avenues); Tel: 838-0177.

THEATRICAL HANGOUTS

If you haven't gotten enough of the cast at the show, you can try to rub elbows afterward. Waiting at the stage door for an autograph is a venerable Broadway tradition, and well worth it if you have the patience. Not only could you meet your favorite performer, but you'll encounter a curious cast of regulars—autograph hunters and photographers—who live in a subculture all their own.

There are also a number of Theater District restaurants where you'll likely find actors unwinding after shows. If you want to go in comfort, **Orso** (322 West 46th Street, near Eighth Avenue) is a pleasant Italian restaurant where you might find the stars of major shows and visiting celebrities. Immortal **Sardi's** (234 West 44th Street, between Broadway and Eighth Avenue) still gets its share of the prominent and would-be prominent. And **Café Madeleine** (43rd Street and Ninth Avenue) gets after-show clientele from both Broadway and Theater Row.

On the other hand, if you'd like to see how most actors really live, try **Barrymore's** (267 West 45th Street, between Seventh and Eighth avenues), a large, dark bar where you'll see a lot of people wearing the nylon jackets emblazoned with logos that Broadway shows issue to their casts and crews. The food won't send you to gastronomic nirvana, but you won't get ptomaine either, and you'll be seeing life as actors live it—or at least actors who are working in the theater. To experience the life of most New York actors, you'd have to go to an unemployment line or become a waiter.

Finally, if you're not satisfied to see the show, wear the sweatshirt, buy the album, get the autograph, and eat next to one of the cast, you can always follow the actors home. The M 104 bus goes up Eighth Avenue and Broadway to the Upper West Side, haunt of many actors. The Seventh Avenue (numbers 1, 2, 3, and 9) and Eighth Avenue (A, B, C, and D) subways are the closest to Theater Row and Broadway. Between 11:30 P.M. and 1:00 A.M. these public conveyances bear many actors (looking incongruous without their makeup, costumes, and stage auras) back to their homes. Try not to stare.

THEATER BOOKS AND MEMORABILIA

Many a city has theaters, but New York has a theater culture. With a little effort, you can find a 1964 Broadway poster, a book on Kabuki, or the script of the new play you saw last night.

Scripts and Books

The city's major bookstores have well-stocked drama sections, but the best place to start hunting (especially for a new play) is in one of the bookstores that cater to the trade. They make an effort to have available everything currently showing as well as thousands of other plays, memoirs, works of scholarship, and such books as *Foreign Dialects* and *How to Market Your Play.*

Many new scripts are quickly published in inexpensive, pamphlet-like editions by one of two major publishers: Samuel French and Dramatists Play Service. **Samuel French** maintains a bookstore of its own (45 West 25th Street, between Sixth Avenue and Broadway), where you can purchase its own editions and other theater books; Tel: 206-8990. **Applause Theatre and Cinema Books** (211 West 71st Street, west of Broadway) bills itself as "the unavoidable source" and offers everything from the essays of Eric Bentley to recently published Australian plays, as well as a wide selection of other publishers' titles; Tel: 595-4735.

For rare theater books and old prints of theater productions, an excellent source is **Richard Stoddard Performing Arts Books** (18 East 16th Street, room 305, between Fifth Avenue and Union Square); Tel: 645-9576. In the theater district itself there are two comprehensive bookstores: the **Drama Bookshop** (723 Seventh Avenue, near 48th Street; Tel: 944-0595), and **Theatrebook** (1600 Broadway, room 1009, near 48th Street; Tel: 757-2834). A good place to hunt for show scores and sheet music is **Colony Records Center** (1619 Broadway, at 49th Street; Tel: 265-2050).

Souvenirs and Memorabilia

New York's theater culture offers a wide selection of souvenirs and memorabilia, ranging from the plastic *Phantom of the Opera* masks sold everywhere around Times Square to framed, original drawings by Hirschfeld, *The New York Times*'s indestructible caricaturist of 50 years.

The most "touristy" of places to hunt souvenirs (but worth a look, nonetheless) is **One Shubert Alley**, a memorabilia-crammed shop tucked between the Booth and Shubert theaters in Shubert Alley. (The "alley" extends between 44th and 45th streets in the block between Broadway and Eighth Avenue.) This is the place for tee-shirts, mugs, postcards, the latest posters, and the like; Tel: 944-4133. Slightly to the west on 44th Street is the **Actors' Heritage** (number 262), which carries photographs, movie stills, programs, posters, scripts, and some records and scores; Tel: 944-7490. **Actors Too** (210 West 45th Street, between Broadway and Eighth Avenue) sells similar merchandise; Tel: 382-0577.

The biggest seasonal break for souvenir hunters, though, is in early October, when Lincoln Center's **Performing Arts Library** (a branch of the city's public library system, with clippings, scripts, scores, recordings, and a vast collection of other material pertaining to the performing arts) has its annual sale. Every conceivable kind of memento relating to theater, dance, opera, and music is offered at prices that begin at 25 cents. The sale items are not merely the library's castoffs: Theater people often donate things (the proceeds help the library). The library's sale is one of the best sources in the city for one-of-a-kind theatrical souvenirs. For information, Tel: 870-1670.

Finally, for the serious collector (spending serious money) there are a number of galleries that offer posters and original drawings. Two that have a strong emphasis on theater are the **Triton Gallery** (323 West 45th Street, between Eighth and Ninth avenues; Tel: 765-2472), featuring Broadway and foreign posters; and **Margo Feiden Galleries** (699 Madison Avenue, between 62nd and 63rd streets; Tel: 677-5330), which has, among other things, those Hirschfeld drawings.

LITERARY NEW YORK

By Ingrid Nelson

Ingrid Nelson is a freelance writer living on Manhattan's Upper West Side.

Few writers have character strong enough to write in New York. For all the hoo-haw that surrounds it, writing is the least glamorous of professions: It is slow, laborious, and ultimately solitary work. To attempt it in a city as distracting as New York can be disastrous, and while there have been times when writing has flourished here, the names of the talented writers who have died from overindulging in Manhattan's fleshpots could also serve as a reading list for a survey course in American literature. Writers with sense head for tamer spots, like Chicago, when there's work to be done.

Nonetheless, New York is essential to American writers for two reasons: It provides inspiration and it promises fame. Nowhere else is such a variety of human beings and human pursuits packed into such a small area; the inspirational potential of this pure human concentrate is boundless. And once words have been set down on paper the city becomes the writer's marketplace.

New York is the seat of publishing, the home base of most important magazines and journals, the headquarters of the country's largest wire service (the Associated Press), the stage upon which playwrights make their reputations, and the country's chief forum for the dissection, analysis, and judgment of literature. The novelist Thomas Wolfe, whose relationship with New York was as ambivalent as any writer's has ever been, described the city he adopted in *From Death to Morning:* "The great vision of the city is burning in your heart in all its enchanted colors just as it did when you were twelve years old and thought about it. You think that some glorious happiness of fortune, fame, and triumph will be yours at any minute, that you are about to take your place among great men and lovely women in a life more fortunate and happy than any you have ever known—that it is all here, somehow, waiting for you."

THE EARLY DAYS OF PUBLISHING

In the beginning—that is, before 1850—there wasn't much that was literary about New York. Publishers lived in Boston. Writers were from elsewhere. One exception was Washington Irving, who had been born in lower Manhattan in 1783. This was merely an accident of birth; after he gained his early and considerable fame from humorous essays about New York society, Irving moved to Europe, which he far preferred, and stayed there for much of his adult life. When it came time to retire he installed himself and his extended family in an eccentric mansion called Sunnyside, in Tarrytown, about 25 miles north of Manhattan. (Sunnyside is now a house museum, open to visitors; see the Day Trips chapter.)

Around 1850, however, publishers began to migrate south from Boston, drawn by New York's growing population (and thus, pool of book purchasers). With them came editors, illustrators, and the usual literary hangers-on. The city was ripe for this cultural migration. Having made money in trade, wealthy New Yorkers were ready to invest it in less tangible assets: They were endowing museums, amassing art collections, and reading for pleasure.

MELVILLE AND POE

At the time, New York was also the occasional home of two genuinely great writers: Herman Melville and Edgar Allan Poe. Neither prospered from his writing, nor did either find the city to be a sympathetic place. There was something about New York, even in these early days, that didn't like writers.

Herman Melville was born in lower Manhattan, in 1819. When he was 12 his father died. A few years later, Melville ran off to sea and lived the adventures he described in two early books, *Typee* and *Omoo*. Both were wildly successful, and Melville purchased a farm near Pittsfield, Massachusetts, and settled in to write his masterpiece, *Moby-Dick*. It was a complete flop, denounced by the critics and ignored by the public. Destitute and discouraged, Melville returned to New York. He moved his family into a brick house at 104 East 26th Street and took a job as a customs officer at a dock on the Hudson River. The pay was about four dollars a day. He died 28 years later, in 1891, having written a series of brilliant but unrecognized novels and stories. Melville is buried at Woodlawn Cemetery in the Bronx, under a headstone engraved with a blank scroll. During his career he earned less than $8,000 from his writing; in his obituary *The New York Times* called him Henry.

Edgar Allan Poe was born a Bostonian, but in 1844 he moved to Greenwich Village with his child bride, Virginia, and took a job at the *Evening Mirror* newspaper. Although a collection of his tales was published in this period, and he wrote several well-known poems, including "Annabelle Lee," the Poe family was impoverished, and Poe himself was regarded more as a hack critic than as a real artist. Virginia suffered from consumption, and by 1846 she was so ill that Poe rented a house (now the **Edgar Allan Poe Cottage**, at Kingsbridge Road and the Grand Concourse; open to visitors) in Fordham, in the Bronx, where the air was then clean. The rent was $100 a month. This put such a strain on his precarious finances that Virginia's mother (who lived with them) had to beg the neighbors for food. Virginia died in 1847. Two years later Poe himself died during a trip to Baltimore; he was found in an alcoholic stupor outside a voting booth where presumably he had been earning a few dollars as a repeating voter.

EDITH WHARTON AND THE EUROPEAN CONNECTION

Fortunately for literature, New York City's next great writer chose to live abroad. Edith Wharton was born here in 1862 and grew up in a brownstone at 28 West 25th Street. She married Teddy Wharton in a church across the street, and the affluent young couple embarked on a comfortable but ultimately stultifying life together. In her mid-40s Edith fled to Europe and eventually settled in Paris. Her novels, however, are wicked dissections of the city she left, set in and around her old neighborhood. In *The Age of Innocence,* the Archer family lived in a brownstone on West 28th Street, where similar buildings still stand. Of them Wharton wrote in *A Backward Glance:* "the narrow houses so lacking in external dignity, so crammed with smug and suffocating upholstery... the little low-studded rectangular New York cursed with its universal chocolate-colored coating of the most hideous stone ever quarried."

Whatever it was about early New York that drove these writers to Europe or to their deaths—perhaps the city's crass materialism or its stuffy provincialism—was about to change. The first wave of European immigrants arrived in Manhattan in 1850 or so. The contribution they have made to this city, and this country, is incalculable—they brought vitality to New York, and they formed a bond between America and Europe, a kind of vibrating chord linking the Old World to the New. They also created a whole new social climate, one in which teeming slums existed cheek by jowl with uptown brownstones. In succeeding decades the city became a different place altogether, and as such it was the geographical center for a remarkable group of writers, men and women of enormous energy, sophistication, optimism, and humanity, all imbued with a strong social conscience.

WALT WHITMAN AND THE SOCIAL CONSCIENCE

An early member of this group (actually, a precursor) was Walt Whitman of Long Island. Whitman was an editor of the *Brooklyn Daily Eagle,* among other newspapers, for many years. In his free time he roamed through lower Manhattan and composed some of the poems that would eventually make him one of the best known of all American poets; poems about the Brooklyn Bridge and "Mannahatta," written with exuberance, sensuality, and a strong sense of individualism. Unfortunately, the New York curse on writers was still partially in evidence, for Whitman never achieved in his lifetime the fame that came to him after his death.

The writers of the next few decades did, however. O. Henry (William Sydney Porter), who lived on Gramercy Park, wrote a story a week for the *New York World* newspaper, and earned $100 for each—remarkable affluence for a New York writer. The legend goes that he wrote "The Gift of the Magi" in **Pete's Tavern**, still just around the corner from the park, on Irving Place at 18th Street.

THE LITERARY ENCLAVES

Something of a writer's colony grew up around Washington Square in Greenwich Village, the New World's closest equivalent to the Latin Quarter. Theodore Dreiser and Sinclair Lewis both struggled with naturalistic novels here early in their careers. Stephen Crane explored the nature of war and of heroism; Lincoln Steffens, the New York journalist for whom the word "muckraker" was coined, lived in the Village too. Proclaiming that "the city is human nature posing nude," he travelled throughout the country recruiting like-minded writers to join him in New York. One who did was John Reed (author of *Ten*

Days That Shook the World). Reed lived at 42 Washington Square (now the address of New York University's law school), and wrote a poem about his apartment:

> In the winter the water is frigid,
> In the summer the water is hot;
> And we're forming a club for controlling the tub
> For there's only one bath to the lot.
> You shave in unlathering Croton,
> If there's water at all, which is rare—
> But the life isn't bad for a talented lad
> At Forty-Two Washington Square.

Reed belonged to a small theater group called the Provincetown Players. It may have been the most talented amateur theatrical group in history—other members were Edna St. Vincent Millay, Sherwood Anderson, e. e. cummings, and Eugene O'Neill.

Another group of writers, critics, and wits congregated uptown, at a round table in the Rose Room of the **Algonquin Hotel** on West 44th Street. Robert Benchley, Alexander Woollcott, George S. Kaufman, and the riveting Dorothy Parker formed the inner circle. One afternoon, Mrs. Parker was asked to use the word "horticulture" in a sentence. "You can lead a whore to culture," she instantly replied, "but you can't make her think."

And, farther uptown, the **Harlem Renaissance** was just getting underway. It was, as the name suggests, a new birth of black writing; it owed much to W. E. B. DuBois, a Harlem-bred scholar and writer who wrote, as early as 1903, that "The problem of the twentieth century is the problem of the color line." DuBois was also an organizer of the NAACP. Countee Cullen was part of the renaissance; the poet Langston Hughes was an usher at Cullen's wedding in a Harlem church and a disciple of his work.

THE 20TH-CENTURY LITERARY SCENE

All these literary stirrings and rumblings in New York attracted more writers, some of whom came here to write about someplace else. Sherwood Anderson was physically present in New York City while his imagination populated small towns in the American Midwest and evoked them in several novels. The novelist Willa Cather lived at 5 Bank Street and later on Park Avenue and wrote about Nebraska; at the Society Library on East 79th Street she once ran into Truman Capote, another writer from elsewhere (Alabama) who had come to make his reputation in New York. Capote wrote that Cather's appearance "rather mesmerized me—her eyes especially: blue, the pale brilliant cloudless blue of prairie skies." At their first meeting, and before they exchanged names, she asked Capote what writers he liked. He named several, then added, "I really like Willa Cather. Have you read *My Mortal Enemy?*"

"With no particular expression," Capote recalled, "she said, 'Actually, I wrote it.' "

The subjects and styles of these uptown, downtown, and out-of-town writers differed; they were not always familiar with one another's work, or even aware that one another existed. Nevertheless, they existed together in this city, and together they created a literary community, the first New York had known. They were drawn here by New York's growing sophistication and variety; they in turn gave to the city the two essentials of lyricism and passion.

New York's literary community would prove to be lasting, although its hospitality to writers turned out to be a fleeting thing. After World War II rents began to rise, and many of the writers who had been dispersed by the war moved to cheaper places. But the template of a literary community remained, and it wasn't long before a new group of New York writers emerged.

The term *beatnik* seems curiously outdated; its literary equivalent, Beat, is hardly ever heard now. And Allen Ginsberg and his fringy, offbeat contemporaries—Gregory Corso, Jack Kerouac, and William Burroughs—are practically grand old men of mainstream American letters today. When they started out, however, they shuttled between the Upper West Side (where Ginsberg was a student at Columbia University) and the Lower East Side (where they took their various pleasures) like ragged urchins. Nobody believed that the free-form, experimental writing they were touting as poetry would last. It did, of course. However, the Beat poets did not stay for too long in New York; the whole movement shifted to the West Coast and San Francisco.

In postwar Harlem, James Baldwin, the son of a preacher and a preacher himself for a brief period, brought the original Harlem Renaissance into a more militant phase with his uncompromising and beautifully written book *Go Tell It on the Mountain.* But Baldwin too left New York, and settled in France.

The handful of writers who did try to work in New York had, often as not, sadly truncated lives. Notable among them are the poet Delmore Schwartz, who died an alcoholic in 1966, and Dylan Thomas, who perished in 1953 in St. Vincent's Hospital in the Village after a monumental drinking binge. Clearly there was still something about New York that drove certain writers to Europe or to their deaths.

It's worth mentioning that the exact opposite was true of New York's intellectual community. The city is and has long been a haven for thinkers of all persuasions. Edmund Wilson and Lionel Trilling are two American critics who found employment and success in New York. Philosopher Hannah Arendt and art critic Meyer Schapiro were both refugees from Europe; Arendt taught at the New School for Social Research in the Village, and Schapiro at Columbia University; both became essential parts of the New York intellectual landscape.

THE PUBLISHING BUSINESS

Of course, where there are writers there are also editors, and New York's publishing industry thrived from the early 20th century. Practically every important American publisher was based in Midtown Manhattan, close to former speakeasies turned literary watering holes. (The "21" Club, on West 52nd Street, is one, but it has since degenerated into an expensive see-and-be-seen hangout.)

Publishing for the most part is a fairly dull business conducted by penny-pinching businessmen, but occasionally an editor will come along who is as much an artist as the writers he works with. Great editors, it has been said, are artists whose medium is the work of other artists. One was Maxwell Perkins, who, during much of this period, worked for Scribners. Perkins's other artists included Ernest Hemingway, F. Scott Fitzgerald, and Thomas Wolfe.

What of the current literary situation in the city? Where are the presses hottest, the writers most talented, the poetry most modern? For one thing, publishing houses have moved downtown in recent years, to the lofts and low office buildings around Union Square.

Lunching is a large part of the business. If you were to wander into the **Union Square Café** at one o'clock or so and see a pair of diners, one casually but carefully dressed, the other looking slightly disheveled, you are probably witnessing an expense-account meal between editor and author. If that evening you wish to go to a real literary watering hole, you should know that there aren't any left in New York. There are those with historic interest—the **White Horse Tavern**, at 567 Hudson Street, in the West Village, where Dylan Thomas hung out; the **Lion's Head**, at 59 Christopher Street, which has long been a meeting place for journalists from the *Village Voice;* and **Chumley's**, a former speakeasy at 86 Bedford Street, also in the Village. But young writers in New York today tend to frequent the posh restaurant and club scene—those establishments that are photographed for the latest issues of *New York* magazine and *Vanity Fair.*

Instead, one of the best ways to get a good feel for literary New York is to visit bookstores. Few cities have so many that are so good. If you frequent the idiosyncratically stocked shops scattered throughout Manhattan, you will discover the part of New York where ideas are wealth and talent is currency. And this may very well be the real soul of the city. Below is a highly selective list of some of New York's best bookshops.

BOOKSTORES

Downtown

The **Academy Book Store** (10 West 18th Street) is a used-books store. It is not nearly as large as the Strand (see below), and, as a consequence, the books out on the shelves (about 100,000 at any one time, with 200,000 in reserve) are carefully chosen and rotated regularly. The tone here is generally quite serious; humanistic subjects such as philosophy and history are stressed. The Academy also has a superb collection of used records, including some classic recordings that are unavailable elsewhere. Tel: 242-4848.

Barnes & Noble (105 Fifth Avenue, at 18th Street; 128 Fifth Avenue, across the street; and 2926 Broadway, at 115th Street, at Columbia University) has about a dozen branches around town, but these three are among the best stocked. (See also the Barnes & Noble "superstores" in the "Uptown: East Side" and "Uptown: West Side" listings, below.) The main store, at 105 Fifth Avenue, has a really remarkable collection of books: shelf upon shelf of the newest fiction and nonfiction in both paperback and hardcover; a large room full of the latest in medical books; and a rear annex of university texts. The sales annex across the street has terrific prices on current books and an uneven, but immense, selection of over-stocks and out-of-prints that are even cheaper. The 115th Street branch serves as the Columbia University book-store, but nonstudents are welcome, and the paperback fiction collection is wonderful. Tel: 807-0099 at 105 Fifth Avenue; 633-3500 at 128 Fifth Avenue; 854-4131 at Columbia University.

The **Biography Bookshop** (400 Bleecker Street, near 11th Street) specializes in people—books about people, that is. Biographies, autobiographies, diaries, letters, and anything else pertaining to lives both famous and obscure can be found here. Tel: 807-8655.

Bob Fein Books (150 Fifth Avenue, room 623, near 20th Street) has a wonderful collection of books, new and old, about the Indians of North and South America. Mr. Fein also sells photographs, prints, and lithographs with Indian themes and has a revolving collection of small sculptures for sale. Tel: 807-0489.

Books of Wonder (132 Seventh Avenue, at 18th Street) is a children's bookstore with a collection so good that adults will almost certainly find something to read, too. There is a small case of first editions and fine bindings and a nice selection of posters and cards. Tel: 989-3270.

East West Books (78 Fifth Avenue, at 14th Street; 67 Cooper Square, at the intersection of Third and Fourth avenues in the Village; and 568 Columbus Avenue, at 87th Street) deals in philosophy, spiritualism, and self-help. The emphasis here is on Eastern writers and thinking and New Age material; the atmosphere in these small stores is appropriately serene and contemplative. Tel: 243-5994 at Fifth Avenue; 475-4459 at Cooper Square; 787-7552 at Columbus Avenue.

Esoterica (61 Fourth Avenue, near 9th Street) deals in tomes and accessories that are religious, occult, and generally esoteric. They claim to have the largest selection of Tarot cards this side of Ursa Minor; the shop is scented throughout with the evocative incense of the Far East. Tel: 529-9808.

Forbidden Planet (821 Broadway, at 12th Street) doesn't look like a bookstore. In fact, it looks a bit like the alien bar in the first Star Wars film. The resemblance must be intentional, for the specialty here is science fiction and fantasy (with a sideline in comics). Tel: 473-1576.

Granary Books (568 Broadway, suite 403, at the corner of Prince Street) has no real counterpart in the city. It is part art-book shop, part art-book publisher (whose offerings are, of course, available here), and part dealer in painted books and one-of-a-kind art books. As you might expect, prices are steep. Tel: 226-5462.

Jaap Rietman (134 Spring Street, second floor, between Wooster and Greene streets) is one of the city's oldest sellers of art books, located now in new quarters conveniently placed next door to Jeffrey Ruesch, a dealer in contemporary prints and posters. Tel: 966-7044.

Judith's Room (681 Washington Street, between West 10th and Charles streets) sells books by or about women, along with magazines and newspapers that address women's concerns. Tel: 727-7330.

Macondo Books, Inc. (221 West 14th Street, between Seventh and Eighth avenues), has one of the city's largest collections of Spanish-language books—poetry and prose, classic and contemporary, fiction and nonfiction. Tel: 741-3108.

mosaicBooks (167 Avenue B, near East 10th Street) has a carefully chosen selection of contemporary fiction and poetry by Native American, Mexican, African, and South American writers. Some titles are in Spanish; art exhibits with a similarly multicultural theme are often mounted. Tel: 475-8623.

Oscar Wilde Memorial Bookshop (15 Christopher Street, at the corner of Gay Street) claims it is the oldest gay and lesbian bookstore in the world. At more than 25 years old, it may very well be. The collection here consists of books by or about gay people; all titles costing more than $10.95 are discounted. Tel: 255-8097.

Pageant Book and Print Shop (109 East 9th Street, between Fourth and Third avenues) offers a good selection of old prints and maps, and a remarkable variety of used books ranging in subject from Plutarch to the Beat poets. Tel: 674-5296.

A Photographer's Place (133 Mercer Street, south of Prince Street) is a trove for the photographically inclined. Its quarters are packed with cases of antique cameras, stacks of new (and old) technical journals, how-to books, postcards, and, of course, photo collections with publication dates spanning the past several decades. You'll be greeted upon entry with a stack of bumper stickers reading: "Honk if you love Stieglitz." Tel: 431-9358.

Revolution Books (13 East 16th Street, between Fifth Avenue and Union Square West) is the largest revolutionary bookstore in the country. Around a core of tomes on Marxist, Leninist, and Maoist theory is a collection of books describing the struggles of oppressed peoples all over the world. Many titles are in Spanish. Tel: 691-3345.

Russica Book and Art Shop (799 Broadway, near 11th Street) is not set up for browsers. However, its collection of books in the Russian language, books published in the former Soviet Union, and books about the former Soviet Union is unrivaled in the West. Tel: 473-7480.

St. Mark's Bookshop (12 St. Mark's Place, between Third and Second avenues) had a near brush with bankruptcy recently but is flourishing again. The collection of fiction and literary journals here is so good that New Yorkers from as far away as the Upper West Side trek down here to shop. Tel: 260-7853.

St. Mark's Comics (11 St. Mark's Place, between Third and Second avenues) sells comics, old and new, along with baseball cards, video tapes, and other accoutrements for the playfully inclined. Tel: 598-9439.

Samuel French, Inc. (45 West 25th Street, between Sixth Avenue and Broadway), deals in single-volume editions of plays and musicals (including scores). Just about any play or musical currently in production, or ever in production for that matter, is available here. Tel: 206-8990.

Science Fiction Shop (163 Bleecker Street, between Thompson and Sullivan streets on the second floor) is tiny and packed as neatly as a submarine with (mostly paperback) science fiction. Tel: 473-3010.

Skyline Books and Records, Inc. (13 West 18th Street, between Fifth and Sixth avenues) is a relatively new establishment with an excellent collection of used books and records, and some new ones, too. Tel: 759-5463.

Spring Street Books (169 Spring Street, at West Broadway) has several racks of magazines up front. In keeping with this neighborhood of galleries, the selection of art magazines is terrific. In the rear is a well-chosen collection of fiction and nonfiction. Tel: 219-3033.

The **Strand Book Store** (828 Broadway, at 12th Street) claims to have eight miles of books—used, overstocks, out-of-prints, reviewer copies, and some of the oddest paperbacks that have ever been printed. But how anyone could measure anything in this rabbit-warren of a place is a mystery. Whatever the mileage, this is New York's biggest used-books store, and thus the biggest in the country. By mysterious means, previously owned books from as far away as China find their way here. They are arranged by subject, the staff is adept at negotiating the maze of shelves to find what you may be looking for, and you can spend hours browsing through the splendid selection. There is also a section of fine bindings and rare books. Tel: 473-1452.

Three Lives & Co. (154 West 10th Street, between Sixth and Seventh avenues) is one of the superb general-interest bookstores in New York. Usually, such bookstores mirror the special interests of their owners; here, these happen to be fiction and art. Tel: 741-2069.

Village Comics (163 Bleecker Street, between Sullivan and Thompson streets), which sells comics old and new, is frequented by scholarly looking teenage boys, a sure indication of the quality of its inventory. Tel: 777-2770.

Midtown

Antiquarian Booksellers International, Inc. (125 East 57th Street, Gallery 48 in the Place des Antiquaires, between Park and Lexington avenues), is a store/showroom that was founded by a group of rare-book dealers. Browsers are welcome, though, and the books, prints, autographs, maps, and manuscripts on display will provide a brief introduction to the fascinating subject of rare books and incunabula. Tel: 751-5450.

Argosy Book Store (116 East 59th Street, between Park and Lexington avenues) has a vast collection of used books, which range in price from less than a dollar to several hundred times more. Prints are also available here, notably many Audubons, as well as some autographs. Tel: 753-4455.

B. Dalton (666 Fifth Avenue, at 52nd Street), the huge chain with outlets across the country, has its flagship store on Fifth Avenue between 52nd and 53rd streets. There is an up-to-date selection of current titles here, as well as a good stock of standard titles, especially in paperback. Tel: 247-1740.

Brentano's (597 Fifth Avenue, near the corner of 48th Street) occupies the landmark Scribner's building, with its wrought-iron façade and airy, two-story interior. It stocks books of every kind; the business and art-book selections are particularly broad. Tel: 826-2450.

Charles Colin Publications (315 West 53rd Street, between Eighth and Ninth avenues) is a venerable family-owned shop that specializes in brass and jazz ... of the musical variety, that is. They stock a broad selection of how-to and instructional books about jazz, brass instruments, and big bands. Tel: 581-1480.

Coliseum Books (1771 Broadway, at 57th Street) has an amazing number of books, mostly paperback, on all subjects. This is a great place to browse; even if you don't find what you're looking for you will certainly find something you want. Tel: 757-8381.

The **Complete Traveller** (199 Madison Avenue, at 35th Street) specializes in travel books. It stocks most of the Nagel guides—expensive but authoritative—and also has a terrific selection of maps. Tel: 685-9007.

Doubleday (724 Fifth Avenue, just south of 57th Street) has branches, but it's best to shop in the main store, at 57th Street. The selection of new fiction is excellent—occasionally, books are on sale here before the official release date. The reference section is also particularly good, and in the store's other special sections, spread out over three floors, you'll find most standard books in stock. The store is open until midnight, six days a week. Tel: 397-0550.

The **Gotham Book Mart** (41 West 47th Street, between Fifth and Sixth avenues) has a sign over the awning that says, "Wise men fish here." Indeed they do, and even the unwise may learn something here. The Gotham has made no concessions to fleeting fashion or modern marketing in its 50 or so years of existence. It remains a book-lover's bookstore, with a new and used collection of poetry, fiction, journals, and books on film and the theater that reflects the taste and interests of its founder, the late Frances Steloff, who was an early reader and supporter of James Joyce, Ezra Pound, Henry Miller, and Dylan Thomas, among many others. Give yourself an afternoon, at least, for the Gotham. Tel: 719-4448.

Hacker Art Books (45 West 57th Street, between Fifth and Sixth avenues) bills itself as the largest art-book shop in the world. Size aside, its collection is probably the broadest—every period of fine and applied art is represented here. Tel: 688-7600.

Hagstrom Map & Travel Center (57 West 43rd Street, between Fifth and Sixth avenues) sells books related to travel and world geography. They stock atlases and travel guides and offer a wide selection of maps, from local street maps to topographic, nautical, aeronautical, and decorative wall versions. Tel: 398-1222.

Librairie de France (610 Fifth Avenue, in the Rockefeller Center Promenade) sells French and Spanish books, tapes, guides, and posters, and English books in translation. Tel: 581-8810.

The **Museum of Modern Art** store (44 West 53rd Street, between Fifth and Sixth avenues) has a good selection of books about modern art, catalogues of museum exhibits, and some eye-popping posters, writing paper, and post-cards of works from the museum's collection. Tel: 708-9700.

The **Mysterious Book Shop** (129 West 56th Street, between Sixth and Seventh avenues) is a chummy spot stocked with mysteries of every genre and populated by mystery lovers of every description. Hardcover and paper-back, new and used whodunits are available. Tel: 765-0900.

New York Bound Bookshop (50 Rockefeller Plaza, in the lobby) limits its merchandise to things pertaining to New York City, old and new. As this collection demon-strates, however, there is no limit to the ways that writers, artists, and photographers have described and depicted New York. Tel: 245-8503.

Patelson (160 West 56th Street, between Sixth and Seventh avenues) is just behind Carnegie Hall and, appro-priately, stocks the city's largest collection of books on classical music and musicians, as well as sheet music and recordings. Tel: 582-5840.

Rand McNally Map & Travel Store (150 East 52nd Street, between Lexington and Third avenues) offers a wide range of travel books, accessories, and paraphernal-ia. In addition to guides for any destination, the store sells travel videos, which will give you a preview of your vacation spot. They also carry small travel items, such as clocks, and a large selection of maps and globes. Tel: 758-7488.

Rizzoli (31 West 57th Street, between Fifth and Sixth avenues) is a handsome store where the oak shelves groan under the weight of the finest art, photography, and fashion books published in the United States and Europe. On hand here, too, is one of New York's finest selections of foreign periodicals. Rizzoli's stores at 454 West Broad-way (between Houston and Prince streets) and 200 Vesey Street (downtown in the World Financial Center) have a similar though smaller selection, with an emphasis on art. Tel: 759-2424 at 57th Street; 674-1616 at West Broadway; 385-1400 at Vesey Street.

Traveller's Bookstore (75 Rockefeller Plaza, in the lobby) is a good place for both real travellers and arm-chair travellers. The standard guides are available, as well as a good collection of travel writing, old and new, fanciful and factual. Tel: 664-0995.

United Nations Bookstore (at the United Nations, 46th Street and First Avenue entrance) stocks many UN publications and reports, as well as a genuinely international selection of children's books. Tel: 963-7680.

Urban Center Books (457 Madison Avenue, at 51st Street) is suitably located in the historic Villard Houses, former private residences that are now part of the New York Palace Hotel. The store is run in part by the Municipal Arts Society and stocks 4,000 titles on anything that has to do with cities: architecture, historic preservation, and the like. Tel: 935-3592.

Uptown: East Side

Appelfeld Gallery (1372 York Avenue, near 73rd Street) is a bibliophile's delight. It's a charming, somewhat creaky shop that deals, appropriately, in charming old books that are rare and out of print. Tel: 988-7835.

Barnes & Noble (1280 Lexington Avenue, between 86th and 87th streets) is one of the two so-called superstores the chain has opened in the city. The store is vast and attractive, with acres of polished wood and shelves that are well stocked with an inventory that leans more heavily to popular, current titles than it does to backlist and university presses. Tel: 423-9900.

Books & Co. (939 Madison Avenue, at 74th Street) has won a wide following probably because it's carefully designed to appeal to a toney crowd—classical music plays softly in the background; books about art, philosophy, and literature (with a capital L) are stressed; and there's a well-bred mien to the salespeople. Despite all this niceness, the books here are really quite good, and it's a wonderful place to browse. Tel: 737-1450.

Burlington Book Shop (1082 Madison Avenue, near 81st Street) is a snug, cheerful spot where pets are welcome, smokers are unharassed, and books—a startlingly good selection on a wide range of subjects—are the focus of everyone's attention. Downstairs is a quirky toy store with glass cases full of toy soldiers; upstairs is a used- and rare-book department that keeps somewhat eccentric hours. Tel: 288-7420.

Kitchen Arts & Letters (1435 Lexington Avenue, near 93rd Street) stocks cookbooks of every persuasion and the work of food writers of every kind. Tel: 876-5550.

The **Metropolitan Museum of Art** bookstore (Fifth Avenue at 82nd Street) has a strong collection of art books. But what's best here are the imaginative and beautiful books produced by the museum staff and illustrated with images from the museum's vast holdings. Tel: 535-7710.

Military Bookman (29 East 93rd Street, just west of Madison Avenue, in a brownstone, ground floor) carries books about military history, from the taking of Troy to the present, although the emphasis is on classic battles of earlier wars. Some of the books are rare and quite valuable, posters and periodicals are in stock, and the salespeople here are nice as well as knowledgeable. Tel: 348-1280.

Uptown: West Side

The **American Museum of Natural History** bookshop (Central Park West at 79th Street) deals in books about anthropology, American Indian lore, and the natural world. Best is the selection of books for kids, which is both fun and instructive. Tel: 769-5100.

Applause Theatre and Cinema Books (211 West 71st Street, between Broadway and West End Avenue) deals mainly in drama—British, American, and European—in anthologies, annotated versions, and single-play books. Although there is an emphasis on British drama, it is not necessarily serious; it's possible to find, for instance, a collection of Monty Python skits. Applause also has a large number of books on the cinema. Tel: 496-7511.

Bank Street College Bookstore (610 West 112th Street, at Broadway) has an extensive inventory of books relating to the Bank Street College of Education's curriculum (early childhood development, museum education programs, and so on) upstairs. The ground floor is dedicated to children's books and literature (with selections for pre-toddlers through teenagers), and the staff is exceedingly helpful and knowledgeable. Tel: 678-1654.

Barnard Bookforum (2955 Broadway, at 116th Street) serves the Columbia University–Barnard College community but offers university press books, scholarly texts, classics, and a good selection of fiction for students of all ages. The staff is well read and helpful and will order academic texts that are not currently in stock. Tel: 749-5535.

Barnes & Noble (2289 Broadway, between 82nd and 83rd streets) occupies a whole city block and, with a café, frequent readings, and cozy library tables where customers can sit and read as long as they wish, represents a "bookstore as event" phenomenon. The vast stock doesn't dip too far into esoteria, but the inventory is appealing enough to keep the store hopping right up until closing at 11:00 P.M. weeknights, midnight on weekends. The children's section and the selection of periodicals are especially good. Tel: 362-8835.

Black Books Plus (702 Amsterdam Avenue, on the corner of 94th Street) carries books by and about blacks: fiction and nonfiction, and the largest collection of black children's books in the city. Tel: 749-9632.

Endicott Booksellers (450 Columbus Avenue, near 82nd Street) offers many good titles from which to choose, along with comfortable couches for relaxed browsing. Tel: 787-6300.

Gryphon Bookshop (2246 Broadway, near 80th Street, with an annex across the avenue at 246 West 80th Street, fourth floor) sells used books and records. The selection is good, particularly in the children's section, where all (it seems) of the Oz books are available in any edition you would care to own. Used records are also on sale; in the annex some of the books have been marked down. Tel: 362-0706.

Murder Ink (2486 Broadway, between 92nd and 93rd streets) sells mysteries, new and used. The books are no longer arranged according to the old impenetrable shelving system, but are now alphabetical. Business hours are eccentric, so call in advance; Tel: 362-8905.

Papyrus Books (2915 Broadway, at 114th Street) is not worth a special trip uptown, but if you are in the neighborhood you should certainly stop by. It has a good collection of new and used fiction, particularly paperbacks, but it has a truly amazing collection of periodicals. Tel: 222-3350.

Pomander Bookshop (955 West End Avenue, at 107th Street) is an airy, well-lighted room full of out-of-print and used books. It is an exceedingly pleasant place to shop. Tel: 866-1777.

Shakespeare & Company has an uptown and a downtown shop (2259 Broadway, at 81st Street, and 716 Broadway, at Washington Place). The 81st Street location is an Upper West Side institution, and on sunny Sunday afternoons it gets almost as crowded as nearby Zabar's (though the new Barnes & Noble up the street has thinned the throngs here a bit). The stock of new fiction and nonfiction here reflects the neighborhood: eclectic, offbeat, and brainy. Tel: 580-7800, uptown; 529-1330, downtown.

LITERATURE AT NIGHT: READINGS

In recent years, the spoken word—or, specifically, the words spoken by the writers and poets who create them—has become increasingly popular as entertainment in New York. Venues range from quiet, wood-paneled bookstores where authors read to hushed and properly appreciative admirers, to rollicking theaters and cafés where the audience may be just as appreciative but vocally so, and the praise (or condemnation) is immediate and unconstrained. Poetry and prose readings take place on a largely irregular basis so you'll need to do a bit of research to find out what's on. You should start with the *New York City Poetry Calendar,* a monthly broadsheet (not published in July and August) that lists readings about town. Copies are free, and available in many of the bookstores listed in this chapter; if you can't find one, telephone the *Calendar* at 475-7110. The *Village Voice* newspaper also provides a weekly listing of readings.

Some general rules do apply, however. There are very few readings during the summer months; writers, presumably, take vacations too. Bookstores that host readings do not, as a rule, charge admission and, depending on the largesse of whatever publishing house is involved, may spring for snacks. Theaters and cafés generally ask that you purchase a ticket or make a donation and, of course, are perfectly happy to sell customers a beer or two as well. Finally, people of all types attend readings in New York. Don't be discouraged by fears of an impossibly intellectual or elite crowd. That said, we include here a few of our favorite spots.

Readings in Cafés and Theaters

If you're searching for both fun and enlightenment, you would do well to stop by the **Nuyorican Poets Café** (236 East 3rd Street, between Avenues B and C). The poets here are hip, the crowd demanding, and the Friday night "poetry slams" provide some of the best entertainment in town. Tel: 505-8183.

More subdued is the **Poetry Project** at St. Mark's-Church-in-the-Bowery (131 East 10th Street, at Second Avenue). New poets read from their work on Monday, Wednesday, and Friday evenings (closed July through September). Tel: 674-0910.

The Knot Room in the **Knitting Factory** (47 East Houston Street, between Mott and Mulberry streets) offers an eclectic selection of poetry readings during most weeks. Tel: 219-3006.

At **La MaMa Experimental Theater Company** (74A East 4th Street, between Third and Second avenues) a room called La Galleria hosts both poetry and prose readings on a regular basis. Tel: 475-7710.

The **Symphony Space** theater (2537 Broadway, at 95th Street) offers Selected Shorts, a very popular short-story series, read by professional actors and broadcast on National Public Radio, every other week from January through May, and celebrates Bloomsday in June with readings from James Joyce. Tel: 864-1414.

The **92nd Street Y** (1395 Lexington Avenue) sprinkles a wide sampling of readings among its year-round concert and discussion series. Tel: 427-6000.

Readings in Bookstores
Bookstores, by their nature, provide a more consciously literary setting for readings, and many of those recommended in this chapter organize soirees with whatever writer or poet happens to be in town. They include the downtown establishments of **Judith's Room**, **Rizzoli** in SoHo, **mosaicBooks**, **A Different Light** (not in our listings but one of New York's excellent gay and lesbian bookstores; 548 Hudson Street, between Charles and Perry streets, Tel: 989-4850), and **Granary Books**. In Midtown, **Brentano's** hosts 10 to 15 readings each month. **Endicott Booksellers** on the Upper West Side and **Books & Co.** on the Upper East Side both maintain a lively schedule of readings.

SHOPPING

By Lynn Yaeger

Lynn Yaeger is the author of a biweekly column in the Village Voice *on antiques and collectibles and was also a contributor to* The Village Voice Guide to Manhattan's Shopping Neighborhoods. *A resident of New York City for more than 20 years, she has written on fashion for* Cosmopolitan, Mademoiselle, *and other publications.*

It stands to reason, New York City being as it is a home base for eccentric, offbeat, oddball citizens who have emigrated here from all over the globe, that attendant unusual shops have sprung up to meet their peculiar needs. "There's a nut for every street lamp in New York," as the saying goes, and often enough there's a store shimmering under that light as well. People only visiting us will want to avail themselves of our profusion of one-of-a-kind, out-of-the-way venues in order to carry back to their peaceful homes talismans of Manhattan life.

In the first section of this chapter we cover a broad range of merchandise: furniture, housewares, ethnic imports, hobby and collectible items, dolls and toys (for kids and adults), sports equipment, and various other sundries, such as stationery, buttons, and pipes. In the **Antiques and Collectibles** section you will find vintage versions of most of these items. We wind up with a segment on **Fashion**, which encompasses clothing, shoes, and handbags, cosmetics, and other accessories. Other specialty shopping items can be found in other chapters: books in Literary New York; cameras and lenses in Photography and Filmmaking; food, tabletop, and cooking items in Food, for a few examples.

FURNITURE

Those shoppers who would rather equip their homes than themselves face an almost endless selection of domicile-related shops in New York. They'll find furniture to suit every lodging from basement flat to loft to veritable castle—there are no limits placed on the consumer's imagination (only on his or her credit cards).

Traditional Furniture

Shoppers seeking voluminous comfort should go to **Shabby Chic** (93 Greene Street, between Prince and Spring streets), where the faded floral divans have the saggy-springed look of yesteryear. At **George Smith** (73 Spring Street, between Crosby and Lafayette streets) the oversized, overstuffed sofas are imported from cozy old England. **Carlyle Custom Convertibles** (1056 Third Avenue, between 62nd and 63rd streets) features fringed brocades and velvets as well as more conservative interpretations for the lived-in living room. Over at **E. J. Audi** (317 East 34th Street, between First and Second avenues), Mission is the byword—the stock comprises fanatically faithful line-for-line reproductions of L. and J. G. Stickley designs.

Modern Furniture

At **Maurice Villency** (200 Madison Avenue, corner of 35th Street) there are up-to-the-minute armoires (lots of mirrors, burled wood, and hidden handles) as well as suede sectional couches and Art Moderne coffee tables. **Palazzetti** (246 West 80th Street, between Broadway and West End Avenue; and 515 Madison Avenue, on 53rd Street) features a roster of big-name European designer classics bearing fairly reasonable price tags.

Avant-Garde Furniture

For the ultimate in avant-garde discomfort, the gallery/shop **Modern Stone Age** (111 Greene Street, near Prince Street) features slabs of rock converted into modern pieces of Fred Flintstonian furniture. Minimalist Italian efforts (Milanese Memphis and beyond) are for sale at **Modern Age** (795 Broadway, near 10th Street).

Inexpensive Furniture

A whole host of stores serves the needs of Manhattan's space-starved and budget-wise apartment dwellers. The **Door Store** (123 West 17th Street, between Sixth and Seventh avenues, and other locations), **Workbench** (470 Park Avenue, at 32nd Street, and other locations), and **Bon Marché** (55 West 13th Street, between Fifth and Sixth avenues) all sell shelving and small-scale furniture that is more than decent looking and quite cheap. To accessorize rooms with breathtaking thrift, try the **Bombay Company** (1018 Madison Avenue, between 78th and 79th streets, and other locations), which has lots of amusing pieces (camp desks, dressing tables, miniature chests of drawers) at ridiculously low prices. Wicker furnishings, having recently expanded their scope beyond the exclusivity of the summer porch and now bedecking rooms for all seasons, are in good supply at **Deutsch** (31 East 32nd Street, between Madison and Park avenues) and at the remarkably inexpensive **Pier I** (461 Fifth Avenue, at 41st Street).

DECORATIVE ITEMS AND HOUSEWARES

Old-Fashioned Decor

Shoppers who wish to buy into the English country-home look (that of late is smothering rooms all over America under oceans of chintz, mottled and faded carpeting, and hairy dogs) should head uptown to **G. Elter** (740 Madison Avenue, between 64th and 65th streets), where antique reproduction picture frames can be purchased. Fortuny-inspired Venetian pillows from **Portantina** (895 Madison Avenue, at 72nd Street), a narrow, velvet-encased shop, are fine for reclining on after a day of shopping. Possessors of ill-shaped windows, who travel with or have memorized the dimensions of their unfortunate vitrines, can order custom-made lace-patterned French-style curtains from the always charming **Wolfman-Gold & Good** (116 Greene Street, between Prince and Spring streets).

Modern Accessories

The notoriously abrupt owner at **Bridge Kitchenware** (214 East 52nd Street, between Second and Third avenues) will nonetheless condescend to sell you some of the finest pots and pans big money can buy. Both **Zabar's** (2245 Broadway, at 80th Street, upstairs) and **Broadway Panhandler** (520 Broadway, at Spring Street) are considered equipment heaven by fledgling and gourmet cooks alike.

The more prosaic offerings at **Conran's Habitat** (2–8 Astor Place, just east of Broadway; 2248 Broadway, at 81st Street; and 160 East 54th Street, at Third Avenue) and **Pottery Barn** (250 West 57th Street, at Eighth Avenue, and many other locations) include stacks of cheerful, colorful bath, table, and pantry accessories. (Also see "Cookware" in the Food chapter.) The brand-new **Bed & Bath & Beyond**, occupying one of the enormous old Ladies' Mile shopping emporiums (620 Sixth Avenue, at 19th Street), goes *way* beyond, stocking virtually everything you might need for your home. Unusual telephones (in the shape of, say, juicy puckered lips, Snoopy dogs, or cheeseburgers) are for sale at the **Phone Booth** (12 East 53rd Street, between Fifth and Madison avenues).

Linens
Linens are the specialty at **E. Braun** (717 Madison Avenue, near 64th Street), an old-fashioned holdover from the days when Madison Avenue was just the local shopping street for rich people. **Descamps** (just up the avenue at number 723) has modern, very popular sheets, towels, and pillowcases from and for upper-crust France. Everything in SoHo's **Terra Verde** (120 Wooster Street, between Prince and Spring streets) is ecologically correct, including the unprocessed, undyed, natural cotton sheets, pillow sleeves, and duvet covers.

Flatware
At **Christofle Pavillon** (680 Madison Avenue, near 60th Street) silver-plated flatware and other more elaborate items appeal to the conservative good-taste crowd, while across the street **Georg Jensen** (number 683) purveys the Scandinavian design items that have been staples of the ritzy (but unglitzy) home for more than 40 years. If the duke and duchess and their 15 progeny are ambling over to dinner, matching silver for incomplete sets of flatware may be located at **Jean's Silversmith** (16 West 45th Street, between Fifth and Sixth avenues).

China, Crystal, and Pottery
Top-of-the-line classic crystal from France is the draw at **Baccarat** (625 Madison Avenue, between 58th and 59th streets), while Postmodern minimalist Japanese crystal is the specialty at **Hoya** (450 Park Avenue, at 57th Street), where the severe atmosphere makes even the most delicate visitor feel like the proverbial bull in a china shop. Those who subscribe to a rather more slap-dash style of home decoration may prefer the whimsical offerings at the **Mad Monk** (500 Sixth Avenue, between 12th and 13th streets), a hand-thrown-pottery store (it also sells Zen books) at the northern end of the West Village. Utilitarian restaurant china and glass, not usually sold on a per-piece basis, can be found at **Fishs Eddy** (889 Broadway, at 19th Street).

Lighting

At **Jerrystyle** (380 Lafayette Street, between East 3rd and 4th streets) the verdigris sconces, lamps, and chandeliers might have just emerged from a Roman tomb (had the Romans had electricity). More aesthetically accessible lighting fixtures are available from **Lee's Studio Gallery** (1755 Broadway, at 56th Street). The various offerings include high-style Deco, pop art, neon, and halogen.

Tiles

Thrillingly pretty hand-painted tiles from southern Europe—that might make you wish to immediately demolish your perfectly serviceable kitchen and bath and start over—are available down in Chelsea at **Country Floors** (15 East 16th Street, between Fifth Avenue and Union Square). The artists' limited-edition offerings at **Tiles** (42 West 15th Street, between Fifth and Sixth avenues) have a similar effect on the nascent home-renovator.

FABRICS, BUTTONS, AND NEEDLEWORK

A whole shop, **Tender Buttons** (143 East 62nd Street, between Lexington and Third avenues), splendid as an art gallery, is devoted to these humble items—antique, vintage, and new—sometimes made up into cuff links or earrings, but most often left in their natural state to adorn your most prosaic garments. Wholesale ribbons, laces, and trimmings, for much less, are available in the area of **Sixth Avenue** in the high 30s, where cardboard boxes showcase the wares, and trading, though brisk, will tolerate the retail customer. For fabrics, investigate **Jerry Brown** (37 West 57th Street, between Fifth and Sixth avenues), where reasonably priced yard goods, from taffeta to tweed, crowd the heavily traversed selling floor. If you care to purchase leather skins straight off the animal's back, go to **Grosz Leather** (245 West 29th Street, between Seventh and Eighth avenues), a shop selling ordinary to obscure hides. Your castle walls, albeit sagging beneath the groaning display of oil-painted Irish setters and someone else's dead relatives, should include some of mummy's needlepoint, which can be made up from kits purchased at **Erica Wilson Needle Works** (717 Madison Avenue, near 64th Street). Stop by the small, charming **Yarn Connection** (218 Madison Avenue, near 36th Street) if you're searching for a particular yarn or to browse through the high-quality inventory.

STATIONERY

Exquisitely marbleized Venetian papers, in the form of stationery but also made up to cover a wide range of desk accessories, are for sale at **Il Papiro** (1021 Lexington Avenue, between 73rd and 74th streets, and in the World Financial Center, 200 Vesey Street). The correct pen and/or pencil for the scholarly-journal underliner can be found at **Arthur Brown** (2 West 46th Street, just west of Fifth Avenue).

Fetishistically proper monogrammed note cards (as well as wedding invitations) can be custom ordered at **Tiffany & Co.** (727 Fifth Avenue, at 57th Street) and **Cartier** (653 Fifth Avenue, at 52nd Street). Only slightly less conservative are the offerings at **Dempsey and Carroll** (110 East 57th Street, between Lexington and Park avenues). More sprightly visitors wishing to send silly, charming greetings to faraway friends should head downtown and check the card racks at **Farfetched** (110 Fourth Avenue, between 11th and 12th streets) and **Alphabets** (115 Avenue A, between 7th and 8th streets).

Visitors desperately thrashing in the throes of wretched homesickness should pull themselves together long enough to visit **Hotalings**, the gigantic news dealer smack in the middle of Manhattan (142 West 42nd Street, between Broadway and Sixth Avenue). If there's anyplace in town that carries a copy of your home-town paper, this is it.

PIPES AND CIGARS

The right cigar for late-night musing can be chosen at **Nat Sherman** (500 Fifth Avenue, at 42nd Street). When nothing but the professorial puff of a pipe will do, visit **Pipeworks & Wilke** (16 West 55th Street, between Fifth and Sixth avenues).

ETHNIC SHOPPING

Despite varying tendencies among New Yorkers to alternately embrace and deny their immigrant origins, shops catering to merchandise from the old country abound. In addition, disparate nationalities continue to arrive and, once here, open specialty shops importing goods associated with the life left behind.

Although in no way comparable to their numbers 50 or even 30 years ago, there are still plenty of Irish in Manhattan whose ancestral longings can be assuaged by a visit to **Shamrock Imports** (in the sixth level of A & S Plaza, at 33rd Street and Broadway), where, among a selection of emerald-green ephemera, hand-knit fisherman sweaters, wide caps, and *claddagh* rings are available. Fiercely nationalist remnants of the Ukrainian community, still hanging on in the rapidly gentrifying East Village, go to **Surma** (11 East 7th Street, between Second and Third avenues) for traditional painted Easter eggs and embroidered linens. Though burgeoning Chinese immigration is pushing northward beyond Canal Street and spilling into the **Little Italy** area, the Mulberry Street corridor continues, for the time being, to sell ornate Italian pottery, posters of Sophia Loren, and cappuccino machines. **Chinatown**'s endurance as a tourist attraction, meanwhile, supports the type of (souvenir-laden) stores you would anticipate.

The needs of those recently arrived from India are met by a variety of stores located in **Little India**, the area of Park Avenue South and Lexington Avenue in the high 20s. Sari fabric off the bolt and sticks of incense are always available, and there are numerous other products less immediately accessible to the North American consumer. Those other Indians—the ones Americans like to watch on TV westerns—are an almost strictly imaginary community in New York City. Their indigenous merchandise, however, is available at a number of venues, among them the Village's **Common Ground** (19 Greenwich Avenue, between Christopher and 10th streets), which handles baskets, weavings, and silver and turquoise jewelry.

Tibetan textiles, mirrored caps, silver charm bracelets, and other accessories from Tibet's far-flung outposts have found a peaceful home in the heart of the West Village at **Tibet West** (19 Christopher Street, between Sixth and Seventh avenues). Visitors whose taste remains deeply entrenched south of the equator will like **Craft Caravan** (63 Greene Street, between Spring and Broome streets), which sells African handcrafted tin toys among other artifacts. From this hemisphere, both **Back from Guatemala** (306 East 6th Street, between Second and First avenues) and **Pan American Phoenix** (153 East 53rd Street, at Lexington Avenue, in Citicorp Center) import handwoven textiles and hammered-tin housewares as well as long, gathered skirts and homespun smocks, suitable to lounge in while leafing through the pages of old *National Geographic*s. For a huge selection of small, intriguing items from around the globe, visit the **United Nations Gift Shop** (First Avenue and 46th Street entrance), but be warned: This place is especially arousing for children.

DOLLS, TOYS, GAMES, AND GADGETS

Although there remain in Manhattan a number of toy stores dedicated exclusively to a clientele composed of the under-12 set, many such places cater to an adult audience that can't seem to get enough of this merchandise. (We cover antique dolls and toys in the Antiques and Collectibles section.)

Dolls and Dollhouses

At **B. Shackman** (85 Fifth Avenue, at 16th Street) the specialty is reproduction Victoriana manifested in bisque-headed dolls, paper ephemera, and miniatures, including dollhouse furniture. Prices are always inviting. Those readers obsessed with the diminutive (and this includes the growing number of adults who like to play with dollhouses) should visit **Dollhouse Antics** (1343 Madison Avenue, at 94th Street) for a full line of stunted furniture and accessories.

Magic, Gags, and Sci-Fi

Children who enjoy annoying adults by performing tedious magic tricks (and who among us does not know at least one of these small persons) will benefit from a trip to **Hornmann Magic Co.**, located upstairs in the office building at 45 West 34th Street (between Fifth and Sixth avenues). Youngsters (as well as certain older persons) whose idea of a brilliant practical joke rests at the level of the whoopie cushion should head for **Jimsons** (28 East 18th Street, between Broadway and Park Avenue South), where kindred items crowd the chaotic shelves.

The young science and science-fiction fanatic should visit **Forbidden Planet** (821 Broadway, at 12th Street), where comic books and merchandise pack two stories in an atmosphere that can only be described as scholarly. Dungeons and Dragons partisans will enjoy the **Compleat Strategist** (11 East 33rd Street, between Fifth and Madison avenues), a place filled with stimulating boxed mind-games and patronized by a passionate group of devotees of all ages.

Toys

The **Last Wound-Up** (1595 Second Avenue, at 83rd Street), which sells mechanical toys in an exhaustive range of prices, sizes, and models, is as popular with adults as with kids. Way down on the Lower East Side, **Little Rickie** (49½ First Avenue, at 3rd Street), with its

1960s ephemera, Barbie-related accessories, and one of the last extant black-and-white photo-booth machines in town, appeals to the laugh-riot crowd. The younger set is wild about the toy-shop-gone-mad atmosphere at the famous **F.A.O. Schwarz** (767 Fifth Avenue, at 59th Street). Assuming you can abide the giant singing clock at the entrance ("Welcome to our world, welcome to our world of toys"), you'll find the scope and selection, which goes far beyond toys, to be more than impressive. And you'll find yourself wondering about the tiny recipients of the life-size rocking horses and the infant- and toddler-size gold lamé pouf dresses and black-velvet evening gowns costing hundreds of dollars.

Toy shopping in New York does not have to be a hair-raising experience. The **Museum of American Folk Art Gift Shop** (Columbus Avenue at 66th Street) sells old-fashioned, very inexpensive simple toys that nevertheless often receive an outsized reception. Tiny infants (are there any other kind?) can be mollified with a cozy, affectionate stuffed toy, the kind that grandma used to make, still handmade by anonymous grandmas at the charitable **New York Exchange for Woman's Work** (1095 Third Avenue, at 64th Street). The **Lighthouse** (800 Second Avenue, between 42nd and 43rd streets), which sells items handcrafted by the visually impaired, has extremely inexpensive crocheted farm and barn animals, of which the pastel kangaroo-en-famille is especially engaging. Visitors seeking to take a break from mental activity can indulge themselves at **Big City Kites** (1201 Lexington Avenue, between 81st and 82nd streets), where the merchandise, once properly assembled, will (presumably) soar.

Games

The **Game Show** (474 Sixth Avenue, between 11th and 12th streets) has games and puzzles from around the world (many from museum shops), most of which are geared for grown-ups. Shoppers in search of the lost world of bohemian Greenwich Village may be inspired, after an interval of watching the perennial chess players at the southwestern corner of Washington Square Park, to purchase a chess set of their own, available in an impressive range of styles and prices from the **Village Chess Shop** (230 Thompson Street, between West 3rd and Bleecker streets).

Gadgetry

Shoppers interested in high-quality gadgetry should visit **Hammacher Schlemmer** (147 East 57th Street, between Lexington and Third avenues), famous for upper-class items on the order of bun-warming frankfurter steamers and solar-charged garden sprayers. Less rarefied though still amusing items can be examined at the **Sharper Image** (4 West 57th Street, between Fifth and Sixth avenues). More old-fashioned souls might gravitate toward **Rita Ford's Music Boxes** (19 East 65th Street, between Fifth and Madison avenues), a 19th-century sort of place featuring obviously tuneful, if not inexpensive, merchandise.

HOBBIES AND COLLECTIONS

People will collect or make a hobby of anything, and residents of New York City are no exception. Indeed, with the availability and accessibility of just about every imaginable collectible or hobbyist item, this city's collectors are probably among the more devoted in the world. (See also Dolls and Toys in the Antiques and Collectibles section, below.)

Baseball Cards and Comics

The inveterate collector of baseball cards can visit **Jeff's** (150 Second Avenue, between 9th and 10th streets) and the huge **Collector's Stadium** (214 Sullivan Street, between Bleecker and West 3rd streets). Both of these places can also provide information about upcoming card-trading fairs. Comic-book collectors can browse through the selection at Jeff's but should afterward head straight to the much-acclaimed **Forbidden Planet** (821 Broadway, at 12th Street). Devotees of comics of the past will find their heroes (Dagwood, Porky, Goofy, and Archie) emblazoned on sweatshirts and sundries at **Too Cute** (113 Prince Street, between Greene and Wooster streets).

Models and Trains

The **Red Caboose** (16 West 45th Street, sixth floor, between Fifth and Sixth avenues) and the **Train Shop** (23 West 45th Street, on the same block) will serve the serious collector of trains as well as the casual hobbyist. Model sets, ranging from simple balsa-wood planes to stunningly intricate hardwood tall ships (some of which take thousands of hours and nerves of steel to put together) can be found at **Jan's Hobby Shop** (1557 York Avenue, at 82nd Street).

Bones to Butterflies
The American Museum of Natural History neighborhood provides a suitable setting for **Maxilla & Mandible** (451–455 Columbus Avenue, between 81st and 82nd streets), where you might pick up a bleached animal skull to complete the southwestern motif in your living room and where collectors of such things can find fossils, mounted bugs, and other creepy-crawly stuff (be sure to pay heed to all the scolding signs: Do Not Touch, Do Not Breathe, etc.). Younger visitors will undoubtedly enjoy the thought-provoking widgets at the **Nature Company** (8 Fulton Street, in the South Street Seaport area). Those preoccupied with the pursuit of supine butterflies and moths will not want to miss the pleasant **Mariposa** (also at South Street Seaport, at Pier 17, second floor).

Music and Movie Memorabilia
Old radios and phonographs (Edison wind-ups through the Art Deco years) are for sale at **Waves** (32 East 13th Street, between Fifth Avenue and University Place). Contemporaneous movie posters, lobby cards, and other motion-picture ephemera are available at **Jerry Ohlinger's Movie Material Store** (242 West 14th Street, between Seventh and Eighth avenues).

Stamps, Coins, and Autographs
Collectors with a passion for tiny squares of paper and/or small, round pieces of metal should visit **Stampazine** (119 West 57th Street, second floor, west of Sixth Avenue) and/or **Ideal Stamp and Coin** (460 West 34th Street, tenth floor, between Ninth and Tenth avenues).

Larger scraps of paper with names scribbled on them—some are menus, programs, and even cancelled checks—are beautifully mounted and framed at **James Lowe Autographs** (30 East 60th Street, between Madison and Park avenues) and **Kenneth Rendell** (in the Place des Antiquaires, 125 East 57th Street, between Lexington and Park avenues).

SPORTS EQUIPMENT
Despite its concrete-and-steel exterior, Manhattan is home to thousands of sand-and-sea, mountain-air, wind-

blown-links, and locker-room enthusiasts. **Paragon Sporting Goods** (867 Broadway, at 18th Street) is the best all-around sports store in the city. It's got enormous ranges in prices and selections, from good, basic equipment to top-of-the-line stuff for professional athletes. Paragon will equip and outfit you for swimming, weight lifting, aerobics, boxing, every type of ball game, bird-watching, kayaking, camping, hiking, water skiing, and every other sport imaginable.

Eastern Mountain Sports (611 Broadway, at Houston Street; and 20 West 61st Street, west of Broadway) and **Tents & Trails** (21 Park Place, between Broadway and Church Street) provide the necessities for excursions to woods, lakes, and mountains. Those who want to do a little hunting (whether big game or bunnies) in the great outdoors can locate fashionable supplies at the chic **Hunting World** (16 East 53rd Street, between Fifth and Madison avenues). **Orvis** (355 Madison Avenue, at 45th Street) accoutres both shooters and anglers, the latter of which will want to visit **Capital Fishing Tackle** (218 West 23rd Street, between Seventh and Eighth avenues).

If you like to take your exercise on the open road you might prefer the offerings at **Bicycle Habitat** (172 Seventh Avenue, between 21st and 22nd streets). Lean and mean, equipmentally correct cyclists go to **Toga** (110 West End Avenue, at 64th Street), but recreational cyclists are pretty much snubbed there. Those ambitious and trendy athletes with superior balance and poise can find the latest in-line skates at **Blades** (105 West 72nd Street, off Columbus Avenue, and 160 East 86th Street, off Lexington Avenue). Many of the runners rounding the path that encircles the Central Park Reservoir shop at **Super Runners** (1337 Lexington Avenue, at 89th Street; 1170 Third Avenue, at 68th Street; 416 Third Avenue, at 29th Street; and 360 Amsterdam Avenue, at 77th Street), whose running shoes and clothes are sold by a knowledgeable and helpful staff. **Island Windsurfing** (1623 York Avenue, between 85th and 86th streets) will equip misplaced Californians who believe that since Manhattan *is* an island you should logically be able to buy windsurfers, surfboards, wet suits, and skateboards here.

Old-fashioned types whose idea of a workout is a morning on the Central Park bridle path can purchase leather riding gear at **M. J. Knoud** (716 Madison Avenue, between 63rd and 64th streets), **Kauffman & Sons** (419 Park Avenue South, at 29th Street), or **Miller's** (123 East 24th Street, between Park and Lexington avenues), all of which are equestrian stores selling boots, bits, feed bags, jodhpurs, and fashionable riding habits. Tennis players can count on sound advice while they choose from a line of high-quality, well-priced rackets, including the latest high-tech models, at **Mason's Tennis Mart** (911 Seventh Avenue, near 57th Street). The huge **New York Golf Center** (131 West 35th Street, between Seventh Avenue and Broadway), has everything a golfer could want, whether a $75 set of clubs or a $5,000 set, at competitive prices. If you can't find what you're seeking here, you probably won't find it anywhere.

Fans of indoor sports can pick up the latest in aerobics wear at **Women's Workout Gear** (121 Seventh Avenue, near 17th Street), also offering more-down-to-earth styles as well as shoes.

OBJECTS OF WORSHIP: TRADITIONAL AND ARCANE

Readers who have long since acknowledged that a gadget or game won't solve their problems and are still searching for answers can investigate the **Magickal Childe** (35 West 19th Street, between Fifth and Sixth avenues) or **Enchantments** (341 East 9th Street, between First and Second avenues), both of which sell ritualistic equipment to New York's active witch and warlock community. Those attracted to the more traditional faiths should visit **Altar Egos** (110 West Houston Street, between Thompson and Sullivan streets), where sacred objects and ephemera of every religion crowd the ecumenical shelves.

ANTIQUES AND COLLECTIBLES

Whether the collector is visiting New York for a few months or a fortnight, whether he or she is an avid accumulator of objects from the past or maintains a purely academic, scholarly interest in such items, New York City provides a scope and variety of antiques, antiquities, and collectibles probably unrivaled in the world today. (Did somebody say London? But London is full of old English things. New York City is full of old things from *all* over.)

Anywhere you go in New York you are likely to run into antiques and collectibles shops, nestled in the shadows of the Washington Square Arch and buried in the small streets radiating from the major museums. Certain areas, however, have clusters of stores, and the serious shopper should head to these places first to get an idea of what is currently popular in the Manhattan antiques world and what prices the New York City market will bear.

Serious money might begin its tour with the axis of 57th Street and Madison Avenue. On **57th Street** proper, between Fifth and Lexington avenues, are a number of antiques dealers with internationally known names, displaying goods (mostly furniture and decorative accessories) of exquisite manufacture and rigorous provenance. Turn up **Madison Avenue** and you will find a number of additional prestigious shops, most of which have been at their addresses far longer than the foreign fashion stores snuggling up next to them. Their aristocratic presence is felt in varying intensity up to about 96th Street, where Madison Avenue sheds its golden glow and begins its rapid decline.

A visit to the Madison Avenue antiques shops stuns all but the wealthiest antiques hunter into shocked, impoverished silence. But it's easy to jump on the Lexington Avenue downtown local subway (number 6) and alight at the Spring Street stop in SoHo, which, while not inexpensive, gives the ordinary working person at least a fighting chance at shopping survival. (Concentrate your attention particularly on Lafayette, Greene, Wooster, Thompson, and Sullivan streets and the cross streets Prince, Spring, and Broome.) The mood down here is rampant Art Deco and French bistro, and there is a growing enthusiasm for Mission oak and the Arts and Crafts movement. The atmosphere is relaxed, and even when the price tag is astronomical the salesroom will lack the pin-drop hush of 57th Street.

From SoHo, the inexhaustible visitor might walk northwest to **Greenwich Village**, where on Hudson Street or Greenwich Avenue he or she will find lots of furniture stores with jumbled-up stock that looks inexpensive but isn't, really. Higher priced things are for sale on Bleecker Street between Christopher and Bank streets, where for some reason the shops seem equally divided between delicate, austere French and Biedermeier furniture on the one hand and folk art—quilts, Beacon blankets, and moth-eaten dolls—on the other.

Wholesale Only or To the Trade signs hang on the doors of the huge repositories of furniture, lamps, bronzes, and so on in the **wholesale antiques district**, also located in the Village, up and down Broadway and University Place and intervening streets between 8th and 14th streets. Though you are neither dealer nor decorator, a tough-talking demeanor and the willingness to pay quickly and in cash may succeed in getting you past the door.

Those young urban professionals who do not mind being identified as such can hop on the Seventh Avenue train (numbers 1, 2, 3, or 9) to West 72nd Street and stroll with their compatriots up **Columbus Avenue** (to about 92nd Street) and back down **Amsterdam Avenue**, where a selection of stores sell old and antique furniture and accessories that are appropriate for the furnishing of one's new co-op or first home in Westchester.

Specific recommendations regarding individual antiques and collectibles stores have built-in limitations: The stock in any given store may vary enormously, and antiques buyers tend to rely on the inspiration of the moment. Furthermore, the assiduous antiques shopper is ever on the lookout for that one-in-a-million baby in a five-and-ten store and may in fact turn up nothing of interest in any store described below, but rather find his or her heart's delight in some alleyway hovel unknown to us. (Note: Be sure to check the other shopping sections, where a number of additional stores specializing in collectibles are described. Vintage-clothes wearers, for instance, will find their haunts listed in the Fashion section.) Keeping all of the above in mind, we suggest the following.

FURNITURE

A huge and intense variety of styles, periods, countries of origin, and prices exists in New York City, and shopping for antique furniture and other decorative accessories is serious business here. (In fact, it is difficult to ascertain which preoccupation is more intense among New Yorkers: their personal appearance or the way their houses look.)

American Antique Furniture

In SoHo, **Bertha Black American Antiques** (80 Thompson Street, near Spring Street) sells small pieces of hand-painted furniture that evince a Hudson River School influence. At **Peter Roberts Antiques** (134 Spring Street, between Greene and Wooster streets) the hunky, chunky look of Mission oak is much in evidence. **Alice's Antiques**

(505 Columbus Avenue, between 84th and 85th streets),
on the Upper West Side, specializes in 19th-century American iron beds.

European Antique Furniture

If you have money to burn, proceed uptown in a taxi to
such establishments as **Stair & Company** (942 Madison
Avenue, between 74th and 75th streets), **Didier Aaron,
Inc.** (32 East 67th Street, between Madison and Park
avenues), and **Dalva Brothers** (44 East 57th Street, between Madison and Park avenues), where the finest of the
finest English and French 17th- to 19th-century antique
furniture is for sale.

Downtown, in SoHo, visit **Eileen Lane Antiques** (150
Thompson Street, between Houston and Prince streets)
to choose among the endless examples of flawless Scandinavian Biedermeier. Unusually interesting 19th-century
Portuguese and Spanish furniture is for sale at **Cobweb**
(116 West Houston Street, between Thompson and Sullivan streets). You'll find French working-class pieces such
as bistro tables and caned chairs at **T & K French Antiques** (120 Wooster Street, between Prince and Spring
streets).

Country Pine

Investigate Scandinavian country pine (lots of massive
Old World armoires) at **Evergreen Antiques** (120 Spring
Street, between Greene and Mercer streets, and 1249
Third Avenue, at 72nd Street). On the Upper West Side
Better Times Antiques (500 Amsterdam Avenue, at 84th
Street) can provide likely companion pieces in English
pine.

Art Deco Furniture

Those preferring sleek, polished examples of the Art Deco
period should dip down to SoHo and investigate **Alan
Moss Studios** (88 Wooster Street, between Spring and
Broome streets). At **Depression Modern** (150 Sullivan
Street, between Houston and Prince streets), streamlined
upholstered living-room settees and glass-and-chrome occasional tables sport fairly reasonable price tags.

1950s and 1960s Furniture

Collectors of the newly fashionable mid-20th-century designer furnishings will be serviced by **Fifty/50** (793 Broadway, between 10th and 11th streets). At **Full House** (133

Wooster Street, between Houston and Prince streets) the stock begins with the optimistic era of the boomerang coffee table and scurries quickly through the television decades, stopping gently just before the ascension of the lava lamp.

Less Expensive Vintage Furniture

If your eyes are wider than your pocketbook, don't despair; visit **ABC Antiques** (888 Broadway, between 18th and 19th streets) or the **Salvage Barn** (523 Hudson Street, between West 10th and Charles streets), both of which sell interesting pieces (mostly late 19th and 20th century) from various countries for reasonable prices.

JEWELRY

Jewelry is one collectible category traversed even by those who otherwise shy away from antiques and collectibles. Much interesting jewelry is available from the variety of dealers at the fairly affordable **Manhattan Art and Antiques Center** (1050 Second Avenue, at 55th Street) and at its more glamorous, less affordable sister, the **Place des Antiquaires** (125 East 57th Street, between Lexington and Park avenues). For more on these noble places, see the Antiques Centers section later in this chapter.

Expensive

Edith Weber and Company, in Place des Antiquaires, has a distinguished collection of English lovers' eyes (painted on ivory, under glass) from the turn of the 18th century. **Fred Leighton** (Trump Tower, Fifth Avenue at 56th Street; and 773 Madison Avenue, at 66th Street) has Cartier Art Deco diamonds and other signed pieces of early-20th-century jewelry, as do **Primavera** (808 Madison Avenue, between 67th and 68th streets) and **Macklowe Gallery & Modernism** (667 Madison Avenue, between 60th and 61st streets). **A La Vieille Russie** (781 Fifth Avenue, at 59th Street) carries jewels that look as if they would have fallen out of the czarina's Gladstone had she crossed the border into Finland. **James Robinson** (15 East 57th Street, between Madison and Fifth avenues) has wonderful fine jewelry in its street-level store; take the elevator up to six for more affordable Edwardian and Victorian paste, cut steel, and Scottish agate.

Less Expensive

Still less expensive antique jewelry may be found in the Village, where the **Antique Buff** (321½ Bleecker Street, between Christopher and Grove streets), **Claudia Kable Antiques** (106 MacDougal Street, between Bleecker and West 3rd streets), and its next-door neighbor **Den of Antiquity** (number 108) all offer a range of late-19th- and early-20th-century possibilities. Over at **Ouch** (96 Greenwich Avenue, between 12th and 13th streets) there is a showcase of fairly reasonably priced ancient-world rings. A few blocks to the southeast, the miniature **Once Upon A Time** (36 East 11th Street) sells old jewelry at encouraging prices. Fans of the rather overblown costume jewelry of Miriam Haskell will want to know that there are always many pieces available at **Norman Crider Antiques** (Trump Tower, Fifth Avenue at 56th Street).

Watches

Those interested in acquiring a vintage wristwatch are advised to visit **Time Will Tell** (962 Madison Avenue, between 75th and 76th streets) or **Aaron Faber** (666 Fifth Avenue, between 52nd and 53rd streets). Prices will be higher here than at the flea markets, but the shopkeeper will at least provide a guarantee.

FOLK ART

American folk art has burgeoned in popularity over the last several years, and with it has come an attendant boom in fakes and reproductions. Foreign visitors, who may never have seen a drunkard's-path quilt or yellow-ware bowl close up should exercise special caution when considering items such as these at outdoor markets. The following shops will, of course, provide annotated receipts assuring the quality and provenance of your purchases.

Downtown

At **Susan Parrish Antiques** (390 Bleecker Street, between Perry and West 11th streets) the stock approximates a veritable museum of hooked rugs, indigenous textiles, Adirondack furniture, Indian souvenir beading, and various other items in the folk-art fashion. **Cynthia Beneduce** (281 Lafayette Street, between Prince and Houston streets), in SoHo, carries much the same merchandise.

Uptown

Laura Fisher, in the Manhattan Art and Antiques Center (1050 Second Avenue, at 55th Street), is a nice person who sells hundreds of quilts and knows a lot about them. **Thos. K. Woodard** (835 Madison Avenue, between 67th and 68th streets) and **Judith James Milne** (506 East 74th Street, second floor, just east of York Avenue) both tempt the well-fixed collector with spectacular quilts and other examples of folk artistry. **Hirschl & Adler Galleries Inc.** (21 East 70th Street, at Madison Avenue) is a serious gallery where browsing is expected and purchasing is a more private affair.

CLOCKS AND LAMPS

A man walked into a New York City clock shop some years ago, looked around, saw something he favored, and brought it over to the shopkeeper. "I'll give you $300 for it," the man said. "Well, I'll tell you," said the proprietor, "I'm not going to sell it for that—Mr. Fanelli on Madison Avenue will give me at least $400 for it." "I am Mr. Fanelli," said the first gentleman, "and I will give you $300." Mr. Fanelli's shop, **Fanelli Antique Timepieces, Ltd.** (1131 Madison Avenue, near 85th Street), is the only place to go.

With the comforting tick-tock of your grandfather clock in the background you'll be tempted to spend your evenings curled up under a Victorian lamp with an issue of *The Smart Set.* Appropriate illumination can be purchased at **Louis Mattia** (980 Second Avenue, at 52nd Street) or **Barry of Chelsea** (154 Ninth Avenue, between 19th and 20th streets).

SILVER

Tudor Rose (28 East 10th Street, off University Place) and **Nelson & Nelson** (1050 Second Avenue, between 55th and 56th streets) have a sizable stock of English and American silver, including many small items (boudoir accessories, picture frames), at exceptionally reasonable prices. **Alice Kwartler Antiques**, in the Place des Antiquaires (125 East 57th Street, between Lexington and Park avenues), sells a rigorously curated collection, with a lot of things at the level of signed Tiffany dresser sets. Antique silverplate and sterling coffee and tea services, along with early flatware (sold individually or in sets), are among the specialties at the venerable **S. Wyler Inc.** (941 Lexington Avenue, at 69th Street).

ANTIQUITIES

Collectors of ancient art and objects of antiquity must pay a visit to **Royal-Athena Galleries** (153 East 57th Street, between Third and Lexington avenues), where more than 1,500 ancient sculptures, vases, and other objects (Greek, Roman, pre-Columbian, etc.) are for sale by an enthusiastic staff. In the rarefied reaches of upper Madison Avenue, between 75th and 76th streets, **Antiquarium Fine Ancient Arts Gallery** (number 948) and the **Safani Gallery** (number 960) might be worth looking into as well. **Ares Rare** (down the avenue at number 605, fourth floor), among its other jewelry offerings, features authentic ancient Greek and Roman bibelots.

RUGS AND TEXTILES

Cora Ginsburg (19 East 74th Street, third floor, between Madison and Fifth avenues; open by appointment only, Tel: 744-1352), usually whispered to be the high bidder at textile auctions, presents a scholarly collection of early examples (including rare 18th- and 19th-century day clothing, shoes, and lingerie) at her gallery. For carpets and tapestries the toney name is **Doris Leslie Blau** (15 East 57th Street, between Madison and Fifth avenues), where exceptionally high tariffs justly reflect the quality of the merchandise.

Shoppers with less money who are forced to be more flexible in their requirements might find an acceptable antique floor covering across town at the **Rug Warehouse** (220 West 80th Street, at Broadway) or just to the east at **Central Carpet** (426 Columbus Avenue, near 80th Street). Both these places usually have on hand an assortment of desirable 1920s Chinese Art Deco rugs.

Those looking for something cozy that need not be treated like a museum piece will find that the vintage Pendleton blankets and charming cushions sold at **Paula Rubenstein** (65 Prince Street, between Lafayette and Crosby streets) will bring a welcome dose of warmth to their cold-water flats.

DECORATIVE GLASSWARE AND POTTERY

A revival of interest in Tiffany, Gallé, Daum, and other art glass has priced most examples right out of the market, but those who like to look at these things should visit **Minna Rosenblatt** (844 Madison Avenue, between 69th and 70th streets). French and English cameo glass and highly collectible glass paperweights are specialties at **Leo Kaplan** (967 Madison Avenue, between 75th and 76th streets).

For the less moneyed, flea markets and travelling antiques shows remain excellent sources for early-20th-century glass and porcelain, but a careful and prudent eye is advised. (The tiniest chip, of little interest to the casual user, can devalue the object considerably.) **Susan P. Meisel Decorative Arts Gallery** (141 Prince Street, between Sullivan and MacDougal streets) holds down a corner of the world market of the British Art Deco chinaware by the eccentric artisan Clarisse Cliff.

KITCHEN AND TABLEWARE
Those collectors wishing to emulate the buying habits of the late Andy Warhol should head for **Kaleidoscope Antiques** (636 Hudson Street, at the corner of Horatio Street), where hundreds of gaudy figural cookie jars are for sale. Mid-20th-century kitchen kitsch (vegetable-shaped salt and pepper shakers, kitty-cat cruets) is sold at **Dullsville** (143 East 13th Street, between Third and Fourth avenues) and **Zero to Sixties** (72 Thompson Street, between Spring and Broome streets). Utensils for the unrenovated prewar pantry are available at **Kitschen** (15 Christopher Street). Shoppers desiring depression-era proto-American Fiestaware dishes are advised to visit **Mood Indigo** (181 Prince Street, between Thompson and Sullivan streets), where stacks in several colors and sizes are always on hand at reasonable prices.

ORIENTALIA
Bargains on authentic examples in this area may be ferreted out by experts—we have the ability only to recommend highly reputable if costly outposts. **Ralph M. Chait** (12 East 56th Street, between Fifth and Madison avenues) specializes in Chinese pottery, porcelains, and hard stones dating from the Neolithic period (2500 B.C.) through the heady days of the early 18th century. **Flying Cranes Antiques** (in the Manhattan Art and Antiques Center, 1050 Second Avenue, at 55th Street) sells cloisonné, satsuma, bronzes, and the like from both Japan and China from 1690 to 1890. Nestled in a corner of the Carlyle Hotel is **Michael B. Weisbrod** (987 Madison Avenue, between 76th and 77th streets), who carries fine Chinese works of art, including inlaid lacquer. You may require a few stiff ones at the

hotel's well-known Bemelmans Bar before you garner the confidence to sign the enormous check.

LUGGAGE

If you are perpetually on the road, visit **Eclectiques** (483 Broome Street, at Wooster Street), where you will find a large selection of rare vintage Louis Vuitton suitcases as well as antique hatboxes, Pullman cases, and other bags covered in a variety of exotic animal skins, from ostrich to elephant. You can hide your eiderdowns and hand-me-downs in a well-weathered trunk from **Home Town** (131 Wooster Street, on the corner of Prince Street).

ARCHITECTURAL SALVAGE

Furnishings that once graced the interiors of now-defunct barbershops, saloons, and ice-cream parlors now grace **Urban Archaeology** (285 Lafayette Street, between Houston and Prince streets). Smaller items in a similar vein (world's-fair standing ashtrays, old Coney Island peep-show machines) can be found down the street at **Lost City Arts** (275 Lafayette Street). Up the block and around the corner (14 Second Avenue, at East Houston Street) is an authentic urban archaeological site: **Irreplaceable Artifacts**, a market that harks back to the sack of Rome with architectural remnants, broken pediments, claw-footed bathtubs, and even the odd church pew strewn about.

Howard Kaplan's Bath Shop (47 East 12th Street, between Broadway and University Place) sells museum-quality vintage bath fixtures for shoppers who wish to perform their ablutions in the tubs, sinks, and vanities of 19th-century ruling-class France. For less precious plumbing, say a replacement knob for the hot-water faucet of your prewar pedestal sink, try **George Taylor Specialties Co.** (100 Hudson Street, near Franklin Street). Taylor's is especially helpful if you need to adapt an old fixture to modern hookups.

If you're thinking of decorating your domicile in the manner of the American home circa 1935—be it a cottage with sagging porch and cabbage-rose wallpaper or an oilcloth-covered Sears & Roebuck–furnished Bronx apartment—you will find authentic rolls of wall-coverings and linoleum at **Second Hand Rose** (270 Lafayette Street, at Prince Street).

DOLLS AND TOYS

Aficionados of old toys, games, dolls, and assorted childhood memorabilia are among the most zealous visitors to
flea markets and antiques shows, where genuine bargains
may still surface and careful searching can really pay off.
Those interested in visiting stores that specialize in this
sort of thing should take in **Second Childhood** (283
Bleecker Street, between Sixth Avenue and Seventh Avenue South) for tin toys, soldiers, and interesting, small
Celluloid dolls. **Darrow's Fun Antiques** (1101 First Avenue, near 59th Street), in the shadow of the 59th Street
Bridge and under the intermittent gaze of the Roosevelt
Island tram, sells vintage games and rarer items like big
1930s toy zeppelins.

A jumbled-up but excellent selection of dolls is for sale
at the **Antique Doll Hospital of New York** (787 Lexington
Avenue, between 61st and 62nd streets), where the proprietor is a real craftsman. ("Can I repaint a doll's eye? I can
fix anything. I am an artist.") Boyish types of any age will
probably like the **Soldier Shop** (1222 Madison Avenue,
between 88th and 89th streets) and/or **Classic Toys** (69
Thompson Street, between Spring and Broome streets),
both of which specialize in highly collectible, but not
inexpensive, antique toy soldiers and military miniatures.

ANTIQUES CENTERS

Somewhere between the unrestrained jumble of collectibles for sale at outdoor markets and a full-fledged antiques store lies the province of the antiques center—a
collection of glass-enclosed booths owner-operated by
individual dealers. There are two major centers in New
York City. The **Manhattan Art and Antiques Center** (1050
Second Avenue, at 55th Street), with 104 galleries, sells
everything from toys to rugs to objects of virtue, with a
heavy concentration on fine jewelry. The newer, smaller,
and very elegant **Place des Antiquaires** (125 East 57th
Street, between Lexington and Park avenues) contains 64
miniature shops showing admittedly expensive merchandise.

There are also a number of small, fairly diverting antiques malls in town. On weekends in Chelsea the **Metropolitan Arts & Antiques Pavilion** (110 West 19th Street,
between Sixth and Seventh avenues) offers high-quality
jewelry and other collectibles. If you find yourself strand-
ed in that shopping desert known as the East 30s, you can

seek temporary relief at the **City East Antiques Center** (201 East 31st Street, between Second and Third avenues).

AUCTION HOUSES
Those visitors possessed of steel nerves who disdain paying preordained prices for anything might care to try their hand at a Manhattan auction. These occur at **Christie's** (502 Park Avenue, at 59th Street; Tel: 546-1000 or 371-5438), **Christie's East** (219 East 67th Street, between Second and Third avenues; Tel: 606-0400), and **Sotheby's** (1334 York Avenue, at 72nd Street; Tel: 606-7000 or 606-7245) at least weekly (see also the Art chapter), and there are often interesting items at **Doyle Galleries** (175 East 87th Street, between Lexington and Third avenues; Tel: 427-2730) and **Phillips** (406 East 79th Street, between First and York avenues; Tel: 570-4830) as well. Check the advertisements in *The New York Times,* paying careful attention to notices of Christie's Collectibles or Sotheby's Arcade auctions, as these often feature lower priced, more amusing merchandise. Downtown, free-wheeling, more eclectic auctions (frequently comprising the contents of estates) take place at **Lubin Galleries** (30 West 26th Street, between Broadway and Sixth Avenue; Tel: 924-3777) and **Tepper Galleries** (110 East 25th Street, between Park and Lexington avenues; Tel: 677-5300).

MARKETS
Of course, many people eschew conventional antiques stores and the upper-class hush of auction houses entirely in favor of flea markets, antiques shows, and public auctions. For these collectors, the thrill is in the chase and the serendipity.

There are a number of year-round weekend markets in Manhattan, the most recommended being the one located in two adjacent parking lots on **Sixth Avenue** between 24th and 26th streets. Although this market is open on Saturdays, the offerings then are paltry, because for three decades this has operated mainly as a Sunday market, and dealers are by nature creatures of habit. Half the market is cordoned off and requires that you pay one dollar admission, presumably to discourage diamond thieves who might otherwise enter and have a field day. On weekends in **SoHo** a newer market at Broadway and Grand Street is developing a loyal following. Other markets include one in the schoolyard of **Public School 183**

(York Avenue and 67th Street) on Saturdays, and its superior cousin on Sundays at **P.S. 87** (Columbus Avenue and 77th Street). Both of these also have small, depressing indoor sections in school cafeterias still redolent of lunches but transformed for the weekend into collectibles dens.

SHOWS AND STREET FAIRS

There are any number of specialty shows (paper ephemera, dolls, baseball cards, etc.) and street fairs that make their way to New York City. For current listings of these, buy the Friday and Sunday editions of *The New York Times* and check the antiques classified advertisements. Shows of a more general, eclectic nature spring up all the time as well. Highbrow ones take place in fall, winter, and spring at the **Park Avenue Armory** (the winter show, in January, is the fanciest), and there is a wonderful show of more than 600 dealers held on three **Hudson River piers** each year in November and March. Once a year (March also) a huge and highly regarded collectibles show takes place on the boardwalk in **Atlantic City**, easily accessible from New York City by the buses that shuttle thousands of unregenerate gamblers to and from the Atlantic City casinos on a daily basis.

FASHION

From its earliest days as a metropolis New York displayed an enthusiasm for the culture of beauty, the cult of fashion, and the vagaries of style quite out of proportion to the circumstances of most of its residents. "I have known young ladies supporting themselves," wrote one Anne Royall in the early years of the 19th century, "sit up 'til 12 o'clock at night, to complete a suit of clothes, the proceeds of which was to purchase a fine cap, or a plume of feathers, to deck herself for church. Hundreds of those females thus maintain themselves in a style of splendor; no ladies in the city dress finer. A ten dollar hat, a thirty dollar shawl, with silk and lace, is common amongst the poorer class of females."

By the middle of the 19th century A. T. Stewart, considered the first true department store in the United States, had opened on lower Broadway, employing good-looking gentlemen to shepherd the ladies from counters of the finest European laces and linens to the revolutionary displays of ready-made cloaks and mantles. Other dry-goods stores were also expanding (many dispensing with the traditional custom of selling "wet" goods—rum—on one side of the establishment and necessities for the ladies on the other), including Lord & Taylor, which had a great currency during the Civil War years at the now almost irredeemable intersection of Grand and Chrystie streets.

As the century progressed the big stores moved uptown, erecting towering cast-iron emporiums along "Fashion Row" (Sixth Avenue from 14th to 23rd Street) and the "Ladies' Mile" (Broadway in the same area). "Meet you at the fountain!" shoppers said to one another in 1895, referring to the waterworks in front of Siegel-Cooper Dry Goods Store, Sixth Avenue at 18th Street, years before the clock at the Biltmore Hotel came into fashion. But no sooner had Fashion Row and the Ladies' Mile become firmly entrenched in the shopper's imagination than the stores pulled up stakes and moved again. (Lord & Taylor, having left the Lower East Side in 1869 for Broadway and 20th Street, packed up again in 1906 and relocated to its present Fifth Avenue location.)

Of course, not everyone dressed in silks and proper bonnets, genteelly attempting to ape their betters. There were those, then as now, who stuck their stylistic tongues out at the passing show and elected a wildly bohemian style. The Bowery G'hirls of the 1840s, with their garish yellow shawls, scarlet dresses, and giant feathers and boas, scandalized society with bold manners and ankle-length skirts (floor-dragging being the only respectable length). Now their spiritual descendants, in torn black leather, nose rings, and spiked hair, tread the same streets with identical *épater les bourgeois* intentions occupying their youthful minds.

Why is it that New York remains at the crossroads of style and fashion, decade after decade? Is it because for 150 years Manhattan has been a center of clothing manufacture, of design, of intense wholesale and retail activity? By the 1920s the clothing business had moved from its squalid cottage-industry origins to large-scale factories in the neighborhood once known as the "Tenderloin," now known as the **Garment District**—Sixth to Eighth avenues in the 30s. A noontime visit to this area will dispel any doubts the reader may harbor that Manhattan has somehow passed its peak as the apex of the fashion industry. Choking racks of clothing impede all but the hardiest pedestrian, trucks with screaming drivers stall aggressively at loading docks, and the whir of 10,000 sewing machines is dimly audible in the distance.

Today as yesterday young designers fresh from fashion school in Manhattan apprentice themselves to established designers or set up storefront couture houses on their own here. And when the time comes to show the fashion collections of the major designers, there are no "American" or "United States" collections for the press and society to flock to. The only important fashion showings this side of the Atlantic are the appropriately named, aptly situated, and justly famous New York collections.

The range and scope of fashion and fashion-accessory shops in Manhattan can overwhelm even the most stalwart shopper. In this section we have broken down the enormous number of choices into manageable subsections. We cover department stores first, because they can serve as a fine introduction to the amazing varieties of goods available in New York and are very convenient for those in town on only a flying visit. We then proceed to cover shopping by neighborhood, concentrating mainly on women's fashion. Then follow sections on men's clothing, children's fashion, discount shopping, vintage clothing, and furs. A section on shopping for accessories encompasses handbags, shoes, lingerie, scarves, hats, eyewear, umbrellas, and cosmetics. The section ends with a selection of jewelry stores.

DEPARTMENT STORES

A visitor overwhelmed by the number of small stores in New York, or desiring a crash course in the scope, price ranges, and general diversity of merchandise in Manhattan, should plunge headlong into Manhattan department-store shopping.

Those who desire hair-raising excitement can elect to visit **Macy's** (34th Street and Sixth and Seventh avenues) first—purportedly the world's largest department store and containing departments covering all of humankind's basic needs in every price range and to suit every taste. There are floors of inexpensive merchandise, but lots of less democratically priced high-fashion goods as well.

Reeling from the mobs at Macy's? Seek refuge a block south, at the new **A & S** store (899 Sixth Avenue, between 32nd and 33rd streets), which, hoping to break the curse that kills New York department stores, has optimistically opened in the spot once inhabited by the now-deceased

Gimbels. Farther north, on Fifth Avenue, **Lord & Taylor**
(424 Fifth Avenue, between 38th and 39th streets) tries
valiantly to hang on to its superlative reputation, but the
inelegance of the surrounding neighborhood has taken
its toll, and the old girl (despite an excellent collection of
American country-style clothing) is a shadow of her
former self. **Saks Fifth Avenue** (611 Fifth Avenue, between
49th and 50th streets), luckier in its location across Fifth
Avenue from Rockefeller Center and across 50th Street
from St. Patrick's Cathedral, offers a predictable cross-
section of high-quality merchandise.

Bloomingdale's (59th Street and Lexington Avenue),
which started life as an East Side bargain basement, has
transformed itself, especially over the past 20 years, into
the epitome of glamorous new-wave fashion. The entire
fourth floor is given over to individual boutiques, and the
big names—Chanel, Ungaro, St. Laurent, plus more obscure avant-gardists such as Romeo Gigli and Workers for
Freedom—evince a merchandising sensibility not to be
trifled with. The new and ultra-fashionable **Barney's**, at
Madison Avenue and 61st Street, will be giving Bloomie's
a run for its money.

Bergdorf Goodman, for years a dependable if fading
flower on the corner of 57th Street and Fifth Avenue, has
recently blossomed with a burst of excellent European
and American designer merchandise (Gaultier, Donna
Karan) in its newly renovated interior. **Henri Bendel**,
longtime home of the moneyed anorexic set, still features
lots of one-of-a-kind obscure merchandise in its innovative street-of-shops format. Bendel's new, larger quarters
in the former Rizzoli and Coty buildings (712–714 Fifth
Avenue, between 55th and 56th streets) feature spectacular Lalique window panels uncovered during renovation;
these remain on display for shoppers who like to mix a
bit of art appreciation with their pursuit of fashion. Lastly,
Francophiles are breathless at the arrival of the first
American **Galeries Lafayette**. This venerable Parisienne
occupies the empty shell of the much-mourned Bonwit
Teller (10 East 57th Street, just east of Fifth Avenue).

UPPER EAST SIDE

Holding strong at the center of the East Side shopping
firmament is **Madison Avenue**, the street of dreams for
those who wish for the best clothes from the fanciest
shops with the most uncompromising service. From 59th
Street up to 96th Street there are several stores scattered

along each block of Madison as well as on adjoining streets and some of the other avenues. To get the most out of an Upper East Side shopping tour you'll want to canvass the area on foot—taking frequent breaks for coffee (or Sherry)—then grab a taxi home or back to your hotel.

Young and Hip

For the youthful shopper there is a judiciously edited collection of European items at **Betsey, Bunky, Nini** (980 Lexington Avenue, between 71st and 72nd streets). **Joseph Tricot** (804 Madison Avenue, between 67th and 68th streets) can provide properly unserious knitwear; veer slightly off the avenue for **Emilio Pucci** (24 East 64th Street), whose garish tights and slinky, silky knits are, after more than two decades of hibernation, suddenly at the height of fashion again.

Upscale

The marginally more mature shopper cruising along Madison Avenue might prefer to buy her pullover at **Cashmere Cashmere** (number 840, between 69th and 70th streets), where styles are casual but the materials at hand are almost insufferably elegant. Down the street **Sonia Rykiel** (number 792, corner of 67th Street) plies her snug, knitted costumes (considered quite revolutionary at their introduction some 20 years ago) from a comfortable, busy store. And the phenomenally well received shoes of **Robert Clergerie** inhabit their own shop a half block off Madison at 41 East 60th Street.

Designer

Although the well-fixed but not unhip matron will probably head next for **Giorgio Armani** (815 Madison Avenue, at 68th Street) and **Gianni Versace** (number 816, across the street), both of which sell famous, luxuriously appointed Italian separates, she should also consider heading several blocks north to **Milan D'Or** (number 910, at 73rd Street), which offers less well known Italian designs, so she won't see herself coming and going at embassy cocktail parties. From his flagship town house just off Madison Avenue (21 East 69th Street) **Romeo Gigli** sells his distinctive, drooping, muted Milanese clothing. Back on Madison Avenue, **Yves St. Laurent** (number 855, between 70th and 71st streets) and **Emanuel Ungaro** (number 803, between 67th and 68th streets) offer their labels in relatively close proximity to one another. Just to the east you will find shoes by **Maud Frizon** (19 East 69th Street, between Madison and Park avenues), internationally renowned for their blend of grown-up gamin (round toes, bows) and glamour girl (gold kid, high heels).

Americans experiencing a burst of civic pride (and foreign visitors weary of encountering the same old designer merchandise in all the major cities on the globe) should visit **Polo/Ralph Lauren**, sequestered in the old Rhinelander mansion at the corner of Madison Avenue and 72nd Street (867 Madison), of interest to students of architecture and interior design as well as those in search of fashion. The old mansion still sports its original interior, the lower floors being full of Lauren clothing interspersed with antiques (both fine and homely), while the upper floors, where Ralph sells furniture and decorative accessories, stand ready with their old-fashioned bedsteads, travel trunks, lace panels, and even the occasional birdcage.

FIFTH AVENUE / 57TH STREET AREA
The area around 57th Street and Fifth Avenue, sunk deeply in myth from the time that Zelda swam in the Pulitzer Fountain and the morning Holly broke fast at Tiffany's, remains for many the cosmopolitan center of the universe, and the shops fanning out in all directions do nothing to disabuse them of this notion.

Fifth Avenue North from 50th Street
Those who wish to approach this zenith from a southerly direction should begin their walking tour at **Saks Fifth Avenue**, on Fifth Avenue between 49th and 50th streets. With St. Patrick's Cathedral across 50th Street and Rockefeller Center rising across the avenue, this area gives the shopper plenty of opportunities for sightseeing as well. Though this stretch of Fifth Avenue lacks the stupendous allure it once held, there are still some excellent shops, including **Mario Valentino** (number 645, at 51st Street), **Ferragamo** (number 717, at 56th Street), and **Fendi** (number 720, across the street), all featuring Italian clothing and leather goods. At **Goldpfeil** (number 711, at 55th Street) hued Gladstones from Germany gladden the fashionable arms of the wealthy, worldly set. Anglophiles should visit **Aquascutum of London** (number 680, at 54th Street) to pick up one of the firm's indestructible raincoats. Directly off Fifth Avenue, at 15 West 55th Street, the

international coterie that follows the fancy footwork of the shoemaker **Manolo Blahnik** will find a shop devoted to his designs. Shoppers devoted to the shriekingly chic regardless of cost should visit the legendary **Martha** (720 Fifth Avenue, at 56th Street), where the attentive *vendeuses* act as if they've just stepped out of an Audrey Hepburn movie.

Readers as yet unconvinced that Mr. Mencken spoke the truth when he asserted that "no one ever lost money underestimating the taste of the American people" can dispel any lingering doubts with a visit to **Trump Tower** (725 Fifth Avenue, at 56th Street). This pink marble and waterfall-encrusted edifice, attended by embarrassed-looking security guards dressed in Gilbert and Sullivan costumes, actually contains a few not uninteresting shops (Asprey, Charles Jourdan, etc.). And you can now escape directly into the French department store Galeries Lafayette (see Department Stores, above) and then into the pleasant greenhouse atmosphere of the IBM Building's atrium.

Along 57th Street

A half-block detour to the west of Fifth Avenue will lead you to **Charivari 6**, at 18 West 57th Street, considered by many connoisseurs to be the best of the Charis, with four floors of designer merchandise plus the video screens, good-looking salespersons, and blaring music some people consider indispensable company when they spend their money. Next door, at **Susan Bennis Warren Edwards** (number 22), suitably exotic, expensive footwear is dispensed.

East of Fifth Avenue, 57th Street easily maintains its reputation as one of the city's prime shopping areas. **Chanel** (at number 5; the company waited a long time for this particular address) sells its famous collarless brass-buttoned suits, but there is also a full range of makeup and accessories available (including the quilted bag) for those wishing to commit a few hundred rather than a few thousand. The popular **Ann Taylor** (number 3) has reasonably priced, stylish clothing, a glass elevator, and a highly regarded shoe department. **Laura Ashley** (number 21) specializes in the maid-of-the-moors look, with its flowery prints, high-waisted dresses, puffy sleeves, and sashes. For a more androgynous appeal, turn instead to **Burberry's Ltd.** (number 9) or **Jaeger** (number 19), both of which will accoutre the serious person, with not a sprig in sight. At **Matsuda** (just north of 57th Street, at 465 Park Avenue) the clothes are World War I as filtered through the artistic sensibility of modern Tokyo; while the palette is sober and conservative, the prices are not.

UPPER WEST SIDE

Once, not so long ago, the Upper West Side was a shabby-genteel neighborhood, full of butcher, hardware, liquor, and shoe-repair shops. Then came the co-ops, and the traditional stores found themselves replaced by boutiques selling antiques and arugula. Lately the more esoteric of these shops are beginning to disappear, in favor of branches of European clothing chains and fancy ice-cream depots.

Charivari 72 (corner of 72nd Street and Columbus Avenue) deals in high-priced men's and women's big-name European clothing from its triplex shop. (The Charivari shops were among the first fancy stores to open on the Upper West Side and have since reaped the profits of their prescience.) Among the other offerings spread out along **Columbus Avenue** you might like **Sacha London** (number 294, at 74th Street), for interesting shoes with low prices, or **French Connection** (number 304, between 74th and 75th streets), for hip, collegiate clothing. Those with more exotic tastes should look into **Street Life** (number 422, at 81st Street), which has a house line of oversize cotton shirts and smocks, with a lot of items in the rare under-$100 range. At **Angel Heart** (number 410, between 79th and 80th streets) full-cut folksy country-girl garments predominate. **Charivari Workshop** (number 441, across the street from the American Museum of Natural History) is especially strong in the area of gender-neutral clothing from Japan. Over on Amsterdam Avenue **Nana** (number 414, between 79th and 80th streets) sells Dr. Martens and other post-punk bohemian footwear.

CHELSEA

Chelsea has experienced something of a renaissance lately, and now qualifies as a fairly serious hunting ground for the fashion-minded traveller. **Barney's** (Seventh Avenue and 17th Street) remains the most important reason to travel to Chelsea for shopping (Barney's recently opened a store at 660 Madison Avenue, between 60th and 61st streets, so uptowners needn't make the trek at all), and although its six floors of very stylish, very desirable European and American clothing, shoes, and accessories for men and women are intriguing, the consistently high tariffs have left tourists and natives alike stampeding to the elevators and into the street. Still, all the major (and a lot of the minor) labels are represented, and the physical setting is impressive. If you're down here to sightsee rather than shop, you won't want to miss Barney's store-window displays. The decidedly secular holiday-season windows are so wild they often make the evening news.

After Barney's, you can walk east a few blocks to **Fifth Avenue** in the teens, an area that is experiencing definite retail revival. The avenue boasts two recently opened sartorial palaces: **Emporio Armani** (number 110, at 16th Street), with its house line of somewhat less expensive (but hardly inexpensive) Armani clothing from Italy, and the even newer flagship shop of **Matsuda** (number 156, between 20th and 21st streets), featuring high-priced, but undeniably interesting, avant-garde Japanese clothing. Here you will also find **Joan and David** (number 104, at 16th Street), selling their wildly popular, yet classic, footwear; and the excellent **C. P. Company** (number 175, at 23rd Street), where racks of Italian men's clothing hang on hallowed ground—the apex of the Flatiron Building.

WEST VILLAGE

For almost a hundred years the words "Greenwich Village" have conjured images of bedraggled painters starving in attics, bearded poets ranting in parks, and bohemian wine parties of astonishing debauch. Visitors in search of this lost world will reel in horror at the reality of streets full of squeaky-clean suburban teenagers and nice respectable couples pushing baby carriages where once the middle classes feared to tread.

Still, it is possible, with a little determination, to uncover a few interesting shops in these confines, especially along **8th Street**, which is crammed with tiny clothing stores and innumerable affordable and highly stylish shoe stores. **Patricia Field** (10 East 8th Street, between Fifth Avenue and University Place), despite its proper-sounding name, has some of the weirdest, most uncompromising getups to be found around town (clothes like this must be in demand, as there's a new Patricia Field shop nearby, at 408 Sixth Avenue, between 8th and 9th streets). At **Untitled** (26 West 8th Street, between Fifth and Sixth avenues) the items are upper-crust British rock star, and the designs lean heavily to the brocaded waistcoat and the odd, displaced ruffle. **Capezio**'s upper floors (177 MacDougal Street, just off 8th Street) contain appropriate outfits for the aspiring ballerina or black-clad modern dancer.

Various other Village outposts can outfit visitors of differing types. **Ibiza** (42 University Place, between 9th and 10th streets) sells clothing suited for the rich hippie whose taste is rooted in yesteryear, such as 1930s-influenced printed rayon dresses and long skirts. For reasonably priced, stylish, youthful clothes, you should not miss the huge and justly famous **Reminiscence** (74 Fifth Avenue, between 13th and 14th streets), located at the very northernmost tip of what is considered Greenwich Village, but well worth the walk.

EAST VILLAGE

The undeniably shabby East Village, with its tottering tenements, luncheon counters, and crackpots of every persuasion, nonetheless pulls like a magnet at the heart of every would-be hipster from Bangkok to Bailey's Beach. The shops, as you would expect, are tiny, eccentric, ever-changing holes-in-the-wall—some cluttered, some streamlined by recent art-school graduates, all selling things either stitched up on the home sewing machine or hammered together in a garret (or perhaps specially ordered from the wilds of punkdom in the United Kingdom).

Ian's (5 St. Mark's Place, between Second and Third avenues) is home to the heavy-metal aficionado, though it may be possible to turn up something like a fuchsia mohair sweater mixed in with the spikes and chains. **Ponica** (325 East 5th Street, between First and Second avenues), comfortingly located next to the local police precinct house, sells transparent, drifting dresses suitable for the Mad Hatter's tea party.

SOHO

Once purely a center for painting, sculpture, and performance art (and, for a century before that, a warehouse district with a lingering reputation of 19th-century licentiousness), SoHo in the past few years has come to rival Madison Avenue as a place to view, purchase, and parade around in expensive, interesting clothes. Stores open, close, and replace one another with dizzying rapidity down here, because of the spiraling rents and the shifting buying moods of the crowd.

A shopping tour of SoHo might begin on West Broad-

way and proceed south, with forays to the east on Prince
and Spring streets. Thompson Street, one block west of
West Broadway, also has some likely stops for the visiting
shopper. Most of the best shopping in SoHo is north of
Spring Street, but there are also a handful of decent shops
below.

West Broadway and Points East

Your first stop on West Broadway as you descend into
SoHo might be **If** (number 470, near Houston Street),
which features an outstanding selection of European
clothing, with labels running the gamut from Azzedine
Alaïa to Zoran, with Clergerie shoes and Gaultier corse-
lets wedged between. **Nicole Farhi** (435 West Broadway,
at Prince Street) has Frenchified clothes for a woman who
works as an executive in the towering glass monsters of
Montparnasse. Suitable clothing for this entrepreneur's
secretary, or her lycée-attending daughter, is available at
Agnès B. (116–118 Prince Street, between Greene and
Wooster streets). Also on Prince Street, **Tootsie Plohound**
(number 110, at Greene Street) sells clunky beribboned
clodhoppers, many with the obligatory serrated rubber
sole, which many people think look great with droopy,
flappy Japanese costumes. Even wilder shoes are available down the street at **John Fluevog** (number 104, between Mercer and Greene streets), where the platformed
monstrosities shriek Saturday Night Fever on Carnaby
Street.

   Visitors anxious to spend more money should head
westward a block and a half and then down Wooster Street,
where **Comme des Garçons** (number 116, between Prince
and Spring streets) holds forth with its world-renowned
collection of Rei Kawakubo–designed esoterica, including
oddly shaped and sized coats, shirts, dresses, and accessories. The enpixilated American clothing at **Morgan Le Fay**
(151 Spring Street, between Wooster Street and West
Broadway), fashionable in an otherworldly way, would suit
a giant sprite who moonlights as an office worker. Head up
Wooster to find **J. Morgan Puett** (number 140, near Houston Street), which specializes in giant linen smocks, perfect for the shopper who takes her fashion cues from
Millet's *Gleaners*.

West of West Broadway

Thompson Street, one block west of West Broadway, features a number of smaller shops with growing reputa-

tions. **Betsey Johnson** (number 130, between Prince and Houston streets) sells weird skintight clothes for shoppers young enough to be amused by such things. The offerings at **FDR Drive** (number 109, between Prince and Spring streets) include fine gabardine 1930s- and 1940s-influenced separates and oversize, unisex printed rayon shirts, all of which are made from authentic vintage fabric. **Peter Fox** (number 105, on the same block) carries shoes with curved court heels and delicately laced napes. Not far to the east is **Agi Brooks** (192 Spring Street, between Sullivan and Thompson streets), which specializes in round-collared, padded-shoulder affairs for a Joan Crawford-as-Claudine-à-l'école look.

South of Spring Street
Head south on Thompson to reach Broome Street, where you'll find **Pastec** (number 459, between Mercer and Greene streets), whose exquisitely delicate Italian pullovers and cardigans lie supine on huge wooden display tables. A couple of blocks southeast, **Yohji Yamamoto** (103 Grand Street, on the corner of Mercer Street) features a line of clothing similar in price and drape to the oddments at Comme des Garçons (though fans of the two will turn purple with rage at the allegation that these two giants are at all comparable).

Broadway
If you choose to work your way out of SoHo by walking north up Broadway, you'll find the offerings slightly scruffier than those along its western counterpart. **Street Life** (number 470, between Broome and Grand streets), which has colorful drapey blouses to top leggings, and **Canal Jean Co.** (number 504, between Spring and Broome streets), featuring tee-shirts and cotton jerseys in every color imaginable among its countless offerings, are two good stops.

MEN'S CLOTHING
Traditional
The main line of gentlemen's clothiers is in the area of Madison Avenue in the lower 40s. Here are **Brooks Brothers** (346 Madison Avenue, at 44th Street), justly famous, predictably conservative, surprisingly affordable; **Paul Stuart** (southwest corner of Madison and 45th Street), more ambitious merchandise; and **F. R. Tripler** (366 Madison, at 46th Street), for old-fashioned items including the hard-

to-find gentleman's Edwardian nightshirt. If you are looking for the loud, off-center style peculiar to the American country-club denizen, investigate **Chipp** (342 Madison, near 44th Street), for club ties depicting 90-plus breeds of dogs, or **J. Press** (7 East 44th Street), for indescribable madras-plaid patchwork baggy trousers.

Farther uptown, the **Custom Shirt Shop** (618 Fifth Avenue, between 49th and 50th streets, and other locations) makes chemises to order, as the name would indicate. At **Sulka** (430 Park Avenue, at 55th Street) the extremely refined goods are strictly for the silk-undies set. Cashmere robes here are $700 plus, but an ascot might prove affordable—and makes a lovely souvenir. **Burberry's Ltd.** (9 East 57th Street) has the plaid-lined raincoats synonymous with its name. The gentleman traveller should be aware that **Bergdorf Goodman** has opened a huge new men's store directly across the street from their flagship at 57th Street and Fifth Avenue. The offerings include boutiques devoted to Charvet (France), Turnbull and Asser (England), and Romeo Gigli (Italy). Mildly eccentric, but by no means ridiculous, sports clothes are available at **New Republic Clothiers** in SoHo (93 Spring Street, between Broadway and Mercer Street).

Designer

For a new shirt to wear home visit the American outpost of English designer **Paul Smith** (108 Fifth Avenue, at 16th Street), which specializes in oversize shirts with unusual details. For the blue-blooded American prep-school look—studied but chic sloppiness—drop by **Polo/Ralph Lauren** (867 Madison Avenue, at 72nd Street), where you'll feel as if you've stepped into your ancestral home. Profligate guys who must be the cynosure of all eyes can fulfill that intention with a new outfit from that wildly admired Italian, **Giorgio Armani** (815 Madison Avenue, between 68th and 69th streets). For Armani-philes with rather smaller purses, **Emporio Armani** (110 Fifth Avenue, at 16th Street) has less serious, less expensive items, while **A/X Armani Exchange** (568 Broadway, at Prince Street) sells the cheapest and most casual Armanis of all.

Hip

An entirely different sort of man, who looks as if he rolled out of a haystack dressed in the same black sweat shirt and jeans you've seen him in for 20 years, may also be a secret shopper—albeit of a radically different persuasion.

His requisite leather jacket can be purchased at the **N.Y. Leather Co.** (33 Christopher Street, between Sixth and Seventh avenues). On the rare occasion (his wedding day?) that this guy dresses up, he might consent to wear a neo-1940s outfit (pleated pants, gabardine shirt) from an excellent in-house collection at **FDR Drive Men** (80 Thompson Street, at Spring Street).

Surfer guys with biker tendencies will like the baggies, caps, and leathers at **Stüssy** (104 Prince Street, between Greene and Mercer streets). **Ian's** (5 St. Mark's Place, between Second and Third avenues), which he will surely saunter past on his nocturnal treks to the East Village, will happily accoutre the aspiring rock star. If he suddenly wins the local lottery or has a successful day at the races, the visitor might enjoy a shopping trip to the elegant, austere **Comme des Garçons** (116 Wooster Street, between Prince and Spring streets), **Yohji Yamamoto** (103 Grand Street, at the corner of Mercer Street), or **Matsuda** (461 Park Avenue, between 57th and 58th streets, and 156 Fifth Avenue, between 20th and 21st streets), all of which feature expensive, extreme, avant-garde designs from Japan.

Finally, the man whose sartorial style was fixed for all time during his freshman year at the University of Wisconsin circa 1968 (or the University of London, or Sydney, or the Sorbonne) will find everything he requires down among the canteens, gas masks, and goggles at the **New York Army & Navy Stores** (221 East 59th Street, between Third and Second avenues, and other branches) or at **Weiss and Mahoney** (142 Fifth Avenue, at 19th Street).

See the Discount Shopping section, below, for lower-priced menswear.

CHILDREN'S FASHIONS

The fairly recent but undeniably virulent national obsession with childbirth, babies, and their attendant requirements has spawned a serious increase in the number of stores serving small persons in Manhattan. Wee shops with teensy, adorable names are springing up all over, and autos with Baby on Board signs trudge from the East River to the Hudson and back in search of the perfect snowsuit and the most elegant bunny pajamas.

If you are travelling with a child or know one at home you'd like to buy something for, you will soon find that the New York kiddie market divides itself into two distinct branches: one approximating the taste of the (pre–Fergie and Di) British royal family—a lot of tartan plaid, velvet collars, and patent-leather Mary Janes—and its polar opposite, a sort of 1960s redux, with the prevailing themes being tie-dyed or painted tee-shirts and bib overalls.

Traditional

Those shopping for the former style should visit **Liberty of London** (630 Fifth Avenue, at 51st Street), where printed smocked dresses with round collars and sashes are available for fruity little girls. **Cerutti** (807 Madison Avenue, between 67th and 68th streets) has French and Italian items as well as things from England, and will suitably attire the luckless little pretender to one or another royal throne. Miniature men can be happily fitted out at **Boy Oh Boy** (18 East 17th Street, between Broadway and Fifth Avenue), not far from the discount menswear shops strung along lower Fifth Avenue. Readers who resent spending a week's wages on an outfit consisting of a quarter-yard of fabric should stop down at **Klein's of Monticello**, on the Lower East Side (105 Orchard Street), where heavily discounted, high-toned European children's clothes have been available for years.

Funky

Converts to the Woodstock school of children's fashion will find diminutive hipster clothing at **Space Kiddets** (46 East 21st Street, between Park Avenue and Broadway). **Dinosaur Hill** (302 East 9th Street, at Second Avenue) is a preeminent tee-shirt source, and **Peanut Butter & Jane** (617 Hudson Street, between 12th and Jane streets) will outfit a child appropriately for West Village life. Miniature Bianca Jaggers who wear baby Maud Frizons and seek outfits to match may like the selection at **Bebe Thompson** (98 Thompson Street, between Prince and Spring streets).

The **Upper West Side**, every other resident of which seems to be pushing a pram, sports a number of likely children's emporiums, including **Greenstones et Cie** (442 Columbus Avenue, at 81st Street), which specializes in whimsical hats and elfin slippers, and **Shoofly** (465 Amsterdam Avenue, just north of 82nd Street), featuring an array of shoes ranging from the silly-but-serviceable (green rubber boots with frog faces) to the whimsically sensible (bright red Mary Janes embroidered with letters of the alphabet).

DISCOUNT SHOPPING

Visitors who are incorrigible, incurable bargain hunters, or those temporarily overawed by the bold, unblinkingly high price tags that pass for normal in Manhattan, will be happy to know that there is a shadow world of shopping in New York, where bare metal racks and dusty linoleum floors yield delectable merchandise at genuinely encouraging prices.

Chelsea

In these hidden districts of the city, no one ever pays full price for anything. Tentatively acclimate yourself to lower prices by visiting the area of lower Fifth Avenue between 16th and 23rd streets for off-price menswear, where **Moe Ginsburg** (number 162) is prototypical. In the same area, but not solely for men, is **Daffy's** (111 Fifth Avenue, corner of 18th Street), whose motto is "Clothing Bargains for Millionaires." The three full floors may indeed yield possibilities for intrepid hunters who don't mind communal fitting rooms. Try West 14th Street for extremely cheap, appealing children's clothes, especially **Bunnie's Children's Department Store** at number 116 (between Sixth and Seventh avenues).

Lower East Side

Thus primed, plunge headlong into the land that time forgot, the bargain center of the universe—the creaking but thriving, ancient Lower East Side neighborhood of **Orchard Street**, where the impoverished and the savvy bargain hunter have met for the past 100 years. (For the most part, the district is open every day but Saturday; Sunday is the day for lovers of hyperactive crowds and screeching, henpecked proprietors.) Lots of the neighborhood's stores confine themselves to ordinary merchandise, but a few break out with high-class, high-style European designer goods. Extraordinarily chic shoes, all heavily discounted if not absurdly cheap, are carried by the **Lace-Up Shoe Shop** (110 Orchard Street, at Delancey Street). Shoppers willing to stand in line (sometimes extending outside the door) may reward themselves with a name-brand off-price handbag from the famous **Fine & Klein** (119 Orchard Street, just off Delancey Street).

Discount Stores

Of course, some people blanch at the highly charged atmosphere of the Lower East Side. These visitors might prefer several of the other discounters scattered throughout Manhattan. Young women, or those who have preserved the physiques of their younger selves, might like the offerings at **Strawberry** (129 East 42nd Street, at Lexington Avenue, and all over town) or **Joyce Leslie** (20 University Place, at 8th Street, and numerous other locations), both of which specialize in very inexpensive, up-to-the-minute imitations of designer merchandise. The offerings at **Bolton's** (27 West 57th Street, between Fifth and Sixth avenues, and other locations) are usually more grown up.

The more bohemian reader will prefer the **Canal Jean Co.** (504 Broadway, between Spring and Broome streets), a cavernous hole-in-the-wall near New York University with an immense collection of hip, cheap things. Young gentlemen of the painter-writer-filmmaker persuasion can purchase suitable outfits here as well. Lots of New Yorkers, regardless of age, income level, and fashion philosophy, seem to love the basic sportswear for sale at the multitudinous **Gap, Gap Kids**, and **Baby Gap** stores— though the Gap is not a classic discount house, prices are wonderfully low and the back-to-basics clothing is extremely well made. Some of the larger Gap outlets are at 86th Street and Broadway on the Upper West Side, 86th Street and Madison Avenue on the Upper East Side, West 57th Street between Eighth Avenue and Broadway, and Sixth Avenue and West 4th Street in the Village.

Fashion connoisseurs with more taste than money might wish to investigate the unpretentious **Dollar Bill** (99 East 42nd Street, between Park and Lexington avenues), specializing in off-price Italian fashions. The shop is not breathtakingly cheap, but it does feature impressive merchandise. More adventurous visitors should stake out **Century 21** (22 Cortlandt Street, between Broadway and Church Street, in lower Manhattan), where, despite a frustrating no-trying-on-allowed policy, the high-style French and Italian merchandise is snapped off the racks.

Shoppers who wish to experience a genuine Third World bazaar atmosphere while remaining on the isle of Manhattan should head for one of the **Conway** stores (225 West 34th Street, at Eighth Avenue, and other locations), where overstuffed hausfraus and irascible teenagers compete for groaning racks of ridiculously inexpensive merchandise. The offerings spill right out of the giant plate-glass, garage-type doors, covering adjacent sidewalks and encroaching on neighboring storefronts. The resultant bulging pink paper shopping bags can be seen draped over the arms of bus and subway riders all over town.

VINTAGE CLOTHING

The popularity of vintage clothing, which began its world-wide ascendance in the 1960s, has hung on with surprising tenacity in New York City. Many of the locals pride themselves on dressing funny and find that their innate taste and "ideas" about clothing, usually crippled by their lack of funds, can find full expression at the secondhand store.

Greenwich Village

There are fine antique clothes (1920s through 1940s, excellent condition and presentation) at **Stella Dallas** (218 Thompson Street, between Bleecker and West 3rd streets), **O'Mistress Mine** (143 Seventh Avenue South, at the corner of Charles Street), and the vintage racks at the always appealing **Reminiscence** (74 Fifth Avenue, at 13th Street).

Visitors too young to remember the 1960s might be seduced by some fashions from that long-lost decade. Stacks of these wearables are available at the inexpensive **Screaming Mimi** (22 East 4th Street, near Lafayette Street). **Cheap Jacks** (841 Broadway, between 13th and 14th streets) features lower-priced rough-and-tumble merchandise whose condition is often dubious—but you are sometimes able to uncover a diamond in the rough.

SoHo

Harriet Love (126 Prince Street, between Greene and Wooster streets), the grandmother of antique-clothing stores in New York, now stocks a variety of new clothing along with the special old pieces (beaded jackets, cashmere sweaters, rayon dresses) for which she is so justly famous. Madame Liza of **Liza's Place** (132 Thompson Street, between Houston and Prince streets) boasts that her shop sells authentic Chanels and Schiaparellis, but even when these are not in evidence you will find unparalleled beaded flapper dresses among her permanent collection. (By appointment only; Tel: 477-6027.) At **Alice Underground** (481 Broadway, between Broome and Grand streets, and 380 Columbus Avenue, at 78th Street, on the

Upper West Side) the surroundings are more casual and price tags are extremely reasonable.

Uptown
At **Jana Starr/Jean Hoffman Antiques** (236 East 80th Street, between Second and Third avenues) there is a preponderance of Victorian white-work and hard-to-find accompanying accessories such as boudoir caps and early satin dancing shoes. (These ladies outfit a lot of weddings, graduations, and christenings, and thus provide a high level of service—with prices to match.)

East Village
Shoppers seeking to spend very little money will be quite happy visiting **Andy's Chee-Pees** (16 West 8th Street, between Fifth Avenue and MacDougal Street), where the quality is often commensurate with the price. Among the other inexpensive possibilities in this neighborhood is the long-lived **Love Saves the Day** (119 Second Avenue, at 7th Street).

FURS
The fur coat, once strictly the province of the moneyed classes and once emblematic of female sophistication and implied indolence, is no longer synonymous with the life of leisure. It has been embraced by the working woman, the gentleman stroller, and even the (fur) swaddled babe in arms. Though animal-rights activists demonstrate and pass out leaflets all winter long, the first cool day in New York City still finds a segment of the populace bundled neck-to-ankle in fur.

Less Expensive Furs
Reasonably priced middlebrow coats are available all over town, but the stoical of heart are urged to take on the **fur district**, a shabby stretch of Seventh Avenue in the high 20s where office buildings bursting with innumerable showrooms and workshops sell coats in various price ranges, depending on the skins in question and the complexity of design. The fur district has the aura of a wholesale-only operation, but many (most) of the businesses are more than happy to entertain the retail customer. **Steven Corn Furs** (145 West 28th Street, ground floor, between Sixth and Seventh avenues) is huge and bustling and will keep the undecided customer occupied for hours. At **Harry Kirshner** (307 Seventh Avenue, fourth

floor, between 27th and 28th streets), a typical factory/ salesroom operation, the service is unusually cordial and solicitous. Uptown, the **Fur Vault** (41 West 57th Street, between Fifth and Sixth avenues) sells a wide range (from under $1,000) of fur jackets and coats; some of the less expensive models are conspicuously stylish.

Expensive Furs

Shoppers intent on owning one of the shearling sheepskin coats that are now popular should visit **MacDouglas** (645 Madison Avenue, between 59th and 60th streets) for high-fashion styles from France, or **New York Leather Co.** (33 Christopher Street, at Waverly Place), which features *outré* shearling outerwear to suit the adventurous dresser of either sex. Those who wish to disguise their politically incorrect lust for fur should head to the venerable **Sprei Frères** (725 Madison Avenue, between 63rd and 64th streets), where there are sportif woollen anoraks with hidden fur interiors. To examine the dramatic, groundbreaking designs that have left fur fanatics breathless over the past several years, don't hesitate to visit the coats at **Fendi** (720 Fifth Avenue, at 56th Street), even if potential purchase (never under $10,000) remains remote.

ACCESSORIES

If, as has been alleged, God is in the details, then surely your outfit, whether at home or abroad, would benefit from a few distinguished accessories. These popular items (scarves, hats, gloves, handbags, etc.) have an additional benefit as souvenirs, since any size will fit the recipient; they are available over the complete spectrum of prices, and, most important, they are usually small and travel well.

Handbags and Briefcases

Because of their currency in both business and fashion, handbags and briefcases of surprising beauty and interest are available all over town.

Traditional. If utility is paramount: **Coach** (342 Madison Avenue, at 44th Street; and South Street Seaport) has softly tailored American leather products, and **Lederer** (613 Madison Avenue, at 58th Street) has classic French styles. At **Ghurka** (41 East 57th Street, between Park and Madison avenues) the baggage and handbags seem to have been faintly influenced by the tastes of long-lost colonial Britain. The adored status symbol known as the

Kelly bag is available (well, you may have to back-order it) at the stratospheric **Hermès** (11 East 57th Street, between Madison and Fifth avenues). Savvy New Yorkers know that **J. S. Suarez** (26 West 54th Street, between Fifth and Sixth avenues) sells the most convincing replicas of these bags, although prices here aren't exactly bargain-basement either. At the old-line **Crouch & Fitzgerald** (400 Madison Avenue, at 48th Street) traditional styles crowd the first floor, while upstairs the complete line of Louis Vuitton items waits in chains. (Crouch was the first place in town to carry L.V., years before it assumed its current popularity.)

High-Fashion. Higher-priced fashionable bags are available from **Bottega Veneta** (635 Madison Avenue, between 59th and 60th streets), which also carries especially impressive small leather goods (wallets, card cases, etc.)—but beware of scorching prices. Likewise, **Loewe** (711 Madison Avenue, at 63rd Street) and **Prada Milan** (45 East 57th Street, between Park and Madison avenues) stock distinctive, expensive handbags, attachés, and smalls. More youthful designs are sold by the famous French house **La Bagagerie** (727 Madison Avenue, at 64th Street). The even more ambitiously stylish should seek out the Italian **Furla** (just down the street, at 705 Madison Avenue). Downtown, **Il Bisonte** sells its signature bleached-calf accessories in SoHo (72 Thompson Street, between Spring and Broome streets). Among an impressive array of items made up from quilted, printed Provençal fabrics, **Pierre Deux** (870 Madison Avenue, at 71st Street) offers commodious duffel bags suitable for weekends in the Hamptons. And for those willing to cash in their airline tickets and stow away for the trip home, **Bergdorf Goodman** (Fifth Avenue and 57th Street) carries Barry Kieselstein Cord's incomparable reticules, made of the finest alligator skins and embellished with gold-plated lizard heads and four miniature splay-toed gold feet.

Shoes

It sometimes seems that even if each resident bought a thousand pairs, the combined effort would not be able to support the number of shoe stores flourishing in Manhattan. Although quite a few booteries are scattered elsewhere throughout this chapter (mainly in the neighborhood sections), the true shoe enthusiast should not fail to visit **West 34th Street** between Fifth and Sixth avenues and **West 8th Street** between the same avenues. Both thoroughfares are crowded with shoe shops, and while styles there are always up-to-date, corresponding price tags are unassuming.

Custom-made Shoes. Shoe-lovers who have come to New York expressly to find items they can't locate at home will find a number of venues that specialize in the creation and fitting of custom-made footwear. At **Vogel**, staked out in the same location for more than a hundred years (19 Howard Street, near Lafayette Street, just north of Canal), the specialty of the house is made-to-measure boots. For exquisite slippers, the likes of which you rarely see outside of a Marlene Dietrich movie, go to **Mathias** (17 East 45th Street, fourth floor, between Fifth and Madison avenues). Bring thousands, not hundreds.

Lingerie

Visitors who possess a sentimental longing for underthings of the past will enjoy the neo-Victorian, neo-hippie look of lingerie at **Michelle Nicole Wesley** (26 West 17th Street, between Fifth and Sixth avenues). Plenty of pristine white cotton, tiny satin bows, and seed pearls are in evidence, and there is usually a corner piled high with crushed velvet items as well. Exquisite hosiery—forest green cashmere tights, nearly transparent scarlet stockings—is the specialty at **Fogal** (with stores at 510 and 680 Madison Avenue, near 53rd and 62nd streets, respectively). The specialty is handmade pure-silk camisoles and drawers at **Montenapoleone** (789 Madison Avenue, between 66th and 67th streets), popular with daughters of deposed dictators, and **La Lingerie** (792 Madison Avenue, at 67th Street), beloved by movie stars and/or wives of movie moguls. If you have insufficient funds for those, you should visit **Victoria's Secret** (34 East 57th Street, between Park and Madison avenues), where items in satin and faux silk materials are glamorously cut and reasonably priced. Saucier readers might prefer **Enelra**, in the East Village (48½ East 7th Street, between First and Second avenues), specializing in naughty but friendly garter belts and bustiers.

Scarves

For that prototypical souvenir, the silk scarf, many travellers visit **Hermès** (11 East 57th Street, between Madison and Fifth avenues) or **Gucci** (685 Fifth Avenue, at 54th Street), where the haut bourgeois merchandise is always dependable. The slightly more original shopper might prefer to travel down to the East Village, where a few surviving nativist shops still sell brightly colored, floral printed, wool challis Ukrainian peasant scarves out of piles of cardboard boxes stacked up on ancient, creaking showcases.

Hats

Though only a decade ago it seemed as if the custom millinery business in New York was all but dead and buried, the corpse has in fact been resuscitated over the past few years, and a couple of establishments can actually be described as thriving. **Lola Millinery** (2 East 17th Street, just off Fifth Avenue), in particular, has a number of appealing designs—ranging from the winsome to the downright strange—and will listen to and attempt to incorporate your suggestions into her work.

Eyewear

Horn-rimmed or tortoiseshell-framed spectacles (as well as some other examples of the most stylish eyeglasses in the city) are available at **Joël Name** (65 West Houston Street, between Wooster Street and West Broadway; and 353 Bleecker Street, between Charles and West 10th streets), **Robert Marc** (190 Columbus Avenue, between 68th and 69th streets; and 1046 Madison Avenue, between 79th and 80th streets), and the extremely fashion-forward **Alain Mikli** (100 Fifth Avenue, at 15th Street). Sinister sunglasses can be selected from an array at **Shades of the Village** (33 Greenwich Avenue, near West 10th Street), for those who prefer to appear inscrutable.

Umbrellas

The best stop for umbrellas in all of Manhattan is an easy choice, **Uncle Sam** (161 West 57th Street, between Sixth and Seventh avenues), which has been unfurling them for almost 130 years. You can also pick up a distinguished-looking walking stick or cane here.

Cosmetics

Boyd Chemists (655 Madison Avenue, between 60th and 61st streets), despite its elegant location, is anything but subdued—the wildly enthusiastic, overly made-up sales staff will push products on you no matter how reluctant you are to buy. The selection is impressive (it includes hard-to-find foreign brands), and there is a spectacular array of hair accessories, leaning heavily toward the fake tortoise and rhinestone variety and hailing mainly from France.

Downtown at **Kiehl's** (109 Third Avenue, between 13th and 14th streets), considerations of health outweigh those of glamour. The store sells a house brand of potions and ointments, and many New Yorkers swear by their efficacy. The new **Origins Natural Resources** store (767 Fifth Avenue, between 58th and 59th streets) sells a popular line of crèmes and lotions to suit the moods of the most capricious skin. **Caswell-Massey** (518 Lexington Avenue, at 48th Street), the oldest pharmacy in the city, also has a private label and the accompanying claque of enthusiastic fans.

To renovate your complexion with a complete and rigorous workout, call for an appointment at **Georgette Klinger** (501 Madison Avenue, between 52nd and 53rd streets; Tel: 744-6900) or **Janet Sartin** (480 Park Avenue, between 58th and 59th streets; Tel: 751-5858); either of these ladies will slather, slap, and massage your face in accordance with her particular expensive regimen.

JEWELRY

Fifth Avenue Gems

Many of the old-line jewelry houses may claim at least partial responsibility for lending the words "Fifth Avenue" their international connotation of wealth and glamour. **Cartier**, snug in its landmark building at the corner of 52nd Street, remains hushed and intimidating to all but the most brazen and well-heeled shopper. **Tiffany's** (at the corner of 57th Street), by contrast, exudes a bustling, almost egalitarian air. (Take the elevator to two for less expensive silver items, still packaged in the famous Tiffany blue box and brought to you from the stockroom by an antiquated system of dumbwaiters and pneumatic tubes.) **H. Stern**, also on upper Fifth Avenue (number 645, between 51st and 52nd streets), is a specialist in the innovative use of colored gemstones. The venerable **Harry Winston**, to whom Ms. Monroe alludes when she asserts that diamonds are a girl's best friend, also occupies a site on Fifth Avenue (number 718, at 56th Street).

Discount Jewels

Intersecting Fifth Avenue at 47th Street is the **Diamond District**—one solid block (west to Sixth Avenue) of stores, booths, workshops, and showrooms dedicated to the design, renovation, repair, but mostly the sale, of diamond, colored gemstone, and gold jewelry. Though it looks and behaves like a wholesale area, most of 47th Street talks retail enthusiastically. Bring cash and prepare to bargain. And remember: *caveat emptor.* A similar, but smaller and less boisterous, wholesale-retail **jewelry district** exists downtown in the area of Canal Street and the Bowery; proximity to Chinatown accounts for its interesting supply of high-karat red-gold charms and chains.

Fabulous Fakes

Shoppers attracted to Fifth Avenue gems but lacking corresponding funds should consider visiting **Kenneth Jay Lane** (in Trump Tower; Fifth Avenue at 56th Street), who made his reputation with beautifully executed copies of high-priced pieces. Those who leave the real thing in the vault, or wish to appear as though they do, should stop at **Jolie Gabor** (699 Madison Avenue, between 62nd and 63rd streets), where individual pieces can be copied or "fabulous fakes" bought off the shelf. Much less expensive is **Gould Jewelry** (611 Madison Avenue, at 58th Street), whose imitation baubles would be perfectly illuminated by the dim light of dusk on an ocean-liner deck.

Pearls

If it's pearls you're after, you might try **Mikimoto** (608 Fifth Avenue, between 48th and 49th streets), the veritable inventor of the cultured variety. **Buccellati** (in Trump Tower) will seat you on a comfortable chair and spread before you individual specimens of heartbreaking luster and intensity, to be strung at your behest. Stagger out of Buccellati to the nearest magazine stand, from whose wooden frames many news dealers are selling one-dollar strands of ersatz pearls—just to make sure these things truly become you.

Watches

For a wristwatch, head to **Tourneau Corner** (500 Madison Avenue, at 52nd Street) for a staggering collection of watches, ranging from reasonably expensive to rarefied Rolex. An entirely different world of watches is available at **Swatch** (500 Fifth Avenue, between 42nd and 43rd streets), whose wacky designs become collector's items minutes after they hit the market. For oversize, comical, bubble-headed watches, travel downtown to West 8th Street, where **Savage** (number 59, just off Sixth Avenue) sells a likely selection.

Everyday Jewelry

People who want some unusual jewelry but still have to work for a living will find amusing but wearable examples at **Ylang Ylang** (4 West 57th Street, between Fifth and Sixth avenues). Francophiles longing for a souvenir of Paris will be glad to know that **Agatha** (610 Fifth Avenue, near 50th Street at Rockefeller Center) features items on the order of Tour Eiffel earrings. Animal lovers should visit **Malvina Solomon** (1122 Madison Avenue, at 84th Street) for sterling charm bracelets—feline and canine themes predominate.

Modernists who don't mind spending a bit may prefer **Artwear** (456 West Broadway, between Prince and Houston streets). Such unusual metals as titanium are experimented with here; the results (by designer Robert Lee Morris) often decorate the mannequins at prestigious fashion shows. At **Charles' Place** (234 Mulberry Street, in Little Italy, between Prince and Spring streets) rhinestone-bedecked animal earrings (the gamboling pigs are nice) can be custom tailored to your specifications or bought ready-made. Gentlemen who are looking for shops that will sell them a single earring will want to know that the stretch of **8th Street** between Fifth and Sixth avenues, as well as eastern **Greenwich Avenue**, should prove particularly fruitful.

Lastly, shoppers in search of something completely different (as well as those who find themselves temporarily in queer street) might benefit from a visit to **Gem Pawnbrokers** (608 Eighth Avenue, between 39th and 40th streets), a classic place (three balls outside, glass window) with a surprisingly comprehensive display of "out of pawn" offerings.

FOOD

By Bonnie Rothman Morris

Bonnie Rothman Morris is a writer and television producer who has contributed to 7 Days, Food and Wine, Cosmopolitan, and Allure. Although she recently moved out of New York City to the suburbs, she continues to shop for food here.

If you have a yen for any food item in this city—be it a bagel, a brioche, or some beluga—just about any New Yorker can tell you where to get the best of it. Trouble is, no two answers will be alike. But then again, with the abundant culinary treasures that are available here, no two answers will be wrong.

In New York, the quest for a culinary experience can border on the sublime—or the ridiculous, however you choose to see it. A few years back, for instance, Bloomingdale's began selling mounds of ice at seven dollars a pound—plain ice, the kind made by freezing water.

The hitch? The ice was imported from the North Pole, was more than 100,000 years old, and was guaranteed to be free of pollution.

That the city loves its food is evident in the labor expended to get it. Most New Yorkers prefer specialty shops over supermarkets. After all, why buy, say, olive oil at the supermarket when you can choose from 25 varieties at one of the big five specialty shops: Zabar's, Grace's Marketplace, Balducci's, Dean & DeLuca, or Macy's Cellar? New Yorkers will go to one shop for *ficelles,* to another for fresh ravioli stuffed with shiitake mushrooms, and on to a third for plump Roma tomatoes. Most residents consider food shopping to be an outing rather than a chore. Any serious shopper drags along a wire cart, squeezing it through the narrow aisles of old-time shops and bumping it against the legs of the throngs poking through the produce at the city's greenmarkets. Food shopping is one of the city's most sacred rituals.

SEASONAL FOODS

For all the city's sophistication, New Yorkers' stomachs are keenly attuned to the seasons. In fact, many New Yorkers anticipate the appearance of the first stalks of fresh fall broccoli in the markets as passionately as they await the opening of the opera season or some other urbane event. A fairly easy way to determine what seasonal food is capturing New York's attention at any particular time is to look at the specials offered by restaurants, or, if you care to do a little sleuthing, see what foods shoppers are standing in longer-than-usual lines for as they go about their daily shopping rounds.

In spring this seasonal bounty, hauled from the local waters and trucked fresh into the city daily from the farmlands in the surrounding countryside of Connecticut, New Jersey, New York State, and Pennsylvania, includes shad and shad roe, often taken from the Hudson River. Deep-water halibut also comes into the fish markets in spring (and fall), and by April tender, thin spears of asparagus poke up in vegetable bins, as do fiddlehead ferns from the forests of the Northeast. Soft-shell crabs (recently molted blue crabs that taste best sautéed and, to the disdain of visitors accustomed to Dungeness crab from the waters of the Pacific Northwest, are eaten shell and all) usually begin showing up in the markets in mid-May, along with the first cherries and blackberries from Upstate New York orchards. A summer morning at a large New York produce market, such as Fairway on the Upper West Side (see below), can be a mob scene, as shoppers clean out supplies of corn and vine-ripened tomatoes—often picked just a few hours before—by early morning. Apples, pears, and cider are plentiful fall through winter, when butchers sell fresh game (including fresh Long Island duck) and the fish markets serve up oysters.

If you really want to indulge in indigenous food from the city itself, Steve "Wildman" Brill will give you a free tour of Central Park, pointing out foods that can be harvested there—mushrooms, carrots, nectarines, mustard greens, various berries, and the like. It doesn't get any fresher. (Call Steve at 718-291-6825.)

FOOD SHOPPING BY NEIGHBORHOOD
New York is a city comprising distinct neighborhoods, each of which has a distinct personality that is ever evolving. Many New York neighborhoods cling to their roots through their specialty food shops. The upper reaches of the Upper West Side, for example, boast their share of Latin markets such as **Stop One** (210 West 94th Street, between Broadway and Amsterdam Avenue), where

dried chiles can be found in a dozen varieties. Tucked into the Upper East Side are vestiges of the Eastern European community that settled there a century ago—such places as Orwasher's Bakery and Rigo Hungarian Viennese Pastry (both on East 78th Street, between First and Second avenues). The Lower East Side, although its Jewish immigrant population has thinned out significantly, still offers the best knishes and pickles in town.

The city's ubiquitous Korean groceries unify the New York food shopping experience. It seems that the wares of these markets—neatly stacked towers of oranges and apples sharing cramped space with salad bars and freezer cases loaded with five brands of gourmet ice cream— spill out onto every block in town. With many staying open 24 hours, they're the city's version of 7-Eleven stores, only better.

Upper West Side
Columbus Avenue. A walk north up the Upper West Side, beginning, say, in the neighborhood of ABC's network headquarters at Columbus Avenue and 66th Street, will bring you to one famous food mecca after another. You'll first come to **Muffins** (220 Columbus Avenue, at 70th Street), which offers three dozen varieties of its eponymous product (the berry ones are best) as well as buttery scones. An Upper West Side coffee war began a couple of years ago when **McNulty's Tea & Coffee Company**, long entrenched in Greenwich Village, set up a branch shop at 247 Columbus Avenue (between 71st and 72nd streets), just around the corner from the long-standing **Sensuous Bean** (66 West 70th Street, at Columbus Avenue). While the shopkeepers in both stores are happy to guide you to the latest in exotic coffees, they'll also help you find a blend that you'll want for every day. The chocolatier **Godiva** is just up the street at 245 Columbus Avenue (between 71st and 72nd streets). The tiny **Silver Palate** (274 Columbus Avenue, between 72nd and 73rd streets), birthplace of three best-selling cookbooks, has been sold by its founders but still turns out the simple and delicious fare such as wild-rice salad and chicken Marbella that made it famous.

Broadway. To make the rounds like a neighborhood resident, wend your way west toward Broadway. **Nevada Meat Market** (2012 Broadway, between 68th and 69th streets) is an old-fashioned butcher shop with superb cuts of meat, an array of *wursts* and cold cuts, and plump, fresh free-range poultry. **Acker Merrall & Condit** (160 West 72nd Street, between Broadway and Columbus Avenue) is a well-stocked and snazzy wine shop with salespeople to match. **Adriana's Bazaar** (2152 Broadway, at 75th Street) offers exotic spices and condiments, and has a superb takeout section that sells food from local restaurants, mostly Indian and Far Eastern. Across Broadway is **Fairway** (2127 Broadway, between 74th and 75th streets), a dizzying produce market known for its exotic and local fruits and vegetables, bounteous cheeses and breads, and thick crowds of typical neighborhood residents, blue-suited executives next to actors in blue jeans. Although Fairway can resemble a jungle dense with produce and people, the traffic flows and service is swift. The signs are terrific, too ("Fresh Figs, Raw Sex, Same Thing," for example). **Citarella's**, practically next door (2135 Broadway, at 75th Street), sells a glistening array of fresh seafood and employs full-time one fishmonger whose sole responsibility is to construct a window sculpture out of raw fish. A new window display is unveiled around noon each day. Citarella's recently expanded to the terrestrial and now sells prime meats as well.

The culinary hot spot on the Upper West Side is **Zabar's** (2245 Broadway, between 80th and 81st streets), arguably the best food (and kitchen equipment) store in the world. It's famous for top-quality smoked fish, sausages, caviar, coffee, bread, and cheeses; a staggering cookware selection; and a take-out deli where grilled quail is as easy to come by as roast turkey. When it's open, it's busy, and when it's busy, it's a nuthouse. It is one of the few mandatory stops on a New York City food-shopping tour.

Bagels can be gotten warm from **H & H Bagels** (2239 Broadway, at 80th Street), said by many to be the best in the city; H & H will ship anywhere. **Sarabeth's Kitchen** (423 Amsterdam Avenue, between 80th and 81st streets) makes a heavenly lemon pound cake and is a nice resting spot for a pot of tea.

North of 85th Street. If the wait for smoked fish is too long at Zabar's, there are two other acclaimed purveyors on the Upper West Side: **Barney Greengrass** (541 Amsterdam Avenue, between 86th and 87th streets), with a restaurant where you may find yourself eating your lox next to Woody Allen or other celebrities who have made the place famous, and **Murray's Sturgeon Shop** (2429 Broadway, between 89th and 90th streets), renowned also for its caviar. **Mondel** chocolates (2913 Broadway, at 114th

Street, near Columbia University) makes the best diet chocolate you're likely to find anywhere, and the fattening stuff is good, too.

Upper East Side

Up until 40 years ago or so the carriage trade on the Upper East Side employed cooks to prepare its sumptuous meals. Today, the plethora of specialty caterers offering prepared foods has supplanted large household staffs.

North from 80th Street. Setting the tone is **E.A.T.** (1064 Madison Avenue, between 80th and 81st streets), a white-tiled lair where one small raspberry tart can cost more than an outfit from the Gap. E.A.T.'s near-perfect breads, particularly the raisin-nut rolls and sourdough baguettes, are available in other city markets.

Lorenzo and Maria's Kitchen (1418 Third Avenue, between 80th and 81st streets) are caterers who sell prepared dishes from their tiny wood-paneled shop. Any Park Avenue matron would be proud to serve their marinated vegetables and filet mignon brochette. **Likitsakos Market** (1174 Lexington Avenue, between 80th and 81st streets) has a Greek flair, offering *taramosalata,* focaccia, and other Mediterranean specialties in a homey setting.

Yorkville, as the neighborhood in the far east 80s is called, is the home of an old Eastern European enclave. Cooks of Hungarian and Czech descent stock up at such shops as **Paprikas Weiss** (1572 Second Avenue, between 81st and 82nd streets), the best source for Middle European spices. **Ottomanelli Meat Market** (1549 York Avenue, at 82nd Street) is known for game and for its helpful butchers, who will tell you how to prepare it. If you want to see where prime beef and prime real estate share the same price structures, check out **Lobel's Meat and Poultry** (1096 Madison Avenue, at 82nd Street).

The 70s south to Bloomingdale's. The chrome-and-glass design of gourmet grocers and caterers **Neuman & Bogdonoff** (1385 Third Avenue, between 78th and 79th streets) makes a perfect backdrop for the glass bottles of milk, gigantic scones, and such prepared dishes as stuffed chicken breasts, haricots verts, and asparagus vinaigrette.

Great bakeries flourish on the Upper East Side, notably two on East 78th Street between First and Second avenues: **Orwasher's Bakery** (number 308) for bread, especially the pumpernickel and rye, and neighboring **Rigo Hungarian Viennese Pastry** (number 314) for rich pastries. (The friendly staff behind the counter at Rigo is likely to tell you that eating pastry is good for you, "rounds you out.") **Sant Ambroeus** (1000 Madison Avenue, at 77th Street) has Italian sweets, while **Bonté Patisserie** (1316 Third Avenue, between 75th and 76th streets) has a smashing assortment of French pastries and tiny, buttery cookies. **William Poll** (1051 Lexington Avenue, between 74th and 75th streets) is a gourmet market with an old-fashioned feeling that is praised locally for its tea sandwiches. Chocolate lovers will find satisfaction at **La Maison du Chocolat** (25 East 73rd Street, between Fifth and Madison avenues), a branch of the famed Paris chocolatier. **Fraser-Morris** (1264 Third Avenue, between 72nd and 73rd streets) specializes in baskets filled with exotic sweets and nuts.

Grace's Marketplace (1237 Third Avenue, between 71st and 72nd streets) is another New York mega-market with a warm Italian flavor. Grace is a member of the Balducci family, whose Greenwich Village market is an institution, and she carries the family tradition uptown. The selection of produce, meats, cheeses, pastas, and pastries is staggering; the prepared dishes, delicious. For health food that doesn't taste healthful, such as grain-stuffed yams smothered in mushroom gravy and fat-free fudge, and enthusiastic advice on nutrition, try the **Healthy Candle** (972 Lexington Avenue, at 71st Street). For wine, **Garnet Liquors** (929 Lexington Avenue, between 68th and 69th streets) stocks a broad selection at excellent prices.

The hottest bread bakery in town is **Ecce Panis** (1120 Third Avenue, at 65th Street), where the bakers sign each large, dark sourdough loaf with the store's initials. **Hale & Hearty** (849 Lexington Avenue, between 64th and 65th streets) makes terrific soups and salads. The renowned **Sherry-Lehmann** (679 Madison Avenue, between 61st and 62nd streets) has probably the city's best selection of New York State vintners among its superlative selection. East Side shopping always includes **Bloomingdale's** (Lexington Avenue, between 59th and 60th streets), which serves a rich cup of cappuccino along with neat pastries from its 59th Street–side shops that also sell smoked fish, prepared salads, and charcuterie.

Midtown

This heart of corporate headquarters is a great place for lunch—except from noon to 1:30 P.M., when it is impossible to get near any place that's reasonably priced. Before or after the rush try **Piatti Pronti** for sandwiches and Caesar salad adorned with Parmigiano (34 West 56th Street and 37 West 46th Street), or **Savories**, downstairs next to the skating rink/café in the 30 Rockefeller Center concourse, for take-out food of all types. **Focaccia Fiorentina** (in the Crystal Pavilion, 805 Third Avenue, at 50th Street) is the American outlet of a very popular sandwich shop in Florence. **Mangia**, whose grilled vegetables and bean salads push the notion of a salad bar to new extremes, has two locations (54 West 56th Street, between Fifth and Sixth avenues; and 16 East 48th Street, between Fifth and Madison avenues); both draw a devoted clientele for takeout nosh.

At **Between the Bread** (145 West 55th Street, between Sixth and Seventh avenues) the huge muffins and stuffed sandwiches are good stand-ins for the expensive restaurant fare in the area. **Good N Plenty** (410 West 43rd Street, between Eighth and Ninth avenues) turns out a mean vegetarian chili, along with chicken tamale pie and other homey dishes.

Specialty stores attest to the proximity of the United Nations and the presence of international businesspeople: **Caviarteria** (caviar and other piscine fare), 29 East 60th Street, between Madison and Park avenues; **Petrossian** (caviar and smoked fish), 182 West 58th Street, at Seventh Avenue; **Maison Glass** (European spices), 111 East 58th Street, between Park and Lexington avenues; **Nyborg & Nelson** (Swedish and Scandinavian foods), 153 East 53rd Street, at Lexington Avenue; and **Katagiri** (Japanese), 224 East 59th Street, between Second and Third avenues.

At **Morrell & Company** (535 Madison Avenue, between 54th and 55th streets), the helpful staff offers the city's best selection of exotic, rare, and expensive wines. **Galeries Lafayette** (10 East 57th Street, at Fifth Avenue) sells imported French condiments in a lower-level shop, where you can find herbes de Provence and real French Dijón mustards. Squeezed in near the cafés in the lower level of Trump Tower (next door) is **Le Cordon Bleu**, which offers chocolate, condiments, coffee, and tea bearing the cooking school's classic blue label. **Coisa Nossa** (41 West 46th Street, between Fifth and Sixth avenues) specializes in South American fare and hot sauces.

For one-stop shopping try **Macy's Cellar**. It's a selection of "boutique" outlets of small Manhattan specialists such as Ottomanelli Brothers, plus Macy's own departments to fill out the line. You might find a few bargains, but mostly they offer quality and convenience with acceptable service.

Ninth Avenue

Ninth Avenue in the 30s and 40s is in Hell's Kitchen, but for food shoppers this old-fashioned neighborhood is paradise. You can walk this stretch of the avenue and step in and out of dozens of ethnic food shops, picking up provisions for a Pan-Mediterranean dinner.

The Italian presence on the avenue is led by **Bruno**, the self-coronated "King of Ravioli" (number 653, between 45th and 46th streets), whose stuffed pastas are coveted city-wide. (Bruno has opened a branch on the Upper West Side at 2204 Broadway, at 78th Street.) Greek pastries with flaky phyllo are always fresh at **Poseidon Bakery** (number 629, between 44th and 45th streets). **Natura** (number 615, at 43rd Street) is multinational in scope but focuses on the Mediterranean, with grains, dried beans, yogurts, and prepared dishes.

Just off the avenue is the **Little Pie Company** (424 West 43rd Street, between Ninth and Tenth avenues); the sour-cream apple walnut pie is delicious, sold whole or by the slice à la mode in the store. **Empire Coffee and Tea**, back on Ninth Avenue (number 592, between 42nd and 43rd streets), has 75 different kinds of coffee beans, as well as herbs, teas, and spices.

Ninth Avenue International Foods (number 543, between 40th and 41st streets) is owned by a Greek, Sotirios (called Sam), who sells delicacies such as cheeses, olives, and olive oil wholesale to shops all over town and offers the same delicacies, along with dried fruits and coffees, here. His brother, Pete, has an outpost down the block, **Pete's International Grocery and Meat Market** (at number 529, between 39th and 40th streets), where you can find rare dried herbs and imported feta cheeses. **Central Fish Co.** (number 527, between 39th and 40th streets) offers more than 50 varieties of fish. **Esposito and Sons** pork store (number 500, at 38th Street) prepares Italian sausage and suckling pig, which they'll marinate in seasonings of your choice.

Little India

This neighborhood along Lexington Avenue in the 20s houses many inexpensive Indian restaurants, as well as a few places to dig up the staples and exotic spices of that national cuisine. **Kalustyan's** (123 Lexington Avenue, between 28th and 29th streets) sells Indian and Middle Eastern spices and groceries. **Foods of India** (121 Lexington Avenue, between 28th and 29th streets) has the most extensive selection when it comes to cooking utensils and spices, and has an energetic staff.

Murray Hill

Around the corner from Little India is "Little France," a mini epicurean fiefdom spinning off the popular restaurant Park Bistro (414 Park Avenue South, near 28th Street). **Les Halles** (411 Park Avenue South, on the same block) is an authentic French butcher, famous for *boudin noir;* **Park Avenue Catering** (47 East 29th, between Madison and Park avenues) prepares Provençal dishes to go. Both are chic and *cher*.

Italian gourmet items and fresh cheese fill the shelves at **Todaro Brothers** (555 Second Avenue, between 30th and 31st streets). **Karabelas** (630 First Avenue, at 37th Street) specializes in Greek delicacies and has a few tables, if you feel like stopping for a nibble. For wines in the area, **William Sokolin** (178 Madison Avenue, between 33rd and 34th streets) offers the best learning experience for those who want to know more, with reasonable prices.

Greenwich Village

The place to begin an epicurean tour of the Village is Bleecker Street, and the stretch between La Guardia Place and Seventh Avenue South (intersected by Jones, MacDougal, and Cornelia streets) is lined end-to-end with "the best ofs." **Porto Rico Importing Company** (201 Bleecker Street, between Sixth Avenue and MacDougal Street) can create any coffee-bean blend you want. The chocolate-coated beans are incredible. **Faicco's** (260 Bleecker Street, at Sixth Avenue) is an old-fashioned Italian market selling sausage. At **Zito and Sons Bakery** (259 Bleecker Street, between Sixth and Seventh avenues) shoppers line up when the light Italian loaves emerge from the ovens twice daily. Spices and herbs (medicinal and cooking) fill the shelves at **Aphrodisia** (264 Bleecker Street, between Sixth and Seventh avenues).

Just off Bleecker Street is **Florence Meat Market** (5 Jones Street, between Bleecker and West 4th streets), tops in town for veal. Around the corner, at tiny **Murray's Cheese Shop** (257 Bleecker Street, at Cornelia Street), you'll get a contact high from the scent of hundreds of ripening cheeses.

Head up Bleecker to Christopher Street, where **McNulty's Tea & Coffee** sells its exotic blends in an aromatic, old-fashioned shop at number 109 (between Bleecker and Hudson streets). Farther down the block, **Li-Lac** (number 120) has been making a wicked fudge and other chocolates since 1923. Go early for the best selection. Just north of Christopher Street is **Taylor's** (523 Hudson Street, between West 10th and Charles streets), a sliver of a place making its own popovers, muffins, scones, and fresh soups. For trifle mixes, steak and kidney pie, and other English fare, there's **Myers of Keswick** (634 Hudson Street, between Horatio and Jane streets). **Schapira Coffee Company** (117 West 10th Street, between Greenwich and Sixth avenues), another coffee store, roasts their own beans.

Sixth Avenue is another bustling food thoroughfare in the Village. **Jefferson Market** (between 10th and 11th streets) is long on service and expertise, selling reasonably priced meats and fish. **Balducci's**, a block south at 424 Sixth Avenue, is what food shopping in New York City is all about. It's homey, it's crowded, and the selection is exquisite: produce, charcuterie, meats, exotic fish, cheese, prepared foods, baked goods, and condiments are among the finest city wide. Balducci's is run by three generations of an Italian family that strives to be the first to introduce New Yorkers to new culinary delights—and they frequently succeed. On the weekends the place is mobbed and the wares go quickly. Try visiting on the off hours—it's open daily until 8:30 P.M.—but definitely do visit.

A couple of blocks south, **V.P. To Go** (140 West 4th Street, between Sixth Avenue and MacDougal Street) creates harmonious macrobiotic *dim sum*. **Hot Stuff** (227 Sullivan Street, at West 3rd Street) stocks more than 40 hot sauces imported from around the world to spice up burgers, stews, and chili.

Lower East Side and East Village

The old Jewish areas of the Lower East Side (parts of which are now called the East Village) have clung fiercely to their identity, despite the influx of other ethnic groups. Russians, Ukrainians, and Poles mingle on East Houston Street, awaiting the kosher delights of **Yonah Schimmel's** knishes (number 137); **Ben's Cheese Shop**'s cream cheese and farmer cheese (number 181); and **Russ and Daugh-**

ters' Nova, lox, smoked fish, and caviar (number 179).
Once you've stocked up on lox at Russ's, the counterman
will say, "Don't you want a nice piece of herring?" Your
answer: "Yes." (Calvin Trillin singled out Russ's and Ben's
as "Best in Class" for the perfect cream cheese and lox
combo.) Bialys can be had fresh at **Kossar's** (367 Grand
Street), and Ukrainian meat specialties are available at
Kurowycky Meat Products (124 First Avenue, between 7th
Street and St. Mark's Place). Hit the **Second Avenue Kosher
Deli** (at 10th Street) for traditional Yiddish K-rations:
kasha, kugel, kishke, and knaidel. (The *Journal of Gastronomy* quotes an exchange that could have been heard
anywhere around here. Customer: "I don't like the looks of
this whitefish." Waiter: "You want looks, you shoulda ordered goldfish!")

Native Farms (332 East 11th Street, between First and
Second avenues) is a rustic organic food store where
tastings are cheerfully offered. If you want to get into the
environmentally conscious spirit of the place, bring your
own bag. Two doors down is the doyenne of Italian
bakeries, **Veniero's** (number 342), where you'll have a
tough time choosing among the cannoli, pignoli cookies,
and anise toast.

On First Avenue below 11th Street you'll find the East
Village at its schizophrenic best. While not-so-fresh fruit is
sold outside a laundromat, two doors away is the highly
touted sweet shop **Black Hound** (149 First Avenue, between 9th and 10th streets), where chocolate truffles are
tucked into wooden Shaker boxes. Next door is **Angelica's Herbs and Spices** (147 First Avenue), with more than
2,500 varieties of herbs and spices scooped from large
apothecary jars by sullen young women wearing black
eyeshadow and black clothing.

SoHo and TriBeCa
Dean & DeLuca (560 Broadway, at Prince Street), a tanta-
lizingly trendy shop that has pioneered experiential food
shopping, anchors the SoHo food scene. The throng at
the espresso bar at the front of the store is the very
definition of chic, and in high-tech, lofty surroundings
beyond lie some of the best and most expensive foods in
the city, from breads and baked goods to meat, perfect
vegetables, and spices, as well as cookware and tabletop
items. They do a strong mail-order business, too.

SoHo also has any number of small specialty shops.
Daniel's Market (179 Prince Street, at Thompson Street) is

a butcher shop turned take-out place with a French flair. The **Ravioli Store** (75 Sullivan Street, between Spring and Broome streets) sells funky ravioli, such as black beans and Monterey Jack cheese stuffed into blue-corn pasta. **Raffetto's** (144 West Houston Street, between Sullivan and MacDougal streets) is a friendly, old-time fresh pasta shop where wares are displayed in little drawers.

TriBeCa was "discovered" only in the last decade or so and has become a chic residential quarter for artists and stockbrokers, but it has its food specialists, too. There is **Commodities Natural Foods** (117 Hudson Street, at North Moore Street), featuring a huge selection of organic produce and cookbooks. **Bubby's** (120 Hudson Street, at North Moore Street) has gloppy pies, cinnamon rolls, and an atmosphere that's reminiscent of San Francisco's Haight-Ashbury.

Little Italy and Chinatown

The **Italian Food Center** (186 Grand Street, at Mulberry Street) and the **Alleva** (across the street) are two spots for specialty Italian foodstuffs beyond the pastries that can be found almost anywhere in Little Italy. The first is a complete source for all things Italian, the second specializes in fresh ricotta and mozzarella. **Piemonte** (just up Grand Street at number 190) makes terrific ravioli (the spinach-cheese is supernal).

Chinatown offers a much more vibrant street scene. Little stands scattered throughout the neighborhood sell a deliciously sweet pastry that can only be described as a Chinese doughnut hole, made for a dollar a dozen right in front of you. Fish markets are plentiful and offer good value, but since many of the signs are in Chinese and the fish may not be familiar to you, don't be afraid to point. **Kam Man** (Golden Gate) department store (200 Canal Street, near Mulberry Street) sells all manner of Chinese foodstuffs and cookware. **Bangkok Market** (10 Mott Street) has herbs and grocery ingredients with a slant toward Thai and Vietnamese specialties. **Poo Ping** (81 Bayard Street, between Mott Street and the Bowery) also offers a profusion of exotic produce; the owner is a congenial man who speaks English.

The Other Boroughs

The people in the outer boroughs are not deprived of the riches offered in Manhattan. Indeed, Manhattanites have been known to traverse bridges and tunnels in pursuit of a particular foodstuff. Thriving ethnic communities, many of which are more tightly knit and authentic than their Manhattan counterparts—which have been diluted by gentrification—keep culinary traditions alive.

Brooklyn. Brooklyn has a Middle Eastern contingent on Atlantic Avenue. **Sahadi** (187–189 Atlantic Avenue, between Clinton and Court streets) offers top-quality spices, grains, olives, nuts, and dried fruits in bulk. A few doors down the street, and down a flight of steps, **Damascus Breads and Pastries Shop** (195 Atlantic Avenue) makes first-rate *spanokopita* (phyllo with spinach and feta) and steamy fresh pitas. The health-conscious set in Brooklyn Heights heads to **Perelandra** (175 Remsen Street, between Clinton and Court streets). The organic supermarket's prepared tofu pies and wild-rice salads are popular lunch fare with people who work in the nearby courthouses. **Bagels and Caviar** (72 Clark Street, between Henry and Hicks streets) in Brooklyn Heights makes what are (arguably, of course) the best bagels in New York City.

Many Italian-American families reside in Brooklyn's Carroll Gardens, and the real **Cammareri Brothers Bakery**, where Nicholas Cage lived and baked in the film *Moonstruck,* is located at 502 Henry Street (at Sackett Street). Lard bread (stuffed with salami and cheese) is the most popular item here. **Pastosa Ravioli,** also in Carroll Gardens (347 Court Street, between President and Union streets), makes superb stuffed pastas.

Brooklyn also has a big Russian community at Brighton Beach, West Indians in Flatbush, a thriving community of Poles in Greenpoint, and three distinct Jewish communities: Hasidim in Williamsburg, Lubavitchers in Crown Heights, and Sephardim on Kings Highway and in the Borough Park area.

Queens. Queens is home to many ethnic groups, and accordingly is a good place to find ethnic food. Greek, Italian, and Chinese grocers on Steinway Street in **Astoria** (near the American Museum of the Moving Image) offer many of the specialties (at incredibly low prices) you'll find in chic food shops in Manhattan.

Jackson Heights is an old-fashioned immigrant neighborhood with a new-fashioned selection of immigrant foodstuffs: The Argentine, Colombian, Cuban, Peruvian, Filipino, Salvadoran, Thai, Indian, and Irish populations all offer up at least a restaurant or two of home-style cooking, and most also have a store that stocks the essentials of their culinary heritage. To get to Jackson Heights, take the num-

ber 7 subway from Times Square or Grand Central to the
69th Street/Fisk stop for the Filipino area, or get off at any
of the next four stops (74th, 82nd, or 90th streets, or
Junction Boulevard) for the Latin areas. Indian, Korean,
and an abundance of Latin American markets and restaurants are alongside each other on **Roosevelt Avenue**. One
of the best-stocked markets here is **La Gran Habana
Carnicera** (76–77 Roosevelt Avenue), whose South and
Central American imports, such as Venezuelan corn meal
and Peruvian potatoes, are rare finds.

Bronx. **Arthur Avenue**, a typical Italian-American shopping street in the Bronx, has the typical good old-
fashioned smells and the familiar sight of cheeses and
salamis hanging aloft.

SHOPPING FOR COOKWARE

When it comes to cookware, New Yorkers have a di-
lemma: There's just not room in their cramped kitchens
for all the enticing cookware that's available around town.
Zabar's (2245 Broadway, between 80th and 81st streets)
devotes its second floor to a huge cookware department,
where you can find just about any cooking hardware you
could imagine. Small appliances, such as Cuisinarts, espresso machines, pasta makers, even irons and ironing
boards, can be had at exceptional prices. **Macy's Cellar**, in
the flagship store at 34th Street and Broadway, also offers
its share of stockpots, wire whisks, and cappuccino makers, along with everyday china, mugs, and serving bowls.
Mixers, food processors, and pasta machines are real
bargains, and the sales are always worth watching. **Bloomingdale's** sixth-floor department called "Main Course"
has little boutiques for knives, pots, and Cuisinarts.
There's an especially large selection of linens, funky serving pieces, and teapots. If you buy J. A. Henckels knives
here, you can bring them regularly to be sharpened.
Broadway Panhandler (520 Broadway, at Spring Street) is
a downtown shop with great service, good prices, and
broad selections of all types of kitchen equipment. If they
don't have what you want, ask; chances are they'll be able
to get it for you. **Bridge Kitchenware** (214 East 52nd
Street, between Second and Third avenues) is the con-
summate cooking-supply shop, with three floors of merchandise: kettles, caldrons, strainers, knives, rolling pins,
baking supplies, and mechanical items. For authentic
chefs toques, jackets, and aprons, **Le Cordon Bleu**, a
boutique located on the lower level in Trump Tower

(Fifth Avenue at 56th Street), offers those preferred by master French chefs. The ecology-minded will enjoy **Terra Verde** (120 Wooster Street, between Prince and Spring streets), where the cookware, made of clay and other biodegradable material, is earth-conscious.

Robin Importers (510 Madison Avenue, between 52nd and 53rd streets) sells a good selection of knives and tableware at discount prices. The three Manhattan outlets of **Conran's Habitat** (in the Citicorp building in Midtown, on Astor Place in the Village, and at Broadway and 81st Street on the Upper West Side) offer specialty cookware, such as clay pots and woks, and the tableware selection will make you want to throw yours out and start anew. **Williams-Sonoma** (20 East 60th Street, between Madison and Park avenues) artfully displays Le Creuset cookware in the color of the moment and other appealing, high-end utensils. **Gracious Home** (1220 Third Avenue, at 70th Street) caters to the carriage trade; prices are high, but the selection of pots, pans, and accessories warrants them.

For the specialist, the **Chocolate Gallery** (34 West 22nd Street, between Fifth and Sixth avenues) brings baking and candy making to high (or low, depending on your waistline) art. Upon entering, you are greeted by hundreds of bride-and-groom cake toppers, candy molds in traditional squares and erotic forms, and every size baking pan known to man. Baking and decorating demonstrations are given upstairs and tastings are encouraged.

There is a street of suppliers where the pros go for kitchen equipment, and if you want the very best deals, you should go there, too: the Bowery, between Houston Street and Cooper Square. The neighborhood is a bit gamey, and you should not visit it alone, but **King Glassware** (112 Bowery, at Grand Street) can be worth it. From major appliances to small gadgets, everything is at hand here, and most of it for just 10 percent above wholesale. Top chefs call it the best source, period. Bring cash.

FOOD FESTIVALS

The city that makes such a to-do about shopping for food also makes festivals out of eating it. Two of the most popular (and crowded) are the **Feast of San Gennaro**, held for two weeks at the end of September in Little Italy, and the **Ninth Avenue International Festival** (along Ninth Avenue in the 30s and 40s) in May. San Gennaro is immortalized by Calvin Trillin, New York's favorite food writer, in his essay "Confessions of a Stand-Up Sausage Eater." Trillin's images of the streets of Little Italy being stuffed with people eating stuffed sausage-and-pepper sandwiches while playing carnival games in the hopes of winning stuffed animals ring true for all New Yorkers. That description also fits the Ninth Avenue fair, but the sandwiches here are more likely to be served on grilled pita bread than on hard, crusty rolls. About 60 other food festivals are held each year; you can find them in the Weekend section of Friday's *New York Times,* or call the New York Convention and Visitors Bureau at 2 Columbus Circle (59th Street between Broadway and Eighth Avenue; Tel: 397-8222) to find out what's scheduled (see also our Useful Facts section).

FARMERS' MARKETS

Among the most engaging sights in the asphalt jungle are the ubiquitous produce stands, whose wares spill onto city sidewalks on almost every block. A city-sponsored program called **Greenmarket** takes the concept to rustic extremes, supporting a network of open-air farmers' markets that operate in parks, schoolyards, and empty lots in 17 locations around the city. Farms from the surrounding countryside sell fresh fruits and vegetables, organic meat and poultry, cheese, honey, fresh-baked bread, flowers, and other bounty—which by law must be raised, grown, or produced by the sellers, who really are farmers come to market.

The largest and most popular of these markets operates in **Union Square** (Broadway at 16th Street) Mondays, Wednesdays, Fridays, and Saturdays, year round. You may well want to include the market on your sightseeing itinerary—it's a pleasant 20-block walk down Fifth Avenue from the Empire State Building, for instance, and just north of Greenwich Village. The sight of New Yorkers poring over lettuce with the same determination with which they once attacked the sales tables of the now-defunct Klein's department store across the square is a sight to behold indeed. Other popular farmers' markets are: 57th Street and Ninth Avenue in Midtown, held Wednesdays, Saturdays, and Sundays; 77th Street and Columbus Avenue (in connection with an antiques fair) on the Upper West Side, Sundays only; Hudson and 14th streets in the West Village, Saturdays only; and the World Trade Center, Tuesdays and Thursdays. For more information, Tel: 477-3220.

COOKING SCHOOLS

Peter Kump's New York Cooking School, widely considered the city's best, offers weekend workshops and Sunday classes as well as longer-term courses. The school's specialty is French techniques, but the dozens of courses offered include instruction in many types of cuisine, including Greek, Italian, Thai, and Vietnamese; techniques, such as bread baking and pastry making; and holiday and seasonal preparations. Some summer classes are offered in the Hamptons, the Berkshires, and Vermont. 307 East 92nd Street (between First and Second avenues); Tel: 410-4601 or (800) 522-4610.

The **New School Culinary Arts Program** offers about 150 courses at any one time, many of which are single session. In addition to classes in basic cooking, ethnic foods, baking techniques, and wine appreciation, the school offers behind-the-scenes afternoons at the city's most famous restaurants and walking tours of such neighborhoods as Chinatown, Greenwich Village, and Astoria, Queens, with lunch. Most courses are given at a landmark Village town house, at 100 Greenwich Avenue (between 12th and 13th streets); Tel: 255-4141.

Natural Gourmet Cookery School teaches natural healthful cooking. Weekend courses range from French techniques to Ethiopian dishes, from soup making to crepes, from Indian to Greek to Mexican to stir-fry meals. 48 West 21st Street (between Fifth and Sixth avenues); Tel: 645-5170.

The **James Beard Foundation** offers one to two cooking workshops a month, mostly demonstrations, some participation, many of which take place in Mr. Beard's kitchen in the **Beard House**. This venerable foundation—probably the New York City culinary world's best-kept secret—also has many special events, dinners, lectures, wine and food tastings, and exhibitions, and publishes a 28-page newsletter each month. All events and workshops are open first to members. 167 West 12th Street (between Sixth and Seventh avenues); Tel: 627-2308.

INFORMATION SOURCES

The Food section of the Wednesday *New York Times* provides extensive and enjoyable coverage of the New York food scene—from seasonal foods come to market to cookware bargains to cooking classes. The "Best Bets" column in the weekly *New York* magazine often alerts readers to good buys in foodstuffs and kitchenware. Every weekday at 12:15 P.M., local cookbook author and restaurant reviewer Arthur Schwartz trades recipes and gustatory experiences with food fanatics over the airwaves on WOR-AM radio, number 710.

Kitchen Arts and Letters (1435 Lexington Avenue, between 93rd and 94th streets on the Upper East Side) is a mandatory stop for any visitor to New York who likes to cook and eat. It is probably the nation's best-stocked food-book shop; Tel: 876-5550. Of the many books on New York food, the Bible these days is the *Zagat New York City Marketplace Survey,* in which a cadre of tough and opinionated food fanatics reviews some 500 shops. *The Food Lovers' Guide to the Real New York* is excellent for finding food shops in the outer boroughs, but its Manhattan coverage is curiously spotty.

FOOD SHOPS BY TYPE

Asian Markets
Bangkok Market (*Chinatown*)
Kam Man (*Chinatown*)
Poo Ping (*Chinatown*)

Bagels/Bialys
Bagels and Caviar (*Brooklyn Heights*)
H & H Bagels (*Upper West Side*)
Kossar's (*Lower East Side*)

Bakeries
Bonté Patisserie (*Upper East Side*)
Cammareri Brothers Bakery (*Brooklyn*)
Damascus Breads and Pastries Shop (*Brooklyn*)
Ecce Panis (*Upper East Side*)
Little Pie Company (*Ninth Avenue*)
Muffins (*Upper West Side*)
Orwasher's Bakery (*Upper East Side*)
Poseidon Bakery (*Ninth Avenue*)
Rigo Hungarian Viennese Pastry (*Upper East Side*)
Sant Ambroeus (*Upper East Side*)
Sarabeth's Kitchen (*Upper West Side*)
Taylor's (*Greenwich Village*)
Veniero's (*East Village*)
Zito and Sons Bakery (*Greenwich Village*)

British Fare
Myers of Keswick (*Greenwich Village*)

Cheese
Alleva (*Little Italy*)
Ben's Cheese Shop (*Lower East Side*)
Murray's Cheese Shop (*Greenwich Village*)

Chocolate
Black Hound (*East Village*)
Godiva (*Upper West Side*)
La Maison du Chocolat (*Upper East Side*)
Li-Lac (*Greenwich Village*)
Mondel (*Upper West Side*)

Coffees
Empire Coffee and Tea (*Ninth Avenue*)
McNulty's Tea & Coffee Company (*Upper West Side and Greenwich Village*)
Schapira Coffee Company (*Greenwich Village*)
Sensuous Bean (*Upper West Side*)
Porto Rico Importing Company (*Greenwich Village*)

Deli
Second Avenue Kosher Deli (*East Village*)

French
Daniel's Market (*SoHo*)
Galeries Lafayette (*Midtown*)
Les Halles (*Murray Hill*)
Maison Glass (*Midtown*)
Park Avenue Catering (*Murray Hill*)

General Groceries
Balducci's (*Greenwich Village*)
Bloomingdale's (*Upper East Side*)
Dean & DeLuca (*SoHo*)
Fairway (*Upper West Side*)
Grace's Marketplace (*Upper East Side*)
La Gran Habana Carnicera (*Queens*)
Jefferson Market (*Greenwich Village*)
Macy's Cellar (*Midtown*)
Zabar's (*Upper West Side*)

Greek/Mediterranean Markets
Damascus Breads and Pastries Shop (*Brooklyn*)
Karabelas (*Murray Hill*)
Likitsakos Market (*Upper East Side*)
Natura (*Ninth Avenue*)

Ninth Avenue International Foods (*Ninth Avenue*)
Pete's International Grocery and Meat Market (*Ninth Avenue*)
Poseidon Bakery (*Ninth Avenue*)
Sahadi (*Brooklyn*)

Herbs and Spices
Adriana's Bazaar (*Upper West Side*)
Angelica's Herbs and Spices (*East Village*)
Aphrodisia (*Greenwich Village*)
Foods of India (*Little India*)
Hot Stuff (*Greenwich Village*)
Kalustyan's (*Little India*)
Maison Glass (*Midtown*)
Paprikas Weiss (*Upper East Side*)

Indian
Foods of India (*Little India*)
Kalustyan's (*Little India*)

Italian Gourmet Shops
Alleva (*Little Italy*)
Italian Food Center (*Little Italy*)
Todaro Brothers (*Murray Hill*)

Kitchen Supplies and Cookware
Bloomingdale's Main Course (*Upper East Side*)
Bridge Kitchenware (*Midtown*)
Broadway Panhandler (*SoHo*)
Chocolate Gallery (*Flatiron District*)
Conran's Habitat (*Greenwich Village, Midtown, Upper West Side*)
Cordon Bleu (*Midtown*)
Gracious Home (*Upper East Side*)
King Glassware (*Lower East Side*)
Kitchen Arts and Letters (*Upper East Side*)
Macy's Cellar (*Midtown*)
Robin Importers (*Midtown*)
Terra Verde (*SoHo*)
Williams-Sonoma (*Upper East Side*)
Zabar's (*Upper West Side*)

Meats/Fish/Poultry
Central Fish Co. (*Ninth Avenue*)
Citarella's (*Upper West Side*)
Esposito and Sons (*Ninth Avenue*)

Faicco's (*Greenwich Village*)
Florence Meat Market (*Greenwich Village*)
Jefferson Market (*Greenwich Village*)
Kurowycky Meat Products (*East Village*)
Les Halles (*Murray Hill*)
Lobel's Meat and Poultry (*Upper East Side*)
Nevada Meat Market (*Upper West Side*)
Ottomanelli Meat Market (*Upper East Side*)
Pete's International Grocery and Meat Market (*Ninth Avenue*)

Natural Foods/Organics
Commodities Natural Foods (*TriBeCa*)
Healthy Candle (*Upper East Side*)
Native Farms (*East Village*)
Perelandra (*Brooklyn*)

Pasta
Bruno (*Ninth Avenue and Upper West Side*)
Pastosa Ravioli (*Brooklyn*)
Piemonte (*Little Italy*)
Raffetto's (*SoHo*)
Ravioli Store (*SoHo*)

Produce
Balducci's (*Greenwich Village*)
Dean & DeLuca (*SoHo*)
Fairway (*Upper West Side*)
Grace's Marketplace (*Upper East Side*)
Jefferson Market (*Greenwich Village*)

Smoked Fish/Appetizers
Barney Greengrass (*Upper West Side*)
Caviarteria (*Midtown*)
Fairway (*Upper West Side*)
Murray's Sturgeon Shop (*Upper West Side*)
Petrossian (*Midtown*)
Russ and Daughters' (*Lower East Side*)
Yonah Schimmel's (*Lower East Side*)
Zabar's (*Upper West Side*)

Spanish/Latin Markets
Coisa Nossa (*Midtown*)
Le Gran Habana Carnicera (*Queens*)
Stop One (*Upper West Side*)

Specialty Gourmet and Take-Out Shops
Adriana's Bazaar (*Upper West Side*)
Between the Bread (*Midtown*)
Black Hound (*East Village*)
Bubby's (*TriBeCa*)
Caviarteria (*Midtown*)
Coisa Nossa (*Midtown*)
Daniel's Market (*SoHo*)
E.A.T. (*Upper East Side*)
Focaccia Fiorentina (*Midtown*)
Fraser-Morris (*Upper East Side*)
Good N Plenty (*Midtown*)
Hale & Hearty (*Upper East Side*)
Katagiri (*Midtown*)
Lorenzo and Maria's Kitchen (*Upper East Side*)
Mangia (*Midtown*)
Neuman & Bogdonoff (*Upper East Side*)
Nyborg & Nelson (*Midtown*)
Park Avenue Catering (*Murray Hill*)
Petrossian (*Midtown*)
Piatti Pronti (*Midtown*)
Sarabeth's Kitchen (*Upper West Side*)
Savories (*Midtown*)
Silver Palate (*Upper West Side*)
Taylor's (*Greenwich Village*)
V.P. To Go (*Greenwich Village*)
William Poll (*Upper East Side*)

Wines and Liquors
Acker Merrall & Condit (*Upper West Side*)
Garnet Liquors (*Upper East Side*)
Morrell & Company (*Midtown*)
Sherry-Lehmann (*Upper East Side*)
William Sokolin (*Murray Hill*)

AFTER
HOURS

DINING

By Andy Birsh

Andy Birsh is a contributing editor at Gourmet, *for which he writes a monthly column on New York dining. For a decade he edited and published* The Restaurant Reporter.

The standard estimate of the number of restaurants in the city of New York is 12,000. Even by limiting the word "restaurant" to mean just those places where gracious and potentially enjoyable full meals are served, the number is still in the low four figures. In other words, there are years and years of interesting lunches and dinners to be had in New York—and one of the amazing things about longtime New Yorkers is the number, and the variety, of these meals that they have consumed. New Yorkers virtually live in restaurants, and restaurants easily outstrip any other sort of public place when it comes to where New Yorkers spend their often hard-won free time.

The Restaurants

What follows is a selective survey of places to eat in Manhattan (with some forays to other boroughs). These are restaurants that please New Yorkers and convey the flavor of the city as well as the flavors of the many culinary styles that have made a home for themselves here. Missing are establishments whose tables are filled mostly with weary tourists, and missing, too, are many fine places that could easily have been included had space permitted.

Exact prices are not quoted, but general levels of expense may be gauged from the descriptions of the restaurants. Bear in mind that eating out in New York is more expensive than eating out nearly anywhere else. An ample meal that is inexpensive in relative terms will probably cost $25 to $30 per person, once drinks, sales tax, and an expected gratuity of at least 15 percent are factored in. Dinners in the middle of the local range are liable to run $40 to $60 per person (on the bottom line), and dinners at the topflight places can easily top $100 per person without anyone's ordering caviar or Champagne.

Only the most expensive restaurants expect their male customers to wear ties and jackets, and these places are also rather strict on banning jeans and sneakers. No matter. There are countless places to go in comfortable, casual clothes. It is, on the other hand, impossible to be overdressed in New York. Should you be all done up in evening clothes and jewels while eating at a pizzeria, the staff and the rest of the customers will barely lift an eye to notice. They'll figure you're going on to a fancy party with lousy food.

But while New York's restaurants can reveal the city at its most extravagant, they can also show it at its wisest and simplest; they preserve its oldest ways and make some daring stabs at the future; some exemplify the city's competitive, fame-seeking edge, while others offer blessed relief from it. They can also provide travellers from anywhere on earth with what may be the most delightful mealtimes they will ever know.

Telephone numbers are included for almost every place mentioned, and calling ahead is a good idea, whether it's to book a table or, at the very least, to ascertain that your plans are in sync with the restaurant's hours of operation. All restaurants listed are in Manhattan (telephone area code 212) unless stated otherwise.

Wine Lists

The diversity of bottles of wine available in New York City probably outstrips that of any other place in the world. Virtually every viticultural zone on earth is represented not only in encyclopedically stocked retail stores, but also in many restaurants. This lucky state of affairs is not just a result of the city's own ethnic diversity, but also a result of how ready many nations are to compete for the status of world-renowned winemaker. With these aspirations go an increasing similarity in style and a reliance on some widely popular grape varietals, such as Chardonnay and Merlot.

For restaurant-goers this means that there are now many options for enjoyable drinking at prices lower than are currently being asked by the great wineries of France, Italy, and California. Spanish wines, for example, are showing up on more lists than just those of Spanish restaurants, and with good reason. Many excellent Spanish reds, such as Rioja, are available fully mellowed and matured at a fraction of what Bordeaux of the same vintage would cost. Chilean wine making, too, is no longer a backwater operation nor a refuge for cheapskates; these, too, are now a fine value in restaurants. German white wines are overcoming not only a long-lasting prejudice against many things German, but those who promote them have done a good job of letting the world know that not all German wine is sweet. Indeed, dry, light wines with the Kabinett classification may be one of the best matches for nearly all foods that complement white wine. These, too, have begun to appear on restaurant lists for far less money than is asked for comparably enjoyable bottles from elsewhere.

ITALIAN

It would be fair to say that although the competition is fierce, the most enjoyable eating in New York is to be found in Italian restaurants. This is no surprise when you consider how very much Italian restaurants have to offer: meals that can be either quick, light, and sustaining, or grand feasts; ingredients that ought to be, and usually are, of the most evident freshness; plenty of genially affordable wine (except in the loftiest places); and, of course, pasta, veal, garlic, olive oil, *calamari,* crusty bread, tomatoes, exotic mushrooms, beautiful cheeses, and on and on. New York's Italian cooking has its roots in every corner of Italy, and regional digressions go a long way to keep New Yorkers interested in the subject. Travellers to the city are usually amazed by the vast difference in variety and quality between Italian food here and that in most of the rest of America.

Little Italy

The portion of the Lower East Side that is still called Little Italy (in spite of the near-total relocation of Italian-

Americans to the suburbs) teems with Sicilian and Nea-
politan restaurants, many of which, unfortunately, serve
dreary food. There are exceptions. **Teresa and Mimmo**, at
181 Grand Street (near Mulberry Street), has huge paintings of Naples, mirrors, and a penchant for using good,
fresh ingredients in such old-fashioned must-order dishes as large, handmade ravioli filled with cheese; fennel-
flavored sausages with roasted peppers; and long, grease-
less strands of deep-fried zucchini. The menu is very long
indeed, which is their way of saying they'll make whatever you like. Tel: 966-6862.

Far newer is **Taormina**, a spacious, bright, immacu-
lately maintained establishment nearby, at 147 Mulberry
Street, that is somewhat more expensive than other
family-style places down here. Big tables convey a sense
that families of 12 are always welcome, and the circulating antipasto cart is a nicely dated touch. The very exacting chef-proprietor is descended from cooks in the noble
houses of Naples. Tel: 219-1007.

People—well, mostly guys who have been waiting all
week, or all their lives, to behave disgracefully in public—
head unerringly for **Puglia**, at 189 Hester Street (near
Mulberry Street). The kitchen does nothing to distract
them from the rowdiness at hand, and the management
has the decency to charge very little for what it sends out.
Tel: 226-8912.

Greenwich Village and South

There are more small, affordable Italian restaurants in
Greenwich Village than would be easy to count. Of particular note at the moment is **Arlecchino**, at 192 Bleecker
Street (between Sixth Avenue and MacDougal Street), in
the heart of the espresso-sipping, folk-song-remember-
ing, poetry-pondering world south of Washington Square.
Fanciful images in all media of the harlequin figure from
commedia dell'arte cover the walls and shelves, but the
menu sticks to and succeeds with the basics: first-rate
pasta, golden chicken *scarpariello,* and tender veal chops.
As should be expected, the coffee is superb. Arlecchino
keeps very long hours. Tel: 475-2355.

Several restaurants in the area have had their doors
open for decades, such as the readily affordable **Grand
Ticino**, at 228 Thompson Street (near West 3rd Street; Tel:
777-5922), and **Minetta Tavern**, at 113 MacDougal Street
(on the corner of Minetta Lane; Tel: 475-3850). Others are
part of a Florentine tide of eateries that has brought real

trattoria fare to an area that ought to have real trattorias. **Cent'Anni**, at 50 Carmine Street (between Bleecker and Bedford streets, just west of Sixth Avenue), has simple decor and a tiny kitchen, but is justly renowned for its cooking. Wild mushrooms, handfuls of fresh herbs, and rich, fruity olive oils find their way into a remarkable range of dishes, which includes perhaps the best bowl of soup in New York. Add some rare Tuscan wines and the check will start to climb, but most of the customers are in raptures over their meals and don't care. Tel: 989-9494.

Da Silvano, an older Florentine standout, at 260 Sixth Avenue (between Bleecker and Houston streets), is priced higher than Cent'Anni but has a more worldly, fashionable air and some sidewalk tables for the good weather. The place gets quite busy in the evening, but when the midday customers (some of whom are SoHo art dealers) carefully work on their artichokes, a sophisticated leisureliness prevails. The printed menu provides only a portion of the news on what's available. Tel: 982-2343.

Some newcomers seem to be here to remind New Yorkers that Italy stands for sleek design and that pasta is an art form and not just a chore for mamma. **Rosolio**, at 11 Barrow Street (off Seventh Avenue near Sheridan Square), doesn't require customers to appear in Milanese tailoring, but they do anyway. Low-slung black leather chairs allow for lingering conversations after the consumption of superb hand-cut pasta. Tel: 645-9224.

New generations have revitalized some other, older places. **Rocco**, at 181 Thompson Street (between Bleecker and Houston streets), is now in the hands of the former boss's sons, and they have refreshed the look of the place and awakened the somnolent waiters. Family atmosphere still prevails. Tel: 677-0590. **Ballato**, at 55 East Houston Street (near Mulberry Street), a sort of gateway to Little Italy, is also still a family operation, only the family has changed. The former owners were courtly Sicilians who befriended Andy Warhol, Leo Castelli, and other art-world luminaries. Now this venerable storefront (with a little courtyard in back) is run by the sons of Anthony Macagnone, the owner of Sal Anthony, a long-running establishment near Gramercy Park. The old modern art is gone, but good food is still easy to come by here. Tel: 274-8881.

It may well be true that there is a good Italian restaurant out there for everyone. The well-heeled downtown art crowd takes its calamari and *tiramisù* at **Arqua** and

Barocco, 281 and 301 Church Street (a few blocks below Canal Street), respectively. Both are modishly stark and very noisy, and both belie their black-clad patrons' apparent disenchantment with life. Cooking as good as this can put a song in the heart of the most studied nihilist. Tel: 334-1888 for Arqua; 431-1445 for Barocco.

Chelsea

The Florentines have set down in Chelsea, too. **Chelsea Trattoria**, at 108 Eighth Avenue (south of 16th Street), is snug and small and friendly and serves food that is far better (and a little costlier) than its unassuming façade suggests. Tel: 924-7786. **Le Madri**, at 168 West 18th Street (near Seventh Avenue), is large, airy, rarefied, and fashionable. Its name, "The Mothers," refers to the Tuscan owner's policy of importing trios of Italian women who are known for their cooking to act as advisers to the kitchen for six-month stints. The results are impressive, if expensive. Wildly imaginative fresh-fruit-and-vegetable sculptures substitute for flowers. Tel: 727-8022.

Southern Italian

For the most part, the American public recognizes a distinction between Northern and Southern Italian cooking. Southern is synonymous with "tomatoey," and Northern means "kind of expensive." In its deep fascination with Italian cooking, New York has pushed beyond this simple formula. The cooking of Southern Italy is not only preserved (to some extent) in Little Italy but is also celebrated in stylish new places that have introduced something of a second wave of Southern Italian cuisine.

A Sicilian chef named Maria Sindoni owns a pair of very good restaurants, **Azzuro** and **Baci**, on opposite sides of town, that have fairly extensive menus and vie tenaciously for the eggplant crown. Sautéed *pleurotes* reach an apogee at these places, and Sindoni's cold orange *zabaglione* with strawberries may be the stuff of future legends. Baci, at 412 Amsterdam Avenue (near 80th Street), is the more casual of the pair—no reservations or credit cards, and it is open midday. Tel: 496-1550. Azzuro, at 245 East 84th Street (between Second and Third avenues), where nearly everything is indeed a vibrant blue, serves dinner solely. Tel: 517-7068.

Homage to the vacation playgrounds of the Amalfi Coast is offered at **Sistina**, a snug, superior outpost of traditional cooking at 1555 Second Avenue (between 80th and 81st streets), and somewhat the same theme prevails at **Positano**, a far larger establishment at 250 Park Avenue South (at 20th Street). Both can promise superior risotto, seafood, and the traditional chocolate-and-almond dessert *torta di mandorle*. Tel: 861-7660 for Sistina; 777-6211 for Positano.

Northern Italian

Northern Italian comes in many different shapes and sizes. Apart from the Florentines, there are Venetians, Milanese, Piedmontese, and some culinary free agents who have built styles of their own. While not necessarily cooking by the old rules, these innovators would make centuries of traditional Italian cooks proud. Some of these places also have the questionable distinction of being the most expensive Italian restaurants on earth; no meal in Italy could possibly cost as much.

Primavera brings Old World comfort to an otherwise characterless corner of Yorkville, at 1578 First Avenue (at 82nd Street). Park Avenue's denizens have no trouble negotiating the distance east from their co-ops when the late autumn brings white truffles from Alba to Primavera and the waiters are shaving the precious fungi onto steaming bowls of fettucine. When the season ends, the gang gets by with meltingly tender *capretto* (baby goat), sweetly delectable veal, and game birds. An expensive outing but a great one. Tel: 861-8608.

Palio, at 151 West 51st Street (near Seventh Avenue), not only has a major kitchen, but is also a design tour de force. The downstairs bar is dominated by a four-sided depiction of *il palio,* the reckless annual horse race run through the main piazza of Siena, painted by the Italian Neo-Expressionist Sandro Chia. The upstairs has an almost Japanese orderliness, and tables are set with the sort of fine wafer-thin crystal that can't possibly go into dishwashers. Risottos are to be adored here, and so is venison. Pre-theater menus are offered daily, although it's a toss-up whether or not Palio is the better show. Tel: 245-4850.

Nearby but less expensive is **Remi**, which takes its inspiration in looks and cooking from Venice. Remi is also quite large and, like Palio, is installed in a new skyscraper, one misleadingly called 1325 Avenue of the Americas that is actually on West 53rd Street, closer to Seventh Avenue. One wall is glass and looks out onto a *galleria*-style arcade, and although the light that consequently pours in may not qualify as Venetian, the jaunty stripes on much of the decor certainly do. Seafood and rice and other traditional specialties share the menu with the chef's inventions (such as whole-wheat spaghetti tossed with wild mushrooms and *speck,* Italian smoked ham). The wine list, helpfully categorized by price levels, goes on forever, in an array of Italian names that maybe 90 people in the world can discriminate among. A point is made about Italy's bounty and sophistication. Tel: 581-4242.

The Upper West Side now has a major entry in the field in the form of **Carmine's,** which has been installed (to look old) in a vast space at 2450 Broadway (between 90th and 91st streets). The food could be described as "retro Italian-American," for here one finds brimming platters of linguine and meatballs, chicken *contadina,* lobster *fra diavolo,* and that old favorite, veal parmesan. The brimming platters are meant for sharing by two or more, so the total cost can be light indeed. Tel: 362-2200.

The installation of a primitive-looking wood-stoked oven gives the charmingly understated **Mazzei,** on the Upper East Side at 1564 Second Avenue (near 81st Street), a culinary advantage. Instead of making pizza in the special oven, the house primarily uses it to give delicately smoky character to small casseroles of *calamari* or wild mushrooms or *radicchio* with smoked mozzarella. These can happily precede pan-braised swordfish or roasted chicken with very hot Tuscan peppers. Mazzei keeps the butter to a minimum and serves fresh *ricotta* with a tomato-topped bread (a version of *focaccia*) that is baked in the charcoal oven. Tel: 628-3131.

A worthwhile escape from luxury and novelty may also be found on the Upper East Side at **Triangolo,** 345 East 83rd Street (near First Avenue), a smart, one-room restaurant with a long list of very good pastas (mostly housemade) and short lists of everything else. Welcome low prices prevail, but payment is in cash only. This is the sort of place that ought to be in every neighborhood in every city, but few others are so lucky. Tel: 472-4488.

Italian in Brooklyn

For those willing to travel, an expedition to Coney Island, where Brooklyn meets the Atlantic Ocean, can be an experience to treasure. Take either the B or the F subway all the way to the end (about an hour), or drive along the Belt Parkway, passing under the Verrazano-

Narrows Bridge, until the skeleton of the old parachute-jump tower appears on the horizon. At 2911 West 15th Street (between Surf and Mermaid) is **Gargiulo's**, a monument to the generations-old tradition of having a really big dinner. In case Coney Island doesn't whet your appetite for seafood (Coney Island was prettier 80 years ago), the giant plaster octopus stretched across Gargiulo's ceiling should bring seafood to mind. Share a Deep Sea Royal (plenty of seafood, plenty of pasta), lotsa wine, and pray that you pick the lucky number from 1 to 90 that means dinner is on the house. It happens at least once a night. Then hit Surf Avenue and its clackety, terrifying landmark roller coaster, the Cyclone. Your car should be quite safe behind the high brick walls (topped with jagged glass) in Gargiulo's lot. Tel: (718) 266-4891.

Coney Island is also home to **Totonno's Pizzeria Napolitana**, 1524 Neptune Avenue (at West 16th Street), a shrine to masterful brick-oven pizza-making. The rules are rigid here—whole pies only (no slices sold)—and the prices are high by pizzeria standards. The payoff is card-thin crusts, very fresh toppings, and no pizza bellyache afterward. Tel: (718) 372-8606.

The cult also thrives far closer to Manhattan at **Patsy's**, 19 Old Fulton Street (between Front and Water streets), in the shadow of the Brooklyn Bridge. Almost as great a treat as the pizzas is a jukebox there devoted in large part to Frank Sinatra. Tel: (718) 858-4300.

Italian in the Bronx

The Bronx has a thriving Italian neighborhood centered on Arthur Avenue, not far from the Bronx Zoo. From Manhattan take the Metro-North train on the Harlem Line from Grand Central Station to Fordham Road; walk four blocks east to Arthur Avenue. By car, cross the Willis Avenue Bridge to the Bruckner Expressway, take that to the Bronx River Parkway, and then take the Bronx River to Fordham Road, which meets Arthur Avenue at a gas station.

There are shops here that make traditional sausages, salamis, cheeses, and pastries, and several restaurants that whip it all up into finished dishes. One is **Dominick's**, at 2335 Arthur Avenue (between 186th and 187th streets), which is so informal that customers all sit packed together at long communal tables and waiters heft platters of food over heads. They never prepare nearly enough divinely good stuffed peppers. No reservations, no credit cards; Tel:

(718) 733-2807. Across the street is **Mario's**, at 2342 Arthur
Avenue, which has tablecloths, printed menus, and waiters
with note pads. Prices are higher, but the food equals
Dominick's in gusto, and no one's windbreaker is in your
linguine. Tel: (718) 584-1188.

FRENCH

Bistros

Cutting more and more deeply into the devotion New
Yorkers feel for their Italian restaurants are the carefully
replicated French bistros. This may well be because bistros have the reputation for bringing a certain gladdening
vigor to everyday eating. Whatever the cause, they're all
over town, and new ones crop up constantly. Never has so
much *cassoulet, choucroute garni,* and *rillettes* of pork
been dished out in Manhattan.

In its own way, the West Village has the charm of a
Parisian *arrondissement.* It seems natural, then, to find
some of the city's best bistros wedged in among the
shaded, crooked streets of this neighborhood. "**14**" (formerly known as Quatorze), at 240 West 14th Street (near
Eighth Avenue), is a classic: a quaint and handsome setting with relaxed atmosphere and lusty, authentic bistro
food. It is also fairly inexpensive (a big salad with *lardons*
is easily enough for two as a first course) and therefore
crowded. Reservations are essential; Tel: 206-7006. An
offshoot, **Quatorze bis**, has opened on the Upper East
Side, at 323 East 79th Street (near Second Avenue), with
the same menu and prices. Tel: 535-1414.

A wooden girl in traditional French country dress announces the entrance to **Chez Jacqueline**, at 72 MacDougal Street (between Bleecker and Houston streets). She
holds the menu card for the day, which may list such
delights as roast leg of lamb with flageolet beans or roast
pork with Dijon mustard. Other house specialties are
solidly Niçoise (as are the owners), so look for *pissal-
adière* and *brandade de morue*. The restaurant inside is
handsome and comfortable, the service and wine list
exemplary. Tel: 505-0727.

Chez Jacqueline's creators have opened another cozy,
agreeable spot a few blocks away at 18 King Street (at
Sixth Avenue). Called **Le Pescadou**—Niçois for "the
fisherman"—this establishment proffers specialties that
almost all come from the sea. Look not only for potent
bouillabaisse, but for garlicky *bourride,* another great

Provençal seafood stew. Also not to be missed are classic tarts made with fruits of the season. Tel: 924-3434.

The French peasant farms of yesteryear are evoked by **La Métairie**, at 189 West 10th Street (near Seventh Avenue). Flowers, country furnishings, and bare floors add up to a look that accords well with duck dishes, hearty salt-cod dishes, *chèvre* salads, lamb, and homey desserts. The wine list is long and wide-ranging. Tel: 989-0343.

"Straightforward" is the word for **Café Loup**, a loyalty-inspiring bistro in roomy digs at 105 West 13th Street (near Sixth Avenue). Warmed rounds of garlic sausage, steaks with slender *pommes frites,* and a selection of fruit tarts are always on hand, as are a museum-grade display of photographs and a changing list of intriguing wines (at merciful prices that may make them seem even more intriguing). Tel: 255-4746.

A recent arrival on the bistro scene is the huge and very admirable **Steak Frites**, at 9 East 16th Street. Initially, the menu was to consist almost solely of grilled rib-eye steaks with French-fried potatoes, but this began to seem rather like an act of stinginess from a kitchen that could easily do more. Now the fries are great, and so are steaks, roasted herbed chicken, wintertime *pot-au-feu,* and summer salads. The midday hamburger is arguably the best in New York, and the *profiteroles*—cream-puff pastry filled here with praline ice cream and topped with chocolate sauce—are inarguably the best in town. Tel: 463-7101.

Florent, 69 Gansevoort Street (between Hudson and Washington streets), was once a meat-packing-district diner and is still open 24 hours a day. Downtown types now sit elbow-to-elbow with Wall Streeters here, and they all seem to enjoy the flow of wine and the rough country cooking. Tel: 989-5779.

Farther uptown is **La Colombe d'Or**, 134 East 26th Street (just off Lexington Avenue). Its rooms have the feeling of a country inn. Large parties can sit at a big round table in the back of the room. The Provençal cooking has recently improved in a big way, so it's worth a visit for more than the pots of *tapenade*—olive and anchovy paste—to spread on the delicious yeasty bread. Tel: 689-0666.

A French chef with very lofty credentials, Jean-Michel Diot, and a couple of his buddies have teamed up at **Park Bistro**, at 414 Park Avenue South (between 28th and 29th streets), a jolly, crowded little joint whose kitchen produces some splendidly fancy stuff at bistro prices. Lunches feature the delectable cold arrays—*assiettes*—of hams, veggies, etc., that every bistro ought to sell. Tel: 689-1360. Their success has produced two offshoots, an even less formal eatery and butcher shop called **Les Halles**, which is directly across Park Avenue South from the bistro and is rip-roaringly popular (Tel: 679-4111), and **Brasserie des Théâtres**, at 243 West 46th Street (between Broadway and Eighth Avenue), a welcome addition to the Theater District that keeps long hours and looks like Paris in 1910 (Tel: 719-5588).

The winds of fashion have whipped up to gale force at **Jo Jo**, at 160 East 64th Street (near Lexington Avenue), another outpost for a chef, Jean-Georges Vongerichten, fleeing employment in a multi-starred kitchen. Vongerichten, who is Alsatian, may turn out the very best roast chicken during an era when New Yorkers can't seem to get enough of this basic dish, and he eschews sauces in favor of flavorful broths and tiny amounts of infused oils. The calories thus saved can be blissfully ingested at dessert (chocolate cake with warm chocolate mousse, for instance). Tel: 223-5656.

Chez Napoleon, 365 West 50th Street (between Eighth and Ninth avenues), is a popular place to come before or after the theater. After decades of service the decor is a little frayed but nevertheless comfortable, and the food is always dependably good and affordable. Tel: 265-6980.

Another popular theater restaurant is **René Pujol**, at 321 West 51st Street (between Eighth and Ninth avenues). There is nothing chic about this place, but the food is reliable, the service friendly, and you'll be in your theater seat on time. It is a bit more cushy than a bistro, but the food still has gusto. Tel: 246-3023.

Chez Josephine, 414 West 42nd Street (between Ninth and Tenth avenues), set amid a group of playhouses called Theater Row, is named for Josephine Baker and is run by one of her adopted French children, Jean-Claude. Her semiclad likeness hangs everywhere, and her *joie de vivre* lives on in cooking that cheerfully varies between bistro and Deep South. The house's well-thumped piano is, in fact, the same instrument Ms. Baker practiced with in Harlem before her epochal trip to Paris in 1925. Tel: 594-1925.

French Restaurants

French restaurants, as in the phrase "fancy French restaurant," have a shorter history in New York than you might suspect. A hundred years ago, in the city's first heyday of grand public eating, the action was controlled by Germans and Italians. There were traditional French influences on the highest-priced meals, and an evocation of Paris was always good for a few extra pennies on the right-hand column of the menu, but proud, authoritative French cooking was little known here until after World War II.

Even then there was not much of the real thing. Good little bistros that specialized in the cuisines of rigorous French frugality (plenty of tongue, kidneys, and mussels on the menu, beef and birds fit for stewing in the pots) dotted Manhattan, but *haute cuisine* meant some mushrooms and a little wine in the sauce for the Chateaubriand and, for a big occasion, lobster Thermidor—the cooking, in fact, not of the restaurants of France but of the first-class dining rooms on ocean liners.

The lighter, fresher, more delicate manner of cooking that emanated from the kitchen of Fernand Point of La Pyramide in Vienne took hold only later, at the legendary Le Pavillon (which was a holdover from the French pavilion at the 1939 World's Fair). For more than 30 years Le Pavillon was considered the best restaurant in New York, and even now, two decades after the place's extinction, former employees still work many of the best dining rooms and kitchens in the city. Le Pavillon was one of a kind for many years, until other equally ambitious restaurant owners began to open places that played variations on Pavillon's theme of restrained richness of decor, exacting, laborious cooking, waiters trained in Europe, daily attention to costly flower arrangements, and prices that were unapologetically stiff. For many Americans, Le Pavillon was the only place they had ever been where their dinner gave them a thrill.

The pattern set by Le Pavillon was picked up by the newcomers La Grenouille, Lutèce, La Caravelle, and La Côte Basque (the less formal offshoot of Le Pavillon, installed in the original site when Le Pavillon moved).

La Grenouille has always been and remains more fashion conscious than the more puritanical, and more famous, Lutèce (see below), and its mood is also more notably Parisian. Housed in a town house at 3 East 52nd Street (just east of Fifth Avenue), La Grenouille is well known for filling nearly every cranny with great eruptions of fresh flowers (the place closes Mondays because it takes a full day to do all the arranging). Despite the restaurant's association with fashion designers and their latest creations, its menu has changed very little over the past 30 years and seems never to have needed a major update. Something about the scrupulous care the owners take with everything in their environment—the sparkling crystal, the burnished silverware, the virtually flawless cooking—has seemed to lift the restaurant out of time altogether. An amber glow of nostalgia hangs over a room where women will still wear hats to lunch. Tel: 752-1495.

Despite its worldwide reputation as the best restaurant in New York (an endlessly debatable point), **Lutèce** is a cozy place, an out-of-the-way restaurant that is essentially a mom-and-pop operation (Mr. and Mrs. André Soltner) in which Pop, who could be overseeing legions of cooks in some huge, frightfully posh hotel, would rather just cook (or oversee the cooking) for a few people a day and keep things cheery, personal, and actually on a higher standard than you can hit in one of those hotels with so many people coming and going.

In fulfillment of all this, Lutèce is set in a relatively unassuming town house at 249 East 50th Street (near unfancy Second Avenue). Even after a recent redecoration, the rooms still feel like those in a town house and the meal like a well-catered party. The food has gotten lighter, but only in ways that are hard to detect (sauces haven't been thinned out to broths, although they are no longer so rich as to constitute a food in their own right). Should you go to Lutèce when you have only a relatively short time to spend in New York (assuming a reservation can be obtained)? Only if some very pampered time-travel is in order, or if you know you'd like an escape from hard-driving New York while you're still in the city. Tel: 752-2225.

La Côte Basque, at 5 East 55th Street (between Fifth and Madison avenues), has had its culinary ups and downs, but every time things start to ossify, owner Jean-Jacques Rachou revamps his menu and restores the plea-sure. Some might feel that this is his civic duty, because the sprightly, luminous murals of waterfront life in Basque country still form a backdrop to what is certainly one of the ritziest rooms in town. Come hell or high water, the frontmost tables at lunch are still occupied by the latter-day equivalents of the ladies who headquartered here in Truman Capote's venomous unfinished novel *Answered Prayers*. They have the Dover sole and skip dessert. Tel: 688-6525.

Through much of the 1980s **La Caravelle**, at 33 West 55th

Street (between Fifth and Sixth avenues), held on as the stodgiest of the pack. But after some key retirements and shifts in ownership—to André Jammet, son of the founder of the great Hôtel de Bristol in Paris, and his wife, Rita—La Caravelle has emerged as something of a salon, a most welcoming and well-run salon. The Jammets have freshened the look of the dining room, lightened the menu, and attracted a new, sophisticated clientele. This is probably the only one of the topflight French restaurants where one is likely to overhear some good conversation. Lunches at La Caravelle are now sold à la carte, but dinners are still at a fixed (high) price on a par with the other grand restaurants. Special goodies generally add a few dollars to the bill, and a useful rule of thumb is to estimate that each person's meal—with drinks, wine, tax, and tip factored in—will come to about twice the menu's fixed price. Tel: 586-4252.

The creative resurgence in cooking in France that started way back in the 1970s and shows no sign of slowing down has influenced New York in many ways (right down to goat cheese on salads in bars). But it is most keenly felt at some of the city's French outposts.

Lespinasse, at 2 East 55th Street (between Madison and Fifth avenues), in the beautifully refurbished St. Regis Hotel, has a kitchen overseen by a young chef, Gray Kunz, who is actually Swiss, but who was trained by the world-acclaimed master Fredy Girardet. In the best contemporary manner, Mr. Kunz has explored Asia (he commanded a great restaurant in Hong Kong, speaks some marketplace Cantonese, and lived in Singapore as a boy) as well as Europe, and now has come to respect fine American ingredients, too. Thus he will sauté his New York State duck *foie gras* in a Chinese-style taro-root batter or surround his pale ivory fillets of East Coast black sea bass with a sauce infused with Thai-style *kaffir*-lime leaf— neither of which violates the tenets of *haute cuisine*. The dining room in which these lovely meals are served is hushed and spacious, and tables are set with plates commissioned from Tiffany—a style meant to suggest the heyday of John Jacob Astor (the builder of the St. Regis, who gallantly went down with the *Titanic*). Tel: 339-6719.

Le Bernardin, at 155 West 51st Street (between Sixth and Seventh avenues), was at first intended to be the New York branch of a very successful seafood restaurant in Paris owned by a brother and sister, Gilbert and Maguy Le Coze. But given an instant blast of acclaim in New York (and a kitchen that is a professional chef's most glorious dream come true), the Paris operation seemed like old hat and was sold. Now the Le Cozes' unusual cult of fish and shellfish (meat is served grudgingly and only on special request) is centered in Manhattan and has easily as many adherents as it had across the Atlantic. Descended from Breton fishermen, the siblings sell sparkling fresh aquatic fare that has the cold brightness of sashimi and the oceanic goodness of a dockside grill. The food is presented simply, but the dining room is plush and formal, and wonderful genre paintings (heroic fishermen, still lifes of crustaceans) hang on the walls. Desserts are state-of-the-art lovely and yummy. Some people find the seafood regimen more to their liking at midday than in the evening. Very expensive. Tel: 489-1515.

If you have the time or the resources for but one lavish meal in New York, you might well consider **Le Périgord**, a veteran establishment at 405 East 52nd Street (off First Avenue), whose kitchen is in the hands of yet another tireless young genius, in this case Antoine Bouterin. Why here? Well, because the menu reaches in every direction: some very current light food; some conscious throwback dishes; creative *menus gastronomiques;* dessert-lovers' desserts—all served with abundant good humor. It could be the answer to what virtually everyone looks for in a splashy French restaurant. Tel: 755-6244.

AMERICAN

For the purposes of dining out, "American food" has come to mean cooking prepared by chefs with classical training using ingredients that most (or at least some) Americans are familar with, but that would force a normally parochial European to do a bit of head scratching.

This outlook has been raised to a highly individual art by American chef Larry Forgione at his eatery **An American Place**, at 2 Park Avenue (at 32nd Street). He gained attention initially by vowing not to use imported European ingredients (not something New York chefs rely on heavily in the first place), but his talent has been for taking such American vernacular items as corn relish, beef jerky, and apple brown betty and turning them into dishes that lift the senses as vigorously as French cooking will with its own best ingredients on hand. Naturally the wine list is entirely American, too. The best thing about An American Place is that years after proving his point about American food sources, Mr. Forgione keeps using them with love and gusto. Tel: 684-2122.

Looking approvingly, one imagines, over Mr. Forgione's shoulder is Leon Lianides (both men were championed by the cooking authority James Beard), whose **Coach House**, at 110 Waverly Place (a block south of 8th Street, between Sixth Avenue and Washington Square), has been serving gracious American meals (with overtones of the South, although Mr. Lianides is a Greek) for more than 40 years. Rather than spin out new dishes, Mr. Lianides has spent his career perfecting a set of American basics that includes paradigmatic crab cakes, corn sticks, black bean soup, roast rack of Kentucky lamb, steak au poivre, chef's custard, and, for a few special autumn weeks, quince pie. The staff is all in the near-retirement years, and so a meal is not rapid-fire. Tel: 777-0303.

The fires of youth burn elsewhere, most strongly at Bouley and Park Avenue Café, two gracious establishments that are firmly under the control of young American chefs. **Bouley** is the last name of chef David Bouley, and he has fashioned in a southern TriBeCa warehouse zone, at 165 Duane Street (between Greenwich and Hudson streets), a nearly perfect re-creation of the sort of provincial French restaurant where a lovely hedge border protects a parking lot full of large Mercedes-Benzes. Bouley's ceilings are gracefully vaulted, and a dignified calm reigns. The cooking, much of which is very exciting, is French-derived, but with an increasing reliance on local producers of fine ingredients. The chef's geographic center has been moving westward, and the tastes of his customers have been driving him further into seafood. He makes a proud display of his French souvenirs (including an 18th-century walnut front door), but his style is his own. Tel: 608-3852.

Park Avenue Café takes up much of the ground floor of a swanky Park Avenue apartment house (entrance at 100 East 63rd Street) and is home to the adventuresome and often unforgettable cooking of David Burke. The menu is full of intriguing twists and turns (Burke likes, for example, to hide little extra morsels in the lids of dishes), but the chef does not lose sight of basics. Portions are large, and desserts are spectacles—such as an igloo of baked Alaska with a blown-sugar penguin paddling by on a banana kayak. Tel: 644-1900.

For nearly a decade **Chanterelle**, at 2 Harrison Street (at the corner of Hudson Street), in TriBeCa, kept a nightly vigil in a lonely corner of SoHo that somehow remained untouched by the neighborhood's art and apparel boom.

In new, slightly enlarged quarters, David Waltuck continues to turn out long, exquisite meals, while Karen Waltuck presides in front. The Waltucks also have a following among leading artists, many of whom have designed menu covers. These friends of the house include Merce Cunningham, John Cage, and Eric Fischl. (The late Virgil Thomson scored an original number for the Waltucks called "Intensely Two.") David Waltuck's own art has to do with such fine things as seafood sausage in beurre blanc and some surprisingly glamorous approaches to pork and to venison. Chanterelle also offers one of the most extensive cheese boards in the known world—a staggering variety, mostly farm-made, all in peak condition. The evening costs about as much as a minor work of art, but it might hold your affection for longer. Tel: 966-6960.

Chefs are a nomadic lot, and New Yorkers carefully scan the press for the not unexpected news that a cook they admire has just given notice and will soon be appearing at a new stove. Thus when one of these talented drifters finds a place to call true home, the town tends to applaud. Tom Valenti, who opened and left some very good restaurants, has settled down, it would seem, at **Alison on Dominick Street**, a small gem west of SoHo at 38 Dominick Street (between Varick and Hudson streets)—an obscure location that baffles even life-long Manhattanites (although with a move to Midtown in the offing, that problem will soon be erased). It is run by the stylish actress-proprietress Alison Hurt, and she and Mr. Valenti go for the cooking of Southwest France in a big way, hence lentils, lamb shanks, and ducks are treated with special care, and the wines are robust and affordable. Tel: 727-1188.

Some similarly great food can be found these days at vastly reduced cost at a place called, aptly enough, **Prix Fixe**, in a cavernous space at 18 West 18th Street (between Fifth and Sixth avenues). Dinners here run $24 and $36 (including everything but beverages) and lunches for $13.50 and $18.50. It verges on the miraculous that a $24 dinner can commence with *sashimi* tuna "tart" with marinated fennel and black-olive vinaigrette; follow with *tournedos* of salmon with a light horseradish crust; and finish with a chilled dessert soup of berries around a ginger pudding with a big splash of Champagne. The tradeoff is bistro-style service and some noise, but for people for whom food is foremost, Prix Fixe is paradise. Tel: 675-6777.

Some of Manhattan's most daringly different kitchen work is done in a tiny Federal-era corner house east of SoHo that now quarters **Savoy**, 70 Prince Street (at Crosby Street). Peter Hoffman and his wife, Susan Rosenfeld, work closely with farmers who supply the city's network of open-air Greenmarkets, and they devise menu items based on what the markets have to offer. People who get testy when a dish arrives unsalted (the chef is trying to highlight the other tastes) or when their trout comes stuffed with fruit should stay away. The broad-minded will be very pleased. Tel: 219-8570.

More conventionally gratifying is **Lora**, in an old town house at 104 West 13th Street (near Sixth Avenue). Lora Zarubin is a genius at the wood-stoked grill, and all the meats she sells come from chemical-free ranches in California (the animals eat grain fit for human consumption). Her style is bold and direct, and her simple, elegant bar and dining room are hung with fine photographs. Tel: 675-5655.

Anne Rosenzweig gained notice at Vanessa, in Greenwich Village, which has now changed names and hands. Along with a business partner, she opened **Arcadia**, at 21 East 62nd Street (just off Fifth Avenue), one of the smartest small restaurants in the city (it sports a charming panorama of the seasons by Paul Davis), where she has achieved success with such inventions as a lobster club sandwich (lunch) and "chimney-smoked" lobster (for dinner). Tel: 223-2900. She and her business partner Ken Aretsky also took on executive positions at the refurbished **"21" Club**, the posh, hulking Establishment hangout, at 21 West 52nd Street (just off Fifth Avenue), that has slowly but surely emerged from the bygone days when its executive/sportsman clientele was fueled by martinis. Ms. Rosenzweig has little to do with daily operations, leaving the long and ever-expensive menu in the capable hands of Michael Lomonaco, who has gotten his customers off meat and potatoes (and lifeless chicken hash) and into some lively contemporary cooking. Tel: 582-7200.

A similar rejuvenation has been wrought by a chef named Andrew D'Amico at the famously beautiful (and formerly scorned) restaurant **Sign of the Dove**, at 1110 Third Avenue (on the corner of 65th Street). A few years ago, masses of bric-a-brac went heave-ho, and now simple wrought iron, exposed brick archways, skylights, roomy tables, and a barroom inspired by Josef Hoffmann's designs are part of this long-running establishment's attraction. The house-made sourdough is one of the best loaves in town and it may quite conveniently be used to absorb the last drops of Mr. D'Amico's lovely light sauces. During good weather the skylights open, but the cuisine is a lure year-round. Tel: 861-8080.

LOCAL PHENOMENA
There are some restaurants that could happen only in New York, because anything more modest than the ambitions of this city probably could not have propelled them into existence.

At the figurative epicenter stands the **Four Seasons**. Philip Johnson designed it 34 years ago under the eye of Ludwig Mies van der Rohe as a part of Mies's Seagram Building on Park Avenue (the restaurant's entrance is at 99 East 52nd Street). In its looks and manners the Four Seasons may be the purest statement of wealthy, confident Modernism anywhere; it pioneered sans-serif flatware and stemless brandy snifters and elevated basic American foodstuffs to international recognition. Grandly spacious and luxurious in spite of its rigorous geometry, the Four Seasons is something of a law unto itself. Menus and greenery still change on the first day of every season. Hordes of well-attired customers troop past the huge Picasso in the corridor linking the dining rooms or sip drinks beneath Richard Lippold's sculpture comprising thousands of suspended brass rods. Given the size of the place, the kitchen is staggeringly good. The Pool Room, which is named for the square, burbling fountain in its center, offers more elaborate meals than the Grill Room, which is well known for its high-profile clientele at midday (who tend to order the same simple things every time) and its chic and less-expensive suppers at night. The Pool Room has a long menu (which always includes a superb roast duckling), and its waiters perform the carving and plate arranging at tableside. Luscious desserts are wheeled from table to table on a cart that someone, someday, is going to hijack. Tel: 754-9494.

Recessed into the lower level of Grand Central Terminal is the **Grand Central Oyster Bar & Restaurant**, since 1913 a mecca for seafood lovers, commuters, business folk, and those remaining few travellers who expect a celebratory send-off before a train trip. About 2,000 people a day are served under its vast vaulted ceilings, at tables, along counters, and at the granite-topped oyster bar itself, where imperturbable chefs prepare the likes of oyster "pan roasts" or Ipswich clam stews, one portion at a time, wearing what looks like lab gear. Briny fresh oysters (bluepoints, Chincoteagues, Wellfleets, Malpeques, and so on) are pried open all day long to be savored raw, and the kitchen carefully prepares an almost confounding array of the freshest fish, such as yellow perch, Montauk bluefish, smelts, and wolffish, in addition to Atlantic salmon, lemon sole, tuna, halibut, and many more. The Oyster Bar also offers a similarly all-inclusive list of American white wines. Tel: 490-6650; closed on weekends.

Rockefeller Center, between Fifth and Sixth avenues off 50th Street—the visionary office complex in the heart of Midtown—has dramatic eateries at its pinnacle and at its base. At the very top of the RCA Building (now officially the GE Building) is the legendary **Rainbow Room**, a triumph of Style Moderne, recently restored to its 1930s ebullience, with a revolving inlaid dance floor, big-band music, cigarette girls, and fancy, authentically mediocre nightclub food. Many of the dancers on the floor really know their moves; they can fox-trot as gracefully as some of the ice skaters, 65 stories below, can glide. Black tie is never out of step. Tel: 632-5000. (By day the Rainbow Room is a private club.)

Adjacent to Rockefeller Center's sunken rink is the handsomely appointed, spacious **SeaGrill**. It lists far fewer fish than the Oyster Bar but prepares them more elaborately. In the months when there is no skating some of the Lower Plaza is given over to umbrellaed outdoor tables (sharing the territory with the less expensive and less commendable American Festival Café). Very properly suited types inhabit SeaGrill by day, and their very properly dressed families come in at night. Tel: 246-9201.

The magnificent view from the **River Café**, moored in the shadow of the Brooklyn Bridge on the Brooklyn side (at 1 Water Street), takes in Wall Street's towers and the bay and river that almost lap at their edges. The restaurant is a pair of barges in the East River and is rightly famous for its sophisticated American cooking. The stove's current overseer is a young chef named John Loughran, the latest in a distinguished line at the River Café. He succeeds Larry Forgione (see An American Place) and David Burke (see Park Avenue Café). Given the panorama out the windows, the restaurant would fill if it sold only cheese and crackers, and so the excellence of the cooking just serves to make it a tougher booking. The solution: a weekday lunch. An error: trying to get in on Mother's Day.

To reach it by car or cab from Manhattan, take the first exit off the Brooklyn Bridge and follow the road that curves back down to the water. The restaurant will summon a cab or notify a car service, on request, for the return trip. Tel: (718) 522-5200.

The River Café and countless other specks on the cityscape can be pointed to from the restaurant complex **Windows on the World**, which is on the 107th floor of 1 World Trade Center (the north tower). Dinners served in "The Restaurant"—enough table linen here for a tent city—are passably good, but dinners served in the tiny room called **Cellar in the Sky**, which offers a single lengthy, imaginatively orchestrated wine-and-food blowout (with one seating, at 7:30), are marvelous. The catch is that you are cut off from the view. The tower restaurants are closed indefinitely, due to damage sustained in the World Trade Center bombing of February 1993. Tel: 938-1111.

Tavern on the Green, in Central Park at West 67th Street, does more business than any other restaurant in New York, so "tavern" is somewhat misleading: Tabernacle on the Green might come closer. In any case, it is also the city's leading purveyor of hoopla (tens of thousands of firefly-size lights in the trees, chandeliers galore, an unashamed leaning toward desserts). Birthdays are to Tavern on the Green as Christmas is to Macy's. People who think hard about their food go elsewhere, but the spectacle is unrivaled. Tel: 873-3200.

Another local spectacle is the fabled **Russian Tea Room**, best known perhaps for its slogan, "Slightly to the Left of Carnegie Hall," which translates into 150 West 57th Street, near Seventh Avenue. It is home to the czars and czarinas of show business, who assemble here at lunchtime to do business. This must give the nonindustry people who watch them a delicious thrill—they could not possibly be here for the food, which is quite expensive and is doled out with very un-Slavic stinginess. The decoration is indeed cheery, and the caviar and blinis are a delectable splurge after a concert, but if the crummy little pastries that pass for dessert were shown to a real czar he'd call the executioner. Tel: 265-0947.

A few years ago Nikko Hotels, a major Japanese chain, took over the aging Essex House, an Art Deco pile on Central Park South near Seventh Avenue. The firm has restored and in some ways amplified the grandeur of the building. One step was to install a new, very small, uncompromisingly luxurious French restaurant and to call it **Les**

Célébrités (also the name of the restaurant in the Hôtel Nikko in Paris). The chef is Christian Delouvrier, who has brought honor to a number of kitchens in Manhattan. The dishes he has devised look very good on (partially) gilded plates. The name refers to the amateur artists whose paintings adorn the walls; they are celebrities from other fields (most act) who like to paint. The roster includes James Dean, Gene Hackman, Elke Sommer, and Peggy Lee. None of their work detracts much from the pleasure of the meal. Dinner only. Tel: 484-5113.

New York Delis

It has long been pointed out that no all-American city is complete without something called a New York–style deli in which certain facets of traditional Jewish-Romanian party food are sold at varying stages of deep frost. But are there New York–style delis in New York?

"In name only" are the words that might come to the lips of most longtime New Yorkers, for deli food has fallen on hard times, at least as far as eating out is concerned (stunningly fine fare is still available from many sources to carry back to your lair—it's the deli-as-public-accommodation that has suffered lately). The death of Leo Steiner, a voluble, fanatical, corned beef–apotheosizing promoter was a deep blow to the noshing community. Within weeks of Steiner's passing the word was out that his headquarters, the **Carnegie Delicatessen and Restaurant**, at 854 Seventh Avenue (between 54th and 55th streets; Tel: 757-2245), had taken advantage of his unavoidable absence and "changed the coleslaw." It was deemed sweeter, more luncheonette-like, and missing its more difficult, sinus-clearing edge. If they could let the slaw go, might not Steiner's whole legacy be trashed?

The next realization was that aside from the Carnegie, most delis hadn't been very good anyway. They let their meats dry out; the yellow in their chicken broth looked suspiciously industrial; and the chopped liver was clearly made by people who had no idea what it was supposed to taste like. The Carnegie Deli, the **Second Avenue Kosher Deli** (at 156 Second Avenue, at 10th Street), **Sarge's Delicatessen and Restaurant** (at 548 Third Avenue, near 36th Street), and a bunch of others remain busy and popular, but the boasts about their cooking ring very hollow now. Steiner, who had an awesome temper, must be truly beside himself somewhere.

If money is no object, then a kind of feast of Jewish

nostalgia may be held at the **E.A.T. Café**, at 1064 Madison Avenue (near 81st Street). Mushroom barley soup, meat-based borscht, pot roast with a side order of kasha *varnishkas* (steamed buckwheat with onions and bow-tie pasta), and truly magnificent house-baked *challah, mandelbrot,* and *rugelach* are all available in a pretty, rather Parisian-looking setting. That side order of kasha *varnishkas* is eight dollars, so this is a very pricey Memory Lane. The proprietor is Eli Zabar, a member of the family that owns Zabar's, the renowned West Side food store. Though his relatives are famous for bargains, Eli goes the other way—but what he makes is excellent. Other parts of the menu are French and Italian, and E.A.T. Café is easily the best place to eat near the Metropolitan Museum of Art. Tel: 772-0022.

Theater District Dining

The Broadway Theater District has recently undergone a dining renaissance; now avoiding the tourist traps is easy. The two most prominent additions are **Ollie's Noodle Shop & Grill** and **Carmine's**, both branching out from the Upper West Side originals. One is Chinese and the other is Italian, but they are virtually neighbors, at 190 and 200 West 44th Street, respectively (on the same block as the still-infamous Sardi's and Mamma Leone's). Ollie's serves a simplified version of Chinatown *dim-sum* and noodle fare along with rice dishes and soups—a good, cheap, fast meal. Carmine's (see the Italian section) imitates, very persuasively, the family-platter, eat-until-you-burst philosophy of dining that scoffs at the five-perfect-ravioli manner of expensive Italian restaurants. Both Ollie's and Carmine's are dodgy about reservations—their low prices mean they won't hold tables open—so it's best not to try to squeeze in immediately before a show. Tel: 921-5988 for Ollie's; 221-3800 for Carmine's.

Not as immediately successful, but ideal for right before the theater, is **Le Max Restaurant**, at 147 West 43rd Street, a cavernous new place rather astonishingly painted with trompe l'oeil murals and set up to look older than anywhere else in the neighborhood. The food is basic, with a French emphasis, and fairly priced. Tel: 764-3705. **Century Café**, across the street at number 132, recently hired a well-qualified chef who has made this large and decor-free restaurant an attractive place for pastas, salads, grilled chicken, and other everyday fare. It has become a favorite with Broadway performers. Tel: 398-1988.

At the uptown end of the Theater District, an almost incredibly sweet man named Rosario Carvelli has opened **Trionfo**, at 224 West 51st Street (between Broadway and Eighth Avenue), a handsomely appointed Italian restaurant with refined cooking and Mr. Carvelli's brand of service (the antithesis of Carmine's). Adult female customers are not normally permitted to leave without being gently flattered and solicitously looked after. Old World in the best sense. Tel: 262-6660.

The area's officially designated **Restaurant Row**—West 46th Street between Eighth and Ninth avenues—used to be a dining mine field, but now is worth a look. There are still a handful of old-fashioned, cozy French restaurants that are best appreciated for the motherly attention of the waitresses than for *la cuisine*. The best of these is **Café Beaujolais** at number 364. Tel: 974-7464.

The block also supports what is surely Manhattan's only Chinese restaurant, **Pomaire**, at number 371. Named for an artisanal Andean mountain town, the restaurant prepares a number of dishes in clay pots from there. Chilean cooking has affinities with Spanish style and reveals some native traits as well. Meals here are invitingly inexpensive, even with the excellent Chilean wines. Late on Fridays and Saturdays the house offers a big stew, *curanto,* and provides live Andean music in the background. Tel: 956-3055.

On the far side of Ninth Avenue from Restaurant Row is **Zen Palate**, at 663 Ninth Avenue, one of the prettiest vegetarian restaurants ever to open in New York City (there is a modicum of dairy on the menu). The place seems in accord with how a good many non-meat-eaters feel about themselves, for a change. The menu is a bit of the East and a bit of the West and includes bean curd given many rather delicious twists and some lovely salads and noodle fantasies—*shiitake* mushrooms and bean sprouts with pan-crisped green pasta appears in the listings as "Dream-Land." Quite charming. Tel: 582-1669.

CHINESE

The golden age of going out for Chinese food lasted from about the time that President Nixon stood on the Great Wall of China until approximately the time of the bicentennial of United States trade with China, a little more than ten years later. These were the years when hot, spicy, colorful, tangy dishes from Szechwan and Hunan provinces appeared in the city, and many dedicated diners had simply never in their lives eaten so well (and for so little money).

The golden age ended as the Grand Openings of Chinese restaurants started to outnumber, by an enormous factor, the chefs with even the most modest talent (Chinese restaurants even appeared to outnumber dry cleaners on the avenues of Manhattan). Five thousand years of culinary greatness declined rapidly into the stuff that New Yorkers sat in front of the TV eating on rainy nights.

Visits to Chinatown (or to the few relatively expensive places outside Chinatown that can afford a real chef) are now the only ways to relive the heyday. Nearly any New Yorker who swears that the take-out place on the corner is very good is really talking about how well the place maintains its delivery bikes and not how well it maintains its cuisine.

Chinatown

Manhattan's Chinatown, however, will provide some magnificent eating. As the neighborhood has grown—it has essentially swallowed up Little Italy and the old Jewish Lower East Side—it has changed from a tourist attraction into a Chinese city (the eventual transfer of Hong Kong from Britain to the People's Republic has sparked a financial boom here that makes Chinatown seem like wall-to-wall banks). With many, many Chinese people to feed, the newest, biggest restaurants no longer promote such Western concerns as "our Cocktail Lounge" and don't care that their English-language menus hopelessly misrepresent what their kitchens really produce.

The way around this is simply to eat the way Chinese people eat. Gather a group of anywhere from eight to a hundred people, walk into a big, busy Chinatown restaurant at the very busiest time, and order a fixed-price banquet, which might cost $180 but will handily feed ten people. It's still $180 whether you are eight people or twelve people; the quantity of food is not adjusted until your group becomes *two* tables. Even if every dish doesn't meet with universal acceptance, there is still more than enough food to send the gang rolling home.

98 Mott Restaurant, at 98 Mott Street, is the sort of place to go for a huge evening banquet (no prior arrangement necessary), and so are the **Silver Palace**, at 50 Bowery, the **Golden Unicorn**, at 18 East Broadway, and the

Nice Restaurant (which has a particularly adept kitchen), at 35 East Broadway. You need the names of all three of these places because one or more are liable to be booked solid with big parties. The meal generally begins with savory hors d'oeuvres, moves through a velvety soup (often made from winter melon), and usually pushes on through shellfish, duck, chicken, beef, bean curd, and, last but not least, a glorious whole fresh fish. Coke, Sprite, Tsing-Tao beer, and tea are the beverages of choice.

From early morning until about 4:00 P.M. all of these restaurants offer *dim sum,* the small plates of dumplings, fritters, meat morsels, and sweets that are meant to accompany tea, gossip, and newspaper reading (ask for the *better* tea; it's worth the $1.50). Women circulate through the restaurants pushing carts, each laden with several different dishes. **Triple Eight Palace**, at 88 East Broadway, has an outstandingly broad and well-prepared selection. **H.S.F.** (for Hee Seung Fung), at 46 Bowery, offers its daytime *dim sum* along with explanations for the inexperienced, and consequently a long line can form at peak times on weekends. You pay in cash based on a tally of your empty plates (the range is from two to four dollars per plate, and four or five small dishes will satisfy most people).

Diners unable to summon legions of companions have their Chinatown options, too. Very good and very up-to-the-minute Hong Kong–style food is offered at **Wong and Kwong**, 11 Division Street (near Chatham Square). Seafood is a big deal here, especially when there are live shrimp to be netted from a tank and steamed to order— great as a first course with Chinese beer. The house has a knack for introducing authentic Cantonese dishes to Westerners whose notions of Cantonese cooking were ruined in childhood by bad take-out. Tel: 431-1040. Less guidance is offered at the cacophonously boisterous **Oriental Garden Restaurant**, 14 Elizabeth Street (near Canal Street), but the fresh fish and other items from the sea are superbly and very inexpensively prepared. Stays open until 2:00 A.M. Tel: 619-0085.

Soups are the main topic on the menu at **First Taste**, 53 Bayard Street (near Elizabeth Street), and they are exceptional—pure, deeply flavored, and nourishing. These meals-in-themselves are brought to the table in big bowls for sharing in little bowls, and a great variety of ingredients can add flavor and substance to the basic broth. First Taste is also one of the few places in Chinatown that gives a hoot about the aesthetics of eating—the Formica and linoleum basics are augmented by modest display cases of antiques and *objets d'art*. Tel: 962-1818.

Great Shanghai, at 27 Division Street (between East Broadway and Bowery), has playful Postmodern decor and offers do-it-yourself hot-pot meals with a marvelous sauce you blend to your liking from 12 ingredients. You select the seafood, meats, and vegetables to slip into the bubbling hot pot from a long list—each item is priced individually—and the more you select the more complex and aromatic the cooking liquid becomes when you drink it as the meal's last touch. Whole fish are also prepared particularly well here, and the best dessert in Chinatown, a hot "eight-treasure" rice gâteau (*ba bo fan*), is on hand, too; place the order for it at the beginning of the meal. Tel: 966-7663.

Chinese Elsewhere in Manhattan

Away from Chinatown are the myriad Hunans (Lake, Park, House, Tower, Cottage, Balcony, and so on) and Szechwans, but few serve food worth stopping for. Good food, matched with handsome surroundings, is to be found in **Chin Chin**, at 216 East 49th Street (between Second and Third avenues), which is run by two brothers named Chin. Elegantly framed studio photos of their Taiwan boyhood line the walls, and the back room is one of the most austerely lovely eating salons in the city. Just the place to gnaw delicately tea-smoked duck. Tel: 888-4555.

Exactingly executed Cantonese cooking is the reason to visit **Fu's**, at 1395 Second Avenue (between 72nd and 73rd streets). The decor is hard-edged glitz, and the staff is less than chummy, but there is no argument with the kitchen and its way with glistening fresh seafood. Tel: 517-9670.

Some old hands in the business recently opened **Our Place**, at 1444 Third Avenue (at 82nd Street), and the Italianate minimalist decor (black chairs, white walls) is so bare that anything heartier than mineral water seems out of place. But the cooking is good and the kitchen makes an effort to cook with the seasons and to show off the freshness and color of its ingredients. Tel: 288-4888.

Basic black is used to dramatic effect in the West Side's **Shun Lee**, at 43 West 65th Street (near Columbus Avenue), which has a black-on-black main dining room (expensive) encircled by a wonderful crinkly fiberglass dragon. A side room, **Shun Lee Café** (not expensive), offers a limited menu of *dim sum* and noodle dishes, which makes it a fine choice for pre– or post–Lincoln Center suppers. The café is done up in a striking black-and-white checker pattern that M. C. Escher would have loved. Tel: 595-8895.

Almost as bold looking is the very successful new **Chiam**, at 160 East 48th Street (near Third Avenue). There is an air of celebration about the place, as if Chinese New Year were just about to begin, but the cooking has been conscientiously lightened in the fat and salt departments, making it suitable for nonindulgent occasions. Tel: 371-2323. The heights of luxury (and cost) may be scaled at **Tse Yang**, 34 East 51st Street (between Madison and Park avenues), a reassuringly dark and private enclave that offers, among other things, the best Peking duck in the city—they remove all the fat from the undersides of the "lacquered" skin and wrap it in the sheerest of Chinese pancakes. Tel: 688-5447.

JAPANESE

Real Japanese food came to the city not to provide Americans with something new to eat but to supply much-needed tastes of home to the growing numbers of Japanese businessmen dispatched to the New York office. For their sake, Japanese restaurants (down to the actual building materials) were shipped (stamped "Midtown Manhattan," it seemed) across the Pacific. The surprise was that curiosity about a sushi bar or a warren of tatami rooms or buckets of noodles would pull New Yorkers in off the streets as well, and that they would come back for more.

Sushi and sashimi were the Japanese specialties that attracted the most attention, and eating raw fish, like jostling for lox at Zabar's, became a rite of passage for newcomers to the city. The ability to order individual portions of sushi or sashimi in passable Japanese was a badge of worldly sophistication. This fashion for raw fish has waned among the non-Japanese, which must come as a relief to homesick Japanese businessmen who now can peacefully soak up some of the raffish conviviality that characterizes sushi bars in the old country. To this end, the Japanese flock to **Sushiden**, at 19 East 49th Street (just off Madison Avenue), an architecturally pleasing spot with two long counters made of traditional Japanese cypress as well as some regular tables. It's best to order "piece by piece" (actually two pieces at a time) at the counters. Tilefish, ark shell, yellowtail, and *toro* (the richest cut of tuna) all have their seasons, and the chefs behind the counters will gladly point out what is best at the moment. At the tables it is customary to order a large assortment of sushi or sashimi for communal delectation. There are also some hot dishes on the menu. The waitresses are as adept and polite as their counterparts in Japan. Tel: 758-2700.

Of longer standing and in perpetual struggle for the number one spot in the "best of" lists are **Hatsuhana**, with branches at 17 East 48th Street (just west of Madison) and 237 Park Avenue (in an arcade between 45th and 46th streets), and **Takesushi**, with only one venue, at 71 Vanderbilt Avenue, which is the street bordering Grand Central Station to the west. Both cater to an interestingly international clientele and have a busy, no-nonsense air that makes you feel you are in the right place. Tel: 355-3345 and 661-3400 respectively for Hatsuhana; 867-5120 for Takesushi.

Another intriguing option is New York's first *okonomi-yaki* joint, a type of small restaurant found all over Japan, and especially in Osaka. The term means "as you like it," and that which is made to your liking is a chunky crêpe binding together various combinations of seafood, veggies, pork, and even eggs and noodles. Customers sit at counters lined with big griddles or at tables with a wooden edge and a griddle in the center. At night, *teppanyaki,* the artful carving and quick cooking of sirloin (primarily), takes place on the same surface. The "crêpes" are one of the cheap, sustaining meals (under $10 at lunch) that have made Japan great. **Chibo Okonomiyaki**, at 47 East 44th Street (between Madison and Vanderbilt avenues), is more pleasingly decorated than most of its counterparts in Japan, and service is eager and prompt.

In New York (as opposed to Tokyo), other Japanese specialties such as sukiyaki, tempura, yakitori, and so forth are usually served under one roof. An example of this is **Nippon**, a large and fairly formal establishment at 155 East 52nd Street (between Lexington and Third avenues), which has a bustling sushi scene but also provides as much culinary variety as perhaps ten restaurants in Japan. It has a short menu of savory little bar treats meant to go well with liquor or *sake,* and tables where people come to eat sukiyaki (the sweet, oniony stew) and *shabu-shabu* (the Mongolian-inspired boiled dinner of beef, many vegetables, and sloppy, slippery noodles). There are also tatami rooms (with wells under the tables to prevent leg cramps in the unpracticed), where long, multicourse banquets can be served in dignified privacy. Tel: 355-9020.

More lavishly lovely is **Seryna**, at 11 East 53rd Street (between Fifth and Madison avenues), which, in the spirit of the grandest restaurants in Japan, has very good art, demure, overqualified waitresses, and tiny portions of luxurious food, some of which is cooked at the table on a heated rock. Tel: 980-9393.

Diners looking for the serene, beautiful side of Japanese life (free of commerce, kitsch, and that Japanese specialty, commerce *in* kitsch) tend to seek out **Omen**, at 113 Thompson Street (between Spring and Prince streets in SoHo). The cooking is delicious and the pottery is also worthy of contemplation. The crowd is young, poised, and wears its basic black attire in a way that is somehow not glum. Tel: 925-8923. A most welcome addition both to SoHo and to Japanese dining in New York is **Honmura An**, beautifully installed in a walk-up loft space at 170 Mercer Street (near Houston Street). The specialty of the house is *soba* cuisine, which mainly takes the form of hand-cut buckwheat noodles and dumplings—a food that is simple, nourishing, satisfying, and linked for centuries with Zen practice. Soba is also oddly delicious, and the family behind Honmura An has been in the business in Tokyo for generations. Tel: 334-5253.

The centerpiece of **Umeda**, at 102 East 22nd Street (near Park Avenue South), is a *sake* bar offering about 30 brands of rice brew and its grain-based relative *shochu*. The *sake*s range from bone-dry to lightly sweet and can be served heated, iced, or at room temperature. Delicious tidbits emerge from the kitchen to accompany the tastings at the bar (the raw beef with a dab of ginger-chili relish is not to be missed), and there are also regular tables and a pair of *tatami* rooms for full meals that are a progression of these small savories. Westerners can be cold-shouldered at *sake* bars in Japan, but that's never the case at Umeda. Tel: 505-1550.

It virtually had to happen: A Japanese corporation had to open the sort of privileged, deeply luxurious restaurant that is so expensive that even rich Japanese think twice about it. The essence of such places is often the beauty of the architecture and the decoration rather than the cooking, so when Chinzan-So New York failed, it left behind a gorgeous shell, perched on stilts on the New Jersey side of the Hudson River. It is now inhabited by a branch of an excellent and affordable sushi-and-tempura chain from Japan called **Hero Chan**. Among things to try here are "dynamite rolls"—a crisp seaweed wrapper filled with ingredients that include grated radish soaked in hot chile sauce. One rarely gets to eat such sociable food in so refined an environment. The restaurant is at 595 River Road, in Edgewater, New Jersey, about 3 miles south of the George Washington Bridge (take the Lemoine Avenue exit) or 3 miles north of the Lincoln Tunnel (take the Weehawken exit). Tel: (201) 945-9450.

SPANISH AND LATIN AMERICAN
Spanish cooking has a long history in New York, and many denizens of the city fondly remember the Spanish restaurants of their youth, places where brimming pots of paella or *mariscado* fed them amply for very little money on their first big dates. The encouraging thing is that the Spanish restaurants of almost everyone's youth are still in business and still feed all comers heartily.

Most typical of the venerable spots is **Sevilla** in Greenwich Village, at 62 Charles Street (near West 4th Street, west of Seventh Avenue). The room is dark and filled with music, the Spanish wine flows freely, and waiters practically buckle under the weight of the pots of food they carry to the tables. The big decisions are whether to have seafood or land food in the paella and whether to try to go it alone or split the main course two ways. Whichever, the prices are an act of mercy. Tel: 929-3189.

Café San Martín, at 143 East 49th Street, is blessedly undim. In fact, its charming host, Ramon San Martín, could easily brighten the place himself. While still an excellent value, dinner here is more elaborate than in the Village places, and the roast meats and splendid desserts are actually to be preferred to filling up on a big rice dish. Some house specialties include *chorizo* sausage braised in red wine, and a genuine delicacy: baby eels from Spain flash-cooked with garlic and hot pepper flakes. Tel: 832-9270.

Adventuresome diners may want to try **Río Mar**, a little splinter of Bilbao among the trucks of the meat-purveying district, at 7 Ninth Avenue (near Little West 12th Street). The specialty here is phenomenally low-priced juicy steaks with huge fried potatoes, but the bar serves up real *tapas,* the little tidbits meant to foster drink sales, and was doing so long before *tapas* became chic. You are more than welcome to toss your peanut shells on the floor. Tel: 243-9015.

Probably the best bar-scene-with-*tapas* at the moment is to be found at **Solera**, 216 East 53rd Street (between Third and Second avenues), a handsome newer place with a zigzagging bar where the *tapas* are convivially downed by an after-work crowd that may, by now, know a thing or two about the great Sherries Solera has to offer. The unusually multiregional dining-room menu has been assembled by a fine American chef with a driving passion for Spanish cuisine. Tel: 644-1166.

Brazilian

Brazilian cooking can be found in generous supply and close concentration along two blocks west of Fifth Avenue in Midtown. A pleasant introduction can be made at **Via Brasil**, at 34 West 46th Street (between Fifth and Sixth avenues). Spit-roasted chicken and the Brazilian "national dish," a dark, starchy ham-and-sausage stew called *feijoada,* are the usual things to order, after hearts of palm and shrimps cooked a variety of ways. To finish: guava jelly with cream cheese and, of course, a cup of Brazilian coffee. Tel: 997-1158.

Not far away, at 123 West 45th Street (between Sixth and Seventh avenues), is **Cabaña Carioca**, a joint where music reigns and the menu includes a few Portuguese dishes, as well as the Brazilian standbys. The portions of food are gargantuan, which you might not notice after a few shots of *cachaça,* the Brazilian white-lightning sugar-cane liquor (also used in the "Brazilian margarita," the *caipirinha*). People come here to make noise, and the place is built to take it. Tel: 581-8088.

Argentine

The IRT number 7 subway train can whisk you from Times Square or Grand Central in Midtown Manhattan out to Jackson Heights in Queens, where at the intersection of Roosevelt Avenue and Junction Boulevard (which is the name of the stop at which you detrain) there is a concentration of Argentine enterprises that includes several good restaurants. One of them is **La Cabaña Argentina**, at 95-91 Roosevelt Avenue. A gigantic wood-stoked grill in the front window should give it away that platters of juicy meats and sausages, the traditional *parillada,* are the house specialty, which is meant to be washed down

with robust Argentine wine—all an excellent value to
boot. Dinner only. Tel: (718) 429-4388. And what do many
Jackson Heights Argentines like for dinner? The spectacu-
larly good *paella* at *their* local Spanish restaurant, **El
Bodegon**, 40-20 Junction Boulevard (near 41st Avenue).
This may be one of the great affordable feasts in all New
York. Tel: (718) 457-0121.

STEAKS

You could always get a good steak in New York, from the
time when slaughterhouses lined the piers of the East
River and the best cattle in the West were sent to New
York, where they could command a higher price than
anywhere else in the country. The slaughterhouses have
been replaced by the United Nations and the leafy tranquility of Beekman Place, but New Yorkers are still willing
to pay exorbitant prices for a good cut of meat.

What **Christ Cella** (pronounced Cri-SEL-la), 160 East
46th Street (near Third Avenue), lacks in decor, it makes
up tenfold in service and the quality of its cooking.
Attention is paid to the simple requirements of meat and
potatoes as well as to shellfish. There are no menus, so
listen carefully to the waiter's catalogue of appetizers
and entrées—it's not long, but you don't want to miss a
single thing. Tel: 697-2479.

Peter Luger is worth a trip to Williamsburg in Brooklyn, where it is located at 178 Broadway. Left behind in
what was once a prosperous commercial neighborhood,
the restaurant is surrounded by the massive Romanesque
hulks of great banks that now serve as social-service
centers. But stepping into the restaurant transports you
back to a more prosperous time. The waiters, one and all,
are good-natured characters, and the steaks—sized for
one, two, or three large appetites—are perfect. Reservations are required for dinner; at least a week's notice for
weekends. Lunch is less hectic and full of businessmen
who have cabbed over from Wall Street. To find Peter
Luger look for the big signs at the end of the Williamsburg Bridge. Tel: (718) 387-7400.

Despite Italian origins, **Palm** and **Palm Too** (between
44th and 45th streets at 837 Second Avenue and 840
Second Avenue, respectively) are noted for their steaks.
There is sawdust on the floor and there are cartoons on
the walls, but the loud and at times raucous crowds have
been coming here for a good part of this century mostly
for the delicious chops and T-bones. But the Italian

specials—linguine in clam sauce, for one—are not to be forgotten, either. Tel: 687-2953 for 837 Second Avenue; 697-5198 for 840 Second Avenue.

The best steak house opened during most people's lifetimes is **Sparks**, 210 East 46th Street (just east of Third Avenue). The dining rooms are plush in a manly way, and the brothers Cetta, who own and run the place, have amassed one of the nation's great restaurant wine cellars—the American offerings are something of an honor roll, and their red Bordeaux collection puts most French places in the shade. This is one-item-per-plate cuisine: The steak comes on one plate, the spinach on another, and so on. Many serious wine types believe that food this simple (and excellent) is what the really complex bottlings need for a foil. In keeping with the times, Sparks has added more fish to the menu—fish that can be served in a steak-y manner, such as swordfish and salmon. Here, as at the two Palms, lobsters huge enough for a horror movie are dug into by ambitious eaters in neck-to-waist bibs. Tel: 687-4855.

The **Post House**, at 28 East 63rd Street (between Madison and Park avenues), is a very handsome place with a ritzy clientele that comes for the genteel atmosphere and the excellent wine list. Nothing is a bargain here, but the cooking is carefully done and the restaurant is quiet enough to allow you actually to get some work done or hold a conversation that requires concentration. Tel: 935-2888.

Sammy's Rumanian Restaurant, at 157 Chrystie Street (a few blocks south of Houston Street), is in yet another desolate part of the city, this time the Lower East Side. But the luxury cars are still parked, unmolested, outside, and on winter nights fur coats drape across the backs of chairs and lap into the aisle. It's an experience just to squeeze into this tiny basement room. Dinner is served from 4:00 to 10:00 every night, and you are expertly hustled in and out. Cuts of beef stick out over the edges of plates, but no one seems to need a doggy bag. Jars of U-Bet chocolate syrup, seltzer, pickles, and chicken fat threaten you from the center of every table. Tel: 673-0330.

SEAFOOD

Every place serves fish and shellfish these days; it's what New Yorkers like to eat. Thus the old boundary between restaurants that do best by meat and restaurants that do best by fish has blurred. An institution such as Spark's

Steakhouse sells virtually as much seafood as it does beef. And yet a special allure clings to a place that conjures up sea imagery, and even if the cuisine is no better than it is in less specialized establishments, there is still something joyful in a communal gathering over the bounty of the oceans.

For some of the very best: Refer to the French Restaurants section for Le Bernardin; to Local Phenomena for the Grand Central Oyster Bar & Restaurant and the SeaGrill; to Japanese for a number of sushi bars; and to Chinese for the Chinatown addresses, where the standards of freshness may be the highest in the city. Here are other aquatic-oriented places.

Gage & Tollner, at 372 Fulton Street in Brooklyn's re-emerging downtown, is a perfectly intact souvenir of the Gaslight Era, and for all of its 114 years it has held a special franchise on shellfish—old menus listed over 50 ways the restaurant served clams (some of these recipes are now lost). The divine broiled soft-shelled clam "bellies" are still served nightly, but Gage & Tollner has been revitalized by the arrival of chef Edna Lewis, the dean of Tidewater and Carolina cookery. The lure of, for example, her catfish stew, scalloped oysters, and Charleston she-crab soup has brought hundreds of new faces through the ancient door. Yes, the gaslights are still working, and the menu has plenty to offer the landlubber. From Manhattan, take the number 2 or 3 subway train to Hoyt Street–Fulton Mall, or take the number 4 or 5 train to Borough Hall. By car, cross the Brooklyn Bridge and drive straight ahead, as far as the beautifully restored Borough Hall, but look to the left to spot G & T. Tel: (718) 875-5181.

Closer to the Midtown office towers is the **Manhattan Ocean Club**, at 57 West 58th Street (between Fifth and Sixth avenues). The chef, Jonathan Parker, perfected his seafood technique at Le Bernardin, but he works in a more exuberant style here and will often let his customers have their swordfish, for example, prepared as many as three different ways. Maine lobsters may be ordered very plainly steamed (for purists) or stuffed with excellent lump crab meat and baked (for people who like to upset the purists at their table). He also makes a clam chowder that could explain why New Englanders came to love chowder in the first place. Tel: 371-7777.

In the skyscraper across East 45th Street from the Helmsley Building, the MetLife Building (200 Park Avenue), there are several fairly awful restaurants and one that has become superb under the guidance of a talented young chef, Ed Brown. He was handed a theme—anything suggested by the name **Tropica**—and a decorative scheme (upscale Key West), and he has spun gold from them. Seafood is the heart of his menu, and his inventions—combining salmon fillets with various seaweeds, improving on "jerk chicken," and zapping conch chowder with hot pepper—are among the most satisfying dishes to eat in New York these days. Lovely presentations, too. The flavors of Hawaii and other parts of the Pacific are also explored. Tel: 867-6767.

There are two branches of **Dock's Oyster Bar**, one on the Upper West Side at 2427 Broadway, near 89th Street, and the other in Midtown on Third Avenue at 40th Street. Both cater to a lively, youngish crowd that doesn't mind a fairly long wait for some fairly ordinary seafood. But the prices aren't bad, the white-tiled floors are correct, and the white wine is tossed back merrily. Tel: 724-5588 at the Upper West Side location; 986-8080 in Midtown.

Similarly lively, and stronger in the stove department, is **Claire**, at 156 Seventh Avenue (near 20th Street) in Chelsea. Claire has a sister restaurant in Key West, and so the mood is subtropical. The Bahamian conch chowder is zesty with pepper, the fish list changes daily, and the Key lime pie wraps it all up nicely. This is also the only place in town where the menu credits the designer of the waiters' shirts. Tel: 255-1955.

For a big, messy crab feast, you may tie on your bib and wield your mallet at **Sidewalkers'**, on the Upper West Side at 12 West 72nd Street, across the way from the Dakota apartment house. The crabs are heaped on your brown-paper-covered table with the Old Bay spices still clinging to them. After a while your fingers may be scratched and weary, but the feeling in your belly is a happy one. An array of other, very decent seafood is available, too. Tel: 799-6070.

If only the news were better concerning the seafood available within a short walk of the city's huge, bustling Fulton Fish Market, adjacent to the South Street Seaport in lower Manhattan. **Sweets** and **Sloppy Louie's**, the real old-timers (at 2 Fulton Street and 92 South Street, respectively), serve fish that is only passable, on a good day. Attempts at a large-scale fish place in one of the seaport buildings seem to run aground every year. In this part of town the best bet is probably to order lots of fried *calamari* in one of the bars and wash it down with some interesting suds. Tel: 344-9189 for Sweets, 509-9694 for Sloppy Louie's.

SPICY FOOD

There are a slew of places around town that cater to the craving for spicy food. Some are straightforward, serving the cuisine of countries such as Mexico and Indonesia, where spices are an intrinsic part of cooking. Others are a hodgepodge of styles—Tex-Mex, Southern, Soul Food, Cajun—where the food is often great, but the atmosphere and action are even better.

Greatly enjoying its moment is **Mesa Grill**, which is in a big, colorful converted garment showroom at 102 Fifth Avenue (near 16th Street). The Southwest represented here is highly imaginary, but the chef, Bobby Flay, puts genuine fire into his salsas, relishes, jalapeño jellies, *pozoles,* and other derivations from the U.S.–Mexican vernacular. Mr. Flay also has a way of making his plates of food look very fashionably mussed and nonchalant, but behind the fun is much highly precise culinary skill. His blue-corn-meal *biscotti* with pistachios, for example, turn out to be irresistibly good cookies. Tel: 807-7400.

In contrast, **Rosa Mexicana**, at 1063 First Avenue (at 58th Street), aims, very successfully, for true Mexican cooking. This is a real sit-down establishment where the almost mandatory guacamole is made to order, at tableside, in a rough stone *molcajete*. It really tastes incomparably better this way. Proprietor Josefina Howard also sees to it that her tortillas are handmade, to order, that her *mole* sauces are fresh and complex, and that her special margaritas with freshly pressed pomegranate juice are highly destabilizing. Her chocolate cake inflected with jalapeños makes for a perfect finish. Tel: 753-7407.

More of a kick-up-your-heels mood prevails at **Zarela**, a duplex joint at 953 Second Avenue (near 51st Street). Zarela Martinez's dishes are less rigorously authentic but hardly less delicious, and her side plates of *arroz con crema* and *torta de arroz* are required eating, especially to bank the fires in some of the other items. Tel: 644-6740.

Nusantara, at 219 East 44th Street (between Second and Third avenues), is a startlingly beautiful restaurant filled with art treasures from Indonesia. The food is intriguing, subtly spiced, and deeply flavorful, and the place is convenient to the United Nations for the Indonesian diplomatic corps who entertain here. Tel: 983-1919.

Tommy Tang's, 323 Greenwich Street (between Duane and Reade streets, not far from the river), is both culinarily and stylistically hot. Thai food provides the spice and TriBeCa patrons bring the funk. The food is good, though expensive, but portions are shared so a little goes a long way. Tel: 334-9190.

One of the oldest Thai restaurants in the city is still one of the best. It's called **Thai Restaurant**, and it has occupied the same spot in Chinatown, 106 Bayard Street (at the corner of Baxter Street), for as long as anyone remembers. Arrestingly spicy cold dishes, such as beef salad and squid salad, find a calming counterpoint in ultra-thin noodles that come either soft or crisped. Every new generation rediscovers this good place (and its endless supply of quaffable Thai beer). Tel: 349-3132.

A free hand with the Thai peppers can be found at the small but dedicated establishment **Shaliga Thai**, at 834 Second Avenue (near East 45th Street). The "curries" (rather liquid stews in the Thai manner)—red, green, yellow, or Muslim—pack a punch. The unassuming grace of the staff perhaps makes the food taste all the hotter by contrast. Tel: 573-5526.

Acme Bar & Grill, 9 Great Jones Street (near Lafayette Street and the big NoHo emporiums), proclaims its theme with hot-sauce bottles—all makes and origins—lined up on shelves around the room. You can even grab one and douse the already spicy Cajun–Gulf Coast food with a little more fire. This is a place to kick back and down a few beers. Tel: 420-1934.

Something of a law unto themselves are the two **Benny's Burritos** (one in the Village at 113 Greenwich Avenue, on the corner of Jane Street, and the other in the East Village at 93 Avenue A, near 6th Street). Gently steamed foot-wide flour tortillas with delicious, healthful fillings—some vegetarian—are eagerly consumed under a not unpleasant barrage of rock music, amid 1960s *objets* and some rather more contemporary margarita gulping. Benny's rather blunt slogans are "No Preservatives, No Lard, No Microwave, No MSG," and "Ours are bigger than yours." Very fresh food and very kicky *salsa* at an easy price: Thus, quite a crowd forms at prime hours. Tel: 727-3560 (the Village) or 254-2054 (Avenue A).

Sylvia's Restaurant, at 328 Lenox Avenue (between 126th and 127th streets in central Harlem; take the 2 or 3

IRT subway to 125th Street), is unequaled in the city for its Southern cooking. Black-eyed peas, collard greens, fried chicken, barbecued ribs, and superb ham are served in great heaps in a casual, homey atmosphere. Pies, sweet potato in particular, are pretty darn good, too, and the breakfasts are life enhancing. Tel: 996-0660.

You can also get some fine soul food at **Jezebel**, 630 Ninth Avenue (at 45th Street). The room is decorated with lace, funky antiques, and lavish flowers. Smothered pork chops and spare ribs are excellent. Tel: 582-1045.

CROWD SCENES

With the exception of a few hushed gastronomic laboratories, all of New York's restaurants are sociable places, but some go a step beyond and are dominated by people who have turned nightly socializing into a craft, or possibly a cause, one that they pursue with more ardor than they do their daytime activities. In some, the clubbishness of Wall Street, the media, or sports devotion transforms the jammed-in conditions of a subway at rush hour into many people's idea of a good time.

Almost every night of the week, a very hip, aggressively dressed crowd packs the booths at **Coffee Shop**, 29 Union Square West (at 16th Street). Tight tee-shirts, rolled up jeans, and personal talismans hanging on leather strips— the off-the-job apparel of fashion models—gives Coffee Shop a mock-brooding mood against a background of loud music and a foreground of Brazilian-esque food. The malaise of all these gorgeous youths might stem from the models despairing that they'll never be taken seriously and the serious ones despairing that they'll never be models. Tel: 243-7969.

Not quite so accessory oriented, but very much the place to be seen, is **TriBeCa Grill**, at 375 Greenwich Street (at the corner of Franklin Street). This former food-wholesalers building has been converted to film-industry offices by Robert De Niro, and this is his restaurant (in partnership with Drew Nieporent). The food and service are miles better than they need to be, considering the celebrity glut at the tables, the wide-eyed gawkers at the bar, and the papparazzi on stakeout in front. But then, De Niro never puts in a bad performance. Tel: 941-3900.

After many years without the sort of intriguing and forward-thinking restaurants that would seem to fit a setting famous for intriguing and forward-thinking art, SoHo has caught up with itself. **Boom**, at 152 Spring

Street, near West Broadway, is most stridently of the moment and is SoHo's most recent hit. The reasonably priced cuisine is a forced melting pot of styles from the world over (the "BBQ Chinese duck *confit* sandwich," for example), and the floral centerpiece, at least lately, is made of leaves gathered from the floor of an endangered rain forest and strung on heavy vines. Tel: 431-3663.

From noon until 4:00 A.M. **Lucky Strike** offers some choice hanging out in SoHo, at 59 Grand Street (off West Broadway). A simple, modestly priced bistro menu is part of the allure, but the real roughed-up charm of the place comes from the customers themselves, these lithe kids in, yet again, jeans and tee-shirts that are as scrupulously fitted as *couture* suits. No reservations taken, no matter who in the world you may be. Tel: 941-0479. Quite nearby, at 337 West Broadway (at the corner of Grand Street), the scene at **Jour et Nuit** is almost as lively, if a little more European and dressy and concerned with interesting food than Lucky Strike. The upstairs half of this pretty duplex restaurant seems to be where the action is. Tel: 925-5971. Now there to catch the overflow from Lucky Strike and Jour et Nuit is **Félix Bar & Restaurant,** at 340 West Broadway. When the weather is good, the scene spills out onto the street, and it is hard to know who is a customer and who is just visiting from one of the other places. The vivid bistro fare at Félix is better than the scene might tolerate. On a big night, the skimpy costumes, the table-hopping, and the polished sports cars and Harleys out front add up to a vision of St-Tropez in the high season. Tel: 431-0021.

After wandering around NoHo (around Broadway north of Houston Street) for a while or flipping through the racks at Tower Records on Broadway and East 4th Street, check out **Bayamo,** up the street at 704 Broadway. The place is huge and often filled to the rafters with New York University students pledging allegiance to their first well-made cocktails and talking up a storm. The rafters themselves are hung with examples of huge, wacky East Village sculpture. The cooking is based on the Cuban-Chinese style of the barrios and happens to be delicious. Tel: 475-5151.

Gonzalez y Gonzalez also attracts a big crowd of beginning carousers, and no one can deny there's a party going on around here (live music!). The guests of honor are bottles of beer from Mexico. The Mexican food is strictly an impulse buy but turns out better than you might expect. Gonzalez takes up a vast block-wide space a few streets south of Bayamo, at 625 Broadway (between Houston and Bleecker streets). Tel: 473-8787.

In some places first-rate food is just one element in the sort of lively scene that captures New York at its best. The archetypal downtown hangout the **Odeon**, at 145 West Broadway (at the corner of Thomas Street), in TriBeCa, has a fine kitchen under the command of Stephen Lyle, but the good cooking doesn't occasion the kind of reverential hush that falls over the tables in many other places. The discovered and undiscovered artists, the loft-dwellers, the people with defiantly original wardrobes, and the more worldly Wall Streeters can get the place hopping even without the engaging and reasonably priced fare. Tel: 233-0507. And the same is true for the Odeon's slightly more expensive Upper West Side sequel, **Café Luxembourg**, at 200 West 70th Street (just west of Broadway). This loving re-creation of 1930s Paris—zinc bar, rattan café chairs, tiled and mirrored walls, plenty of noise—offers rather more ambitious cooking, which is in the hands of a self-effacing Chinese-American chef named Tony Shek. Ordering the day's fish dish is the direct route to something memorably delicious, and it's no surprise that the place is packed all night long. Reservations are crucial. Tel: 873-7411.

A crowd scene of foodies—those folks who organize their lives around what exactly will be for lunch or dinner and then love to talk about it—gathers at **Union Square Café**, just west of the square at 21 East 16th Street. This big, airy, well-run establishment serves its own up-to-date hybrid of Italian, American, French, and grandmotherly cuisine, and it is only modestly expensive. Really, foodies love it, but many other people feel lost here, like the uninitiated watching a game of go. They simply don't see how a plate of perfect mashed turnips could mean so much to anyone. Tel: 243-4020.

B. Smith's is a beacon of civility at the fairly grimy intersection of Eighth Avenue and 47th Street, near the Theater District. It is not only a good place to eat, with a wide-ranging menu, but is also a gathering place for members of New York's soigné black elite, who have coalesced around the gracious and quite beautiful Barbara Smith, a former actress and fashion model, who lends her presence to the place most nights. Many of the impeccably dressed customers have perfected the art of occupying a table with such relaxed, almost Parisian confidence that the act of conversing seems transcended. Tel: 247-2222.

The Upper East Side is dotted with places that have their almost religious adherents among the very-well-to-do who live nearby. **Mortimer's** (at the corner of Lexington Avenue and 75th Street), **J. G. Melon** (at the corner of Third Avenue and 74th Street), **Jim McMullen** (on Third Avenue near 76th Street), **Elaine's** (on Second Avenue near 88th Street), and many others might strike newcomers as overcrowded, uncomfortable, and charmless, but to many of the locals they are kitchen, pantry, dining room, and clubhouse rolled into one. All serve a reliable hamburger, decent salmon, and respectable salads (or sturdy Italian fare at Elaine's), but their social cachet stems more from what they lack (the obvious trappings of luxury) than what they provide (which is a hearty welcome to the regulars). None is terribly pricey. Tel: 517-6400 for Mortimer's; 744-0585 for Melon; 861-4700 for McMullen; 534-8103 for Elaine's.

Younger East Siders and young Europeans love to shoehorn themselves into places that specialize in pastas and dressy little pizzas. **Mezzaluna**, on Third Avenue near 75th Street, and **Baraonda**, on Second Avenue at 75th Street, are always hopping, even though tables are so close together you might mistake the neighbors' conversation and food for your own. The style has spread to SoHo, in the form of **Mezzogiorno**, at the corner of Spring and Sullivan streets. The meals in these places are usually simple and delicious, but service is often infuriatingly muddled, and no one speaks with a soft voice. Tel: 535-9600 for Mezzaluna; 288-8555 for Baraonda (no credit cards); 334-2112 for Mezzogiorno.

INDIAN

Around East 6th Street

The nearly elbow-to-elbow Indian restaurants on East 6th Street, between First and Second avenues, have both contributed to and benefited from the redevelopment of the East Village. The nearby side streets, once dark and grungy, are now well lighted, with fashionable clothing stores and galleries open late into the evening. The restaurants themselves, as befitting the neighborhood's new prosperity, have been spruced up and are very welcoming indeed.

The best restaurant on the strip is **Mitali**, at 334 East 6th Street. Except for very large groups, reservations are not taken—hence the long line outside the door on weekends. Arrive before 7:00 or after 9:00 and the wait won't be as long. Once you are inside the low-ceilinged room, which is hung with tapestries and billowing cloth, such dishes as quail stuffed with almonds and ground meat or coriander-infused *dansak* curry take precedence. Beer is the drink that helps with the spices. Tel: 533-2508.

The attraction at both **Romna**, at 322 East 6th Street, and **Bombay**, at 320 East 6th Street, is the live music. Sitar and drums heighten the authentic taste of the curries and tandoori specialties. Tel: 533-3662 for Romna; 260-8229 for Bombay. **Passage to India**, at number 308, has the most attractive folkloric decor on the street and is also a contender for the prize for the most irresistible fresh hot Indian breads (*poori, chapati, naan,* etc.). Tel: 529-5770.

Around the corner, on First Avenue, a lavish banquet for a crowd can be had for very little money at **Royal Indian**, at 93 First Avenue. The two long, narrow rooms fill quickly on most nights. The food is a blend of Bengali and southern styles; the first includes cream-based specialties such as *tikka* chicken *mahani* sweetened with pineapple, and the second means fiery heat, as evidenced by the Madras Special's combination of chiles and aromatic spices that have been rubbed deeply into pieces of tender lamb. Tel: 473-9673.

Meanwhile, around the other corner at 100 Second Avenue, Abu Ahmed, the owner of the above-mentioned Mitali, has opened the neighborhood's first truly elegant Indian restaurant, **Haveli**. He has cleverly employed an ancient Gujarati architectural formula for a celebration house, and the results are a sort of thank-you note to the East Village, for here the denizens may dine in fine style at the prices they are used to. The *dosai* (crêpes) and some southern Indian specialties are truly outstanding. Tel: 982-0533

Lexington Avenue: Little India

Another pocket of Indian cooking is on and near Lexington Avenue between East 27th and 29th streets. The sharp, almost sweet scent of heady seasonings fills the air from the many spice shops in the neighborhood.

Annapurna, at 108 Lexington Avenue, is a little fancier than other restaurants nearby. The room is very attractive, and delicious regional specialties are served in a friendly manner. Tel: 679-1284.

The most comfortable spot in the neighborhood is **Maurya**, at 129 East 27th Street (near Lexington). They do an especially careful job with chicken, lamb, and shrimp cooked in the wood-stoked tandoor oven. Tel: 689-7925.

Midtown

As you head uptown, Indian restaurants become more lavish and seem to compete with one another for grand decor and genteel service. **Darbar**, 44 West 56th Street (between Fifth and Sixth avenues), has long been considered the most elegant, with its intricately carved screens and luxurious velvet covering the walls. The food is also exquisite. A buffet of wonderful dishes is provided at lunch in the upstairs portion of the restaurant and it is a real bargain. Tel: 432-7227.

Dawat, 210 East 58th Street (between Third and Second avenues), is a very spacious and formidably serious addition to the scene. Madhur Jaffrey, star of films by Ismail Merchant and James Ivory and a renowned cooking teacher and cookbook author in her own right, developed the dishes on the menu. Here you'll find *bhel poori,* a plate laden with crisp wafers, puffed wheat, and sweet chutneys that is a re-creation of the legendary street snacks of Bombay; and *rogan josh,* goat simmered in a cardamom-infused sauce until it falls deliciously off the bone. These are classic, authentic dishes, beautifully rendered. Tel: 355-7555.

KOREAN

The West 30s off Fifth Avenue form the center of Korean cooking in Manhattan. Surrounded by businesses connected with the Korean community, the restaurants on these streets fill with businessmen on the weekdays and families out on the town on the weekends.

New York Kom Tang House, at 32 West 32nd Street (off Broadway), is noted for its beef barbecue. The diner sits at a table with a metal well in the middle, where a hibachi is placed. The waitress brings a pile of marinated short ribs of beef and spreads it onto the grill. Once the meat is cooked, the diner rolls the meat in a lettuce leaf along with a garlic clove and sliced hot pepper, and dabs it with *miso* sauce. Bowls of *kim chi*—pickled vegetables—and soup precede the meat; fruit and a stick of gum follow, along with the very reasonable check. Be sure to sit upstairs. Tel: 947-8482.

Nearby is **Kang Suh** at 1250 Broadway (at 32nd Street). Downstairs is a Japanese-style sushi bar; upstairs are the tables with wells. Barbecued pork is the specialty—be sure to let the edges burn to a savory crispness. Tel: 564-6845.

Woo Lae Oak of Seoul, at 77 West 46th Street (between Fifth and Sixth avenues), is handy for pre-theater dining, so make a reservation, especially on the weekends. The large room fills up quickly with families and, later, with big groups of young people, all having a boisterous time as the room fills with smoke from the table grills and the air becomes scented with warm, delicious aromas. Tel: 869-9958.

MEDITERRANEAN AND MIDDLE EASTERN

Many purveyors of Middle Eastern food have come to feel uncomfortable with that designation lately. Somehow the heading "Mediterranean" fits more agreeably, and the justification comes from the interrelatedness of cuisines from Morocco to Turkey to Greece. Fortunately the change hasn't compromised their spice-loving, vibrant style of cooking.

One of the embodiments of it is Andrée Abramoff, who, along with her husband, Charlie, runs the charming little **Café Crocodile**, at 354 East 74th Street (near First Avenue). The crocodile motif stems from Andrée and Charlie's youth among the cosmopolitan Jews of Egypt (she occasionally offers a selection of appetizers that she calls an "Alexandria Quartet"). Her family was of French nationality, and so she claims Pan-Mediterranean rights as a cook. Her style is earthy but subtle, and Charlie stocks very good, very affordable wines (several bottles can go down for the price of one bottle elsewhere). Tel: 249-6619.

Greek food is not the ready-to-hand specialty here that it is in a number of American cities, despite the huge Greek community in Astoria, Queens. But one bright spot is **Periyali**, at 35 West 20th Street (between Fifth and Sixth avenues). It has an uncluttered Aegean atmosphere and lovingly prepared food, some of which is set out on a display table for all to admire. Tangy, garlicky flavors predominate, and dishes such as moussaka are rescued from heaviness by a deft kitchen. Reserve well in advance if possible. Tel: 463-7890.

A strip of little Israeli and Lebanese spots along Mac-Dougal Street in Greenwich Village caters to those in search of vegetarian nourishment and those in search of an inexpensive piquant meal. The street might well be renamed Pita Place someday. Most of the restaurants here are undecorated storefronts where falafel and gyros and salads are ready in a jiffy. You can sit down and spend a little more time in the **Olive Tree Café**, 117 MacDougal Street, a short stroll south from Washington Square, and still enjoy the same restorative, easily affordable cooking. A comedy club beckons from downstairs. Tel: 254-3630.

Couscous, those gentle, nourishing granules rolled from semolina flour, may be chic among the French now, but the real (inexpensive) Moroccan-Tunisian thing is to be found in little places like **Lotfi's Couscous**, in the Village at 28 Cornelia Street (between West 4th and Bleecker streets). Whether laden just with vegetables or with everything in the kitchen, the couscous makes a pleasing and most mercifully priced meal. Tel: 929-3693.

Brooklyn Middle Eastern

Along Atlantic Avenue, between Court and Henry streets, and a few blocks from Brooklyn's Borough Hall (and easily reached from Manhattan via the 2, 3, 4, 5, N, and R subway lines), there is a high concentration of Middle Eastern shops and restaurants. Jars of spices, nuts, and grains line the shelves of the shops, and from the baker-ies come the smell of honey and ground pistachios and the warm fragrance of baked phyllo dough.

It's impossible to walk down the avenue and not be-come incredibly hungry. Head for **Moroccan Star**, 205 Atlantic Avenue, for some *babaganouj* (smoked eggplant with tahini, garlic, and lemon juice) or *hummus* (mashed and spiced chickpeas), *tajine* chicken, and lamb kebabs. All wonderfully inexpensive. Tel: (718) 643-0800. Or swing around the corner to Court Street for **Almontaser**, at num-ber 218, and ask for the stuffed grape leaves as part of a meal of lots of shared appetizers and salads. Then summon forth an array of flaky phyllo pastries for dessert with thick, jolting Middle Eastern coffee. Tel: (718) 624-9267.

A long and beautiful wooden boat is moored inside the **Tripoli**, at 156 Atlantic Avenue. At night when the lights are low the room seems magically out at sea. The lamb dishes are very good here, and so is the service. Tel: (718) 596-5800.

NORTHERN AND EASTERN EUROPEAN

Lower East Side

Like many groups before and after them, the German and Slavic immigrants who came in the great wave that hit American shores in the latter half of the 19th century settled on the Lower East Side. What remains today of their early efforts in this new land are a few good restaurants that serve honest home cooking at a very reasonable price.

Chief among these places is the **Ukrainian Restaurant**, at 140 Second Avenue (near 9th Street). You enter through a long, drab hallway into a spartan dining room, where the tables are filled with Ukrainian families and the new, more prosperous (or artistically bent) residents of the neighborhood. Bring a healthy appetite. Portions are large, and the food—pickled herring, borscht, variously stuffed pirogi, and stuffed cabbage, to name a few specialties—is hearty. To wash this all down try one of the rich dark beers. No credit cards are accepted. Tel: 529-5024.

The **Veselka Coffee Shop**, at 144 Second Avenue (on the corner of 9th Street), is a neighborhood landmark. The swirling murals inside and outside the restaurant depict shop owners and old residents of the area. The pirogi here are excellent, as are the blintzes—with plenty of sour cream. Veselka is open late and becomes very lively with a good cross section of the East Village population all forking down the poppyseed cake. Tel: 228-9682.

Leshko Coffee Shop, on the corner of Avenue A (number 111), across from Tompkins Square Park, has very good borscht and stews. People tend to linger long in the comfortable booths and watch the street scene through the large windows. Tel: 473-9208.

Yorkville

When the *General Slocum,* an excursion steamer, capsized on June 15, 1904, more than a thousand people from the Lower East Side lost their lives. The victims were mostly of German descent, and the disaster forced the surviving grief-stricken families to move to other parts of the city. One of the areas they settled in was **Yorkville**, on the Upper East Side. There they joined Czechs, Slovaks, Hungarians, and a smattering of Irish. Sadly, everyone's favorite old German pastry shop, Café-Geiger, closed recently. Nonetheless, a few Teutonic and Slavic spots remain.

The **Red Tulip**, 439 East 75th Street (between York and First avenues), is a very lively and pretty Hungarian restaurant. This is no place to go if you're in a quiet mood; the dining room becomes very crowded and gay, with strolling musicians dressed as gypsies. Stuffed cabbage, grilled Hungarian sausage, and crackling duck here are exceptional. Tel: 734-4893.

Midtown

Scandinavian cooking was once a staple of the New York dining scene—especially the lavish smorgasbords at such long-gone destinations as the Gripsholm and the Three Crowns. The gap left by their disappearance was partly filled a few years back by **Aquavit**, a multi-storied, elegant establishment in a historic limestone-fronted former Rockefeller town house at 13 West 54th Street. The closest one may come to a smorgasbord is a sampler, prepared in the kitchen, of Scandinavian hors d'oeuvres. But authenticity is assured by a steady supply of ingredients flown in mainly from Sweden. The many forms of herring here are a must, even for those not normally pleased by herring, and so are such items as hazel grouse, Arctic venison, and desserts with lingonberries and cloudberries. Rather expensive but a fine meal. Tel: 307-7311.

The owners of Aquavit recently branched out by opening a pretty but less expensive offshoot called **Snaps** (which is slang for aquavit, the flavored Scandinavian liquor that is inseparable from the word "*Sköl!*"). The new restaurant is in the Helmsley Building, at 230 Park Avenue (at 46th Street). The menu here is less conventionally Scandinavian than at Aquavit, but there is no mistaking the origin of peel-and-eat shrimp with Västerbotten cheese or warm Baltic herring with cod roe and cream. Snaps is meant to appeal mainly to Midtown business folk, but it gives them something rather better than they normally find so close to work. Tel: 949-7878.

Russian Dining in Brighton Beach

Brighton Beach, Brooklyn, has come to be known as "Odessa by the Sea" because of the thousands of Russians who have emigrated and settled here. The restaurants in the area not only serve terrific Russian food but offer a crash course in a very lively culture.

The D train stops right in the heart of Brighton Beach, which is also the name of the stop, and the **Odessa** (at 1113 Brighton Beach Avenue, between 13th and 14th streets) is close by. Don't come any earlier than 9:30 on a weekend night or you are liable to have the whole garishly decorated room to yourself. And don't order from the menu; have the buffet at about $32 (it goes up, but only slightly, with the quality of the evening's musicians). The price includes a bottle of vodka for a party of four, two trays' worth of cold and hot appetizers (anything from homemade ham to smoked fish to ribs with potatoes), main courses (lamb kebab, roast chicken), and dessert. The music is lively, and everyone dances. It makes for a memorable night. Open Friday through Sunday. Tel: (718) 332-3223.

The action at the **National**, at 273 Brighton Beach Avenue (between 2nd and 3rd streets), begins even later, but, as at the Odessa, it goes on and on. The National holds 200 people and on a good weekend it seems to hold more. Open Friday through Sunday. Tel: (718) 646-1225.

Gastronom Moscow, on the Brighton Beach boardwalk near 6th Street, is a dimly lit boardwalk café that serves tea and vodka, a bleakly poetic place to linger and watch the ocean, especially when the beach crowds are gone. Tel: (718) 934-7418.

People all over Russia love to eat Georgian cooking, partly because Georgia is a land of plenty, and also because lively, spicy dishes and hearty hospitality are longingrained customs. **Primorski**, at 282 Brighton Beach Avenue (on the same block as the National), is the place to go for shish kebab, *pasturma* (lavishly spiced meat), and split grilled *tabaka* chicken. Unlike the big party joints, Primorski is open every day from 11:00 A.M.—to "who knows?" as the boss there says. Tel: (718) 891-3111.

GREEN DINING

Mealtime options for those who eschew meats—or for those who are very particular about how the things they eat are grown—have never been wider or more promising. Quite a few of the most elegant and highly regarded restaurants now have items on their menus that are meatless, such as elaborate plates of grilled vegetables and various pasta inventions. Risotto, couscous, and salads are also common enough these days so that vegetarians need not feel out of place in practically any establishment.

Chinese culture has always honored meatless eating, partly because of Buddhism and partly because traditional medicine dictates that meat should be avoided at certain times. Well named is **Vegetarian Paradise**, in

Greenwich Village at 144 West 4th Street (near Sixth Avenue). This is paradise not only because the choice is so wide and affordable, but because this is cooking for people who not only eat veggies and bean curd, but like them. Tel: 260-7130.

Two Indian vegetarian places of high repute are **Madras Woodlands** and **Madras Palace**. Both specialize in the complex, earthy staples of southern India, with its 17 types of lentils and its love for chiles. Rich-tasting items such as cauliflower with ginger and coriander and potato patties stuffed with lentils and chiles make up for a lack of not only meat and fish but dairy and eggs (they do use a little butter in the desserts) as well. An example of the urban melting pot at work, both restaurants have been rabbinically certified as kosher. Madras Woodlands is at 308 East 49th Street (between First and Second avenues); Tel: 759-2441. Madras Palace is at 104 Lexington Avenue (between 27th and 28th streets); Tel: 532-3314.

There are two branches in Manhattan of a restaurant called **Souen**, which has a varied Japanese-influenced menu but does a brisk business in brown-rice dishes, bean curd, and *miso* (fermented soy paste with a delicious nutlike flavor). Because the policy here is macrobiotic—a bit of fish is allowed, but no sugar or dairy—the crowd here tends to be rather more ascetic-looking than in some other places. One branch is at 210 Sixth Avenue (at Prince Street); Tel: 807-7421. The prettier one is at 28 East 13th Street (just off Fifth Avenue); Tel: 627-7150.

Visually indistinguishable from most other attractively designed Postmodern eateries is **Luma**, at 200 Ninth Avenue (between 22nd and 23rd streets). Here the menu usually offers a game bird and plenty of fish, and any meats they serve are from organically raised, free-range animals. The menu partly devotes itself to strictly vegetarian items, including the best eggless pasta around. The rules here are no dairy, no eggs, and no sugar; and banished, too, are the heavyweight recipes and the grim atmosphere most people associate with "health food." Tel: 633-8033.

Similarly pleasant is the bluntly named **Nosmo King** (i.e., "No Smoking"), at 54 Varick Street (just south of Canal Street). Here, too, the specialty is organically grown produce and game birds (and, of course, fish). The mood is a bit more boisterous than at the tonier Luma, but the kitchen is just as concerned with hitting the mark gastronomically. Many vegetarian options. Tel: 966-1239.

Less strict about dietary matters but still environmentally sensitive is **Time Café**, a large and popular spot in a fine 19th-century edifice at 380 Lafayette Street (corner of Great Jones Street). Vegetarian dishes are sufficiently numerous to please nearly anyone, with special attention warranted by small pizzas with whole-wheat crusts. Adjacent to the dining room is a shop that carries take-away baked goods and reputedly nonpolluting grocery items. Tel: 533-7000.

Grand occasions need not mean breaking one's dietary resolves. The **Four Seasons** (see Local Phenomena) has for years offered its trademark Spa Cuisine—gorgeous and inventive plates, several offered every day, that minimize calories and maximize nutrients. Some of the offerings are meatless.

Saturnia, in the Doral Park Hotel (70 Park Avenue, between 38th and 39th streets), is a New York outlet for the fancy low-calorie, low-sodium, low-fat cuisine of the swank Doral Saturnia International Spa and Resort in Miami. It would be hard to find a splashier, more luxurious setting for minding the waistline. Less emphasis is placed here on organic food sources. Tel: 983-3333.

A PROPER TEA

Not everyone stops for teatime in New York, but those who do don't mind being different. It leaves more room for them. At four o'clock these days it's not just maiden aunts and their visiting relatives who settle down with their cups and plates, but businesspeople, too, who find the calm and elegant surroundings of the best tearooms to be conducive to the closing of a deal. Tea is the relaxed and perfect setting for catching up with friends, cooling your heels after a day's shopping, or simply recharging for the evening ahead.

The **Mayfair Hotel Baglioni** (formerly the Mayfair Regent), at 65th Street and Park Avenue, provides a perfect tea. At four the ivory-colored velvet settees and armchairs slowly fill with an elegant clientele. Potted palms and silk lampshades reflecting soft lights give the room an intimate feeling. There are seven kinds of teas to choose from, such as Lapsang Souchong, Russian, and jasmine. Finger sandwiches are delicious, especially the smoked salmon and chicken, and the scones . . . well, it's hard not to eat a stack of them. Tel: 288-0800.

The problem with the **Rotunda**, where tea is served at the Pierre Hotel, at Fifth Avenue and 61st Street, is that there are only eight tables nestled in this lavishly decorated room. But once you are seated upon a coveted sofa or in the arms of an overstuffed chair, the focus is on the table spread. A three-tiered silver tray is brought to the table, laden with savory sandwiches, Dundee fruitcake on occasion, scones, and tarts. The wide choice of teas almost seems to be an afterthought. Reserve a table. Tel: 838-8000.

The **Gold Room** at the New York Palace, at 455 Madison Avenue (near 50th Street), is even more stately than the Pierre. The room was designed by Stanford White as part of the 19th-century Neo-Renaissance Villard Houses and modeled after the Palazzo della Cancelleria in Rome. The tables are set with gold-trimmed china, and, on an overhead balcony, a harpist plays. Eighteen teas are offered with the three-course menu. First there are the properly thin finger sandwiches. Next come warm scones with Devonshire cream and fruit preserves. Last is a tray of fruitcakes, tarts, and pastries. Tel: 888-7000.

For a bit more fun during tea, repair to the **Gallery** at the Carlyle Hotel, 35 East 76th Street (at Madison Avenue). Nestled to the side of the lobby, the comfortable arrangement of velvet love seats and upholstered armchairs gives a bird's-eye view of the interesting comings and goings in the lobby. The offerings are not as lavish here as at the three places above, with only a few types of teas available, but everything is quite good. Slipping into the cocktail hour with a sherry is encouraged. Tel: 744-1600.

Nearby, at the Mark Hotel, at 25 East 77th Street (between Fifth and Madison avenues), an especially tasty tea is served among the potted palms and rose-velvet banquettes in **Mark's Restaurant**. Pastry chef Susan Boulot produces elegant French pastries, including lemon tartlets and strawberry barquettes as well as scrumptious scones served with fresh *mascarpone*. Tea sandwiches are also offered. Tel: 879-1864.

Downtown at Barney's New York clothing store there is **Le Café**, at 106 Seventh Avenue (at 17th Street). On the lower level, in a charming garden setting—complete with a rustic fountain of frogs and hand-painted palm frond mirrors—Le Café offers a buffet of cold seafood, smoked fish, egg salad, and Polish ham. There are also luscious cheeses and many, many cakes and sweets, such as poppyseed, flourless chocolate cake, and profiteroles. And not everyone is sipping tea: A nice wine list is available, too. Tel: 929-9000.

FOR ALL AGES

"In America, there are two classes of travel," Robert Benchley wrote. "First class, and with children." The same could be said for dining out. Given enough money and a few years of rigorous training, it's possible that a parent could walk into the finest restaurant in the city with his or her children in tow and have a pleasant meal. But the evening would do little to promote how much fun eating out should be, and it would do less to improve the quality of family relations.

Better to take the kids to a place where everyone can truly enjoy themselves, like the **Hard Rock Café**, at 221 West 57th Street (between Seventh Avenue and Broadway). Everything is here: the constant beat of music, personable, good-looking young help, big hamburgers, and gooey desserts. There is often a long line outside the door to endure before you're allowed in to wait still longer for a table, but once inside you can get a drink at the bar and stare at the memorabilia: Joan Jett's black high-top sneakers, Prince's purple cape, Elvis's guitar, and stacks of Gold Records. Tel: 489-6565.

Don't like the looks of the line at the Hard Rock? Well, it's bound to be longer not far east on 57th Street in front of **Planet Hollywood**, at number 140 (between Sixth and Seventh avenues). This Planet has many of the same principal players as the Hard Rock, plus financing from some of filmdom's richest stars. The memorabilia here is from cinema rather than rock-'n'-roll, and the decor sprang from the mind of Anton Furst, who created the *noir*ish look of *Batman*. Kids for whom the movie left-overs mean little will, no doubt, get with the program when they see that pizza is on their menu (along with a big salad called a Hollywood Bowl). Tel: 333-STAR.

Across town there is **Serendipity**, at 225 East 60th Street (between Third and Second avenues). Young "society" girls who didn't want to go to the Village in the 1960s used to hold court amid the exuberantly funky decor of this toy shop–restaurant. You'll still catch them here, but now they bring their children and discreetly chow down on bowls of chili, hamburgers, and foot-long hot dogs. No one passes on dessert, especially "F-f-f-frozen hot chocolate." Tel: 838-3531.

Rusty Staub's on 5th, at 575 Fifth Avenue (at 47th Street), might be the perfect spot for training young people in how to dine in a relatively formal restaurant. The food is both approachable and really good—there are chili and ribs along with filet of fresh tuna, the staff is easygoing, and the kids are likely to meet a genuine hero, Rusty Staub, "Le Grand Orange," smacker of 296 major-league home runs and a respected wine connoisseur. Tel: 682-1000.

Outside **Two Boots**, at 37 Avenue A (between 3rd and 2nd streets on the Lower East Side), there's a brightly painted seal balancing a ball on the tip of his nose. A ride on him will cost a quarter. The very good Cajun-Italian food served inside is only slightly more expensive. A hip East Village crowd fills the place on most nights. Tel: 505-2276.

What the **Boathouse Café** on Central Park's Lake, on the East Drive north of 72nd Street, sorely lacks in culinary delights it makes up for in charm. Selections from the Northern Italian menu should be kept simple. Better yet, come for drinks and dessert, then a row across the lake (boats are rented right next door). Tel: 517-2233.

If you've been wandering around the city and you need a respite, give the children a bellyful of good things to eat at **Sarabeth's Kitchen**, at 423 Amsterdam Avenue (at 80th Street, not far from the American Museum of Natural History), and at 1295 Madison Avenue (between 92nd and 93rd streets). Prices are moderate, and the room is homey and relaxed. Brunch is particularly good; for munching later, stock up on the brownies and cookies from the case up front. Tel: 496-6280 for Amsterdam Avenue; 410-7335 for Madison Avenue. Sarabeth has now taken over the restaurant in the Whitney Museum of American Art, at Madison Avenue and 75th Street—a possibly effective bribe to get the little darlings to see some art.

Hamburger Harry's also has more than one location: 145 West 45th Street (between Sixth Avenue and Broadway) and 157 Chambers Street (south of Canal Street). A battalion of cooks man charcoal grills on a raised station in the back of the room and flip big, juicy meat patties at an astonishing rate. To go with the burgers there are interesting toppings as well as great french fries. Kids will like to drink the lime rickeys and may even want to give the turkey burgers a try. Tel: 840-2756 for West 45th Street; 267-4446 for Chambers Street.

Another good bet are pasta restaurants. **Sorrentino**, at 813 Eighth Avenue (at 49th Street), serves big bowls of noodles, generously sauced. For children who clean their plates, the restaurant has been known to add an extra dollop of whipped cream to desserts. Tel: 307-5484.

South Street Seaport

The second floor of the main market building in the South Street Seaport is filled with stalls that offer food of every description. Long curls of french fries, oysters and clams on the half shell, barbecue, deli, pastries—it's a glutton's (or growing child's) delight.

Across the square, at the corner of Fulton and South streets, is the **Northstar Tavern**. Housed in one of the oldest buildings in the city (where slave runners used to congregate), the tavern offers a large selection of domestic and imported beers for adults, and simple, English pub–type food for the young people. Tel: 509-6757.

For dessert, or to hold you over until the next meal, stop in at **Die Fledermaus**, across the square from the main market building at Front Street. There are salads and tiny sandwiches, but they're incidental compared to such Viennese pastry delights as chocolate mousse cake, lemon swirl, and raspberry tarts. Tel: 269-5890.

A few blocks north of the seaport is the **Bridge Café**, a down-to-earth joint that many New Yorkers consider an antidote to the seaport's hype. The oldest restaurant building in the city, it predates City Hall (which went up in 1811). Salads, pastas, fish—good straight stuff—and the help tells the kids some very convincing ghost stories. The Bridge Café may be found by sauntering away from the seaport, toward the Brooklyn Bridge on Water Street. It's at the end, 279 Water Street, on the corner of Dover Street. Tel: 227-3344.

BRUNCH

Brunch: gathering to eat at a time when so many needs must be met. Perhaps you crave some breakfast (although it's past noon) while the rest of the crew has already been out and about and needs lunch; or perhaps you need cover for ordering a drink—a Bloody Mary, for instance, to set things back to rights. Some in the group may be famished, others might be a little peaked and would prefer just tea and toast. It was probably all these divergent demands of modern life that put an end to big Sunday dinners (the daylight kind) in New York. Well, it's an interesting subject, the evolution of brunch. Maybe *The New York Times Magazine* will take it up, and we can all read about it over brunch one Sunday. In the meantime, gather up the sections of the paper you like to read and toddle over to any of the following.

The epicenter of brunch has long been recognized as **Café des Artistes**, at 1 West 67th Street (just off Central Park West). It may have to do with the awakening effect of looking at the sisterly cavorting nudes that Howard Chandler Christy painted all over the walls. Indeed, this is one of the best-looking restaurants in town, and brunch dishes and desserts are the kitchen's strong suits. It is also one of the few places in the city that offers truly superior fresh fruit as a final course for those disinclined to eat pastry. This is a dressy and somewhat expensive brunch, but it may be the nicest (and reservations are crucial). Tel: 877-3500.

Another vigorous wake-up call is sounded at **Lola**, at 30 West 22nd Street (between Fifth and Sixth avenues), a deservedly popular spot for any day of the week that offers a rousing Gospel brunch on Sundays. Just as you might be tucking into your Caribbean-influenced waffles, a dynamic woman in a choir robe steps up beside a piano and, well, hallelujah! The music, the Cayenne onion rings, and the overall cheer of the place should repair any damage wrought by the night before. Tel: 675-6700. A short menu of Southern specialties from Edna Lewis—all are quite heavenly—is offered every Sunday afternoon from September to June at **Gage & Tollner**, at 372 Fulton Street in Brooklyn (see Seafood for more on their offerings), for an admirably low fixed price.

It might be soothing indeed to watch the river flow while you eat a light meal at the **Water Club**, docked on the Manhattan side of the East River at East 30th Street. A drink outdoors is permitted in good weather, and tables for large groups are easily obtained. The menu will include something pleasing for all tastes. Tel: 683-3333. And, of course, there is also Sunday brunch at the **River Café** (1 Water Street, Brooklyn; see Local Phenomena).

There are branches of **Elephant & Castle** (named after the London underground stop) in the Village, at 68 Greenwich Avenue (near Seventh Avenue), and in SoHo, at 183 Prince Street (between Sullivan and Thompson streets). E & C specializes in affordable breakfasts all week long, so no major gears need to be shifted to turn out fluffy omelets and bowls of fruit-laden yogurt frou-frou on Sundays. Both provide simple, snug surroundings in which it is permissible to read the paper. Tel: 243-1400 for the Village; 260-3600 for SoHo.

Many of the major hotels offer big buffet brunches, a fact that most New Yorkers seem unaware of, and so these fine opportunities for grazing are patronized mainly by out-of-towners. Nevertheless, an "all-you-can-eat" for a fixed price is being held weekly in the **Barclay Restaurant** in the Hotel Inter-Continental, 111 East 48th Street (at Lexington Avenue; Tel: 755-5900); and overlooking Fifth Avenue in **Restaurant Adrienne** at the Peninsula New York, at the corner of 55th Street (Tel: 903-3918); and, most elegantly, in the ever-stylish confines of the **Café Carlyle** in the Hotel Carlyle (from September to June only), Madison Avenue and 76th Street (Tel: 744-1600). These generally commence at noon and last until 2:30.

Other ideas for brunch include **Sarabeth's Kitchen**, the baking and preserve specialists (see For All Ages), any of the restaurants in Chinatown that offer *dim sum* (see Chinese), and the delis (see Local Phenomena). For a most intriguing departure, try an Indian brunch. The two branches of **Mitali**—the original on East 6th Street (see Indian) and the offshoot, **Mitali West**, in the Village at 296 Bleecker Street (near Seventh Avenue South)—both have Sunday buffets and the kind of hearty, spicy food that might be just right before a big afternoon around town.

Should brunch be required on a *Saturday,* **Union Square Café** (see Crowd Scenes) offers an innovative and diverting Greenmarket Brunch, which takes its name from the popular open-air market held every week on that day in Union Square, a few feet from the restaurant's door. The chef always includes dishes that he improvises from the produce that the Greenmarket farm stands have to offer, some of which is quite exotic. But that's just on Saturdays.

OUT LATE

If you're up past midnight there are many places around town where you can still get a good feed. Some are scenes unto themselves, and just getting admitted to them may take until the wee hours of the morning.

Nell's, 246 West 14th Street (between Seventh and Eighth avenues), **Temple Bar**, 332 Lafayette Street (at Bleecker Street), and **Au Bar**, 41 East 58th Street (between Madison and Park avenues), are just such places. Nell's began the trend—mock gentlemen's clubs, decorated in English style—but the differences between them can sometimes be detected only by the chosen few who attend regularly. In all you'll find good music, a very stylish crowd, a lot of posing, and, surprisingly, some darn good food (especially at Nell's). Reservations for dinner allegedly help, and there is, of course, a cover charge if you're fortunate enough to be chosen by the nice men at the doors. Tel: 675-1567 for Nell's; 925-4242 for Temple Bar; 308-9455 for Au Bar.

The phrase "supper club" suggests beautifully dressed people who never feel weary and for whom caviar is a staple source of protein. **Laura Belle**, at 120 West 43rd Street (between Sixth Avenue and Broadway), opens her discreetly unmarked doors to them with late, elegant meals, at tables bordering a dance floor, from 9:00 P.M. to 1:00 A.M. (the whole club stays open till 4:00 A.M.). Responsible for this is Michael O'Keeffe, owner of the River Café and the Water Club restaurants. To keep the evening alive, Laura Belle stocks numerous brands of Champagne, rare brandies, and plenty of premium cigars. Need it be said that jeans and sneakers are stopped at the door? Tel: 819-1000.

Taking much the same glamorous tack is the **Supper Club**, where the band comes on at seven, then makes way for a small orchestra in the later hours, when the dance floor really comes to life. The management is serious about the "supper" part—they want their patrons to eat well. Food is available until 2:00 A.M. The space was designed years ago as a bona-fide nightclub, in the Theater District's Hotel Edison, at 240 West 47th Street (between Broadway and Eighth Avenue). You can get in the swing of things there just by remembering the phone number: 921-1940.

Acme Bar & Grill, 9 Great Jones Street (near Lafayette Street), is a good restaurant that serves fiery Southern cooking (see Spicy Food, above). But past midnight the crowds come more to drink and mingle than to eat. Tel: 420-1934. This is also true at the **Great Jones Café**, 54 Great Jones Street. Cajun martinis and the very good jukebox fuel the frenzy. The cooking is tasty, too. Tel: 674-9304.

For just a good hamburger and beer in a convivial setting there is the **Broome Street Bar**, at 363 West Broadway (at Broome Street) in SoHo. There's a long bar in front and a pleasant, dimly lighted back room. Tel: 925-2086.

On the edge of SoHo, the **Moondance Diner**, at 80 Sixth Avenue (at Grand Street), serves improvements on standard American road food at a decent price. The diner is open until midnight on weeknights, 24 hours on weekends. It gets busy at lunch, then again after midnight on weekends when the clubs let out. Tel: 226-1191.

Breakfast begins at 1:00 A.M. at the **Empire Diner**, 210 Tenth Avenue (at 22nd Street). An assorted clientele from all parts of the city congregates for scrambled eggs and hash browns or a very rich and satisfying sundae. Tel: 243-2736.

What's bad about going late to the **Hard Rock Café**, 221 West 57th Street (between Seventh Avenue and Broadway), is the line out front. It can get longer and longer as the night progresses. Once inside, and once you're seated (another wait; see For All Ages, above), it's like being at a good loud party, provided you're young and you like your music strong and uninterrupted. Good, hefty hamburgers, chicken club sandwiches, and desserts. The food keeps coming until 4:00 A.M. Tel: 489-6565.

Of course, chefs, waiters, bartenders, and maître d's need to eat, too, and so a group of the city's top young culinarians banded together to open a restaurant called the **Chefs Cuisiniers Club**, a pleasantly decorated, lively joint that serves imaginative, quite substantial, top-quality dinners until 2:00 A.M. on weekends. Also open for lunch. The address is 36 East 22nd Street (between Broadway and Park Avenue South). Tel: 228-4399.

RESTAURANTS BY NEIGHBORHOOD
The following is a list of New York restaurants organized by neighborhood; for descriptions, addresses, and telephone numbers, consult the preceding listings, organized by type of food and special interest.

Lower Manhattan
Arqua (Italian)
Barocco (Italian)
Bridge Café (seafood and pasta; see For All Ages)
Bouley (American)
Cellar in the Sky (Continental; see Local Phenomena)
Chanterelle (American)
First Taste (Chinese)
Die Fledermaus (dessert; see For All Ages)
Golden Unicorn (Chinese)
98 Mott Restaurant (Chinese)
Great Shanghai (Chinese)
H.S.F. (Chinese)
Hamburger Harry's (burgers; see For All Ages)

Nice Restaurant (Chinese)
Northstar Tavern (pub food; see For All Ages)
Nosmo King (healthy food; see Green Dining)
Odeon (American; see Crowd Scenes)
Oriental Garden Restaurant (Chinese)
Sammy's Rumanian Restaurant (Steaks)
Silver Palace (Chinese)
Sloppy Louie's (Seafood)
Sweets (Seafood)
Thai Restaurant (Thai; see Spicy Food)
Tommy Tang's (Thai; see Spicy Food)
TriBeCa Grill (American; see Crowd Scenes)
Triple Eight Palace (Chinese)
Windows on the World (Continental; see Local
    Phenomena)
Wong and Kwong (Chinese)

Downtown above Canal Street
Acme Bar & Grill (Cajun; see Spicy Food and Out Late)
Alison on Dominick Street (American)
Arlecchino (Italian)
Ballato (Italian)
Bayamo (Cuban-Chinese; see Crowd Scenes)
Benny's Burritos (Cal-Mex; see Spicy Food)
Bombay (Indian)
Boom (international; see Crowd Scenes)
Broome Street Bar (see Out Late)
Le Café (see A Proper Tea)
Café Loup (French)
Cent'Anni (Italian)
Chefs Cuisiniers Club (see Out Late)
Chelsea Trattoria (Italian)
Chez Jacqueline (French)
Claire (Seafood)
Coach House (American)
Coffee Shop (Brazilian-esque; see Crowd Scenes)
La Colombe d'Or (French)
Elephant & Castle (see Brunch)
Empire Diner (see Out Late)
Félix Bar & Restaurant (bistro food; see Crowd Scenes)
Florent (French)
"14" (French)
Gonzalez y Gonzalez (Mexican; see Crowd Scenes)
Grand Ticino (Italian)
Great Jones Café (Cajun; see Out Late)
Haveli (Indian)

Honmura An (Japanese)
Jour et Nuit (Continental; see Crowd Scenes)
Leshko Coffee Shop (Slavic; see Northern and Eastern European)
Lola (Caribbean; see Brunch)
Lora (American)
Lotfi's Couscous (Moroccan; see Mediterranean and Middle Eastern)
Lucky Strike (bistro food; see Crowd Scenes)
Luma (healthy food; see Green Dining)
Le Madri (Italian)
Mesa Grill (Mexican; see Spicy Food)
La Métairie (French)
Mezzogiorno (Italian; see Crowd Scenes)
Minetta Tavern (Italian)
Mitali (Indian; see also Brunch)
Mitali West (Indian; see Brunch)
Moondance Diner (American; see Out Late)
Nell's (see Out Late)
Olive Tree Café (Mediterranean and Middle Eastern)
Omen (Japanese)
Passage to India (Indian)
Periyali (Greek; see Mediterranean and Middle Eastern)
Le Pescadou (French)
Positano (Italian)
Prix Fixe (American)
Puglia (Italian)
Río Mar (Spanish)
Rocco (Italian)
Romna (Indian)
Rosolio (Italian)
Royal Indian (Indian)
Savoy (American)
Second Avenue Kosher Deli (delicatessen; see Local Phenomena)
Sevilla (Spanish)
Da Silvano (Italian)
Souen (Japanese vegetarian; see Green Dining)
Steak Frites (French)
Taormina (Italian)
Temple Bar (see Out Late)
Teresa and Mimmo (Italian)
Time Café (vegetarian; see Green Dining)
Two Boots (Cajun-Italian; see For All Ages)
Ukrainian Restaurant (Ukrainian; see Northern and Eastern European)

Umeda (Japanese)
Union Square Café (multinational; see Crowd Scenes and Brunch)
Vegetarian Paradise (Chinese vegetarian; see Green Dining)
Veselka Coffee Shop (Slavic; see Northern and Eastern European)

Midtown: 27th Street to 59th Street

Restaurant Adrienne (see Brunch)
An American Place (American)
Annapurna (Indian)
Aquavit (Swedish; see Northern and Eastern European)
Au Bar (see Out Late)
Barclay Restaurant (see Brunch)
Le Bernardin (French)
Brasserie des Théâtres (French)
B. Smith's (American; see Crowd Scenes)
Cabaña Carioca (Brazilian Portuguese; see Spanish and Latin American)
Café Beaujolais (French; see Local Phenomena)
Café San Martín (Spanish)
La Caravelle (French)
Carmine's (Italian; see Local Phenomena)
Carnegie Delicatessen and Restaurant (delicatessen; see Local Phenomena)
Les Célébrités (French; see Local Phenomena)
Century Café (American; see Local Phenomena)
Chez Josephine (French)
Chez Napoleon (French)
Chiam (Chinese)
Chibo Okonomiyaki (Japanese)
Chin Chin (Chinese)
Christ Cella (Steaks)
La Côte Basque (French)
Darbar (Indian)
Dawat (Indian)
Dock's Oyster Bar (Seafood)
Four Seasons (American; see Local Phenomena and Green Dining)
Gold Room (see A Proper Tea)
Grand Central Oyster Bar & Restaurant (seafood; see Local Phenomena)
La Grenouille (French)
Les Halles (French)
Hamburger Harry's (burgers; see For All Ages)

Hard Rock Café (burgers; see For All Ages and Out Late)

Hatsuhana (Japanese)

Jezebel (Southern; see Spicy Food)

Kang Suh (Korean)

Laura Belle (see Out Late)

Lespinasse (French)

Lutèce (French)

Madras Palace (Indian; see Green Dining)

Madras Woodlands (Indian; see Green Dining)

Manhattan Ocean Club (Seafood)

Maurya (Indian)

Le Max Restaurant (French; see Local Phenomena)

Nippon (Japanese)

New York Kom Tang House (Korean)

Nusantara (Indonesian; see Spicy Food)

Ollie's Noodle Shop & Grill (Chinese; see Local Phenomena)

Palio (Italian)

Palm (Steaks)

Palm Too (Steaks)

Park Bistro (French)

Planet Hollywood (American; see For All Ages)

Le Périgord (French)

Pomaire (Chilean; see Local Phenomena)

Rainbow Room (American; see Local Phenomena)

Remi (Italian)

René Pujol (French)

Rosa Mexicana (Mexican; see Spicy Food)

Russian Tea Room (Russian; see Local Phenomena)

Rusty Staub's on 5th (American; see For All Ages)

Sarge's Delicatessen and Restaurant (delicatessen; see Local Phenomena)

Saturnia (spa cuisine; see Green Dining)

SeaGrill (seafood; see Local Phenomena)

Seryna (Japanese)

Shaliga Thai (Thai; see Spicy Food)

Snaps (Swedish; see Northern and Eastern European)

Solera (Spanish)

Sorrentino (Italian; see For All Ages)

Sparks (Steaks)

Supper Club (American; see Out Late)

Sushiden (Japanese)

Takesushi (Japanese)

Trionfo (Italian; see Local Phenomena)

Tropica (Seafood)

Tse Yang (Chinese)
"21" Club (American)
Via Brasil (Brazilian; see Spanish and Latin American)
Water Club (see Brunch)
Woo Lae Oak of Seoul (Korean)
Zarela (Mexican; see Spicy Food)
Zen Palate (vegetarian; see Local Phenomena)

Upper East Side

Arcadia (American)
Azzuro (Italian)
Baraonda (Italian; see Crowd Scenes)
Boathouse Café (Italian; see For All Ages)
Café Carlyle (see Brunch)
Café Crocodile (Mediterranean and Middle Eastern)
E.A.T. Café (delicatessen; see Local Phenomena)
Elaine's (Continental; see Crowd Scenes)
Fu's (Chinese)
Gallery (see A Proper Tea)
J. G. Melon (bar food; see Crowd Scenes)
Jim McMullen (bar food; see Crowd Scenes)
Jo Jo (French)
Mark's Restaurant (see A Proper Tea)
Mayfair Hotel Baglioni (see A Proper Tea)
Mazzei (Italian)
Mezzaluna (Italian; see Crowd Scenes)
Mortimer's (bar food; see Crowd Scenes)
Our Place (Chinese)
Park Avenue Café (American)
Post House (Steaks)
Primavera (Italian)
Quatorze bis (French)
Red Tulip (Hungarian; see Northern and Eastern European)
Rotunda (see A Proper Tea)
Sarabeth's Kitchen (American; see For All Ages and Brunch)
Serendipity (burgers and sweets; see For All Ages)
Sign of the Dove (American)
Sistina (Italian)
Triangolo (Italian)

Upper West Side

Baci (Italian)
Café des Artistes (see Brunch)
Café Luxembourg (American; see Crowd Scenes)

Carmine's (Italian)
Dock's Oyster Bar (Seafood)
Sarabeth's Kitchen (American; see For All Ages and
  Brunch)
Shun Lee (Chinese)
Shun Lee Café (Chinese)
Sidewalkers' (Seafood)
Tavern on the Green (American; see Local Phenomena)

Harlem
Sylvia's Restaurant (Southern; see Spicy Food)

OUTSIDE MANHATTAN

The Bronx
Dominick's (Italian)
Mario's (Italian)

Brooklyn
Almontaser (Mediterranean and Middle Eastern)
Gage & Tollner (Seafood; see also Brunch)
Gargiulo's (Italian)
Gastronom Moscow (Russian; see Northern and Eastern
  European)
Moroccan Star (Mediterranean and Middle Eastern)
National (Russian; see Northern and Eastern
  European)
Odessa (Russian; see Northern and Eastern European)
Patsy's (Italian)
Peter Luger (Steaks)
Primorski (Russian; see Northern and Eastern Euro-
  pean)
River Café (American; see Local Phenomena and
  Brunch)
Totonno's Pizzeria Napolitana (Italian)
Tripoli (Mediterranean and Middle Eastern)

Queens
El Bodegon (Argentine; see Spanish and Latin
  American)
La Cabaña Argentina (Argentine; see Spanish and Latin
  American)

New Jersey
Hero Chan (Japanese)

BARS

By Edward Hernstadt and Helen O'Connor

Edward Hernstadt, who contributed the Greenwich Village section of this guide, spends just enough time in bars to remain sane. The late Helen O'Connor was a freelance writer from Ireland who contributed frequently to the Daily News, New York *magazine, and other publications.*

New York City is all things to all people, and nowhere is this more evident than in the infinite number and variety of establishments where the natives go to drink, chat, and be seen. From the neighborhood dive to the exclusive hotel bars with the dangerous ultra-chic designer furniture, you'll find just the place in New York to crook your elbow. In fact, the bar you choose as yours will effectively say who you are. If it's a downtown club scene you're after, there are fewer than half a dozen bar counters you should be leaning against. If you want to ride the crest of the latest trend, there will be only one or two bars where you'll dare to show your face. You're not a real New Yorker until you know the discriminating difference.

In New York, bars have another distinct function: They're somewhere to go when you're awake in the city that never sleeps. When the restaurants have put the chairs up on the tables, you can still find a bar that won't say go until 4:00 A.M. or later.

The following highly selective listing is a completely arbitrary attempt to open the doors of New York bars to the uninitiated newcomer. Bear in mind that the definition of a bar is very loose and open to interpretation, and that the categories below are equally haphazard. Many places mentioned here are drinking-only establishments, while others include the options of food and entertainment. All the bars listed are located in Manhattan.

CLASSIC NEW YORK BARS

In a marked affront to all the change around them, some New York bars stubbornly refuse to change at all. One of the very best of these is the completely unassuming **Ear Inn** (326 Spring Street, between Greenwich and Washington streets), so called because somebody once blacked out the curved parts of the first letter in the original sign that read BAR. This neighborhood mainstay has evolved from whorehouse to speakeasy to longshoreman's local and is still going strong. It's low-slung and run-down enough to feel like home, but the cook is definitely not Mom: Beware the food. If you're Irish, this is the place to sample one of the best pints of Guinness in Manhattan. If you're a poet, show up and declaim at the weekend poetry readings.

If you ever watched the opening credits of the old "Late Night with David Letterman," you've been on a swooping tour of the **Old Town Bar** (45 East 18th Street, between Park Avenue South and Broadway). That millions of people zoom through the bar every weeknight is ironic, given the management's desire to keep the place unknown and unchanged. And unchanged it seems to be. It is obviously one of the oldest and architecturally most original bars in Manhattan, with towering ceiling and cut-glass panels between the treasured booths. The burgers and fries are great here and provide much-needed ballast, but to order anything else is suicidal. And be forewarned: The place has been discovered by a regular crowd of local advertising executives and photographers.

In the same mold is **Fanelli** (94 Prince Street, at Mercer Street). Not as big as the Old Town but just as original, this SoHo place serves better food to an artier crowd. On the weekends it's largely overtaken by tourists, and most evenings with folks from various outlying areas, but on afternoons and off nights it's the local pub for those lucky enough to live in the neighborhood.

Imbued with a similar Prohibition-era feel, **Peter McManus** (152 Seventh Avenue, at 19th Street) is one of those local bars whose worst flaw is being too popular. The long, curved bar is generally packed with a mix of serious-drinking regulars, retired frat boys fresh from the softball fields, and Chelsea theatergoers and actors, while the comfortable booths in the back remain empty. It is a tribute to the spirit of McManus that these oil-and-water crowds generally get along swimmingly. There are great burgers and local beers on tap (this is one of the few places in town where you can still get pitchers).

As if pressed between the pages of a 1950s brochure, the bar at the **Gramercy Park Hotel** (2 Lexington Avenue, at 21st Street) is a throwback, complete with sample case–toting travelling salesmen, grannies in town to shop wholesale, and such odd folks as Sinead O'Connor. The windows are draped in heavy red velvet, and barely lit chandeliers dangle over tables clustered around a faintly off-key crooner in a Nathan Detroit suit tinkling the ivories. The bartender, whose sense of humor is as creaky as he is, presides over a lovely oak bar, while huge mirrors and wood paneling form an unlikely frame for the television set. A grand place to meet for cocktails.

The **Grassroots Tavern** (20 St. Mark's Place, between Second and Third avenues) has been around nearly forever, tucked neatly down half a flight of stairs from the riot of shops, restaurants, and street vendors lining St. Mark's Place. The appearance of everything—floor, chairs, carved-up tables, and patrons—in this long, low, dark bar, with a vintage black tin ceiling, gives new meaning to the phrase "beer-soaked." A broad cross-section of the colorful folks who make the neighborhood home come to enjoy the loud if chancy jukebox and pitchers of beer.

Nearby, and almost never worth the walk, is **McSorley's Old Ale House** (15 East 7th Street, between Second and Third avenues). Allegedly the oldest bar in New York (according to the bartenders), it was certainly the last one to allow women to enter its seemingly hallowed portals (by court order in the early 1970s). Unfortunately, McSorley's still draws that type of piggish, priggish crowd—and lots of them—so whatever charm history generally imparts to a bar is crushed by the hordes of loud collegians who will say anything once they've poured a few brews down their throats. On weekends people actually wait in line to stuff themselves in. On the bright side, if you wander in of a rainy afternoon you can enjoy this tavern's plentiful character in peace while tucking into a ploughman's lunch and downing a few brace (they are sensibly dispensed only two at a time) of the excellent home brews.

An old-time bar that does triple duty as businessman's hangout, maturing frat boy's beer joint, and age-indifferent pickup parlor is **P. J. Clarke's** (915 Third Avenue, at 55th Street), a Midtown institution aptly famous for its longevity as much as anything else. It's *the* classic New York bar. As the surrounding neighborhood has evolved from residential to skyscraper-dominated business district, countless beers and hamburgers have continued to pass over its well-worn counter. Through it all, no matter what shenanigans have gone on in front of the bar, there has always been one constant: an Irish barman to cast a cold eye over it all.

Finally, we include here two bars that are not classic so much by dint of their perseverance or preservation but because of their immutably New York character. The **Corner Bistro** (331 West 4th Street, at the corner of Jane Street, near Eighth Avenue) serves, quite simply, the best bar burgers in the city. Small and dark, with a slightly dingy wood interior, this tavern fills nightly with a mix of Yuppies seeking to evade that moniker and older locals who come to quaff the excellent tap beers (featuring McSorley's brew, if you happen to skip that bar) and to attempt to work the giant burgers and BLTs into their eager jaws. Not always the prettiest sight, but worth enduring.

A very good bar in a questionable neighborhood, the **Parkside Lounge** (317 Houston Street, at Attorney Street, between avenues B and C) flies flags above the piano-key tiling that runs along the walls at table height representing all the countries supplying immigrants to our fair city. Scattered among them is a menagerie of stuffed animal heads, stuffed fish, and stuffed parrots. One of the only bar bowling machines in town graces one corner, and a remarkable "Star Trek" pinball machine (featuring Scottie chortling "Aye Captain" when your quarters have been accepted) the other.

NEIGHBORHOOD BARS
New York has a blessed plenitude of the kind of neighborhood bars in which folks congregate to talk, hang out, seek solace, or just drink. Not so different in spirit from the classic bars above, these taverns tend not to have the additional glamour of an Old New York look or feel, nor do they attract the yahoos that charm and beauty unfortunately but inevitably draw. Nonetheless, they embody that rare mix of darkness and character that is the thumping, glorious heart of any true tavern.

The **Spring Lounge** (48 Spring Street, at Mulberry Street in Little Italy), known to regulars as the "Fish Bar" because of the large stuffed sharks and swordfish on the wall, is a small, dark, comfortable joint with an appealing mix of regulars. This is the kind of place to go with a group of friends and see what happens. The jukebox is solid and drinks properly priced.

Puffy's (81 Hudson Street, at the corner of Harrison Street) is always a good stop on a downtown bar crawl.

Because of Puffy's location in TriBeCa, which accounts for the high tin ceilings and pounded wood floors, the crowd is slightly more well-to-do and successful here but nowhere near prissy. Talk to Susan, the bartender, formerly of the Raccoon Lodge. She's O.K.

Despite the "great" in its name, the **Great Jones Café** (54 Great Jones Street, east of Lafayette Street) is just a hole-in-the-wall off the Bowery. But its tasty and reasonable Cajun food, intimate seating, and lively clientele from the Off Off Off Broadway theaters on 4th Street have attracted locals and names as big as Bruce Springsteen. Crowded with diners early; the bar scene really gets going after 11:00 P.M., when all the regulars show up. You know you've found the right place when you see the bust of a disheveled and sad-eyed Elvis in the window.

Another local tavern known as the "Fish Bar" because of its ubiquitous piscatorial decor, **Kastro's** (237 East 5th Street, between Second and Third avenues) is the regular haunt of waiters, waitresses, and chefs liberated from their night shifts in the toney restaurants of the Village. A minuscule place fronted by what looks like a garage door with glass panes, Kastro's doesn't get going until late, and then it goes hard, loud, and strong. It has one of the largest food selections in town, chiefly because its menu comprises all the take-out menus of the surrounding restaurants.

A handful of bars in a three-block radius in the East Village offers a range of experiences. One of the best vantage points from which to observe the stirring parade of bikers, posers, leather queens, hard-core and semi-hard-core punks, artistes and artists, bums, and true-life stories that is the East Village is the sidewalk terrace at **Sidewalk** (94 Avenue A, at 6th Street). Some people eat here, but most come to make their own scene or check out what's on in the neighborhood while sucking down the huge and excellent frozen margaritas.

The **Big Bar** (73–75 East 7th Street, between First and Second avenues) is a tiny room housing what passes for a beautiful crowd in this neighborhood. Cocktails are the rule of thumb and conversation tends to be muted and design-oriented. Design is a motivating force rather than a topic of conversation at the **Gold Bar** (345 East 9th Street, between First and Second avenues), which also attracts a more financially comfortable set of the neighborhood's denizens. Sheets of steel provide flooring over the sand-covered basement, which is visible between the cracks in the floor. The regular art exhibits are usually architectural installations (concrete stools on rollers, for example). The German-American owner, Roberta, offers a selection of real German beers (not Becks), including, when that season is upon us, Oktoberfest beers, which may explain the bar's popularity with German speakers. Wednesday is "fräulein night," when Teutons and other regulars hang out at the bar and an interesting crew of East Village lesbians takes over the rest of the place.

Counterpoint (237 East 9th Street, just west of Second Avenue) is a new arrival whose overwhelmingly red decor is interspersed with black tables and a beautiful gold bar. Although the lace and velvet curtains further the look of a bordello run by the French during the waning years of the czar, the place has a Latin sensibility, featuring the mambo on Sunday evenings.

A bizarre mix of camp and grit typifies the **Reno Bar** (155 Second Avenue, between 9th and 10th streets). Although the tap-dancing waiter in the spangled vest is no longer with us, his spirit still guides this two-story home-away-from-home for those obsessed with Marilyn and Marlene—as well as the eclectic neighborhood crew that stops in nightly for a few hours. The upstairs is usually uncrowded and offers a rare, peaceful view over the bustle of the street below, while downstairs belongs to the now almost exclusively gay regulars.

Even more bizarre is the **Village Idiot** (160 First Avenue, between 9th and 10th streets), the constantly changing sign in front of which has read "Live fast, die young, drink beer." In the afternoons this is a sanctuary for people who are truly out of luck and time. At night Pabst Blue Ribbon in a can remains the *cocktail maison,* but the patrons could afford more if they wanted it. You are confronted then with make-believe derelicts, fresh-faced groovoids, and hard-core biker-rockers, all of whom take a break from their imbibing to belt out sing-alongs to country classics, taking their cue from the bouncing-ball pumping fist of the petite bartender. (The for-all-purposes-unconscious fellow with his pants hovering mid-crack who anchors the bar and sustains the realness of the afternoon crowd is the owner.) If you are stuck on the West Side and either unwilling or unable to stagger crosstown, try out the Idiot's meat-packing-district companion bar, **Hogs and Heifers** (859 Washington Street, at West 13th Street).

If you are a very loud youth inclined to alternate your quarts of beer with shots of Jaegermeister (a death-dealing German schnapps), try out the **Bear Bar** (2156 Broadway, between 75th and 76th streets). This bar is a kind of German spa–frat house combination that features a truly stellar and national selection of local American beers. The huge stuffed bear outside alerting you to the bar's presence sets the level of subtlety you will find throughout—one young female patron observed that the habitués include the "dumbest guys I've ever met." But there is a place for that sort of baseball-capped mind set from time to time, and the nightly beer specials, foos-ball machines, and bear tracks leading to the facilities signal that this is such a place.

PINTS

A handful of neighborhood gems feature Guinness Stout, which though a pale shadow on these shores of the miraculous and holy pint found in Ireland is still a mighty beverage to sit behind of an evening. Generations of underage drinkers have been received into the welcoming arms of Bacchus at the **Dublin House** (225 West 79th Street, between Broadway and Amsterdam Avenue). Although the current bouncer, Bernie (whose business card reads "Professional Anti-Host"), takes care to exclude the pre-adolescent, this longtime neighborhood icon still maintains an exquisite mix of customers that seems to decrease in age by the decade as you move deeper into the bar: Crusty pensioners near the entrance give way to graying regulars in the heart of the bar, giving way in the back room to boisterous youth. The jukebox houses an outstanding selection of Motown and classic rock, and the Guinness is fine, if on the chilly side.

A no-frills pub capping the East Village, **O'Hanlons** (349 East 14th Street, west of First Avenue) is the kind of bar at whose doorway you stop briefly on weekend nights to take in the din of discoursing patrons, lame 1970s music, and shattering glass before being swept into its raucous maw. On weeknights, however, the place wears the face of comfortable local and is an inviting spot to catch up with an old friend over a few pints. A new look and changes in the bar staff have lowered the charm level—and the quality of the Guinness—somewhat, but it's still a decent bar.

Two pubs within a block of each other offer mild variations on the Irish theme. **Molly's** (287 Third Avenue, between 22nd and 23rd streets) is dark and perhaps a hair too self-conscious, evidenced by the superfluity of sawdust on the floor and the confusing decor: odd nautical props, wrought-iron candelabra, and wood ceiling beams of questionable provenance. But the bar is on the whole a comforting place, lined with solo drinkers of venerable aspect and down-at-heels businessmen, and the waitresses are authentically hard-eyed. The pint is quite good, although a step behind that pulled at the **Glocca Morra** (304 Third Avenue, just north of 23rd Street). The atmosphere is basic Irish-American, featuring a breathtaking collection of tasteless Irish-iana behind the long and truly oak bar. Tiffany lamps clash with dart boards, the soundless television is tuned to sports, and people actually dance to the jukebox beneath an impressive black air duct that runs the length of the bar. Live music—Irish folk groups, including the popular Black 47 from time to time—is an occasional bonus.

Rounding out this collection is the motley **Tom Milanos** (51 East Houston Street, between Mott and Mulberry streets), a narrow sliver of a beer-soaked pub. The eclectic decor focuses on New York baseball players and Irish-American politicians of bygone eras. Some of the regulars verge on the scary—they are genuinely desperate and probably at least vaguely involved with the IRA. The pints are good, although the pipes could use a cleaning, and the bartender is a polite tie to reality. Best in the deserted afternoons.

BARS WITH JUKEBOXES AND POOL TABLES

Here follow a few places that are high in comfort and low in effort, cost, and pretension—part of a highly developed subgenre of the neighborhood-bar species. Invariably "downtown" in attitude, and for the most part in location, they'll give you a local nod, some cynical chat (if you're up to it), and most probably, if you fit in, every third glass on the house. This category disproves anyone who says New York is an unfriendly, faceless place.

Vazac's (known locally as 7B because of its location on the corner of 7th Street and Avenue B) has been around longer than anyone can remember, yet it constantly crops up as a favorite neighborhood bar. Buried deep in Alphabet City (that's what locals call the Lower East Side where beyond First Avenue the avenues turn from numbers to letters), it's pretty run-down-looking from the outside. But you're in no danger. Once inside you can sit under the purring ceiling fans at the same gigantic wooden horseshoe bar where Paul Newman sat in one of the early segments of the movie *The Verdict,* drink cheap beer all night, and benefit from the wonderfully well stocked jukebox, which boasts more than its fair share of 1960s and 1970s hits. Here you're as likely to meet a gang of suited Wall Streeters on the rampage as a group of British artists checking out America. This is a laid-back place where you can hug a beer all night and nurse a broken heart or meet some new and interesting friends.

The same can be said for what has to qualify as Lower Manhattan's seediest bar, the **Dugout** (108 Third Avenue, on the northwest corner of 13th Street). This drinking den is literally dug out of the sidewalk, and a sign above the door bears the legend "On this day in 1897, nothing happened." This is a bar to frequent if you ever find it difficult to sleep at night. Sit at the run-down, Formica-topped bar, sip a Schlitz, watch the giant-size CNN screen for as long as you can hold your chin on your arm, and, oh, yes, continue the house tradition—do nothing.

If it's strictly pool you're after, though, wander back east to the other side of Tompkins Square and call in at **Blanche's** (135 Avenue A, between 8th and 9th streets), a small room with a pool table under a single parlor lamp in the back, where seasoned locals will be putting their names in line for a game late into the night. Get one of them to introduce you to the fearsome woman who runs the place (her name's not Blanche); if you're lucky she'll grace you with a free shot of throat-scorching Polish vodka. Not far from Blanche's, **Mona's** (224 Avenue B, between 13th and 14th streets) will give you a dose of the same downtown dive atmosphere.

If you want to settle in for a night of running tables in a more mellow atmosphere, reverse your steps to **Joe's Bar** (520 East 6th Street, between avenues A and B). You know you are home the second you first stride across its red-and-black-checked linoleum floor, settle in at the bar, and, torn between resting your eyes on the red tin ceiling or the sign depicting Elvis goosing Santa Claus, order your first beer. The juke is excellent, too, packed with tasty country tunes from all the masters, from George Jones to Tom.

For an ever-so-slightly more respectable pool experience, head back west to the **Blue and Gold** (79 East 7th Street, east of Second Avenue) or its neighbor, the **Holiday Cocktail Lounge & Restaurant** (75 St. Mark's Place, between First and Second avenues), a pair of old-fashioned pubs with miniature bars and low ceilings, quaintly lost somewhere in the 1950s but fashionable for those in their 20s.

For something a little more on the quiet side, try the **Edge** (95 East 3rd Street, just west of First Avenue), which has two pool tables and a much-pocked dart board. The crowd here is more professional and trendy than at Blue and Gold, Holiday, or Aces & Eights—there's a definite feeling that the people may well have real jobs—but the big glass windows that front the establishment and the interior red-brick walls give it an air of openness and friendliness that's hard to come by. Even the Hell's Angels who wander in from their New York headquarters a few doors down are friendly, though less so on the street; and more than a few late-night brawls have frightened the Edge's mellow patrons.

If you're one of those people who's sorry that punk passed away, **Max Fish** (178 Ludlow Street, just below Houston Street) will make you believe that you've died and gone to Heaven. The atmosphere here is outrageous, raucous, in-your-face hip. Apart from the requisite pool table and ear-splitting jukebox, you'll find the walls covered in graphic, bordering-on-obscene cartoons (some donated by local artists, some left by regulars) and three blinking pinball machines at the door.

Farther downtown is the funky and cool **Raccoon Lodge** (59 Warren Street, between Church Street and West Broadway). Although the decor's attempt to suggest an atmosphere somewhere between a he-man hunting cabin and a big-boy tree house is a bit studied, it's a good place for some serious pool under the lights of the high ceiling. There's now a Raccoon Lodge uptown, too, at 83rd Street and Amsterdam Avenue, but it's crowded with a mix of 21- to 23½-year-old Wall Street scamps and semi-tough bikers (no wonder they advertise clean bathrooms). It's not pool they're thinking of, but rather young love under the lights of the Upper West Side.

A couple of Upper West Side places on Amsterdam Avenue between 81st and 82nd streets have very crowded pool tables. The **Quarter Moon Saloon** is a fairly pleasant, surprisingly characterless Western-theme bar with many 20-ish folks in white tee-shirts and caps, while the **Insomnia Hotel Bar** is not a hotel but a bar opened by a couple of insomniacs. It offers different drink specials on most nights, and draws a lot of local bartenders and waitresses—so they are doing something right here.

The couches tucked away in corners seem to remain refreshingly isolated even when the room is wall-to-wall people.

THE SINGLES SCENE

It won't surprise you to know there's a whole slew of bars in New York that hold out the mysterious and vague promises of love, eternal or otherwise. Look into the throbbing **Live Bait** (14 East 23rd Street, between Broadway and Park Avenue South) any time after nine o'clock any night of the week. With a pretty good Cajun restaurant at the back and a noisy, squirming bar up front, the name isn't a misnomer. It's one of the liveliest checkout scenes in town.

A similar bait-box on the Upper West Side is **Lucy's Retired Surfers Club** (503 Columbus Avenue, near 84th Street). The packed bar is a draw for less-than-rich editorial assistants and baby bankers. The young patrons here wade about in an inch of what one hopes is beer, having all the devious thoughts their mothers warned them about before they migrated to the Big Apple. Expect a line from here to tomorrow. It's easier to get into the **Outback** (1668 Third Avenue, between 93rd and 94th streets); the **Shark Bar** (307 Amsterdam Avenue, between 74th and 75th streets); **Gonzalez y Gonzalez** (625 Broadway, between Houston and Bleecker streets), an enormous pickup joint with a Mexican flavor; or **Ruby's River Road Bar and Café** (1754 Second Avenue, at 92nd Street), which has made a specialty out of getting everyone lubricated before the mating game begins with its infamous Jell-O shots, two-dollar dollops of gelatin made with schnapps or vodka. Other concoctions guaranteed to get you in the mood are the pickled pineapple (drawn from silly giant glass vats of vodka and pineapple that command attention at one end of the bar) at **Memphis** (329 Columbus Avenue, between 75th and 76th streets), which attracts a slick, good-looking, early-30s crowd, and the mulled apple cider at the **Dive Bar** (732 Amsterdam Avenue, at the corner of West 96th Street).

"Ridiculous" is one word to describe **Chaz and Wilson's** (201 West 79th Street, at Amsterdam Avenue), where prematurely faded preppies cavort under rose lights to (surprisingly good) doo-wop music. **Hi-Life** (477 Amsterdam Avenue, between 82nd and 83rd streets) is a 1950s dream with figured aluminum and black Naugahyde walls decorated with pink flamingos. Correct martinis are served in wonderfully flaring glasses to a rather beautiful crowd busily getting to know each other. The terrace is a charm in the summer.

Downtown toward Lincoln Center you can try your luck at the **Saloon** (1920 Broadway, at 64th Street). The bar is large and commodious, and even offers those displaced from the bar itself an area to stand in. The drinkers at the Saloon are young, rowdy, and often single; you might leave with a date for your next theater event. When the weather is warm the staff breaks out the sidewalk tables, creating one of the finest people-gazing spots in the city.

Sfuzzi (58 West 65th Street, between Columbus Avenue and Central Park West) is part of a nationwide chain, all presumably featuring the same faux-Pompeii look with terra-cotta floors, partial frescoes on exposed brick, uncomfortable Italian-design stools, and confusingly placed columns. The well-dressed (and monied) after-work crowd is perhaps drawn by the huge containers of vodka and fruit; there are often free early evening appetizers laid out on Mondays and Tuesdays.

Downtown, and also notorious for its heavy-duty singles scene, especially after work on Friday nights, is the touristy **South Street Seaport**. By day the area is crammed with Wall Streeters lunching and out-of-towners visiting the museum, boarding the ships, and sampling from some of the dozens of eateries in the area. But at night, when the Brooklyn Bridge sparkles like a glittering harp and the surrounding shores of the East River wink with lights, the Seaport draws herds of young men and women braying to the god of beer on their rowdy quest for love. **Pedro O'Hara's** (89 South Street) packs a big, lively crowd.

BARS FOR THE RICH, THE BEAUTIFUL, AND THE WANNABES

New York is a fickle town. Its changing moods, seasons, tastes, and fashions will always have the natives scurrying to catch up and keep up. Bars open, are "totally cool" for six months, and fade away when a new hot spot lights up. It's dicey business taking the pulse of the current Manhattan bar scene, but here are the very latest, hottest, chic-est places around town. Remember, though, they may be dead tomorrow.

Leader of the pack is **Coffee Shop** (29 Union Square West). A sure sign of the rejuvenation of the once drug-ridden and dangerous Union Square, Coffee Shop is certainly now firmly established as *the* preserve of the beautiful people. Pseudo-Brazilian in feel, food, and decor, this is a place where nothing other than Armani or leather will suffice. You've seen the women somewhere before, like maybe on the cover of last month's *Harper's Bazaar*. If you have any doubts whatsoever about your poise, your cool, or your looks, don't even think about coming here. You have to be thin, tall, and young to feel comfortable sitting at the long, black, winding bar. So popular is this night spot that the owner recently decided to keep it open round the clock, and it teems all the time. When the weather is warm, sidewalk tables are just as valid a place to be seen.

The Fez, entered through the eternally chic Time Café (380 Lafayette Street), is a very stylish bar with a highly romanticized Moroccan decor, drawn more from repeated viewings of *Casablanca* than from any familiarity with the real thing. Fashions are nearly as high as the cheekbones on the extremely attractive clientele, but the atmosphere is surprisingly low-key and unpretentious. Dandy jazz shows downstairs on most nights.

Another whistle stop in Beautifulpersonville is **Tatou** (151 East 50th Street, between Third and Lexington avenues). The name is French for "bugle call." Tatou is a summons to hunt in the elegant evening. A two-room throwback to the days when women dressed for dinner, this club is glamorous: the drapes, the individually illuminated tables, the circular bar, the two-tiered dining area, the raised stage for live jazz. Stake your spot in the inevitable after-work rush and catch some smooth jazz early in the evening. If you stay long enough, the floor will clear for disco. It's not inexpensive, though. Be prepared to part with a minimum of five dollars per drink. Figures will soar into the three figures for dinner, which is worth it thanks to the truly excellent and imaginative cuisine.

You'd pass right by **Temple Bar** (332 Lafayette Street, at Bleecker Street) if you didn't know it was there. Only the ceramic skeleton of a chameleon-like creature and a pair of smoky green lights indicate the existence of life within. Once inside, you're transported into another world. Mahogany paneling, Oriental rugs, and luxurious draperies lend an air of seriousness and importance. The successful-looking, 30-ish clientele sips Champagne cocktails and martinis and exchanges tasteful chatter that you can almost, but not quite, overhear. Music is low, tones are muted, and while the mood is low-key, there is enough action to keep an evening here interesting. Prices are high and the service haughty, slow, and overbearing. These flaws, however, dissolve before the bar's nearly perfect beauty.

For a similar dose of elegance, wander any night past midnight into the lobby of the **Royalton Hotel** (44 West 44th Street, across the street from the Algonquin). A very rich and often very beautiful, self-assured crowd congregates in the space-age **Vodka Bar**—a sort of *Sleeper* pleasure chamber/"Star Trek" transporter-room environment —or perches on the pointy "chairs" reading novels, playing chess, or just looking good. Providing a home to a younger, chic-er generation of Eurotrash (the Condé Nast delegation at the Royalton writes about them) is the refurbished **Paramount** hotel (235 West 46th Street, between Broadway and Eighth Avenue), designed by the same ultra-modern French designer, Philippe Starck. Head for the eclectic and trendy **Whiskey Bar** or mount a magnificently broad staircase from the lobby to the quieter cocktail lounge.

Some bars garner a reputation even before they open. Such was the case with **TriBeCa Grill** (375 Greenwich Street, at Franklin Street), of which actor Robert De Niro is a co-owner. So heavy was the hype surrounding the grand opening that for the first two months it was impossible to get in. Dustin Hoffman, Martin Scorsese, Nelson Mandela, and others have filled these tables. The bar, which has a social life distinct from the restaurant's, is the circular centerpiece of the large dining area, a good vantage point from which to stand and sip (bar stools are very scarce) while you stare. If you're a nobody and you decide to corral a table, though, be forewarned—they may put you in a back room where no one can see you.

Lucky Strike (59 Grand Street, off West Broadway) is one of those rare bars that manages to rate favorably on the "cool" stakes but still treats you nonjudgmentally. It doesn't matter who you are, if you want to sit down and eat, you still have to get in line for one of the tables in the back. While you're waiting, you can savor the compressed, raucous atmosphere of the bar in this French-style bistro. It's always jolly and jumping, and the mix is usually fun and interesting. No one type of crowd, no one age group frequents the place. It's inexpensive and always full, and the food is really just an afterthought.

Taking advantage of the crowds that always seem to be milling around Lucky Strike, two new bistros opened down the street in the last year, and they seem to be doing a formidable job of taking care of the overflow. Next door, **La Jumelle** (55 Grand Street) weighs in as a dumpier, but pleasant, version of Lucky's. For more of the same, try **Jour et Nuit** (337 West Broadway, at the corner of Grand Street). An art venue that's currently chic is **Nick & Eddie** (203 Spring Street, at the corner of Sullivan Street), a reconverted neighborhood bar and grill that serves solid American home cooking and hosts a hopping bar scene. Not as trendy, but as plentifully stocked with beautiful arts-and-crafts types, is the new **Grange Hall** (50 Commerce Street, at Barrow Street). A sincere effort is made with the food, but the gorgeous, softly lit bar, imported from some out-of-town gem, and other design features are really the focus here.

If you like wine, **I Tre Merli** (463 West Broadway, at Prince Street), a cavernous SoHo Italian restaurant lined with racks of delectable vintages, is heaven neatly packaged and sent to earth. And no matter what night you venture here, every woman in the place is model perfect and beautiful.

Starving artists themselves, as opposed to the people who are in the business of selling art, are likely to be found at **Life Café** (343 East 10th Street, on the northeast corner of the city's infamously funky Tompkins Square Park). Dishing up delicious, and cheap, Tex-Mex fare as well as house margaritas at the bar, it's called Life because the walls, the ceiling, and all the tables are decorated with a collage of illustrations from old *Life* magazines. Sit outside and catch some real-life street life.

Appearances are certainly deceiving when it comes to **Flamingo East** (219 Second Avenue, near 13th Street). The darkened and tattered awning outside looks as inviting as a gateway to a coal mine. But don't be confused. The new owners left the awning and name of the restaurant that previously occupied the space just to mystify the uninitiated and cultivate the air of external tackiness. Once you enter, you're in a futuristic playpen of the rich and famous. The music is eclectic, the menu expensive, and the decor 1950s. A black bar looms large at the front of the room, and the huge, high-ceilinged upstairs room has the feel of a faded ballroom.

LESS COOL BUT RESPECTABLY TRENDY BARS

The fundamental rule for trendy bars in Manhattan is that the longer they're around, the less fashionable they become. Nevertheless, some joints, the epitome of "cool" in their day, have somehow dug roots deep enough to outlast fashion.

At one time it was nigh on impossible to jump the velvet rope into **Nell's** (246 West 14th Street, between Seventh and Eighth avenues), the faux-Edwardian lounge that spearheaded the 1980s retro look in dance clubs. Though the stylish crowd that once infested it has largely moved on, this place is not dead yet. Nell's red reclining sofas, glittering gilded mirrors, and dark rich carpets against a wood-paneled background all combine to make you feel a little glamorous for the night. The club is divided into rooms geared to dancing, eating, and just talk. You still have to pass the entrance exams of the goons at the door, though, and pay an entrance fee of $20 or so.

These restaurants have cultivated an independent bar scene as well. The **Odeon** (145 West Broadway, at Thomas Street), too, was once a bright light in the social circle of happening New Yorkers. Formerly a 1950s-style cafeteria, it still retains its Art Deco atmosphere. A spacious interior, high ceiling, and long, elegant bar make you want to sit and shoot the breeze all night long. The bar's clientele has grown up somewhat in the past few years, but you're still likely to star spot: Mick Jagger eats here when he's in New York, for one. For marginally more upscale food and atmosphere in an uptown version, try **Café Luxembourg** (200 West 70th Street, between Amsterdam and West End avenues).

The **Gotham Bar and Grill** (12 East 12th Street, between Fifth Avenue and University Place) is a maze of columns, marbles, and sunken eating areas. The beautiful people have marched on, but the restaurant still has a stalwart collection of regulars who come for the elegant bar and outstanding cuisine. It's no longer an essential place to be seen but, rather, a nice spot for a drink in magnificent surroundings befitting a modern-day Cleopatra.

Sam's Café (1406 Third Avenue, at 80th Street), named after and founded by actress Mariel "Sam" Hemingway, is another bar that has withstood the test of time. A down-to-earth and pleasant spot that opens onto the sidewalk during the summer, it defiantly retains a casual feel that somehow grates with the swankier Upper East Side bars that surround it. This is a place for singles and casual dates.

In the depths of the meat-packing district, just south of West 14th Street, is one of the oldest, most authentic, and best *tapas* bars in town, **Río Mar** (7 Ninth Avenue, near Little West 12th Street), where you can have a glass of Rioja and forget you're in New York. Down the street is **Florent** (69 Gansevoort Street), a 24-hour diner with excellent food, plenty of vino, and elegant company at all hours of night and day. But remember, they don't call it the meat-packing district for nothing—transvestite hookers roam outside after dark.

TOP-HAT BARS

If you're looking for bars where you can impress an out-of-towner with the wonder, riches, and splendor of New York City, this category is for you. Tuxedos and evening gowns would not be amiss at any of these places. Make sure there's money in your bank account.

The bar of choice for the city's lunchtime power brokers is the **Four Seasons Restaurant** (located in the Seagram Building, at 99 East 52nd Street, just east of Park Avenue). Wealth, opulence, grandeur, the feeling that, yes, maybe money can buy anything, will envelop you and your guests as you take your place among the city's heavyweight politicos and business tycoons. Try to look important and dress for success.

If your taxi driver mistakenly brings you to the Four Seasons Hotel instead of the restaurant, grab the opportunity to enter this brand-new I. M. Pei skyscraper (57 East 57th Street, between Madison and Park avenues) that will soon be a New York classic, along the lines of the Flatiron and Chrysler buildings. Pass through the stunning three-story-high lobby to the almost breathtakingly beautiful bar, decorated with inlaid wood and sketches of the Central Park Carousel, circa 1925. The latest word is that the bartender is a whiz at martinis, attracting a fairly sophisticated after-work crowd.

Although she is currently serving time as a guest of the people, Leona Helmsley is the persona behind **Harry's New York Bar** (in the New York Palace Hotel, at Madison Avenue and 50th Street). The actual bar is sedate and understated, but to see Leona at her decorating best, venture beyond into the **Gold Room**, gaudily gold all over, or the **Hunt Room**, a Helmsleyan mock-Tudor English gentleman's parlor, or, last but not least, the **Madison Room**, a bronze and marble creation that looks as if it were designed by Liberace.

For a little more elegance and refinement—after all, this is where the supremely debonair Cary Grant was mistaken for a spy in *North by Northwest*—try the Plaza Hotel's **Oak Bar** (Fifth Avenue at 59th Street). Authentically dark and woody, it's the place after a hard day's shopping on Fifth Avenue to find a nice leather-upholstered booth, sip a Kahlua and cream, look out on Central Park, and breathe in the eternal romance of the room.

Top of the Sixes (666 Fifth Avenue, between 52nd and 53rd Streets) is a homey retreat right up the street from St. Patrick's Cathedral. A voluminous 39th-floor restaurant and bar, carpeted in red, with wall-to-ceiling velveteen drapes on each window, it captures a spectacular Midtown view of New York at night. True, the place is not terribly sophisticated, the food isn't great, and it's expensive, but the service is pleasant and old fashioned.

Since we're talking tall: The ultimate overview of the city by night is to be had from the **Hors d'Oeuvrerie**, at Windows on the World, 107 stories from the ground, atop One World Trade Center. Though expensive (there's a cover charge after 7:30 P.M.), the bar is well worth a visit for a special treat or occasion. If the weather is good, it's the most effective way to send a visitor home on a high. (Note that the World Trade Center's top-floor bars and restaurants are closed indefinitely; for information, Tel: 938-1111.)

If you're the type of person who can dance real dances (like waltzes and tangos and two-steps), you should include the **Rainbow Room** (30 Rockefeller Plaza) on your New York itinerary. The legendary Art Deco dance club at the top of the RCA Building (now officially named, after its new tenant, the GE Building) was the reigning dance palace in the sky during the 1930s. Recently restored, it now has a revolving dance floor, a big band, and wall-to-ceiling windows staring Midtown in the face. It's a luxurious and glamorous slice of old New York, inviting you to dance and romance—one of the few remaining places you can really dress up for. You can wine here or dine here, or both.

For another slice of the old city, one that has miraculously, despite its prices, survived intact and unscathed through the decades, check out the **"21" Club** (21 West 52nd Street, between Fifth and Sixth avenues). Step down past the row of haughty miniature jockeys standing guard at the entrance and enter another luxurious world. Deep-pile carpets, attentive service, a cigar counter, and one of the most expensive, one-step-removed-from-pedestrian menus in the city all add up to the feel of a New York that's all too quickly diminishing.

Old-time service and prices are also the norm at the **Bull and Bear**, the bar addition to the swank Waldorf-Astoria, on Park Avenue at 49th Street. An after-work Midtown hangout for stockbrokers and financial whizzes, this multilevel establishment has an ever-running ticker-tape machine, so its clients feel right at home. Prices are bullish, but if you're a visiting businessman on an expense account staying at the Waldorf and you'd like something a little on the old-fashioned side, it's certainly worth investing a look.

The **Café des Artistes** (1 West 67th Street, off Central Park West) is a highly praised restaurant, so its bar is often overlooked. This is a good thing, for the bar, though small, is very cozy. Dress here is stylishly conservative; clothes worn for the theater are probably just fine. Middle-aged men and women discuss the performance they just saw in refined, hushed tones, and the service people glide by so as not to disturb the avid conversation. During warm weather out-of-towners and natives alike can be found sipping aperitifs on the brick patio café of **Tavern on the Green** (in Central Park at 67th Street). Ignore the touristy types and the creepy feeling that you are in a coffee commercial: This establishment is indeed a New York institution.

LITERARY BARS

Some people maintain that there's no such thing anymore as a literary bar in Manhattan. That can't be quite true, because almost everybody in the following places has a novel or just a bit of doggerel up their sleeve. You may not find Tom Wolfe at the **Lion's Head** (59 Christopher Street, near Seventh Avenue), but you may well run into *Daily News* or *Village Voice* journalists who look as if they've seen it all, or one of the many writers whose book jackets adorn the walls. The food in the back is good, tending toward burgers and salads, but the main attraction is an older, educated clientele, who like to belly up to the lovely old front-room bar and talk about books, boating, and the general state of the world.

Similar in flavor is **Chumley's** (86 Bedford Street, enter through a courtyard around the corner on Barrow Street), a bit hard to find because it has no sign. It's easy to imagine this bar in its old days as a speakeasy. Inside there's a snug little bar adjoining a slightly larger dining area, quite cozy in the wintertime with the fire going. As at the Lion's Head, the walls are lined with book jackets. Chumley's is at its best during the week; weekends it's packed.

Probably best known as the place where Dylan Thomas drank himself to death, the **White Horse Tavern** (567 Hudson Street, at 11th Street) is still a good place for Guinness aficionados, because it serves one of the better pints in the city. On weekends the main room, with its handsome original back bar, is packed, as are the sidewalk tables outside. But if you stick to weekday afternoons, you can generally escape the masses that have sucked this landmark dry of charm, and enjoy a few hours in the more modern rooms off to the side. Likewise, at off hours the outside café can be a pleasant place to enjoy a hamburger or a tuna melt; it's an interesting summer spot from which to watch the passing West Village parade.

Moving uptown and out of literary bohemia, be sure to visit the **Algonquin Hotel** (59 West 44th Street, between Fifth and Sixth avenues), long regarded as the lunchroom of *The New Yorker* magazine. At the Round Table in the back of the dining area once sat the best wits of the 1920s, including Dorothy Parker, Alexander Woollcott, and George S. Kaufman. Here they traded quips and honed their barbs. The decor has changed so little their ghosts should still feel at home here. Have a drink in their memory in the pleasant sitting area opposite the main desk, or in the oak-paneled Blue Bar (the *new* one, to the left of the lobby), where you might well find yourself sharing a corner with a reporter from *The New York Times*. The offices of the Gray Lady aren't too far away.

The tabloid press, on the other hand, will be found lobbing headlines and one-liners at the **Fleet** (203 East 45th Street, at Third Avenue), or **Maguire's Café** (800 Second Avenue, at 42nd Street, just across from the *Daily News* building). Try Maguire's in particular if you're interested in catching up with your favorite columnists. You might even persuade them to give you a tune behind the mike on *karaoke* (sing-along) night—Thursdays, winters only, though.

BARS WITH MUSIC

Some places showcasing live music that call themselves bars are not in their hearts bars at all, but venues. This is said not in a spirit of derision, but in the vigorous pursuit of truth in drinking experiences (see our Nightlife chapter for places where the emphasis is on the music). Others, however, retain their essential character as bars even though bands, instead of jukeboxes, supply the tunes. One of the best of these is **Dan Lynch's** (221 Second Avenue, near 13th Street; Tel: 677-0911), once one of the few bars in the city to feature blues exclusively. And even though in the past few years it's been joined by a half-dozen other joints that also sing the blues in earnest, Lynch's, the shabbiest of the bunch, is still the city's blues cathedral. Some of the performers here are as good as you're going to hear anywhere this side of Chicago. The setup is very intimate—all that separates you from the band is a well-worn bar rail. There's no cover and musicians are supported by passing the hat. A few doors down, the **Nightingale** (213 Second Avenue, corner of 13th Street; Tel: 473-9398) has a gritty, local clientele and seemingly no musical policy at all. In one night you may be exposed to heavy-metal radiation, all-original surfer rock, and an Allman Brothers cover band. Wait long enough and you'll hear something you like.

Candy-B1 (240 East 9th Street, between Third and Second avenues) is New York's premier low-rent, live-music *karaoke* bar. 'Nuff said. The **Spiral Bar** (244 East Houston Street, between avenues A and B) is a good place to check out if CBGB (see the Nightlife section) is too crowded. The pseudo and actual drug abusers who frequent this locale are less serious about music than they are dedicated to their tattoos, leather, chains, and facial rings. The generally punk music seems to have a synthesizer track mixed in, which is as innocuous as the fresh-faced lass who's usually behind the bar.

Moving north in the East Village, you will discover that a pair of almost ludicrously unmatched bars are near-neighbors off Tompkins Square Park. **Café Sin-é** (pronounced "shinay"; 122 St. Mark's Place, west of Avenue A; Tel: 982-0370) features what is currently New York's freshest, most earnest, and best-performed folk music. You will experience the odd clunker, but even then the Irish immigrant pub-cum-coffeehouse atmosphere and palpable sense of community make a trip here worthwhile.

Alcatraz (132 St. Mark's Place, at the corner of Avenue A) is a bit grittier. There is no live music here, but the jukebox—jam-packed with old and new heavy-metal classics—is cranked up so loud it usually takes a while to realize there isn't. Tattoos are de rigueur, though head-banging and lying on the floor to make out are optional. Unquestionably the best metal bar in town.

If loud Southern rock and country is more your speed, check out **Blondies** (2180 Broadway, at 77th Street; Tel: 362-4360). Live music is scheduled Sunday through Wednesday, and the rest of the week it is an unpretentious non-meat-market joint with pitchers of beer, friendly bartenders, lots of Lynyrd Skynyrd, and "atomic" chicken wings. A pleasantly real hangout in a neighborhood known for lamely trendy bars.

If jazz is your thing, **J's** (2581 Broadway, second floor, north of 97th Street; Tel: 666-3600) features top-drawer musicians in a regulars-only environment. Luckily, the sharp-eyed weekend bartender Danny has a great memory, so one trip may be enough to qualify you for that tag. Wrecked old-timers with arrays of drained shot glasses before them circle the bar, chatting with hot young horn players too young to drink legally. Deadly serious jazz aficionados and less intense music lovers fill the seven-dollar-minimum tables three steps down on the main floor. At press time, J's has closed, possibly temporarily, but possibly permanently.

Manny's Car Wash (1558 Third Avenue, between 87th and 88th streets; Tel: 369-2583) is a popular enclave for young fans of blues-rock. Busy and bopping, it's a place to *party.* If you drink anything other than beer, though, expect to go thirsty. If you eat anything other than White Castle hamburgers or Domino's Pizza warmed up in a microwave, expect to go hungry.

THEME BARS
For lack of any other sensible grouping, the following are termed "theme" bars, though nothing unites them except their uniqueness or, perhaps, their oddity.

At **Sugar Reef** (93 Second Avenue, between 5th and 6th streets), one of the first places in the city to feature Caribbean food, bar business seems to have taken on a life of its own. Almost every night of the week it's packed until the wee hours with people knocking back Red Stripe and Panama beers and swaying to the loud calypso beat. The decor is flashy and trashy, featuring lots of colorfully painted 55-gallon drums and colored lights. It's more Caribbean than the Caribbean itself.

What Sugar Reef is to Jamaican food, **Brothers Barbeque** (228 West Houston, at Varick Street) is to barbecue and Southern cooking. Dominated by the long, curving bar, the decor of this joint is so overpowering that somehow the food and the beer taste more authentic because of all the flour sacks, pictures of barbecue stands, and soda-pop signs on the walls. The atmosphere is Southern and lazy, except when a countryish band kicks in and gets the joint jumping. For the Upper West Side version, though a little tonier, there's **Yellow Rose Café** (450 Amsterdam Avenue, between 81st and 82nd Streets). Also in the Southern vein, **Fannie's Oyster Bar** (765 Washington Street, at West 12th Street) is a narrow, two-story place with a tiny back room and outdoor terrace (a joy in the summer) and a long, low, down-and-dirty bar in the basement. Excellent crab cakes and quite respectable jambalaya or red beans and rice mesh well with ice-cold beer and the frequent live bands doing odd 1920s and 1930s numbers.

Delia's (197 East 3rd Street, between avenues A and B) is one of the least probable bars in the city. Neither its blackened exterior nor its slightly scary East Village location gives you any idea of what lies inside. Half of the magic of this place is its shock value. Pulling back the black curtain at the door, you unveil an Anglo-Irish country home, with gilded mirrors, salmon-colored walls, waist-high moldings, and a genteel Irish hostess—Delia herself. Head straight for the bar and watch the varied clientele. You'll see white-haired Irish businessmen sitting cheek-by-jowl with heavy-metal rockers. Skip the expensive food. Sit and ponder the lesson of Delia's: If an Irish aristocrat fallen on hard times can open up a country house in the middle of the burnt-out East Village, then truly anything is possible in New York.

There's one street in Manhattan where every bar on the strip is a singalong. Its name? Grove Street. Every night, but especially weekends, hundreds of New Yorkers and visitors pack themselves into the tiny underground clubs and sing themselves into morning. Some people tout **Arthur's Tavern** (57 Grove Street, west of Seventh Avenue across from Sheridan Square; Tel: 675-6879) for good jazz. But a favorite of many is the last on the row, the **Five Oaks Restaurant** (49 Grove Street, west of Seventh Avenue; Tel: 243-8885), where a cynical old black pianist called Marie alternately cajoles and coddles her audience into having a memorable night. Marie's friends are always turning up to lend a tune, and they include everyone from opera stars to jazz greats. This is a great place to enjoy yourself and impress your entourage.

GAY BARS

Visitors who pop into New York for a few days and want to spend their evenings checking out the gay scene should take heed: In this richly complex city the social milieu isn't so clearly drawn on sexual lines as it is elsewhere. While there is no shortage of bars and clubs that are exclusively gay—and within that category exclusively male and exclusively female—many clubs and bars cater to a compatible mix of straights and gays, and many "straight" venues put out the welcome mat to a largely, but by no means exclusively, gay clientele one or two nights a week. The Gold Bar, for example, has a lesbian night, while the Reno Bar's downstairs room pulls in a mainly gay clientele (see the Neighborhood Bars section, above, for both).

Nor does geography define New York's gay turf: Christopher Street in the West Village is arguably the epicenter of gay New York, but there are few neighborhoods, in Manhattan at least, that don't have sizable gay populations with attendant bars and clubs where gays make up at least part of the mix. Following are but a few of the city's more popular gay bars and clubs. For the latest on gay entertainment, check out the *Village Voice* or *New York Native;* both are weekly newspapers with extensive listings and reviews.

Uncle Charlie's, a large, noisy bar in the heart of the Village at 56 Greenwich Avenue (at Seventh Avenue), is, if you will, the Cheers of New York gay bars—it's been around forever, it's comfy, and just about anyone who walks through the door (whatever your sex and sexual persuasion, but especially if you're a gay man) is going to feel comfortable here. Somewhat of the same amiable atmosphere prevails at **Ty's**, another long-standing, still-popular, predominantly male domain at 114 Christopher Street (between Bleecker and Houston streets). **The Monster**, 80 Grove Street (at Seventh Avenue), is a different animal—the emphasis is on noise and crowds, especially on the subterranean dance floor.

The Village's venerable lesbian hangout—venerable as

in it's been around awhile and is frequented by older regulars—is **DT's Fat Cat**, a comfy piano bar at the corner of West 4th and West 12th streets. **Henrietta Hudson**, formerly the Cubbyhole (438 Hudson Street, at Morton Street), draws a hip lesbian crowd, young and old. The **Duplex**, 61 Christopher Street (just off Sheridan Square), is another Village institution, with a convivial piano bar downstairs and musical revues and comedy acts upstairs; many, but certainly not all, of the performers here—amateur and professional—are gay. Across town in the East Village, **Boybar**, 15½ St. Mark's Place (between Third and Fourth avenues), perennially draws an eponymous, early-20s clientele.

The **Roxy**, 515 West 18th Street (just west of Tenth Avenue), is a commodious and appealing dance club that's enjoyed a long run of popularity. It is one of the aforementioned places that draws a predominantly gay crowd some nights (usually Saturdays, Sundays, and Tuesdays), but whatever your sexual taste, you'll probably feel comfortable here any time (see also our Nightlife section). Before you wander into **Rawhide**, 212 Eighth Avenue (at 21st Street), be forewarned that the name provides a clue to the leanings, sartorial and otherwise, of the clientele—you'll feel weird in a suit here, out of place if you're not gay, and like an alien if you're a woman.

Don't Tell Mama, appropriately located in the Theater District at 343 West 46th Street (between Eighth and Ninth avenues) spotlights gay performers; this is a good place to catch some budding, first-rate cabaret talent. Singing waitresses are a fun, campy touch in the piano bar, and there's a pool table to accommodate the neighborhood types (many actors and actresses) who hang out here. Befitting it's East Side location, **The Townhouse**, 236 East 58th Street, seems like a well appointed private club, and this reserved, nicely appointed room does serve as an after-work watering hole for many Midtown executives. In fact, this may be the only gay bar in the city where you're expected to show up in a coat and tie. **The Works** is the Upper West Side's most popular gay bar, at 428 Columbus Avenue (between 80th and 81st streets). The long room looks like many of the other fern bars up here and attracts a gay, neighborhood-appropriate crowd of youngish men aspiring to the bourgeoisie; all proceeds from a much attended, weekly Sunday beer blast benefit the Gay Men's Health Crisis, New York's laudatory AIDS-sufferers' support group.

COFFEE BARS

A format that has not translated well to these shores, the coffee bar, as you might suspect, flourishes best in old-time immigrant neighborhoods. The **Caffè Reggio** (119 MacDougal Street, at the corner of West 4th Street) is a classic Greenwich Village Italian coffeehouse with bitingly perfect espresso, frothy pastries, and a huge brass cappuccino machine. Because it is in the heart of the Village, you may have difficulty finding a table here, but even when this place is busy, the friendly bustle inside is a tonic from the crush on the streets outside.

Little Italy is littered with coffee shops on Mott and Mulberry streets between Canal and Broome. **Le Poeme Corsican** (14 Prince Street, at Elizabeth Street) is probably the very best of them. This self-styled French tearoom does the proper in a pleasant, unrushed, and uncrowded setting. The pastries are particularly tempting.

A charming, never crowded, if somewhat innocuous coffeehouse in the East Village is **Caffè La Strada** (78 East 4th Street, between Third and Second avenues). Whether you are recharging after a bout in one of the nearby Tower warehouses (records, books, video), or from a tour of the neighborhood's many intriguing secondhand shops, this is a tranquil little respite where they will let you nurse your hot or iced cappuccino or coffee for hours. The simple fare is tasty and extremely reasonable.

One can't say that about the notoriously high-priced (the very high quality makes it difficult, though not inaccurate, to call it overpriced) **Dean & DeLuca**, which now offers three shops serving an array coffees, espresso, and cappuccino, as well as a huge selection of ridiculous pastries and cakes. There are the stand-up auxiliary corner in the vast new 560 Broadway shop (at Prince Street); a full-fledged coffee shop in the charming and not so small old store at 121 Prince Street (between Wooster and Greene streets); and the oh-so-chic outlet in the chic hotel Paramount (235 West 46th Street, west of Broadway). Other Dean & DeLuca outposts have been installed at 75 University Place (at 11th Street in Greenwich Village) and at the Guggenheim Museum, freshly opened after a two-year renovation; see the Museums chapter.

If for some reason you are trapped on the Upper West Side and need a jolt of caffeine before fleeing to a more sensible downtown neighborhood, head for the Romanesque **Caffè Monaco** (421 Amsterdam Avenue, at 80th Street), or any of the other coffeehouses that have sprung up along this once shabby avenue. **Zabar's**, the huge food and cookware emporium at 80th Street and Broadway, operates an always-crowded, stand-up coffee bar on its premises.

POPULAR MUSIC AND NIGHTLIFE

By David Frankel

David Frankel, formerly an editor of New York *magazine, has written on music for* New York *and for* Rolling Stone. *He is an editor of* Artforum *magazine.*

Generations of New York nightlife come and go, but having gone they don't necessarily disappear—they just move out of the consciousness of the public, or at least of the particular public that decides which clubs and practices are hot and of the moment. For some, New York club life died in 1973 with the closing of the old Copacabana. For others it was 1980, when the late Steve Rubell and Ian Schrager, the owners of the seminal late-1970s discotheque Studio 54, faced the tax-evasion charges that eventually sent them to jail; or perhaps it was 1982 and the loss, after similar tax charges, of Steve Mass's Mudd Club, a rudimentary below-Canal establishment that began as a kind of artists' and downtowners' bar. Yet not only are people still going out in the evenings, they're going to rooms that are basically similar to those older haunts—or at least to Studio and the Mudd. It's just that they're also going to, and talking about, what came after—or whatever may have come after that by the time you read this book.

The Copacabana is a different story. From the 1940s through the 1960s, the club defined the image of the New York night spot as many imagined it: big-name entertainers, a floor show, glamour. It had its own chorus line, the Copa Girls (a tall dancer was called a show girl; a short one, unimaginably today, a "pony"), and its ever-so-vaguely Brazilian decor—the palm trees were concrete—was for countless Americans the instantly evocative epitome of show biz. In its billing, the Copa found ways to cope with the times, moving from Brazilian bombshell Carmen Miranda in designer fruit-salad hats to a twisting Chubby Checker to Tom Jones, creating lines, the story goes, four times around the block. But the club did not survive Las Vegas. The big casino hotels that went up there in the 1960s hired singers like Jones as part of the bait to lure players in to the tables, and could pay extraordinary fees out of their gambling income. Relatively small rooms couldn't compete. The Copa is now a discotheque, and the only regular chorus line left in town is Radio City Music Hall's Rockettes, who perform in annual Christmas and Easter shows as well as occasional engagements scattered throughout the year.

For many, of course, chorus line–type entertainment isn't such a great loss. Still, New Yorkers who remember the Copa kind of club sometimes malign the contemporary scene: It's all geared for teenagers and the rock 'n' roll crowd; there's nowhere left to eat a good supper in a sophisticated surround and see a big star; and so forth. It's certainly true that rock, disco, and their variants are the popular music of the day, that their audiences tend to be young (though aging all the time), and that their settings take rough wear. It's also true that the economics of nightlife have changed; Frank Sinatra doesn't play supper clubs anymore.

As for the rest of us, New York is a very big town with a long and thrilling tradition in every branch of the performing arts. It attracts singers and dancers, pianists and horn players, cabaret acts, comedians, and rock 'n' rollers from all over the country—as well as rearing its own—and these people expend a great deal of energy, both competitive and collegial, on figuring out how to put themselves in front of a crowd that will listen while they do what they do. If New Yorkers like to appear jaded to the city's nightlife, that may be because there's more of it here than they can possibly see; and if you have to miss a good cabaret act or club date or jazz gig, why not pretend you did it on purpose?

CLUB CLASS

Different modes of night spots from the different eras cohabit, whether or not they're in the spotlight. On 52nd Street—once Swing Street, the Jazz Capital of the World, a night owl's delight of side-by-side jazz clubs from speakeasy days in the 1920s on—a row of high-rises has replaced the clubs. But that only means that jazz spots are diffused around town, from a concentration in the Village to a scattering on the residential Upper West Side.

Cabarets and piano rooms are sprinkled throughout Midtown in the still raffish neighborhoods around Times Square and Broadway, pulling in strollers from the theater crowd; their performers too are sometimes spun out of Broadway, as when singers and musicians from the stage moonlight or just drop in to some loosely organized bar that welcomes anyone with a voice (and some without). The Village still bears traces of its 1960s folk scene, rock 'n' roll is pretty much everywhere, and the discotheques that dominated nightlife in the late 1970s are still laying down their old beat (though maybe complicating it with hip-hop, techno, house, and other, newer musics with a pulse). And in addition, of course, there's whatever superseded these spots—whatever's of the moment at the moment.

The most recent really coherent vogue, now seen as distinctly passé, was what's been christened the Dim Age. This phase was ushered in late in 1986 with the opening of a club called Nell's, far west on 14th Street. Whereas the preceding era of clubs had gone for glitz and light shows and fabulous technology on the one hand, or for hole-in-the-wall funk on the other, Nell's tried to conjure a softly lit sitting-room mood. It may seem paradoxical to line up and pay for something like home, but people did, in a hip, downtown version of 1980s American conservatism. This didn't mean that the old disco palaces emptied out—abandoned by the scene setters, they were simply made available for everyone else. But a number of clubs, notably M.K. and the almost parodistically classy Au Bar (library wainscoting on walls further decorated by polo sticks and croquet mallets), did very well for a few years by following Nell's lead. Judging from the success of the current hot disco Club USA, the trend nowadays is for sweaty high tech with grace notes of de Sade. Still, Nell's and Au Bar hang on (though M.K. is gone), proving that there is always a market for comfort.

WHERE FUNNY MEETS MONEY
All this activity doesn't mean that New York makes life easy for aspiring club owners. An urgent issue is the city's high rent scale, which, despite the recent dip in real-estate values, sometimes seems to people who live here like a threat to all civilized life as we know it. New Yorkers

pay for this all around, in their own living expenses, of course, and (as concerns nightlife) in ever-higher admission fees and cover charges, but also in terms of the community of performing artists here, who need space to rehearse in, experiment in, and to live in—space that is less and less available. New York State's residential rent-control laws tend to make apartments cheaper in relation to the market the longer a tenant has occupied them (the rent increases less when a lease is renewed than when it changes hands), which is fortunate for the town's longer-standing citizens but unhelpful to its newcomers. And because New York's cultural life depends on its centripetal power to attract the newcomers who will contribute to it and constitute it, some worry is attached to the question of whether those people will find a room of their own here.

The early 1980s saw a revealing confrontation with these issues in the East Village, traditionally a part of Manhattan that was low-rent to the extent that large sections of it were derelict (fewer, but still numerous, blocks remain so). The relative cheapness of life there made the area attractive to artists and other low-budget young people, and some of them opened night spots of a kind, in the lineage of the Mudd Club, with names like 8 BC (on 8th Street between Avenues B and C), Darinka, the Limbo Lounge, and the Pyramid. As these logos may suggest, East Village cabarets catered to a crowd that was youthful at least in heart and usually also in actuality. They were small establishments, storefronts and tenements converted to their new use at minimal expense and often rudely and imperfectly—a 1980s version of the "Hey, kids, let's put on a show" movies of the 1930s, and infinitely tackier though just as enthusiastic. The entertainment was of a kind with its location: raw, or at least unafraid to be so. Some East Village performers have gone on to TV careers (Ann Magnuson) or have seen the inner meaning of their work discussed in art magazines and *The New York Times* (Karen Finley). The unpretentiousness of their environment, which was cultivated, and their own Dadaistic familiarity with the shock tactic as stage business have not obscured their inventiveness.

Today, however, most of these cut-rate nightclubs are gone. As Cornelius Conboy, the former co-owner of 8 BC, told *The New York Times* in 1985, when the club closed, the city government hit them with wall-to-wall paperwork: "license fees, certificate of occupancy, cabaret license, lease or bill of sale, nonflammability of drapes, public assembly permit, fire inspection, electric and gas inspection, health permit, liquor license, consumer affairs. . . ." Few of the Lower East Side cabarets were operating on that bureaucratic level. Though a few have survived, an arrest or two for selling alcohol without a license, or the prospect of having to scrape up lawyers' fees to stay open, was enough to fold the rest.

Any visitor to a nightclub has, of course, a justifiable interest in whether the ceiling will collapse and the sprinkler system will work (or whether there *is* a sprinkler system). Still, given the number of basement social clubs operating illegally in New York—unlicensed rooms offering liquor, some of them staying open for years without police action (a fire in one of these bars in 1990 left 87 people dead)—the city's attention to the East Village scene seemed out of scale. And it played a part in the escalation of rents. The unsafe and empty streets of the Lower East Side had discouraged landlords from repairing the area's derelict buildings. With clubs and art galleries attracting crowds to those streets again, developers began to rebuild the neighborhood, and the shoestring operations that had touched off the cycle were pressured to leave—in some cases, conveniently, by the city—so that more lucrative businesses could replace them. The effect was a contribution to the conservative drift defined by Nell's, a reclaiming of the night by establishments with relatively abundant capital. (And after the East Village everyone wanted a little comfort.)

But clubs like 8 BC did set a vital example. Will New York City's current financial state, more perilous in the early 1990s than at any time since the mid-1970s, be compensated for by more affordable commercial rents and a new wave of low-budget cabaret creativity? There are no signs so far that it's getting easier to put on a show, though the Nuyorican Poets Café, a downtown bar and performance space dedicated to creating an audience for, of all things, poetry readings, keeps alive some idea of what the East Village of the 1980s was like.

NIGHT COURT

In one respect the bureaucratic load that night spots bear has lightened lately, with the demise of a cabaret law that had been a consistent source of complaint. Originally passed in 1926 as a tool for crackdowns on speakeasies, the law forbade certain instruments and restricted to three the number of musicians who could perform simultaneously in clubs without a cabaret license. These licenses demanded annual fees and the fulfillment of certain zoning and safety requirements, and many rooms functioned quite well, and quite safely, without one—but they couldn't legally book four or more pieces, or horn players, or even drummers. Bands got around the law by organizing wrestling-type tag teams—you would see players waiting to step onstage as soon as one of the three already there stepped off. The practice was sometimes diverting but more often distracting. It ended on January 28, 1988, when a New York State Supreme Court judge found the law an unconstitutional violation of performers' freedom of expression. That evening bandstands all over town were packed as musicians asked their friends to step up and jam with them. It was a happy night—and, clearing the way for larger bands, it offered more musicians the chance of employment. Now the city is trying to write a new law, one that will restore its lost control through a form of zoning code. "To some people on the city council," said one cabaret owner a while ago, "all music is noise."

Another legal change in the last few years that directly affected nightlife was the 1985 raising of the state drinking age from 19 to 21—a particularly important development for rock clubs and discos, which have a large teenage clientele. Theoretically, anyone 16 or older can go to a club that serves liquor, though they now have to be 21 to be served a drink. Until recently, it was considered easier to keep under-21s out of a disco than to let them in and then try to identify them at the bar. But the teens and twenties are prime club-going years, which owners can't afford to ignore. And good-looking young people, "club kids," are also important to the image of many night spots, particularly discotheques.

So a manager has to be resourceful—he may, for example, let anyone in but rubber-stamp adults' wrists or give them a rubber bracelet once they've proved their age; they have to show the stamp to buy a drink. A dicier way to get around licensing and drinking-age laws has been invented by the sponsors of floating clubs, such as Payday or $100,000 Bar, which are rarely in the same place twice. These liquor-licenseless impresarios scout out basements and halls to take for a night, spread the news by word of mouth (stumbling on one of these events tends to put you in the way of finding out where and when the next one may be), and aim to be gone before anyone complains. Less mobile organizations set aside rooms for under-21s where no liquor is served, or open only to teenagers on selected nights of the week. This last wrinkle puts the newly 21-year-old in a novel position: Having spent the last several years trying to persuade a club's bartenders that he's old enough to drink there, he now has to persuade the club's doorman he's young enough to be let in at all.

AND MAY I SEE YOUR PASSPORT?

Club doormen have a very up-and-down reputation in New York—doted on by some, loathed by others. The doorman has absolute say as to whether or not you're admitted. And the fashionable clubs, particularly dance clubs (you won't find this problem in jazz or cabaret rooms), use the door as a tool: Creating a crowd outside is the approved way of letting the city know the place is hot. Stories are told of waiting outside the velvet ropes in front of some new venue only to enter at last and find the place half empty. And those who are allowed in, at least when a club is of the moment, are carefully chosen: If the crowd hanging around outside is engineered to create an impression of the club's exclusivity, and of how desperately people want to be there, the crowd inside is the main attraction and has to be worth the wait.

Most Manhattan clubs have regulars, a set that goes there all the time and never worries about admission. People outside those cliques tend to show up looking their best (but what should that be? Some doormen have been known to reject, for example, anyone wearing loafers) or at least dressed for maximum self-confidence. They arrive early rather than late—late being after midnight, when the clubs fill up, early varying from place to place but probably not after 11:00. They may go on a weekday rather than a weekend. They may try calling in advance to make a reservation, which some establishments accept depending on the positions of the planets. And they try not to take things personally.

In the summer of 1991 a Los Angeles judge ruled that a nightclub's use of doormen to decide who was "interesting" enough to admit was a violation of the state civil rights act. "Said policy is nothing more than a smokescreen for blatantly discriminatory behavior, with an awesome potential for abuse," he wrote. The judgment has so far shown no sign of impact on the New York club scene. But in any case, the buzz about these nightclubs lasts only for a while; then they cease to be considered "hot," and the crowd moves to somewhere else. The set that once loved the place now complains that it's full of "bridge-and-tunnelers"—off-islanders who, like virtually everyone who wasn't born here, have come to Manhattan by one of those two types of entry. Bridge-and-tunnelers, of course, and every other visitor from outside the club's set, both out-of-towners and New Yorkers as well, are paying guests, and the clubs are in the business of earning money. After making themselves visible by whatever means they can, including invidious door policies, club managements settle down to turnover and emptying the till.

Watching outside the the Palladium (opened 1985) recently, we saw no one forced to wait to get in. Outside Nell's (opened 1986) we saw a few people waiting; outside Au Bar (opened 1988), only a few people were trying to get in, and they were being turned away. On the street outside Club USA (opened 1993) was a patient mob. And even the Limelight had a large crowd at its ropes; though it opened in 1984—eons ago NYNT (New York nightlife time)—it underwent a renovation a while ago, and the improvements (quite perfunctory ones to these eyes) were enough to reinflate its reputation. If you have trouble with the door in any such places (and you may have none), remember it's only a business ploy and go instead to S.O.B.'s, which runs a great live-music program with dancing for a strictly first-come, first-served crowd. Or call the Vanguard, or Bradley's, and see if they can seat you for jazz. It's a big town.

DETAILS, DETAILS

In the descriptions that follow, we haven't tried to provide specific times or prices for the various night spots, as they may change at the drop of a hat. Jazz clubs and cabarets tend to start their programs at 9:00- to 10:00-ish, and run till after midnight. They may open earlier, particularly if they serve food. Dance clubs may not open till 10:00 or 11:00 and close at 3:00 or 4:00 in the morning; or they may move their hours forward on weekdays. Some close in the early part of the week—Sundays through Tuesdays or Mondays through Wednesdays. There is a lively homosexual culture in New York, and a few clubs,

particularly dance clubs, may go all-male on certain evenings; a phone call ahead will help you either avoid or
locate such events, depending on your taste. A lot of jazz
clubs close on Mondays, which may also be a cheap night
at places that stay open. Many charge a cover plus a drink
minimum at your table; it's often worth checking whether
the cover is dropped if you sit at the bar. Some discotheques bump up their prices during the course of the
night—it's cheaper or even free (try the Copa) early on.
(The management's bet is that you'll spend money in the
club while you're waiting for everyone else to arrive.)

A lot of residents here use *New York* magazine, *The
New Yorker,* and the *Village Voice* for listings, ads, and
reviews that will tell them what's going on. These publications also list the larger theaters, such as the Beacon,
the Paramount the Apollo, Radio City Music Hall, Carnegie Hall, Avery Fisher Hall, Madison Square Garden, and
St. Ann's (in Brooklyn Heights), which run popular-
music concerts of bigger acts than fit into the clubs. (We
don't cover those halls here, since their billings are
sporadic. Avery Fisher and Carnegie are mainly classical
concert halls; see the Classical Music chapter. The Garden, a hangarlike modern stadium, shows more sports
than music, but the biggest of the touring rock bands
may play here, or else at the **Meadowlands** arena, across
the river in New Jersey, an easy bus-ride away via the
Port Authority bus station on Eighth Avenue at 42nd
Street. The Beacon and the Paramount feature big-name
popular-music groups that can't—or prefer not to—fill
the really big venues, like the Garden, while Radio City
Music Hall tends to show more established or more
mainstream artists than the Beacon. The Arts at St. Ann's
is an adventurously aestheticized popular-music program run out of a Brooklyn church. And the financially
strapped Apollo tends toward variety-show type acts.)
The Paper is a good source for gossip about whatever
venues are newest and hottest—that, and plentiful use
of the telephone.

We don't talk about a lot of places, just the best or most
interesting in a reasonable range of types with various
types of clientele. Once you're in one that sounds good to
you, you'll have no trouble finding out from fellow revelers about other places to your taste, if you're the restless
type.

The telephone area code for Manhattan is 212.

JAZZ, PIANO, AND SOME FOLK

The Village and South

The **Village Vanguard** is the oldest jazz room in the city—it opened in 1935—and a much-beloved local institution. The music that's been played here over the years seems to have seeped into the walls and furniture to give the place its particular jazz-nirvana feel. It's a basement, down a steep flight of stairs from the street, characterized by dark walls laden with photographs and posters, red banquettes underneath them (more comfortable than the tables crowded together out on the floor), and an informal crowd with high standards in what it expects to hear. 178 Seventh Avenue South, just south of 11th Street; Tel: 255-4037.

A few blocks south of the Vanguard is **Sweet Basil**, a club and restaurant that bills equally classic jazz, if perhaps slightly more eclectically. There's an outer room, a kind of porch, which generally substitutes a view of the street for a view of the stage, though the music is still perfectly audible. Inside, a wood-paneled room under a nice tin ceiling squeezes in half a dozen tight rows of tables full of well-heeled West Villagers and other visitors out for a civilized evening on the town. 88 Seventh Avenue South, between Bleecker and Grove streets; Tel: 242-1785.

The string of clubs along **Bleecker Street** between Sullivan and La Guardia Place is the gradually mutating corpus of the Village's old folk-and-rock scene, now catering to a rowdy mix of tourists, young bridge-and-tunnelers in for the evening, college students from nearby New York University, and neighborhood folk preserving their own corner of the 1960s. Although some New Yorkers see this heavily visited neighborhood as seedy and commercial, it's relatively inexpensive and may well reward an evening's bar-hopping. With a few exceptions there's not much to tell between these places.

The **Village Gate**'s cavernous basement room is large enough to bill significant, mainly jazz, names, and every Monday evening a terrific series of salsa concerts. The Gate, a hallowed Village institution, also has an upstairs theater/cabaret and a pavement-side bar that sometimes features live music. Along the street is the **Village Corner**, a dark and ancient bar (here in one form or another since 1904) with a grand piano; this place is more low-key and comfortable than many of the clubs in the area. The

Village Gate is at Bleecker and Thompson streets; Tel: 475-5120. The Village Corner is at Bleecker Street and La Guardia Place; Tel: 473-9762.

The **Blue Note**'s glass and mirrors, its darkness, and its bluish decor give it an underwater feel. Upstairs there's a gift shop selling Blue Note pens, tee-shirts, spoons, and watches; out in the bar, which you have to pass through to get to the main room, there's a hard stone floor to take the busy milling about that the place seems to attract. Still, the club books good bills, ranging from the R & B side of jazz to (on occasion) such luminaries as Dizzy Gillespie, who can fill halls many times this size. 131 West 3rd Street, just east of Sixth Avenue; Tel: 475-8592.

Zinno takes up the ground floor of a nice old brownstone on a tree-lined street. Inside, it's an elegant but warm contemporary space, and between the bar and the larger main room is an alcove with enough room for a jazz duo or trio to accompany diners through a refined Italian supper. The bar also takes listeners, for the price of two or three drinks, and the music is choice. 126 West 13th Street, west of Sixth Avenue; Tel: 924-5182.

On a good night **Bradley's** may be as close as a bar comes to a concert hall: Jazz pianists and bass players get a beautiful sound here, and the usual restaurant noises of cutlery, talk, and general coming and going seem voluntarily muted so people can listen. The dark wood paneling and low, black-painted tin ceiling somehow help, framing the light in the room the same way a deep double bass frames the clarity of a piano. This is a popular place for serious jazz fans, who stand packed in the bar or who book a table for an unfancy meal. 70 University Place, a block east of Fifth Avenue and just south of 11th Street; Tel: 473-9700 or 228-6440.

The **Knitting Factory**, a bare-bones but friendly walk-up on the western edge of the East Village, is a pleasant reminder of the city's old jazz-loft days and, at the same time, a workshop for the present Lower East Side artist community. The music here may be rock-based, may be jazz-based, may be the guy drinking beer at the bar (which trembles when you lean on it) getting up to play guitar by himself; generally, it's experimental and personal. On the ground floor there's a small restaurant with speakers hooked into the sound system above, and the prices throughout are low enough that people from the neighborhood can easily drop in. The neighborhood is young and *avant*. 47 East Houston Street, between Mott and Mulberry streets, north of Chinatown and Little Italy; Tel: 219-3055.

Canal Street in its western section is a congested commercial strip full of hustling electronics and audio shops and eccentric hardware stores. Sandwiched between the galleries and restaurants of SoHo and Tribeca, this is a recalcitrant holdover from the days when they were both manufacturing districts. Perched on a corner here is a ferny, brick-walled music bar, an advance outpost of one or the other of those two heavily gentrified neighborhoods. Geographically vanguard, the **New Music Café** is musically so as well—the people who play here are often young jazzers making a name for themselves, with a sprinkling of more or less experimental upstarts in other popular forms, and a steady flow of reggae. 380 Canal Street, at West Broadway; Tel: 941-0900.

North of 14th Street

The French *mardi gras* literally means "fat Tuesday," and refers to Shrove Tuesday, the spring day before Ash Wednesday and the beginning of the Christian calendar's 40 days of fasting over Lent. So *mardi gras* was the last chance for a blowout, and in New Orleans and other tropical cultures it became a carnival. In New York, **Fat Tuesday's** is a basement jazz club with a pretty good rep for its bookings. Just north of the Village at 190 Third Avenue, at 17th Street; Tel: 533-7902.

The **Five Spot** is not the famous and long-gone Village jazz club of that name, commemorated in live-album titles and fond memories. It is, it claims, "a different kind of jazz club"—meaning, for one thing, that it boasts an ambitious menu. Had the Five Spot no music it would still be a popular place for dinner. This high-ceilinged room was once the rather grand ballroom of the hotel next door, from which it preserves its Corinthian columns, its gold-leafed acanthus braids on the ceiling, its whole Louis Quinze schtick. Music tends toward the funk-inflected quarter of contemporary jazz; in this tall and echoey space, the quieter, more chamber-music-like groups might fare better. Yet the Five Spot incarnates the jazz club in an unusually comfortable and elegant version. 4 West 31st Street, west of Fifth Avenue; Tel: 631-0100.

Midtown

Just off Times Square, all set to attract visitors looking to extend an evening in the theater district, is the functional but comfortable jazz club **Indigo Blues**. It's a basement, but more spacious and airy than jazz basements often are; there's a sizable bar at the back, often populated with regulars exchanging Broadway gossip. The largish stage accommodates good-size groups of musicians, and the club opened auspiciously with Miles Davis, who usually played much larger halls. But booking has now settled into a variety of mainly more Brazilian- and Latin-oriented stuff. 221 West 46th Street, between Eighth Avenue and Broadway; Tel: 221-0033.

The location of **B. Smith's** may remind you of the grime at the raffish heart of Damon Runyon–land: A block from the rapidly refurbishing Times Square, totally practical for the theater district, this bar-and-restaurant establishment still manages to find itself next door to a pornographic cinema and opposite an X-rated video store in a run-down block. But B. Smith's itself is a sophisticated place in a new, stylishly modern low-rise building, and has become known for its bar—lifted a little from the street, walled mostly with window, it makes the grunge seem glamorous. The effect is doubled in the upstairs music room, **The Rooftop**, one side of which is a kind of greenhouse looking over Eighth Avenue and across the tenements to the hotels and new high-rises of Broadway. Come here weekends and occasional other evenings, when well-heeled urbanites listen to jazz and enjoy their insiderness. 771 Eighth Avenue, at 47th Street; Tel: 247-2222.

Upper West Side

Back in the late 1940s, Allen Ginsberg and Jack Kerouac would drop into the West End Café between classes at nearby Columbia University, where Ginsberg studied English and Kerouac played football. Eventually this made the place known as a beatnik bar, though it really got that reputation simply by catering to the neighborhood community—much of which orbits around academia. Beside the main space was a jazz room, where every now and then Ginsberg would do a reading of his poetry. Now known as the **West End Gate**, the club has been refurbished by new management. It's almost chic—the walls are stripped to bare brick, and the food, which used to be strictly steam table, is, well, better, and still geared to the student pocket. The jazz room is now a black-walled den at the back. It rarely books big names, but some of those who play here have had substantial careers, and there are also open-mike nights that will give you an idea of what's on the minds of those precocious Columbia students. About the only thing left from the old days is the bar, an imposing edifice built in a kind of ring shape to fit the maximum number of under-age undergrads with forged IDs. 2911 Broadway, south of 114th Street; Tel: 662-8830.

CABARET AND SUCH

Midtown

The old Jan Wallman's has now become **Judy's**, but the booking policy—civilized entertainment—seems to be pretty much the same. This welcoming space avoids both the pomposity of some of the hoity-toitier cabarets and the raffishness of its relatives to the west, the Times Square–area piano places. Up front there's a piano bar, and in back a friendly restaurant-cum-cabaret room. 49 West 44th Street, west of Fifth Avenue; Tel: 764-8930.

The **Algonquin Hotel**, where famous *New Yorker* writers used to congregate to cut each other verbally into ribbons (and may still do—the magazine's offices are nearby), recently refurbished its cabaret spot, the **Oak Room**, which tends to run very polished singers of the evening-dress variety. But the Algonquin has its own idea of progress: At a cost of a quarter-million dollars, it replaced the room's handsome old paneling, in oak veneer, with handsome new paneling, in solid oak, for pretty much the same visual look. We are reminded of the 1920s Hollywood director Erich von Stroheim, who insisted that the Austrian cavalry officers in his film *Foolish Wives* wear authentic silk underwear. But those visitors in the know may experience a more tangible sense of luxury. 59 West 44th Street, east of Sixth Avenue; Tel: 840-6800.

The **Russian Tea Room**, right next to Carnegie Hall, has long been a favorite of ladies who lunch, not to mention of the publishing and entertainment-business moguls whose offices are in the neighborhood. Now this rather expensive restaurant—the food gets mixed reviews, though no one we know has ever refused to be treated to blinis and caviar here—has opened a cabaret in an upstairs space that's like a more intimate version of the main room below. The paintings that line the rich green walls include works by Stuart Davis, Reginald Marsh, and John Sloan, which will give you an idea of the general air of luxury. 150 West 57th Street, east of Seventh Avenue; Tel: 265-0947.

The bar of **Michael's Pub** is all dolled up with oak and

old mirrors to look like what a visitor from Ireland might—might!—expect to find in some Victorian remnant back home. This is incongruous, given the building's steel-and-glass exterior, but it makes for a pleasant environment in which to hear music. That last comes from an inner room, a supper club, which takes acts ranging from cabaret and stand-up comedy to serious jazz, and regularly bills big names. The Dixieland band that plays here every Monday is known for featuring Woody Allen on clarinet, though he doesn't invariably show up. If you're not in the mood to sit down (the service here, incidentally, is sometimes brusque), all this can be heard, though not seen, relatively inexpensively from the bar. 211 East 55th Street, east of Third Avenue; Tel: 758-2272.

Some folks must consider **Cleopatra** delightfully campy —a fabulous combination of Egypt and Las Vegas. Outside, large granite bas-reliefs of old gods look down on a street on the edge of the theater district; inside, the carvings are of young Egyptian women doing their makeup. There are mummies, a wall of hieroglyphs, and pharaonic heads set in mirrored walls that reflect a modern (and rather pricey) supper club, complete with candlelit tables, gold trim, and electric stars above the bar. (The club advertises the availability of these extravagant premises for bar mitzvahs— pretty weird for an Egyptian place.) But the band here plays authentic-sounding Middle Eastern music very well. Belly dancers and a whirling dervish are also impressively skilled, and as the night goes on the room tends to involve everyone there in these somewhat unfamiliar entertainments. 327 West 44th Street, east of Ninth Avenue; Tel: 262-1111.

Upper West Side

Following the example of 57th Street's Russian Tea Room, its main New York competitor in a certain pricey yet tinselly corner of the restaurant biz, **Tavern on the Green** has turned over a dining hall to music. The space is this many-chambered institution's Chestnut Room, a name in tune with its supposedly pastoral site, once a deliberately rustic sheepfold built in 1870 not on farmland but in newly constructed Central Park. Never did a sheepfold have so much cut glass, or indeed *any* cut glass, or for that matter any chandeliers, or Christmas lights, or paper lanterns, or brass huntsmen, or topiary. But though Tavern on the Green seems meant mainly for tourist buses, weddings, and overindulgent treats for one's grandchildren, the music billings here are surprisingly hip, even leaning sometimes toward the R & B side of the jazz-recital spectrum. In Central Park at Central Park West and 67th Street; Tel: 873-3200.

Upper East Side

The Carlyle, one of New York's most elegant hotels, runs two music rooms outfitted accordingly. **Bemelmans Bar** is a tenebrous room, full of dark leather upholstery. (The management has sometimes considered redesigning and brightening up the bar, but neighbors have always written enough letters of protest to forestall them, in the Upper East Side version of social activism.) On the walls are the brownish-toned murals of Ludwig Bemelmans, well known as the illustrator of the Madeline children's books. These paintings, which date from 1947, are whimsical and playful, with balloon sellers and bulldogs and snowy skating scenes and kangaroos. In the middle of the room is a piano; the program changes somewhat with the seasons, but a regular here is Barbara Carroll. Next to the bar is the **Café Carlyle**, with more original murals, these from 1955 by the French artist Vertès—a kind of post-Fauvist idyll of harlequins and horses, musicians and birds. Many of the tables here have cushioned love seats instead of chairs. This rather luxurious space is the supper club in which the supremely accomplished pianist and singer Bobby Short has played, again depending on the season, for more than 25 years. Madison Avenue at 76th Street; Tel: 570-7189.

Chelsea

On a rather unprepossessing block in northern Chelsea is a classy, elaborately Continental restaurant and cabaret called the **Ballroom**. Attended by waiters in black bow ties and waistcoats, patrons snack on *tapas* and martinis at the bar, which is decorated with ornamental foodstuffs—smoked hams, plaits of garlic bulbs, dried peppers—and then take their drinks through a mirrored double door to a dark, simply designed room supplied with a sizable stage and a piano. The tables are on gently descending terraces, so everyone gets a good view of the singers and accompanists and good-taste comedy acts the place books. 253 West 28th Street, east of Eighth Avenue; Tel: 244-3005.

The Village

Broadway attracts actors, dancers, and singers to New York, then doesn't hire them all, so the balance have to keep their hand in however they can. **Eighty-Eights**—the name, of course, refers to the number of keys on a piano—is the kind of place where the pianist sings and the waiters sing and people dropping in sing, some of them very well. It's a contemporary room full of blond wood and black glass and dove-gray carpeting; there's a cabaret upstairs. The club has a Midtown cousin, **Don't Tell Mama** (same management), which is much closer to Broadway and much more rowdy and casual.

Eighty-Eights, 228 West 10th Street, west of Bleecker Street; Tel: 924-0088. Don't Tell Mama, 343 West 46th Street, west of Eighth Avenue; Tel: 757-0788.

ROCK AND OTHER LIVE MUSIC

Mostly Rock

It seems symbolic that Bleecker Street, the main drag of New York's 1960s folk scene, should end abruptly on the Bowery at **CBGB**. In the late 1970s this club was the heart of the city's punk-rock movement, which set out to replace everything sensitive and singer-songwriterly in popular music with the abrasive, the aggressive, the loud. Some of the groups that played here back then (the Talking Heads, for example) ended up as arty as rock comes, but CBGB hasn't changed: It's the archetypal dive, dark, worn, graffitied, and odorous of beer. Generally speaking, the bands haven't changed either, so the place can be tough on the ears. But CBGB is historic in its way. Old habitués feel affectionate about it, and sometimes musicians now quite elevated in the world come back to play. The letters of the name, incidentally, are not, as is sometimes thought (given the club's aura and Skid Row location), a riff on "heebie-jeebies"; they stand for *C*oun-try, *B*lueGrass, and *B*lues, none of which has been booked here in years. 315 Bowery, at Bleecker Street; Tel: 473-7743.

The **Bottom Line** is a basic rock 'n' roll club, considerably less raunchy than CBGB, where record companies like to see breaking acts showcased for the influential New York media searchers. It also features long-established people who have sizable followings but may not fill a big hall; singers like Donovan and Laura Nyro regularly pass through. The club is near New York University, so it gets a student audience, and when jazz players like Sun Ra and his Arkestra play here they pull out all the stops to grab the young crowd. 15 West 4th Street, west of Broadway at Mercer Street; Tel: 228-6300.

Sadly, the Lone Star Café lost its lease on the lower Fifth Avenue building it had decorated with a giant rooftop sculpture of an iguana and a banner proclaiming "Too Much Is Not Enough." That leaves us with the **Lone Star Roadhouse**, a Times Square–area room done up from the outside to look like a Greyhound bus. Inside, the club shows the influence of its location: It's a cabaret-type space, with mirrored walls and pictures dotted around, the way rooms in this neighborhood put up pictures of Broadway stars who stop by (though the folks in this little gallery are more Long Tall Sally than Tin Pan Alley). So there's less Texas atmosphere than in the old place, but the acts are still roadhouse rock 'n' roll, R & B, blues, Western swing—anything that sounds like a party. 240 West 52nd Street, west of Broadway; Tel: 245-2950.

Wetlands Preserve is a theme rock 'n' roll club, and the theme is the 1960s—and the 1990s version of 1960s politics. By the downstairs lounge is a black-light corridor peppered with fluorescent posters advertising the Grateful Dead and the Age of Aquarius; there's a health-food menu; and by the main dance floor is a mural of dancing hippies, or perhaps of their imitators among today's college kids. Near the door, a VW microbus doubles as a tee-shirt stand and a billboard for psychedelia. This has to be the only nightclub in New York to run a mini reading room of ecological and antinuke literature, set out alongside petitions to save Tibet. But you know some of the bands that play here just have to be meat-eaters. 161 Hudson Street, at Laight Street—far west, and three blocks south of Canal Street; Tel: 966-4225.

A while ago the **Ritz** moved uptown, from the gorgeous East 11th Street Art Deco–style hall that it gave hard wear to (now reopened as the dance club Webster Hall), to a West 54th Street site that is intriguing in a different way—this is the former Studio 54, a seminal discotheque in New York discotheque history. Somehow these new quarters, once the acme of glamour, now look pretty much the way the Ritz always did. It's as if one forgot, in the old days, that this was simply a made-over theater with the ground-floor seats ripped out, but with the vaulted ceiling, balcony, stage, etc., basically intact.

The Ritz bills all kinds of rock 'n' roll, and it's gentler on the feet than it used to be—there's much more sitting space upstairs to complement the big dance floor below. 254 West 54th Street, east of Eighth Avenue; Tel: 541-8900.

Irving Plaza, a former Polish dance hall near Union Square, seems a constant in the rock 'n' roll life of Manhattan—in ever new incarnations it comes and goes, a space too good to lose yet too small, too simple, to hit nightclub big time, not, at least, without serious renovation. In the 1970s, for just one example, this was Club 57, a downtown artists' congregating place where we remember being served canapés consisting of cocktail sticks stuck through single grains of white rice. Today, not every night but more often than not, the hall opens under the name the **Continental Club at Irving Plaza**, billing some of the more adventurous and important of the mainly younger rock bands. 17 Irving Place, north of 15th Street; Tel: 249-8870.

The **Marquee** is your basic rock club, but the crowd-control people here are perhaps a little gentler than at the Ritz, and the billing tends more toward relatively unfamiliar but interesting bands best known to devotees of American college radio. 547 West 21st Street, west of Tenth Avenue; Tel: 533-4828.

Mostly Latin and Blues

S.O.B.'s—Sounds of Brazil—grew out of a season that owner Larry Gold spent going to Brazilian bars in Paris and wondering why there was no equivalent in New York. Since his club opened, in 1982, the city's enthusiastic dance and music crowd has proven he asked the right question. S.O.B.'s specializes in the rhythms of Brazil, tapping the country's local expatriate community for acts and bringing them up here from Rio and Bahia and beyond. It also explores the music of Africa and the Caribbean, and the purview is gradually expanding. This is a supper club, and a lot of patrons have dinner here—a Brazilian menu—before settling in to samba. The place is noisy and energetic, the music both ambitious and wildly danceable. 204 Varick Street, at West Houston Street; Tel: 243-4940.

A block of 21st Street between Fifth and Sixth avenues has become a peculiar kind of inner-city entertainment mall: Besides the Philippine restaurant and club **Manila** (which seems to book mainly Latin-type jazz, with an occasional touring Filipino pop star), there is a chic, well-lit pool hall called Chelsea Billiards and—an urban rarity, though no great metropolis should be without one—an indoor miniature golf course called Putters Paradise.

On the same block as Manila is **Tramps**, opposite the golf course. Tramps used to be housed in the Gramercy Park neighborhood, when it was known for a while as the home away from home of the singer Buster Poindexter. Now the club has moved to a much larger, unpolished but comfortable loft, and though rock bands we've never heard of often appear, whenever it gets the opportunity Tramps bills the greats of blues, soul, and R & B roots music—if they're playing in the city, they're probably here. 45 West 21st Street, east of Sixth Avenue; Tel: 727-7788.

IRISH HANGOUTS

The **Eagle Tavern** is an Irish bar, a basic kind of place, much more like most of the pubs we remember in Ireland than the more deliberately "Gaelic" drinking spots in which the city abounds. There's a back room decorated, inexplicably, with a maritime motif (eagles swim?), and here, on Friday nights, visiting fiddlers and tinwhistlers and button accordionists spin out jigs and reels. Some of the musicians are Irish-American, some are from the Old Country, and the crowd seems similarly mixed. There are Irish sessions and open-mikes scattered on other nights of the week; Saturday nights are for various acoustic musics of the folk variety, though it's predictable that they should have a Celtic lilt. 355 West 14th Street, between Eighth and Ninth avenues; Tel: 924-0275.

Tommy Makem's **Irish Pavilion** puts a ceramic shamrock over its door to broadcast its national allegiance; inside, a sign reads *Failte* (Welcome), though no Gaelic is needed to read the invitation in the nice old china spirit kegs that decorate the place. Befitting its 57th Street location, the Pavilion is a rather elegant version of an Irish bar, with its brass rails and green walls and gentle light. Downtown is **Glocca Morra**, a darker, homier version of the same institution. (According to the pilfered Irish road sign that is Glocca Morra's principal concession to decor, it is 19 miles from East 23rd Street to Spiddal, County Cork.) Judging from both these rooms' billings, the criteria of Celtic music are a tenor voice and an acoustic guitar. Alongside Irish staples like "Black Velvet Band" and "Johnny I Hardly Knew Ye," singers here may throw in Allman Brothers numbers, or "New York, New York"; but then the Irish have historical connections

with New York, and songs about the American open road
are as popular in western Eire as in the western United
States. In any case, everyone seems to know all the words.
The Pavilion has a musical edge in that Tommy Makem,
the great Irish singer and multi-instrumentalist, appears
here regularly. The Irish Pavilion, 130 East 57th Street, just
west of Lexington Avenue; Tel: 759-9040. Glocca Morra,
304 Third Avenue, just north of 23rd Street; Tel: 473-9638.

With **Café Sin-é**, the Lower East Side coffeehouse goes
Gaelic. Owner Shane Doyle, an Irish expatriate, opened
his tiny musical and literary storefront—which, with its
short menu of salads, sandwiches, and desserts, is marginally a restaurant—because he wanted somewhere sympathetic to hang out. His pleasantly scruffy place was instantly endearing to youthful locals. It got a boost when
Irish rock star Sinead O'Connor began wearing a Café
Sin-é tee-shirt; this was noticed in Dublin, where the
newspapers, says Doyle, "took a liking to the idea of a
Bohemian Irish club in New York." Ever since, he has
played host to a friendly mix of area residents and drop-
in members of Ireland's intelligentsia, particularly the
country's heavyweight popular musicians. The latter like
to make the room theirs when they're in New York, and
they swell out Doyle's limited-budget billings on the little
stage. The program is Celtic-inflected rather than Celtic-
fixated, and includes readings, slide shows, and literate
arguments as well as music. This is a distinctly 1960s-style
meeting place rather than a club—"more of a philosophy," says Doyle, "than a café." Admission is free, and
there's no liquor, just teas (many of them on the herbal
side) and coffees.

You can tell how rooted the storefront-café tradition is
on the Lower East Side by the fact that this block alone
has three more such institutions besides the Sin-é, which,
helpfully, is the one that doesn't put its name up outside,
just the word "Café." 122 St. Mark's Place, west of Avenue
A; Tel: 982-0370.

PERFORMANCE ART, POETRY, ET AL
In the early to mid-1980s, the unpredictable, no-rules
kind of entertainment known as performance art seemed
well rooted in the East Village. The neighborhood then
held a sizable nightclub and gallery scene of young entre-
preneurs evading the high rents of the established art
districts by operating here instead in pocket-sized spaces
where they showed the emerging local talent. Today few

remain, most having either closed or, in the case of many of the galleries, moved to upgraded spaces in and around SoHo. And that improbable storefront nightclub the Pyramid, once one of the most adventurous and fun of the performance spots, has most nights narrowed its focus to a particularly stable section of the local population, the Lower East Side's gay and transvestite community.

But **P.S. 122** endures. This former schoolhouse become neighborhood art center takes some of the same performers and some of the same crowd as the old clubs did, but the mood is more theatrical than clubbish—though with bleacher seating and no air-conditioning in summer. Outside the neighborhood, New York performance fans may go to **The Kitchen**, in Chelsea, which also runs an ambitious contemporary-music program. These places, some of whose income comes from public grant money, are less free-for-all than the clubs were; hey, this stuff is supposed to be art. Nonetheless, performance remains virtually anything the artist in question decides it should be, from the humdrum to the hilarious to the cover-your-eyes-and-pretend-you-didn't-see-that.

P.S. 122, 150 First Avenue, at 9th Street; Tel: 477-5288. The Kitchen, 512 West 19th Street, west of Tenth Avenue; Tel: 255-5793.

The **Nuyorican Poets Café** seems a holdover from the 1980s performance scene on the Lower East Side but, having entered its second decade, actually predates it. ("Nuyorican," incidentally, is local argot, a common combo, at least among the city's Latins, of "New York" and "Puerto Rican.") The highlight in this high-ceilinged, raw-brick-walled room, an exceptionally welcoming place (on a forbiddingly dilapidated block), is the poetry slam, every Friday evening beginning around 10:00. To slam around here is to compete, which poets do by standing up to read their work. Judges in the audience, usually other poets, vote winners. A free-for-all of opinion ensues if the crowd disagrees. These exchanges can be heated but are more often good-humored—the people who come here seem to know they have something unique going. Sometimes relays of slammin' po's virtually chase each other on and off the stand in the rush to read. During the rest of the week the café runs a variety of other poetry- and performance-related events. 236 East 3rd Street, west of Avenue C; Tel: 505-8183.

A little outside the old neighborhood is **Time Café**, an extremely trendy location considering it's a vegetarian restaurant, but then, with its fish and, yes, burgers, this isn't actually a vegetarian restaurant—it's a restaurant with more than the usual proportion of green stuff on the menu. Time was founded to take advantage of the wave of eco-chic that surged at the end of the 1980s. Burgers and all, it's made out very well; pop into the little store beyond the bar, buy some Rain-Forest Crunch (trail mix under a different name), and feel you've done your bit to save the earth. At the back and downstairs is a club with a Moroccan motif, **The Fez**, where a variety of events are staged: poetry and other readings, stand-up comedy, jazz (the great band of the late Charlie Mingus has had a long-running weekly stint here), even, on occasion, karaoke, the Japanese entertainment in which you symbolically murder the singers of your favorite records by having your own voice dubbed in their place. Time Café is walking distance from both the fashionable shops and galleries of SoHo and the hip dereliction of the East Village, and you can tell. 380 Lafayette Street, at Great Jones Street; Tel: 533-7000.

Far west on Spring Street, almost all the way to the Hudson, is **Ear Inn**, a surprising and pleasant little bar and restaurant in a sort of rickety building that is old by New York standards. But the dining room is homey and friendly, fittingly so for this quiet backwater neighborhood just outside the rigorous stylishness of SoHo. Ear Inn supposedly got its name when parts of the letter *B* in the neon sign outside that said "Bar/Inn" were blocked out, transforming the *B* into an *E*. And so the sign remains, but the Ear idea is in any case irreproachable for an establishment dedicated to new and experimental music. It even publishes a magazine on the stuff. The space here is small, and performances tend to be on the quiet and quirky side, including spoken-word artists beside sounds produced instrumentally and otherwise. 326 Spring Street, west of Greenwich Street; Tel: 226-9060.

COMEDY CLUBS
In the late 1970s, when the satiric TV show "Saturday Night Live" was at the height of its cult popularity, stand-up comedy took on a whole new glamour in New York. Young comics achieved for themselves the kind of media stardom that had once been linked mainly with rock 'n' roll—which for many culture consumers had begun to seem either overly well established and safe or, in the hands of the punksters who were trying to make the

music risky again, a little too confrontational for comfort. Part of rock's role has been to offer an identity, a feeling of group community, to whatever generation is growing up at the time. And as music slackened its hold (not that it isn't still popular) comics were the perfect substitute, especially if their humor was of that nervy kind that kids weren't sure was funny, suspected was shocking, but at least knew that their parents weren't laughing at. That moment has to some extent passed, but its legacy is today's comedy clubs, which are full of young comedians looking for their break. Their models are less Henny Youngman and Rich Little than John Belushi and Steve Martin; you can go to hell just for hearing some of their jokes.

On good nights these places are full of fresh energy. In comedy clubs, however, good nights are unpredictable. These rooms are where comics learn as well as practice their craft. Sometimes they fly and sometimes they flop, and the best can flop in front of an audience that just isn't amused. A crowd that goes to see Bill Cosby at Radio City Music Hall goes ready to laugh, wanting to laugh, knowing the night will be funny. A comedy-club crowd expects the quality to vary and can be ungenerous. Two clubs on the Upper East Side sometimes demonstrate this clearly. The Comic Strip and Catch a Rising Star are within walking distance of each other, and people who aren't enjoying the one can easily stroll over to the other to see what's going on. If they do, they may find that a comic they saw earlier in the evening has taken the same walk, and though they just watched him bomb, now he's rolling. His act is probably identical.

Given the proviso of variable evenings, **Catch a Rising Star**, on the Upper East Side, is a good bet for hilarity. It's a popular club (the bigger the crowd, the better the probability of laughter, which is infectious), and it's a comfortable and friendly spot. The **Comic Strip**, nearby, is a barer and less polished room, but not necessarily the less funny for that, and it's nice to sit at the bar here and listen to the comics hanging out and telling stories about horrible audiences they have known. **Caroline's**, a popular club that used to live at the South Street Seaport, has recently reopened on Broadway near Times Square— probably a more appropriate setting for this rowdy act.

A lot of the same performers circulate from one to the other of these clubs—and we've mentioned only a few; check the nightlife ads in the *Village Voice* or the entertainment listings in *New York* magazine for more—which means that the chances for enjoyment are spread around. An evening in any of these places may see a dozen young aspirants chewed up or coming off smiling. And although the clubs may have open evenings when anyone can stand up to take his or her knocks, these are not amateur outfits. Many of the comics who play them are very polished indeed, with a lot of pro experience, and well-known names sometimes pass through.

Catch a Rising Star, 1487 First Avenue, south of 78th Street; Tel: 794-1906. The Comic Strip, 1568 Second Avenue, south of 82nd Street; Tel: 861-9386; Caroline's, 1626 Broadway, north of 49th Street; Tel: 757-4100.

DANCE HALLS, SOIREES, AND DISCOS

Midtown

Roseland is New York's classic Broadway ballroom. It has been where it now stands since 1956, but it opened around the corner on 51st Street in 1919. A renovation in the mid-1980s didn't do too much harm. The decor looks pretty much as always, though the red-rose-studded green carpet is actually new; the dance floor, ringed by a sinuous wrought-iron balustrade punctuated by low lampposts, is still half a block long, and there are clubs in the city that are smaller than its bandstand. The versatility of the lighting system, however, is entirely modern. On Thursdays and Sundays people can dance here for nearly nine hours a day, beginning in midafternoon, principally ballroom and swing. These events can be fascinating, allowing a glimpse of an older Broadway culture. A "wall of fame" on the way in is a display case of the shoes of famous dancers, from Ruby Keeler to Ann Reinking, from George Raft to Gregory Hines. Pop acts in need of a hall with a floor sometimes stop in, but the air still breathes Stan Kenton and the Dorsey Brothers. 239 West 52nd Street, west of Broadway; Tel: 247-0200.

Decorated in blue and gold, moons and stars, the **Supper Club** is a big, old-fashioned space insinuating big-band jazz and the nightlife of an older New York, rather like a smaller Roseland. And big-band jazz is what they do in fact stage here on Saturday evenings, along with more cabaret-like performers and jazz trios on Thursdays and Fridays. The wide floor has tables out for supper, but they can be pulled off for dancing; upstairs there's a smaller, more intimate cabaret, the Blue Room, done up in the same blue and gold, with photos of Broadway performers both familiar and forgotten on the walls. Late weekend nights the Supper Club turns into a conventional contemporary discotheque, and on Monday evenings a discotheque celebrating 1960s and 1970s soul and funk. This used to be the Edison Theater, site of the famous 1960s musical *Oh, Calcutta!* 240 West 47th Street, west of Seventh Avenue; Tel: 921-1940.

The **Rainbow Room** is in Rockefeller Center, and you can reach it from Sixth Avenue and 50th Street, but don't. Take the processional walk in from Fifth Avenue, with your destination, 30 Rockefeller Plaza, brilliantly spotlit in front of you at night above the golden statue of Prometheus. The gentle descent of the pavement pulls you on, and the architecture tells you you're going somewhere big. Inside, the floor continues its easy slope, and you reach the private burl-paneled elevators that will whisk you express to the 65th floor; step out, turn around, and there's a sudden view of the Empire State Building with all of southern Manhattan laid out around it.

The Rainbow Room first opened in 1934, an Art Deco palace in the sky. It reopened at the end of 1987, after a two-year, $20 million renovation, in all its former stylishness, with contemporary design and *objets* artfully complementing the old. The band plays Glenn Miller; the dance floor revolves; the floor-to-ceiling windows frame . . . practically everything. Fred Astaire and Ginger Rogers do not go swinging by, but in the general flurry of evening gowns and tuxedos it's easy to pretend. Dinner and dancing here may run $100 or so a person; from the neighboring bar you can enjoy the same views for the price of a drink, though the music is now remote, and gentlemen still must wear a jacket. A new addition to the place is the Rainbow & Stars, which combines the same views with sophisticated cabaret acts. 30 Rockefeller Plaza, near 50th Street off Fifth Avenue; Tel: 632-5000/5100.

The **Red Blazer Too** is a relaxed dinner and dancing place that specializes in the jazz of the 1920s and 1930s: Dixieland, swing, and the chunkily swinging stuff in between. Some of the bands that run here feature players from those times. There aren't many rooms around anymore in which this music can be heard from a dance floor instead of from a chair, so the people who come to the Red Blazer seem to know both their jazz history and how to get up and enjoy it in the best, nonacademic way—in their dancing shoes. 349 West 46th Street, west of Eighth Avenue; Tel: 262-3112.

For over 30 years, from its opening in 1940, the **Copacabana**, almost always called the Copa, was a hegemonic presence in New York nightlife. Everybody played there, from Frank Sinatra to Chubby Checker to the Supremes and on. A booking here marked a performer as a star, like a stamp he needed in his passport. There are volumes of Copa lore—how co-owner Jules Podell was an associate of underworld crime boss Frank Costello; how Desi Arnaz and Lucille Ball first met in the club, when she was in its chorus line; how Dean Martin and Jerry Lewis both began and ended their career as a comedy team here. After Podell's death in 1973 the club closed its doors. It reopened in 1976 and is now a regular discotheque, open Tuesdays, Thursdays, Fridays, and Saturdays and booking live, mainly Latin, bands. But the downstairs room has been restored rather than renovated and has the same painted Carmen Miranda–headgear mirrors, the same concrete support columns made over into white-enameled palm trees, the same frond-pattern carpeting that made the Rat Pack feel at home. Until recently the Copa had competition in the restoring-the-glamour-of-yore stakes, in El Morocco, on East 54th Street near Second Avenue. From the late 1930s on, El Morocco's zebra-pattern upholstery was a trademark signature in countless photos of the stars out on the town, and it's all still there; but the club, alas, is at this writing an upmarket form of topless bar. Go to the Copa instead, at 10 East 60th Street, east of Fifth Avenue; Tel: 755-6010.

Tatou was built, some 60-odd years ago, as a kind of miniature neighborhood opera house, and it must have been a jewel. Proscenium stage, 30-foot ceiling, ornate balcony, fanlike plan, and huge chandelier all testify to the room's original use. But this is an intimately proportioned space, well suited to its current life as a glamorous evening supper club and nighttime discotheque. (Actually, it wasn't an opera house long; it's been a round of nightclubs, notably the Versailles, where Desi Arnaz led the band and where Edith Piaf opened in New York in the early 1950s.) Tatou is lavishly designed, with antiqued mirrors, enormous floral arrangements, and exotically draped chairs. Light is plentiful but subtle. Architects have played carefully with the space's features so that it feels both theatrical and at the same time like a perfect toy of a theater: The curtain, for example, is artfully rolled down just enough to reveal its Raphaelesque *putto,* and gilded ladies from Greece bear lamp standards on either side. This is an elegant place for supper (and the kitchen is ambitious). For entertainment there is gentle live music for dining, then louder pop for late-evening dancing. There are also stage shows of different kinds, usually in the early half of the week. A good idea here is to make a reservation and arrive early enough for dinner; that way you won't have to worry about getting past the doorman when the place transits from restaurant into nightclub. Broadway theatergoers who eat here before their shows can ask for a card that will get them back in for dancing later on—a sumptuous evening. 151 East 50th Street, west of Third Avenue; Tel: 753-1144.

Nightclubbers who had discovered the richness of dancing to African music loved Kilimanjaro, which booked live African bands both local (a number of Northeastern cities have sizable African-immigrant communities) and touring from the mother continent. Now Kilimanjaro has closed, but it has a successor, the **Club Harambee**, a Times Square–area room that works both as a discotheque—spinning records not only from Africa but from the Caribbean and other black-diaspora regions—and as the place where travelling African bands are most likely to play. Club Harambee is a rather nondescript space, and can seem bleak on a slow night. But the groups that play here can be extraordinary. And how can you not love a place that promises so many different kinds of music you've never heard or even heard of: *charanga, chimurenga, kwela, jit, makassi, milo, palmwine, soukous, juju, rai, ska,* candance, *zouk, soca,* highlife, and on and on down to the dear old rhumba. 127 West 43rd Street, between Sixth and Seventh avenues; Tel: 819-1133.

Club USA, which opened in early 1993 to breathless press accounts of the $8 million it cost to launch, has been designed with an eye on the seedy recent history of its Times Square neighborhood, and indeed of its own building, formerly the Minsky burlesque. (Remember the movie *The Night They Raided Minsky's?*) The large pictorial cutouts above the dance floor include a leather-clad dominatrix wielding a chainsaw, and there are more beleathered mannequins in sci-fi Plexiglas tubes on a balcony, suggesting a kinkier version of *Star Trek.* Neon reads "DRUGS" and "GIRLS," and if you know Japanese you'll see "SEX CHANGE" spelled out on a billboard. Venturing upstairs—the club has five levels—and negotiating a dizzying mirror-walled corridor, you'll find a row of video booths where, for a quarter, you can watch soft porn. Surely in the works are many doctoral theses on the transition of such imagery from the taboo to the camp chic. Their authors are probably bopping at Club USA right now. 218 West 47th Street, west of Seventh Avenue; Tel: 869-6001.

Uptown

Club Broadway is in a heavily Hispanic Upper West Side neighborhood, above a jeans outlet and beside a McDonald's. The blue-velvet ballroom, unpretentious but capacious and comfortable, is open late weekend nights for dancing to splendid Latin big bands. 2551 Broadway, south of 96th Street; Tel: 864-7600.

Downtown

The **Palladium** is housed in a big and battered old theater from 1926 that used to be called the Academy of Music. This discotheque's designer, the Japanese architect Arata Isozaki (creator of the new Museum of Contemporary Art in Los Angeles, among other buildings), has kept large chunks of the original decor. The parts of the interior that were decaying he preserved or even encouraged in their decay, but he mixed them with decisively modern elements. The dance floor, for example, is encased in a high-tech open-sided cube, with built-in lights and video banks, and paintings and designs by significant current artists are scattered about the walls. This is a spectacular space, full of dramatic lighting effects and vistas, jumbling the antiqued with the contemporary, that makes you feel as if you were living out the transition from one kind of world into another. As architecture it's as worthy of a visit, as indicative of its time as, say, Grace Church or the lobby of the Woolworth Building. As a dance club, it's been on the scene a little too long to be called state of the art—it opened in 1985, a long time ago in some circles—but, at least in its visual style, few of the hot clubs of the present day really advance on it, and many of them are in its debt. The Palladium is an almost obligatory stop for nightclubbers, if only for the sake of history. 126 East 14th Street, west of Third Avenue; Tel: 473-7171.

Those who see New York as Sin City, a destroyer of all

Christian values, might surely support their argument by citing the **Limelight**. For most of the years since the 1840s this building was the Church of the Holy Communion; now it's a discotheque. When the Limelight opened, in 1984, the regional Episcopal bishop pronounced himself "horrified," but the church had already been sold into secular use. Now light towers and catwalks scrape the Gothic arches, and dancers pump to disco in the nave. A marble tablet in the vestibule advises them that "this house was created to the honor of God and for the good of His children"; maybe, in their own way, they agree. 47 West 20th Street, at Sixth Avenue; Tel: 807-7850.

When it opened in 1986, **Nell's** was something new under the sun, or at least in the New York club life of the preceding decade. Where discos from Studio 54 on had emphasized a high-tech glamour that reached its peak in the Palladium, Nell's decided to be an Edwardian salon. On the ground floor is a rather beautiful room, all softly lit red-velvet sofas and low coffee tables on faded carpets, with dark wood paneling on the walls and gilt-framed mirrors stretching back under a dim but lustrous chandelier. In the far section of the space you can dine, or you can converse on a couch as if in a more luxurious version of your sitting room, but with a bar. For dancers there's a floor in the basement, so they don't have to go somewhere else. Nell's is one of those clubs that likes to keep people standing outside; but it's not a huge space, and a chunk of its nightly clientele will be the in-crowd "registrants," the regulars who get precedence at the door. You can try to ensure entry by calling ahead, early, to make a reservation. 246 West 14th Street, east of Eighth Avenue; Tel: 675-1567.

In the late 1970s and early 1980s caring New Yorkers could have been in on the birth of a whole new thing in American culture: black hip-hop, not so much a sound as a lifestyle, incorporating everything from dance moves to fashion to music (most notably rap) to political attitude to the way people walked down the street. A roller-skating rink called the **Roxy** was a high-temperature incubator— on weekends it became a very-late-night dance club. Downtown and up, Friday afternoons you'd hear people asking, "Going to Roxy tonight?" Later you'd head over here after midnight when the subways were slow and the streets empty; half the train would get off at 18th Street and walk in a long, straggly crowd west toward the river.

Today there are evenings when the Roxy draws a mainly gay clientele. Judging from one of those nights a while ago, however, no one who feels comfortable in such a crowd is likely to be made unwelcome. 515 West 18th Street, west of Tenth Avenue; Tel: 645-5156.

The **New York Swing Dance Society** has left the rock club where it used to rent time in favor of friendlier digs in the former Polish dance hall known as Irving Plaza. When the society first arrived here the hall doubled as the home of an Off Off Broadway musical with a Chinese theme, and the whole space was suffused with cardboard chinoiserie—a background against which the 1930s big-band music that the dance society exists to cherish seemed perfectly comfortable. Now most of that decor has gone, though some survives in the hallways. Here on Sunday evenings people get together to do the lindy and other steps of that family to live bands. Many of the patrons are regulars, and there's that warm, sociable feeling of a shared, not necessarily fashionable, common interest. Some dancers are old enough to have known the Savoy (a famous Harlem hall torn down in the 1950s, its memory preserved in Chick Webb's "Stompin' at the Savoy"), others waited to be born until after the Beatles broke up. We hope that the next Off Off Broadway musical booked at Irving Plaza provides as congenial a decorating scheme as the last one did. 17 Irving Place, north of 15th Street; Tel: 696-9737 for the Swing Dance Society. Sunday evenings only.

SUMMER IN THE CITY

If you're visiting New York in the summer months you might investigate some of the outdoor music programs that run only then. Perhaps best is **SummerStage**, on weekend afternoons and nights in Central Park, a program of live popular music plus poetry readings and such. The park is also the site of classical-music and opera performances on summer nights. There are usually rock concerts at Jones Beach (on Long Island's south shore, a train ride away from the city). The **Museum of Modern Art** sometimes organizes a jazz or classical program in its sculpture garden, and the **South Street Seaport** often books summer music. Lincoln Center sometimes presents music events outdoors on the plaza. There are also various lunchtime performances at downtown office plazas in the World Financial Center–Battery Park area. All these outdoor programs vary from year to year; some are commercial, some, like SummerStage, are free and depend for their existence on the skill of their fund raisers. So it's best to check the papers (especially the Arts & Leisure section of the Sunday *New York Times*) for times and locations.

CHRONOLOGY OF THE HISTORY OF NEW YORK CITY

When Europeans arrived, the land that is now New York City was peopled by Algonquin subtribes belonging to the Wappinger Confederation (Bronx and Manhattan) and the Delaware Confederation (Staten Island and Brooklyn), who subsisted by hunting and fishing. The Indians greeted the first European arrivals with curiosity and were soon trading furs and wampum (strings of shells) with the newcomers. The harmony was interrupted, however, in the mid-1600s when Dutchman Willem Kieft initiated unprovoked attacks on the Indians. They retaliated, and soon general mistrust and hostility strained relations between Europeans and native Americans.

The Dutch Settle New Amsterdam

- **1524**: Giovanni da Verrazano of Italy sails into New York Bay and anchors in the Narrows; Esteban Gomez, exploring for Spain, follows.
- **1609**: British explorer Henry Hudson drops anchor at Manhattan Island before continuing up the Hudson River.
- **1613**: Dutch captain Adriaen Block winters on Manhattan.
- **1624**: The first Dutch West India Company settlers arrive and dub the land New Netherland; most go upriver, but eight men stay in Manhattan, which comes to be called New Amsterdam.
- **1625**: Large group of West India Company employees, mostly Walloons, arrives on the island, followed by the first blacks, probably Portuguese slaves.

- **1626**: Peter Minuit, the West India Company's director-general, buys Manhattan from local Indians for $24 worth of goods.
- **1628**: The Manhattan settlement has 270 inhabitants, 30 houses, 6 farms.
  First black women (also slaves) arrive.
- **1629**: Dutch West India Company issues land grants (patroonships) to anyone bringing 50 families to New Netherland to settle.
- **1631**: Peter Minuit builds an 800-ton ship (then the largest ever built) to demonstrate uses of local timber to authorities in Netherlands.
- **1632**: Minuit loses his post as director-general; returns to Netherlands.
- **1638**: Willem Kieft, new director-general, imposes first known city ordinances (port regulations, drinking laws) and raises tensions with Indians.
  New Amsterdam's first school opens (for Dutch and black children).
  Ferry begins operation between Manhattan and Brooklyn.
- **1639**: First English immigrants arrive in New Amsterdam.
- **1641**: The Wooden Horse, first tavern, opens.
  New law makes it illegal to drink during church hours.
  At New Netherland's first hanging the rope breaks, and the authorities opt to allow the criminal, a slave convicted of murder, to go free.
- **1643**: Settlers have their first serious clash with Indians.
  Deborah Moody is the first woman to receive a land grant (in Gravesend, Brooklyn).
- **1644**: Some African slaves are set free and given land.
  A new law forbids dumping refuse and urinating in the streets.
- **1645**: A truce is reached with the Indians; selling liquor to Indians is prohibited.
- **1647**: Kieft is replaced as director-general by Peter Stuyvesant, whose first ordinance is to close taverns at nine o'clock.
- **1652**: New Amsterdam institutes the first speeding law (no galloping allowed in the city) and gun-control law (no shooting in the streets).
- **1653**: New Amsterdam forms a new municipal

government, a forerunner of today's city council; its concerns include support of widows and orphans and control of the hogs that roam the streets.

City Hall is established in a tavern.

New Amsterdam's first lawyer is not allowed to practice because there is no one to act as opposing counsel.

The wall that gave Wall Street its name is built to keep out Indians.

- **1654**: The colony's first Jews arrive, from northern Brazil.
- **1655**: Indians attack New Amsterdam, killing and capturing settlers.

  Jews win right to join militia and own homes (against Stuyvesant's protest).

  The first slave ship direct from Africa lands.
- **1656**: New Amsterdam has 120 homes and a population of 1,000.

  Sunday Laws forbid drinking, tennis, dancing, laboring, bowling, and boating during church hours.
- **1657**: The directors of the West India Company uphold freedom of religion in New Netherland after Stuyvesant tries to outlaw all but Dutch Reform.

  It becomes illegal to litter in the streets of New Amsterdam.
- **1658**: First street is paved (Stone Street, with cobblestones).
- **1660**: Settlers and Indians establish peace.

  A hospital is instituted to tend soldiers and blacks.

British New York

- **1664**: The English take over New Amsterdam and rename it New York.
- **1665**: Thomas Willett is the first mayor of New York City.

  Stuyvesant retires to his *bouwerie* (the Bowery).

  New Jersey is colonized.
- **1670**: First merchant exchange is established when businessmen begin meeting Fridays at noon on the bridge over Broad Canal (now Bridge Street).
- **1671**: Society of Friends (Quakers) holds its first meeting in New York—in a tavern.

- **1673**: The Dutch regain New York; it becomes New Orange.
- **1674**: Treaty of Westminster gives New York back to the English; its inhabitants become British subjects.
- **1683**: Thomas Dongan, New York's first Roman Catholic governor, calls a representative assembly.
- **1685**: Dongan Charter, or Charter of Liberties and Privileges, is New York's first constitution.
- **1688**: King James is overthrown and William and Mary ascend the throne; in New York, Jacob Leisler and Jacob Milbourne assume the governing of the city.
- **1691**: William and Mary's governor finally arrives in New York; Leisler and Milbourne wait 24 hours to hand over rule, thus angering the Crown, and are hanged for treason.
- **1692**: City begins landfill at Water Street, eventually creating Front and South streets.
- **1693**: Fearing an attack by the French the city sets up a battery of cannon at the southern tip of the island (the Battery).
  William Bradford opens the city's first printing shop.
- **1695**: Parliament pardons Leisler and Milbourne four years after their execution.
- **1697**: Streetlight law requires every seventh house to hang a lantern.
- **1698**: Census counts 4,937 inhabitants.
- **1702**: New York's governor, Edward Hyde, Lord Cornbury, distinguishes himself by promenading about the city in women's clothes.
- **1705**: First free grammar school is instituted.
- **1712**: Nine whites are killed in slave revolts; 21 blacks are executed.
- **1725**: The city's first newspaper, *The New York Gazette,* is published.
- **1732**: Bowling Green park is fenced off and used for bowling.
- **1733**: *New York Weekly Journal* appears.
- **1735**: John Peter Zenger, imprisoned for criticizing the British government in print, wins his case, the first victory for freedom of the press in America.
- **1741**: After a number of fires and robberies that come to be called the Negro Conspiracy, 4 whites

and 29 blacks are put to death, 71 blacks are transported, and 52 blacks are pardoned.

- **1750**: New York's first theater opens on Nassau Street.
- **1754**: King's College (now Columbia University) is founded.
  New York Society Library is established, first public library.
- **1763**: Ferry service to New Jersey begins.
  West Indian Samuel Fraunces opens his tavern on Pearl Street.

American Revolution and Independence

- **1765**: British pass the Stamp Act; colonists meet in City Hall at Stamp Act Congress and issue Declaration of Rights and Grievances.
- **1766**: British repeal the Stamp Act but impose new taxes on tea, paper, glass, paint.
- **1767**: Britain passes the Townshend Acts, which impose shipping laws and taxes for a militia on the colonists.
- **1770**: Skirmish between British soldiers and colonists on Golden Hill (John Street) predates Boston Massacre by a few days.
  Parliament rescinds duties on everything but tea.
- **1775**: American Revolution begins; George Washington makes Richmond Hill house in Greenwich Village his headquarters; British position themselves around the city.
- **1776**: July: The Declaration of Independence is read publicly from Manhattan's City Hall, and America's flag is flown.
  August 27: Americans retreat after losing Battle of Long Island; British take Brooklyn Heights.
  September: Americans win battle of Harlem Heights and move north; British take possession of New York City (the city remains Loyalist until 1783); American troops and Patriots begin to leave the city.
  September 21: Nearly a fourth of Manhattan is destroyed by fire; losses include Trinity Church.
  September 22: The British hang Nathan Hale, age 22, as a spy, without giving him a trial.

- **1779**: Irish recruited to fight for the British hold New York's first St. Patrick's Day Parade.
- **1781**: The martini, the first cocktail, is invented near Tarrytown.
- **1782**: Loyalists, almost a third of the city's population, start leaving for Nova Scotia.
- **1783**: November 25, Evacuation Day: American troops led by Washington reenter New York, as Loyalists and British leave.
  December 4: At Fraunces Tavern George Washington bids his comrades farewell.
- **1784**: New York State legislature begins to meet at City Hall.
  Bank of New York established (first bank).
  King's College is renamed Columbia University.
- **1785**: U.S. Congress meets in New York City.
- **1786**: First city directory is issued, listing names, addresses, and occupations.
- **1788**: New York ratifies the new U.S. Constitution and becomes the federal capital.
- **1789**: George Washington is inaugurated president on the balcony of Federal Hall in Manhattan.
  Tammany Society, a benevolent organization, is formed.
- **1790**: Federal capital moves to Philadelphia.
  First sidewalks are put down on Broadway.
- **1792**: Forerunner of the New York Stock Exchange is born when brokers begin meeting under a buttonwood tree on Wall Street.
- **1794**: City council changes names of streets and places that have British names.
  The city uses Belle Vue farm to isolate yellow-fever patients.
- **1797**: The state legislature moves from Manhattan to Albany.
  Ordinance against pollution prohibits candle, glue, and soap making inside the city.

The 19th Century

- **1800**: African Methodist Episcopal Zion Church, first church for blacks, is organized by a freed slave.
- **1801**: Alexander Hamilton founds *The New York Post*.

Botanist David Hosack opens the 20-acre Elgin Garden on the site of Radio City Music Hall.

- **1804**: Prominent New Yorkers Aaron Burr and Alexander Hamilton duel in Weehawken, New Jersey; Hamilton is killed.

  New-York Historical Society founded.

- **1805**: The New York Free School Society is instituted to educate children who can't afford private schools.

- **1807**: Robert Fulton begins steamboat service between New York and Albany with the *Clermont.*

- **1809**: Washington Irving publishes *A History of New York from the Beginning of the World to the End of the Dutch Dynasty by Diedrich Knickerbocker.*

- **1811**: Randel Plan is drawn up, dividing most of Manhattan into grids with numbered avenues running north–south and streets running east–west.

- **1814**: War of 1812 ends.

- **1817**: The New York Stock Exchange is chartered.

  The Staten Island Ferry begins running.

- **1818**: Brooks Brothers menswear store opens.

- **1820–1829**: About 4,000 immigrants arrive in New York City per year.

- **1821**: African Grove Theater, first black theater, opens on Bleecker Street.

- **1822**: About two-thirds of the city's population evacuates to Greenwich Village and other country retreats during yellow-fever epidemic.

- **1824**: Fifth Avenue is laid down from Waverly Place to 13th Street (it extends to 24th Street in 1830 and to Harlem by 1864).

- **1825**: The Erie Canal opens, connecting the Hudson River to Lakes Champlain and Erie.

  New York Gas Light Company begins to lay gas pipelines.

  Arnold Constable, the city's first department store, opens.

- **1826**: All white males over 21 who have lived in New York State for one year are given the right to vote.

- **1827**: *Freedom's Journal,* the world's first newspaper published by and for blacks, begins publication.

  New York State outlaws slavery.

- **1828**: New York's first known seller of roasted chestnuts sets up on Broadway at Duane Street.
- **1830**: 14,000 immigrants enter New York.
  The first parade on Fifth Avenue is held, in honor of the 1830 revolution in Paris, starting the tradition of parades on this avenue.
- **1831**: Nonsectarian New York University is instituted as an alternative to Episcopalian Columbia.
- **1832**: New York and Harlem Railroad starts running horse-drawn street cars from Prince Street to 14th Street.
- **1833**: The *New York Sun* begins publication.
- **1834**: Cornelius Van Wyck Lawrence is the first mayor elected by popular vote.
  Steam trains are running on Second, Sixth, and Eighth avenues.
- **1835**: 32,715 immigrants enter New York.
  Great Fire of 1835 destroys most of old Dutch New York.
  Two Democratic party groups, Irish and "native," riot at Five Points.
  The *New York Herald* is first issued.
- **1837**: Financial panic causes a six-year depression.
  The *Daily News* is founded.
  Tiffany & Company opens.
  Samuel Morse demonstrates the telegraph at Castle Garden.
- **1838**: The *New York Herald* becomes the first newspaper to use foreign correspondents.
- **1839**: Samuel Cunard founds his famous shipping empire in New York.
- **1840–1856**: Three million immigrants enter New York, many fleeing potato famine in Ireland.
- **1841**: P. T. Barnum's American Museum opens, featuring curiosities, freaks, and natural-history oddities.
  Horace Greeley founds the *New York Tribune*.
  Brooklyn Democrats found the *Brooklyn Eagle*.
- **1842**: New York City takes over the public schools and discontinues aid to parochial schools.
  Croton Reservoir is built at 42nd Street and Fifth Avenue to supply the city with water.
  The New York Philharmonic is formed.
- **1843**: Brooklyn Institute of Arts & Sciences (Brooklyn Museum) is founded.

- **1844**: New York City Police Department is formed (police refuse to wear uniforms until 1853).
- **1845**: The New York Knickerbocker Baseball Club draws up a formal set of rules for the new game.
- **1846**: Hudson-River Railroad runs along the river from Manhattan to Albany in five hours.
  Walt Whitman takes job as editor of the *Brooklyn Eagle*.
- **1847**: Abolitionist Henry Ward Beecher begins preaching at Plymouth Church of the Pilgrims in Brooklyn.
- **1848**: Manhattan's residential area extends as far north as 23rd Street.
  New York News Agency (later renamed Associated Press) established.
- **1849**: Supporters of English actor Charles Macready clash with those of American actor Edwin Forrest in the Astor Place Riot, leaving dozens dead and wounded.
- **1850**: Hecker & Brothers millers on Cherry Street install the first freight elevator.
  Jenny Lind makes her American debut at Castle Garden under the management of P. T. Barnum.
- **1851**: *The New York Times* begins publication.
- **1852**: William Marcy (later known as "Boss") Tweed is elected to city council.
- **1853**: Manhattan hosts the world's fair.
  Steinway & Sons piano manufacturers opens in Manhattan.
- **1854**: Chester A. Arthur represents Elizabeth Jennings in a suit against Third Avenue Railroad, which had refused to let her ride because she was black; her victory brings an end to official discrimination on public transportation.
- **1857**: Financial panic sets off a depression.
  Construction of Central Park begins.
  Haughwout Store installs Otis passenger elevator, said to be the first in the world.
  The Fenians, the Irish Republican Brotherhood, is formed in New York.
  Joseph C. Gayetty of West 33rd Street invents toilet paper.
- **1858**: The Crystal Palace, a fireproof exhibition hall, is demolished by fire.
  New York Symphony Orchestra is formed.
  New York City has 16 baseball clubs.

- **1859**: Cooper Union, a tuition-free science and arts school, opens.
- **1860**: Abraham Lincoln, seeking Republican nomination for the presidency, gives a speech at Cooper Union.
  Tweed rises to prominence in Tammany Society.
  Four thousand socialites pay their respects to the Prince of Wales (Edward VII) at a spectacular ball at the Academy of Music.
- **1861**: American Civil War begins.
- **1862**: F.A.O. Schwarz toy store opens.
- **1863**: The Draft Riots sweep the city as gangs set fires and attack blacks and abolitionists in protest against military draft; there are many deaths and injuries and many buildings destroyed.
  General Tom Thumb, a famous "exhibit" at Barnum's museum, marries at Grace Church.
- **1864**: Songwriter Stephen Foster dies destitute in the Bowery.
- **1865**: The city staffs its first paid, trained fire department.
  Woodlawn Cemetery opens in the Bronx.
- **1866**: New York establishes a board of health.
  The Black Crook, progenitor of the American musical comedy, begins a 16-month run.
- **1868**: Boss Tweed has virtual control of city and county of New York.
  Elevated railway is erected on Greenwich Street.
- **1869**: Tweed forms the Tweed Ring, putting control of the city in the hands of four men.
  American Museum of Natural History is founded.
  Bellevue Hospital starts horse-drawn ambulance service.
- **1870**: The Metropolitan Museum of Art is founded.
  Alfred Ely Beach builds a wind-powered subway under Broadway, but Boss Tweed prevents him from getting funding.
- **1871**: When citizens meet at Cooper Union to protest Tweed's rule, he makes his famous reply: "Well, what are you going to do about it?"
  The New York Times begins printing articles exposing the corruption of Tammany Hall; with the help of Thomas Nast's political cartoons, it leads to the investigation and downfall of the Tweed Ring.
  The city passes its first Tenement Law, which sets

minimum light and air requirements for tenement apartments.

National Association of Baseball Players is founded in New York; the league includes the New York Mutuals and the Brooklyn Eckfords.

- **1872:** Tweed Courthouse completed; massive cost overrun causes scandal.

  Bloomingdale's opens.

- **1873:** Stock market crashes: Exchange closes for ten days; railroads go bankrupt; six-year depression follows.

  Frederick Law Olmsted designs Riverside Park, and he and Calvert Vaux finish Central Park.

- **1874:** Society for the Prevention of Cruelty to Children is founded in New York.

  Henry Ward Beecher is tried for and acquitted of adultery.

  "Pedestrianism" becomes the new fad in New York; crowds gather at such venues as Madison Square Garden to watch six-day walking races; socialites even join the craze, walking laps around ballrooms.

- **1876:** The New York Legal Aid Society is founded; first such institution in the world.

- **1878:** Boss Tweed dies in debtors prison.

  Elevated trains are operating on Ninth, Sixth, and Third avenues.

  Bell Telephone Company of New York issues its first telephone directory; telephone users are gradually getting used to the new word "Hello," coined as an alternative to "Ahoy!" and "What is wanted?"

- **1879:** Charles McKim, William Mead, and Stanford White found an architectural firm that will change the face of New York.

- **1880:** Electricity lights the city's streets.

- **1882:** Thomas Edison's central electrical plant goes into operation, supplying electricity to homes and businesses.

- **1883:** The Brooklyn Bridge opens the first roadway between Brooklyn and Manhattan.

  First Metropolitan Opera House opens.

- **1884:** The Dakota apartment house lures New Yorkers to the Upper West Side.

  World's first roller coaster is installed at Coney Island.

- **1886**: One million people gather for the unveiling of the Statue of Liberty.

  "Boodle Board" scandal exposes city officials extorting money from a railroad company.

- **1888**: The Great Blizzard dumps 22 inches of snow on the city; falling telegraph and electrical poles and wires prompt the city to move them all underground.

  The city's first deli opens on Delancey Street and introduces New Yorkers to pastrami on rye.

- **1889**: A wooden arch is raised in Washington Square to commemorate the anniversary of Washington's presidential inauguration (the permanent, marble version is erected in 1895).

  Charles Dow and Edward Jones start publishing the daily *Wall Street Journal*.

- **1890**: Federal government takes over immigration and moves the operation to Ellis Island (which opens in 1892).

  Thousands attend the opening of McKim, Mead & White's Madison Square Garden.

  Movies are first shown in New York.

  Jacob Riis's *How the Other Half Lives* exposes the plight of the immigrant poor.

- **1891**: Carnegie Hall opens; Tchaikovsky is one of the first conductors to appear.

- **1892**: Building of the Cathedral Church of St. John the Divine begins (still not completed today).

  The first of Broadway's monstrous electrical signs is lit.

- **1893**: Henry Street Settlement, still active today, opens.

  Stephen Crane's *Maggie: A Girl of the Streets* portrays life in the Bowery.

- **1894**: The city indicts 67 policemen on corruption charges.

  Theodore Roosevelt becomes city police commissioner.

  Yiddish-language daily *The Forward* begins publication.

  Statue of Christopher Columbus is put up in Grand Circle, renamed Columbus Circle.

  Edison opens a Kinetoscope (type of moving picture) theater in Manhattan.

- **1895**: First electric streetcars run.

"White Wings," street cleaners in white uniforms, are a visible part of the city's new sanitation system.

- **1896**: Building of Columbus Park in lower Manhattan eradicates the city's most notorious slum, Five Points.

  Castle Clinton becomes home to the New York Aquarium.

  A Clinton Street baker uses an old German recipe with a Yiddish name, *bagel,* and starts a New York tradition.

- **1897**: Dow and Jones begin monitoring the stock market.

  Oscar Hammerstein's Olympia Theater is the first to open in what is now considered the Theater District.

  Steeplechase Park, an amusement park, opens at Coney Island.

- **1899**: Two million people line Broadway and Fifth Avenue at a parade to welcome Admiral George Dewey back from a victorious campaign in the Spanish-American War.

  Entire stretch of road from lower Manhattan to the Bronx-Westchester line is given the name Broadway.

The 20th Century

- **1900**: Building of subways begins.

  Traffic laws, enforced at specific times of day, come into use in New York City.

  Madison Square Garden hosts the country's first auto show.

  B. A. Macfadden opens the first of his chain of Macfadden Physical Culture Restaurants in New York, promoting what he calls "muscular vegetarianism."

- **1901**: Macy's opens at Broadway and 34th Street.
- **1902**: The Flatiron Building goes up.
- **1903**: C. K. G. Billings gives the famed Horseback Dinner at Sherry's restaurant; the guests sit on horses—sipping the Champagne in their saddlebags through straws—and are served by waiters dressed as grooms.

  The New York Highlanders baseball team (later the Yankees) forms.

- **1904**: The IRT subway opens with trains from City Hall to 145th Street.

  The tradition of New Year's Eve in Times Square (up until now known as Longacre Square) starts at the inaugural celebration of the New York Times Tower.

  The steamboat *General Slocum* catches fire and sinks in the East River while transporting 1,335 passengers, many of them children, to a picnic; 1,051 die and 124 are injured.

  The New York Public Library is built at 42nd Street and Fifth Avenue on the site of Croton Reservoir.

  August Belmont commissions his own private subway car with a bar, washroom, waiters, and its own conductor.

  George M. Cohan's *Little Johnny Jones,* featuring "Give My Regards to Broadway," opens.

- **1905**: George Bernard Shaw's *Mrs. Warren's Profession* is closed by censor after opening night.

- **1906**: Architect Stanford White is killed by Henry K. Thaw, his former mistress's husband, in Madison Square Garden's roof garden.

- **1907**: Stock market panic (Panic of 1907).

  Subway service to Brooklyn begins.

  It becomes against the law for women to smoke in public in New York City.

  The first Ziegfeld Follies show opens.

- **1908**: Eight New York artists (including Maurice Prendergast, John Sloan, and Robert Henri) form group known as the Ashcan School.

- **1909**: Hudson-Fulton celebration commemorates Hudson's 1609 excursion and Fulton's 1807 steamboat.

  The NAACP (National Association for the Advancement of Colored People) is founded and opens its first chapter in New York City.

  Wilbur Wright flies over Manhattan: the first plane ever to pass over the island.

- **1910**: McKim, Mead & White's Pennsylvania Station opens.

- **1911**: After nearly 150 workers (mostly young women) are killed in a fire at the Triangle Shirtwaist Company, changes are made in the city building code and new safety regulations are instituted.

  New York City hires its first black police officer.

- **1913**: Grand Central Station and the Woolworth Building (world's tallest until 1930) open.

  The moving of the old Park Avenue railroad tracks underground is completed, and the avenue begins to assume its current cachet.

  The New York Armory Show, featuring works of Cubist, Fauvist, Futurist, and Postimpressionist artists, introduces modern art to a bewildered America.

- **1914**: World War I begins.

  The Hotel Biltmore opens; "under the clock at the Biltmore" becomes a favorite meeting place.

- **1915**: An explosion during subway construction kills and injures many people and leaves a crater in Seventh Avenue.

  Provincetown Players theater group is founded.

- **1916**: New York passes its first zoning law, which requires tall buildings to have setbacks to let more light to the street.

- **1917**: The city's last horse car is put out of service.

  The Original Dixieland Jazz Band comes to New York.

- **1918**: Allies and Germany sign armistice.

  More than 12,000 New Yorkers die of influenza.

- **1919**: The passage of the 18th Amendment (Prohibition) brings such speakeasies as the Cotton Club, the Stork Club, and the "21" Club into business and contributes to the rise of organized crime.

  The Marx Brothers, Gloria Swanson, Rudolph Valentino, and others are making movies at Astoria Studios in Queens, the movie capital of America.

  A. D. Juilliard's will bequeaths $20 million to start the Juilliard School of Music.

  New School for Social Research opens.

- **1920**: American women get the right to vote.

  An as-yet-unexplained bombing at the Morgan Guaranty Trust Building kills 33 people.

  Paul Robeson makes his professional stage debut with the Provincetown Players.

  Coney Island's boardwalk opens.

- **1921**: First Quota Law is instituted to help regulate immigration.

- **1923**: Yankee Stadium opens; Babe Ruth's three-run homer helps the Yanks beat the Red Sox in the first game.

New York's first birth-control clinic is established.

Saks Fifth Avenue opens.

- **1924:** The *Herald* and the *Tribune* merge to form the *New York Herald-Tribune*.
- **1925:** McKim, Mead & White's original Madison Square Garden is torn down.

  Top-hatted cartoon figure Eustace Tilley graces the cover of the first *New Yorker*.

  Al Hirschfeld's caricatures first appear in *The New York Times*.
- **1926:** James "Jimmy" Walker begins serving as mayor.
- **1927:** New York honors Charles Lindbergh with a ticker-tape parade after his transatlantic flight.

  Holland Tunnel opens.

  Coney Island's hair-raising roller coaster, the Cyclone, still running today, opens.

  The Harlem Globetrotters stunt basketball team is founded.
- **1928:** Arturo Toscanini becomes the conductor of the New York Philharmonic.
- **1929:** Stock-market crash sets off the Great Depression.

  Museum of Modern Art opens with Postimpressionist show featuring works by Gauguin, van Gogh, Cézanne, and Seurat.
- **1930:** Meeting of 10,000 Communists and sympathizers ends in riot in Union Square.

  RCA founds a television station in New York.

  The Chrysler Building is completed, world's tallest.
- **1931:** The Empire State Building, complete with a mooring mast for airships, tops the Chrysler.

  George Washington Bridge opens.

  Ground is broken for Rockefeller Center.
- **1932:** Mayor Jimmy Walker, under investigation for corruption, resigns.

  Unemployment reaches 25 percent in New York.

  Columbia opens its Teachers College.
- **1933:** A quarter-million New Yorkers watch the mayoral election returns on the Times Tower's moving electric sign, singing "Who's Afraid of the Big Bad Wolf," victor Fiorello La Guardia's theme song.

Prohibition ends.

Rockefeller Center's flagship, the RCA Building, is completed.

Douglas Leigh, creator of such classics as the Camel cigarette billboard that blew smoke rings (installed just before World War II), puts up his first Broadway advertisement—a giant, steaming cup of coffee for A & P.

- **1935:** WPA Federal Art Projects begin.

  Alcoholics Anonymous is founded in New York City.

- **1936:** Robert Moses becomes parks commissioner (until 1960) and changes the New York City landscape.

  The bus displaces the electric streetcar.

- **1938:** Orson Welles makes his "War of the Worlds" radio broadcast.

  The Cloisters, a branch of the Metropolitan Museum of Art, opens.

- **1939:** The World of Tomorrow World's Fair is constructed by Robert Moses in Queens on the site of a former dump.

  Municipal Airport (later La Guardia) opens.

  The Sixth Avenue "El" is torn down.

- **1940:** The Eighth Avenue "El" goes the way of the Sixth.

- **1941:** U.S. enters World War II.

  New Yorkers endure blackout conditions and air-raid drills.

  Adam Clayton Powell, Jr., becomes the first black elected to New York's city council.

- **1942:** Gracie Mansion becomes official mayor's residence.

  Idlewild Airport (now JFK) opens.

  The New York Times prints its first crossword puzzle.

- **1943:** Riot erupts in Harlem after a black serviceman is shot by a white cop.

- **1945:** World War II ends.

  Fourteen people are killed when an American bomber crashes into the 78th and 79th floors of the Empire State Building.

  Sixth Avenue is renamed Avenue of the Americas.

- **1947:** Construction of United Nations Plaza begins.

Jackie Robinson signs with the Brooklyn Dodgers and helps them win the pennant.

December 17 snowfall drops 28 inches of snow on the city.

- **1948**: Bus and subway fares go up to a dime.
- **1949**: "Harry Gross Affair" reveals corruption in the police department.

  Yankees win first of five World Series in a row.

- **1950**: Port Authority Bus Terminal opens.

  To facilitate street-cleaning procedures, New York City institutes its ingenious (and infuriating) alternate-side-of-the-street parking law—allowing parking on each side of the street on particular days—forever changing the experience of owning a car in the city.

- **1952**: Edward Steichen curates the wildly popular Family of Man photography exhibit at the Museum of Modern Art.
- **1953**: Dylan Thomas dies of alcohol poisoning at St. Vincent's Hospital in the Village.
- **1954**: Ellis Island immigration center closes.
- **1955**: Last train runs on the Third Avenue "El."

  The *Eagle,* Brooklyn's only daily paper, stops publication.

- **1956**: Maria Callas debuts at the Metropolitan Opera.
- **1957**: New York Giants move to San Francisco and the Brooklyn Dodgers move to Los Angeles.

  New York City's last trolley runs.

  Leonard Bernstein creates the star-crossed lovers of upper Manhattan in *West Side Story.*

- **1958**: Fire damages the Museum of Modern Art.

  The Seagram Building goes up.

- **1959**: Construction of Lincoln Center for the Performing Arts begins.

  City Council considers the feasibility of making New York City the 51st state.

  Frank Lloyd Wright's controversial Solomon Guggenheim Museum opens.

- **1962**: The New York Mets baseball team is formed; New Yorkers love them for their clumsiness.

  The Pan Am Building goes up, changing the Park Avenue vista.

  Eero Saarinen's futuristic TWA Terminal is built at Idlewild (now JFK) Airport.

Nine city newspapers begin four-month strike.

- **1963**: President John F. Kennedy is assassinated.

  Seven hundred are arrested during demonstrations in favor of minority hiring in construction jobs.

  McKim, Mead & White's well-loved Pennsylvania Station is demolished; the New York City Landmarks Commission is founded in response.

  The *New York Review of Books* is founded to take up slack during the newspaper strike.

  The Guggenheim puts on a Pop Art show featuring the works of unknowns Andy Warhol, Robert Rauschenberg, Jasper Johns, and others.

- **1964**: Harlem and Bedford-Stuyvesant are the scenes of race riots.

  The murder of Kitty Genovese in Queens becomes the shocking symbol for New York apathy when it is revealed that 38 neighbors heard her cries for help and did nothing.

  Verrazano-Narrows Bridge, the longest suspension bridge in the world, links Staten Island to Brooklyn.

  The giant globe known as the Unisphere is the symbol of the second world's fair in Queens.

  Shea Stadium is built.

- **1965**: Blackout hits the Northeast; 30 million people are without electricity.

  Black Muslim leader Malcolm X is assassinated in upper Manhattan.

  Students in Brooklyn demonstrate against segregation.

- **1966**: Transit workers go on strike.

  Newspapers strike for nearly five months.

  New York Herald-Tribune stops publication.

  The Brooklyn Navy Yard closes.

  The Metropolitan Opera House opens at Lincoln Center.

  Truman Capote throws a notorious party at the Plaza Hotel to celebrate the publication of *In Cold Blood.*

- **1967**: 700,000 people parade down Fifth Avenue in support of the Vietnam War; Martin Luther King, Jr., then leads march protesting American involvement in Vietnam.

  Warhol releases his film *The Chelsea Girls.*

- **1968**: Martin Luther King and Robert F. Kennedy are assassinated.

  The streets are piled with garbage while city sanitation workers strike for nine days.

  A student sit-in closes Columbia University.

  Valerie Solanis, an actress, shoots Andy Warhol.

  Gerome Ragni and James Rado's counterculture musical *Hair* is staged.

- **1969**: The police raid the Stonewall Inn, a private club for homosexuals in Sheridan Square, and a riot erupts when the club patrons fight back; the annual Gay Pride Day Parade is instituted to commemorate the incident, which gave birth to the gay-rights movement.

  The Mets amaze everyone when they win the World Series.

- **1970**: Explosion in a Greenwich Village house kills three members of the radical group the Weathermen.

  Construction workers beat up antiwar protesters on Wall Street.

  The city grants artists legal permission to move into abandoned buildings in SoHo, which they had been doing illegally since the early 1960s.

  First New York City Marathon is run.

- **1971**: *The New York Times* prints articles exposing a Pentagon study of American policy in Vietnam—the Pentagon Papers.

  New York City police go on strike.

  Off-track betting becomes legal in New York.

  Bill Graham's famous Fillmore East concert hall closes.

- **1972**: The television show *All in the Family* introduces the Bunker family of Flushing, Queens, to America.

  Mafioso Crazy Joey Gallo is shot and killed at his birthday party in Umberto's Clam House in Little Italy.

  Fiddler on the Roof closes after 3,242 performances.

- **1973**: The World Trade Center's twin towers change the shape of the Manhattan skyline.

  Dancers at New York City Ballet strike for job security.

- **1974**: Global inflation strikes.

Price for a seat on the New York Stock Exchange is lowest in 16 years.

- **1975**: New York City nears bankruptcy; secures a federal loan.

  Last American soldiers leave Vietnam.

  Bombings at Fraunces Tavern and La Guardia Airport kill 15 and injure 123.

  Two thousand interns and resident doctors strike at New York City hospitals.

  Metropolitan Opera names its first woman conductor, Sarah Caldwell.

  Beverly Sills debuts at the Met.

- **1976**: In celebration of America's bicentennial, tall ships from around the world sail up the Hudson while six million people watch.

  Carnegie Hall features Leonard Bernstein, Isaac Stern, Vladimir Horowitz, and others at the "Concert of the Century."

- **1977**: Total blackout in New York City area (affecting nine million people) leads to 500 reported fires and the arrest of 3,776 people for looting and vandalism.

  Fatal accident closes the Pan Am Building's heliport.

  Ed Koch is elected to his first of three terms as mayor.

  Rap, a new form of street poetry set to music invented in inner-city neighborhoods, hits the airwaves, and the hip-hop culture is born.

  George Willig scales one of the World Trade Center towers and is fined a penny a floor ($1.10 in all).

- **1978**: The *Post, Times,* and *Daily News* are shut down for 88 days by strikes.

  David Berkowitz, "Son of Sam," gets life in prison for six murders.

  Zubin Mehta is the New York Philharmonic's new director.

  Sex Pistol Sid Vicious murders his girlfriend, Nancy Spungen, in Manhattan's Chelsea Hotel.

- **1979**: New York City passes the so-called Poop Scoop Law, requiring owners to clean up after their dogs in the street—and it actually works.

  The Guardian Angels begin patrolling city streets and subways.

- **1980**: New Yorkers take to bicycles, roller skates, and sneakers during ten-day transit strike.
  John Lennon is shot and killed in front of the Dakota Apartments.
  Graffiti is hailed as the new art form in New York.
- **1981**: Gay Men's Health Crisis is founded in response to the recognition of the AIDS virus.
  Richard Serra's rusted-metal sculpture *Tilted Arc* is installed at Federal Plaza and sets off eight years of protest (it is finally removed in 1989).
  Simon and Garfunkel reunite for concert in Central Park.
- **1982**: Hundreds of thousands attend peace/anti-nukes rally in New York City.
- **1984**: Bernard Goetz, the "Subway Vigilante," shoots four youths on a New York subway.
  The word "Yuppie" (Young Urban Professional) is coined.
- **1985**: Crack cocaine, offering a fast, cheap high, begins to gain popularity.
- **1986**: Corruption scandal in city government breaks within the first three months of Mayor Koch's third term, with charges ranging from bribery to extortion; Queens borough president Donald Manes, implicated in the scandal, commits suicide.
- **1987**: The stock market crashes.
  A young black man is killed and two others are beaten in racial attack in Howard Beach, Queens.
  ACT-UP, the AIDS Coalition to Unleash Power, forms to fight for the rights of people with AIDS.
- **1988**: Demonstrators against a curfew in Tompkins Square Park are attacked and beaten by police.
  Federal government charges New York investment firm Drexel Burnham Lambert and trader Michael Milken with insider trading.
- **1989**: Woman jogging in Central Park is raped and beaten by a gang of teenagers; the brutality of the crime horrifies New Yorkers.
  Yusuf Hawkins, a black teen, is killed without provocation by a mob of white youths in Bensonhurst, Brooklyn; racial tensions flare citywide.
  Hotel queen Leona Helmsley is found guilty of tax fraud; she is later sentenced to four years in federal prison.

David Dinkins beats three-time mayor Ed Koch in the Democratic mayoral primary and goes on to win the election, becoming the first black to hold the position in the city's history.

- **1990:** Eighty-seven people die at the Happy Land Social Club in the Bronx in a fire set by the spurned boyfriend of a club employee.

  Racial tensions mount as trials for the murder of Yusuf Hawkins and the rape of the Central Park jogger get underway; Mayor Dinkins appeals for racial tolerance in an eloquent and historic speech and later calls a rally for racial unity at the Cathedral of St. John the Divine.

  Black South African leader Nelson Mandela, freed after nearly three decades in prison, inspires New Yorkers with his visit.

  A Chorus Line, the longest-running show on Broadway, closes after 6,137 performances.

- **1991:** New York City's budget woes are the worst since the 1970s; city services are threatened.

  Following the death of a black child by a Jewish motorist, riots erupt in Crown Heights, Brooklyn, during which a Jewish man is stabbed to death. The political fallout haunts Dinkins's tenure.

  Five-month strike at the *Daily News* ends, and the paper begins its struggle to win back city tabloid readers.

  Motorman driving under the influence of alcohol causes devastating subway crash; five people die, nearly 200 are injured.

  Reported crime in New York City falls modestly in every category for the first time in 36 years.

- **1992:** Reputed Gambino family crime boss John Gotti is sentenced to life in prison for various mob-related activities, including several murders.

  When a gay and lesbian group is refused permission to march in the St. Patrick's Day Parade, many city and state officials, including the mayor and the governor, decline to join the parade.

  New York gets spruced up for the 1992 Democratic National Convention, held at Madison Square Garden.

- **1993:** International terrorism strikes the city, as the World Trade Center is bombed and a plot to bomb several other sites, including the United

Nations, is uncovered. Doctrinaire Muslim fundamentalists are implicated.

New Yorkers are appalled and charmed by Keron Thomas, a 16-year-old youth who, impersonating a Metropolitan Transit Authority employee, comandeers a subway train for three and a half hours, travelling 45 miles without incident.

After millionaires grapple over it and most of the staff is fired, rehired, fired, and/or promoted, it remains uncertain whether anyone can save the *New York Post,* founded 192 years earlier by Alexander Hamilton.

—*Amy K. Hughes*

INDEX